Proceedings of the Conference on

INTERLIBRARY
COMMUNICATIONS
AND INFORMATION
NETWORKS

Proceedings
of the Conference on

INTERLIBRARY COMMUNICATIONS AND INFORMATION NETWORKS

Sponsored by the American Library Association
and the U.S. Office of Education, Bureau
of Libraries and Educational Technology
held at Airlie House, Warrenton, Virginia
September 28, 1970 - October 2, 1970

Edited by
JOSEPH BECKER

American Library Association

Chicago 1971

The research reported herein was performed pursuant to a contract with the Office of Education, U.S. Department of Health, Education, and Welfare. Contractors undertaking such projects under Government sponsorship are encouraged to express freely their professional judgment in the conduct of the project. Points of view or opinions stated do not, therefore, necessarily represent official Office of Education position or policy.

The final report for a Conference on Inter-Library Communications and Networks was submitted by Information Science and Automation, Reference Services, and Resources and Technical Services divisions of the American Library Association to Division of Information Technology and Dissemination, Bureau of Research, Office of Education, U.S. Department of Health, Education, and Welfare under the title of *Proceedings of the Conference on Interlibrary Communications and Networks*. The Project Number is 9-0288. The Contract Number is OEC-0-9-230288-4235 (095).

Contents

Introduction

The theme of this Conference was "networks." The aim was to explore and study the implications that would follow if a network of libraries and information centers were established in the United States. Today, these institutions are loosely interrelated. However, if maximum communication could be established among them, the resultant interconnection of resources would constitute a unique national information apparatus of immense value to the economic, cultural, and social growth of the country. This was the fundamental thesis examined and discussed by 125 invited participants at the "Conference on Interlibrary Communications and Information Networks," CICIN, held at Airlie House in Warrenton, Virginia, 28 September to 2 October 1970. The Conference was sponsored by the American Library Association and the U.S. Office of Education, with assistance and advice from seventeen professional organizations.

Librarians and information scientists are vitally concerned with network development for a number of important reasons. First, the network concept implies removal of all geographic barriers to knowledge; this is made possible by advances in telecommunications technology. Second, a network implies equal access by any individual for any purpose to the sum total of the nation's knowledge resources; this has been a long-standing educational goal. And third, a network implies positive redirection of the basic professional goals and objectives of librarianship and information science.

Thus in 1969 representatives of the American Library Association, the U.S. Office of Education, and the other library and information professional groups were appointed to an Advisory Board for CICIN. This group met several times in 1969 and 1970 to decide on Conference objectives, organization, and schedule. Dr. Russell Shank, Director of Libraries, Smithsonian Institution, was elected chairman of the Advisory Board. His fellow Board members were:

Pauline Atherton-
American Society for Information Science

Frank G. Burke-
Society of American Archivists

Gary Carlson-
Association for Computing Machinery

Ray M. Fry-
U.S. Office of Education

Marion G. Gallagher-
American Association of Law Libraries

Edwin S. Gleaves-
Association of American Library Schools

Alvin Goldwyn-
American Library Association
(Representative-at-large)

Warren J. Haas-
Association of Research Libraries

Madeline M. Henderson-
Federal Library Committee

John A. Humphry-
American Library Association
(Representative-at-large)

Robert B. Lane-
Special Libraries Association

Calvin N. Mooers-
Institute of Electrical and Electronic Engineers

Herbert F. Mutschler-
American Library Association
(Representative-at-large)

James L. Olsen, Jr.-
National Academy of Sciences

Richard H. Perrine-
American Library Association (RSD)

Irwin H. Pizer-
Medical Library Association

Russell Shank-
American Library Association (ISAD)

John Sherrod-
Federal Council for Science and Technology, Committee on
Scientific and Technical Information (COSATI)

Carl M. Spaulding-
Council on Library Resources, Inc.

David C. Weber-
American Library Association (RTSD)

Edward G. Weiss-
National Science Foundation

Bill M. Woods-
National Federation of Science Abstracting and Indexing
Services

The board was responsible for developing the basic structure
of the Conference, determining the criteria for the selection of
Conference participants, and suggesting the names of participants. The criteria they adopted were: (1) that all interested
professional communities be represented — librarians, educators, information scientists, and computer and telecommunications experts, (2) that all types of libraries and
information centers be represented, (3) that all geographical
areas be represented, and (4) that every effort be made to bring
in "new blood" by extending a special invitation to young
professionals. More than 400 names were reviewed by the Board
and staff for sixty-four vacant participant positions. Of the total
Conference positions available, fifty-six were reserved for Advisory Board members and the authors of commissioned papers.

The charge to the Conference was to "identify and discuss the
propositions fundamental to the establishment and operation of
a national network of libraries and information centers." Specific objectives were:

1.   To study the present state of development of
networks, to identify their strengths and
weaknesses, and to highlight potential
development areas with respect to the needs
of libraries and information centers and their
users

2.   To explore the possibility of meeting these
identifiable needs through the adoption and
expansion of present telecommunications
systems throughout the United States

3.   To examine the application of hitherto unused but
technologically sound methods to facilitate
interlibrary communications and data
distribution

4.   To identify, for in-depth study and resolution,
other problems of an administrative, legal,
physical, social, and technical nature that
must be solved before a national network of

libraries and information centers can be
established

5.   To outline a specific framework within which to
develop a plan for a national network

6.   To inform librarians and others, through the
publication of working papers and
Conference *Proceedings,* of the importance of
networks and the areas of research deserving
further study.

Thirty-one special studies were commissioned and distributed
to Conference participants in advance of 28 September. The
papers examined the key network issues and provided a summary of past experience and work as well as recommendations
for the future. Using the commissioned papers as source material, the 125 participants met during the five-day Conference
to dissect the ideas contained in the papers and to explore the
potential and the implications of establishing a national network of libraries and information centers. It was hoped that the
conclusions reached at the Conference would accelerate bringing a network into reality by detailing the tasks and also the
research required for planning.

The Conference was formally opened at 9:45 A.M. on Monday, 28 September 1970, with a message from President Richard M. Nixon. His message read as follows:

THE WHITE HOUSE
WASHINGTON

September 25, 1970

Those who take part in the Conference on
Interlibrary Communications and Information
Networks perform a vital service in our fast-
moving society. In order to be of maximum
benefit to our people, the achievements we
realize must be constantly and efficiently
passed on to those whose well-being they are
designed to serve.

Your part in this process is indispensable,
and I welcome your continuing contributions
to this increasingly important aspect of
American life.

Richard Nixon

Miss Kathleen Molz, Branch Chief, Research and Program
Development Branch, Bureau of Libraries and Educational
Technology, spoke on behalf of the U. S. Office of Education.
She said:

I felt that this meeting needed an invocation, and in the back
of my mind I contemplated a quotation from John Keats. I
was slightly worried about addressing such an assemblage
with the remarks of a poet; you might, perhaps, think I was
being too literary. But last night when I saw the pants-suits of
the ladies, so reminiscent of the days of George Sand, and the
Regency sideburns on many of the gentlemen, I believed we
might not be altogether removed from the Romantic era, so I
shall ask you this morning to reflect on these words:

"And other spirits there are standing apart
Upon the forehead of the age to come;
These, these will give the world another heart,
And other pulses...."

In a very small way, that is where we are today, upon the forehead of that age which is yet to come, in which new titans, new spirits of thought and ideas, will give the world "another heart, and other pulses."

This Conference is intended to afford us the opportunity of looking at new modes of transferring information and to encourage those among us who handle information to be more generous in discovering methods of expediting the sharing of the nation's knowledge banks and repositories. In an oft-reiterated goal, the Office of Education in the Department of Health, Education, and Welfare has set a high priority on the equalization of educational opportunity. Certainly, those among you who propose a national informational network envision this equalization as one of your own chief aims. It is within this context, that is, the educational benefits that will accrue to the American taxpayer who has made this Conference possible, that your deliberations this week should take place.

On behalf of the office then, its newly appointed Associate Commissioner of the Bureau of Libraries and Educational Technology, Burton E. Lamkin, and the Director of Library Programs, Ray M. Fry, both of whom look forward to joining your sessions this week, I welcome you to this long-awaited Conference at Airlie House. Recognition should also be given to several other Office of Education staff members who worked in many ways to make this Conference possible: F. Kurt Cylke, formerly of the National Center for Educational Research and Development, who served as the project's first program officer, and Paul C. Janaske and Lawrence S. Papier, both of the Bureau of Libraries staff.

For myself, I cannot but wish that the weather will hold clear and the dialogues prove fruitful. A wise Oriental once wrote that a conference should have all the components of a good meal: the substance of rich meat, the seasoning of wit, and the savory of remembrance. All these, the office wishes for you; all these, the office hopes will result in greater opportunities for readers and information users everywhere.

Dr. Russell Shank, Conference Advisory Board Chairman, welcomed the participants and outlined the history and organizational structure of the Conference. He recalled that the project had originally been conceived by three American Library Association divisions—the Reference Services Division, the Information Science and Automation Division, and the Resources and Technical Services Division. He further explained the interests, objectives, and involvement of the many associations and agencies whose representatives constituted the Conference Advisory Board.

The keynote speaker at the Conference was Kenneth Cox, former Commissioner of the Federal Communications Commission and currently Senior Vice-President of Microwave Communications of America. Mr. Cox's address appears in full in the *Proceedings*.

Three tutorials were presented to participants. They provided a common basis for understanding the terminology and concepts of the interdisciplinary groups represented at the Conference. The first tutorial dealt with telecommunications and was presented by Brendon Healey and Charles Brockman of the American Telephone and Telegraph Company. In addition, AT&T provided demonstrations of equipment, including the new Picture-phone, on-line computer inquiry, facsimile, teletype, and touch-tone retrieval. The second tutorial was presented by Richard Darling, Dean of the School of Library Service, Columbia University. He outlined the fundamentals of librarianship and briefly described the principal areas of interlibrary cooperation. In the third tutorial, given by the International Business Machines Corporation, Mr. Dan Jones described computer concepts and explained the relationship of the computer to library automation. Harold Johnson, Vice-President of Western Union Telegraph Company, participated in a panel on communications costs.

The Conference was organized into five Working Groups, each covering a different facet of the network topic. Each had a leader and one or more associate leaders. The Groups, leaders, and associates were:

Networks Needs and Development
  John W. Bystrom (leader)
  Raynard C. Swank (associate)

Network Services
  F. F. Leimkuhler (leader)
  Pauline Atherton (associate)
  Brigitte L. Kenney (associate)

Network Technology
  John W. Meaney (leader)
  Edwin B. Parker (associate)

Network Organization
  Robert Heinich (leader)
  Richard Dougherty (associate)

Network Planning
  Carlos N. Cuadra (leader)
  Calvin A. Mooers (associate)

Each Working Group was asked to examine in detail the commissioned papers pertinent to its area of interest, to discuss salient issues, and to prepare written summary reports of their discussions and recommendations. The Working Groups presented two oral reports: the first, an interim progress report at a Plenary Session on Wednesday, 30 September, and a final report at the Plenary Session on Friday, 2 October. The Working Groups developed their own daily schedules, which included many evening meetings.

The edited summaries of reports developed by each Working Group appear in this book as part of the Conference *Proceedings*. It should be noted, however, that their conclusions generally represent expression of the majority views of each Group rather than the unanimous opinion of all. Everyone clamored for more time to resolve differences, and the Conference could easily have continued for another week given the camaraderie and enthusiasm that developed during the latter part of the week. I feel compelled to include as an epilogue to the *Proceedings* a poem which made the Friday Plenary Session an unforgettable experience.

In keeping with the Conference's emphasis on new methods of communication, it should be noted that the ALA contracted with Herbert Avram, President of STENOCOMP, Inc., to transcribe the Conference papers and Plenary Session discussions using a new stenotype-to-computer transcription technique.

Also, as Conference Director, I wish to summarize some personal observations after editing the *Proceedings:*

1. The Conference, through the commissioned papers and subsequent critiques, produced a gold mine of information about networks. Without a doubt, the papers in this book of *Proceedings* represent the most comprehensive collection of materials of its kind on networks.

2. A national network of libraries and information centers appears to be a viable and attractive concept for the library and information science professions to pursue.

3. The individual is the one who will be served by a national network. As Bob Heinich of the Working Group on Organization said, "Networks are for everybody," and the individual's need for self-enrichment and advancement should be a network's primary goal.

4. The development of the network concept is an interdisciplinary task and there is "readiness" in 1970 among different professional groups to take constructive steps in the common interest.

5. Libraries and information centers will need to become "pro-active" rather than reactive social institutions in order to prosecute network objectives forcefully.

6. Finally, "social engineering" is required to overcome many of the obstacles to network progress. There seems little doubt that technology can aid the process, but the fundamental requirement is to motivate institutions to develop new patterns of organization that will permit consortia and networks to operate effectively. Conference discussions made it very clear that a monolithic network structure imposed from the top down will not work. Meaningful network development requires grassroots motivation and grassroots support.

In viewing networks as a national concern, the Conference went on record with two formal resolutions. The first requested that the new National Commission on Libraries and Information Science be made a focal point for devising a national network of libraries and information centers. (The full text of this recommendation is included below.) The second resolution

was a recommendation to the Federal Communications Commission that *"...in the matter of developing a United States position for the forthcoming World Administrative Radio Conference, that our national position contain a provision for the exclusive allocation of the 2500-2690 MHz band within the United States for space and terrestial non-commercial public and educational services, including library and information services."* The following recommendations relating to the National Commission were culled from the several Working Group summaries. Many other recommendations were made and these will be found in the working group's summaries in the body of the *Proceedings.* The first recommendation (here shown in italics) was the one formally adopted by floor resolution; the others stem from the individual working groups. In many ways the "Conference on Interlibrary Communications and Information Networks" may be viewed as a prologue to the appointment of the new National Commission on Libraries and Information Science by the President.

On January 10, 1971 the Conference Director sent the following letter to President Nixon advising him of the results of the Conference's deliberations and forwarding a formal Conference Resolution with supporting Working Group recommendations to the National Commission on Libraries and Information Science.

INTERLIBRARY COMMUNICATIONS
&
INFORMATION
NETWORKS
CONFERENCE 1970

Sponsored by
AMERICAN LIBRARY ASSOCIATION
UNITED STATES OFFICE of EDUCATION

DIRECTOR: Joseph Becker
6400 Goldsboro Road
Bethesda, Maryland, 20034
Area Code 301-229-1102

The President of the United States
The White House
Washington, D. C. 20500

January 10, 1971

Dear Mr. President:

Your message of September 25, 1970 to the "Conference on Interlibrary Communications and Information Networks" was warmly received and appreciated by the 150 librarians, information scientists, and computer and communications specialists in attendance.

The Conference theme was "networks." And its objective was to explore how libraries and information centers can be organized into a national network so that their combined resources would be available to any individual in the country for educational and personal advancement.

Knowing of your desire to improve the quality of life in America, I felt certain you would be interested in the outcome of our deliberations. Those attending the Conference concluded that a national information apparatus is vital, technically feasible, and compatible with the new telecommunications technology; and, that the resultant interconnection would constitute a unique national resource of immense value to our nation's economic, cultural, social, and scientific progress. The prospect of seeing this become a reality captured the imagination of all present.

While in plenary session the Conference passed two formal resolutions. First, a request that the new National Commission on Libraries and Information Science be made a focal point in devising a national network of libraries and information centers, and second, a resolution to the Federal Communications Commission requesting specific frequency allocations for space and terrestial non-commercial public and educational services, including library and information services.

Submitted herewith for your information is a copy of our Conference recommendations. The complete transcript of the Conference <u>Proceedings</u> will be forwarded to the Chairman of the National Commission on Libraries and Information Science when he is appointed.

Respectfully,

Joseph Becker
Conference Director

Enclosure

RECOMMENDATIONS OF PARTICULAR
INTEREST TO THE NATIONAL COMMISSION
ON LIBRARIES AND INFORMATION SCIENCE

CONFERENCE RESOLUTION ON 2 OCTOBER 1970

That, as a matter of priority, the National Commission on Libraries and Information Science devise a comprehensive plan to facilitate the co-ordinated development of the nation's libraries, information centers, and other knowledge resources.

Further, that action be taken as soon as possible to appoint members of the Commission and fund its activities.

SUPPORTING WORKING GROUP RECOMMENDATIONS

That the National Commission recommend national policy with respect to network development in order to foster integrated action on local, state, and regional levels

That the National Commission, as part of its annual report to the President and to Congress, describe the advances made in network development and pinpoint the strengths and weaknesses of information access among different constituencies, geographic regions, and groups

That the National Commission assure the financial support required for network programs by developing legislative proposals at the federal and state levels, generating a base of understanding within the library and information science professions, and providing a broad base of public understanding of the need for a national network of libraries and information centers

That the National Commission coordinate its programs closely with those of the Office of Telecommunications Policy and the Federal Communications Commission in order to ensure that emerging commercial and governmental telecommunications programs will be capable of accommodating the communication requirements of a national network of libraries and information centers

That the National Commission designate or recommend establishment of a national center to coordinate the creation of standard bibliographic data records for all forms of material

That the National Commission support the establishment of interdisciplinary educational and training programs to equip librarians and information scientists with the technical knowledge required of them in library and information networks at all levels

That the National Commission coordinate the development of national plans for a library and information network with those of other countries in

order to facilitate information transfer on an international basis

That the National Commission be apprised of the discussions, conclusions, and recommendations of this Conference, and be requested to assume responsibility for promoting by all appropriate means the network objectives that have been identified.

This letter was acknowledged by the White House on January 26, 1971 as follows:

THE WHITE HOUSE
WASHINGTON

January 26, 1971

Dear Mr. Becker:

The President has asked me to thank you for your letter of January 10 in which you advise him of the results of the Conference on Interlibrary Communications and Information Networks, which you chaired last September.

I join the President in commending you and the Conference participants for the seriousness of your deliberations and for your constructive recommendations in this important and expanding field.

We will forward the recommendations for the National Commission on Libraries and Information Science to the Commission Chairman when that appointment is made.

With regards,

Sincerely yours,

Leonard Garment

Mr. Joseph Becker
Becker and Hayes, Inc.
6400 Goldsboro Road
Bethesda, Maryland 20034

In closing I wish to express my deep appreciation to Kristy Leivestad Coomes, who served as my administrative assistant. To her belong all the credit and all the kudos for a superb job of organization and planning. Another contributor behind the scenes was Kristy's secretary, Barbara Carleo. Barbara conceived many valuable ideas in the course of the project, and we greatly appreciate her contributions.

Special thanks also are due to Don Culbertson and Russell Shank for their fine support and helpful assistance, and to Kurt Cylke, Larry Papier, and Paul Janaske, who served as project monitors for the Office of Education, and to Ray Fry and other members of the Bureau of Libraries and Educational Technology.

Many thanks go also to the many individuals who gave of their time and talent so willingly — to the Advisory Board members, in particular, the Working Group chairmen and their associates, and of course, to all of the Conference participants.

Joseph Becker
Conference Director

Federal Telecommunications Policy and Library Information Networks

Kenneth A. Cox

In a recent article in *Datamation,* the director of libraries for MIT pointed out that the worldwide outpouring of printed words is going up 8 to 10 percent a year, with about 400,000 books, 200,000 periodicals, and 200,000 technical reports published in 1968. He indicated that among academic libraries, Harvard has more than eight million volumes, and that there are nearly 100 other universities in this country with more than a million. Each of these hundred is buying annually more than 5 percent of the titles published since Gutenberg.

In my own field of the law, the number of articles which appear each year in any specialized field of legal practice is staggering. I had occasion the other day to search through the Legal Periodical Index for articles dealing with certain aspects of broadcasting and was amazed at the enormity of the literature on that rather new subject alone. This is not to mention the vast output of judicial and administrative decisions in the various fields of law, which has given rise in recent years to efforts to design computerized legal retrieval systems to enable a busy lawyer to manage a research problem with a minimum of time and to give a lawyer some assurance that he has available the means for a thorough search of all relevant cases.

Although the phrase "information explosion" may be a hackneyed one which librarians are weary of hearing, I wonder if the public—which must sustain the increasing cost of making a rapid exchange of scientific, technical, medical, and other information available—realizes how vital it is to take advantage of modern communications facilities for an exchange of the library resources now available. Librarians have begun to accept the premise that it is technically feasible for sound, pictures, and digital data stored at distant locations to be made available with relative ease.

Certainly the federal government is becoming increasingly aware that innovations in communications technology are providing new tools for increasing the capacity and versatility of communications networks for these and other purposes. Congress enacted the Higher Education Act of 1968, which includes, in Title IX–Networks for Knowledge, provisions designed to encourage joint programs among institutions of higher learning for the cooperative exploration of the new computer and communications technologies.

Other national developments which are creating demands for expanded library service and for the building of information networks are the State Technical Services Act; the National Library of Medicine's program for regional medical libraries; the Regional Medical Program for Heart Disease, Cancer, and Stroke; the Office of Education's support of libraries; the joint program of the Library of Congress, the National Library of Medicine, and the National Agricultural Library for development of machine-readable catalog data for monographs and serials; and the supporting programs of the National Science Foundation.

During 1967 it became apparent to the National Science Foundation that the developing discipline-oriented information systems in the professional societies, the mission-oriented systems in the federal agencies, and the private institutions and organizations with their specialized information systems would require some kind of coordination and eventual integration into a national information network. These programs have not only produced a new and more favorable climate for libraries and information centers but have also emphasized the critical need for communications among them.

Many states are readying network plans under Title III of the Library Services and Construction Act. Thus far, installation of teletype and telefacsimile networks has received the most attention, but there are also signs of affiliation and amalgamation at the local level due to the availability of the MARC computer tapes from the Library of Congress. MARC tapes are certain to have a consolidating effect on technical processing, particularly among public and school libraries. The concept of a dynamic network involving all types of libraries has been advanced in Washington, New York, California, and other states.

I note that the main purpose of the Conference on Interlibrary Communications and Information Networks is to contribute toward a significant improvement in library service to communities, academic institutions, etc., for which the availability of rapid exchange of information is becoming increasingly vital. I believe that the sense of urgency the sponsors of this Conference feel about the establishment of library networks on a national scale is consistent with the inevitable drive of a highly complex and industrialized society toward the use of the available modern technologies.

There are times when one wonders whether technology is really the magic road to improving the quality of life in an increasingly urbanized world, where many of our ills, after all, are due to modern industry and its depersonalization of work. But there is no turning the clock back, however nostalgic we may be for the days when man's work was closer to the natural rhythm of a less complex agrarian society. The simple sociological fact is that in a complex, interconnected society, the conditions of happiness for the mass of the people—social and economic security, education, equal opportunity, decent housing, medical care, and the like—involve a high degree of collective action through the agency of government, national or local; the same is true with respect to the communications facilities we need to bind us together.

But the things people need are not always available where they live. How many people in rural areas and small towns have died for lack of modern medical attention in their communities? Today there is a national network tied into the NIH Library of Medicine through which physicians can obtain the latest biomedical information. Television networks for broadcasting medical information are becoming more sophisticated so that a surgeon in a small town can tap the knowledge of specialists in a large city hospital. And "networks" of another kind—using base station and mobile radio units—can enable an attendant in an ambulance sent to pick up the victim of a heart attack to transmit electrocardiographic information back to the hospital and receive instructions for treatment to be administered in transit, thereby improving the patient's chances of survival. So communications can play a role in medicine that was undreamed of just a few years ago.

Certainly, the Federal Communications Commission is conscious of the complex issues surrounding the problem of providing an appropriate communications environment within which large, multiaccess systems can develop and grow. For example, the form and speed of the transformation of the telephone industry's voice-oriented nationwide communications network into a general purpose plant that is less hostile to the special requirements of data communications poses difficult questions, especially because of the very high level of investment in existing facilities. This is likewise true of the introduction of satellite technology as an adjunct to the terrestrial network. The commission must pass on these matters, but the competing considerations of public policy are extremely complex, and the judgments the commission will have to make in choosing between conflicting interests would confound the wisdom of a Solomon. I wish you could be present at a commission meeting to get some understanding of the weighing and balancing of interests that go into the formation of commission policy on such matters as the development of the CATV industry, the question of entry of new competing carriers such as Datran and MCI, and so on. I think you would find it interesting—but a bit frustrating—as, indeed, I think most of the commissioners do.

Let me turn now to some of the commission's more important recent decisions in the field of telecommunications and indicate how the rapid and effective transmission of information, hopefully, can be assisted by flexible and imaginative formulation of government policy. It is up to you to take the initiative in developing your capabilities in a society which puts increasing demands on your resources, but it is up to the federal government to develop the communications policies which will provide the opportunity and framework within which you can operate as efficiently and economically as possible. We cannot decide what systems you should use for library networks, but we can try to provide an "open sky" for innovation and can try to

remove unreasonable constraints on growth and development in telecommunications. I hope you will excuse me if I sometimes slip back into the first person in referring to the commission. My new colleagues at MCI frequently catch me in such indications that I really have not quite made the transition back to private life.

In the landmark MCI case, which of course involved my new associates, the commission in 1969 authorized a new carrier to enter the field of intercity microwave service between Chicago and St. Louis. This decision was premised largely on the objective of affording users a wider range of economic choice as to how they may best satisfy their continually expanding needs for communications services. On 17 July of this year, the commission issued a Notice of Inquiry in Docket 18920 to formulate policies and procedures for consideration of applications to provide specialized common carrier service in the domestic point-to-point microwave radio service. The commission has pending before it some 1,900 applications—including those from companies associated with MCI, Data Transmission Corporation (Datran), United Video, New York-Penn Microwave, and others—for authorization to construct and operate microwave and other facilities to provide specialized common carrier services, particularly for the transmission of data and the provision of business communications, in various parts of the country. It is anticipated that numerous additional applications for facilities of a similar nature will be forthcoming.

Datran has proposed a nationwide, switched, digital communications network specifically designed and engineered for data transmission. The initial system would have twenty-four microwave stations in a high channel density backbone trunk which would follow a route connecting San Francisco, Los Angeles, Dallas, Minneapolis, Atlanta, and Boston. Perhaps the easiest way to describe this proposal is to quote two paragraphs from the notice of Docket 18920. The commission said:

7. According to Datran, major economic sectors, individual consumers, and providers of information systems and services in the aggregate have a rapidly expanding need for rapid, accurate, low-cost data transmission services which is largely unmet by present common carrier offerings. Specifically, Datran claims that the costs of existing communications services have not declined in proportion to data processing costs; that existing analog transmission systems require costly modulator-demodulator equipment to convert digital signals to analog and back again; that current switched services often take significant time to establish connections, which detracts from the productivity of data terminal and operator; that transmission systems originally engineered for voice and record transmission do not meet the more demanding reliability standards of digital data transmission; that existing switched services generally cannot handle full-duplex transmission, which leads to reduced throughput and wasteful line reversal time; that the basic switched services, originally intended only for voice and record, provide only two major speed selections whereas many new data applications require faster and more varied choices; that attempts to establish a switched connection for data transmission can be impeded by the high incidence in points and times of heavy user con-

centration; that communication between terminal devices utilizing different line speeds is not possible in most existing major networks; that many data transmissions can be completed in far less than the minimum charge periods now in force; and that while common carriers have recently begun to drop barriers against sharing and interconnection, much confusion and difficulty continues to exist in user attempts to apply this flexibility.

8. Datran attributes many of the asserted unmet needs of data transmission users to the circumstances that the existing switched facilities of common carriers were originally engineered only for voice and record analog transmission services, a constraint which does not exist in its proposed digital system. The three basic integrated components of Datran's proposed end-to-end system (trunking system, switching system, and local distribution system) are engineered specifically for, and dedicated to digital data transmission. Thus, a subscriber need not convert his digital signals to a different (analog) transmission mode, since the system transmits the subscriber's signal in its original form. Moreover, as the signal is transmitted through the system, it is continuously regenerated into a new, clean and conditioned signal without the amplified system noise present in analog system.

Many of these same points are made by MCI and the other specialized carrier applicants.

Datran says that its system will meet current and projected data transmission needs which are largely unmet by the existing carriers—though both Bell and Western Union have recently proposed new offerings in this area. It also asserts that effective utilization of existing data processing technology is constrained by present common carrier communications services and facilities, and that the design and development of new computer applications requiring data transmission is restricted by high cost as well as by unreliable and inflexible service. It contends that the public will not realize the full benefits of existing and potential data processing technology until this situation is remedied.

There also are pending some 700 applications by fifteen MCI-associated companies for regional portions of a proposed nationwide network to provide specialized, private-line communications services between Boston and Miami and San Diego and Seattle and some 135 major cities in between. MCI claims that its proposal offers the following characteristics or procedures which are not available to communications users on existing common carrier facilities:

Communications channels designed especially for data transmission

Specified data error rate of as little as 1 in 10^7

Analog or digital inputs

Data channels starting as low as five cents per mile per month and priced on data speed rather than bandwidth

One-way transmission

Two-way transmission of different bandwidths

Ninety-three different types of channel terminations with seventy-two channel bandwidths ranging from 200 to 960,000 Hz

Half-time use

Sharing of channels.

MCI asserts that a grant of its applications would afford a flexibility in service needed by, but not now available to, an important communications submarket, would cause existing carriers to revise their service offerings to the benefit of communications users, and would stimulate the development of new communications equipment.

In order to resolve the broad policy and procedural questions involved in handling these pending and anticipated microwave applications, the commission has invited comments on the Common Carrier Bureau's analysis of the "threshold" issue of general policy—whether the public interest would be served by permitting new carriers to enter the specialized communications field. If you have views on this question, you may want to file these with the commission. The bureau expressed the view that entry of new carriers into the field could provide a useful regulatory tool which would assist in achieving the statutory objective of adequate and efficient service at reasonable charges. The commission proposed not to hold comparative hearings on issues of economic exclusivity, since there seemed to be sufficient market potential to support more than one applicant in a given area. The bureau noted that the demand for all types of communications services is growing very rapidly and that data communications will probably exhibit very substantial growth over the next decade. It said that the entry of new specialized carriers would help meet the increasing public need for diverse and flexible means for satisfying expanding specialized communications requirements.

I should make it clear that the commission is deferring any determination of its own on the general policy question of permitting the entry of new carriers until it has the benefit of comments by interested parties on the staff's position. There is no doubt, however, that the procedures it has set up will facilitate resolution of the difficult policy and procedural questions presented by the multiplicity of applications. Needless to say, there will be many policy issues to be solved before this proceeding is over—for example, the existing carriers claim that authorization of specialized systems will result in so-called "cream skimming," or the diversion of revenues from the most profitable routes, thereby affecting the rates for service on thinner, less profitable routes, and may also delay the planned construction of high-capacity systems in this decade, thus denying the public potential economies of scale. The applicants for the new facilities deny that any of these dire results will follow because they seek to serve new markets whose needs are not being met by the existing carriers.

I believe the commission has taken a bold new direction in its handling of these competitive applications which so vitally affect national communications policy. While lawyers may differ on procedural niceties, I think the order represents a landmark in its forward-looking effort to avoid years of costly litigation.

In the time left to me, I will try to sketch some of the other areas of federal policy which I hope may be of interest to you.

The FCC as well as the Nixon Administration have been studying the policies which should be established as the framework within which satellite technology may be best applied to our domestic communications needs. On 23 January 1970, the White House sent a memorandum to the chairman of the commission with respect to public policy objectives in this important field. The letter emphasized the need for reliable communications services for public, business, and government use at reasonable rates and the assurance of a healthy environment for continuing innovations in services and technology. The statement of policy points out that the White House has concentrated on the following objectives:

Assuring full and timely benefit to the public of the economic and service potential of satellite technology

Insuring maximum learning about the possibilities for satellite services

Minimizing unnecessary regulatory and administrative impediments to technological and market development by the private sector

Encouraging more vigorous innovation and flexibility within the communications industry to meet a constantly changing spectrum of public and private communications requirements at reasonable rates

Discouraging anticompetitive practices—such as discriminatory pricing or interconnection practice and cross-subsidization between public monopoly and private service offerings—that inhibit the growth of a healthy structure in communications and related industries

Assuring that national security and emergency preparedness needs are met.

On 24 March 1970, the commission issued a Notice of Proposed Rule Making with respect to domestic satellite facilities. Potential applicants and other interested persons were requested to comment on the question of whether the public interest would be better served by authorizing domestic satellite facilities to AT&T without restriction as to the type of service it can provide, or by limiting it to public message service as recommended by the executive branch, or by confining AT&T's participation for an initial period to leasing satellite channels in systems established by others.

The commission also indicated that it would accept applications from all interested parties. The first one was submitted a month or so ago by Western Union. The commission has since fixed 1 December 1970 as the deadline for filing of additional applications. It is expected that Comsat will file in conjunction with AT&T, that Hughes-Teleprompter will apply for a system heavily emphasizing service to the cable television industry, and that RCA and others may file. The MCI carriers also have indicated interest. So it appears that we may soon move on to the next stage in developing a domestic satellite system which will undoubtedly lean heavily on the distribution of network television programming but also can serve data transmission, long-haul telephone, and a wide range of other communications needs—perhaps including some of yours.

The commission also is trying to develop new policies to make better use of cable technology as an integral part of our television system. That process involves many thorny policy questions since cable television has a potential for weakening the basic over-the-air service. But if sound answers as to copyright liability and importation of distant signals can be worked out, the CATV industry may develop a network of broadband facilities extending to 75 or 80 percent of television homes, which would be used for many other communications purposes such as facsimile reproduction of newspapers, security surveillance, meter reading, electronic mail, the checkless society, and so on. Perhaps of more interest to you is the possibility that these facilities may permit children to have access to centrally located teaching machines; may allow their parents to tie into computers for a variety of purposes; and may eventually make it possible for us to dial up regional libraries of printed, filmed, and recorded information and entertainment, scan a list of materials available in a particular area, and then order the transmission of items selected in printed, video, cathode ray tube display, or other form. This is certainly an exciting prospect, and it seems a bit odd that its coming about may depend on policies which are being developed initially to promote more diversified television service.

The commission's Carterfone decision, issued in July 1968, was one of the most noteworthy actions taken in recent years to expand the range of choice available to users in satisfying their communications needs. That decision is significant for several reasons. First, it required the common carriers to delete from their tariffs the restraints they had previously imposed upon their customers' freedom to interconnect private communications systems and terminal equipment of their own choice to the facilities of the carriers. The commission concluded that the carriers' preexisting practices in these respects were unlawful to the extent that they prevented the customer from using his service in a manner that was beneficial to his business or social need or convenience without detriment to the telephone network or its other subscribers. Second, the commission scrapped the so-called case-by-case or "exception" approach implicit in the old tariff provisions. This had required a separate determination as to whether each individual piece of equipment or system was safe and could be authorized as an exception to the general prohibition. This required each individual telephone subscriber or equipment supplier to challenge the tariff restriction separately in a lengthy and costly administrative hearing. More often than not, the process effectively discouraged him from doing so. Third, the commission's decision unleashed the inventive forces of independent development and manufacture of communications- related equipment. This action fertilized a competitive market, which in turn has produced a diverse supply of new and useful consumer apparatus such as data sets, computer ports, speakerphones, and PABXs, among others.

Finally, I would like to say a few words about the commission's Computer Inquiry. On 3 April 1970, the commission issued a Tentative Decision which proposes to establish a policy with respect to the entry of communications common carriers into data processing. It ruled that carriers may not engage directly or indirectly in offering data processing services except through separate corporate entities maintaining separate books and employing separate operating personnel and facilities.

The commission had received comments from every segment of the data processing industry, the communications industry, and commercial users of data systems. As many of you know, we retained the Stanford Research Institute to prepare a comprehensive report on the market structure of the data processing industry, the potential effects on competition of failing to regulate the entry of carriers into data processing, etc. The crucial problem pointed out by the noncarriers was the potential effect of cross-subsidy by carriers who could use their own communications facilities at below cost in the sale of data processing services. Consequently, the commission decided to impose the safeguards on entry indicated above.

Here, again, many problems will remain unsolved for years to come as the competitive forces and market structure of the computer communications industry shift with changing technology. I am impressed with one problem which does not lend itself to easy solution—the matter of the economic power and position of the carriers. Despite all legal safeguards to prevent unfair cross-subsidy, they may nevertheless be able to offer intangible inducements such as superior installation, maintenance service, or equipment which the customer may consider more important than the level of charge for the data processing service itself. I am not sure how the commission can cope with this problem—unless it were to impose a complete bar to carrier entry as it did in excluding telephone companies from providing CATV service in areas where they furnish local exchange service. That is a conclusion which the commission is apparently unwilling to accept at this time.

In conclusion, I think it is important in evaluating our national communications policy to recognize that our system of common carrier communications is one of the few in the world which is privately owned but subject to government regulation. I believe that the initiative of private industry, when stimulated and supervised by effective government regulation, provides a combination which, by and large, has provided the American consumer with services which are efficient and reasonably related to cost. It has been demonstrated that when restraints on innovation develop in our system, they can be removed by government action, with resultant benefit to the public—and ultimately, to the carrier itself. This is the role which I believe the commission has played in Carterfone and MCI, and which I think it will continue to play in the future.

I hope that this process will result in the formulation of policies which will favor the development of interlibrary communications and other information networks of the kind your Conference will consider. Like medical care, our educational and library resources are not evenly distributed throughout the country. If the public is to have fair and equal access to our great reservoirs of information, you must develop techniques of cooperation among the various institutions involved and must be able to call upon the communications industries for the network circuitry—whether terrestrial or satellite, radio or cable—which you will need to interconnect all the parts of a truly national information system. Only in this way can we hope to make the best use of our accumulated knowledge, which is essential if we are to solve the many complex problems which confront us today. This is a most important task in which you are engaged. I wish you success in it, for all our sakes.

Network Needs and Development

Working Group Summary On
Network Needs and Development

Aim: To analyze the need for a national Network of Libraries and Information Centers, and to develop a measure of its viability.

Man is fulfilled as he shares in and enriches his cultural heritage. His survival, his self-realization, and his social enlightment turn upon his knowledge of the concepts, habits, skills, arts, instruments, and institutions of that heritage. In advanced societies his knowledge of that heritage depends increasingly upon recorded information resources. To these resources every man, according to his needs, should have realistic access.

The tremendous growth and diversification of this information resource in modern times are abundantly evident. Less evident is the degree of society's dependence upon this resource for its further welfare, security, and progress. The resource having outreached the capacity of any man, or of all men, to learn and remember, the issue of its preservation and effective use has become critical. The ability of man to save words, sounds, pictures, and other symbols for future recall upon demand is one of his greatest achievements. The product of this achievement has now become a cultural utility of the most compelling significance.

However diverse are the broad social problems that require information for their solution, the human need is basically individual. In nations with large, heterogeneous populations, huge urban centers, and amazingly complex technologies, the individual remains the important unit — to be respected, given a chance to strive toward his own goals, and provided an opportunity to reach his potential. Two basic needs of the individual are survival and self-realization — survival in the sense of food, clothing, health, employment, and adjustment to a changing society; and self-realization in the sense of such aspirations as personal identity, appreciation of arts and letters, philosophic and religious experience, and creativity. There is also the need of the individual to participate in educated ways in the political and social movements of democratic nations.

Working Group Leader: John Bystrom, Department of Speech Communications, University of Hawaii, 2560 Campus Road, Room 131, Honolulu, Hawaii 96822
Associate Leader: Raynard C. Swank, University of California, School of Librarianship, Berkeley, California 94720

THE NEED FOR INFORMATION

These basic needs are felt in some degree by people in all segments of society, regardless of their geographical location, social condition, or intellectual achievement. There is almost universal concern today with such issues as urban decay, racial conflict, poverty, career lattices, early childhood education, drug addiction, minority ethnic cultures, environmental pollution, and war, as well as with technological innovation. Yet the existing inequities of access to library and other information sources are staggering. The doctor, the lawyer, the teacher, the student, or the business man in rural or ghetto America has, as an individual, no less need for information then does his counterpart in middle class, metropolitan America.

Information is needed, moreover, where the individual is — geographically, socially, intellectually, and emotionally. A man must feel identity with his local point of contact with the information resource, and the information that he gets should be immediately relevant to him. He must be able to talk with his sources of information, to exercise his own initative, extend his own choices, control his own searches, change his own mind, and set his own values. In contrast with mass media broadcasting, the information system must offer each man, at his own time and place and in his own manner, private access to any pertinent part of the total information resource. And access should be given to information in any medium, whether book, film, television, or phonorecord, at appropriate levels of urgency and sophistication.

Man always has used information, and since primitive times he has made records of it. By now the records save the most part of all that men have known. Societies that use that knowledge will continue to mature; those that do now will regress. There is no health, economic welfare, national security, or personal fulfillment in ignorance of what centuries of good men have already learned.

UNMET NEEDS FOR INFORMATION

Existing library and information services have channeled growing proportions of the information resource to larger and more varied segments of the populace. The scholarly community probably has been best served, and public libraries have reached far into rural communities. Programs for the socially underprivileged and physically handicapped are now achieving some success. Yet in general, existing information services are still deficient in fundamental ways that deny people at many levels of society access to major information resources.

The information resource is underutilized, in the sense, first, that it has not yet been comprehensively collected and controlled and second, that important parts of it are neither known to nor used to the best advantage by many people. Channels to the information resource are not yet fully open through many libraries and information centers.

There are staggering inequities in the sources of information that are available to people in sparsely populated, economically depressed, or educationally deprived communities, as compared with people in well-to-do, middle- and upper-class, metropolitan communities. This is true of teachers, doctors, lawyers, and engineers, as well as the lay public. For many segments of society, there is no information agency close at hand; the available agencies are weak, or their potential users are unaware of their existence.

Existing libraries and information centers are often unable to provide relevant responses and requests for aid and fail to communicate with many readers in appropriate terms. The problem exists not only in libraries serving the underprivileged but also in those serving communities of scholars.

The personal and human element is often lacking or weak, especially when new technologies are employed. The total information resource is not interpreted for the reader in terms that he can understand and apply to his own problems. Some of the reasons for these failures may be: (a) lack of awareness, (b) economic and political constraints, (c) provincialism and vested interest, and (d) gaps or overlapping jurisdictions among service agencies.

In all parts of this nation, among all ethnic groups, and at all educational and economic levels, there are failures in access to information. Services are too frequently unresponsive, slow, undiscriminating, or based on insufficient collection. They are sometimes insensitive to the wide range of possible responses to particular needs, as when information is needed (now, tomorrow, next week, or when possible), the format in which it is desired (expendable or on loan, graphic, audio, or visual), the level of sophistication (elementary, scholarly), and the access level (select list, abstracts, extensive bibliography, full text) that are appropriate.

In such ways the library or information center often fails, but seldom does it know how badly it fails. The extent to which information needs are in fact being met is suspected more than documented. A social "bridge" is needed to those persons who are unaware of their own need for information, do now know what information exists, or do not know where to go for it.

The assessment of needs for information and of the degree to which present services meet these needs could be analyzed and described by means of a two-variable matrix identifying class of user and type of information function or use. Classes of users might include administrators, scientists, students, educators, professional practitioners, and the "general public." Types of function might include problem-solving, personal interest, education/training, and research. For each user/function one might evaluate, first, apparent needs and second, the present degree of fulfillment of those needs.

The evaluation of each variable might be represented on scales of quality, comprehensiveness, urgency, and availability. For example, need of educators for quality of research information might be rated high but quality of information services, low, which would suggest improvement in services.

The urgency of information needs might be rated as moderate, as might also be the service schedules, which would suggest no need for improvement. Such an analysis of information needs and services with respect to all classes of readers and information uses could help to identify and describe the specific weaknesses of existing information services.

The shortcomings of existing processes for information transfer emphasize that there is indeed a need for improvement. It is equally clear that primary responsibility for providing information will continue to rest with the many agencies and institutions charged with serving individuals directly — libraries of all kinds, broadcasting and television stations, and specialized information centers. These are the true terminals of the nation's information system, and each must be strong, well managed, responsive, and innovative.

THE CHALLENGE OF NEW SYSTEMS

The prospect of providing an additional powerful capability for each of these system components to expand resources and increase service capacity is an attractive one from both the managerial viewpoint and from the prospect of the community of users. A growing, more educated, and more intellectually demanding population coupled with recent advances in technology have given an old and established network concept a new and dramatically promising appeal for many groups of users and for many individuals professionally involved in the complex process of safeguarding and promoting the use of society's most important asset.

Simply acknowledging shortcomings in the process of information distribution is perhaps all that is necessary to justify development and extension of the full range of network techniques so that they might be available to the terminal agencies when they can serve a useful purpose. But the real case grows from another need. It is quality, not quantity, that is in short supply — quality of information, quality of insight. The challenge facing all persons concerned with processes that involve the human record is to protect and promote the best, not the most. Individuals can now have access to the best information — organized in better ways and presented in better forms. Ideally, obstacles of location, economic condition, and lack of knowledge about knowledge can be controlled, and the possibility of the good driving out the bad can be improved. Linking primary sources can reduce redundancy among institutions, stimulate and challenge responsible professionals, and provide one more way to amplify the impact of the best records of discovery and the most exciting kinds of human creation.

The technology — mechanical, electronic, and methodological — that now takes the concept of sophisticated networks possible is only a means to an end. It makes a promise of improved human communication possible, but it does not make that promise real.

Any kind of organizational arrangement must have a goal though this goal need not be fully attainable. Nor is it always susceptible to ultimate justification. It represents a consensus of what those involved in the organized activity consider desirable. If such a goal were articulated, its aim would be to have the several libraries and information systems of the nation, not individually but collectively, provide each citizen with the information he wants, when he wants it, and to do so at a cost sufficiently reasonable to be borne willingly by organized society. This is an ideal, of course, but it is a practical, working ideal.

The United States should work toward a time when the availability of knowledge will not be severely limited by the ability of certain individuals to pay for it, by the fortunes of geographical location, or by associational membership. Knowledge should be treated as a universe, and availability of knowledge should be considered in relation to the total needs of all the individuals and institutions which make up the nation.

There are at least three basic requirements for the system which distributes knowledge and information: (1) The individual should be able to find out where materials are stored; (2) he should be able to receive the knowledge or information he needs once he himself has made that decision; and (3) the form, place, and time of delivery should be suited to his needs, assuming that the resource and techniques are available.

Libraries and other information collection centers cannot achieve these goals on a national scale without cooperation. Cooperation cannot have its full impact without telecommunications and automation. It should be added immediately that this Group has little idea at this time of the degree to which networks and automation can become workable and prove useful. Furthermore, there are many basic needs in addition to networking which must be met, e.g., needs for financing, organization management, and training, which must not be discounted. Nevertheless, cooperation support by technology is a vital ingredient of any general plan such as we have envisaged.

It is physically impossible to provide the cumulative record of man to every human neighborhood in the country. This is the single fact on which a justification for cooperation and networks is based.

Because it carries the promise of extending the availability of information, of bringing the user closer to stores of information, telecommunications must be seriously considered as a means of communication between centers of storage and distribution. Delivery of voice information by telephones to homes in the U.S. is commonplace. However, no electronic method has been applied generally for delivery of printed and graphic information to the home on demand. And even industry is only beginning to use telecommunications information delivery systems for support in decisionmaking.

How can we separate the opportunities of the future from those of the present? The greatest need at this time of the library and information science community is to make a decision to apply networking if it so chooses.

The choice for any particular library is not whether the general concept of technologically supported exchange is desirable but whether a particular arrangement provides benefits that strengthen the service without negative side effects offsetting these benefits.

CONCLUSIONS AND RECOMMENDED ACTION

The greatest need at the moment, therefore, is organization. The capability is needed for drawing together those diverse elements and shaping the many policies which go into a network system, for making judgments as to efficiency and effectiveness of practice, and for providing libraries and other information services opportunities for choosing specific services.

Network-supported cooperation cannot be imposed on the existing system. It will have to evolve out of the existing system and preserve the freedom of choice and local autonomy which allows individual libraries and information services to adapt themselves to the needs of their constituency.

It is essential that networking develop out of the existing system. A national effort (1) should be a composite of many efforts and systems, (2) should be based on successful experience, (3) should continue to be increasingly personal, (4) should extend the choices available to individuals (5) should be responsive to change, and (6) must work.

There is a danger in drift. The rapid increase in the publication rate, the rising need and demand for education, and the increased scope and tempo of change are such that the independent library with only a distant relationship to fellow institutions is not able to serve its local constituency well. And a collection of such institutions will not serve the nation and its citizens well.

A carefully constructed plan of network development is needed. Short-term and long-term actions should be scheduled, and an organized effort sufficient to ensure implementation should be initiated. Specifically:

A. Promote a receptive environment for network development.

1. The general direction of government and private development policy should support, promote, and encourage cooperative efforts between organizations, institutions, and developing networks through:

    a. Freedom of competition and innovation

    b. Maintenance of the widest possible range of options, including the development and operation of new alternative communication systems — public, private, or nonprofit

    c. Unimpeded flow of information without needlessly restrictive communications regulations, copyright, or other government and industrial practices

    d. Technical compatibility for communication among networks, institutions, and individuals by means of translation and/or standardization

    e. Establishment of mechanisms to review development objectives and priorities, and to monitor system performance on a continuing basis.

2.   The professions, industries, and citizens should organize an effective and representative program to increase social concern for improved access to sources of information, to support government and private efforts to this end, and to encourage maximum benefits from the investment.

3.   Federal and other governmental agencies, charged with responsibility for fostering the development of information-handling processes, should assess their progress and extend their efforts to meet established goals.

4.   Nongovernmental agencies concerned with operational aspects of information transfer should expand their efforts and assume the initative to promote national capabilities.

5.   Personal privacy and other human considerations should be protected in the interface with technology, and freedom of access to information without the constraints of censorship should be guaranteeed.

B. Establish an organizational framework.

1.   A "public corporation" along the lines of the Communications Satellite Corporation or the Corporation for Public Broadcasting should be explored as a possible means to stimulate the development of library and information networks to achieve a balance between local autonomy and centralized purpose, direction, and standardization, to provide a versatile mechanism for funding, and to motivate and guide a coordinated program of research and development.

2.   State and local governments should promote the development of networks, including those at present in existence or conceived, or by developing state or regional public corporations.

3.   Organizations operating networks should work toward effective interface with one another.

4.   Professional associations should establish working groups to promote networks and other information system elements. They should assume special responsibility to develop and utilize suitable standards to facilitate interface.

C. Provide financial support.

1.   In order to reflect the pluralistic nature of network organization, financial support should be pluralistic, including the public and private sector as well as foundations. Funding agencies must recognize that the budgets of reference and research libraries are stretched to the limit and that new money is needed for increased extramural services, covering full incremental costs, to enable them to participate in improved information systems.

2.   The federal government, through its agencies (including the proposed Public Corporation), should serve as the major source of financial support for network developments, both (a) directly, by funding a large part of such costs as initial equipment acquisitions, research, development, demonstration and operating costs, and (b) indirectly, through grants or matched fund support of statewide networks or multistate networks.

3.   State governments should pay a substantial portion (the range of support to be dependent on the resource of each state) of the governmental share of network costs including developmental costs, operational funds, and grants-in-aid premised on the development of compatible area wide plans.

4.   A fee structure for services should be considered under arrangements which should not preclude access to information by users.

5.   The library and information science community should promote free or low-cost telecommunication rates for educational purposes as a dividend for taxpayer investment in the development of communications technology.

D. Promote the development of professional expertise and technical skills.

1.   The skills, knowledge, and insights required in network organization and administration must be identified. The National Commission on Libraries and Information Science, professional associations such as ALA and ASIS, and the U.S. Office of Education should take appropriate steps to this end. This effort should include representatives of all interested groups and should address itself to basic professional education, continuing education, and the training of paraprofessionals, taking cognizance of the various staffing requirements of network operation.

2.   Current curricula of library and information science schools should result in the preparation of

guidelines for alternate experimental courses and multidisciplinary curricula. Subsequent demonstrations (as previously indicated), conducted in library and information science schools, will test the guidelines.

E. Undertake research to understand network needs and assess performance.

1. All research should take account of the findings of relevant current and completed research.

2. A nationwide descriptive inventory of networks should be prepared.

3. The performance of existing networks should be assessed in the context of their mission and the elements determining success and/or failure identified.

4. A continuing national assessment should be made of major unsatisfied information needs according to user category in order to identify those needs that might properly be met by networks.

5. A scientific analysis of costs and performance potential of alternative methods of providing information should be made.

6. A study should be made of the content and physical form of recorded information in order to identify areas of redundancy and duplication.

7. A multidiscipline group with strong representation from urban libraries should make a major study of the implications for libraries of the wired city cable systems. Such a study should be pursued in enough depth and be given wide enough dissemination to perform a function in national and local wired city decisionmaking proceedings.

8. Libraries, including the three national libraries, should be encouraged to mount network demonstrations which might be linked to pending applications before the Federal Communications Commission for authorization to private industry to launch communications satellites. Demonstrations of library and information network services on publicly owned and operated satellites also would be desirable.

Interlibrary Cooperation, Interlibrary Communications, and Information Networks—Explanation and Definition

R. C. Swank

The intent of this paper is to state the principal issues and parameters of concern at this Conference on Interlibrary Communications and Information Networks. As I conceive my task, I should map the entire field of our concerns and describe its topography in general terms. I should not analyze specific problem areas, offer solutions, or recommend plans for action; these are the tasks of the papers that follow.

DEFINITIONS

I will begin with definitions of information and communications networks. In my review of the literature, I found the most help in the publications of Carl Overhage, Joseph Becker, and Launor Carter.

Overhage identified five different contexts in which the term "networks" is used.[1] The first is *science literature,* as in networks of situation-linked papers. The second is *organization structures,* as in the ERIC clearinghouses. The third is *cooperative arrangements,* as in interlibrary loans. The fourth is *communications systems,* as in press wire services. And the fifth is *computer-communications systems,* as in the NASA Recon system. Overhage explains that while networks of scientific literature, of organizational structures, and of libraries are all important, none specifically characterizes the communications links to be used. The primary topic of his review of "information networks" was networks of communications and of computer-communications systems which do specify the use of electric signal transmission. For the purpose of his paper, therefore, he adopted the following definition: "...when these [communications] channels are used for the transfer of certain categories of information they are customarily said to constitute an *information network.* In this usage...the essential feature of an information network is the utilization of a set of communications channels through which the information is transferred by electric signals."[2]

Becker and Olsen also noted the varieties of contexts in which the term "network" is used. They then divided the definitions, first by *class of equipment,* as in telephone, teletype, facsimile, and computer networks; second by *form of data,* as in digital, audio, video, and film networks; and third by *functions,* as in financial, library, education, and management networks. The authors continued: "Information networks include some combination of the above three elements, which when coupled with a communications system, provide the desired pattern of information

exchange."[3] The main concepts of an automated information network and they pointed out that none yet existed—would be:

1. *Formal organization:* Many units sharing a common information purpose recognize the value of group affiliation and enter into a compact.

2. *Communications:* The network includes circuits that can rapidly interconnect dispersed points.

3. *Bidirectional operation:* Information may move in either direction, and provision is made for each network participant to send as well as to receive.

4. *A directory and switching capability:* A directory look-up system enables a participant to identify the unit most able to satisfy a particular request. A switching center then routes messages to this unit over the optimum communications path.[4]

Becker and Olsen then noted that the word "network" also is widely applied to"...the banding together of existing information systems into some type of communications cooperative, e.g., referral centers, information analysis centers, industrial departments, airline ticket offices, and police precincts, in order to satisfy a functional goal."[5]

Carter took a somewhat different line in that he included the terms "data base" and "remote users" in his definition:

An information network, or a library network, I think, has the following characteristics. First we have two or more nodes, or centers of intercommunication and of data bases. One node or center, by itself, is not a network.... The nodes are interconnected and are able to use each other's data bases, and that is very important. Each node has a unique data base or capability—in terms of a bibliographical apparatus, in terms of unique holdings, in terms of the power of the computer center—and each one is able to call upon the others for assistance. You have nodes, then, which are interconnected by communications, and that is my second point. Third, each node in this system has remote users—the users are quite separated from the nodal center. Nodes in, say, Olympia, Bellingham, Hoquiam, Vancouver, Spokane, etc., could all be switched more or less automatically to a node in, say, Seattle or some other place. Those, then, are the three characteristics I think of a network as having: It has nodes, with a unique data base at each node; it is of course electronically switchable and has high-speed communications; and it has remote users.[6]

For the purpose of balance, let me add a definition that I used in 1967 with reference not to any particular class of communications equipment or type of data but to what Becker and Olsen called the "banding together of existing information systems"—in this case libraries and information centers.

The network concept includes the development of cooperative systems of libraries on geographical, subject, or other lines, each with some kind of center that not only coordinates the internal activities of the system but also serves as the system's outlet to, and inlet from, the centers of other systems. The concept is also hierarchical in that the centers of smaller systems are channels to centers of larger networks at state, national, and even international levels. A familiar analogy is the telephone service, in which local systems were first coordinated and then hooked up into national and international networks.[7]

Overhage, Becker and Olsen, and Carter, while acknowledging the importance of networks of existing library and information systems, all defined information networks in the modern sense as utilizing communications by electronic signal transmission. This may be appropriate as an ideal but there are two reasons why I do not think that we should limit our discussions to networks that specify particular types of communications channels. First, many of the evolving networks of existing library and information systems tend toward that ideal. In mixed ways, and in varying degrees, they do use electric signal communications through telephones, teletype, and sometimes computer applications. Second, overemphasis on the communications technology sometimes obscures other essential components of information services that are not dependent, strictly speaking, upon any particular technology. For example, Becker and Olsen included "a directory look-up system" in their definition. This to me is an understatement of the central problem of the intellectual organization of documents and data—a problem that grows more and more crucial as information systems are elaborated into networks. Carter included the "data base" in his definition, and this is an abstraction of the tremendous problems of the selection, acquisition, and purging of the information resources to which access is the very reason for networks. Carter also included "remote users," which leads us again into the maze of user studies—the audiences to which network services should be addressed and the needs to be met. The technology changes and grows more powerful, but these problems remain essentially unchanged. The more widely our networks spread, the greater should be our concern about these

indispensable components of all library and other information services.

I like to think of library and other information services as extensions of the home, the office, or the personal library. There a man collects his books, journals, and data files according to his own wishes. When he has so much that he cannot readily find what he wants, he begins to organize his collections—to arrange them systematically on shelves and in file drawers, and to make catalogs and indexes. The breadth and variety of the data bases that are accessible to him are then extended stage by stage through local libraries, information centers, and other communications channels to regional systems and national networks until he ideally should have the world's knowledge at his finger tips. The extensions of his data base are accompanied by corresponding extensions of his powers of analysis through increasingly more comprehensive and sensitive schemes for the intellectual organization of that knowledge. The methods by which he can get his hands on the desired materials—that is, gain physical access—are similarly extended. To accomplish these extensions, larger organizational units of service are created, and new technologies are brought to bear upon the data bases, the schemes of intellectual access, and the methods of physical access. At every stage along the way there is a shifting balance between what the user does for himself and what the system does for him. There are trade-offs between values gained and values lost, as well as between cost and effectiveness. But the perfect information network would be the one that took us full circle to the personal library again—making the world's knowledge an extension of the user's private collection, giving him intellectual access to the whole of it at home, and putting copies of anything he wants on his own desk.

In this perspective, the modern information network would be new and different primarily in its technological power to extend tremendously a set of elemental functions that started at home, that are running the gamut of library and information systems and networks, and that ought sometime to end at home. For present purposes, let me define an information network as having these characteristics:

1. *Information resources* — collections of documents or data in whatever medium; the data bases; the input

2. *Readers or users* — usually remote from the main sources of information

3. *Schemes for the intellectual organization of documents or data* — as directories for use by readers or users

4. *Methods for the delivery of resources* to readers or users—the output

5. *Formal organization* — of cooperating or contracting formations, representing different data bases and/or groups of users

6.   *Bidirectional communications networks* — preferably through high-speed, long-distance electrical signal transmission with switching capabilities and computer hook-ups.

These are the broad areas of concern at this Conference, and I will organize the rest of this paper around them.

THE INFORMATION RESOURCE

I tried once before to say in the most general terms what this commodity, the information resource, is as it relates to the library and information needs of society.[8] What is it that we collect, store, organize, and disseminate? We may think of books, journals, or other texts; of audio or visual documents; or of smaller units of information or data that can be separately manipulated, as by a computer. All of these forms of record comprise parts of the information resource, but it is helpful to perceive that recorded resources are still only a part of a society's general cultural resource consisting of an accumulation of concepts, habits, skills, arts, instruments, institutions, etc., handed down and built upon by each generation. What is worth remembering comes down to us through many channels—parents, teachers, and friends; churches and other social institutions; manners and customs; folk tales and arts; and radio and television channels. In advanced societies a substantial part of the culture also comes down to us in recorded forms of one kind or another, and this is the part that concerns information networks.

I put the matter this way in order to emphasize the crucial role that recorded knowledge plays in advanced societies. Let us hypothesize that the more advanced the society, or the greater the totality of learning, the greater is the dependence upon the record for access to that learning. We can hypothesize further that no society can advance beyond a certain point without effective access to its collective memory of record, or conversely, that an advanced society that loses control of the record will regress. In this perspective, modern information networks might be seen as a late high refinement of societies that depend increasingly upon recorded information for their further advancement.

This basic concern about the social significance of information in recorded form, however, should not be misconstrued as requiring the preservation of the totality of recorded information. A great deal of learning, whether recorded or not, has deservedly been forgotten throughout history, and the act of recording does not of itself make a piece of learning more deserving of preservation. There is a concern, then, about the problem of completeness. The goal of complete coverage of foreign materials of scholarly interest is found in the Farmington Plan and the Shared Cataloging Program under Title IIC of the Higher Education Act.[9] A report of the Committee on Scientific and Technical Information, COSATI, urged that it be "...the Federal Government's responsibility to insure that there exists within the United States at least one accessible copy of each significant publication of world-wide scientific and technical literature."[10] These are reasonably qualified goals, far short of the totality of recorded information. Carter seriously questioned the need of anyone, including scholars, to know the holdings of every library in the country and suggested that information networks be confined to selected research libraries. A nationally integrated computer network might not be required at all, except in certain discipline-oriented fields.[11]

The further problem of preserving the totality of unrefined data in recorded form was dramatically illustrated by James Fava in his account of the massive amounts of raw data accumulated by the space programs.[12] On the one hand, as in archival administration, large packages of related data might have to be calendared as a whole; on the other hand, a line might have to be drawn somewhere between the potentially infinite floods of raw data and the generalizable products of that data after compacting, editing, correcting, merging, and interpreting. Total access to uninterpreted data appears to be a vastly greater chimera than that to unevaluated publications. But still, within narrowly specialized communities of scholars, continuing access to raw data for the purpose of reanalysis and reinterpretation could be essential until better data are produced.

There is the further concern that the information resource, as we should be viewing it, includes documents, or records, in all media.[13] Printed documents, yes, but also audio records, as in discs and tapes; video records, as in films, slides, and tapes; and digital records, as in cores, tapes, and discs. The recording media are becoming increasingly varied through technological extensions of the written word, pictures, and sounds. We need to ensure that information networks of the future are flexible enough to embrace any kind of record that may be useful to society.

Here are three major concerns, then, about the information resource:

1.   The general nature and significance of the recorded information resource to society

2.   The completeness with which the information resource can be usefully acquired and stored for future access through information networks

3.   The varieties of recording media that are utilized as information resources by information networks.

USERS

In talking about the users of information network services, we are concerned primarily with the increasing numbers of users and the growing varieties of their needs, the rights of users to equal access to information services (including realistic access at local points of service), the categories of users to be served, and the general problem of user studies.

I already have noted the growing dependence of advanced societies upon their collective memories of record. Individuals, too, can carry only a limited portion of the world's knowledge in mind even in narrow specializations. The larger the number of people and the greater their dependence upon the record, the greater the burden upon information services. Data on the number of users of science and technology data and documents were published by System Development Corporation, SDC.[14] Similar data should be developed about users in other fields. There is real concern about the ability of future information networks to cope with the demands that will be made upon them. Certainly the present information systems are already in trouble.

Further demands upon information networks, however, could be influenced as much by the democratization of information services as by increasing numbers of special categories of users. In some societies, access to libraries has been a privilege reserved for an educated elite, those who have earned or inherited the privilege, who bear the social responsibilities, and who hold the power. More recently, access to information has been claimed as the right of Everyman for purposes of universal enlightenment, regardless of social class, ability, or responsibility. In Western concepts of democracy, power resides not with a privileged elite but with an educated and informed populace. One could go a step further and postulate that in advanced, technological societies, information becomes not just a privilege or a right but a necessity for essential social and national purposes. A sense of national urgency now pervades many library and information programs not only in the United States but also in certain developing countries where the goal may not be so much to foster individual rights as to train the manpower required for the achievement of national goals, such as health, economic welfare, and security under threat of war. But whether because of individual rights or national imperatives, information should be as widely available as possible to all the people.

One of the goals of library and information networks, therefore, should be more realistic and effective access to information resources for every citizen.[15] Weinstock set a similar goal for special libraries: "Every library should provide every patron with any published information required."[16] As in the acquisition of the total information resource, the ultimate goal probably never can be reached. Not all parts of the total resource probably ever could be made immediately accessible to everyone, but there is a continuum along which each man's opportunity can be measured.

The principle of equality of access to information everywhere raises some real problems. People are accustomed to thinking of local library and information centers as more or less self-sufficient resources to satisfy local needs, and many centers reflect those needs with remarkable sensitivity. But we are still stuck with the notion that the need varies with numbers of people or with the size and wealth of communities. Smaller, poorer communities are presumed to need less; larger, richer communities are presumed to need more. There are certainly valid differences among community needs on the basis of subject interests and emphases, but the principle of "books per capita" should be persuasively investigated. The college freshman, the engineer, the school teacher, the doctor, and the business man in rural, North-Mountain California have no less need, as individuals, of the total resource than do their counterparts in the San Francisco-Bay Area. The basis of need is not political, geographic, demographic, or economic; it is personal. The need finds expression not simply as a relationship between a community and its locally supported library but as one between the

individual, wherever he may be, and the total information resource, wherever it may be.

For people everywhere, moreover, realistic and effective access should mean their ability to discover, at any local point of contact with the information network, what books and information are available from the network, and then to get prompt delivery, also at the point of contact. Here again the ideal never may be fully achievable, but progress could be made along this continuum by means of computer and communications applications to the dissemination of bibliographical information on the one hand and to document delivery on the other.

The existing inequities of realistic access to information throughout the country are staggering,[17] and they merit our most serious study. They involve, of course, many categories of users. Our concern is not only with scientists, engineers, and professionals in other critical fields but also with the lay public, including the underprivileged. We are concerned with nonusers of information as well as with users. We are concerned with education,[18] business, and recreation as well as with research.

For all these categories of users, a further concern is the paucity of data about their information problems and needs. A careful analysis of user studies in the fields of science and technology by SDC revealed a number of useful recent studies but also pointed out the limitations of most of them.[19] Almost all the studies used questionnaires and interviews to ask scientists what they think or say they need at some point of time. One wonders if other methodologies could be developed to assess the needs of scholars, such as, say, an analysis of a field of scholarship itself, its goals, the types of research done, the kinds of data used and the methodologies of their use, the sources of data, and so on. More studies also are needed of other categories of users, such as suburban communities, public schools, rural neighborhoods, small business organizations, and ghettos. Such studies should supply criteria for the design and the evaluation of information networks.

The major concerns, then, in the area of users include:

4. The growth in numbers of users and in the varieties of their information needs

5. Equality of access by individual users to information resources everywhere, including realistic and effective service at local points of contact with the information network; the inequalities of existing access

6. The categories of users and the range of purposes that information networks should serve

7. User studies of the various kinds of readers to be served, as criteria for the design and evaluation of information networks.

INTELLECTUAL ACCESS

The next broad area of concern is intellectual access to documents and data or, in conventional library terminology, bibliographical organization. I will not give much space to this area because of its great complexity, but it is, I believe, the really unique, gut problem of any library or information service. The communications and computer technologies for information network development are already at hand, but the logical means of organizing the information resource for discriminating access are not. The intellectual problems far outweigh the technological.

One way to express this problem is to postulate a direct relationship between the size of the data base and the selectivity required in its intellectual organization through catalogs, indexes, bibliographies, or other schemes. The larger and more varied the information resource to which access is desired, and the greater the numbers and heterogeneity of users who need access, the more refined, sensitive, flexible, and discriminating must be the schemes of intellectual organization. These schemes are like sieves that sort huge quantities of grossly related things into sequentially smaller quantities of more closely related things until what is pertinent to a special need is sifted out. The Library of Congress classification and the dictionary catalog are already tremendously complex sets of sieves, but the schemes that would be needed to sift out for every man, everywhere, the few materials wanted from a nationally integrated network of the total information resource are still almost unthinkable.

This problem, it appears, would be exaggerated by mechanized retrieval systems unless highly reactive, or interactive, schemes became practicable. Our traditional manual schemes permit a user to enter and reenter the system at different points, to narrow or broaden his search strategies, to browse, and to select as many or as few references as he wants. A similar capability must be built into mechanized systems, and indeed, impressive progress already has been made. But there are still bottlenecks in the logic of the structure of very large files and in the programs for reorganizing stored information in response to the differing and changing needs of users.[20]

The reactive process, moreover, must occur where the user is—again, at his local contact with the information network—either by means of manually searched catalogs produced by machine for distribution to local service points or by means of direct interrogation of computer files.

There is a plethora of problems behind these broad concerns: the concepts and terms around which documents and data are organized, and the derivation of those concepts and terms; their arrangement for speedy access; the rules by which documents are entered under them or by which they are assigned to documents; and so on. Automatic associative indexing and question-answering systems are possibilities but still in the future for large-scale applications. Major insights into the logical problems of information organization will be required before the network capabilities of electric signal transmission can be fully exploited.

Our concerns here are primarily:

8. The further refinement of existing schemes, or the creation of new and more sensitive ones, for intellectual access to the hugely augmented information resources that will be available through information networks

9. In particular, the development of reactive, flexible, mechanized retrieval systems that simulate the user's interchange with manual systems.

PHYSICAL ACCESS

By physical access I mean the getting of copies, in whatever form, of the documents or data selected through the process of intellectual access. Our concern is that the information network be able to supply copies, within reasonable periods of time, for users who want them. I suspect that, on the whole, this is a much less critical concern than intellectual access. Many users might want only the bibliographical references or abstracts, and others might be in no great hurry for the full texts. But the modern information network should have as one of its goals the prompt location of desired documents or data anywhere in the country and the delivery of some of them, or parts of them, by such means as long-distance facsimile transmission, computer print-out, or CRT display, as well as by conventional interlibrary loan. The potentially huge volume of traffic along these delivery lines might necessitate rigorous priorities.

In future fully automated networks, physical access might form a single continuum with intellectual access. A reactive system of intellectual access might be able to display not only conventional bibliographical references but also annotations, abstracts, and selected segments of the text (as microfilms are scanned); then, desired parts of the work, or the whole of it, could be printed out. The potential spectrum of representation of a document extends from brief citation to full text. For a long while, however, the practicable methods of physical access appear likely to remain separate from those of intellectual access and to employ different kinds of equipment.

Our main concern is:

10. The prompt location of desired documents or data anywhere in the country and the delivery of copies, within appropriate periods of time, to users at local outlets of the network.

FORMAL ORGANIZATION

The preceding areas were mainly related to objective concerns—the why, the who, and the what of information networks. I now turn to the operating agencies that comprise service systems and networks, and the organizational structures that bind them together. This is a large, practical area that, together with technological concerns, will probably dominate the discussions at this Conference.

To Becker and Olsen, a formal network organization occurs when "...many units sharing a common information purpose recognize the value of group affiliation and enter into a compact."[21] I would add that such organizations often are conceived as having hierarchical levels of cooperating units and affiliations. From any local service point, the search for documents and data might rise, if need be, through several layers of cooperating information systems—local, regional, national, or even international—each system at each level having its own communications center or node. The network idea, in a sense, is the full, modern extension of a drive that began many decades ago to organize larger units of public library service—a drive that has resulted in county, regional, and to a certain extent, statewide public library systems. Characteristically, such organizations consist of centers or nodes of local service that are then affiliated under second-level centers or nodes with higher switching capabilities, and so on. Theoretically, the ultimate national network should have some sort of super-node at the apex of the hierarchy.

One major concern, then, is the conformation of such hierarchical organizations. What, for example, would be the optimum size of systems at each level of the network? What would be the best balance between resources that are locally available from any particular node and those that must be sought through nodes at higher levels? What levels of local sufficiency would be most cost-effective, given varying levels of back-up capability? For network purposes, how should a region be defined? What would be the functions of a regional center or node? Under what circumstances should requests for service by-pass regional or other immediate nodes and proceed directly to coordinate or higher nodes? At what levels of centralization should certain technical processes occur, such as accounting, circulation control, and the production of union lists? There has been a great deal of pragmatic experience with these and similar concerns, but the general conformation of network organizations has, to my knowledge, received very little systematic study.

More attention has been paid to the kinds of formations that should be banded together. Separate cooperative systems may be formed by type of library or information center, such as public, academic, or special libraries; by form or medium of record, such as technical reports, motion picture films, or journals; or by discipline, such as medical, agricultural, or chemical information services. Title III of the Library Service and Construction Act promotes cooperation among all types of libraries. Carter has argued that national networks might be developed most usefully along subject lines.[22] I have argued for mixed networks of geographical systems, embracing public, school, and small college libraries, with separate subject systems of special libraries, and with our great university and research libraries backing up all on a broad contractual basis.[23] The geographical boundaries of public and subject systems might differ greatly. Many patterns are possible; perhaps no consistent pattern is needed as long as the nodes of each system are in communication with each other so that public systems may be served also by subject systems, subject systems by media systems, and so on. The real-life mosaic of special interest systems that will comprise the information network of the future could be very complex indeed.

Another problem is the nature of the compacts that bind governmental units, public and private institutions, and business and industrial organizations together for the common purpose of sharing information. What legal bases have been or could be used for financial and service agreements? What is offered, what is received, and by what accounting?

More fundamental is the problem of overall responsibility for and control of information networks, particularly at the national level. Some sort of central coordination, either by a federal agency or by a national commission, seems needed.[24]

The federal and state governments have a basic responsibility for the equalization of information service opportunities and a financial interest in the performance and promise of information networks.[25] Yet the contributions and interests of the private sector must be respected and protected. No satisfactory formula has been evolved yet for the allocation of these responsibilities, but some observers believe still that modern information networks of national scope are not likely to be built until the federal government has been persuaded to finance them.[26]

Planning at the national level is certainly essential. In the last two decades, wave after wave of national document-handling plans have been advanced by various agencies. Fifteen of the best known plans were reviewed by SDC.[27] Most of them concentrated on the organizational aspects of the national information problem. Few dealt with the acquisition of resources; the needs of users were generally overlooked; relatively little attention was paid to technical problems; and still less attention, perhaps, was devoted to currently operating library systems.

The experience of existing library and information systems should not, I think, be neglected in the design of national networks. SDC analyzed a selection of federal and nonfederal libraries; information analysis centers; publication, announcement, and distribution groups; document generators/users; and administration, policy, and support groups in the fields of science and technology.[28] This analysis is impressive, and similar studies of formations in other fields would be most helpful. Also helpful would be equally thorough studies of the evolving patterns of cooperative systems and networks. Some surveys have been made,[29] and these are revealing even though they are often more discursive than systematic.

The national planners often would impose entirely new networks from above on the assumption that the tortuously evolving efforts from below have failed. The revolutionary tends to by-pass due process. The evolutionary prefers to build upon existing institutions, which are, for better or worse, the only operational ones we know. Perhaps both approaches are needed—planning from above and building from below—each with full appreciation of the other.

In support of the evolutionary approach, certain points can be made. This is the real-life world of information service—the best yet. A national document system that tried to ignore it might wash down the drain because of the absence of grass-roots delivery facilities. The understructure of local facilities, educated and experienced staff, and even informed readers is indispensable. The proof of any network is the goods actually delivered to people who understand what they can ask for from staff who know how to get it through well-developed organizations at the local level.

In support of national planning, certain other points can be made. Existing institutions are bound by tradition and motivated by self-defense. They eschew new ideas and technologies that disturb their sense of security and success. They fail to face the future. The only way to get on with the business is to create *de novo* new systems based on broader concepts that exploit more advanced technologies.

There is some truth, I suggest, in both positions, but not the whole truth in either. Within the realistic economic and social constraints of operating library and information services, new ideas and technologies have, in fact, been readily espoused. But the more revolutionary ideas and technologies that are not achievable yet within these constraints have been understandably resisted. Revolutionary approaches might be possible, but only, and then not likely, by the intervention of such a *deus ex machina* as the federal government.

So, our areas of concern under the rubric of formal organization include:

11. The conformation of network structures; the optimum size of systems at each level; the balance between local and back-up resources; centralized processing; and so on

12. The kinds of information agencies to be formed into systems; geographical, type of library, media, and subject systems; the linking of mixed systems into networks

13. The compacts that bind information agencies together into systems; financial and service agreements

14. Responsibility for and control of information networks; contributions of the governmental and private sectors; the federal government and national network development

15. Planning for national networks; the need of new national structures

16. Evolution of existing cooperative systems and networks; the importance of building upon operational experience.

THE NEW TECHNOLOGIES

Earlier in this paper I noted that the modern information network would be new and different primarily in its technological power to extend tremendously a set of elemental functions that started in the personal, home library. These extensions of power should enable us to amass larger data bases without filling miles and miles of book shelves, to search them more deeply without thumbing millions of catalog cards, and to obtain copies of documents without traveling across the country or sending for them by mail. Telecommunications and computers, in particular, are magnificent tools that should help us in our trade as the hammer helps the carpenter.

There are many kinds of new technological developments in such fields as document miniaturization and reprography, printing, and audio and visual techniques—all of which are of general interest to us. But for network development our primary concerns are telecommunications and computers. These are the particular tools that encourage us to plan toward national information networks that might help us realize the century-old dream of interlibrary cooperation. It is the potential power of their application to information services that has justified this Conference.

Becker gave us a brief description of modern telecommunications devices, classified by type of signal (audio, digital, and video) and by signal carriers (telephone lines, radio broadcasting, coaxial cable, microwave, and communications satellites).[30] For the technological layman, like myself, he also reviewed in simple terms the history and significance of the computer interface with communications. He described the increasing capacities of telephone lines; the advent of wideband facilities that will easily accommodate the language of the TV camera, the facsimile scanner, the teletype machine, and the computer; the role of switching stations; and the nature and potentialities of satellites. He then illustrated the use of communications for remote access to computer-manipulated data bases, including audio as well as digital messages.[31] The wedding of on-line computers with communications networks and remote user terminals is the key to expanding information services through network development.

It would be presumptuous of me to undertake any discussion of these technological developments. The latest developments were covered by Overhage in the 1969 *Annual Review*.[32] Taking my cues partly from him, I will outline briefly the following major areas of our concern:

There is first the general need for the further development of communications and computing capabilities as they relate specifically to large-scale document and data handling systems. I refer particularly to storage capacities, reactive retrieval systems, and high-speed, high data-rate, low-cost communications channels.

Second is the need of further applications to operating information systems at various levels, from relatively simple teletype and facsimile transmission through computer-communications configurations. Such experiments should certainly include mixed systems that might be based, for example, partly on computers, partly on microforms of one kind or another, and partly on conventional texts. A "pure" computer-communications network might never be technically or economically feasible in the field of information services. The most fruitful immediate computer applications appear to be in the area of intellectual access to, or bibliographical organization of, documents and data.

A third broad problem is the compatibility of machine systems. The difficulties of arriving at standards and formats that can be used for the transfer of information between units of a cooperative system or network have been well demonstrated by the MARC project. Recent efforts to reach agreements and guidelines were reviewed by Overhage in his *Annual Review* chapter. A distinction should be drawn, I think, between flexibility in local record-keeping and conformity in the transfer of information among the units of a network.

Fourth is the problem of regulation. Existing communications networks are not well suited to information services, partly because of rate structures. High common carrier tariffs and rigid controls over the use of communications utilities work against information network development. The growing interdependence of computers and communications has further complicated the issues of policy and control.

Fifth is copyright, which is a familiar problem with new twists in the computer field. For example, is the copyright law violated when a document is put into a computer data base or when it is displayed? Even the old issues of fair use and office copying are still unresolved. How, then, should the process of modifying texts, manipulating and consolidating their content, and displaying them in new ways be interpreted under the law?

And finally, there is the problem of educating librarians and information specialists, on the one hand, and the user public, on the other, in the nature, operations, and values of modern technological network extensions of familiar library and information services. What should the library and information science schools contribute? What sorts of continuing education programs should be offered? What is the role of in-service training by operating agencies that are engaged in network development? These considerations, again, are major reasons for building gradually upon alert, experimental, existing agencies that can do the necessary educational job.

In summary, then, some broad concerns in this area are:

17. Further development of communications and computing capabilities for large-scale document and data handling operations

18. Further applications to operating information agencies, including experimentation with mixed, as well as pure, information networks

19. The adoption of compatible machine systems, standard formats, languages, etc.

20. The regulation of communications utilities in such ways as to permit their use by information networks in flexible ways at reasonable cost

21. Resolution of copyright restrictions, including those relating to manipulations of texts by computer

22. The education of librarians, information specialists, and the user public in the nature, operation, and values of modern information networks.

CONCLUSION

I have tried to identify and describe the large areas of concern at this Conference. I have dealt lightly with the technological problems and more heavily with the functional problems because I know less about the former and the engineers among us know less about the latter. We will all have to adjust our attitudes toward information services if the networks of the future are ever to be created.

Those, like myself, who have operated existing services will have to revise our conception of the operative information agency. Our conception of institutional responsibility limited primarily to supportive segments of society will have to give way to that of broader social obligations. While each library must attend to the interests of its own clientele, it can minister fully to

those interests only if it recognizes that their range and depth often extend far beyond the resources locally available. The educational, cultural, and technical interests of a local clientele often will be served poorly by protecting the user's access to inadequate local collections at the expense of access to larger, richer reservoirs of the information resource.

The ideal of independent, locally self-sufficient programs must certainly give way to that of dependent participation in nationally sufficient programs. If national information networks were ever to be built, local libraries and information centers would have to be redefined as selective inlets to and outlets from those networks. The specifications, for example, of local acquisition policy would need to be modified to reflect a new balance between resources that, on a cost-effectiveness basis, should be acquired at home and those that should be acquired only upon demand from various levels of network service. If the information networks could ever in fact deliver the goods efficiently and promptly at local service points, the effects upon the nature of local libraries and information agencies would be profound indeed.

I assume, of course, that somewhere higher up in the network hierarchy, the national resource would in fact be acquired and controlled. This is a precarious assumption. Librarians often have pointed out that the cooperative enrichment of local library resources is a condition of useful cooperative service. A poverty of resources can be shared without information networks.

The information and communications engineers among us might revise their conceptions of the nature and role of information networks by paying more attention to the substantive problems of information service. Information networks are not just a technological challenge. For every advance in technological power, there must follow, if not precede, a corresponding advance in the conception of the functions to be advanced. In the world of library and information services, these functions are and always have been the acquisition of information resources, with all the problems of selection, storage, and purging; the intellectual organization of those resource through catalogs, bibliographies, indexes, and lately, computer-based retrieval systems; and the methods of physical delivery of copies of documents and data, all in the service of users whose needs should determine the goals of the service.

I hope that at this Conference, the engineers will listen to the practitioners who work with the information that networks will communicate, as I also hope that the practitioners will grasp the opportunity created by the engineers to pursue further their crucial social mission.

Our commodity, again, is not just documents and pieces of data; it is that growing part of our culture that is recorded and therefore, capable of being saved for recall as needed—our capacity to learn and remember having reached a human limit. The recorded information resource, when adequately organized and communicated, should become one of the greatest utilities of advanced societies.

NOTES

1. Carl F. J. Overhage, "Information networks," in C. A. Cuadra, ed., *Annual review of information science and technology* (Chicago: Britannica, 1969), p.339-44.

2. Ibid., p.339.

3. Joseph Becker and Wallace C. Olsen, "Information Networks," ibid., 1968, p.209-91.

4. Ibid.

5. Ibid.

6. Launor F. Carter, "What are the major national issues in the development of library networks," *News notes of California libraries* 63:406-07 (Fall 1968).

7. R. C. Swank, *Interlibrary cooperation under Title III of the Library Services and Construction Act* (Sacramento: California State Library, 1967), p.51.

8. ...., "Partnerships in California: how can books and information be mobilized for every Californian," *News notes of California libraries* 63:419-28 (Fall 1968).

9. John G. Lorenz, "Networks for knowledge," *Mountain-Plains library quarterly* 14:3-6 (Spring 1969).

10. A. G. Hoshovsky, "COSATI information studies--what results," in *American Society for Information Science, proceedings, vol. 6,* (Westport, Conn.: Greenwood Publishing Corp., 1969), p.402.

11. Launor Carter, "What are the major national issues...," *News notes of California libraries,* p.415-16.

12. James A. Fava, "A framework for future data centers," in *American Society for Information Science, proceedings, vol. 6,* p.417. The data, for example, of one ionospheric experiment is stored on 340,000 linear feet of microfilm.

13. Joseph Becker, "Tomorrow's library service today," *News notes of California libraries* 63:430-31 (Fall 1968).

14. System Development Corporation, *National document-handling systems for science and technology* (New York: Wiley, 1967), p.116-17, 296-98.

15. R. C. Swank, *Interlibrary cooperation under Title III...,* Newsnotes..., p.47.

16. Melvin Weinstock, "Network concepts in scientific and technical libraries," *Special libraries* 58:330 (May-June 1967).

17. For data on California see R. C. Swank, *Interlibrary cooperation under Title III...,* Newsnotes..., p.7-17.

18. George W. Brown et al., *EDUNET; report of the summer study on information networks,* (New York: Wiley, 1967) 440p.

19. System Development Corporation, *National document handling...,* p.102-12.

20. Launor Carter, "What are the major national issues...," *Newsnotes...* p.408, 416; Joseph Becker, "The future of library automation and information networks," in S. R. Salmon, ed., *Library automation; a state of the art review* (Chicago: A.L.A., 1969), p.1-6.

21. Joseph Becker and Wallace Olsen, "Information Networks," *ASIS proceedings,* p.290.

22. Launor Carter, "What are the major national issues...," *Newsnotes...,* p.410-11.

23. R. C. Swank, *Interlibrary cooperation under Title III...,* Newsnotes..., p.61-68.

24. A. G. Hoshovsky, "COSATI...," in *ASIS proceedings* p.403.

25. William G. Colman, "Federal and state financial interest in the performance and promise of library networks," Leon Carnovsky, ed., *Library networks--promise and performance* (Chicago: Univ. of Chicago Pr., 1969), p.99-108.

26. Launor Carter, "What are the major national issues...," *Newsnotes...,* p.416-17.

27. System Development Corporation, *National document handling...,* p.129-89.

28. Ibid., p.7-69.

29. E.g., G. Flint Purdy, "Interrelations among public, school and academic libraries," in Leon Carnovsky, ed. *Library networks...,* p.52-63; and Willian S. Budington, "Interrelations among special libraries," in ibid., p.64-77.

30. Joseph Becker, "Telecommunications primer," *Journal of library automation* 2:48-56 (September 1969).

31. ...., "Tomorrow's library services today," *Newsnotes* p.429-36.

32. C. F. J. Overhage, "Information networks," in C. A. Cuadra, ed., *Annual review...,* p.339-377.

Telecommunication Networks for Libraries and Information Systems: Approaches to Development

John Bystrom

As this was written, President Nixon signed into law S.1519 creating a National Commission on Libraries and Information Science. Under the statute, which incorporated the major recommendations of the National Advisory Commission on Libraries, the federal government will begin to provide central direction to the growth of libraries.

At the same time, reorganization of federal telecommunication management affairs, including the establishment of the new Office of Telecommunication Policy in the Executive Office of the President, gives promise to greater central direction to national telecommunication policy.

The opportunity for coordination and leadership has special importance to the development of information networks. It has been stressed repeatedly that to solve the problems standing in the way of network development greater coordination of the many independent federal efforts is needed. Central planning and management are critical to the ordering of developmental activities which must precede large-scale library and information network operation. The 1970 Conference on Interlibrary Communications and Information Networks provides an excellent opportunity to consider how many independent activities, public and private, may contribute to the growing coherency essential to progress.

PURPOSE AND DEFINITIONS

The focus of this paper will be on the development of telecommunication networking by library and information networks. With the word "development" I mean to include all the processes necessary to broad application and to encompass the necessary social, political, industrial, and professional responses to technological advancement as well as technological innovation itself.

It is important to stress at the very beginning that telecommunications is a means to an end. Its use is to advance the function of the library. Yet libraries are also a means; their function is to serve the individual by linking him to stores of information and ideas.

The telecommunication network, as a means, can produce diametrically opposite results depending on the communication system it serves. By linking broadcast stations it limits already limited choices. When applied to libraries, however, the telecommunications network expands choice and the power of the individual. By making available the material of many libraries, networks can enhance individual opportunity. As Dan Lacy has said very well:

> The ratio of listeners to one speaker, or readers to one writer, have been astronomically increased by the latest generation of social and technical communications...almost alone among the devices of our society in reversing this ratio and linking the single reader or listener or seeker to myriad sources of information, ideas, and inspirations among which he can choose...is the library. It is our one major communication device that deals with an audience as individuals....[1] The purpose for any telecommunication networking of libraries should be to increase the capacity of the individual to call upon the intellectual resources of the centuries.

During the last year we have seen sharp national debate over the processes by which the gatekeepers of the mass media select and limit our impression of events. What has not always been clear is that mass media inherently selects, and we as users are inevitably limited in the number of available viewpoints.

Our expectations of what libraries can do to counter this tendency can only be modest. Nevertheless, the promotion of libraries and their networks represents a tangible way in which government can recognize the right of the individual to have many points of view available.

Before continuing, let me define the term "network" for purposes of this discussion. I hope it is sufficient to use the term in only two ways. Telecommunication network will refer to an operating electrical transmitting system which links two or more points. Telecommunications is defined by the International Telecommunications Union as:

> ...any process that enables a correspondent to pass to one or more given correspondents (telegraphy or telephone) or possible correspondents (broadcasting), information of any nature delivered in any usable form (written or printed matter, fixed or moving pictures, words, music, visible or audible signals, signals controlling the function of mechanisms, etc.) by means of any electro-magnetic system (electrical transmitting by wire, radio transmission, etc.) or a combination of such systems.[2]

A library or information network refers to a cooperative joining of geographically separated libraries or information systems, using a center for coordination, with the purpose of maintaining a continuing working relationship involving the sharing of information and other joint operations.

The attention to be given to telecommunications does not imply that "wiring together" of libraries is the best available means for transferring information today. The transport of reels, tapes, or films by airmail can be less costly and more effective. The National Education Television network has used the mails almost exclusively for linking affiliate stations. The National Library of Medicine finds the mails quite adequate in its exchanges with medical library computer centers in England and Sweden. Telecommunications are emphasized because their use on any scale will introduce a new set of concerns for libraries and will demand a coherent national development program.

The use of telecommunications is dependent upon cost, system capacity, and availability. These factors are influenced by the running interplay between industry, government, and the consumer. The federal government has highly developed roles and procedures which strongly influence the course of telecommunication system development.

Current use of telecommunications by libraries is relatively small when compared to other users. As a result, libraries are in the position of reacting to and taking advantage of opportunities created for others. A question to be considered is the degree to which, as users of telecommunication networks in the future, libraries should pursue their own course and begin aggressively taking steps to shape a favorable environment for net development.

This paper will examine the telecommunication environment in which library telecommunication networks can develop. The attention of the paper will be on the next several years and on reasonable prospects for accomplishment. The bias is toward action. Long-range predictions are avoided. My plan is to describe some behaviors at federal, state, and local government levels which have affected networking, abstract from this experience elements of special relevance to future development, and conclude with a few proposals for action which build on the experience thus far.

The point will be made that the development of library telecommunication networks of national scope and importance will require many strategies. Fiscal, industrial, political, and rhetorical strategies will be involved in any comprehensive plan of development, along with the accepted practices for problem-solving using research and application projects.

LIBRARIES AND TELECOMMUNICATION TRANSMISSION SERVICES

Currently, libraries are not very demanding on telecommunications. The concepts of role, constituency, and service and the practices which develop from them may demand only modest increases in telecommunication traffic. Both the telephone and the teletypewriter are well suited to the basic processes of libraries. Matters are not entirely satisfactory; facsimile communication seems desirable but too costly, and teletype would be used more if costs were reduced. The current network problems of most libraries, however, are met by the existing telephone and teleprocessing systems.

The amount of coordination and cooperation which develops between libraries is one of the key factors if demand for telecommunication services is to increase. Greater demand will result with the achievement of one of the ultimate goals of a national library plan: "...a nationwide system of service which can be responsive to the legitimate demands from a user of one type of library through use of the resources of another library."[3]

Yet even with a nationwide system, the demand on telecommunication transmission may remain small. Demand will depend on the adoption of certain types of terminal equipment not now in use and on something approaching equal treatment for nonprint materials. Demand also can be increased greatly by a serious effort on the part of libraries to reach the general public through electronic means. Networks may be divided for purposes of discussion into those serving institution-institution relationships, both domestic and international, and those serving institution-client relationships. In the materials on library policy that I have reviewed, there has been much interest in the former. As for the latter, technology to serve researchers has center stage, and applications to meet general needs are largely untouched. If telecommunication networks are ever used to deliver knowledge to the general public, there will be an entirely new level of demand for transmission services.

When we look at the telecommunication transmission system of the country with escalation of library use in mind, we find capabilities of service to be very uneven. The need for new facilities in both rural and urban areas is clear. But will new facilities be developed for library use? Not, in my opinion, without a forceful, mission-oriented national program. If one begins to list some of the questions of library policy which make the future of telecommunication networks for libraries uncertain, the size and complexity of the network development problem become evident. Such questions concern, for example:

1. The role of the library in storing and delivering materials in nonprint forms

2. The rate and degree to which automation will be adopted

3. The final relationship of the libraries to the independent bibliographic, material handling, and archival efforts of the disciplines

4. The development and acceptance of national standards of procedure

5. The extent of new public financial support

6. The effectiveness of the new tools and their availability in forms and at costs which will ensure use in institutions and homes

7. The resolution of outside constraining factors, such as the copyright question

8. The relative utilization by libraries of "off-the-shelf" versus "on-the-line" media delivery systems

9. The role of private industry in the information field

10. And the degree to which libraries show themselves able and willing to attack the geographical and social barriers currently standing in the way of service to many citizens.

While these uncertainties make the nature of library traffic and future requirements for communications difficult to predict, there are equal uncertainties as to the capacities of telecommunications to respond. The telecommunications industry is highly volatile with change effecting change. Library networking will have to conform largely to available transmission facilities and will depend in its growth on the extent to which new telecommunication facilities are constructed for general use. The traffic potential which libraries represent probably is not sufficient in itself to warrant large-scale independent telecommunication systems — as is the case in ETV broadcasting, for example. This is an important assumption in determining the direction of future library network development efforts. Equally important is the assumption that new and desirable library practices will require telecommunication transmission capacities not yet constructed.

The pace of technological advance in telecommunications is greater than ever before and faster than in most lines of industry. It has been estimated that 65 percent of the telecommunication products being manufactured today were introduced in the last decade; only 35 percent of the products available in 1960 were introduced in the 1950-60 period. More than 20 percent of the current sales appear to be made up of products introduced in the last five years.[4]

The technology on which telecommunication networking is based has produced a series of major innovations. Federal policy which determines the pace and direction of development has been a battleground. In the course of these struggles there have been actions designed to shape communication policy in support of education. Attention has focused on noncommercial television broadcasting for a number of reasons.

The capacity of the nation's transmission system for optimum library services is dependent on a number of unpredictables:

1. Federal support policies — the extent to which telecommunication networking is support by comprehensive federal intervention

2. Enlightened use of the spectrum — the extent to which library and information systems will be represented and recognized as valued users of the nation's spectrum of supported telecommunications

3. Growth of transmission and switching capacity — the extent to which private capital is turned into new plants, broadband and digital capacities are increased, satellites are applied effectively, etc.

4. Cost reductions — the extent to which economies of scale and design are passed on — and perhaps even diverted — to library and information systems users

5. User sophistication — the extent to which research and development activities, training programs, and pilot projects are mounted within information and library enterprises

6. Effective marketing — the extent to which industry produces services and equipment which meet library requirements at acceptable costs.

The previous lists are by no means definitive, and there are bound to be differences of opinion, especially on matters of readiness. The point is that the circumstances necessary for application of telecommunication networks to libraries are dependent on a wide range of political, social, industrial, and professional conditions, as well as by technological development.

A major influence on the future will be the extent to which libraries adopt a dynamic posture in their mission and work aggressively to modify the telecommunication environment.

A comprehensive approach to the development of library and information networks must have careful planning and firm direction but at the same time be adaptable and responsive to a sudden turn of events. This should be much easier for librarians to accept than for some others. Libraries are not an independent, tightly bound system. They are constrained by and must be responsive to their sponsoring organizations; they are dependent on the publishing industry and on abstracting and indexing services from outside. In the case of telecommunications, libraries cannot be passive. Their operating processes are too likely to be shaped by the potentialities of telecommunication networks.

Despite the magnitude of network development there is a point at which all activities meet. That is the doorstep of government — federal, state, and local. The federal government has a variety of accepted functions which influence the availability and acceptability of telecommunication services:

1. It is a regulator of interstate telecommunications services through control of the radio spectrum.

2. It is a user of telecommunications which it both leases and owns.

3. It is a promoter of advancement in science and technology and has concern for the flow of information necessary to advancement.

4. In the national interest it supports essential work which cannot be accomplished through the

operation of the free market such as the space program, the subsidy of ETV, etc.

5.   It supports research and development activities in telecommunication development and use.

Add to this the involvement in libraries:

1.   The federal government operates library services in a number of forms.

2.   It promotes development of libraries and information systems through grants and contracts.

3.   It provides leadership in the development of library policy through planning grants and efforts such as the National Advisory Commission on Libraries.

Here is a formidable array of tools to support any efforts to achieve more effective information services of benefit to individuals and to society.

State governments regulate telecommunication within the state, own and operate telecommunications systems in many instances, and lease services in every instance. They lay claim to a leadership function for libraries, public and private, typically involving regulation, and have responsibility for the education system in the state.

Local governments have powers as franchisers of public utilities, which now include telecommunication systems by cable, and are operators of libraries and schools.

At this moment all three levels are deeply involved in decisionmaking affecting the growth of telecommunication networks and will have a direct influence on the basic character of library operations.

In the pages ahead I will describe some of these actions, because the response of libraries to network development must be within the context of what has gone before. The time has come, in my opinion, when the purpose of libraries to serve the knowledge needs of the individual will be advanced by an active concern for telecommunications policies and practices.

FEDERAL TELECOMMUNICATION POLICY

So all-inclusive is federal involvement in the subject of this Conference that it is difficult to be selective. Each of the proceedings included in the following discussion has the potential for favorably influencing the course of library telecommunication network development. Domestic communication satellite policy retains possibilities for triggering a network demonstration. Educational television is a natural ally and may create precedents useful to libraries. Policies to reduce costs may yet be necessary as a basic condition for large-scale networking. And the need for effective scientific and technical communication continues.

NATIONAL COORDINATION OF INFORMATION SYSTEM DEVELOPMENT

Repeatedly over the last several years, attention has been directed to the need for coordination at the federal level if communication technology is to be applied effectively to education and the public services.

Three major national advisory groups have recommended national developmental centers to facilitate the application of systems technology to the more effective dissemination of knowledge. The conclusions of these committees reflect similar earlier recommendations from professional bodies. In addition, within the federal government there have been efforts to mount such a coordinating mechanism –t o my knowledge in the Departments of HEW and Commerce, and the Office of Telecommunication Management. These failed in the face of the usual difficulties confronting interagency cooperation. Coming from so many different quarters, the conclusion that there must be a focusing entity to facilitate development of information systems deserves careful consideration.

The three national advisory bodies each reflected different interests and pressures, but each was concerned with the application of technology to the dissemination of knowledge. The President's Task Force on Communications Policy, made up of representatives at the subcabinet level, was initiated in August 1967 and reported in the closing moments of the Johnson Administration. Its function was "to make a comprehensive study of government policy" in the field of communication.[5] The National Advisory Commission on Libraries is well known to the participants of this Conference. The Commission on Instructional Technology was a response by the U. S. Office of Education to Title III of response by the U.S. Office of Education to Title III of problems of broadcasting were divided from other systems for distributing educational materials. In addition, funds were provided for a study of the impact on education of nonbroadcast communication technology with recommendations to Congress for future action.

The President's Task Force on Communications Policy was struck by "the lack of interdisciplinary research into questions of communication policy" and recommended in its report of 7 December 1968 the establishment within government of a "central source of technical and systems advice and assistance in telecommunications." It proposed "greater multi-disciplinary capability within the Executive Branch" to integrate the variety of policies and interest in communication and to initiate "experimental operations" where needed.[6]

The National Advisory Commission on Libraries in one of five major recommendations made to President Johnson proposed a "National Commission on Libraries and Information Science as a continuing federal planning agency." This proposal became law in July 1970, but the commission was placed in the Executive Office of the President rather than in the Department of Health, Education, and Welfare as recommended.

Another of the commission's recommendations was for "establishment of a Federal Institute of Library and Information Science" within HEW. A principal task was to be "...the system engineering and technical direction involved in the design and implementation of an integrated national library and information system." Beyond that it was to be concerned with the "changing needs of information users and the effectiveness of libraries and information systems in meeting those needs."[7]

The latter recommendation was viewed with enthusiasm in a report completed in August 1969 by the Commission on Instructional Technology. In addition to endorsing the Federal Institute on Libraries and Information Science, the commission proposed a National Institute of Instructional Technology. This was to be a constituent of what was their principal recommendation, a National Institute of Education. (Also visualized in the report was a Library of Educational Resources "...to assist school and college libraries to transform themselves into comprehensive learning centers; and stimulate interconnections among specialized libraries, data banks, schools, and colleges for comprehensive and efficient access to instructional materials and educational management data.")[8]

Additional force was put behind the commission's major recommendation when President Nixon proposed to Congress on 3 March 1970 the creation of a National Institute of Education "as a focus for educational research and experimentation."[9] While this compared to the committee's recommendations, it was also similar to a proposal made during the presidential campaign when Mr. Nixon called for creation of a National Institute for the Educational Future. The President made no mention of an Institute for Libraries; his use of the singular "institute" may be significant.

The three reports are history. What influence they will exert on the new Office of Telecommunication Policy and the National Commission on Libraries and Information Science is to be seen. They stand as evidence of the importance attached to the establishment of a center for information systems development and deserve the active concern of this Conference.

The Communication Satellite

Much of the attention at the federal level directed to the use of telecommunications in education has been based on federal interests in space and the hope that the technological innovations of the space program can result in social benefits. The communication satellite has been viewed as providing an opportunity of breakthrough proportions for the advancement of education throughout the world. The direction of federal policies toward its application and control has been a battleground for nearly a decade.

Of the favorable characteristics claimed for the communication satellite, perhaps the most important is that (1) the factor of distance is separated from the cost of transmission between interconnected points. In addition, (2) the opportunity exists to establish communication with areas of the world previously unserved because of overriding factors of geography, economics or politics. (3) The satellite is adaptable; it can be designed for current special requirements, and its short life span assures continuing redesign and adaptation. (4) The limitations of older established systems may be by-passed by direct point-to-point linkage with service centers. Finally, (5) if the circuit demand can be developed to a point approaching capacity, costs-per-circuit will become very small.

The implications of satellite technology and control to the transfer of information has been a topic of much study and

debate which has focused heavily on its use for television broadcasting. Use of the satellite for educational television attracted wide interest with the proposal of the Ford Foundation in 1966.

President Johnson focused attention on the use of telecommunication technology for libraries and information systems with several speeches in 1967. At the Conference on World Education at Williamsburg on 8 October 1967, he pictured outstanding library facilities being made available any place in the world through development of existing technology. At the signing of the Public Broadcasting Act on 7 November 1967, he looked beyond a broadcasting system to "a great network for knowledge" which would employ "every means of sending and storing information that the individual can use." He pictured an "Electronic Knowledge Bank" comparable in value to the Federal Reserve Bank.[10] Little was to be heard in a concrete way until the Networks for Knowledge section was introduced as part of the Higher Education Act of 1968.

In the meantime a President's Task Force on Communications Policy, made up of subcabinet representatives from major departments, was working on a report requested by the President in his message of 14 August 1967 on the "Global Communications System." One of the top priorities for the task force was to come to grips with the domestic satellite issue and develop a federal posture which would produce a rapid payoff for the public. Nevertheless, in their report filed at the close of the administration, the task force found that data and experience on which to base recommendations was insufficient.

> In light of the various unresolved issues...we consider it premature to fix domestic satellites into a particular institutional and operational pattern....

> The potential benefits of satellites in a domestic setting are not sufficiently comprehended to determine how they might best be shared in the public interest.

> Available data are insufficient to determine the comparative advantages of general purpose vs. specialized system....[11]

The task force recommended a demonstration satellite program to develop information. Television broadcast networks were emphasized as potential users, but also the importance of a wide range of purposes was stressed. In this context the Biomedical Communications Network proposed by the National Library of Medicine was noted.

Policy guidance from the new administration came 23 January 1970, when Peter Flanigan, assistant to President Nixon, directed a memorandum to Chairman Dean Burch of the Federal Communications Commission, FCC, setting forth an "open-sky" position. It was recommended that essentially no limit be placed on applicants for domestic satellite authorizations. And further:

> The most immediate potential for domestic satellite communications seems to lie in long distance specialized transmission service — such as one-way distribution of radio and

television programs or two-way exchange of high speed data or other wideband signals among thinly dispersed users. Common carriers have informed us that satellites do not appear economic at present for the routine transmission of public message traffic.[12]

Thus, emphasis is placed on distance and bandwidth, the strengths of the satellite. The distribution of high-speed data as required by a national library and information network receives attention equal to that given the network needs of television broadcasting.

As this is written the Western Union Telegraph Company has submitted an application to the FCC for a domestic satellite system. It is reported that other corporations will follow.

The opportunity which has existed during the last year for pilot demonstrations in the use of satellites for communication also should be mentioned. The National Aeronautics and Space Administration, NASA, launched a series of Applications Technology Satellites for purposes of research. ATS-1, the first, was launched in 1966 and is in orbit on the equator over the Pacific Ocean. This satellite was made available in 1969 for telecommunications demonstrations. Contracts for demonstrations have been signed with the Corporation for Public Broadcasting and the state of Alaska. The Lister Hill Center at the National Library of Medicine just announced the first group communication via satellite between four medical centers including the University of Alaska, University of Wisconsin, and Stanford University. Voice communication to assist practicing physicians in remote areas was tested and EKG transmissions and slow scan TV are planned.

The University of Hawaii has proposed to NASA that an international consortium of Pacific Basin universities and other educational agencies be interconnected for the exchange of resources in a wide number of areas. Linking of libraries to transmit reference questions by voice with possible use of facsimile is proposed. Scholars in the vast region can benefit by access to the wider collection.

NASA has signed a major contract with the government of India to allow use of ATS-F, now under construction, for a larger scale demonstration extending at least one year. Originally planned for 1972, the project has just been deferred a year.

All of these projects are experimental and do not reflect any permanency of use. Actual operations seem modest when considered against the background of reports, offers, and other rhetoric on the subject. The bright promise held out for the communication satellite can hardly be overlooked entirely by this Conference. What application of this technological achievement, if any, can be made to the long-distance transfer of information?

EDUCATIONAL TELEVISION NETWORK

What I wish to emphasize in discussing educational television is the nature of the campaign. The development of ETV was led by well-organized, well-financed, central leadership outside government. The development policies were drawn so as to support rather than to challenge the motives of private industry.

And fear of government influence forced a series of innovative proposals to permit the benefits of federal financing without the benefits of federal advice.

Initial encouragement of educational television was in the action of the FCC to "reserve" TV channels for noncommercial broadcasters. The action was supported by the commercial networks and individual stations, and was entirely compatible with their economic interests. The effect was to reduce potential commercial competition by removing limited channels from commercial use.

The Ford Foundation became the primary supporter of ETV broadcast development, and its contribution of more than $100 million far exceeds all federal financial assistance combined. The foundation saw a special benefit in national networking and was the major backer of a central network organization, the National Educational Television network, NET. Thus ETV had strong central leadership outside government from the beginning.

Federal support for construction of stations was authorized in 1962 under the Educational Television Facilities Act. The prompt use of television channels for noncommercial purposes was primary. While funds for construction of network interconnections were allowed, there were inhibitions to such grants. Action again was compatible with the economic interests of private industry.

The act reflected the fear that government would control content. It provided funds for equipment only and specifically stated that there would be no government interference in programs.

In 1966 a citizen's commission was funded by the Carnegie Corporation of New York to study educational television and to provide recommendations for future development. In their report the Carnegie Commission on Educational Television recommended establishment of a "private corporation" to be supported by federal funds. It was to be "insulated" from government influence by a financial mechanism which involved a tax on the sale of new TV receivers. The sums raised were to be placed in a dedicated fund and made available to the corporation without annual appropriation by Congress. The corporation itself was prevented from exercising undue central control by restrictions on its capacity to operate facilities or produce programs. It was prevented from operating a network.

The Public Broadcasting Act of 1967 authorizing the corporation, was passed quickly, supported by everyone including commercial broadcasters. The insulating mechanism for financing was not included, however, and the corporation today operates on an annual appropriation basis. Currently, the Corporation for Public Broadcasting, CPB, is moving ahead forcefully to develop a broadcast network with unique features, but as yet a steady-state telecommunication network operation is incomplete.

In shaping aspirations for library telecommunication networks, it is worth recalling that it has taken fifteen years of determined effort to achieve a "real-time" or "live" ETV network without direct federal participation and support. Like the library, the ETV broadcast station lacks a market economy on which to base development. The alternative to the marketplace in the United States is the taxpayer or a foundation.

So high were the costs for the ETV network that there seemed only one source of support, the federal government, but its control over programs was feared. The Carnegie Commission estimated the cost of national interconnecting of state networks — assuming they existed in each state which was not the case — at $9 million annually for leased services from common carrier. If operator-owned, a capital cost of $30 million and an annual cost of $6 million would be required. The Carnegie Commission recommended free or low-cost rates for ETV interconnection. A provision to encourage the FCC to allow such rates was included in the Public Broadcasting Act. This represented one answer.

A second alternative was contained in the Ford Foundation offer of August 1966 which proposed to establish a private satellite corporation to be capitalized by the Ford Foundation. It would lease interconnection services to the three commercial networks and provide channels for an ETV broadcast network. Channels were also to be made available to elementary, secondary, and higher education. In addition, $31 million was to be provided for ETV broadcast programs from the difference in network operating costs and the amount to be charged the three commercial networks.

The originator of the idea of free interconnection for ETV, interestingly, was the American Broadcasting Company who petitioned the FCC for authority to operate a satellite for interconnection of their affiliated stations and had promised free interconnection service and some dollar subsidy to the ETV network. The Ford proposal was in the form of comments to the FCC in response to the ABC request.

The Ford Foundation justified its plan on a principle which can be traced to the conservation movement born during the Theodore Roosevelt Administration. This is the principle that those who profit from use of resources owned by the people should provide a return to the people. The Ford Foundation used the language of a leader in that movement, Senator George Norris, when it declared that the taxpayer who had financed satellite research should receive a "people's dividend" in the form of educational television network programs.

The search for ETV resources has produced a Corporation for Public Broadcasting, statutory authority to undergird negotiations for low transmission rates and a dynamic idea which still may be used by a government serious about recasting national priorities. While ETV networks and library networks are far from analogous, the contributions to public policy made by the former may be helpful to development of the latter.

RATE REDUCTION

A principal deterrent to ETV networking is the cost of interconnections. Eventually in the implementation of library telecommunication networks, the problem takes on the same character, raising funds and reducing costs.

Efforts at the federal level to secure rate benefits have taken three forms. First, free or reduced rates for education have been advocated with limited success. Through the rate-making process the government is in a position to provide special benefits to educational users in the public interest. The effect is to subsidize a high priority function. Costs of transmission are shifted from favored users to nonfavored users, just as post office book rates pass the burden to the general taxpayer or other users. Claims

for educational advantages have been made on the basis of fair return to the taxpayer for profit-producing benefits provided private industry.

A second form of rate benefit is that negotiated by the government as an administrator. Bulk rates made possible through large traffic volume have served to greatly reduce unit costs.

Third, the government operates or leases systems. Military, space research, transportation, law enforcement, and other recognized federal functions use government operated or leased dedicated systems.

There have been no dedicated systems in education, a primary function of the states. It is worth considering, by way of contrast, that since the establishment of the Library of Congress, the federal government has had library and information functions. Furthermore, information transfer may be accomplished in support of many purposes including those in which the federal role is primary.

Library networking can be promoted by using the opportunities existing for reduced telecommunication rates. Consider first the area of government regulation. The policy of the FCC in connection with common carrier charges in interstate commerce has been equal rates for equal service to all comers. Bookies or scholars are treated equally; put a little less cavalierly, no class or subscriber is assessed charges which subsidize another class of subscriber.

The Public Broadcasting Act of 1967 sought to modify the policy. The FCC was authorized to approve free or low-cost rates for the interconnection of noncommercial education television stations. With the activation of the CPB, negotiations involving the corporation, AT&T, and the FCC have produced reduced charges for network interconnection of public television stations.

A provision authorizing the FCC to approve free or low-cost rates for interconnection of institutions of higher education was later included in the Higher Education Act of 1968 (Section 803). The language was not a part of the original higher education bill in which the U.S. Office of Education staff had hastily inserted a "Networks for Knowledge" provision. It was added later on amendment of Senator Wayne Morse and passed with the bill. Although several years have gone by, to my knowledge no college or university has made use of this provision for interconnection costs. Yet the provision applies to all those *eligible* for support under the section.

The principle of fair public return for benefits conferred has been introduced into the developing struggle over public policy for urban cable systems. Free channels for public use have been advanced as one of the necessary requirements for franchises. The power of the FCC to protect the public interest is a potential force for providing what, in effect, are reduced rates.

Second, as a major user of telecommunications, the federal government enjoys rate advantages which could be used under some circumstances for library networks. For example, state governments have been eligible in most instances for federal Telpak arrangements. Yet three years ago when the U.S. Office of Telecommunication Management reviewed state-leased facilities, they found that twenty-seven states were contracting for services at a commercial rate averaging about $4.00 per month per voice-channel mile, while nineteen states were using state

Telpak rates ranging from $1.00 to $1.50. Only twelve states utilized federal Telpak rates averaging forty cents per month per voice-channel mile.

In some instances where federal rate advantages could be very helpful, they cannot be used. Demonstration projects supported by federal grants and involving networks are not eligible, for example. This has proven a major deterrent to the funding of experiments involving telecommunication applications. I know of one proposed project in which the projected line charges exceeded the several millions of dollars allocated for all research in that educational program category. This limitation is not in the interest of the government, education, or industry.

Third, if we are serious about networking we need to review the possibilities of utilizing the federal government's telecommunication services and systems. There is, of course, the FTS system, the basic government long-distance telephone system. Of special interest to libraries is the Advanced Record System, ARS, developed by the General Service Administration and operated under contract by Western Union. The ARS was designed to interconnect not only conventional teleprinter (narrowband) subscriber stations but all known varieties of high-speed terminal devices requiring broadband transmission facilities. The system is capable of forwarding traffic to Western Union's TELEX and the Bell System TWX, of exchange traffic with AUTODIN of the Department of Defense, and of refile to the Western Union Public Message System.

The various federal rate and systems advantages might be captured under a plan by which one or all of the national libraries served as agents for a network of constituent or affiliated libraries.

Certainly, a comprehensive approach to networking will involve concern for costs as well as appropriations. Good housekeepers will demand a careful study of the existing rate advantages for libraries. Statesmen will provide some assistance to those who are seeking to open up the telecommunication systems of the country for educational uses.

SCIENTIFIC AND TECHNOLOGICAL INFORMATION

There has not been the question concerning federal involvement in science that has existed with respect to the federal role in education. This has its effect on information networks. It has been generally accepted that under the American system of distribution of powers the promotion of libraries is grouped with authority for education and is reserved to the states, with the exception of library functions which are an extension of some recognized federal function. Up until recent years, any federal interest in information has been based on some accepted federal power. Science and technology has benefited from the link with defense and industry.

The Executive Office of the President Office of Science and Technology has a history of concern for information flow in general and networks in particular. The federal government is a major supporter of science. The success with which it meets many of its responsibilities is dependent on the products of science and technology, and information has a vital role in developing those products.

In 1962 the Committee on Scientific and Technical Information, COSATI, was organized within the Federal Council for Science and Technology. Made up of representatives from federal information activities, it has focused on improvements in handling scientific and technical information in the government and on development of information systems to store and circulate scientific and technical information to practitioners.

The problem brought on by the rapid increase in amounts of information has been under attack from both the U. S. Office of Education, USOE, and the National Science Foundation, NSF. Grant awards of the two agencies reveal a strong interest in efforts to retrieve and make available the report products of research. The importance attached to networking has increased with the rise of the computer and the recognition that the decentralized system under development for the retrieval of information was difficult to query.

Over the last decade the NSF has committed large resources to increase and decentralize sources of basic information in the scientific disciplines. Abstracting and indexing services have been supported in chemistry, physics, biology, the earth and environmental sciences, mathematics, and others. The application of the computer has been vigorously promoted as a necessary tool.

A problem that has become apparent is the need for access by the scientist on the university campus where the library is not linked to appropriate computerized information systems. Both the NSF and USOE have shown concern for the problem. It has appeared to some that any science information network would have to be linked eventually to a university library network if it were to perform effectively. A number of proposals for funding have sought to test the extent to which a discipline-centered information service could be used by a broader public when made available through a general library.

Both the NSF and USOE have supported the development of networks on a planned or prototype basis. The requests for such support are greatly in excess of the funds available. Thus administrators are faced with the problems of selecting unique applications in order that research and development funds will not be diverted to routine support.

The Library of Congress has voiced concern over efforts directed to producing an independent science information network. Much of the planning has assumed separation of scientific and technical information from the general body of knowledge. The plan of the System Development Corporation, for example, visualized a network for scientific and technological information involving the federal departments, but no mention was made of the Library of Congress.

The Library of Congress position as set forth in its paper for the National Advisory Commission on Libraries took issue with this approach. Science and technology, the library staff said in *Libraries at Large,* is not a definable area for which a network could be constructed. Although recognizing the federal interest in the status of science and technology, it was suggested that other branches of knowledge — law, the arts, the humanities, and the social sciences — should not be overwhelmed by that interest.

A comparable division can be noted in conversations on political strategies for development. One point of view sees the science network as the pacesetter, breaking ground for comprehensive network development. There is the opposite view that says as many interests as possible should be included in the developmental package to increase the base of support and thus, the chance for implementation.

The future of networks for science and technology cannot be foreseen. The time is not far away when the technical potential will exist for networking at reasonable cost, and pressures created by investments in the collection and storing of data will be greater. A national plan is needed which will be accepted generally as the one to best serve both individuals needs and the national interest.

THE STATES AND TELECOMMUNICATION NETWORK DEVELOPMENT

State telecommunication networks are growing in variety. Some are owned and operated by government, some are leased systems, and some use regular common carrier services. They assist many kinds of public activities, including education, law enforcement, forest protection, highway safety, public health, and disaster control. Growth in the last decade has been influenced by demands which include: promotion of greater efficiency and effectiveness in government services, interconnections of educational television stations, sharing of services between related institutions, the development of emergency and backup telecommunication systems to increase disaster protection.

What benefits can libraries obtain from these state telecommunication activities? The hope is expressed on occasion that existing state telecommunications can be utilized by libraries in their networking efforts. State library networking can be envisaged as a necessary part of a future state library system. A state telecommunications network can be essential to the operation of a state library plan where there is differentiation of function or sharing of materials; it can be the key to plans for extending services to the less-populated areas and for expanding functions as might be required by the concept of a community information center.

State information networks have been viewed in two ways. As a primary system for the state or region, such a network has its own identity and is responsive to demands from within the state, both institutional and citizen. It has also been viewed as a node or regional center of a national system, retransmitting to local points. State telecommunications operations are by now sufficiently well established in many states so as to warrant consideration in planning of library networks and information systems. However, there is no certainty that they can be of use.

Three kinds of state network development have relevance. (1) Efforts are being made in some states to develop statewide telecommunication management, with a backbone network for all kinds of administrative purposes. (2) Educational television stations have been interconnected into network arrangements in nearly half of the states. (3) Health and education institution are interconnecting by means of telecommunications for the sharing of services. Each of these trends will be discussed briefly.

Over the last five years there has been a movement to create central state telecommunication authorities sometimes headed by appointed commissions. The state of Nebraska is a leading example; it has a strong central management group and a state telecommunication board. Illinois, Iowa, Massachusetts and California are also examples.

A review of a number of statewide telecommunication plans reveals little input from libraries. There are a number of reasons that can be suggested. Libraries with their Telex and telephone have seen little to gain immediately from state networks. Often state planning has depended for funding on the Office of Civil Defense; for this reason, emergency communication has been a prime objective. And state agencies already operating statewide systems — such as police, forestry, or roads — have a direct, immediate interest and the trained staff to support this interest.

There are basic pressures which may encourage libraries to use state telecommunication systems when they exist. It is argued that joint use of communication systems by many agencies is more effective and less costly. In the words of one state study, "In order to obtain the greatest economic efficiency for a microwave system it is necessary to carry as much information, communication and data as possible. Statewide coordination between departments and agencies is mandatory if costs are to be kept in bounds."[13]

The state ETV network also represents a possible resource. The first state ETV network was started in Alabama in 1955. Now, multistation ETV network systems are operating in twenty-one states, and in six states funds have been acquired and committed for development. Of the 190 ETV stations, 60 percent are licensed to state systems. States without ETV networking are found in the sparsely populated areas of the Rocky Mountains and Great Plains.

State ETV systems may eventually serve as the basis for the development of educational telecommunication networks in some states. As was pointed out in a telecommunication study for the State of Illinois:

> With the addition of the proper terminal equipment, an ETV network, because of its wide frequency band characteristics, can easily accommodate the other types of narrow band educational transmissions such as slow-scan video, high fidelity audio, telephone quality audio, teleprinter and digital data, and distribution of educational radio network programs.[14]

One possible course of development is to have two major networks, a state administrative network and an educational network, each administered separately. In some states the ETV network and the state administrative network may be developed together. The Illinois study concluded that under some circumstances this will be better economics.

A third type of development is the linking of particular classes of institutions. The interconnection of health and education operations for purposes of sharing services and materials continues to move forward. The first interconnection of institutions of higher education was in Texas in 1961 in a project (TEMP) assisted by Title VII of the National Defense Education Act. There are now six major developing educational networks in the state.

There is a steady growth in interconnections linking industrial plants and offices to university centers. In one instance, Stanford University, this involves the over-the-air 2500 MHz service licensed by the FCC, but for the most part common carrier services are used. The interconnection of medical and health centers for television exchange, sometimes two way, has been growing. With strong support at the federal level the future of medical library networks seems assured.

While much of this activity is occurring in the larger industrial states, it is also true that some sparsely populated states have been able to mount networks, seeing it as a way to extend services outward from major centers of population.

These telecommunication interconnections will grow, undoubtedly, as new health and education institutions are opened to serve an expanding and more demanding population. Benefits to libraries will be judged ad hoc by local management, with professional associations playing an important role in the dissemination of experience.

The strong likelihood that in a substantial number of states the link-up of health or education centers will eventually result in a comprehensive statewide educational network service should be recognized in any national strategy for library network development.

On the basis of the state experience thus far, it is possible to hazard a guess about future directions: (1) Special purpose telecommunication networks will be activated within the state for a variety of objectives depending on social appeal, local leadership, and federal participation. (2) The pressures for more sophisticated uses and for economy of operations will result in a grouping of needs and central planning of facilities, either owned or leased. (3) Libraries will not in most cases operate complete systems. They will work instead with state telecommunication entities. (4) The communication needs of libraries will be small initially; however, the availability of network capability will be an incentive for thinking in terms of a statewide system and also will encourage expanded nonprint services. New methods will result in extending services to the general public, to researchers, and to government and industry.

There are several observations to be made about the current level of state telecommunications. First, development varies greatly from state to state. Any effort which seeks to develop a national network on the basis of linking existing state networks has an uncertain future. Second, network development takes time. Work in developing the Nebraska central telecommunication system extended over five years. The Ohio legislature this year voted funds for a state ETV network, culminating over ten years of continuing effort by strong dedicated leadership. It seems unrealistic to expect general application of state telecommunication networks during the seventies. Third, no one has yet determined how national network standards can be gracefully yet rigorously imposed on independent state operations. Private common carrier history suggests the difficulty of maintaining transmission standards without strong central control. Experiences in the development of a national law enforcement network as well as civil defense efforts deserve the attention of developers of national library telecommunications. Fourth, the planning and activation of state telecommunication services have tended to support purposes for which federal assistance and leadership are available. Thus, when state telecommunication networks for libraries are viewed as part of a national system, it seems evident that only strong federal incentives and a pretty firmly directed program can produce the uniformity necessary to units in a federal network.

Yet there is a basis in present development for pilot demonstrations of statewide information networks. In selected states there is the capacity for statewide relay of the signals as part of a prototype national system. Where national library network plans benefit from high social priorities, as could be the case with a national medical communication system, a prototype national service could supply information over interstate links to some states, to be retransmitted over statewide systems to points of need. In some states the telecommunication potential exists for projects like EDUCOM, in which a network of colleges and universities is linked with national libraries. Furthermore, there are the telecommunication resources in a few states to allow for state pilot projects in extending public library services.

There is the question also of how statewide telecommunications will be used to bring better service to more users. Is state library organization and planning sufficiently strong and coherent to create a purpose for state library networks?

Beyond interlibrary loans, centralized reference, and copy transmission, all on a relatively small scale, there are few uses for state telecommunication networks which would not be disputed by librarians on practical grounds. Experience to date does not provide a persuasive basis for risky attempts at massive restructuring of old institutions currently performing functions which the public understands. A carefully programmed effort needs to be considered to encourage conceptualization and testing on libraries of new practical methods distributing information to the public utilizing telecommunication.

MUNICIPALITIES AND THE CABLE SYSTEM

High-capacity cable systems have passed out of the state of technological innovation and are about to be introduced into operating urban society. We are in a period of political and economic innovation. The future position of libraries and information systems in relation to these telecommunication services, along with man's future access to information, is being determined in the process.

The "wired city" concept has appeared in the context of an extension of existing community antenna television service, CATV. This conceals its importance for information systems and libraries, and a distinction should be drawn between two kinds of systems. The CATV system typically has twelve channels for one-way delivery of television programs to home TV receivers. It is both a transmission system and a program service, and lacks the versatility expected of the future urban cable transmission system. It is tied in purpose to the delivery of commercial television programs; other uses are incidental to that purpose.

The hypothetical "wired city" system has many purposes, most of them potential. It represents in concept an effort to exploit fully the increased coaxial cable capacity which technology has made available. Cable systems using present technology are potentially capable of about thirty TV channels. It has been stated as practical to extend the range to fifty TV channels. The Electronic Industries Association visualizes a dual communication system in our cities involving fifty channels with two-way facilities, limited switching, and capability for communication by sound, pictures, data, and facsimile. The opportunity this would open up for information transfer is obvious.

The limited application of high-capacity cable telecommunication systems to large centers of population is a matter of cost. The President's Task Force on Communication Policy concluded that application of cable telecommunications to the nation as a whole was financially out of the question. It has been estimated that capital outlay for systems serving New York City alone will exceed $1 billion.

The probability that urban areas will be served by broadband, versatile cable transmission systems puts before libraries basic questions of institutional character and function. In adapting to this telecommunication development, libraries could become different institutions.

Most of the new tools for the home, such as facsimile recorders, high-speed coders, and stored television displays, require the high-capacity cable systems to be available sometime in the future. This quotation from the presentation of the Electronic Industries Association to the FCC provides a flavor of things to come:

With such a service available (electronic home library service) a reader can request a book or periodical from a large central library, using a narrow-band channel to the library. The desired book is then transmitted from microfiche, microfilm or video tape, page by page, and received via the...network.

Several modes of operation are possible. In one, the entire book or selected article is transmitted at the maximum reception speed of the user's facsimile recorder....

As an alternative, a soft-copy display can be used. Each page is transmitted and stored at the receiver for reading. When the reader has finished one page, he signals for the next page, and this is transmitted in a small fraction of a second with no perceptible delay....

To get a feeling for the capacity of a broad band channel, it is of interest to note that in the demonstration described...the entire text of *Gone With the Wind* was transmitted in facsimile over a television microwave circuit in slightly over two minutes.[15]

The growth of urban cable service is heavily dependent on the decisionmaking processes of municipal government within conditions set by the FCC. This and the requirements for raising investment capital are shaping networks which have the potential of linking libraries and information centers to the home and place of business.

New York City provides a picture of the difficulties in regulating a new technology. It is presently considering the requests of two CATV companies for twenty-year franchises. The access to such systems which libraries will enjoy is to be determined largely by government regulatory action. Thus, it is important that libraries are capable of bringing to focus their future requirements at those moments when government regulatory policies and practices are set.

A Mayor's Advisory Task Force on CATV and Telecommunications in New York suggested guidelines which included the recommendation that a portion of the channels be made available free. Of seventeen channels, eleven would be used for television broadcast station programs, two would be available to the city for government services, and two more would be "public channels" leased to community groups. Last July, hearings on the two franchises were held by the Board of Estimate. It was protested that a twenty-year lease locked the network into existing technology. And it should be added here that it is equally important from the standpoint of libraries that the network is locked into existing forms of use.

Issues which seem of concern to libraries are these: increased number of channels, two-way capacity, terms of the franchise, free use by favored public users, methods of financing, and delay in decision to allow for long-range studies of potential utilization.

After a look at advances in cable technology, the U.S. Office of Telecommunication Management concluded that it is "not clear...just how broadband local distribution systems are likely to develop."[16] Government decisions over the next several years will do much to shape the future. Much interest has been expressed recently. It is reported that the Ford Foundation will launch a new cable task force. The Rand Corporation is currently undertaking a cable study under a Ford contract. Stanford Research Institute is preparing a major report on cable communications in urban centers, and the Alfred Sloan Foundation has just announced a task force on the study of cable communications in the city. What is the role of libraries at this time in the face of what are obviously many unanswered questions?

The limited use made by libraries of the existing 2,300 CATV systems raises questions as to future library participation in a high-capacity, two-way cable system.

Today's CATV operator has a positive incentive to offer a variety of programs and unlike the broadcaster, has sufficient channels to seek to appeal to minority tastes. Where can one get the programs to fill twelve or twenty channels? There is an existing opportunity for a public library program service. Academic meetings such as the annual convention of the American Association for the Advancement of Science have been programmed on public broadcasting stations; uncopyrighted government and archival films can be displayed; the children's story hour and other regular parts of the library service can be distributed; even the Library of Congress recorded books for the blind might be offered. There is the question of how CATV programming fits into library objectives and functions. But also, the question of readiness is raised. How prepared are libraries to take advantage of the service extension opportunities provided by cable systems?

With the emergence of the "wired city," the libraries have two directions of action to consider. One is to determine what uses, if any, the old institution will make of the new. This will require planned study and pilot demonstrations to be properly carried forward. The second is the mounting of strategic and tactical responses to help assure cable systems which will perform effectively in serving library and other information retrieval functions.

The broad position on which the case for libraries rests has been well stated by Sidney Dean. "A metropolis without open communication channels and media cannot function as a market economy, a free society, or a self-governing polity."[17]

It is possible at this stage to determine the qualities of a cable system which open up communication and allow a place for libraries and other as yet underdeveloped information systems. Specifications which best serve libraries can be reasoned from the technical and economic character of the system. For example, libraries cannot engage in economic competition for channels against profit-making industry. Library use will depend on regulatory concessions made to them as a favored user. Concessions will come most easily if the channels are large in number and readily accessible. Libraries are best served by the cable systems with the largest number of channels. Also systems that provide for two-way communication rather than one-way are necessary to information exchange. Systems that are capable of interconnection with other systems and are suited to all kinds of terminal equipment are better than systems that are not. Characteristics desirable for free and rapid transfer of information can determine a national library posture.

At the same time, a clear and convincing picture of the use which libraries and information services will make of the new cable systems is needed. Innovations necessary to the exploitation of future telecommunication capability require the involvement of library management. Predictions must eventually face the rigors of application, with the tests of cost, public acceptance, and operating feasibility.

Pilot projects may be needed which would utilize the most advanced of the existing cable systems. However, the movement of events is such that public policy toward urban cable systems is likely to be determined before the results of such pilots projects come in. The economic base for the new industry will be laid and capital raised on the basis of market methods already formulated. Libraries will stand with hat in hand alongside other educational users who lack the financial bargaining power of an industry in search of markets. The system will be so firmly rooted as to be all but unchangable.

Politics and economics will determine development of cable systems and may foreclose the future. The plan and manner in which the library position is advocated deserves attention now. Restrictions on active participation in political decisionmaking, real and customary, need to be faced and methods found for surmounting them.

The future is also dependent on innovation in utilization. This is a primary responsibility of the library professional, one he cannot meet effectively without the assistance of many disciplines but one that is primarily his task to perform. There is a long road between the forecasts of the future and the practices of the present. Development requires both a prepared case and a social mechanism to bring argument to bear upon the centers of decision.

SOME PROPOSALS FOR TODAY AND THE NEAR FUTURE

If there is an overriding lesson in the several lines of action just described, it is this: The widely dispersed library and information activities of the country are not organized to develop a comprehensive national network system involving telecommunications and automation. The central mechanisms required to control essential conditions are lacking. Despite the advances there remains a need for coordination and subordination to common purposes which will require a number of years to evolve.

The National Commission on Libraries and Information Science will provide a focal point for leadership. Yet I think we should recognize that its impact cannot be felt for several years. The recent action certainly is not intended to provide a basic organization for the implementation and management of a national system of networks. The use of an appointive commission in the Executive Office of the President to operate a network system is out of the question. There have been suggestions for the management of a network system, but no single plan of organization is acceptable to even a substantial minority in the profession.

We are also without a central approach to research. The national institute suggested by the National Advisory Committee on Libraries has not been created to provide for long-range coordination of the research and development required before there can be networks on a large scale.

Really, we are without a plan for national network development. There have been proposals for pieces of a system. But without a broader framework, there is uneasiness as to the effect which implementation of a part will have on efforts to deal with the whole. Specifically, if the needs of the academically elite are served, will it set back efforts to meet the information needs of the general public?

There has been almost no effort to grapple with the problem of financing. The costs not only of telecommunication network operations are involved but also the increased cost of library operations resulting from improved access to materials.

There is as yet no library strategy for the development and use of statewide telecommunication systems and urban cable systems or for international exchange by satellite. The use to which libraries will put these telecommunication systems is a matter of conjecture. And there is no continuing effort to modify the telecommunication environment for the purpose of extending access to materials through working networks. Libraries are inhibited from being as effective as they might be for many reasons.

In these final pages a number of actions are proposed with two purposes in mind: to develop a capacity for central planning and operation without interfering with the essential independence of separate institutions and without subordinating libraries to a line organization, and second, to respond to the rapid changes in telecommunications in a way that is advantageous to information network growth.

A Public Corporation. In the thirties the government used the corporation to open up the supply of financial capital; in the sixties it used the corporation to open up communication. On three separate occasions the corporation has been established to facilitate application of new communication technology to the needs of society:

1. Communication Satellite Corporation was authorized in 1962.

2. Corporation for Public Broadcasting was authorized in 1967.

3. A private corporation to take over the U.S. Post Office Department was approved in 1970.

It seems to me that a fourth entry is a likely possibility:

4. Information Transfer Corporation may be authorized in 1976.

The public corporation is proposed here in the hope that it will stimulate analysis of the basic problem. Yet only a limited number of approaches to the operation of a national network are available. There is the consortium of users, operation by a national government agency, a special service offered by private industry, and the public corporation.

The basic questions which lead to the selection of the corporation form are: Will network functions be managed inside or outside the federal government? And will networks be created by a variety of ad hoc arrangements or be the product of central management and design?

The primary function of the corporation would be *to arrange for* the storage and transfer of information. It becomes a method for channeling public funds into information development. Supported by federal appropriations, it would be able to make payments to institutions for the storage of information used and to copyright holders for the use of information. Its relationships would be with libraries and information storage agencies. It would not become involved in statewide distribution or with urban cable systems. Yet because of its central position it could assure the compatibility of telecommunication systems. The corporation could provide for high-unit efficiency, for it would negotiate bulk rates with private industry for telecommunication and computer services. The major objective would be to increase equal opportunity for information by facilitating the work of libraries.

In its action creating corporations, the federal government has each time recognized the importance to society of open channels for communication. The CPB increased the still limited number of broadcast program choices. The venerable U.S. Post Office Department was faulted because it could not adapt to technological innovation. In neither case could the free market be relied upon to produce the service. In both instances the public corporation was used to avoid the restrictive practices of government administration.

An information transfer corporation would also escape the constraints which are imposed on government operations. I refer to the fiscal and personnel practices, statutory and policy limitations, and constant time-consuming review. It would be free to act wherever the problems occurred — national, state, or local. Particularly important, it could operate outside the United States with the freedom of any industrial corporation. It would be a force in providing visibility and identity to libraries, not as a part of some host institution but as an independent activity determined to preserve and extend the individual right to information. And it would allow for concentration. If this activity were part of a department of government or a national library it would have to bow to the agency's statutory and policy limitations, and march in some degree to the tune of a multipurpose organization.

Because it can collect demand, the corporation becomes a management tool by which library telecommunication requirements can be determined. New uses can be studied and predicted. Industry receives the information needed to warrant investment in response. The corporation is a means by which technological innovations can be introduced into library services.

A corporation makes it possible to plan and mount a general system. It provides central control and the vital power to enforce system standards. This may be accomplished by little more than a contract with a common carrier. But a corporation also has the capability to utilize alternatives: It can operate a totally owned system using government spectrum space, lease a special designed service from a communications company, use a federally operated communication service through a national library facility and others. It can join with other major entities such as the CPB in joint use of services.

A corporation can exploit to advantage the opportunities afforded by regulation of the radio spectrum. Currently, industrial applicants to the FCC for privileged use of the spectrum have been able to provide only token assurances of public service uses, with the very notable exception of industrial offers made to educational television. A corporation could negotiate with industrial corporations as they prepared applications to the FCC, a very timely moment.

The Information Transfer Corporation is not possible for perhaps five years. We have to learn more about costs and about benefits, and foundation support will be necessary for the study. Conceptualization, professional acceptance, and congressional action all require time. I refer to the experience of the CPB. A year was spent in developing the interest of the government and the profession; the Carnegie Commission required something over a year and Congress something less. The first appropriation came well over four years after the campaign began. I think in this case it would take longer.

But there is not much reason for concern over the delay. The time to treat a national network with the seriousness a corporation implies has not arrived. A telecommunications network will not operate until such time as a standard record has been developed and received acceptance along with a universal language for an automated bibliographical control system. The Library of Congress looks to sometime in 1972 or later for this product. Nevertheless, the ETV experience indicates that if we are interested in an operating national telecommunication network for libraries during this decade it is not too early to begin organized study of ways and means.

In the intervening period the momentum of network development should not be allowed to decline. The need for coordination of research and development requires a central source of direction and the struggle over telecommunication policies, a base from which to exert influence on current decisionmaking.

Research Institute Passage of S. 1519 (establishing the National Commission on Libraries and Information Science) without provision for an institute leaves libraries without a mechanism to coordinate the detailed technical planning and research and demonstrations which the National Advisory Commission on Libraries recommended as essential to the development of a national library system. A strong network development program should be initiated now, if at all possible. This may be an extension of an existing program, such as the Institute for Library Research, or an entirely new program may be desirable with the primary objective to direct research on problems of automation and telecommunication associated with networking.

In my opinion, a private effort would have advantages at this time over a government activity. Many of the reasons listed earlier in support of a nongovernment corporation apply. But a primary reason is the greater possibility today for a private entity to raise adequate funds; that is, if a favorable opinion supports this goal.

The establishment of the National Commission on Libraries and Information Science does not leave groups totally free to take leadership in developing a private institute, even if it were regarded as timely. Yet all initative should not be surrendered. It would be ill-advised to establish an institute without positive interest by the Executive Office of the President and the new national commission. However, the necessary agreement of leading private groups and the assurance of private funding should be explored.

Action Center. Issues which ultimately effect the cost of telecommunications and the access of libraries to users or to other libraries are determined at a number of points: municipal agencies, state commissions, FCC, General Services Administration, Interagency Radio Advisory Committee, and the Congress of the United States.

As potential users of state networks, urban cable systems, and satellite interconnections, libraries have basic interests in these determinations. Some attempts to create a favorable telecommunication environment for education have been described. While one can properly advise that the local library director lead a fight for public channel concessions at a cable franchise hearing, to base national development entirely on the separate actions of hundreds of independent institutions is not likely to assure full exploitation of opportunities or a uniformly high level of access to new telecommunication systems.

Latecomers to the spectrum regulation game are at a severe disadvantage and have difficulty in demonstrating effective use without experience to fall back on. They have much to learn, and because of the volatile character of telecommunications today, they must learn it quickly. Most decisions are made on the basis of arguments presented by self-declared parties of interest. Basic application patterns for the new transmission technologies will be set over the next five years and most often in response to the "squeaky wheel."

In bringing to bear the requirements of libraries for telecommunications, no behavior coming from within government can substitute for strong, organized citizen action outside government. A small investment in an action program now could produce important dividends for libraries, far in excess of the investment.

A National Action Center could be organized with the function of creating a telecommunication environment favorable to the growth of information networks. As a private entity, it could move easily at all levels of government and have a general maneuverability which government agencies lack. It would be designed for effectiveness in adversary relationships and would be a source of information and support in local libraries. While drawing on the expertise of the library profession, it should be regarded as independent of the profession and backed by citizens of national stature.

Finance Study. I have been impressed in my reading with how little attention appears to be paid by the profession to the matter of federal financing. The opposite side of the coin, the control of costs, is often considered in the literature.

There is agreement that an increased proportion of funding must come from Washington. In the past decade the federal programs for libraries followed the general pattern for the new health and education programs. Categorical programs for construction, research and development, professional improvement, and services were broken down by classes of institutions and populations to be served. No steady-state network system is possible under an extension of existing funding patterns.

Financing a national network system involves much more than the costs of technology and its operation. Large-scale exchange of materials between independently supported institutions is not workable when it drains the haves to support the have-nots. Already there is some strain on that point. What will happen when natural barriers to interlibrary loan requests are at a minimum?

Is a national library system based on networking possible without federal financing to support the performance of that mission? Library cooperation and networking can develop to a certain degree along market lines. Ideally, the pattern of funding for a national system should promote the achievement of primary objectives. The Carnegie Commission on Educational Television recommended a plan which reinforced their principal concern, insulation from political influence. One form of library funding might be geared properly to encourage the collection and circulation of materials. A federal funding program for the support of circulation could not be developed without a much clearer picture of operating costs. There are enormous difficulties in the way of cost accounting as is made clear in the paper on library operations costs prepared for the National Advisory Commission on Libraries. Adequate information is lacking and may never become available in ideal form.

Something approaching a market situation might nevertheless become workable. Perhaps it will be as simple as a federally supported fund for reimbursement of national circulation, with libraries drawing payments from the fund for library loans, based on a schedule which would allow a "profit" over actual operating costs.

Obviously, careful study of many alternatives is required. A serious approach to networking cannot neglect the subject of financing. Such a study involves the whole of the library and information service enterprise. Reliance on the present federal patterns of block and formula grants or committee-approved special grants is not conducive to system growth and operation.

The findings of the study should include recommendations for federal financing designed to increase information opportunities for the user. These could remain in the wings awaiting an appropriate opportunity and would be insurance against a program of library funding constructed from general formats by an overworked staff of the U.S. Office of Education.

MAINTAINING MOMENTUM

There should be no let-up in exploring the application of telecommunications to library services. "a program of action" prepared for the National Advisory Commission on Libraries and included in *Libraries At Large* advises, as an approach to technological development in the foreseeable future, a process of identifying and supporting selected "high impact" activities. I would like to add some candidates to the list. These have particular relevance to the future application of telecommunications and reflect events which have occurred since the preparation of that program.

Urban Networks. What, if any, will be the effect of the "wired city" on libraries? A multidiscipline study group with with strong representation from urban libraries might examine the implications of cable systems for libraries. The opportunity would be provided for conceptual meshing of urban library policies and operations with the technological potential of the wired city system. Such a study should be pursued in enough depth to perform a function in national and local wired city decisionmaking proceedings. It seems unlikely that a pilot library project involving cable systems could be successfully initiated for some time. However, the need for such a project should be recognized, and the necessary conditions set forth in the study so as to lay a basis for future industrial and foundation assistance.

Statewide Networks. The planning of library services using statewide telecommunication networks might be funded in selected states. Superior effects would merit further funding for the preparation of detailed plans. If warranted, and if the necessary technical and organizational conditions existed within the state, the future funding of a few demonstration projects might result. It is evident that even a single demonstration would be very costly if carried over a period of a few years and should be undertaken only if there is promise of extending proven practices to other states.

National Prototype Projects. The three national libraries should receive the active support of the profession in efforts to mount national network demonstrations. The National Library of Medicine has developed plans for a national health system. It may be possible that this library system could be linked to an industrial application to the FCC for authority to operate a communication satellite system. There are other possibilities. The National Agricultural Library and EDUCOM are jointly developing plans for a university network. The Library of Congress looks to an automated national network based upon its developing automated central bibliographical system.

A Satellite Strategy. Libraries should actively participate in all efforts to extend the principle of free or low-cost rates for education. This particularly applies to actions under existing statutory language. But it applies also to organized efforts to use the opportunities afforded by requests to the FCC for authorizations to operate communication satellite systems.

National network forecast. There have been several national network models prepared which would serve particular information objectives. No national development schedule based on alternative priority arrangements has been attempted, and it may well be impossible. However, without making explicit the costs, benefits, manpower needs, and general operating requirements for alternate methods to meet the nation's information needs, it is difficult to begin to arrange the political, financial, and operational conditions necessary to future development.

In the interest of favorable support, it is desirable to reduce internal conflict which may weaken confidence. A plan of development which recognizes all legitimate needs and proposes to accommodate them at some point in the future can serve as a basis for unified effort. The good sense of having such information available is clear, but the extent to which it is feasible to get it is the question.

NETWORKS AND THE FEDERAL ROLE, A PERSONAL VIEW

The sad truth is that there are many unresolved problems standing in the way of a national system of library telecommunication networks. Certainly we have reached the point where a more orderly, more coherent, and more effective approach to the development of information systems should be considered. A number of important efforts such as that by the National Task Force on Automation and other cooperative services are clearing away the problems relating to messages. Yet the status of telecommunication development —statewide networks, urban cable systems, national prototype projects — provides no assurance that the normal progression of events will accommodate the probable future needs of libraries. The impression is quite the contrary.

Nor does the commendable growth in sharing between libraries, documented elsewhere, give us assurance that lacking greater direction these separate cooperative programs will inevitably evolve into a well-integrated and equitable national library network. A new level of activity is needed, broader in scope, more coherent in plan, and with much greater involvement by the public and private forces in the field.

Development of library use of telecommunication networks can be viewed in two phases: Creation of the essential conditions, involving an array of actions over the next five years, and initiation and expansion of a steady-state national system sometime thereafter. The earlier phase would use existing federal resources augmented by foundation aid and would encompass programs of research and development to solve technical and operational problems, programs of public action to shape government policy so as to permit educational application of telecommunication, and the development and authorization of a steady-state plan. The latter phase would demand an entirely new level of federal financial support and new operating and management mechanisms. Throughout, the power of the federal government would be paramount.

A principal question in the course of future development is the desirable role to be assumed by the federal government. Stated another way, what are the limits to be placed on federal action in this area of individual communication?

A second major question concerns the nature and goals of private organized effort. The resources of government will be captured only with the help of organized activity outside government. Only with private action can the environment created by government practices, such as the regulation of cable systems, be successfully modified to allow for optimum library network development. Organized private action will be required also if developmental and financial roles of government are to be expanded.

In considering national library and information networking, I think we can easily underestimate the problem. The present library system is representative of an earlier era of more or less autonomous units serving clusters of people, with relationships between units tending to be personal as much as institutional. We are considering marrying this highly autonomous library system to library telecommunication networks which require a great amount of integrative behavior with consistency and conformity by participants. In the process the problems also change from those primarily determined locally or within the institution to problems which require national solutions and national mechanisms to implement solutions.

As far as libraries are concerned, telecommunication networking is not simply one more technical advance. A functioning network heralds the entry of the library into the industrial age. A national network requires central planning and control of the elements needed to assure function of an apparatus which is a national instrument and yet made up of parts which continue to reflect local needs.

We will observe a process which has been repeated many times during the industrialization of the nation, the application of technology to hand methods resulting in increased availability of services. It is a process also in which the small unit often fails or is merged with the larger unit.

The term "network" can signify many forms and degrees of cooperation. To achieve major goals of the National Advisory Commission on Libraries, one can envisage a national library network system made up of regional or state library network systems. Essentially, all locations are provided with access to information on total national and international holdings and access within prescribed limits to the materials contained in the total holding. Telecommunications in this national library system are used routinely for cooperation in acquisitions, technical processing, organizing and maintaining library collections, as well as in sharing resources to meet service demands and in providing access to the total national store. It is a system that uses state or regional telecommunication networks for rapid response and urban cable systems for convenience to the client.

If this, or something approaching this, is a goal, the library will have to increase institutional power. Organized control will be required over far more of the surrounding environment.

A working telecommunication network demands more than a will to cooperate between entities. Sufficient control over the future is required to provide adequate financial resources, enlightened regulations, sound technology, operational competence, and effective articulation with user needs and habits. A national library system will be able to plan cooperative action and exercise the control needed to apply the plans and measure results; these powers are nonexistent in today's laissez faire system.

Evidence of the importance of central control in the operation of telecommunication systems are the two most effective operators today, the telephone company and the U.S. government.

As John Kenneth Galbraith in the *New Industrial State* points out, a major factor in the progress and low cost of telephone service in the United States has been the dominance by comprehensive planning at all points of the system. By way of contrast, he points to the poor performance of U.S. mass transit systems where government policy has precluded central direction.

The military so entirely controls their communication environment, even including the spectrum, that they, as users of communication, can define their requirements and provide a market incentive for industry to solve the problem. The needs for communication go in search of the technology.

Experience surely suggests that the operation of a national library telecommunication network will require strong central operating controls. To date, no operating national telecommunication network has been established outside the market economy except with firm federal direction.

The greatest obstacle to system development according Nelson Associates, Inc., is the library's fear that autonomy will be lost. The library has a number of protections, anchored as it is to a host institution, dependent on local funding, public and private, and protected under state and local statutes. Yet the effect of a national service on local autonomy is a question that cannot be set aside. How can we construct and gain operational effectiveness for a coherent set of national objectives and practices while at the same time preserving as much as possible the ability of individual library units and small systems to adapt to the special needs of their community? An answer must be found to satisfy the individual library if it is to agree to participate in national networking.

Traditionally, the federal government has used the taxing power and gained conformity of the smaller unit through financial inducements. Networking will result probably in greater library operating costs, the formula being increased access equals increased circulation equals greater costs. While libraries as agents of host institutions will continue probably to receive major support from the budgets of their hosts, national networks will surely require increased federal support to libraries.

Federal control of operations need not be a price for additional federal support, however, three private communication corporations established over the last decade by government action are recognition that the superior tax power of the federal government is not to be equated with superior administrative capacity.

On the other hand, Congress has every right to know what it is receiving for expenditures to weigh them against other demands. Measures of performance become a necessary tool to protect management freedom.

It is said that since libraries do not determine content as in the case of television there need be little concern over government influence. Yet libraries do determine access to information. Access can be influenced indirectly by apathetic administration, adherence to old processes, failure to understand the needs of the users, and it can be influenced directly by funding priorities. For different reasons, the question of federal control is as real for libraries as it is for the mass media.

Our problem is to produce a system of funding which serves a creative purpose and does not suppress the very function which it is designed to perform, namely to increase availability of relevant knowledge.

If the federal government were to manage a national library network there would be, it seems to me, some danger that the system would respond best to knowledge requirements growing out of the directions and purposes of established bureaucracy. The federal government is not only a source of finance but also it is an interested party. It includes within its house a great many information users and library institutions. Can any of these honestly speak for the varied needs of the general citizen? The special functions of government — economic development, social control, scientific growth — will receive emphasis while the general needs of man for knowledge to control himself, his environment, his society, and his nation will face a subtle neglect. Will the needs of science and technology for which the federal government provides large resources be emphasized over the humanities and the arts for which the federal government provides only the smallest token of assistance?

The power of the federal government needs to be offset by solid increases in organized power and initative outside government.

Increase in power outside government is desirable for a second reason. It is usually overlooked that a national library network would not be supported by a market economy out of which steam for development can come. Libraries have been told to imitate the network practices of industry. Unlike industry, there are no profits for libraries to be generated with expanded networks. If anything, networks may produce losses when used to increase circulation of materials, unless they are linking units of a single central system. Therefore, the big libraries have good reason to reject networks.

What source is to supply the steam? In the absence of a market economy, the only power available for advancement of a national pattern of networking is the national government. How is the federal power to be evoked? We have observed examples of presidential leadership, foundation leadership, and pressure from science and industry, each seeking to link federal powers to development of a network. What will constitute a sufficiently powerful motivating force to support such leadership? Nothing less, I suggest, than the combined forces of those who would benefit — industry, government, the information using disciplines, the citizen, joined by the private foundations and the library professional — all sharing in a campaign of program planning and persuasion.

I would dispute those who think the national climate to be poor for advancement. There is good reason for the national administration to turn a friendly hand to the improvement of libraries and information services. With recent appointments there are within the Executive Office of the President unusually strong abilities in the area of telecommunications. The administration, furthermore, has rather successfully challenged the highly centralized character of our mass media. It has been met with the charge that its attack, far from representing a concern for the citizen's access to all kinds of opinion, is exclusively concerned with its own public exposure. There could be no such

confusion in the promotion of libraries as the communication medium which provides full and free access to the opinions of the world.

Perhaps out of this Conference can come a temporary steering committee made up of individuals with experience and ties representative of the many facets and interests touched by a national program for information system development. Such a group could lay the basis for a more comprehensive and solidly based approach to the problem, and assure that the momentum of this Conference will not be lost.

NOTES

1. Dan Lacy, "Social change and the library: 1945-1980," in D. M. Knight and E. S. Nourse, eds., *Libraries at large* (N.Y.: Bowker, 1969), p.12.

2. The International Telecommunications Union is an agency of the United Nations. The definition is that approved by the Union.

3. U.S. Office of Education, "The United States Office of Education: Progress and potentialities of its library programs," in D.M. Knight and E.S. Nourse, eds., *Libraries at large,* chap. XI, p.481.

4. U.S. Executive Office of the President, Office of Telecommunications Management, "Significance of technical trends in telecommunications," 22 Jan. 1968. Mimeo.

5. Lyndon B. Johnson, "Special message to the Congress on communications policy," *Public papers of the presidents,* 14 Aug. 1967, (Washington, D.C.: Gov. Print. Off., 1968), p.763.

6. President's Task Force on Communication Policy, *Final report* (Washington, D.C.: Gov. Print. Off., 1968), Chap. IX, p.2-7.

7. National Advisory Commission on Libraries, "Library services for the nation's needs," in D.M. Knight and E.S. Nourse, eds., *libraries at large* p.518

8. U.S. Congress, House, Committee on Education and Labor, Committee on Instructional Technology, *To improve education,* (Washington, D.C.: Gov. Print. Off., 1970), p.45.

9. President Richard Nixon, "Message on educational reform to the Congress of the United States," (Washington, D.C.: Office of the White House Press Secretary, 3 March 1970). Mimeo.

10. Lyndon B. Johnson, "Remarks upon signing the Public Broadcasting Act of 1967," *Public papers of the presidents,* (Washington, D.C.: Gov. Print. Off., 1968), p.996.

11. President's Task Force on Communication Policy, *Final report,* (Washington, D.C.: Gov. Print. Off., 1968), Chap. V, p.14, 17, 36.

12. Peter Flanigan, "Memorandum for the Honorable Dean Burch, Chairman of the Federal Communications Commission, from Peter Flanigan, Assistant to the President," 23 Jan. 1970.

13. South Dakota, Governor's Ad Hoc State Communications Committee, *Communication system planning for the state of South Dakota,* p.25. Mimeo.

14. Illinois, *Telecommunication study,* Report C, (Santa Monica, Calif.: System Development Corporation, 15 Feb. 1969), p.82.

15. Electronic Industries Association, Industrial Electronics Division, *Comments on Docket No. 18397, Part V,* (Washington, D.C.: The Association, 27 Oct. 1969), p.20. Unpublished.

16. U.S. Executive Office of the President, Office of Telecommunications Management, "Significance of technical trends," p.51.

17. Sidney Dean, "Hitches in the cable," *Nation* (20 July 1970).

Emerging State and Regional Library Networks

Genevieve M. Casey

John Cory, speaking at a conference on library networks held at the University of Chicago in the summer of 1968[1] identified four generations of library organization, each achieving increasing levels of capacity, effectiveness, complexity and versatility, and decreasing unit cost. The four generations are:

1. A single library of a single type — a public, college, school, or special library

2. A system or network of several libraries of the same type (such as a public library system)

3. A combination of several library systems or several libraries of different types

4. A combination of various types of libraries and nonlibrary agencies concerned with related activities.

This paper will concern itself with the third generation which represents the growing edge of librarianship today — that is, with state and regional networks combining resources of several types of libraries. It is based largely upon reports from the states on their administration of the Library Services and Construction Act, LSCA, filed with the Bureau of Libraries and Education Technology of the U.S. Office of Education, and on information received directly from state library agencies. Special thanks are due to Dorothy Kittel of the bureau and to the state library personnel who took time to respond to our queries.

INTERLIBRARY COOPERATION

Several official policy statements released by the American Library Association, ALA, reflect the consensus of the library profession that no one library and no one type of library can be self-sufficient in serving its users.

With the exception of the School Media Standards,[2] which encourage districtwide, regional, and state instructional media centers but seem to be unaware of the existence of other types of libraries to which schools might beneficially relate — all the other statements of standards and objectives by major types of library divisions in the ALA refer specifically to the importance of interlibrary cooperation. The Public Library Association makes a fundamental commitment to interlibrary coordination in that its most recent standards are *Minimum Standards for Public Library Systems*.[3] In addition to assuming that adequate library service can be provided *only* through larger units, which except in large cities are achieved by multijurisdictional public library systems, the standards also underscore the responsibility of the public library to take leadership in the fostering of interlibrary cooperation between the various other libraries — school, academic, special — in the community. In fact as early as 1956, the public library standards stated: "Libraries working together, sharing their services and materials can meet the full needs of their users. The cooperative approach on the part of libraries is the most important single recommendation."[4]

The most recent standards for college libraries, adopted by the Association of College and Research Libraries in 1959,[5] include a strong statement on cooperation with other college, university, school, and public library agencies in the community, region, state, and nation for the benefit of students and faculty, and also on the college library's responsibility to help in providing reference service to readers beyond the campus. The *ALA Standards for Junior College Libraries* [6] contains a similar statement on interlibrary cooperation with the emphatic proviso that cooperative arrangements with other libraries ought not to be viewed as a substitute for an adequate library in the junior college itself.

At the state level, the task of fostering the coordination of library resources and services throughout the state is identified as one of the major roles of the state library. Of the eight chapters detailing state library responsibility contained in the most recent standards,[7] three are concerned with "The State and State-Wide Library Development," "State-Wide Development of Resources," and "State and Information Networks." Underlying the entire statement of standards and objectives is the conviction that "the total library and information resources of the state must be developed, strengthened and coordinated as a whole,"[8] and that the emerging systems of public, school, and academic libraries within the state must be "linked in a defined relationship with each other and with other information services to form 'networks of knowledge' ".[9]

In addition to the mandates for interlibrary coordination carried in the standards for various types of libraries, in June

1967 the boards of directors of four ALA divisions, the Associations of Public, State, School, and College and Research Libraries, approved a joint statement on interlibrary cooperation.[10] The statement set forth "the imperative need for cooperation" (generated by such factors as changes in American education and culture which have resulted in increasing and accelerating reader demands upon libraries, changes in quantity and variety of published materials, and developments in technological applications for libraries, plus rising costs of materials, equipment, and service) and principles for attaining effective cooperation. Within the assumption that "no one library can be self-sufficient" and that "libraries acting together can more effectively satisfy user needs," the statement outlines the prerequisites for fruitful interlibrary cooperation: (1) that primary responsibility for each type of library to its special clientele must be defined before interlibrary cooperation can be established to augment service; (2) that effective cooperation depends upon adequate resources, administrative capability, and efficient communications; (3) that although the primary responsibility of each library must be respected, each library must realize its responsibilities to the network and assume its appropriate share of responsibility; (4) that all libraries must maintain an attitude of flexibility and experimentation.

LIBRARY LEGISLATION

Much of the federal library legislation of the sixties reflects the concern of the library profession and of Congress for the coordination of resources and services. The Higher Education Act of 1965, PL89-329, under Title II A provides funds for "combinations of institutions of higher education which need special assistance in establishing and strengthening joint use facilities."

In the amendment to the act in 1968, Title VIII, Networks for Knowledge, was added "to encourage colleges and universities to share to an optimal extent, through cooperative arrangements, their technical and other educational and administrative facilities and resources and in order to test and demonstrate the effectiveness and efficiency of a variety of such arrangements." Eligible projects include "joint use of facilities such as classrooms, libraries or laboratories, access to specialized library collections through preparation of interinstitutional catalogs and through development of systems and preparation of suitable media for electronic or other rapid transmission of materials." Unfortunately, funds have never been appropriated to implement this very promising legislation.

The Elementary and Secondary Education Act, Title II, requires in its regulations that state plans include some provision for coordination between school libraries and public library programs at both state and local levels.[11]

The most significant encouragement to interlibrary cooperation came with the addition of Title III to the Library Services and Construction Act in 1966 although statewide planning for library development really began in most states with the passage of the original Library Service Act of 1956, which provided funds to the states continent upon a plan for the improvement and extension of public library services. Under the Library Services Act and its successor, the Library Services and Construction Act, public library systems were established in most states and became the nuclei of subsequent third-generation library organizations.

Title III of the Library Services and Construction Act provides funds to the states to "establish and maintain local, regional, state, or interstate networks of libraries for systematic and effective coordination of the resources of school, public, academic, and special libraries or special information centers." Funds are to be spent according to a plan devised by the state library agency with the help of an advisory council representative of all library interests in the state. Projects need not be statewide but must include a "mix" of library types. Funds can be spent for equipment, personnel, and leasing of space but cannot be used for the purchase of library material — a wise restriction since it forces the linkage of existing resources and services, and a more creative approach to the cooperation than the traditional purchase of a collection of expensive and/or esoteric material for the use of all libraries in a state or region. Federal funds, according to the act, must be matched on an equal basis with state or local funds although Congress later resolved to suspend the matching requirement through June 1968.

The first appropriation under LSCA Title III was made by Congress in 1967. The act authorizes appropriations of $5 million in 1967, $7.5 million in 1968, $10 million in 1969, $12.5 million in 1970, and $15 million in 1971, but actual appropriations never have enabled more than a basic grant of approximately $40,000 to each state, a sum which if matched at the minimum level, as is common in most states, cannot fund the massive programs needed to make all the library resources of any state available to all its citizens.

Despite its minimal funding, Title III has resulted, in forty-nine of the states, in serious planning between libraries of all types and in a comprehensive look, often for the first time, at all of the library resources in each state from the point of view of the user. Some linkage of resources in major libraries in each state has been accomplished. An evaluation of the total impact of Title III and of what remains to be achieved now is urgently needed.

Funds available under LSCA Title III, supplemented often by state money or Title I, have supported numerous studies of statewide library resources, weaknesses, and needs.

SURVEYS AND STUDIES

A most useful bibliography of statewide studies from 1956 to 1967 compiled by Gale Rike[12] of the University of Illinois Library Research Center should be updated. These studies are an unparalleled record of the growing edge of the profession and usually are available only in limited quantity from the contracting state library agency.

Most of these studies, like Michigan's *Reference and Research Library Needs in Michigan*[13] (which actually antedated LSCA III) are statewide in scope. Maryland, for example, reports "studies to discover new approaches in library planning to meet changing requirements of society, to take advantage of appropriate technologies and provide for the orderly implementation of library development plans." Maine is conducting a comprehensive study of total library resources of the state, including factual data on resources as well as a survey of use and public opinion about libraries in three selected communities. Hawaii commissioned a broad study of all library services on the islands, including an investigation into patterns of library use as well as some research about the nonuser.[14] This study led to a comprehensive, long-range plan for library development which is now being implemented.

One of the most extensive surveys was conducted in Indiana under the direction of Dr. Peter Hiatt and is soon to be published.[15] This study, which began almost two years ago, includes numerous in-depth studies by a wide variety of researchers including: *Response to Change: American Libraries in the Seventies,* by Virginia Mathews and Dan Lacy; *The Role of Libraries in the Cultural History of Indiana,* by Robert Constantine; *Library Usage of Children and Young Adults,* by Philip Wilder and Phillip Mikesell; *A study of Adult Information Needs in Indiana,* by Jack Wentworth and Charles Bonser; *General Economic and Demographic Background and Projections for Indiana Library Services* and *Regional Supply and Demand for Library Services,* by James Foust; *Economic Aspects of Library Services in Indiana,* by Jerome Milliman and Richard Pfister; *A Survey of Library Services for Indiana's Handicapped,* by John McCrossan; *Library Services to Residents of Indiana State Institutions, The Indiana State Library: A Preliminarily Study, Structuring the Indiana State Library for Interlibrary Coordination,* and *Information Services to Indiana State Government,* by Genevieve Casey; *Survey of User Service Policies in Indiana Libraries and Information Centers,* by Edwin E. Olson; *A Survey of Indiana Special Libraries and Information Centers,* by Brigitte Kenney; *Centralized Processing for Indiana Libraries,* by Rothines Associates; *Directory of Special and Subject Collections in Indiana,* by Donald Thompson and Michael Rothacker; *Management and Use of State Documents in Indiana,* by Genevieve Casey and Edith Phillips; and *Historical Archival Programs of the Indiana Historical Society,* by Gerald Ham. A summary volume discussing the key findings of the total study and a long-range program for implementation is being published by Dr. Hiatt. In addition to their unusual scope and depth, the Indiana studies demonstrate a uniquely fruitful partnership between a state library and a library school.

In 1968 Ralph Blasingame completed a comprehensive study of Ohio's library needs[16] which led directly to new state legislation mandating a network of area library service centers and a statewide reference network. In addition to the Blasingame study, a recent issue of the Ohio State Library newsletter lists five other major studies commissioned by the State Library within the past five years.[17]

Supplementing comprehensive, statewide surveys, other states have conducted feasibility studies on some specific aspects of interlibrary cooperation. North Carolina commissioned a feasibility study on a statewide central research library facility. Illinois is investigating how school library programs might relate to other libraries, especially public libraries, and has contracted for a survey of interlibrary cooperation throughout the state to be finished in fall 1970. Nebraska is considering the feasibility of a statewide processing center for all libraries of all types. Other states, like Louisiana, have prepared for the third generation by conducting surveys to identify subject strengths, both in print and microform, in all the libraries of the state.

Evaluation of the emerging networks is understandably just beginning to take place. One of the first evaluation studies is the analysis of the first eighteen months of the Oklahoma TWX Network, OTIS,[18] which ties together the various regions of the state through ten transmission sites, mostly in public libraries, with the five resource libraries of the state: the State Library, the public libraries of Tulsa and Oklahoma City-County, and the two state university libraries. The study estimated the unit cost of the network, both to resource libraries and to TWX center libraries, its benefits in terms of user satisfaction (success in locating and supplying material and turn-around time), and the extent to which the network achieved fringe benefits such as the fostering of better development and use of local library resources, and broader coordination between libraries of various types on a state and local level. The study revealed that access to wider resources brought people into local public libraries who had never used them before and universally encouraged the selection of a higher level of material in the local libraries. The study also documented that the strongest libraries of the state made greatest use of the network. (The public library systems in Oklahoma accounted for more than one-third of the network's requests. The two university libraries accounted for 19 percent of the network's traffic.) The Oklahoma evidence refutes the fear, often expressed, that opening all resources in a state will tend to weaken incentives for local libraries to build collections. OTIS experience also underscores the vital importance of adequate bibliographical competence at the state library, the hub of the network.

The Texas State Library has recently published the second evaluation of its statewide reference network.[19]

The New York State Library continues to lead the nation in the intelligence and sophistication with which it discharges its obligations of leadership and planning. Studies too numerous to list have laid the groundwork for New York's emerging Reference and Research Resource Network, for the statewide cataloging and processing service, and for the New York State Interlibrary Loan Network, NYSILL. Careful research and planning, as well as continuous evaluation of progress, has typified New York State Library efforts. A bibliography of twelve 3R's studies commissioned by the New York State Library between 1962 and 1968 is included in a 1969 summary report by the library's Division of Library Development.[20] A second study evaluating NYSILL and two regional interlibrary networks established in fall 1968 to supplement the statewide network was published by Nelson Associates in 1969.[21] A study of the third phase of NYSILL has just been completed, documenting great improvements in the efficiency of the network and the volume of its use.

INTERLIBRARY LOANS

As some limited funds became available under LSCA III and as statewide studies documented growing needs for better access to materials not locally available, telecommunication networks have been established in almost all of the states. Teletypewriters to connect individual research libraries have been in use since 1927, as Herbert Poole indicates in his state-of-the-art report.[22] Interlibrary loan is as old as the second century before Christ, when Alexandria loaned books to Pergamum. However, these emerging networks are effecting significant changes both quantitatively and qualitatively in interlibrary loan as it traditionally has been practiced.

The National Interlibrary Loan Code most recently revised by the Reference Services Division of ALA in 1968[23] has always taken the view that "the purpose of interlibrary loan is to make available for *research* materials not owned by a given library." It is conceived as a privilege to be sought only for faculty and graduate students, and limited to unusual items which the borrowing library does not own and cannot readily obtain at moderate cost. Ordinarily excluded are U.S. books in print of moderate cost; serials when the item can be copied at moderate cost; rare materials, including manuscripts; basic reference materials; genealogical, heraldic, and similar materials bulky or fragile materials which are difficult and expensive to pack, e.g., newspapers; and typescript doctoral dissertations when fully reproduced in microfilm and readily available.

In 1968 when it promulgated the latest national interlibrary loan code, the Reference Services Division also released for comment a "Model Interlibrary Loan Code for Regional, State, Local or Other Special Groups of Libraries."[24] This code was intended to complement the national code and recognized the need for fundamental changes in interlibrary borrowing and lending practices to accommodate the growing needs of the American people and the new patterns being developed in state and regional networks. In order to provide for full utilization of state and regional resources, and thus to avoid over-use of a few very large national collections, the proposed code recommended a much more liberal lending policy within state networks. As summarized by Marjorie Karlson, chairman of the ALA Reference Services Division Interlibrary Loan Committee, the principal differences between the model regional code and the national code are:[25]

1. Borrowing is not limited to research purposes.

2. There is no borrower statement — anyone presumably is eligible.

3. Almost anything can be requested; however, there is a brief list of materials that should not be requested.

4. There is a strong statement on the responsibility of any library to develop collections adequate to meet its normal needs; freer interlibrary loan should not diminish local efforts to build resources.

5. Requests to borrow should be channeled through some central agency, often the state library, where requests can be serviced in some cases, screened, and the load on other libraries distributed equitably.

6. Funding of state plans is considered.

7. Standard ALA forms may be used, but it is likely that most states will use TWX or Telex installations, thereby simplifying and speeding up procedures; many state plans may pay for these installations through the state library.

8. All types of libraries may be included.

9. Participation presumably will be voluntary, and contracts for services are foreseen.

10. Agreements or contracts among or with individual libraries are not precluded.

Although, as stated in the third point, "almost anything can be requested," the code does recommend that libraries do not ordinarily request (*a*) "books in current and/or recurring demand, (*b*) bulky or fragile materials, (*c*) rare materials, (*d*) large number of titles for one person at any one time, (*e*) duplicates of titles already owned, (*f*) materials which can be copied cheaply, (*g*) materials for class reserve or other group use."[26]

The model code was conceived as subject to change or modification before adoption by any local, state, regional, or other group of libraries. As stated, its fundamental purpose was to provide for the maximum use of local resources and thus to minimize pressure upon the large research libraries of the nation.

Nevertheless, the liberalizing of interlibrary loan privilege as recommended in the *Model Interlibrary Loan Code for Regional, State or Other Special Groups of Libraries* and as practiced in most of the emerging state networks has alarmed some members of the Association of Research Libraries. A position statement on the model code, proposed for ARL by Arthur McAnally, director of the Oklahoma University Library, affirmed continuing commitment to the principle of ready access to information by all who need it; however, he emphasized that the increasing volume of interlibrary loan activity was placing unduly heavy burdens on libraries with nationally important collections —to the point where these libraries might have to terminate interlibrary lending altogether or curtail it drastically unless some method of reimbursement is provided. Dr. McAnally proposed the following guidelines for research libraries participating in state or regional interlibrary loan systems:

1. The needs of the library's own clientele and its obligations to the authorities who established and support it must come first. No library should agree to participate in a regional or state interlibrary loan system to an extent that would reduce the quality of service to its own legal or basic clientele.

2. After its obligations to its own clientele, the next level of obligation of a research library of national strength is to the nation, that is, to the National Interlibrary Loan Code. Participation in a regional or state system should not be at the expense of fidelity to the National Interlibrary Loan Code.

3. Any regional or state interlibrary loan code must contain a statement on the necessity for all libraries to continue to make vigorous efforts to develop library collections adequate to meet the normal, everyday needs of their own basic clienteles.

4. Any regional or state interlibrary loan code should contain provisions which will assure that the burden of interlibrary lending will be distributed as equitably as possible and that it will not fall on just a few libraries, with the exception of a state library. (It is recognized that in some interlibrary loan systems contracts may be negotiated with research libraries to serve as "resource libraries" for the system.) Research libraries should be used as supports to any regional or state interlibrary loan system in which they decide to participate, rather than as the basic supplier of library materials for the system.

5. To secure an equitable distribution of the interlibrary lending burden, a central state agency should screen all interlibrary loan requests submitted through the system. In most states the logical screening agency will be the state library. The screening process should be done by professional librarians. It should restrict requests to research libraries chiefly to those items needed for research which are not available elsewhere in the state or region.

6. As a condition of participation in a regional or state interlibrary loan system, a research library must be able to designate those categories of users which it will serve, the type of materials which it will lend, and conditions of loan.

7. Any research library which participates in a regional or state interlibrary loan system should be reimbursed for loans or photocopies made through the system. The amount of reimbursement may vary from state to state and region to region and may take a variety of forms. But the principle of reimbursement should be recognized and adhered to. If it is not, research libraries will not be able to bear the additional costs which will result from expanded interlibrary loan effort and consequently, will not be able to participate in any proposed system.

8. Any research library should reserve the right to conduct its own interlibrary borrowing and lending programs directly with other research libraries, either in or out of the state or region served by the system.

9. Any research library which participates in a regional or state interlibrary loan system should do so on the basis of a formal, written contract which specifies the conditions of participation. This contract should be submitted to the governing board of the library for approval.

These guidelines were approved by the executive board of the Association of Research Libraries at its annual meeting in January 1969,[27] with the addition of a paragraph which stated: "The Association of Research Libraries recognizes that any ultimate solution to the general problem of expanded library services, including interlibrary loans, will probably require federal financial support to research libraries which serve as national as well as local or regional resources."

SYSTEMATIC UTILIZATION OF RESOURCES

The majority of the state networks, like Oklahoma's, use TWX to link the major public libraries with the resource (academic) libraries and the state library in order to facilitate the rapid and systematic utilization of all resources with the state. Commonly, as in Texas, a combination of long-distance telephone (linking the smaller libraries with the major public library centers) and TWX is used, with the state library assuming the cost of the telephone lines.

Most states have available to them wide-area telephone service (WATS) from the state capitols to key locations. A few states, such as Michigan, Arkansas, and Mississippi, have chosen to use the telephone as the sole communication device. Michigan's hotline project, begun before LSCA III, is an example.[28] The State Library telephones all public library systems headquarters every working day at the same hour to receive requests which cannot be filled in the region. School libraries enter the network through their local public library. The hotline was later extended to the community colleges of the state, and plans were made to include direct calls to the reference departments at each of the state's four-year colleges. The State Library undertook to handle all requests within twenty-four hours and to refer those not available in the state library's collection to the other resource libraries in the state and outside if necessary. The advantage of the hotline over TWX is that during the same daily telephone call, a report can be given on the previous day's requests and questions can be quickly clarified on substitutions, subject requests, etc. A major advantage is that the hotline tends to get a network started quickly with maximum volume since initiative is not left with the local library to use the network. The disadvantage is that it is costly in personnel (a TWX station can be unmanned) and sometimes leads to audio-confusion, especially if clerical rather than professional staff man the telephone. Iowa reports the use of Dataphone, which provides voice contact as well as facsimile transmission.

In most of the networks, the state library acts as the switching center and the bibliographical hub of the system. There are a few exceptions to this rule, such as Maryland which uses the

Enoch Pratt Free Library, Colorado which contracts with the Bibliographic Center for Research, Rocky Mountain Region, to manage the state network, and Kansas where Topeka has been designated as the network's center. In general, the effectiveness of the networks depend in great measure upon the competency of the state library to fill and refer requests.

Delivery of materials is usually done by mail although some states, like Connecticut, use LSCA III funds to maintain a truck for delivery. Many of the New York 3R's systems are delivering materials to member libraries either by truck or parcel delivery. These systems commonly articulate their delivery systems with the public library systems in the area.[29] After complaints that libraries were encountering long delays in delivery of material, Michigan made a study of mail service and discovered that most of the delays were occurring in the State Library, itself, and in the borrowing library (material delayed overnight, over a weekend in the library shipping room, material bottlenecked in the charging operation, etc.). The post office in Michigan was in fact making deliveries most of the time within twenty-four hours throughout the state.

The best known experiment with facsimile transmission was conducted by the New York State Library and abandoned as too costly and not technically satisfactory.[30] California also has experimented with facsimile transmission. Few people doubt that some form of facsimile transmission will become available to library networks within the near future.

Most states have arranged to use the major public and university libraries as resource libraries to fill requests not available at the state library itself. State library capacity to act as significant resource libraries varies widely from such states as Maryland and Colorado which do not aspire to research collections to distinguished research libraries in states like New York, Michigan, and California. In no state, however, can the state library hope to be the only resource.

COSTS AND COMPENSATION

The question of how to compensate the other resource libraries, whether university or large public libraries, is one which deserves serious study. Various patterns are being used, ranging from no compensation to a payment of $5 per transaction worked out in Connecticut and a flat fee paid to each of the resource libraries in Oklahoma, Pennsylvania, and other states. Michigan has taken a different approach by contracting with the University of Michigan for an "access office." Believing that the major cost to a university library is not so much for materials (many of the requests are for periodical, document, and report literature which can be photocopied, and thus duplication of materials is not a significant problem) as for staff, Michigan provides a reference librarian, supporting clerical staff, a telephone, and photocopying equipment by contract to the University of Michigan Library. The function of the access office is to receive and expedite requests for materials not available among the one million volumes at the Michigan State Library. All requests are filtered through the State Library. Michigan's Title III Advisory Council recommended that as funds become available, additional access offices be opened at the three other major resource libraries in the state —Wayne State and Michigan State Universities, and the Detroit Public Library.

New York State is unique in that it enters into contracts with resource libraries in the NYSILL network, compensating them for the state-appropriated rather than federal funds.

The library profession desperately needs definitive studies on actual costs to the resource library, the extent to which duplication of material is necessary, the actual personnel requirements (in terms of volume of requests), and the extent to which the use made of the state network by the resource library (usually a university library) itself outweighs or balances its contribution to the network. The study of interlibrary loan being proposed by the Association of Research Libraries may supply some of these answers.

INTERFACE OF NETWORKS

At least one state, Ohio, has used its (limited) LSCA III funds to establish a subject network linking the art collections in the state. Several states, such as Oklahoma and Indiana, are implementing some interface between the regional medical networks in operation within the state and the statewide reference network. As networks, both geographic and subject, develop and proliferate within states, regions, and the nation, the problem of interface will become acute.

New York and California already have recognized the serious problem of interface. S. Gilbert Prentiss, former state librarian of New York, speaking at the Chicago network conference in 1968, identified as a major problem the articulating and funding of New York's "networks within networks" with a minimum of conflict, competition, overlapping, and other waste motion.[31]

The excellent evaluation of the New York public library systems conducted by the New York State Department of Education in 1969 also emphasized the "need for coordinating library service of all types at all levels"[32] as well as the "need for intersystem coordination."[33]

New York's emerging network — which includes all public library systems, nine Reference and Research Resource systems (linking the public library systems with academic and special libraries in a broad area), and the top-level NYSILL system providing access to the major research collections of the state — is by far the most advanced state network in the nation. Added to the problem of coordinating this hierarchical series of networks are the complications of articulating with the numerous subject networks, national and state, in New York and the need to exploit the values of the data bank being created by the statewide cataloging project.

The council of California Library Association in December 1969 approved a *Master Plan for Total Library Services*,[34] which proposes both geographic networks in which all types of libraries within a given area are coordinated and subject networks linking together all libraries regardless of type which have strong subject emphasis expressed in highly specialized collections and staff. The plan recognizes that a given library may be a part of a geographic network as well as a part of one or more subject networks. The California plan places responsibility for coordinating the two kinds of networks with the California State Library, including "the administration of appropriate State and Federal assistance programs, provision of consultation services to all types of libraries, the maintenance of a centralized cataloging service available to all libraries, and the collection, analyses, and dissemination of library statistics to reveal trends and needs in service. The plan also charges the state library to build resources at the state level, develop specialized bibliographical tools, conduct and promote resource programs, provide leadership in the field of public relations and maintain a continuing education program in cooperation with the library schools of California and other appropriate schools."

BIBLIOGRAPHIC TOOLS

In addition to telecommunications, networks require bibliographical tools to locate materials for borrowing. More than half of the states report expenditures for some form of union list. Many other states have union catalogs which antedate LSCA III but are now being reevaluated. Ohio, for example, has maintained at the State Library a union catalog of the holdings of thirty-two public libraries, one college, and two special libraries since the thirties. At Case Western Reserve University, the forty libraries in the Cleveland area (twenty-seven academic, two public, and eleven special libraries) contribute to a union catalog.[35] In addition to these (card) catalogs, a data base on magnetic tape is being created by the Ohio College Library Center. The State Library has been engaged in studying the value, overlap, and possible coordination, if not amalgamation, of the three data bases as the keystone of Ohio's projected statewide reference network. Smaller states, such as North Dakota, Nebraska, and North Carolina, have undertaken union catalogs of all the holdings of major libraries of the state. North and South Dakota are creating a joint catalog of the serials in forty-seven North Dakota and twelve South Dakota libraries. Indiana is using Title III funds to enlarge the scope of a union list of serials in major Indiana universities to include the holdings of the State Library and several larger public libraries. Oregon, Virginia, and Tennessee are undertaking union catalogs of materials held by a group of libraries in one region of the state. MARC tapes are now opening up new possibilities in capturing information about location of materials, and several state libraries, including Kentucky and Oklahoma, are beginning to experiment with MARC.[36] Other states, such as Delaware, Louisiana, and Maryland, are going the less expensive and less precise route of creating catalogs of subject strengths rather than union catalogs.

A New York State Union List of Serials—using as master checklist the *SUNY Union List of Serials* and the *Central New York Union List,* and including in Phase I the serials holdings of the American Museum of Natural History, the Engineering Societies Library, the New York Public Library Research Libraries, the New York State Library, and the Teacher's College and Union Theological Seminary — was begun in 1968.[37] This list was conceived of as a prototype for the development of regional lists by the emerging 3R's systems.

When one considers the whole question of location tools for improved interlibrary loan, the experience of two major bibliographical centers in the nation — the Pacific Northwest Bibliographical Center located at the University of Washington in Seattle and the Bibliographic Center for Research, Rocky Mountain Region, located at the Denver Public Library — is relevant. Both centers began more than thirty years ago, both maintain author-entry card files of holdings of major libraries in

several states (PNBC: Washington, Oregon, Idaho, and Montana; Rocky Mountain center: fifteen states from Arizona and New Mexico to North and South Dakota). Both centers have massive files. PNBC estimated seven million cards as long ago as 1961, and the Rocky Mountain center now estimates more than three million cards. Both centers are partially subsidized by regional library associations — the Pacific Northwest and the Mountain-Plains Library Associations — and by the institutions in which they are housed — the University of Washington and the Denver Public Library. Both centers are supported largely by user fees, and both are in financial difficulty, finding the massive card files (rapidly growing as acquisition has accelerated especially in the university libraries in the region) more and more expensive to maintain and to query. Both centers have, within the past year, conducted studies of their future roles and financial structure, and find themselves facing a somewhat uncertain future.[38] Recommendations from both studies are remarkably similar. Massive catalogs in card form are increasingly impractical to maintain and to query. With the availability now of the MARC tapes, it would seem necessary to convert the retrospective catalogs to some distributable form (print or microform) and begin a new data bank in machine-readable form which can produce as a byproduct state union lists —tools for which the emerging state networks are discovering a need. Effort and money presently tied up in the maintenance and querying "by hand" of the present catalogs then could be spent in creating a whole universe of bibliographic tools which the networks and growing university libraries need — union lists of serials and periodicals, microfilm, film, state documents, as well as the union lists of holdings in major libraries of each state. That there is still a place for a regional bibliographical center is documented by the fact that the Rocky Mountain center is rapidly growing in volume of requests (80 percent between 1964 and 1968, and 74 percent between the first quarter of 1968 and the same period in 1969), and that it locates more than 94 percent of the material requested, 72 percent of the items in the Rocky Mountain Region. Both centers have traditionally accepted as members individual libraries of all types. Both are now moving away from multiple relationships with hundreds of individual libraries to contracts with the emerging statewide networks. Both studies recommended that the centers become the hub of a regional network of statewide libraries.

The plight of the regional bibliographical centers underscores the need for definitive answers to many questions in network design: How does the high cost of multiple locations in union catalogs balance against the cost of subsidizing a few major resource libraries? How does the cost in time and money for querying a bibliographical center balance against the "hit-or-miss" approach in interlibrary loan? How does the cost/benefit ratio of catalogs of subject strength compare to the cost/benefit ratio of the vastly more costly union catalog? For example, the Ohio Union Catalog maintains literally hundreds of entry cards for titles on Bibles in the Cincinnati Public Library which are queried rather seldom. Is the simple understanding that Cincinnati Public Library has the best collection in Ohio on biblical literature enough?

In addition to establishing statewide networks which link libraries of all types with some form of telecommunication, and creating and maintaining a variety of "union lists," or location tools, many states under LSCA III have initiated projects for the centralized acquisition, cataloging, and processing of materials. Frequently, as in Arkansas, Mississippi, and Montana, these include service only to school and public libraries in partnership with the state library. Other states, such as Delaware, North Dakota, and Utah, include all types of libraries in their plan. Some states, such as Oregon, Arizona, and Mississippi, include only a portion of the state; others, as in Utah and Nebraska, aspire to a single center for the entire state. Hawaii's central processing center serves all school and public libraries on the islands. New York is moving toward a single state cataloging center for all public library systems in the state.

PERSONNEL

An informed and competent staff is the key to the success of any network. Recognizing this, several western states have banded together in a unique project using LSCA III funds to contract with the Western Interstate Commission for Higher Education, WICHE, headquartered in Boulder, Colorado, to provide continuing education for librarians in the region. WICHE plans to conduct a series of conferences for librarians and library workers that will "encourage dialogue between public and school librarians and administrative personnel," and upgrade librarians through various programs of continuing education. The WICHE project involving several western state libraries is one of the most ambitious programs for library continuing education in the nation. It differs from many projects in that it integrates an entire region, making possible a level of training which would not be within the reach of any one state and it enables orderly, long-range planning rather than short-term fragmented focus.

The Southwest Library Association held a meeting in September 1970 to explore a wide variety of cooperative activities to fully utilize the resources of material and professional personnel in that region.

Many obstacles remain before we reach our goal of an integrated library service organized and administered to meet all the library and information needs of all the American people. Despite our fine phrases of commitment, despite the now documented need to share resources, the encouragement of federal and — in some states — state legislative programs, and the exciting possibilities of new communication devices, the National Advisory Commission on Libraries in its report of October 1968 revealed that present arrangements for the coordination and sharing of library resources and services are slow and inefficient, and that planning at all levels is urgently needed to ensure American citizens access to publications and vitally needed information.

In an effort to identify barriers preventing the development of cooperative activities among libraries of all types, the American Library Association, in fall 1968, held a series of ten one-day meetings in various parts of the country to which were invited librarians, library trustees, school administrators, and others. Participants at these meetings identified forty-six major barriers to interlibrary cooperation which Orin Nolting[39] summarized under five major headings: (1) *psychological barriers* (fear of loss of local autonomy, clash or personalities, inertia and indifference,

unwillingness to experiment, etc.), (2) *lack of information and experience* (lack of knowledge of the needs of users, unpredictability of demands on the library by its legitimate users, failure of small libraries to realize the value of resources of larger libraries, lack of public interest, unawareness of successful cooperative efforts in other states), (3) *traditional and historical barriers* (lack of adequate funds, fear by large libraries of being overused and undercompensated, inadequacy of libraries to serve their own needs, limitations on access to academic and special libraries, institutional competition between school and public libraries), (4) *physical and geographical barriers* (distance between libraries and distance of users from libraries, difference in size of collections, lack of space in public libraries to serve students, delays in satisfying needs and requests of users), (5) *legal and administrative barriers* (too many government units, lack of communication across jurisdictional lines, lack of bibliographical tools and controls, incompatibility of equipment and procedures and rules between libraries, lack of properly trained staff, lack of appropriate state enabling legislation, lack of creative administrative leadership, etc.).

SUMMARY

Libraries are now moving toward the third generation of library organization — the combination of several types and/or systems of libraries. Statewide networks are developing in most states, and multistate or regional bibliographical centers which have been in existence since the thirties are now reevaluating their structures and moving toward more fruitful articulation with the state networks.

The profession has reached, officially at least, a consensus that interlibrary coordination is not a fringe activity but a central component of adequate library service. The profession recognizes that self-sufficiency for any library is a myth no matter how large its resources or small its constituency. In statements of standards and objectives by most types of libraries and in the *Model Interlibrary Loan Code for Regional, State, Local or Other Special Groups of Libraries,* the library profession has articulated the rubrics for state and regional networks.

In surveys and studies on resources, services, and needs, many states now have gathered for the first time vitally important data upon which to base future activity.

Important beginnings have been made in the establishment of telecommunication networks. Experience has been gained from experiments such as the New York Facsimile Transmission System to begin to provide a realistic appraisal of the present technical feasibility and cost of our dream of "instantaneous availability."[40] Data is also emerging about patterns of use in the statewide networks, on the major user groups, on the kinds of materials being requested, on the factors governing turn-around time, on the unit cost of transactions, on the role of the state library as a switching center, on the cost/benefit of a variety of location tools, on the adequacy of resources within each state, on staff training and public information as critical factors in the success of any network.

Experience also is being gathered on the effectiveness of acquisition-cataloging-processing centers which cut across geographic, jurisdictional, and type-of-library boundaries. Most especially, the use of MARC tapes on a statewide basis for a variety of bibliographical services is beginning. Until these experiments are conducted widely, and evaluated, the American people cannot realize the benefits of their not inconsiderable investment in the MARC project.

RECOMMENDATIONS

On the basis of our limited experience with emerging state networks and the obstacles articulated by Mr. Nolting, the next steps are obvious: to bring our third generation of libraries into full and productive maturity and to move into the fourth level — a "combination of various types of libraries and non-library agencies concerned with related activities."

1. LSCA III should be renewed, with authorization and appropriation of funds far beyond the minimal level at which it has become mired. Basic grants of $40,000, or basic expenditures of $80,000 (with state matching), cannot be expected to produce significant, statewide results.

2. Networks for knowledge should be renewed and funded.

3. States should assume greater responsibility for encouraging, with legislation and funds, the development of statewide and regional networks. Ohio's recent law providing state-aid to area library service organizations and a statewide reference network might be a model, as is New York's yet to be passed 3R legislation.

4. State libraries must be strengthened to provide stronger leadership, more sophisticated bibliographical and processing capacity, and more effective evaluation of the present statewide networks.

5. State libraries, library associations, and library schools should work together to provide long-range, carefully planned staff development. The WICHE project may provide a model of areawide continuing education.

6. School librarians, teachers, and administrators must understand the importance for their students of access to resources beyond the school media center. More effective use of statewide networks by teachers and students needs to be achieved.

7. Public libraries should be more aware of their responsibility for leadership in the coordination of the resources and services in all types of libraries in their communities.

8. Careful, in-depth cost/benefit studies should be made on (*a*) patterns of interlibrary loan, (*b*) compensation to resource libraries in statewide networks, (*c*) time and money saved by union catalogs against the cost of creating and maintaining such lists.

9. Studies should be made on how adequately undergraduates are being served in college and university libraries and what use they could and should make of statewide networks.

10. Studies should be made of actual and potential use made of statewide networks by major resource libraries within the states and what it is costing research libraries to contribute to state networks.

11. State libraries and administrators of state and regional geographic networks should focus attention on how best to articulate with state and national subject networks, and with second-generation networks within each state and region.

NOTES

1. John Mackenzie Cory, "The network in a major metropolitan center," in L. Carnovsky, ed., *Library networks promise and performance* (Chicago: Univ. of Chicago Pr., 1969), p.91.

2. American Library Association, American Association of School Librarians, and National Education Association, *Standards for school media programs* (Chicago: ALA, 1969), 66p.

3. ...., Public Library Association, *Minimum standards for public library systems, 1966* (Chicago: ALA, 1967), 69p.

4. ...., Public Library Association, *Public library service: a guide to evaluation, with minimum standards* (Chicago: ALA, 1956), p.7.

5. ...., Association of College and Research Libraries, Standards Committee, "Standards for college libraries," *College and research libraries* 20:274-80 (July 1959).

6. ...., Association of College and Research Libraries, Standards Committee, "Standards for junior college libraries," *College and research libraries* 21:200-06 (May 1960).

7. ...., American Association of State Libraries, Survey and Standards Committee, *Standards for library functions at the state level* (Chicago: ALA, 1970), 48p.

8. Ibid., p.10.

9. Ibid., p.14.

10. ...., Public Library Association, *Interlibrary cooperation* (Chicago: ALA, 1967).

11. *Title II regulation* (Code of Federal Regulation. Office of the Federal Register, Title XLV: Public Welfare, No. 117.6), p.307.

12. Galen Rike, *Statewide library surveys and development plans: An annotated bibliography, 1956-1967* (Springfield: Illinois State Library, 1968), 105p.

13. Nelson Associates, Inc., *Reference and research library needs in Michigan* (Lansing: Michigan State Library, 1968).

14. Hawaii Department of Education, Office of Library Services, *Planning for libraries in Hawaii* (Honolulu: Hawaii State Dept. of Education, 1968), 290p.

15. "The Indiana library studies: a list," *Focus on Indiana libraries* 24:86-88 (June 1970).

16. Ralph Blasingame, *Survey of Ohio libraries and State Library services* (Columbus: State Library of Ohio, 1968), 188p.

17. *News from the State Library* 108 (8 July 1970).

18. Genevieve Casey, *OTIS: an evaluation of the Oklahoma Teletypewriter Interlibrary System* (Oklahoma City: Oklahoma Dept. of Libraries, 1969), 116p.

19. Texas State Library, *Evaluation number two - Texas state library communication network* (Austin: Texas State Library, 1970).

20. *The 3R's: reference and research library resources* (Albany: New York State Education Dept., Div. of Library Development, 1969), p.10.

21. Nelson Associations, Inc., *Interlibrary loan in New York State* (Washington, D.C.: The Author, 1969), 300p.

22. Herbert Poole, "Teletypewriters in libraries: a state of the art report," *College and research libraries* 27:283-86 (July 1966).

23. American Library Association, Reference Services Division, Interlibrary Loan Committee, *National interlibrary loan code* (Chicago: ALA, 1968).

24. ...., Reference Services Division, Interlibrary Loan Committee, "Draft of a model interlibrary loan code for regional, state, local or other special groups of libraries," *Special libraries* 59:528-30 (Sept. 1968).

25. Ibid., p.528.

26. Ibid., p.530.

27. Association of Research Libraries, *Minutes of 73rd annual meeting, January 26, 1969, Washington, D.C.* (Princeton: The Association, 1969), p.31.

28. James G. Igoe, "The 'hotline' in Michigan," *Library journal* 93:521-23 (1 Feb. 1968).

29. E. J. Josey, "A summary of the reference and research library resources systems' progress reports," *Bookmark* 29:294-8 (May 1970).

30. Nelson Associates, Inc., *The New York State Library's pilot program in the facsimile transmission of library materials: a summary report* (Albany: State Dept. of Education, 1968), 85p.

31. S. Gilbert Prentiss, "Networks; promise and performance," in L. Carnovsky, ed., *Library networks - promise and performance* (Chicago: Univ. of Chicago Pr., 1969), p.86.

32. New York (State) University, *Emerging library systems: the 1963-66 evaluation of the New York State public library system* (Albany: State Education Dept., Div. of Evaluation, 1967), p.237.

33. Ibid., p.241.

34. *Master plan for total library services* (Sacramento: California Library Association). Mimeo.

35. Yadwiga Kuncaitus, *Comparative study of the Cleveland and Columbus union catalogs* (Cleveland: Case Western Reserve Univ., School of Library Science, 1967).

36. Kenneth Bierman and Betty Blue, "Processing of MARC tapes for cooperative use," *Journal of library automation* 3:36-64 (March 1970).

37. *The three R's: reference and research resources library systems* (Albany: New York State Education Dept., Div. of Library Development, 1969), p.7.

38. Genevieve Casey, *The future role and financial structure of The Bibliographical Center for Research, Rocky Mountain Region: a reconnaisance study* Wayne State Univ., Office of Urban Library Research, Research Report No. 6 (Denver: the Center 1969), and Lura Currier, *Sharing resources in the Pacific Northwest* (Olympia: Washington State Library, 1969).

39. Orin F. Nolting, *Mobilizing total library resources for effective service* (Chicago: ALA, 1969), 20p.

40. "New York facsimile project judged a failure," *Library journal* 93:1566 (15 April 1968).

Limits of Local Self-Sufficiency

Richard E. Chapin

Among the myriad of lapel buttons appearing at recent gatherings of librarians, one stated that "Networking is not a fairy tale." If not a fairy tale, certain aspects of networking — the traditional programs of library cooperation such as interlibrary lending, union lists, centralized cataloging, and bibliographic services — have been around long enough to acquire some characteristics of a fairy tale. That these traditional forms have not made sharing of resources comparable with local ownership has forced libraries to assume the insurmountable task of attempting to provide their users with an ever greater portion of the scholarly record.

Any consideration of library networks, however they are defined and developed, must take cognizance of the seeming failure of our present programs for sharing resources. With interlibrary lending, with the known location of a higher portion of requested materials, and with copying devices, why have the users insisted on local ownership? If networks are teletype and telefacsimile in lieu of interlibrary loan, then nothing new has been added, with the exception of speed, and the user is still likely to demand copies in his own library. If networks are central computer storage of the location of materials in lieu of union lists, then nothing new has been added, with the exception of updating, and the user is still likely to demand local self-sufficiency. If networking is not a fairy tale, then it must be more than new devices for the time-honored, traditional practices.

Verner Clapp, in presenting the Eighteenth Windsor Lecture in Librarianship, noted that local self-sufficiency requires all materials needed for research to be immediately at hand. That this is impossible, especially for a general research library, is obvious; less obvious, but perhaps equally true, is the fact that most libraries will make every effort to be self-sufficient for a high portion of all users. This may be due to the nature of the discipline; to the inefficiencies of our present system of physically sharing resources, forcing the user to limit his use to materials on hand; or to an overexpanded and inefficient bibliographic system which denies the user information as to what is available — either locally or at some other source. For whatever reason, the user demands that the librarian provide local access to more books, more journals, and more reports.

If libraries are to strive for local self-sufficiency, it is necessary to draw a distinction between physical and bibliographic self-sufficiency. Physical self-sufficiency refers to the ability of the library to produce from its own collections, or from its immediate area, a bibliographic unit or a piece of information that is demanded by the user. Bibliographic self-sufficiency, on the other hand, refers to the ability of the library to provide bibliographic identification and location of any one of a variety of research materials.

Inherent in the system of American librarianship is the attempt to provide the necessary book, article, report, or information for any user from local collections. In many libraries, and for a large number of users, the libraries have been surprisingly successful in this attempt. The basic concepts of librarianship — book selection, organization of materials, and reference service — are geared to providing specific information to a user upon request. In most cases we even have ignored worthwhile cooperative projects and the facilities of interlibrary loan in order to be self-sufficient for our users.

We have not been nearly as successful in the matter of providing our own bibliographic services on the local level. It would be foolhardy for any library to make a solo attempt to provide bibliographic access to all of the units in the collection. We cannot get along without the printed and machine-readable catalog copy from the Library of Congress or from the other sources of centralized cataloging. The analytics necessary to provide access to the periodicals and journals are presently available through the indexes and the abstracting services, and cannot be produced on a local level to any degree of satisfaction. Bibliographic self-sufficiency is impossible for any one library.

Since bibliographic services cannot be provided individually, it is this area that offers the greatest potential for networking.

This paper will be concerned with the degree of success that libraries have in providing physical access to materials on the local level. Libraries do provide a large percent of items requested from their own collections. If bibliographic access to collections were improved, then it is likely that local libraries would become even more self-sufficient than they are today.

SELF-SUFFICIENCY BY TYPE OF LIBRARY

If the library is described as a collection of graphic materials organized for effective use, then it is obvious that some libraries can be totally self-sufficient. The housewife, with her shelf of cookbooks, can find more information than she wants to plan and prepare her three meals a day; a specialized research library, limited in its areas of concentration, with a small number of users, can respond favorably to most demands; a general research library, on the other hand, which must provide a multitude of materials to meet an ever-increasing variety of demands, finds it more difficult but not necessarily impossible to do so from local collections.

The libraries in our country range from the large research to the small, one-room school libraries. It is unnecessary to think in terms of networks connecting all libraries to provide equal access to all recorded information for all users. School libraries, for instance, are responsible only for the curricular needs of a limited number of students and do not require access to another three, four, or five million volumes that would be made a-vailable through a networking program. Of course, there are a few advanced students, writing some term papers, who do not have their needs met on the local level. These cases are rare indeed. It is safe to assume that our school libraries, particularly in those states where an emphasis has been placed on their development, are largely self-sufficient. If they are not, then it is from a lack of interest and lack of initative on the local level. A networking scheme is not likely to make these libraries no-ticeably more effective at providing physical access to materials.

Public libraries, excluding those libraries responsible for research materials in the large metropolitan areas, also can be said to be largely self-sufficient. The public library meets the informational and recreational reading needs of a rather small number of people in the local community. It might even be considered as a library for the minority — with most needs being met by a well-selected but limited number of books and periodicals. Recreational reading can be well satisfied at the local level. The information needs of professional men, busi-nessmen, and students are more varied; however, present pro-grams of state support for local libraries should meet even these informational demands.

Extended public library service to those not now being served is possible on the local level. Such extended service requires more in the way of imagination and leadership than it does in the way of physical resources. Proposed library networks to make more materials available will add little for public li-braries. The needs of these libraries which are not met locally or through the state systems are not likely to need access to a large number of additional volumes.

State libraries have a variety of information demands. Not only do they attempt to backstop the local public libraries but they also have responsibilities to their own agencies and to their own legislatures. State libraries do provide adequately for some of these responsibilities, but less so for others. For instance, the public library extension program, coordinated through a state library, can be nearly self-sufficient on the local level. The demands for information through the state type of network are not so sophisticated as to be impossible to meet on a local level. The research needs of the legislature and of the legislative agencies are more difficult. In all cases, however, the state libraries can and do work through the university and other research collections available in the state. If information is not immediately available on a local level, meaning in the state capitol, then it should be identified and made available through other state sources. State libraries, therefore, can be considered self-sufficient.

State libraries may be most important in network planning, especially if the plans as they are developed envision extended service to school and public libraries. Many state libraries, of course, serve as the principal node in state networks and may well serve as connectors in a national scheme.

College libraries are responsible primarily for the support of curricular needs of their institutions. Such needs can be met with a minimum number of volumes in a basic collection and an adequate annual expenditure for books and periodicals. If local collections fall short of supporting curricular needs, this is not the fault of traditional library programs but is the result of priorities established by the college. Such faults can and should be corrected locally rather than depending on the grand net-working scheme of tomorrow.

College libraries are generally self-sufficient; if they are not, then they should be. The demands of the bright undergraduate or the research demands of the faculty are likely to require only occasional use of a network that would provide access to several million more volumes.

University libraries range from small collections of one-hun-dred thousand volumes to great collections of more than eight million volumes. The smaller university libraries are not unlike the college libraries: They can and should be largely self-suf-ficient.

University and other large research libraries, including the metropolitan public libraries, face ever-increasing demands for more and more materials. To meet the local curricular or recreational needs takes only a small portion of the library budget; the remaining portion of the budget is devoted to fulfilling the research needs of the institution. In all cases, this remaining portion always seems insufficient. The variety of demands that are made upon university and other research collections make them difficult to classify in degree of success in providing information. Some users are always satisfied with local collections while others have demands that must be sup-plemented by external sources.

Special libraries, particularly those of research institutions, have an advantage over university and research libraries in terms of the degree of specialization of the user. If the mission of the library is defined and limited, then the library can be self-sufficient.

SELF-SUFFICIENCY BY DISCIPLINE

Libraries are developed, maintained, and supported in order to provide information as requested by their readers. The function is the same whether, it is the limited needs of a school library or the multiple needs of the university library. The measure of success is the degree to which the libraries provide the informational needs of the potential users. Perhaps this can be understood better if we were to look at our success in meeting the needs of physical and natural scientists, humanists, and social and behavioral scientists.

As we look at the disciplines, it is necessary to repeat that we are considering only physical accessibility of materials; the degree of bibliographic accessibility in all fields leaves much to be desired. It is safe to assume that our libraries can provide more physical accessibility than bibliographic accessibility. The large number of journals and research reports for which we have no bibliographic access is scandalous. For all practical purposes, many items on the shelves of our research libraries are not physically accessible to the potential user unless we have bibliographic access. At this point, however, we are concerned only with the degree of providing access to a book, an article, or a report once it has been identified by the user.

The following thoughts are based upon a large number of assumptions, most unproven. These assumptions have been developed over the years by observation, by analysis of use studies, and by conversation. They are presented only as a point of reference, not as a definitive statement on literature use.

The physical scientist, with the exception of the mathematician, makes limited use of library resources. He is likely to be more interested in having the current periodicals on the shelves two days before they are published rather than having twenty years of the backruns of these periodicals. An increasing number of physical scientists are relying upon sources other than libraries for their information. Preprints, symposia, and research reports are as important as the current periodicals. If these materials can be identified and if we can organize ourself in such a way as to get this material on our shelves in a rapid fashion, then we can satisfy most of the known needs of the physical scientist. The unknown needs — the materials which the scientist himself does not even know he wants — are more difficult. In some cases an information analysis center may be more important to him than a library.

The literature of the biological sciences differs from that of the physical sciences. The biological scientist requires long runs of a large number of periodicals. Once something has been described and classified, it stays described and classified. It is more difficult to provide bibliographic identification of the description than physical accessibility to it. The biological scientist may want more periodicals and journals than most libraries can possibly provide, and he wants complete runs. He also demands a variety of printed and machine-readable bibliographic services. The monographic literature is important in terms of the classics and the landmarks, but it is less important for research purposes than are the journals.

The social sciences are undergoing great change, especially in terms of library use. In times past it was thought that the social scientist needed the current monographs, that is, those monographs published during the past twenty-five to thirty years, and large collections of familiar pamphlets and ephemeral material. He used the periodical literature to a degree, but not as much as he used the other types of collections. In recent years, the social scientist has become more of a behaviorist and relies more upon the difficult-to-come-by research reports and processed materials. His laboratory now has become the community, and he is not the library user as he was in the past. The old concept of political economy has given way to the new concept of community survey. This would seem to indicate that the libraries cannot be self-sufficient for the social scientist. As a matter of fact, we are probably more self-sufficient than we used to be because of the limited use being made of the libraries by social scientists. This is especially so if we consider the library use of the historian and anthropologist as being more like the humanist than the social scientist. Give the economist his statistics and give the behaviorist his research reports, and they will be mostly satisfied.

The humanist has an insatiable appetite for research materials, and no one library can satisfy all of his needs. The humanist needs everything and anything that has been published, plus large collections of unpublished materials. Most of these exist in copies of one, so the humanist will go to the source rather than have the source brought to him. We can state with certainty that libraries are not self-sufficient for the humanities.

SOME UNTESTED HYPOTHESES

From the points of reference above — self-sufficiency by types of library and by academic discipline — the needs that would be met by a library network dedicated to providing only physical access to materials are limited. A cost/benefit analysis might well show that returns for dollars spent would not be beneficial.

Further research is necessary before any major networking plan is undertaken. Perhaps the following hypotheses would be worth testing:

Hypothesis 1: "Eighty percent of current research relies upon or reports only those materials published or otherwise made available in the past ten years." An analysis of current research being conducted throughout the country might well show that a large portion of library materials used has been published in the past few years. The 80 percent might well be 60 or 70, and the ten years might well be eight or fifteen. Nevertheless, it seems obvious that a large percentage of library materials used by scholars and researchers are of recent origin. The use studies and other available studies of the literature show a high degree of concentration in titles and in time. If this is so and if a library has had an efficient effective program for acquiring recent research materials, then it can be stated that the libraries effectively provide materials for a large portion of the research users. One might even conclude that some of the newer and some of the smaller research libraries are nearly as effective and as good for the research use of many of the users as are some of the older and large libraries.

Hypothesis 2: "Noncopyrighted materials do not enter the bibliographic chain until such time as they are unavailable for acquisition." Libraries are creatures of habit. They acquire those things that are listed in bibliographies; they acquire those things for which announcements are received; and they acquire things on a standing-order basis. Most of these materials have gone through the regular copyright channels in this country or in countries abroad. These materials are not difficult to acquire, and they are the materials in heaviest demand.

An ever-increasing amount of material being cited in the research literature are the research reports, the ephemera, and other materials that do not go through the normal bibliographic channels. When these are brought to the attention of the library, either through the subject specialist or through bibliographies, the materials are often no longer available. If this is so and if these materials are important, particularly for the physical or the behavioral scientist, then the degree of self-sufficiency of our libraries is limited. In order to stem this trend, it is necessary that libraries make a concerted effort to acquire or to have copies reproduced of the noncopyrighted materials that do not flow through the normal bibliographic channels.

FACTORS LIMITING SELF-SUFFICIENCY

There are certain obvious factors which may limit the self-sufficiency of libraries. Fremont Rider points to the problem in 1944 when he projected the future size of the Yale University card catalog. The limitation of dollars, of course, is one of the first factors that face us when we talk about local collections. But it is possible to identify an amount that will permit us to purchase all materials of potential research interest that have been published through the normal copyright channels of the various countries. This figure for 1970-71 is probably in the neighborhood of $1 million for one copy of the necessary books, periodicals, and reports required for research, not curricular, needs. Certainly one can argue that a serials budget alone could amount to such a sum; however, it is my contention that all libraries subscribe to a large number of serials that are little used for research. The problem is complicated by the fact that serial titles seem to have as much tenure as faculty members. Several studies show that a large portion of the citations in the literature are to a surprisingly small number of periodical titles. We talk in terms of thirty to forty thousand serial titles, while the use studies show that the number being used is much more limited.

If the first hypothesis noted above is correct, and we will assume so for the time being, then a library that will spend $1 million, in terms of today's dollars (not an impossible sum), for books and periodicals will be able to supply requested copies of materials for most of its users over the next few years. The longer this expenditure remains at a high level, the more self-sufficient the library will be. Dollars for the total library program can be a limiting factor for research institutions, but dollars for materials should not stop us from attempting a high degree of self-sufficiency.

The information explosion — or whatever term you use for the large number of books and periodicals being published — is of prime concern when we talk in terms of an individual library supplying copies on demand. What saves libraries from being completely inundated with requests for materials is the lack of bibliographic identification. We should not put too high a priority on acquiring large numbers of books and periodicals for which we do not have bibliographic access. Unless they are properly indexed, we can expect little or no demand for these items. That there are forty thousand, one-hundred thousand, or even two-hundred thousand serial titles being published is of little concern if the user cannot identify those specific materials needed for his research.

Another limiting factor, or what could be considered a limiting factor in terms of self-sufficiency, is that of space. All libraries are constantly faced with the problem of more and more room for books and readers. In the technological sense, however, this matter does not need to be of prime concern. We know that the theoretical reduction ratio is phenomenal; we can put a large number of bibliographic units into a very small space. If we are not satisfied with the 20 to 1 reduction of standard microfilms, then we can go to the 200 to 1 reduction of ultramicroforms. If either reduction ratio is used, space required for materials is of little importance. If the problem of space is measured against the ease of use by the user, then it is another matter. The question is one of the inconvenience of use of a reader for the little-used research materials as opposed to the ever-increasing physical size of our libraries. This is a problem that can cause user frustrations, but it should not be a matter limiting the self-sufficiency of local libraries.

Perhaps the most important thing which will limit the degree of self-sufficiency in our libraries is the lack of expertise in selecting and weeding the collections. A few years ago it was assumed that the faculty members were the primary book selectors on the university campus. Today this is no longer true. More and more, the major research libraries are developing a large staff of bibliographers whose primary responsibility is the care and nurturing of research collections. The expertise that is necessary for this type of project is phenomenal. Not only must the bibliographer be as familiar as the faculty with the subject areas for which he is responsible, but he must be a person with that undefinable book sense. Not only do the collections have to be built, but they must be maintained. The older copies and the outworn copies must be discarded, and other copies added to the collections. Of all of the factors affecting the self-sufficiency of the library, probably the matter of bibliographic expertise is the most important and the most self-limiting. If we cannot or will not staff our libraries with trained bibliographers, then it will be necessary to reinvolve the faculty or find other alternatives for the development of research collections.

There may be an optimum collection size that can be effectively managed in libraries. How many titles can be handled in one central serials record file? Is there an optimum size before the system breaks down? How effective is a very large card catalog as opposed to several smaller catalogs providing access to the collection? We continue to act as if there were no size limitations on our library procedures and practices. The cost of adding materials to collections of five million volumes may be more limiting than the cost of purchasing materials. A million-volume library can handle its technical processes much more effectively and efficiently than a five-million-volume library. Perhaps there is a maximum size which will be the breaking point in our operations.

Another matter limiting local self-sufficiency is that of the unavailability of materials requested by a user. They very well may be in the system, but they are not available for his immediate use. In some cases this lack of availability is tantamount to a lack of ownership of a desired item. Some recent studies show that from 30 to 50 percent of the items requested in major research libraries are not on the shelf and immediately available at the time of request. This seems to give some credence to an earlier assumption that a relatively small number of titles receive a large amount of use. Nevertheless, this lack of physical accessibility, even when the item is owned, is a matter of increasing concern to the researcher and other library users. Does self-sufficiency mean providing a copy upon demand, or does it mean having a card in the catalog? If it is the former, then our libraries are becoming increasingly less self-sufficient.

FACTORS FAVORING SELF-SUFFICIENCY

If there are a number of factors that limit the self-sufficiency of libraries, then there are others that encourage us in the attempt to provide all materials locally. The technology of microcopying, of course, is the most important. Now it is possible to have an edition of one. If an item can be located in any library, then an edition of one can be made available to another library. This type of availability makes it ever more possible for a library to respond to the requests of the users.

A new dimension of library self-sufficiency has been added recently with ultramicrofiche. The real breakthrough is not in terms of the 200 to 1 reduction but rather with the ease of making additional copies of these materials. If a million volumes can be produced for one library, then copies from the master film can be reproduced quickly and inexpensively for other libraries. It is not unreasonable to assume that the collections of Harvard, the New York Public Library, and the University of Illinois will soon be made available rather inexpensively to all other libraries in the world.

The most pressing factor pushing libraries to strive for self-sufficiency are the demands of the user. Most library users are more concerned with the immediate access of materials than they are in the cooperative endeavors. There is a constant pressure on the library to acquire for on-campus use those materials which are demanded by the students and by the faculty. They care not that the library is part owner of a copy in Chicago; they want full ownership of a copy on the local campus. This factor, coupled with institutional pride, might well lead one to believe that cooperation and networking are fine in theory but not useful for an individual campus. It is almost as easy to design an overall system of dissemination of information than to tell a faculty member or student that his book will be available from some other source at some later time. Not only will our users not wait a week, or even overnight, for an item, but they are frustrated if they must wait five minutes.

SUMMARY AND ALTERNATIVES

As one reviews the various disciplines and looks at the types of libraries, perhaps we have been overly critical of our efforts to provide research materials to our users. It is reasonable to assume that most of our libraries are self-sufficient for most of their users.

What we are concerned with, therefore, is the small percent of demands which cannot be met from our local collections. Before we develop grandiose networking schemes, at great expense, perhaps we should have a better idea as to what needs are not being met by traditional programs. It is likely that for an expenditure of a few more dollars we could more nearly approach complete self-sufficiency with our present system than

we could with a network that was designed to provide physical access to materials.

If we include in our definition of self-sufficiency the concept of interlibrary loan, either by traditional means or with the new electronic devices, then we will find that our libraries are even more self-sufficient. At the 1962 automation conference it was suggested that some 80 percent of all interlibrary loan requests to National Union Catalog — and this is often a last resort — are located. If we put this 80 percent together with an earlier assumption that we are already 80 percent self-sufficient, then it leaves a very few items with are not currently being provided to the library user.

It becomes obvious that the major emphasis of library networking should be on providing better bibliographic access rather than physical access to materials. The libraries of today score very high in terms of physical access. We do need help from the new technology to improve bibliographic access. Any networking scheme must give this top priority.

As alternatives I would offer two possible schemes of networking which might provide the final small percent of physical access and could greatly improve our bibliographic access.

The first of these can be described "collections of excellence." In libraries scattered throughout the country there are collections that excel all others. These collections should be identified and described. A mechanism could be developed to direct the user to the definitive collection in his area of interest. The library responsible for a particular collection of excellence should be encouraged to provide detailed bibliographic access to the collection. Also, the library would assume continued collecting in depth. The collections might conceivably develop through the years as information analysis centers.

Another networking concept which should be given consideration is that of collections of materials by types. There should be one place in the country where we could go for all periodicals; there should be another place where we could go for all state documents; and still another for research reports. This concept can be expanded as far as definitions can be made for types of materials. The great advantage of this networking concept lies in the ability of a library to know where materials can be found. No elaborate switching mechanism is necessary to direct the library or the patron in the right direction. These collections by type of material also could provide bibliographic listing and searching in their specialized fields.

Returning to our lapel button "Networking is not a fairy tale" perhaps it will be a fairy tale unless every effort is made to design a network that is more than new devices for current services. Elaborate schemes, at great expense, that do little more than make the last 3 or 4 percent of materials available are likely to be rejected by librarians and the public.

Telecommunications Programs Affecting Network Development

Frank W. Norwood

In a recent issue of *Fortune,* the leading article carried the predictive title, "The Coming Shake-Up in Telecommunications."[1] Increasingly, the attention of the business community and the general public is being called to the emergence of such new and potentially revolutionary communications technologies as community antenna television, CATV, and communications satellites. Most reports focus upon the impressive technical prowess of such new highways for electronic communication and the ways in which the wonders they can work will likely shape the lives we lead and the world in which all live in the future. In his *Fortune* article, Dan Cordtz documents the consequences which new technologies already are having in the world of communications policy and regulation. Adding new ingredients to the communications mix has a strong catalytic effect, releasing powerful forces which churn up established and long-stable policy matters, raising new questions and reopening old ones.

The purpose of this paper is to examine those regulatory, technical, and program developments which are a part of the "shake-up in telecommunications," and to explore their implications for those planning library and other "public-service-oriented" communications networks. Such consideration must include recent and proposed changes in Federal Communications Commission, FCC, rules and procedures; plans for new commercial special service common carrier networks; the predicted evolution of CATV into a national system of broadband cable communications; and developments in the satellite field. In addition, it will be important to see what other public and semipublic agencies are interested in network development, to examine their experience and plans for the future, and to explore what opportunities for cooperative effort and mutual benefits may exist.

FEDERAL COMMUNICATIONS COMMISSION DECISIONS

The climate for the development of new services and new networks is substantially improved under recent and proposed actions by the Federal Communications Commission. The first such landmark ruling from the FCC was the commission's "Carterfone Decision."[2]

Carter Electronics Corporation is a small Texas firm manufacturing a device which permits mobile radio users to couple their two-way radios into the conventional telephone system. Thomas F. Carter, the company's president, initiated antitrust action in the federal courts to end the telephone companies' long-standing ban on the use of such "foreign attachments" as the Carterfone. In phone company terminology, a "foreign attachment" is any device (whether made in Texas or Tokyo) not leased by — or at least approved by — the phone company. Introducing such devices into the phone system could subject the phone company's network and its customers to a source of potential interference and degradation over which the phone company would have no control. So, at least, the rationale ran. The result, however, was not only to reduce potential sources of interference but also potential freedom of choice by telephone subscribers who found themselves limited almost exclusively to those devices which the phone company was willing to provide on a lease basis.

The courts referred the case to the FCC, which, in a unanimous vote in June 1968, found little reason for the carriers to enforce any blanket prohibition. The burden of proof regarding interference with the integrity of the telephone network is now upon the phone company rather than upon the subscriber. In general, the telephone company must establish that a foreign attachment will be harmful before it can prohibit the customer from using it; whereas before, the telephone subscriber had the difficult task of demonstrating to the phone company's satisfaction that it would not degrade the telephone service.

The Carterfone Decision has opened to competition the broad field of telephone attachments. The user may now choose among a vast array of telephone instruments, ranging from the pseudo-antique to space-age modern, transistorized switchboards for office use, and data modems among other attachments. Equally important, the subscriber may often have the freedom to buy such terminal devices outright instead of having to lease terminal gear from the carrier.

The ability to combine new equipment with existing carrier facilities has resulted in some innovative efforts to develop and market new communications services. An example of such service is "telemail," or intercity facsimile service for hire. Like crocus buds after a spring rain, a number of "telemail" companies have sprung up since the Carterfone Decision. Some appear to have suffered from financial and perhaps, manageral malnutrition, and none is yet very large. The service they attempt to perform does, however, appear to fill a genuine need, and one or more public facsimile networks may yet find market viability. Such services are born of the marriage of commercially available facsimile ("fax") equipment and the public telephone network.

For some years such companies as Alden, Xerox, Graphic Sciences, and others have offered machines which permit the transmission of "hard copy" between points interconnected by telephone line. Typically, a memo, graph, or engineering drawing is clipped around the drum of a desk-top device while at the receiving end a blank sheet is inserted in a similar machine. When the start button is pressed on the sending fax terminal, both drums turn in synchronization, and in a few minutes, the original document is reproduced at the receiving location. Greatest users of such devices have been those concerned with intracompany communications. The new entries in the communications field have added the flexibility of multiple address capacity.

The user of a public facsimile network might be a business man in Las Vegas anxious to return a signed copy of a contract to the main office in Los Angeles, an engineering consultant in New York wishing to discuss specifications with a manufacturer in Chicago, or an architect wishing to get his artist's renderings into the hands of a potential client. The common need is to move graphic materials from one point to another with greater speed than the U.S. mails can assure and at lower cost than courier service entails.

The customer takes his document to the local office of the fax network or has it delivered by messenger. The fax service notes the destination and places a long-distance call to the proximate network office or franchisee. The telephones are placed in the acoustic coupler on each fax machine, and the document is transmitted. The receiving fax network station calls the addressee to advise him that there is a message to be picked up, or it is delivered by messenger. Typical total time between delivery of the original document to the sending station and delivery of the copy to the addressee is one and a half hours; typical cost is a few dollars a page, plus the cost of the long-distance phone call. Some public fax networks will store-and-forward, sending documents at low volume times when late-night phone rates apply.

There are still objectives to be met. Facsimile machines are not standardized, and so different networks using differing equipment cannot interchange messages. The U.S. Post Office has many more post offices than any existing facsimile network has stations. Transmission speeds will need to be raised and costs lowered before "telemail" becomes a conventional means of sending messages rather than merely being a helpful device in a crisis.

Whatever shortcomings such a service may manifest in its infancy, the technique of combining available technology and the public telephone system would not have been possible in the same way before the Carterfone Decision. Both the principle and the specific example should provide food for thought to planners of interlibrary communications.

Of equal or greater importance is the FCC'S "MCI Decision," which authorized construction of the first of what many expect to be a whole new class of common carrier networks.

Intercity traffic on the AT&T system is carried both by wire and by microwave relay. Operating at frequencies far higher than those which carry broadcast radio and television signals, microwave systems can carry impressive payloads of information, from multiple telephone conversations to television signals. Since the late 1940s, the rural spaces between our cities have sprouted a substantial crop of tall red-and-white towers. Many belong to the American Telephone and Telegraph Company and are an essential part of Bell's Long Lines system. The FCC has also licensed others to private users although few enterprises can support or fill the capacity of a private system. The growth of community antenna television systems resulted in the FCC giving its approval to the establishment of a third category of license, community antenna relay systems. CARS, as the trade calls them, pick up the signals of big-city television stations and carry them — sometimes hundreds of miles — to the CATV system for delivery to subscribers. Thus, cable TV subscribers in Lafayette, Indiana, see not only the signal of the city's lone TV station but also those of the stations in Indianapolis and Chicago.

"MCI" is the acronym for Microwave Communications, Inc., then a fledgling company which applied for a microwave system paralleling the route between St. Louis and Chicago long ago granted to AT&T. While the basic premise of common carrier as a regulated monopoly opposed duplicative routes, MCI argued that it would be the nation's first "special service common carrier," offering new services for higher reliability and lower tariffs than currently offered by the Bell System. The MCI service would be point-to-point, like private lines, between two or more plants or offices designated by the customer; while voice (and even video) service would be available, the primary target of the MCI proposal is service to computer users. With service "customized" to fit the particular needs of each client, MCI proposes channels as narrow as 200 cycles for costs as low as five cents a mile. Other options not regularly available from the traditional carriers would include asymmetrical circuits (broadband-high capacity in one direction, narrowband voice or teletypewriter in the other), lease of circuits on less than a full-time basis, pooling of service among customers, and the like.[5]

The FCC grant of the St.Louis-Chicago route to MCI represented a policy swing in favor of admitting new carriers offering new services. While the Bell System and the existing telephone companies may continue to be the "only telephone company in town," they may not continue to be the only "anytime, anything, anywhere" network.

The FCC approval of the MCI application came only after a bitter fight from AT&T and was a considerable surprise to those observers of communications regulation not given to placing heavy bets on the underdog, no matter how attractive the odds. More significant than the looks of surprise which resulted from the FCC action was the spate of new microwave common carrier applications which loosening the floodgates unleashed.

By mid-July 1970 more than 1,700 applications for specialized microwave service had been received by the commission. Chief among the applicants were those from Microwave Communications of America, a company which interlocks with MCI, and the Data Transmission Corporation. Each proposed a brand new coast-to-coast microwave network. MCA is the keystone in a group of regional companies, including MCI. Together these locally owned regional operators would comprise a national, special service common carrier network, with Microwave Communications of America acting as national sales agent.

Data Transmission Company, Datran, is a wholly owned subsidiary of University Computing Company. Datran proposes to build a $375 million network, linking thirty-five major metropolitan areas. The Datran system would provide terminal-to-terminal switched service, designed specifically and exclusively for the transmission of digital data. At very least, such proposals offer the planner of interlibrary networks the prospect of new services, greater flexibility in acquiring communications channels well suited for his particular needs, and the additional hope of more attractive prices.

The development of the special service common carrier field is presently suspended between present disappointment and future promise. At this writing, Microwave Communications, Inc., has yet to construct its first tower for the St. Louis-Chicago route, the only special service common carrier authorization which the FCC has made. AT&T, whose opposition is undimmed by the commission's grant to MCI, is still seeking court action to block the actual construction of such a system. All of the other applications — from Microwave Communications of America's associated companies, University Computing's Datran, and other, less-than-national, applications — are just that, applications. Some appear to be mutually exclusive and most, if not all, are opposed by the existing common carriers: AT&T, Western Union, the independent telephone companies, and others.

On 17 July 1970 the commission issued "Notice of Inquiry to Formulate Policy, Notice of Proposed Rule Making, and Order" in Docket No. 18920.[6] The purpose of the inquiry is to resolve broad policy and procedural questions in handling the present and anticipated special service microwave applications. In essence, the notice makes public an in-house analysis prepared for the FCC by its Common Carrier Bureau. The "threshold" question is stated this way:

Whether as a general policy the public interest would be served by permitting the entry of new carriers in the specialized communications field...[7]

The Common Carrier Bureau holds that the answer to the "threshold" question is affirmative since in its view, competition appears to be "reasonably feasible." As summarized in the FCC's announcement:

In support of its position that the entry of new carriers into the field of specialized communications would serve the public interest, the Bureau noted that the demand for all types of communications services was growing very rapidly, and that data communication would probably exhibit very substantial growth over the next decade, It said that the entry of new specialized carriers would help meet the increasing public need for diverse and flexible means for satisfying expanding specialized communications requirements. The Bureau also stated that new entries would have the effect of 'dispersing somewhat the burdens, risks and initatives involved in supplying the rapidly growing markets for new and specialized

services; 'might stimulate technical innovation' and could 'provide a useful regulatory tool which would assist in achieving the statutory objectives of adequate and efficient services as reasonable

If the threshold question is resolved in the manner suggested by the Common Carrier Bureau, the commision might then be free to dispose of the need for holding comparative hearings among the various applicants and decline to hear arguments about the economic impact new carriers might have upon old carriers or upon each other. The FCC could move expeditiously to grant the applications of all applicants who meet basic legal, technical, and financial tests, and let the economic forces in the market place determine which systems are built and operated by whom. The commission noted that Datran's proposed system differs substantially from the others in being all digital and switched, and should, in any event, be considered separately.

The entry of new carriers into the communications field may be expected to have at least two effects which should be beneficial for developers of library and information networks. On the one hand, the potential availability of alternate choices promises the network planner greater flexibilty and freedom of choice, and offers the hope of securing network facilities closely tailored to the user's needs. "Shopping for best price" also may be possible to a degree not now known. The second effect which is already being felt is the restructuring of offerings and tariffs by the Bell System in response to the same growing needs which the new carrier applicants reflect. Some new options, such as sharing of long-distance circuits, are now available, and it is reasonable to expect that more will be offered.

COMMUNITY ANTENNA TELEVISION

Another area of rapidly changing regulation by the Federal Communications Commission is that of cable television. CATV, as it has generally been known to this point, had its origins in the small towns of Oregon and Pennsylvania where enterprising retail television set dealers installed receiving antennas atop the nearby hill and brought the signals of the distant city TV stations into the previously "shadowed" valley communities. Community antenna television still consists, basically, of a well-located antenna installation (now often both sophisticated and expensive) and a web of coaxial cables which transport the signals from the "head end" to the subscriber's set.

While CATV was limited to extending the range of broadcast TV stations into distant small towns, neither the FCC nor the broadcast stations took more than a passing interest. Now, however, the picture has changed in two ways: One, the growth of cable television systems in such cities as San Diego, California, has given indication that CATV may be viable, even where local television signals are available off the air. Cable television systems are either in operation or planned for New York, Los Angeles, Chicago, Philadelphia, and most of the nation's largest cities. Two, the evolution of CATV into a much more significant communications system is widely predicted. CATV uses coaxial cable, about the diameter of a pencil, to carry the signals of local and distant television signals to the homes of subscribers. The capacity of coaxial cable is far from exhausted by such use, and the basic CATV system might, with relatively minor modification, be used to provide the electronic pathways for a wide variety of additional services.

In light of both these facts, the Federal Communications Commission has launched a complex investigation of what role the FCC should appropriately take in regulating the growth of cable communications.[9] One hard knot in the complex of problems is that of untangling the regulatory roles of the municipalities and the states vis-a-vis federal control and in relation to each other. Several states, including Nevada, Connecticut, New York, and Virginia, have passed or are considering asserting state jurisdiction. The interrelationships among the various levels of governmental regulation are the subject of another FCC inquiry.[10]

In yet another docket, the commission seeks comments on the technical standards to which cable systems should be built.[11] The commission notes that it "must consider the future possibility of a nationally as well as internationally connected cable grid which will cater to a variety of sophisticated communications needs."[12] This same Notice of Proposed Rule Making also makes clear the FCC's intention to require that cable operators so design their systems as to provide the possibility of two-way communication. Some of the services which might be possible over an interconnected cable network with two-way capability were suggested by the commission in its First Inquiry and Notice of Proposed Rule Making:

It has been suggested that the expanding multi-channel capacity of cable systems could be utilized to provide a variety of new communications services to homes and businesses within a community, in addition to services now commonly offered such as time, weather, news, stock exchange ticker, etc. While we shall not attempt an all-inclusive listing, some of the predicted services include: facsimile reproduction of newspapers, magazines, documents, etc.; electronic mail delivery; merchandising; business concern links to branch offices, primary customers or suppliers; access to computers, e.g., man to computer communications in the nature of inquiry and response (credit checks, airlines reservations, branch banking etc.), information retrieval (library and other reference material, etc.) and computer to computer communications; the furtherance of various governmental programs on a Federal, State and municipal level, e.g., employment services and manpower utilization, special communications systems to reach particular neighborhoods or ethnic groups within a community, and for municipal surveillance of public areas for protection against crime, fire detection, control of air pollution and traffic; various educational and training programs, e.g., job and literacy training, pre-school programs in the nature of "Project Head Start," and to enable professional groups such as doctors to keep abreast of developments in their fields; and the provision of a low cost outlet for political candidates, advertisers, amateur expression (e.g., community or university drama groups) and for other moderately funded organizations or persons desiring access to the community or a particular segment of the community.[13]

One area of particular interest to those concerned with the development of library networks is that of access to such systems for public and noncommercial services. The Canadian government now requires that CATV systems make available at least one channel for the presentation of educational and instructional programs by local authorities. In this country, the Joint Council on Educational Telecommunications, JCET, and others have urged that 20 percent of the capacity of each cable system be made available without cost to noncommercial users.[14] The JCET chose the phrase "20 percent of system capacity" carefully to reflect the interest of what may be broadly defined as "the educational community," not only in conventional television but in such other services as the commission, itself, suggests in the paragraph previously quoted. Not all of our present needs and still fewer of our future requirements are likely to be definable in terms of "television channel."

SATELLITE COMMUNICATIONS

If our future communications option will be expanded greatly by the development of cable communications along and under the ground, the other development of overwhelming significance will surely be 22,300 miles above the equator —the "parking orbit" for geosynchronous communications satellites. The technology of communications satellites is already well developed, as any viewer of the evening news on television can attest. In international communications, satellites already have established their place. The use of satellites for communications within the boundaries of our own nation has yet to begin on any but an experimental basis. The questions to be answered are not technical but regulatory.

Since 1966 the FCC has been considering the questions which it raised in Docket 16495 on domestic communications satellites. In essence, they deal with such matters as whether the Communications Satellite Act reserves to Comsat the entire field of satellite communications, or only the international segment, whether others may be permitted to operate domestic systems, and if so, what others. On several occasions, it has appeared that the FCC would issue some tentative or final word, but each time the President asked for time to study the matter within the executive branch. Lyndon Johnson, in a message to the Congress on 14 August 1967, established a President's Task Force on Communications Policy and charged it with exploring this and other important policy questions.[15] The task force's report was delivered to the President after his announcement that he would not run again and was never endorsed or act upon by the Johnson Administration.

A new administration provided an opportunity for yet another look at the matter, and an in-house study group within the Nixon Administration was appointed under the chairmanship of Dr. Clay T. Whitehead, then staff assistant to the President and now director of the new Office of Telecommunications Policy.

The LBJ task force recommended that a pilot program be undertaken with Comsat acting as trustee until final ownership questions could be resolved. The Whitehead committee took a different view. A White House memo to FCC Chairman Dean Burch suggested that free entry into the market be maintained and that there appeared to be little reason not to allow any entity, including user consortia and governmental agencies, from entering the domestic satellite field so long as they could demonstrate fiscal and technical capability.[16]

The FCC is an independent regulatory agency, and it need not follow the dictates of the White House. Its Notice of Proposed Rule Making, however, did heed, at least in part, the White House suggestion.[17] The commission has "opened the door" to applications for a domestic satellite system, reserving judgment until such applications have been reviewed as to whether it will ultimately grant one, some, all, or none. At this writing, only one such application has been submitted, that from Western Union. A wide variety of other parties have informed the FCC that they also intend to submit plans. The group includes Comsat; AT&T, which will submit its own proposal or may choose instead to be Comsat's chief customer; Hughes Aircraft, the leading builder of communications satellites; and Teleprompter Corporation, leading cable TV concern (separately or jointly); and both of the leading special service common carrier applicants, Datran and Microwave Communications of America.

Favorable commission action on any of these applications could, at very least, increase competition in the carrier field and perhaps offer alternative choices for national network development. One interesting consideration is that satellite communications (at least their space segment) are essentially distance independent. That is to say that any two earth terminals within view of the satellite can be connected at equal cost. A "hop" from Washington to Baltimore or from Washington to Fairbanks is much the same in technology and in cost.

Yet another important policy decision appears on the horizon. In June 1971 the International Telecommunications Union, the United Nations-affiliated body which deals with allocation of radio spectrum, will hold a World Administrative Radio Conference on Space Telecommunications. The WARC-ST, as it is known, will hammer out agreement among the 190-plus member nations regarding the frequencies that are to be used in satellite services and for what purposes. Much of the deliberation will involve sophisticated questions of electronics and satellite engineering, but the resolution of such questions will have an effect upon the potential uses and users of space-borne communications.

Not all frequencies are equally satisfactory for satellite communications use. The JCET and others have been urging that the American delegation support the allocation of 2500-2690 MHz for noncommercial communications, including but not limited to ETV transmission to communicate receivers and terrestrial ETV stations. Data and facsimile transmission are specifically suggested, and communications among libraries could become a significant type of traffic.

The case put forth by the Joint Council on Educational Telecommunications rests upon three contentions:

1. These are very efficient frequencies for space transmission and would permit the development of ground terminals within the reach of the educational community, perhaps as low as $150 to $750 in quantity production.

2. The opportunity for experimentation is close at hand, NASA already having received a proposal for an experimental ETV transmitter which could deliver a powerful signal in this band. The experiment could be carried out on NASA's ATS-G satellite.

3. The 2500-2690 MHZ band is now allocated in this country to the noncommercial Instructional Television Fixed Service, ITFS, and by allocating the same frequencies to education for space and terrestrial use, interference to existing ITFS systems could be minimized, and beneficial trade-offs negotiated among parties with common interests.

Education's fight for these frequencies is by no means won, either in this country or at the international level. The opportunities which could be opened for low-cost distant-independent communications should be as attractive to library and information science specialists as to those interested in educational and instructional TV.

An examination of the regulatory framework within which telecommunications exists reveals, then, that "the coming shake-up" will include new answers to some presently pressing questions. As the Federal Communications Commission already has cast aside previous restrictions upon what devices the system user may connect to the public telephone network, it appears also to be moving toward admitting to the common carrier field a host of new entities which will be offering new and different services in an expanding communications market. Most of the issues have yet to be resolved in the special service common carrier field; the same may be said even more emphatically with regard to cable communications and to domestic satellites. It is already clear, however, that any one of these developments would have enormous impact in the communications field. Such technological developments coming at the same time assure that it will soon be "a whole new ballgame" in which there are not only new players but new rules of play. Any forward planning for library and information networks which ignores such developments can only find itself out of date before it can be implemented.

TECHNICAL DEVELOPMENTS

The technical developments which give rise to such pressing regulatory questions are of interest in their own right. The technical capacities likely to be offered by new carrier networks, cable communications, and satellites already have been suggested, but a brief look at each would not be out of order.

The development of coaxial cable-based community antenna television brings to the CATV-connected home or office a technology of considerable power. While most present CATV systems carry only twelve channels of TV, the capacity of the cable, itself, is considerably greater. The present "bottleneck" is the tuner of the TV set, designed to tune only twelve VHF channels, numbered 2 to 13. The cable, itself, can carry frequencies from a few cycles per second to approximately 300,000,000. In TV terms, what would provide some channels below Channel 2, more between Channels 6 and 7, which, although numbered consecutively, "jump over" enough room for nine more channels, and above Channel 13. The capacity of present cables is impressive, and it is not unlikely that future systems will be able to transmit UHF as well as VHF frequencies.

To escape the problem of the conventional TV set's limited ability to retrieve all that the cable could offer, some CATV systems have gone to twenty or more channels, issuing to each subscriber a small tuning device which sits atop the TV set like a UHF convertor of the 1950s. While each CATV cable may someday be able to carry a wider range of frequencies, it is possible right now to install more than one cable. Two cables, side by side, will carry twice as many signals, and all the viewer need do is to throw a switch on his CATV tuner which connects him to cable A or cable B. In San Jose, California, a system is now under construction which will use this simple solution to provide a total of forty-two channels. If such communications capacity does not appear to be sufficient to meet your wildest dreams, one might consider the fact that one Rand Corporation expert predicts systems of better than 400 channels.

Four hundred channels of television may appear more likely to stupefy than to inspire. With the possible exception of those TV fans who would welcome the prospect of choosing any *I Love Lucy* episode they might wish to see at any hour of the day or night, 400 channels of TV may appear to be more than the good of the human race actually requires. The more rational view, of course, lies in the fact that such immense communications capacity need not all be devoted to entertainment TV. Some of the communications options, especially with two-way communications, already are suggested in the previous quotation from the FCC's Docket 18397. The comments by the Industrial Electronics Division of the Electronics Industries Association in Docket No. 18397 are illuminating. EIA envisions a broadband communications network, BCN, which would include a minimum 300 MHz "...'pipe' to provide many information services for home, business and government such as broadcast video, first-class mail, and educational material, plus others....The BCN should provide limited return bandwidth for receiving and tabulating specific requests and responses by individual users of the cable or cables."[18]

Such a return circuit would permit the user to order and control what information was sent him. One example is described in the following quote:

The principal elements of the BCNX electronic mail can also provide a new service to the home or business user. This may be called the electronic home library service (designated BCNL). With such a service available a reader can request a book or periodical from a large central library, using a narrow-band channel to the library (a phone circuit of the BCN network itself). The desired book is then "transmitted" from microfiche, microfilm, or video tape, page by page, and received via the BCN network on a dedicated wide-band channel.

Several modes of operation are possible. In one, the entire book or a selected article is transmitted at the maximum reception speed of the user's facsimile recorder. Several hundred simultaneous transmissions in time-division multiplex

are possible with 6-BCN channels and reasonable recorder speed.

As an alternative, a soft-copy display can be used. Each page is transmitted and stored at the receiver for reading. When the reader has finished one page, he signals for the next page, and this is transmitted in a small fraction of a second with no perceptible delay. This is another form of sharing of the broad-band channel.

To get a feeling for the capacity of a broad-band channel, it is of interest to note that in the demonstration described in Reference 5, the entire text of "Gone With the Wind" was transmitted in facsimile over a television microwave circuit in slightly over two minutes.

In its early stages a library service would undoubtedly be limited in quality of the recorded images. The goals of graphic arts quality, color reproduction, and other refinements will gradually be attained as technology advances and as public demand develops. BCN offers a favorable transmission medium in bandwidth and propagation characteristics for such growth in image quality.[19]

Furthermore, it has been suggested that the introduction of computer-based switching into such a system could add greatly to its flexibility and utility. The computer could store an "interest profile" for each subscriber, based upon the user's own statement of his information needs plus the computer's memory of what he has ordered in the past. Each night, the computer would search its record of the day's new acquisitions, match them against the interest profile of each subscriber, and print out at each terminal a list custom-tailored to the individual needs of the subscriber, including, perhaps, a *precis* for those items judged likely to be of greatest interest to the subscriber.

The near-miracles promised by a cable communications system sound impossible to resist, but it is also clear that there are costs, economic and political, which would have to be met. The barriers to the widespread development of cable communications and the economic costs which would be entailed were examined by Harold J. Barnett and Edward Greenberg in a paper prepared for a 1967 conference sponsored by Resources for the Future, Inc., and the Brookings Institute. These Washington University economists coined the name, "the Wired City," which has been widely used to describe the potential of cable communications.[20]

SATELLITE COMMUNICATIONS

If it appears that the full implications of cable communication were not foreseen by those who pioneered in CATV, it is equally true that the potential of communications satellites was clearly seen by Congress when it passed the Communications Satellite Act of 1962. In creating Comsat as this nation's chosen instrument in the field of satellite communications, the legislation clearly intends that Comsat should serve this role in the international communications field. The application of communications satellites to domestic communications then appeared so wildly futuristic that the subject is not even discussed in the act.

The Communications Satellite Corporation, to give Comsat its full name, was chartered as a nongovernmental corporation, the stock of which is held by both the international common carriers and public stockholders. By international agreement, Comsat also serves as manager of the International Satellite Consortium, Intelsat, the multinational agency which operated the international communications satellite system. Educators and librarians, and indeed, any private party, are barred from dealing directly with Comsat by the "authorized user" regulation which restricts Comsat to the role of communications wholesaler, providing satellite services only to authorized common carriers. Thus, to lease a circuit between London and New York, the television networks deal with AT&T here and the British Ministry of Posts and Telegraph at the other end of the circuit.

The domestic communications satellite proposal which the FCC has received from Western Union bears a strong technological resemblance to the present Comsat-Intelsat configuration: relatively small multichannel, multipurpose satellites, working into a small number (five in the WU plan) of large and expensive earth terminals. Such communications satellite systems are termed "relay" satellites.

Engineers distinguish "relay," "distribution," and "broadcast" satellites. Relay satellites, including those now in use, are designed to handle point-to-point traffic on high-density routes, as between North America and Europe. The traffic begins and ends its journey via terrestrial common carrier systems so that only a few ground terminals are needed, each connecting to a terrestrial web for carrying the messages onward.

True broadcast satellites could beam radio and/or television programs directly to the home. Such programs would be received on conventional receivers with, perhaps, minor modifications and special outdoor antennas. At present no broadcast television satellites exist. The technical problems may take five to twenty years to solve; the political problems, inherent in any system which would make it possible to beam TV directly both to and from unfriendly nations, may never find solution.

Between these two extremes lies the "distribution" satellite, the next logical step in communications satellite development. That step already is possible and is planned for some time in the 1973-74 time frame. NASA's Applications Technology Satellite F will carry, among other experiments, a solar-powered 80-watt TV transmitter; the transmitter's power will be concentrated by ATS-F's thirty-foot antenna into a relatively narrow, intense beam which will be focused upon India. There, under an agreement between the governments of India and the USA, schools and community centers in 5,000 Indian villages will receive educational television programming for children and adults on special TV receivers which will cost, in those quantities, something on the order of $500. The programs, produced by the Indians themselves, will be beamed up to the satellite from near Bombay and retransmitted to sets in the villages.

There are technical reasons why that particular experiment cannot be carried out in the United States, largely having to do with the fact that the ATS-F will broadcast its signals in the UHF frequencies. There is no ground-based UHF television in the Indian subcontinent. Here, the satellite would be a potential source of interference with American TV stations on Channels 14 to 83. However, at least one proposal would offer the possibility of a parallel experiment for the USA — including, perhaps, Alaska and/or Hawaii.

ATS-G is scheduled to follow ATS-F by eighteen months to two years. The ATS-G proposal would provide an even more powerful TV transmitter in the 2500 MHz band, a set of frequencies so desirable for educational communications that the JCET, the Department of Health, Education, and Welfare, and others have urged that they be made available on an operational basis.

This ATS-G proposal would permit TV or other broadband communications (such as high-speed data transmission) from the satellite into simple receiving antennas estimated to cost approximately the same as those in the Indian experiment. One important addition in this case would be the option of adding two-way communications from any receiving point. The return channel would not be capable of television but could accommodate voice transmission — allowing a viewing student in Kodiak, Alaska, to ask a question of his TV teacher in Los Angeles — or such other narrowband communications as teletypewriter signals. Both computer access and facsimile transmission would be well within the range of possibility.

The importance of such an advance in communications satellites for library and information network planning is immediately obvious. Since satellite communications are distance independent, this communications technology makes the task of interconnecting five libraries that have similar specialized collections but are geographically dispersed exactly the same as that of interconnecting five libraries in a single state. When connected via satellite, the terrestrial distances between terminals is simply not significant. The President's Task Force on Communications Policy pointed out that there are two characteristics of communications satellites which have no exact terrestrial equivalent: their ability to provide multipoint distribution via a single relay point and their ability to reallocate communications capacity flexibly and rapidly among a number of individual routes. Such flexibility increases as the number of ground stations increases.

Such a system might well prove economically and operationally attractive for establishing a variety of specialized communications "networks" such as multiple-access, variable information rate data exchange service, computer-aided educational services, and occasional, specialized video "networks."

In addition to television distribution, uses of communications satellites in the foreseeable future might thus include: (a) relay of bulk communications such as multi-channel voice/record trunks, high speed data, and video programs among a limited number of points; (b) networking of specialized communications such as voice, data, and graphics among dispersed or mobile users, such as aircraft, ships, computer and information centers; and (c) various scientific and meterological data collection, distribution and exchange services. Satellites might, therefore, open new horizons in the dissemination and exchange of economic, medical, scientific and educational information among businessmen, doctors, students, teachers and others, and lend added impetus to progress in many areas.[21]

To provide service to low-cost earth-based terminals, a communications satellite system must be able to develop satellites of higher power than has been heretofore possible. For a whole complex of reasons, the choice of transmission frequencies used from space is an important factor, and proposals for NASA's ATS-F and ATS-G satellites demonstrate that greatly increased levels of signal strength can be achieved if frequency selection is optimized. It is for this reason that the work of next year's World Administrative Radio Conference on Space Telecommunications will be of critical importance. Thus, the Joint Council on Education Telecommunications, the Department of Health, Education, and Welfare, and others are urging that the best choice of frequencies not be denied to services such as those outlined by the President's task force.

One final word on satellite communications is in order. On 13 June 1969 the National Aeronautics and Space Administration held a meeting at which it announced the availability of two early satellites in the Applications Technology series. The experimental programs for which ATS-I and ATS-III were originally launched had been substantially completed, and NASA invited parties interested in undertaking new experiments and willing to fund the programmatic costs involved to prepare and submit proposals. At the meeting, a series of proposals was put forth by John W. Macy, Jr., on behalf of the Corporation for Public Broadcasting, of which he is the president, the Ford Foundation, the Joint Council on Educational Telecommunications, the National Association of Educational Broadcasters, and National Educational Television.

The proposals of the ad hoc Satellite Task Force deal not only with use of the satellites for television transmission but also for an experimental radio network as well.[22] Of great significance to planners of library and information networks is the fact that these satellites can receive and transmit such narrowband traffic as voice or data through the use of simple, relatively inexpensive earth terminals. Like the public broadcasters, the state of Alaska and the Lister Hill National Center for Biomedical Communications, National Library of Medicine, also have received NASA's agreement to use ATS-I or III for experimental purposes. Opportunities for interlibrary communications via satellite are already available and demonstrate feasible costs. The idea of a library and information network experiment on ATS-I and III would appear much worth pursuing. Plans might be made directly with NASA, or as a part of one of the experiments already proposed by public broadcasting, the state of Alaska or the Lister Hill Center.

The most important lesson to be learned is of far greater importance than the satellites themselves. It is that planners of interlibrary networks need not, and should not, labor alone. This Conference on Interlibrary Communications and Information Networks is an important step toward exploring new opportunities for mutually beneficial cooperation.

EDUCATIONAL BROADCASTING COMMUNITY

Outside the federal government itself, the educational broadcasting community has been the most visible and probably, the principal user of public service-oriented networking. A brief review of some of the major entities, their acronyms, and their activities in networking may help to put educational broadcasting in perspective.

National Educational Television, NET, has been the most familiar organization in public television since the early days of ETV. (The term, "public television" was first applied by the Carnegie Commission in an attempt to find a substitute for the more academic and forbidding "educational TV.") For most of its existence, NET has not been a "net" in the true sense of the word but a producer and distributor of videotaped programming. NET, long based in New York City, is now in the process of merger with New York's local public television station, WNDT (TV). The surviving corporation will be the WNDT licensee, the Educational Broadcasting Corporation, but the NET presence will be echoed in the station's call letters, which are to be changed to WNET.

The stations, themselves, are members of the National Association of Educational Broadcasters, NAEB, the pioneer organization in educational radio and television. The NAEB's membership includes educational radio and television stations, schools and universities, and individual practitioners in the field. Its Educational Television Station, NAEB/ETS, division serves the nation's public television station and through the ETS Program Service, acts as a clearinghouse of the exchange of programs produced by individual stations. NAEB's radio division, National Educational Radio, has for many years operated a program service "network" distributing radio programming on tape.

In both radio and television, some true intrastate and interstate public broadcasting networks exist. All of the state of Wisconsin is served by its pioneering, state-owned FM radio network. Several states operate statewide television networks, and one, South Carolina, combines both closed-circuit television to the schools with a network of broadcast ETV stations. The principal state agencies are represented in NAEB's Council of State Educational Telecommunications Authorities, COSETA.

Genuine networking, in the form of live coast-to-coast real-time interconnection for public broadcasting, is an old dream but a relatively recent reality. The Ford Foundation (long ETV's strongest supporter) backed this nation's first, true public television network in a two-season project called the Public Broadcasting Laboratory. PBL has passed from the scene, but the experimental one-night-a-week interconnection of ETV stations has expanded to six nights a week and to more stations. The networking is accomplished over leased Bell System facilities. While the Public Broadcasting Act clears the legal decks for "free or reduced rate" service, the debate over the degree of cost reductions has not yet been completed. Support for the present network comes from the Ford Foundation and the Corporation for Public Broadcasting.

The Corporation for Public Broadcasting, CPB, was created in response to the recommendations of the Carnegie Commission on Educational Television. Although chartered by Congress, the CPB is not an agency of the government. Its board of directors is appointed by the President, and it receives the major share of its funding by congressional appropriation. Its task is to promote the development of noncommercial radio and television as a national resource. To carry out that mandate, it makes grants to stations and regional networks, and has played a key role in the establishment of other national agencies in public broadcasting. Of particular interest to planners of information networks are two new agencies on the public broadcasting scene:

The Public Broadcasting Service, PBS, has been created to assume operational responsibility for the public television interconnected network. The function, begun by the late Public Broadcasting Laboratory and more recently administered by NET, will become the full responsibility of the new PBS. While the Corporation for Public Broadcasting Board of Directors is appointed by the President of the United States, the PBS board consists principally of public television station managers, elected by their peers from across the nation. Although yet in the process of recruiting its own staff, PBS has exhibited an interest in the broadly developing field of networking and is mindful of the fact that new technical and regulatory developments may directly affect its options in providing the nation's public television stations the flexible interconnection service they require.

While noncommercial educational radio is as old as broadcasting itself, the growth of public radio has been obscured by developments in the world of television. The responsibility to develop public broadcasting as a national service, however, requires that the full potential of the older sound medium be realized as well. Noncommercial radio's dream of a national network is older than those persons now charged with making the dream a reality. Again with impetus provided by the Corporation for Public Broadcasting, 1970 saw the establishment of National Public Radio, NPR.

National Public Radio will act as the nexus of national noncommercial radio development. Its initial list of member stations includes those educational radio outlets which serve the needs to the total community in range of their signals. Excluded are noncommercial radio stations whose primary purpose is to serve a college campus as student voice and training ground for future disc jockeys. Noncommercial stations which are primarily evangelistic voices of their church-related licensees or instructional media beaming school programming at classroom audiences are likewise outside the definition of "public radio."

Almost 100 noncommercial stations have the signal strength, the professional staff, and the commitment to serve a general audience which defines public radio. NPR's responsibility will be to develop a national schedule of radio programming through production of new programming and acquisition of programs from such outside sources as the radio networks of other nations. Donald R. Quayle, NPR president, describes the new network as "event-oriented," leaning heavily toward the live coverage of such public affairs as congressional hearings. NPR also expects to provide meaningful background information and interpretation of events, drawing upon the insights of journalists and other experts and observers from many points around the country.

To meet such goals, NPR will require an extensive and flexible radio network of Bell System lines, with provision to reach all of the nation's public radio stations and the capacity to originate programming from many points on the network.

The prospect of new networks for public broadcasting, including both radio and television, ought at very least to suggest to other network planners new participants in a broadened dialogue. Interstate networks, especially those involving state-owned intercity relay, may provide some opportunities for expansion of service. The state of Wisconsin's FM network is made up of stations which are capable of transmitting special nonbroadcast communications via multiplexed subcarrier signals. While the general audience hears the broadcast program, the multiplexed signal is received simultaneously by a smaller audience equipped with special receivers. The Wisconsin network's "background" channel has been used for medical seminars and other communications with professional interest groups. Experiments also have been undertaken in using the subcarrier system for the transmission of facsimile graphics.

The National Association of Educational Broadcasters' Council of State Educational Telecommunications Authorities looks toward increased service in nonbroadcast communications. In the mid-1960s the NAEB undertook a broadscale examination of the ways in which educational radio and television networks might become the basis for the development of widely useful educational communications systems.

While not so well known as the Interuniversity Communications Council's (EDUCOM) report of its 1966 Summer Study on Information Networks,[23] the NAEB's *Educational Communications System: Phase III* presents detailed analysis of three communications system "models," an intrastate model located in Oregon and based upon that state's existing television network; an interstate model projected for the Midwest; and a "resources model" which would tap the information sources in universities, government, and industry in the Boston-Washington corridor for the benefit of the other two model systems.[24]

Two factors common to both EDUCOM's EDUNET, and NAEB's ECS: Phase III are apparent. One is that each gives clear recognition to the principal that the opportunity to aggregate communications needs can provide the possibility of cost reductions and increased network efficiencies. The concept remains as valid now as it was five years ago. What also is apparent from a rereading of each study is that the context for educational communications networks has changed substantially. The possibility of new nontelephone microwave networks between cities, the prospect of a domestic communications satellite system, the opportunities for broadband communications via coaxial cable are indications of the ways in which the choices for network planners have been increased radically since these two reports appeared.

Such developments are of especial interest to the Joint Council on Educational Telecommunications. The JCET was founded in 1950 as the Joint Committee on Educational Television. Its concern then was to alert education to the need to secure its option in the emerging communications field of television. Now, the cutting edge (or more accurately, "edges") in communications lie in satellites, cables, and the like. The JCET continues its pursuit of the same goal: to alert the educational community to such developments and to help secure the public benefits which such developments can offer.

The JCET is now, as then, a consortium of nonprofit educational organizations. Its member organizations include the leadership in the educational establishment and in the expanding field of public television which the original JCET helped to establish. That such member organizations as EDUCOM and the Indiana Higher Education Telecommunications System are interested in the broad range of "educational telecommunications" is, like the JCET's present name, indication of increasing recognition of the interdependence of all types of public service-oriented communications. The JCET serves not only the twenty-five organizations which are its present members but also the total educational community, and beyond it those entities within and without government interested in public communications planning and policy.

The twenty-year experience of the Joint Council on Education Telecommunications clearly indicates that the enlightened self-interest of those who plan communications networks requires, as does the public interest, that parochialism give way to broader vision and that acute specialization be tempered with cooperation. Each new development in communications — new technology; new policy decisions to be made by the FCC, the Congress, the White House, the International Telecommunications Union; new programs in communication in such allied fields as public broadcasting and public health — offer an increasingly favorable climate for the development of library communications and other information networks. Library and information specialists can help themselves, and others, if they will seek to pool their interests and cooperate fully in the pursuit of the new opportunities which are now increasingly within our common grasp.

NOTES

1. Dan Cordtz, "The coming shake-up in telecommunications," *Fortune* 81:69- (April 1970).

2. Federal Communications Commission, Docket Nos. 16942, 17073.

3. President's Task Force on Communication Policy, *Final report.* (Washington, D.C.: Gov. Print. Off., 1968), Chapt. VI, p.26-28, 37-42.

4. Federal Communications Commission 69-870m re *Microwave Communications, Inc.,* Docket 16509.

5. Federal Communications Commission, Docket No. 18920, p.6-9.

6. Victor Block, "Inside the FCC common carrier bureau," *Telephony* (15 August 1970).

7. Federal Communications Commission, Docket No. 18920, p.13.

8. Federal Communications Commission, "Procedures and policies for handling microwave applications for specialized common carrier services proposed by FCC," Report No. 90 (51530), 15 July 1970, p.2.

9. Federal Communications Commission, Docket No. 18397.

10. Federal Communications Commission Docket No. 18892; see also Leland L. Johnson, *The future of cable television: some problems of federal regulation,* Memorandum RM-6199-FF (Santa Monica, Calif.: Rand Corp., Jan. 1970).

11. Federal Communications Commission, Docket No. 18894.

12. Ibid., p.2.

13. Federal Communications Commission Docket No. 18397, *Notice of proposed rule making and notice of inquiry* (FCC 68-1176), p.5.

14. Joint Council on Educational Telecommunications, *Comments,* (12 May 1969) in FCC Docket No. 18397.

15. "The President's message to the Congress, 14 Aug. 1967," in *Weekly compilation of presidential documents* 3:33, p.1146-1154.

16. Peter Flanigan, "Memorandum for the Honorable Dean Burch, Chairman of the Federal Communications Commission, from Peter Flanigan, Assistant to the President," 23 Jan. 1970.

17. "Sky's the limit on satellite bids," *Broadcasting* 78:42 (30 March 1970).

18. Electronic Industries Association, *Comments* in FCC Docket 18397, Part V, p.2 (28 Oct. 1969).

19. Ibid., p.20-21.

20. Harold J. Barnett and Edward Greenberg, "A proposal for wired city television," *Washington University law quarterly* 1:1-25 (Winter 1968).

21. President's Task Force on Communications Policy, *Final report.* (Washington, D.C.: Gov. Print. Off., 1968) Chapt. V, p.5-6.

22. "A proposal for experimental use of ATS," in J. W. Meaney and C. R. Carpenter, eds., *Telecommunications: toward national policies for education* (Washington, D.C.: Joint Council on Educational Telecommunications, 1970), p.146.

23. George W. Brown et al., *EDUNET* (New York: Wiley, 1967), 440p.

24. John P. Witherspoon et al., *Educational communications system: phase III,* Final Report of Project 450A (Washington, D.C.: U.S. Office of Education, Bureau of Research, October 1966), 300p.

Survey of Interlibrary Cooperation

David C. Weber and Frederick C. Lynden

DEVELOPMENTS AND TRENDS BY TYPE OF ORGANIZATION

MUNICIPAL AND COUNTY DEVELOPMENTS

Public library cooperation has come about gradually over many decades. The most significant and persistent among developments has been the enlarging of administrative units. During the latter half of the nineteenth century, the municipal library was generally a small independent unit supported by local taxes. About 1890, when Massachusetts created a separate agency for the sole purpose of offering library extension services, the state became involved in encouraging the enlargement of library units.[1] It has been the county movement which has produced the most important early cooperative developments in the public library field.

The county movement began in 1900 when libraries in Ohio and Maryland were organized for county service.[2] By 1926, laws permitting the provision of county library service had been enacted in thirty-one states and the territory of Hawaii. California led the country with forty-three counties out of a possible fifty-eight participating. By 1936, forty-five states had plans in which county or regional libraries were a common feature.

A metropolitan, county, or regional "system" consists of several library units connected by a central administration which can provide the services which the individual units find difficult or impossible to provide separately. In a 1969 survey of 491 multijurisdictional public library systems which served 44 percent of the population in the United States, more than a third provided multicounty service, and nearly half, countywide service.[5] Just under half of the multicounty and countywide systems were founded before 1945. The survey noted that "five important services — systematic referral of information requests, centralized processing, centralized purchasing, systemwide users' privileges, and bookmobile service — are provided by more than three-fourths of the system."[6] Therefore, the cooperative developments in public libraries can be attributed in part to the enlargement of units.

Significant encouragement to the county movement resulted from state-aid, studies by the American Library Association, ALA, and efforts of the Works Progress Administration. The ALA Committee on Library Extension compiled a study in 1926 which recommended that the basis for adequate rural public library service be the county or other large unit, and suggested more active participation by state library extension agencies in every state. County service demonstrations, begun in seven southern states in 1929, were sponsored by WPA projects in the thirties and later put on a permanent basis.[7] One of the major problems of the public library extension movement has been the inequalities of service. By 1944, only a quarter of all U.S. counties had county libraries.[8]

In metropolitan areas a major problem has been the lack of systems. Development of library systems has been hampered by the multitude of independent public libraries in suburban areas governed by a variety of political units and by the use of older central city facilities by suburban residents not paying taxes to the city. Both Detroit and New York have established metropolitan systems through independent commissions which do not depend solely on city taxation. The library in Detroit is operated by the Detroit Library Commission, chartered by the state of Michigan rather than the city government.[9] A similar independent commission, the New York Metropolitan Reference and Research Library Agency, METRO, was established in 1964, the first of the nine 3R systems in New York. METRO already has set up a central Advisory and Referral Service for the New York Metropolitan Area.[10]

According to the public library systems survey by Nelson Associates, the greatest obstacle standing in the way of system development is fear of losing autonomy. A "characteristic weakness...[of county systems is]...unwillingness of the better established municipal libraries to become part of the system for fear of dissipating their resources."[11] Other problems frequently encountered in developing systems are shortage of staff and inadequate financial support. Insufficient funding, sometimes due to state legal limitations on taxes, appears to be the worst problem facing current systems. Yet despite these circumstances, library directors generally favor expansion and further consolidation with other systems.[12]

DEVELOPMENT AT THE STATE LEVEL

Until recently, states were not able to provide a great deal of leadership and encouragement for system development because neither the incentives nor the coercive power necessary to accomplish this objective were readily available. The Library

Services Act of 1956, LSA, changed this situation. One requirement for receiving federal aid under LSA was that the state agency develop a state plan for rural library services; it was permissible to spend funds for urban libraries if they were included as part of the entire plan.[13] The Library Services and Construction Act of 1964, LSCA, also channeled its funds for public library construction through state library agencies. Title III of the amended LSCA (1966) specifically encouraged states to plan system development.[14] Despite federal assistance, however, the development of state systems has been uneven because of the inequalities of state funds. "As of 1967, nineteen states have no state-aid programs; of the remainder, eleven states account for all except a fraction of the total, $34,700,000."[15]

Since 1956, three states have used federal monies to produce strong and comprehensive statewide systems. These states are Hawaii, Pennsylvania, and New York.

Hawaii's system is truly a statewide, state-governed library system. LSA funds made possible the survey which established the Hawaii pattern for the statewide system, passed by its legislature in 1961.[16] The entire state is serviced by a network of thirty-four branch libraries using uniform loan regulations and operated from the State Library without local funds.

The Pennsylvania state system, inaugurated in 1962 following a plan developed with LSA funds, has a hierarchical system of thirty districts, each with a state-supported headquarters library and four regional resource centers.[17]

Between 1946 and 1962, 700 public libraries in New York State became part of twenty-two systems. In 1960 the New York State Department of Education set up a Committee on Reference and Research Library Resources, 3R's, which recommended a hierarchical system: the county systems, nine Reference and Resource councils, three geographical referral centers, and nine subject referral centers, all of which are research libraries. Reference questions and interlibrary loan requests pass through various levels until answered. The entire system is monitored by the State Library. In 1967 New York State also experimented with a Facsimile Transmission System, FACTS, which was discontinued after six months because of technical difficulties and high costs.[18]

Other states have used teletype facilities to link their libraries for interlibrary loans. For example, Oklahoma's teletypewriter system, OTIS, links public, academic, and special libraries as well as the State Library. In Texas, a statewide information network was established in 1968 to handle interlibrary loans via telephone and teletype facilities.[19]

In addition to statewide services in reference and interlibrary loan, some states have developed statewide technical processing. Georgia has had a state catalog card service since 1944, and by 1958 this service was furnishing thirty regional public library systems with catalog cards.[20] Hawaii has statewide centralized processing for both public and school libraries. In 1966 Missouri State Library expanded two existing processing centers into a single technical processing center for all public libraries except those in the Kansas City and St. Louis areas.[21]

According to the 1969 Nelson survey of public library systems, the greatest economies from centralization occur in cataloging rather than purchasing and physical preparation. It should be noted that one of the greatest disappointments of system service has been the slow delivery of books by centralized processing.

The evidence can lead one to be very critical of states for the lack of suitable legislation, as well as the lack of adequate financial support, planning, and leadership. A problem facing all states is the lack of public library standards for different kinds of systems as well as the lack of detailed information on existing public library systems.

COOPERATION AMONG SPECIAL LIBRARIES

Special libraries have cooperated in several ways to make the most efficient use of their resources. Larger corporations have developed centralized services for their branch libraries. General Motors Corporation has twenty-two company libraries; however, since 1927 all interlibrary loans have been handled through its central library.[22] Using remote on-line terminals, IBM has a technical processing network, based in Poughkeepsie, in which seven of its far-flung libraries voluntarily participate, preserving individual library autonomy while achieving economical sharing of the system.[23] Smaller corporate libraries have developed arrangements with other corporate libraries. In Minneapolis, six small companies formed a cooperative library association and by 1963, had coordinated their buying, encouraged interlibrary loans, and discussed other mutual problems.[24] As another example, the Associated Science Libraries of San Diego, established in 1963, includes corporation libraries, universities and colleges, public libraries, government agencies, and museums. It has produced a union list and facilitates research through referrals.[25]

The federal government has encouraged cooperation of special libraries through the State Technical Services Act of 1965, which contributed matching federal funds to state programs in order to make scientific and technical information available to business.[26] These funds have made possible, for example, a "Regional Information and Communication Exchange in Houston, the Industrial Information Service in Dallas, and a program in California that links the State Library, UCLA, and public libraries in the Fresno County area — all to serve industry."[27]

The State University of New York Biomedical Communication Network is an example of special library cooperation using the latest technology. Operational since 1968, it links the four medical centers of the state university, SUNY, with the medical library facilities of ten agencies. Computer-based bibliographical files maintained in Syracuse contain the National Library of Medicine Catalog, 1966 to date; five years of MEDLARS records; the records of three SUNY medical libraries; and selected entries from the Harvard University medical library. This file can be accessed via typewriter terminals.[28]

College and research libraries also have made special arrangements to cooperate with special libraries. In 1958 Stanford University Libraries established a separate library office which now serves more than 300 industrial and commercial firms. Regular members pay for each citation delivered, and the membership provides reading room use, loans, photocopy service, interlibrary loans from outside Stanford, and the right to recommend purchases. Thus, the Technical Information Service provides a switching service between a major research library and local special libraries.[29] Massachusetts Institute of

Technology also maintains a similar formal program of services with an annual fee for corporate users.[30]

The unique problems of independent special libraries are their frequently small, mission-directed collections and their necessarily cost-effective evaluation. They are not of a scale to compare with the large special libraries or academic libraries, yet the best of them are noted for providing useful, aggressive, and highly competent service. Because of these facts, however, the balance of interlibrary loan requests is on the side of the special libraries which must depend on outside resources for frequent assistance. A survey of interlibrary lending among industrial corporation libraries showed that a library borrowed an average of 335 volumes a year and lent 57 volumes a year.[31] "Several studies note that special libraries are filling nearly 100 percent of all requests made of them with considerable reliance on other libraries."[32]

Therefore, networks which will provide rapid transfer of information, when needed, may offer the best solution for satisfying the needs of special libraries.

ACADEMIC LIBRARY COOPERATION

Cooperation among academic and research libraries has taken many forms: acquisitions, cataloging, interlibrary lending, and automated services. These are treated below by function. By definition, interinstitutional cooperation includes informal and "...formal agreements between wholly independent libraries, contractual arrangements between two or more libraries, merging of two or more libraries, and reorganization of state institutions of higher education into one system and unification of their libraries."[33] In sharp contrast to municipal, county, state, and special libraries, where the vast majority of significant interlibrary developments have come in the past the fifteen years, academic and research libraries have had major programs for seventy years — with substantial expansion in type of programs during the past forty years.

An example of an informal arrangement among several institutions is the Cooperating Libraries of Upper New York, CLUNY. Formed in 1931, it included Buffalo University, Colgate University, Grosvenor Library, Hamilton College, Syracuse University, Cornell University, and Union College. This group functioned until 1939 as a clearinghouse for mutual problems and cooperated on a union list of periodicals and the joint purchase of microfilm of early English publications.[34] Three of the original members of CLUNY (Buffalo, Cornell, and Syracuse) are now part of Five Associated University Libraries, FAUL, which has compatibility of computer systems as a chief emphasis.[35]

An example of a formal agreement between independent libraries is the Duke/North Carolina Inter-Library Project. In 1931 Duke University and the University of North Carolina decided upon special collecting areas. With a grant from the General Education Board of North Carolina, the libraries were able to exchange author cards from their catalogs; in 1935 a messenger service was inaugurated. Two more North Carolina institutions joined in 1955, and full borrowing privileges were extended to all members.[36]

An example of contractual arrangements among several libraries is the Joint University Libraries founded in 1938 by Vanderbilt University, George Peabody College, and Scarritt College. Operating under a joint board of trustees, the facility is an independent entity, jointly owned and financed by the participants.[37] Another example is the Claremont College library system which began in 1931 when a contractual arrangement among Claremont Graduate School, Pomona College, and Scripps College established a joint order and catalog department to serve the three libraries.[38] There is now a common facility the Honnold Library, which serves six Claremont Colleges: Claremont Graduate School and University Center, the Claremont Men's College, and the Harvey Mudd, Pitzer, Pomona, and Scripps colleges.

An example of the merger of two or more libraries is the Atlanta Center Trevor Arnett Library in Atlanta, Georgia. Built with a grant from the General Education Board in 1932, it serves six colleges of Atlanta: Atlanta University, Morehouse College, Spelman College, Morris Brown College, Clark College, and Gammon Theological Seminary.[39]

Another variation of interinstitutional cooperation — unification of research libraries under state control — was pioneered by the Oregon State Board of Higher Education in 1932. The board appointed one director of libraries for the entire state system, established the principle of free circulation among all state institutions, and set up a central order division which now takes the form of "...a combined author list of all books and periodicals in the State System...maintained in the Order Department of the Oregon State University Library in Corvallis to...eliminate unnecessary duplication of materials."[40]

The University of California at Berkeley *Author-Title-Catalog*, published in 1963 to share research resources, and the UCLA catalog, which came later, were part of the broad program of cooperation among the campuses of the University of California recommended by the All University Faculty Conference and formalized by the regents in September 1961. The State University of New York, SUNY, established in 1948, has sixty colleges and centers presently in operation. In 1966 the central SUNY administrative staff drew up a program for library development including the establishment of a universitywide communications network; a computer-based union catalog for holdings of the entire system; and a processing center for the acquisition, cataloging, and physical preparation of new material.[41]

More recent forms of interinstitutional cooperation will be discussed in the consortia section of this paper. None of the above developments is frequent enough to discern a distinct trend. However, major identifiable needs are standards or criteria for assessing progress, compilations of detailed data on existing arrangements, additional funds to provide experimentation, and greater efforts by librarians to design more effective cooperative endeavors.

FEDERAL LIBRARIES AND LEGISLATION

Nationwide library cooperation efforts have been stimulated by centralized services provided by the "national" libraries, from their efforts to standardize the automation of libraries and from federal legislation aimed at coordinating the efforts of libraries.

The Library of Congress, LC, provides significant instances of centralized services for the nation in acquisitions, cataloging, and interlibrary loan. The Library began acquiring foreign government documents in 1867 through cooperation in an international exchange program and took on one aspect of a national library in 1870, when it was required that two copies of every work copyrighted in the United States be automatically deposited in the LC collection. In 1965 LC began acquiring a more comprehensive collection of foreign publications through a cooperative program, the National Program for Acquisitions and Cataloging, NPAC, which will be described later in this paper. The Library of Congress made printed catalog cards publicly available for every book it cataloged after 1901. It also began building the National Union Catalog in 1901, the expansion and publication of which is reviewed below.

The Library of Congress, in addition to its centralized acquisitions and cataloging services, maintains a vast interlibrary loan program. "Materials from the Library's collections that are not at the moment in demand by Congress and the rest of the Government, and that cannot be obtained otherwise, are now lent to other libraries in this country and abroad when there is a genuine scholarly need."[42] According to the annual report of LC, there were a quarter million volumes loaned during 1968.

The National Library of Medicine, NLM, mechanized its indexing services in 1960, and three years later it began storing these citations on the computer for use in the Medical Literature Analysis and Retrieval System, MEDLARS, which produces twenty-one major indexes including *Index Medicus,* a monthly index to 2,200 of the world's biomedical journals. As a result of the Medical Library Assistance Act of 1965, MEDLARS tapes are made available on a regional basis for bibliographic searching. There are presently eleven MEDLARS stations and eight regional medical libraries participating in an informational network offering bibliographic and reference services and interlibrary loans. The National Library of Medicine has a massive interlibrary loan program, making loans available in photocopy form. A major problem created by the large-scale photocopying is the possible violation of copyright; a 1968 legal suit, currently in the courts, was brought against the National Library of Medicine in this regard.

The Department of Agriculture Library was designated as a national library in 1962, becoming the National Agricultural Library, NAL. It compiles a comprehensive listing, the *Bibliography of Agriculture,* and produces *Pesticides Documentation Bulletin,* a bi-weekly indexed of worldwide literature. Both NLM and NAL have made their catalogs available in book form. In 1967, the first volumes of the *Dictionary Catalog of the National Agricultural Library,* 1862-1965, were published. In addition, both NLM and NAL began issuing a current book catalog in 1968.

The Federal Library Committee was established in 1965 by the Library of Congress and the Bureau of the Budget for the purpose of concentrating the intellectual resources present in the federal library and library-related information community: (1) to achieve better utilization of library resources and facilities, (2) to provide more effective planning, development, and operation of federal libraries, and (3) to promote an optimum exchange of experience, skill, and resources.

In 1963 a basic overall plan was adopted for automation of the Library of Congress's bibliographic system. The plan is now known as the King report: *Automation and the Library of Congress.* One of the long-range purposes of the LC automation program was "...to enhance interlibrary cooperation and secure for the individual user the benefits of the community of library resources."[43] In June of 1967 a National Libraries Task Force on Automation and Other Cooperative Services was announced by the directors of the three national libraries. The task force was to establish a national bank of machine-readable cataloging and serials data as well as to work toward compatibility in subject headings and classification schemes used by the three libraries. Several of their recommendations on standardizing of automation procedures already have been accepted, including a standard format for communication of bibliographic data, MARC — Machine Readable Cataloging.[44]

National legislation also has played an important role in increasing cooperation. In 1938 the Library Services Division was created in the U.S. Office of Education to act as "...a central clearinghouse for library planning and statistics gathering, and a source of information and guidance for all types of libraries."[45] The Higher Education Act of 1965 initiated the National Program for Acquisitions and Cataloging program which directed the Library of Congress to acquire, on a comprehensive basis, currently published foreign scholarly material and to catalog it promptly.[46] The next year, President Lyndon B. Johnson established a National Advisory Commission on Libraries whose final report recommended the establishment of a Federal Institute of Library and Information Science, which "...should have as one of its major responsibilities the system engineering and technical direction involved in the design and implementation of an integrated national library and information system...."[47] This recommendation has not yet been implemented. The Higher Education Act was amended in 1968 to include Title VIII, Networks for Knowledge (as yet unfunded), which encourages the sharing of resources by cooperative arrangements among colleges and universities.[48]

Problems of cooperation on a national level include: (1) the possibility of even more limiting copyright laws and the many unanswered questions as to whether computer data files are copyrightable, (2) tremendous costs of technological innovations necessary for future maintenance of adequate library service, (3) the lack of a really strong congressional mandate for the Library of Congress to exert national leadership, and (4) the lack of a strong Presidential support for a permanent National Commission on Libraries to promote full, coordinated, and effective library services to all of the nation.

COOPERATION FOSTERED BY PROFESSIONAL ORGANIZATIONS

Cooperative effort has been a prime focus in the programs of the American Library Association, the Medical Library Association, the American Association of Law Libraries, the Special Libraries Association, and others. One that has contributed notably to cooperative efforts is the Association of Research Libraries, formed in 1932. Its object is "...by cooperative effort to develop and increase the usefulness of the research collections in American libraries." A Council of National Library Associations was deemed necessary in 1942 "...to promote a closer relationship among the national library associations of the U.S. and Canada." In 1969 two library associations specifically designed to promote cooperation were founded. One, the Association of Cooperative Library Organizations has the aim of providing "...a channel for the exchange of information on cooperative ventures and to disseminate information about significant developments in library programs." The other, the Association of Caribbean University and Research Libraries, hopes "...to develop cooperation among member libraries as one of the first steps in interinstitutional cooperation."

Within the American Library Association many units have played a significant leadership role in promoting cooperation. Since 1877 its committees have developed several editions of national cataloging codes. As early as 1896, ALA's publishing section printed catalog cards. It was an ALA committee which in 1901 encouraged the Library of Congress to begin its card service. The ALA Cooperative Cataloging Committee, in conjunction with the Library of Congress, initiated a program in 1932 for LC to receive and edit card copy from cooperating libraries for new foreign books and monographs, state and city publications, and dissertations.[49] The ALA's Committee on Coordination of College Libraries passed the first interlibrary loan code in 1917.[50] This code has since been revised several times, and a standard form devised. The Resources and Technical Services Division of ALA presently has a Forms Standardization Committee and has developed photographic, bibliographic, book catalog, and reprinting standards. ALA has published standards for public libraries, as well as junior college and college libraries.

The Special Libraries Association has issued four national directories of special libraries and three directories of resources, and has encouraged union lists of serials. SLA also has promoted book exchanges by a routine for circulating lists of duplicate materials.[51]

The Association of Research Libraries has participated in a large number of cooperative projects in the areas of centralized cataloging, cooperative acquisitions, interlibrary loans, joint microfilming projects, union catalogs, and bibliographic centers. ARL was the major force behind the Cooperative Acquisitions Project which obtained material from Europe during World War II and later became the Farmington Plan.[52] It also created the cooperative Foreign Newspaper Microfilm Project, the prototype for the above endeavors.[53] ARL's Shared Cataloging Committee was largely responsible for developing the NPAC program which in 1965 accelerated processing and encouraged more comprehensive collection acquisition programs on the part of LC.[54]

Three years ago the ALA Council adopted as one of its "Goals for Action" the development and support of a national system for information retrieval. It was through the initative of the ALA Resources and Technical Services Division, the Information Sciences and Automation Division and the Reference Services Division, and with the cooperation of eleven other professional organizations that the U.S. Office of Education Bureau of Research funded an ALA proposal for the present invitational "Conference on Interlibrary Communications and Information Networks."

Professional associations are as strong as their membership. Cooperation among associations has been all too scarce. Funds for research come almost entirely from outside agencies or foundations. Improved financial support is highly desirable since associations have accomplished, and can accomplish, so much to advance interlibrary cooperation for more effective information services.

COOPERATION AT THE INTERNATIONAL LEVEL

American library associations have played an important role in international library cooperation ever since 1877 when several librarians, who had attended the first ALA convention, went to London to attend the founding conference of The Library Association.[55] The first international organization to achieve any influence in librarianship was the International Federation for Documentation, FID, founded in 1895 as the International Institute of Bibliography.

In 1924 the League of Nations established the Institute of Intellectual Cooperation which arranged international conferences of librarians and was responsible for bibliographies such as *Index Bibliographicus* and *Index Translationum*. The next organization to be founded was the International Federation of Library Associations, IFLA, created in 1927. Since World War II the United Nations Educational, Scientific, and Cultural Organizations, UNESCO, has been responsible for an ambitious program of publications which have assisted libraries in all countries. The *UNESCO Bulletin for Libraries*, begun in 1947, is devoted to library matters of international interest. The Florence Agreement of 1950, concluded under the auspices of UNESCO, facilitated the free circulation of international publications by reducing or eliminating trade and tariff barriers. In addition, UNESCO has supported FID in its work in developing the Universal Decimal Classification, and "...IFLA has succeeded in achieving important stages in international cooperation, as, for instance, the agreement on international interlibrary loan in 1954 and the International Conference of Cataloging Principles held in Paris in 1961 with the help of UNESCO...."[56]

Another international organization, the International Atomic Energy Agency, IAEA, has developed a cooperative scheme to disseminate atomic energy information — the International Nuclear Information System, INIS — to begin operation in 1970. Member states will put into a data bank the full text of articles on nuclear science with a bibliographic description, keywords, and an abstract. This information will then be made available from the IAEA on magnetic tape or microfiche.[57] The Pan American Union and the Asia Foundation also have contributed much to interlibrary developments.

Most countries have significant examples of interlibrary cooperation, but only a few examples from one country will be mentioned. Great Britain has developed a number of cooperative programs among its libraries.[58] The comprehensive British National Bibliography, BNB, established in 1950, is a product of cooperation among the British Museum, The Library Association, the Publishers' Association, and seven other bodies.[59] In 1950 the British subject-specialization scheme was developed whereby libraries in a region of England are assigned a specific subject and agree to buy every book listed in the BNB in their assgned subject. An interregional coverage scheme, an expansion of the above, began in 1959 to coordinate all the regions into a national system.[60] In 1967 British publishers adopted a Standard Book Numbering System which will undoubtedly have an effect on interlibrary cooperation throughout the world.[61]

International cooperation has resulted chiefly from the efforts of UNESCO which has the funds available to promote co-operation and the authority to call conferences. Unfortunately, on a national level, resolutions resulting from such conferences generally have only the effects of a recommendation. The major problems confronting international cooperation of libraries is the voluntary nature of commitments. Every member country must accept the standards of the group on a voluntary basis.

DEVELOPMENTS AND TRENDS BY FUNCTION

BIBLIOGRAPHIC COOPERATION

One of the most important trends fostering interlibrary co-operation has been the development of bibliographic com-pilations. American libraries have developed resource lists, union lists, bibliographic centers, book catalogs, and union catalogs.

The earliest national resource list, indexed by subject and describing library collections and catalogs, is William C. Lane and Charles K. Bolton's 1892 *Notes on Special Collections in American Libraries.* This resource directory was followed by a large number of similar directories.

A union list has been defined as "A complete record of the holdings for a given group of libraries of material of a given type, in a certain field or on a particular subject." The first major national union list was Henry C. Bolton's *A Catalogue of Scientific and Technical Periodicals,* published by the Smithsonian Institution in 1885; however, this list did not give exact state-ments of holdings. Following the Bolton list, suggestions for a comprehensive national list, indicating exact locations, cul-minated in 1927 with publication of the *Union List of Serials ...,* containing entries for 75,000 serial titles and listing holdings for 225 libraries. "It was rightly hailed as the most notable bib-liography ever sponsored by American libraries...."[62] The third edition of the *Union List of Serials ...,* published in 1965, contains 157,000 entries locating journals in 956 libraries.

In addition to union lists of periodicals, American libraries have cooperated to produce union lists of newspapers, foreign serial documents, microfilm, and manuscripts. These union lists have all had a pattern of development similar to that of the *Union List of Serials.* They have used previous lists in compiling their list, have invited cooperation of large numbers of libraries, have been aided by a foundation grant, have been sponsored by an association, and have received assistance from the Library of Congress.

Union catalogs are an important form of bibliographic co-operation. In 1901 the Library of Congress began building the first national union catalog by collecting cards from government libraries in Washington, D. C., the New York Public Library, Boston Public Library, Harvard University Library, the John Crerar Library, and several others. By 1909 when the con-tributions of cards from nine libraries had accumulated, the union catalog was arranged in a single author alphabet.[63] In 1927 the American Library Association secured a grant from John D. Rockefeller, Jr., to finance a major expansion of the union catalog.[64]

The first major regional union catalog was organized in 1909 in California primarily incorporating public library catalogs. However, major union catalogs increased sharply in number between 1932 and 1940 when seventeen catalogs were es-tablished, many through the assistance of the WPA.[65] A number of these regional catalogs were added to the *National Union Catalog* so that by 1968 it contained more than 16,000,000 cards, representing about 10,000,000 titles and editions.[66]

During the 1930s, with the assistance of WPA, another form of bibliographic cooperation was developed — the bibliographic center. These centers maintain union catalogs for their re-spective area and serve as centers for the exchange of in-terlibrary loan information. They have maintained large col-lections of printed bibliography, including LC catalogs. The centers depend upon financial support from their member institutions. The Bibliographical Center for Research, Rocky Mountain Region, Denver, was established in 1934 as a bi-bliographical collection which would serve the needs of Col-orado libraries. The Pacific Northwest Bibliographic Center, Seattle, was founded in 1940 with a Carnegie grant of $35,000 to the Pacific Northwest Library Association. One of the problems of these centers is the possibility they will atrophy if they do not improve accessibility through regional union catalogs in book form or on-line terminal access for recent materials.

Another trend has been the increased use of book catalogs. The first printed catalog of an American library was the Harvard College Library catalog published in 1723. The size of collections and the cost of book catalogs were major factors in deterring more widespread use between the 1870s and the 1950s. Probably the most important book catalog yet published is *A Catalog of Books Represented by Library of Congress Printed Cards Issued to July 31, 1942,* published by Edwards Brothers, Inc., of Ann Arbor, Michigan, for the Association of Research Libraries.

When the ALA's Board of Resources Subcommittee on the National Union Catalog urged an expanded printed author catalog which would include entries of other libraries, LC began in 1956 publishing the *National Union Catalog* in book form.[67] In 1963 the ALA and LC decided to publish the *National Union Catalog* (prior to 1956) in book form and contracted with the firm of Mansell/Information Publishing Limited in England for its publication. The first volumes of *The National Union Catalog Pre-1956 Imprints* were published in 1968. There are presently more than 500 libraries participating; therefore, the publication of this catalog will be a culminating effort of union catalog development.

The trends in bibliographic cooperation seem to point to lists of resources which cover more titles and record the holdings of more libraries, the development of bibliographic centers on a regional basis, a more comprehensive national union catalog, and finally, a pattern of computer-based indexes and abstract services.

ACQUISITIONS COOPERATION

Libraries continue to purchase publications that will serve the needs of their particular communities. However, as librarians have become better informed of national resources through the aid of union lists, union catalogs, and resource lists, they have begun "...to think of their holdings within a larger frame of reference, as segments of a national resource...."[68] Some forms of acquisitions cooperation are specialization agreements, co-operative buying programs, centralized buying programs, exchange arrangements, photocopying of important research material, and shared book storage centers.

An early specialization agreement was made between the New York Public Library and Columbia University Library in 1896 whereby certain subject areas were allocated to one or the other library.[69] In the same year, the Chicago Public Library, the John Crerar Library, and the Newberry Library divided subject responsibilities in acquisitions.[70]

A major change in the the attitude of institutions toward national specialization agreements occurred as a result of World War II. Due to great concern directed toward the feasibility of acquiring European research materials, the Library of Congress sponsored a conference at Farmington, Connecticut, in 1942. As a result, a committee headed by Keyes Metcalf was appointed to develop a plan which later became known as the Farmington Plan, the first nationwide specialization agreement.[71] The proposal establishing the plan, "Proposal for a division of responsibility among American libraries in the acquisition and recording of library materials," was approved by ARL and was used by the 1946 LC mission to Europe (the Cooperative Acquisitions Project) through which 115 libraries ultimately received 800,000 volumes according to subject allocations.

The experience of the Cooperative Acquisitions Project stimulated acceptance of the Farmington Plan. Begun in 1948 with three Western European countries, the plan was designed to acquire at least one copy of each new foreign publication according to a subject scheme, to list it in the *National Union Catalog*, and to make it available for interlibrary loan. By 1961 the plan covered 146 countries, and libraries had country and/or subject responsibilities.[72] The plan is now being reassessed in view of the Public Law 480 and NPAC program.[73]

In 1954 Public Law 480 made available surplus agricultural products to soft-currency nations. These countries purchased produce with their local currencies, which accumulated unspent. In 1961 the Library of Congress, supported by ARL and the American Council of Learned Societies, sponsored legislation for a plan to acquire publications of India, Pakistan, and the United Arab Republic using the unspent currencies. The Public Law 480 Plan expanded to six countries by 1965, and 1,531,745 items were sent to American libraries. The Library of Congress maintains overseas selections teams in the countries involved and publishes accession lists for these acquisitions, and the libraries contribute funds for cataloging.[74]

The Library of Congress initiated a major centralized acquisitions program when in 1965 Title IIC of the Higher Education Act authorized federal funds "...for the purpose of 'acquiring, so far as possible, all library materials currently published throughout the world which are of value to scholarship.' "[75] The NPAC program has also established regional offices in underdeveloped areas of Asia and Africa, and these offices have published accession lists and helped libraries to secure publications not available in the trade.[76]

In 1941 a group of Colorado college librarians proposed centralized book buying. However, no project resulted until 1967 when a study indicated the feasibility of establishing a centralized processing center for Colorado academic libraries.[77]

With the support of a National Science Foundation grant, the Colorado Academic Libraries Book Processing Center began a one-year experiment in 1969. The center processes book orders, catalogs these books, and physically prepares them for nine participating institutions.

Centralized buying for research libraries also has been accomplished through agents. In 1944 Keyes Metcalf proposed a documents expediter — an agent who would help secure documents which were not issued through the U.S. Superintendent of Documents — since there was concern on the part of libraries that they would not be able to secure declassified documents from the war period. In 1946 a documents expediting office was set up in the Library of Congress, sponsored jointly by the ALA, ARL, SLA, and AALL.[78] For 1967-68, the Library of Congress reported that 142 subscribers to this cooperative centralized service received some 241,000 items.

Sending agents to foreign countries for the procurement of library materials may have had its beginning in 1911 with Walter Lichtenstein's buying trips to Europe and Latin America on behalf of Northwestern University and other American libraries. Much later Seminars on the Acquisition of Latin American Materials, SALAM, recommended that a commercial agent be used to procure Latin American materials for academic libraries, and as a result, the Latin American Cooperative Acquisitions Project LACAP, was organized in 1960 by the University of Texas, the New York Public Library, and Stechert-Hafner, Inc. Currently there are thirty-eight libraries subscribing to the plan, and the Library of Congress is providing rush cataloging for LACAP materials.[79] A total of 19,791 imprints from Latin America were shipped to this country during 1960-65 under the LACAP plan.[80]

Exchange arrangements are another important form of cooperation in the area of acquisitions. The first suggestion for an American exchange came from a French citizen, Alexandre Vattemare, in 1839. In 1848 the Smithsonian Library sent its first publication out to institutions throughout the world; by 1850 Mr. Henry, the secretary of the Smithsonian, reported that "...most of the distinguished foreign literary and scientific societies have placed the Institution on their list of Exchanges."[81]

Library associations have had exchange systems since 1899 when the Medical Library Association established its exchange operation. The Association of College and Research Libraries, ACRL, established the Periodical Exchange Union in 1940, now called the Duplicate Exchange Union. It functions by circulating lists of duplicates to libraries in the order of the size of their collections.

The most active exchange organization in the world is the U.S. Book Exchange, which succeeded the American Book Center for War-Devastated Areas. It was established in 1949 with the assistance of a Rockefeller Grant.[82] The four million-item stock is sufficiently large to allow both American and foreign libraries to send and receive duplicates.

One of the more important trends in acquisitions has been the cooperative microfilm projects for domestic and foreign dissertations, foreign newspapers, office gazettes, and archival materials. A prototype was developed in 1938 when Harvard University secured a grant from the Rockefeller Foundation for the purpose of currently microfilming a number of major foreign newspapers, and positive copies were offered for sale to other institutions. After fourteen years this project was transferred to ARL as a shared-copy plan.[83] Another important effort has been the attempt to register in one list all the master microfilm copies.

In 1965 a Center for the Coordination of Foreign Manuscript Copying was established at the Library of Congress with a grant from the Council on Library Resources. It has proved effective as a clearinghouse for microfilm projects since it enables libraries to cooperate in the microfilming of manuscripts, thus lowering the costs and avoiding duplicate efforts.

In 1902 President Eliot of Harvard advocated a storage facility for little-used materials; it was in Boston in 1939 that this idea was discussed informally again. Two years later the Massachusetts legislature chartered such an institution: the New England Deposit Library, NEDL, which opened in 1942 as a storage library owned and operated by eight libraries.[84] The primary purpose of the depository was low-cost storage. By 1960 there were eleven Boston-area members of NEDL.

John Fall and Keyes Metcalf carried out a survey for thirteen university presidents in the Midwest which recommended a storage facility. This facility was incorporated in 1949 as the Midwest Inter-Library Center, Chicago, with the aid of grants from the Rockefeller Foundation and the Carnegie Corporation, totaling $1 million, and opened in 1951 with ten university libraries as members. Now called the Center for Research Libraries, it is located in Chicago. Its original purpose was to house, organize, service, and under certain circumstances, own, infrequently used materials.[85] This last purpose has been the most important facet of the center's work. The American Association of Research Libraries recently urged all of its members to join the center, which presently has fifty full and associate members and a collection of approximately 2,750,000 volumes.

A third storage center, the Hampshire Inter-Library Center, was established in 1951 by Amherst, Mount Holyoke, Smith College, and the University of Massachusetts. This center is primarily a storage center for little-used serials, and it has a small acquisitions fund for expensive sets and rarely consulted serials.[86] Recently, another storage center was established for medical libraries in New York, the Medical Library Center of New York.[87]

Acquisitions cooperation is not possible without strict adherence to specialization agreements which require some monitoring. Even formal agreements do not have the standing of a binding contractual agreement; furthermore, the only agreements that are viable are those among consenting parties continuingly convinced of their merits.

CATALOG COOPERATION

The general trend of interlibrary cooperation in cataloging has been toward centralized cataloging. There have been four major developments: centralized cataloging, cooperative cataloging, cataloging-in-source (now called cataloging-in-publication), and shared cataloging. The Library of Congress has been involved in all of these developments.

Centralized cataloging, or cataloging done by a central agency, has had a long history starting with the Smithsonian Institution in 1853. The Library Bureau offered centralized

card services to libraries in 1894, and ALA took over these services in 1896. In 1897 R. R. Bowker suggested that the Library of Congress undertake a centralized card service, and the ALA Publishing Board and the Library of Congress reached an agreement in 1901 whereby the latter was to supply printed cards for current books. In 1967-68 the LC Card Division reported that approximately 25,000 libraries, firms, and individuals bought nearly seventy-nine million cards.

Cooperative cataloging, or the supplying of copy to a central agency, began in 1901 when the Library of Congress received copy from other libraries for the printing and distribution of cards. The library of the Department of Agriculture was the first library to contribute. In 1910 LC asked the libraries receiving LC card sets "on deposit" to supply copy for the card service, and about one-third agreed to assist the Library of Congress. A cooperative Cataloging Division was formed at LC in 1932, but recently libraries have submitted copy directly to the National Union Catalog Project.[88]

Cooperative processing on a local and regional level is on the increase. There has been a large increase in public library regional processing centers since 1958. At a typical processing center, original cataloging is kept to a minimum, and LC proof sheets are used for cataloging. Unfortunately, increasing costs and delays in cataloging are current problems which these centralized units face.[89]

Another cataloging trend of particular importance to public and school libraries, is the increase of commercial cataloging services. The first commercial firm to offer such a service was the H. W. Wilson Co. in 1938. In 1958 one firm was offering both catalog cards and book preparation, and by 1968 more than fifty firms were in the commercial cataloging business.[90] This increase can be attributed to government support of library purchases; the majority of firms serve school libraries.

The Cataloging-in-Source Program of 1958-59 was a one-year experiment designed to expedite LC cataloging. After LC had cataloged from page proofs, a facsimile of the catalog card was published in each title. Although this program was much in demand as a cooperative venture, it was abandoned as financially and technically unfeasible.[91]

The Shared Cataloging Program, the culmination of the centralized cataloging movement, was developed as a part of NPAC under the Higher Education Act of 1965. In 1964 an ARL survey revealed that forty-seven research libraries had reported that an average of 46 percent of titles acquired received original cataloging. Therefore, the ARL Committee on Shared Cataloging suggested that the Library of Congress expand its cataloging program. As a result, Title IIC of the Higher Education Act was passed specifically for the purpose of acquiring books on a worldwide basis and assuring prompt cataloging. In April 1966 LC officials met with officials of the British National Bibliography, BNB, to arrange both for advance copies of BNB and blanket-order deliveries of current British imprints. With such an arrangement LC is able to use the data prepared by BNB and thereby, speed up its own cataloging process. When this agreement proved successful, the Library of Congress immediately set up procurement centers overseas.[92] The Shared Cataloging Program presently involves a blanket-order arrangement with a dealer in each of the twenty-two countries, advance copies of the national bibliography of the respective countries, prompt cataloging of titles based upon the catalog from the national bibliography, and rapid distribution of cards to more than eighty participating research libraries.[93]

INTERLIBRARY LOANS

One of the most important facets of interlibrary cooperation — interlibrary lending — is markedly increasing.

The first recorded note of interlibrary loan agreements in the United States occurred in the *Library Journal* of 1876. Samuel S. Green, librarian of the Worcester Free Public Library, suggested that lending books between libraries would increase the usefulness of the collection. He further suggested that libraries rather than individuals engage in the lending. In 1917 the ALA Committee on Coordination of College Libraries drew up the first interlibrary loan code. It is interesting to note that the code state: "If a photographic reproduction would be a satisfactory substitute, librarians should always state the fact."[94] This code was revised in 1940, 1952, and 1968. A standard interlibrary loan form was adopted in 1951.[95]

As a clearinghouse for the location of books wanted on interlibrary loans and with the agreement of ARL, LC began in 1936 the system of circularizing research libraries for books not in LC and adding information to the *National Union Catalog* when a copy of a title was found. As reported in the 1968 LC *Annual Report*, about 82 percent of requests now are filled by locating the titles in the National Union Catalog and for those not found, by circularizing in the "Weekly List of Unlocated Research Books." The National Library of Medicine began its photoduplication service in 1939; by 1956, when it was filling about 85,000 orders annually, it decided to treat photoduplication and interlibrary loans as a single service.[96] The Library of Congress began conducting an experiment last year with a regional switching center for interlibrary loan. The Bibliographical Center for Research, Rocky Mountain Region, will handle requests via teletype transmission on a regional basis. The requests are switched to LC if they cannot be filled regionally.[97]

The teletype now is widely used in this country. One of the first teletype hook-ups was between the public libraries of Racine and Milwaukee in 1949.[98] A library telecommunications directory, updated through July 1968, contains 416 listings of libraries in the U.S. and Canada using teletype and interlibrary communications.[99]

The teletype is only one of the many new forms of telecommunication which are being used for interlibrary loan service. "The first library demonstration of facsimile transmission was in 1948, when an RCA system called Ultrafax was used to transmitted microfilmed text of *Gone with the Wind* to the Library of Congress in two minutes and twenty-one seconds by microwave."[100] The Atomic Energy Commission developed another telefacsimile system in 1950 using broadband transmission equipment. About ten years later, a number of experiments began under the sponsorship of the Council on Library Resources. These experiments have tested closed-circuit television, the Xerox Telecopier, Stewart-Warner dictaphone equipment, and Xerox LDX (long-distance Xerox). Several major problems of these systems have been identified: low quality of copy, high cost, inability to copy bound volumes, copyright difficulties, and the human factors of considerable

time required to bring the book to the copier and a surprisingly long time for the requester to come in to pick up his copy. Until some of these difficulties can be overcome, telefacsimile will not be widely used for interlibrary loan.

Interlibrary loan has several inherent problems in addition to frequently inaccurate citations. First, the privilege has been abused often enough so that the code specifies that requests are to be "limited to the unusual items which the borrowing library does not own and cannot readily obtain at moderate cost." Second, there is some risk of copyright infringement under present laws since it is now common to photocopy materials rather than send the original. Third, as the population increases, the level of education in this country rises, libraries' costs rise sharply, and more books go "out of print," libraries will be pressed to serve a wider and wider audience demanding more and more specialized material. Thus, a heavier burden will be placed on the national libraries and the research libraries with extraordinary collections, thereby raising the possibility of further restrictions or fees for borrowing. It will be necessary to develop formal local or regional lending networks and rely on telefacsimile to avoid an imbalance in use of the national library's resources. The development of international interlibrary lending codes, first developed in 1954 by IFLA, also will play an important role in alleviating the inequities in access to information.

COOPERATIVE EFFORTS IN AUTOMATION

Interlibrary cooperation in this area is too new to evaluate historically. Several hundred institutions are making efforts and having some success. Yet, due to the very large additional expenditures required for major coordinated achievements, the principal contribution to such cooperation is the result of federal efforts. The previous federal libraries section described LC's King report and the MARC projects. In March 1969 a regular MARC distribution service was inaugurated covering all English-language publications cataloged by LC. Seventy-eight libraries are currently participating.[101] Due to the success of MARC, a project to convert all 1968 and 1969 English-language records into machine-readable form was inaugurated in mid-1969. This program, called RECON (Retrospective Conversion), will also test the possibilities of converting older English and other Roman alphabet publications.[102]

The New England Library Information Network, NELINET, a regional library automation project, is sponsored by the Council on Library Resources and is administered by the New England Board of Higher Education. On the basis of a system study of the six New England state universities, the regional center began in 1967 to provide three main services to these libraries: a machine-readable catalog data file; catalog data file searching; and the production of catalog cards, book pockets, and book labels. The requests are processed in the central processing center in Cambridge, Massachusetts, over Dataphone lines, and the products are mailed to the libraries. MARC is the network's communications standard.[103]

The first major collaborative effort in automation has been discontinued. The Columbia/Harvard/Yale Medical library Computerization project which ran from 1962 to 1966 was the first cooperative on-line information retrieval system among universities. The project was designed to use an on-line system for both production of catalog cards and retrieval of bibliographic information. "Harvard officially withdrew because of other priorities at its library; Columbia did some cataloging. Yale has continued on its own."[104] Yale ultimately stored more than 12,000 titles and used the information for accession lists and catalog card production. The departure of the project director, storage costs, and technological problems were other factors which contributed to the project's demise.

The second project, the Chicago/Columbia/Stanford Collaborative Library System Development project, CLSD, was funded by the National Science Foundation to experiment with the feasibility of designing generalized automated systems through cooperative effort on elements of monograph acquisitions system. The eighteen-month project will conclude in fall 1970. Because of geographic separation, the libraries have found scheduling of meetings to be difficult and communication awkward. Other problems were technical terminology, currency and completeness of written documentation, library procedural differences, differences in hardware and operating systems, individual project timetables, and limited availability of senior staff. On the plus side, understanding grew markedly, and it was found that systems design specifications could be jointly developed, design components were defined, pitfalls were avoided, and considerable detail was exchanged.[105]

Eleven libraries currently are participating in the SUNY Biomedical Communications Network previously described in the section on special libraries. This network is designed to provide: a computerized union catalog of textbooks and monographs on a consortium of libraries, lists of journals currently received, bibliographic searches of MEDLAR tapes, production of MeSH subject-heading guide cards, current awareness or SDI services, recurring bibliographies, and direct interlibrary communication. The success of this substantial effort has been a result of "great drive, ingenuity, firm development support from IBM, and a commitment of funds by the State of New York...."[106]

To date, the experience in automation cooperation has indicated that it is necessary to determine precise attainable goals, have strong continuing administration, have financial support from a foundation or agency, and use technically feasible systems.

Consortia

A consortium is defined as a contractual arrangement "...whereby two or more institutions...agree to pursue between, or among, them a program for strengthening academic programs, improving administration, or providing for other special needs."[107] Such cooperation is not new, but the concept has had rapid growth in recent years. In 1934 a study of interinstitutional agreements indicated there were 113 such agreements.[108] By 1965-66 there were 1,017 consortia in existence with 123 of these having the library as the field of cooperation.[109] With increased enrollments in institutions of higher learning, more interdisciplinary courses, and funds stretched to the limit, universities and colleges have found reason to cooperate. This trend has been aided by the development of regional associations which have encouraged

cooperation and federal legislation which has made funds available for cooperative efforts.

Most consortia are established for special purposes. The Southwest Academic Library Consortium was established in 1967 for the purposes of coordinating serial purchases, developing union lists, and improving interlibrary loan. Twenty academic libraries are participating, and it has received a federal grant for its work.[110] Eight Texas colleges and universities signed a 1969 agreement to form a consortium for the purpose of filming Mexican provincial archives. Each institution is responsible for filming in a geographical or functional area in collaboration with a Mexican institution. They will then share this film through interlibrary loan. Seven Minnesota college libraries and the James Jerome Hill Reference Library, St. Paul, formed in 1969 a nonprofit corporation, Cooperating Libraries in Consortium, Inc., CLIC, which will support joint purchasing of materials.[111]

An example of a consortium to improve administration is the 1969 agreement by Iowa State University, the University of Iowa, and the University of Northern Iowa to appoint a coordinator of Automated Library Services to study areas where coordinated system development might be possible. He is responsible to an Inter-institutional Committee of Librarians, and the universities share the expenses.[112] And in Ohio, the Ohio College Association created a Library Center in 1967 to establish a computerized network center for Ohio's academic libraries which would ultimately become part of a national electronic network for bibliographic communications.[113]

All of the above consortia are local or regional arrangements. The first effort to create a national consortium was the Interuniversity Communications Council, EDUCOM, formed in 1964. EDUCOM is a consortium of more than ninety universities; its prime purpose is to promote the application of communication sciences in support of higher education. EDUCOM studied the desirability, feasability, and design of an educational communications system, EDUNET, at a summer service in 1966 which proposed a national network connected by multimedia telecommunications and facsimile transmissions. EDUCOM has done research for the National Library of Medicine and recently has completed a study on the technology required to establish a National Agricultural Land-Grant Information Network.[114]

The real significance of this trend toward consortia is the contractual nature of the cooperation, including a means for members to resign from the group when the group's purposes are no longer relevant for a particular institution. Most consortia ask for membership fees from the participating institutions, yet they are generally supported by federal money or a foundation grant. A distinct benefit of a consortium is the modest cost of participation for a much greater extension of resources and services. Thus, the consortium is an important form of library cooperation.

CONCLUSION

The history of interlibrary cooperation makes it evident that there are several conditions necessary for effective cooperation. First, there must be innovative individuals to identify the need for cooperation and to recommend a course of action, often through a strong library association. Quite obviously the need must be clear and the anticipated results worth the effort. Second, the cooperative program needs the acceptance and leadership of at least one major institution. Third, the proposals for action need the monetary support of foundations or assistance from federal grants with realistic plans for continued financial support. Most forms of cooperation require rather modest funds — but not those based on sophisticated technology. Fourth, a suitable technology must be available when needed. Finally, the program needs the willingness of the participants to surrender a certain amount of self-sufficiency and independence. When all of these conditions are met, there appears to be no obstacle to cooperation.

One major problem facing interlibrary cooperation is geographic in nature. In order for libraries to store an increasing amount of material at distant locations, it is incumbent upon the librarian to assure that this material is locally available as quickly and as economically as possible.

Another constraint on the development of interlibrary cooperation is political in nature. Public support of libraries is still inadequate. Enabling legislation is limited, and funding is generally modest. The fear of loss of independent action, personal status, and institutional pride also is strong in local and state institutions. Copyright is another legal constraint.

Cost is another major problem facing interlibrary cooperation. Where budgets are already stretched, any sizable innovation carries incremental costs that require additional appropriations — new revenue must be found rather than existing funds diverted. For instance, in order to benefit from the developments of computer technology, is necessary to have very considerable additional funds. A large number of major innovations in cooperation since 1956 have been funded by the Council on Library Resources, a private corporation created and funded by the Ford Foundation; by the National Science Foundation; and by the U.S. Office of Education.

Technological barriers are another problem preventing more interlibrary cooperation. The lack of inexpensive computer storage, telefacsimile devices, a cataloger's camera, and inexpensive telecommunications have prevented the rapid local use of centralized collections and services or shared bibliographic data.

One more problem facing interlibrary cooperation is widely differing standards. Local variations in forms, cataloging codes, statistics, and professional standards make interlibrary cooperation difficult. Many libraries using LC cards, for example, make costly changes in the data because they are unable or unwilling to accept it as a local standard.

The history of interlibrary cooperation has indicated some of the serious problems which still hamper interlibrary cooperation; it also has revealed some possible solutions. Some of the trends noted in this paper can suggest directions interlibrary cooperation might take in the future. Prototypes may be found in the Center for Research Libraries, the SUNY Biomedical Network, LC's MARC service, the Rocky Mountain Bibliographical Center, and the consortium type of structure. It is important for libraries to be aware of cooperative needs and to work together to develop extended services. Their future may depend upon it. Although there are several fiscal, technical, and political limitations to interlibrary cooperation, the trend of

library history has been toward increasing interlibrary cooperation and when conditions are right, there appears to be no theoretical limit to such cooperation.

NOTES

1. Carleton B. Joeckel, ed., *Library extension problems and solutions* (Chicago: Univ. of Chicago Pr., 1946), 260p.

2. Eleanor Hitt Morgan, "The county library," in C. B. Joeckel, *Library extension...*, p.59-74.

3. American Library Association, Committee on Library Extension, *A study of public library conditions and needs* (Chicago: ALA, 1926), 163p.

4. Nelson Associates, Inc., *Public library systems in the United States: a survey of multijurisdictional systems* (Chicago: ALA, 1969), 368p.

5. Ibid., p.32.

6. Nelson Associates, Inc., *Public Library systems in the United States* (Chicago: ALA, 1969), p.32.

7. Eleanor Hitt Morgan, "County library," p.59-74.

8. Paul A. T. Noon, "The role of the state agency in library extension," in C. B. Joeckel, *Library extension*, p.160-170.

9. H. C. Campbell, *Metropolitan public library planning throughout the world* (Oxford: Pergamon, 1967), 168p.

10. John Mackenzie Cory, "The network in a major metropolitan center (METRO, New York)" *Library quarterly* 39:90-98 (Jan. 1969).

11. Nelson Associates, Inc., *Public library systems*, p.16.

12. Ibid.

13. Karl Brown, "The Library Services Act, Public Law 597," in *American library annual* (New York: Bowker, 1958), p.121-131.

14. Nathan M. Cohen, "Library Services and Construction Act, as amended," in *The Bowker annual of library and book trade information, 1968* (New York: Bowker, 1968), p.208-213.

15. Nelson Associates, Inc., *Public library systems...*, p.254.

16. U.S. Department of Health, Education and Welfare, Office of Education, Library Services Branch, *State plans under the library services act, supplement 3: a progress report - the first five fiscal years, 1957-61,* Bulletin 1963, no. 14 (Washington, D.C.: Gov. Print. Off., 1963), 187p.

17. Warren J. Haas, "Statewide and regional reference service," *Library trends* 12:405-412 (Jan. 1964).

18. S. Gilbert Prentiss, "The evolution of the library system (New York)" *Library quarterly* 39:78-89 (Jan. 1969).

19. Russell Shank, "Networks," in *The Bowker annual of library and book trade information, 1970* (New York: Bowker, 1970), p.291-296. and book trade information, 1970 (New York: Bowker, 1970), p.291-296.

20. Virginia Drewry, "Georgia state catalog card service," *Library resources and technical services* 2:176-180 (Summer 1958).

21. Sarah K. Vann, "Southeastern Pennsylvania processing center feasibility study: a summary," *Library resources and technical services* 10:461-78 (Fall 1966).

22. Eugene B. Jackson, "The General Motors research laboratories library: a case study," *Library trends* 14:353-362 (Jan. 1966).

23. Bernard M. Wolpert, "A working library network," *American libraries* 1:570-72 (June 1970).

24. Ted Miller, "Six Minneapolis 'insiders' build unique cooperative," *Special libraries* 54:295-97 (May-June, 1963).

25. William S. Budington, "Interrelations among special libraries," *Library quarterly,* 39:64-77 (Jan. 1969).

26. Chris G. Stevenson, "A librarian looks at the State Technical Services Act," *Special libraries* 59:183-85 (March 1968).

27. Russell Shank, "Cooperation between special libraries and other types of libraries," in C. E. Thomasen, ed., *Cooperation between types of libraries: the beginnings of a state plan for library services in Illinois* (Urbana, Ill.: Univ. of Illinois, Graduate School of Library Science, 1969), p.66.

28. "Biomedical communication network," *Bookmark* 28:105-107 (Jan. 1969).

29. David C. Weber, "Off-campus library service by private universities," in Association of Research Libraries, *Minutes of the sixty-second meeting* (Chicago: The Association, 1963), p.25-38.

30. Natalie Nicholson, "Service to industry and research parks by college and university libraries," *Library trends* 14:262-72 (Jan. 1966).

31. Russell Shank, "Cooperation between special libraries...."

32. Nelson Associates, Inc., *Public library systems...*, p.63.

33. Mildred H. Lowell, *College and university library consolidation* (Eugene: Oregon State System of Higher Education, 1942) p.31-32.

34. Ibid., 136p.

35. Stephen A. McCarthy, "Research library cooperation," *Bookmark* 28:75-80 (Dec. 1968).

36. Merton W. Ertell, *Interinstitutional cooperation in higher education; a study of experience with reference to New York State* (Albany, N.Y.: State Education Dept., 1957), 118p.

37. Ibid.

38. Mildred H. Lowell, *...Library consolidation.*

39. Ibid.

40. Oregon, State University, *Bulletin; catalog issue, 1968/69* (Corvallis: Oregon State Univ., 1968), p.10.

41. Carl R. Cox, "Library cooperation in a state university system," *Bookmark* 28:114-17 (Jan. 1969).

42. U.S. Library of Congress, "The Library of Congress as the national library: potentialities for service," in D. M. Knight and E. S. Nourse, eds., *Libraries at large* (New York: Bowker, 1969), p.459.

43. Gilbert W. King, et al., *Automation and the Library of Congress: a survey sponsored by the Council on Library Resources* (Washington, D.C.: The Library of Congress, 1963), p.3.

44. Samuel Lazerow, "The U.S. national libraries task force: an instrument for national library cooperation," *Special libraries* 59:698-703 (Nov. 1968).

45. Elmer D. Johnson, *A history of libraries in the western world* (New York: Scarecrow, 1965), p.330.

46. William S. Dix, "Centralized cataloging and university libraries - Title II, Part C of the Higher Education Act of 1965, *Library trends* 16:97-111 (July 1967).

47. National Advisory Commission on Libraries, "Library services for the nation's needs: The report of the National Advisory Commission on Libraries," in D. M. Knight and E. S. Nourse, eds., *Libraries at large,* p.518.

48. Carl F. J. Overhage, "Information networks," in C. A. Cuadra, ed., *Annual review of information science and technology, Vol. 4* (New York: Wiley, 1969), p.339-377.

49. Robert B. Downs, "American library cooperation in review, *College and research libraries* 6:407-15 (Sept. 1945).

50. Constance Winchell, *Locating books for interlibrary loan, with a bibliography of printed aids which show location of books in American libraries* (New York: Wilson, 1930), 170p.

51. William S. Budington, "Interrelations...."

52. Association of Research Libraries, *Minutes of the forty-fifth annual meeting* (Chicago: The Association, 1940).

53. ...., *Minutes of the sixtieth annual meeting* (Chicago: The Association, 1955).

54. ...., *Minutes of the seventieth annual meeting* (Chicago: The Association, 1965).

55. George Utley, *Fifty years of the American Library Association* (Chicago: ALA, 1936), 29p.

56. Curt D. Wormann, "Aspects of international library cooperation -- historical and contemporary," *Library quarterly* 38:347 (Oct. 1968).

57. John E. Woolston, "The international nuclear information system (INIS)," *UNESCO bulletin for libraries* 23:125-138+ (May-June 1969).

58. George Jefferson, *Library co-operation* (Rev. ed.; London: Andre Deutsch, 1968), 172p.

59. Madeline M. Henderson, et al., *Cooperation, convertibility and compatibility among information systems: a literature review* (National Bureau of Standards Misc. pub. 276 [Washington, D.C.: Gov. Print. Off., 1966]), 140p.

60. Ralph T. Esterquest, "Cooperation in library services," *Library quarterly* 31:71-89 (Jan. 1961).

61. *Standards book numbering,* (New York: Bowker, The Standard Book Numbering Agency, 1968), 13p.

62. *Union list of serials in libraries of the United States and Canada,* (3rd.ed.; New York: Wilson, 1965), preface.

63. Ernest C. Richardson, *General library cooperation and American research books,* (Yardley, Pa.: Cook, 1930), 144p.

64. George A. Schwegmann, Jr., "The National Union Catalog in the Library of Congress," in R. B. Downs, ed., *Union catalogs in the United States* (Chicago: ALA, 1942), p.226-63.

66. Gordon R. Williams, "History of the National Union catalog pre-1956 imprints," in *The National Union Catalog pre-1956 imprints* (Chicago: Mansell, 1968), p.vii-x.

67. John W. Cronin, "The National Union and Library of Congress catalogs: problems and prospects," *Library quarterly* 34:77-96 (Jan. 1964).

68. Robert B. Downs, "American library cooperation....

69. W. Dawson Johnston, "The library resources of New York city and their increase," *The Columbia University quarterly* 13:163 (March 1911).

70. Lowell A. Martin, *Library response to urban change* (Chicago: ALA, 1969), 323p.

71. Edwin E. Williams, *Farmington plan handbook, revised to 1961 and abridged* (Ithaca, N.Y.: ARL, 1961), 141p.

72. Ibid.

73. "Current notices on the Farmington Plan," *Farmington plan newsletter* 29:6-7 (May 1969).

74. James E. Skipper, "National planning for resource development," *Library trends* 15:321-334 (Oct. 1966).

75. L. Quincy Mumford, "International co-operation in shared cataloging," *UNESCO bulletin for libraries* 22:9-12 (Jan-Feb, 1968).

76. U.S. Library of Congress, Processing Department, *National program for acquisitions and cataloging, progress report,* no. 10 (Washington, D.C.: Library of Congress, 1970), 8p.

77. Lawrence E. Leonard, "Colorado academic libraries book processing center: a feasibility study," *College and research libraries* 29:393-99 (Sept. 1968).

78. Association of Research Libraries, *Minutes...,* 1946.

79. Marietta D. Shepard, "Cooperative acquisitions of Latin American materials," *Library resources and technical services* 13:347-60 (Summer 1969).

80. M. J. Savary, *The Latin American cooperative acquisitions program...an imaginative venture* (New York: Hafner, 1968), 144p.

81. U.S. Library of Congress, Processing Department, *National program...,* p.10.

82. Arthur M. McAnally, "Recent developments in cooperation," *College and research libraries* 12:123-32 (April 1951).

83. David C. Weber, "Foreign newspaper microfilm project, 1938-1955," *Harvard library bulletin* 10:275-81 (Spring 1956).

84. Keyes D. Metcalf, "The New England Deposit Library," *Library quarterly* 12:622-28 (July 1942).

85. Margaret Mary Fischer, "Library cooperation," *Catholic library world* 39:332-37 (Jan. 1968).

86. Helen Joanne Harrar, "Cooperative storage warehouses," *College and research libraries* 25:37-43 (Jan. 1964).

87. Frederick G. Kilgour, "Research libraries in information networks," in M. Rubinoff, ed., *Toward a national information system,* (New York: Spartan, 1965).

88. John M. Dawson, "The Library of Congress: its role in co-operative and centralized cataloging," *Library trends* 16:85-96 (July 1967).

89. Peter Hiatt, "Cooperative processing centers for public libraries," *Library trends* 16:67-83 (July 1967).

90. Barbara M. Westby, "Commercial services," *Library trends* 16:46-57.

91. U.S. Library of Congress, Processing Department, *The cataloging-in-source experiment; a report to the Librarian of Congress by the director of the processing department*, (Washington, D.C.: L.C., 1960), 199p.

92. L. Quincy Mumford, "International co-operation...."

93. U.S. Library of Congress, Processing Dept., *National program...*

94. Constance Winchell, *Locating books...*, p.14.

95. Margaret D. Uridge, "Interlibrary lending and similar extension services," *Library trends* 6:66-86 (July 1957).

96. William H. Kurth, *Survey of the interlibrary loan operation of the National Library of Medicine* [n.p.] (U.S. Dept. of Health, Education, and Welfare, Public Health Service, 1962), 49p.

97. "The Bibliographic Center for Research," *Library of Congress information bulletin* 28:246 (6 May 1969).

98. Margaret D. Uridge, "Interlibrary lending...." extension services," *Library trends* 6:66-86 (July 1957).

99. Carl F. J. Overhage, "Information networks...."

100. David Heron, "Telefacsimile in libraries: progress and prospects," *UNESCO bulletin for libraries* 23:8-13 (Jan.-Feb. 1969).

101. "The MARC editorial office," *Library of Congress information bulletin* 29:178 (16 April 1970).

102. "Grant to Library of Congress RECON pilot project," *Publishers' weekly* 197:34-5 (6 April 1970).

103. William R. Nugent, *NELINET: the New England Library Information Network* (Cambridge, Mass.: Inforonics, Inc., 1968), 4p.

104. "Ups and downs of information retrieval," *Datamation* 14:129 (Jan. 1968).

105. Paul Fasana, "The collaborative library systems development project: a mechanism for inter-university cooperation," *Proceedings of the Conference on Library Automation, 6 Jan. 1970,* (Albany, N.Y.: Education Div. of the State of New York, to be published).

106. Willis E. Bridegam, Jr. and Erich Meyerhoff, "Library participation in a biomedical communication and information network," *Bulletin of the Medical Library Association* 58:105-11 (April 1970).

107. Raymond S. Moore, *Consortiums in American higher education: 1965-66; report of an exploratory study* (Washington, D.C.: U.S. Office of Education, 1968), p.4.

108. Daniel Sanford, Jr., *Inter-institutional agreements in higher education; an analysis of the documents relating to inter-institutional agreements with special reference to coordination* (New York: Columbia Univ. Teachers College, Bureau of Publications, 1934), 112p.

109. Raymond S. Moore, *Consortiums....*

110. "Southwest academic library consortium," *Mountain plains library quarterly* 13:28 (Spring 1968).

111. "Consortium (of Minnesota college libraries)," *Library journal* 94:2548 (July 1969).

112. "Iowa University libraries coordinate automation," *Library journal* 94:2546 (July 1969).

113. "College library center to be created in Ohio," *Library journal* 92:726 (15 Feb. 1967).

114. "NAL/land-grant network plan completed," *EDUCOM bulletin* 4:1-3 (Oct. 1969).

Network Services

84

Working Group Summary On
Network Services

Aim: To explore those information and library services that have the greatest potential for networking.

The Working Group on Network Services benefited considerably from the detailed papers prepared for their use. Discussions covered the topics of organization and intercommunication of bibliographic data, and analogously, of microforms, audio and visual materials, and the newer media. In like manner, public services, such as reference inquiries, location referrals, interlibrary and personal borrowing, analysis and summary of data, and compilation of bibliographies were critically assessed and considered in a network mode. Another major area of discussion concerned new types of information services, which though not yet commonplace, may well become so as network activity expands. These included study of the emerging data bank industry, remote access to bibliographic data, and the delivery of information products to the home.

The development of plans for national or regional networks cannot be discussed realistically without prior consideration of the functions and services of such networks. The Working Group on Network Services was accordingly charged with four tasks:

1. Delineate those library and information services which would be enhanced by network development

2. Rank in order of priority those services which could be improved by a national information network, if they existed

3. Specify the problems which stand in the way of improving and extending library and

information service capabilities in the United States

4. Make and justify specific recommendations for research, development, training, and action in the establishment of more extensive interlibrary communication in order to improve information services.

In addition, the Group reached substantial agreement on certain fundamental propositions with respect to the network concept:

1. That the seeker of information in the United States today has a right to the information he seeks unless there are legal or proprietary restrictions on the use of this information. If he is not at present served, this fact should be recognized so that he can be served. If he himself is not aware of his needs, the aim of a network should be to help him become so aware.

2. That it is legitimate for every library or information center to call upon networks to identify, locate, and make available all forms of materials and services, and to provide efficient and dependable information delivery services. This implies freer interinstitutional communication and a more effective organizational structure.

3. That networking is a necessary development that can make possible an enormous increase in the amount, kind, and quality of information service to society.

4. That the network concept will facilitate the development of the kind of technical facilities — both hardware and software — which are necessary if information services are to be expanded.

Working Group Leader: F.F. Leimkuhler, School of Industrial Engineering, Purdue University, Lafayette, Indiana 47907
Associate Leaders: Pauline Atherton, School of Library Science Syracuse Library, Syracuse, New York
Brigitte Kenney, Graduate School of Library Science, Drexel University, Philadelphia, Pennsylvania 19104

5.   That networks will introduce a greater degree of bibliographic standardization through common identification of all forms and greater dependence on the creation of centralized bibliographic records and MARC-type services.

6.   That the major goal in the provision of information services through a library network should be to facilitate *learning* in the broadest sense. Whether contained in separate packages or in data banks, the information needed to meet identified learning needs can best be met through cooperative information exchange. Libraries and other information centers are at the present time able to provide service to a limited number of patrons who can clearly express their information needs. Success reinforces use, and disappointment leads the patron to seek elsewhere or to let his needs go unfulfilled. A service network must take the initative by making its services known to potential users. It must develop the means and take a more active role in identifying and defining a patron's need for information. These may be called *awareness* services.

The first function is that of translation of the need for information into the provision of the data to meet that need. This *mediation* function includes the interpretation of the need and the utilization of whatever knowledge, systems, and services are required for the eventual delivery of the information needed. Thus, the second function to be performed by a service network is the provision of bibliographic or intellectual *access* to data.

In addition to bibliographic access, there must be provision for physical access by *delivery* systems which make information and materials available at the place and time and in the form best suited to the need, as well as under conditions that are acceptable to the user. A delivery system implies the existence of a whole array of technical services for the production, selection, acquisition, processing, storage, distribution, and even disposal of information. It is recognized that problems of resource management and control in a network may be exceedingly complex; nevertheless, these problems must be solved primarily in order to deliver information as equitably and expeditiously as possible. Finally, the network must provide an *evaluation* service. Feedback mechanisms at all levels will provide awareness of changing patterns of need and use so that the network can be modified for more satisfactory performance.

These services — awareness, mediation, access, delivery, and evaluation — describe the user-system interface in terms of the benefits to be provided by an information network. Since the term "user" is meant to include elements in the the network itself (i.e., those elements which need to "know"), these services describe how the network functions as well as what it does. Taken together, they define what can be called a general-purpose *learning environment* which is capable of reflection and

subsequent adaptation. This is analogous to the idea of a conventional library, except that the latter is circumscribed by its dependence on the larger bibliographic world for the services it renders.

In the learning environment created by a fully operational information network, the following services would be provided.

1.   *Awareness* of the universe of information in the light of its relevance to the specific needs of users in the manner of selective dissemination systems. Such awareness is a precondition to a demand for information and the formulation of inquiries.

2.   *Mediation* of user requests, whereby action by the network is initiated and sustained as long as the user chooses to interact with the network. While it may be theoretically possible for mediation to be accomplished by an automated interactive system, it is expected that this particular service will have a significant amount of human monitoring and intervention by skilled practitioners who will serve as network ombudsmen and professional consultants.

3.   *Access* to the universe of recorded information for the purpose of identifying information sources and services which are relevant to user needs. Also, locating these sources and establishing their availability as to timing and as to the conditions under which they may be obtained. The communications system which is established in support of this service must have an unusually high degree of accuracy and speed in sending, receiving, and interpreting access messages throughout the network.

4.   *Delivery* of information media of all kinds to all points within the network in the manner required for the satisfaction of the client. Most of the direct costs of network activities are likely to accrue in this category of service because of its tangibility and ease of measurement. One method of recovering service costs would be to charge the client for what he receives. However, considerable care must be exercised in charging for such services on the basis of direct cost, because serious inequities may arise if the distribution of information services is made not according to need but only according to the ability to pay.

5.   *Evaluation* of the services provided by the network and adaptation to the changes indicated by the evaluation process. This implies the

existence of an accepted set of forms, standards, or criteria for determining the quality of network performance, predetermined procedures for comparing actual performance with the performance desired, methods of assessing the risks of making mistakes in judgment, options to be followed when deviations from the norm are found, and methods of evaluating the evaluation process itself. The evaluation service is intended to maintain the credibility of the network in the eyes of those for whom the network is created.

Based on the above assumptions and considerations, the Working Group organized into subgroups in order to exploit the contents of the commissioned papers on services. Subgroups concentrated on bibliographic services, reference, interlibrary loan, new media, data banks, archives, and audiovisual and library education.

It was realized that while each of the elements represented by these categories are essential in a network, they were not all like elements. For example, bibliographic recording activities are the *sine qua non* of the effort to organize resources for the purposes of other network services. Library education is not a network service but rather a requirement for network development *and* a special clientele to be served by a network. Audiovisual and other "new" media are not separate entities but other forms of information storage. All network services must be considered to include nonbook as well as book materials — hence the use of the term "media" in the remainder of this report.

Finally, four basic categories were identified as principal components of a network of libraries and information centers: (1) Bibliographic Access to Media, (2) Mediation of User Request to Information, (3) Delivery of Media to Users, and (4) Education.

BIBLIOGRAPHIC ACCESS TO MEDIA

Basic to all library and information network services is bibliographic access. The term "bibliographic access to media," as defined by the Group, comprises the identification, location, and conditions of use of all types of informational materials, including books, serials, audiovisual materials, and data archives. All three key words are to be construed in the broadest possible framework. Thus, identification includes the bibliographic description, all access points, and a standard identification number for each item. Location includes identification of those libraries or organizations holding an item, within that system, and the availability of that item. Conditions of use will specify any special availability aspects such as rental or limited use.

For the attainment of effective network services, bibliographic services of the network need to be organized in such a way as to provide:

1.   A standard bibliographic record for each item that can be utilized for all types of bibliographic services (such as library and union catalogs, trade bibliographies, and abstracting and indexing services) in order to avoid the waste and the incompatibility that result from the establishment of multiple records for the same item.

2.   A timely bibliographic record that will be available for publishers' announcements, selection, and acquisition. (Timeliness is not only important to network services as such, but will promote acceptance and use of the standard record by individual organizations, which will in turn contribute to smooth functioning of the network.)

3.   A comprehensive system for recording and disseminating information on the location and availability of all materials ensures maximum ease of user access.

Establishment of a network on any level also requires the standardization of the basic components of the data base. These standards must be acceptable to all generators of the data base and must allow for the special needs of each group. The three components requiring standardization are:

1.   *Structure:* The physical representation of data on a medium (e.g., tape or disc), regardless of the form of material being described

2.   *Content designators:* The tags or labels which explicitly identify or categorize information

3.   *Content:* The data itself (e.g., names, subject headings).

A standard format structure is already in existence in the form of the American National Standards Institute, ANSI, format for the interchange of bibliographic data on magnetic tape.

Standardization of content designation has been accomplished within certain systems, but little has been done to standardize such designation across systems.

Agreement on content also implies common rules, across systems as well, for the generation of the descriptive record and the identification of names associated with the work, both as they appear on or in the work and in their established form of entry. Also implied is a standardized approach to subject analysis based on common rules for the development of thesauri and the greatest possible compatibility and convertibility among major indexing vocabularies, both general and specific.

Standards range from the relatively simple to the extremely complex. They require persons with ability, experience, and the perseverance to "endure" the democratic review process and the constant revision necessary to transform the proposal into a standard.

The benefits of standardization as well as knowledge of the slowness and difficulty of the process of developing standards must be made known to both the creators and the users of library and information services in order to obtain participation by all user groups and the commitment by these groups of staff and money resources.

MEDIATION OF REQUESTS FOR INFORMATION

Mediation service consists of the facilitation of the interface between the seeker of information (henceforth called the user) and the sources of information available to satisfy the user's need. In libraries this service is typically called reference service and in its fullest development, consists of the following component services:

1. Assistance to the user in formalizing and articulating his information need

2. Assistance to the user in the identification of potential sources of information to meet this need

3. Assistance to the user in devising a strategy for obtaining information from these sources

4. Assistance to the user in progressing through the steps necessary for obtaining information and manipulating it

5. Assistance to the user in evaluating the information obtained in relation to his need

6. Assistance by the user in providing feedback information to the system for its potential improvement.

For each of the above components, the level of service can range from the provision of simple instructions to the mediator's actually performing the task on behalf of the user. The level of need by a user for such services at a given transaction can vary from nonexistent to absolutely essential. However, a fairly high level of need seems quite widespread across the various classes of users.

Evidence indicates that the most successful operation of this service involves a high degree of interaction between the mediator and the user throughout the process (however many of the above components are involved in a given transaction). The requirements for offering such services are:

1. Knowledgeable and skillful personnel

2. Bibliographic resources to provide the mediator and user with the intellectual access to potential answering sources

3. Communication facilities to enhance mediator/user/information interaction, e.g., telephones and interdepartmental communications facilities.

Networking offers a mechanism by which this service can be made available to the greatest number of users with the most economical use of human and other resources. In addition, something at least analogous to such service (e.g., referral and switching mechanisms) must be provided *within* a network which is attempting to provide any of the other services discussed in the report of this group.

It appears that the successful provision of mediation by and within a network would involve the same categories of requirements as that of a library, as outlined above, i.e., human capabilities, bibliographic resources, and communications facilities.

The communications capabilities necessary for the provision of mediation service by the network are those that will allow the mediator to be in interactive contact with users on the one hand and with the information sources on the other, in a manner that approximates the face-to-face mode. This seems mainly a matter of technology, economics, and system design.

The bibliographic resources required are those that will provide the mediator with knowledge of the existence, location, and use constraints of potential answering sources. The provision of this category of network resource is a service discussed in another section of the report.

The human attributes required for mediation service in the network include:

1. Attitudes toward information services that have the network, rather than the single outlet, as the frame of reference

2. Knowledge of information users and sources

3. Skill in communication with users, including the use of network communications technology; and skill in the exploitation of information resources, including the manipulation of bibliographic tools.

DELIVERY OF MEDIA TO USERS

A successful media delivery system includes the following components:

1. Increased availability through shared resources and cooperative acquisitions

2. Methods for determining the location and availability of any desired informational unit

3. Personnel trained in packaging information to meet specific user needs

4. Transmittal and display of all varieties of media to meet the user's information need.

This will require the following network activity:

1. Organization of an integrated bibliographic control, location, and circulation system capable of communicating the status of a desired item at any given time

2. Training of network personnel on all levels in packaging information to meet specific user needs, including machine-mediated access to data bases and harnessing the specialized competencies of the "invisible colleges"

3. Removal of organizational barriers preventing or inhibiting delivery between different jurisdictions and between profit-making and not-for-profit information-handling organizations

4. Development of decisionmaking tools to determine cost-benefit relationships among different delivery modes (e.g., first-class mail versus facsimile)

5. Development of hardware and software configurations for transferrability in internodal network delivery

6. Continued effort to reduce cost of communications and transmission links, such as techniques for squeezing signals

7. Development of inexpensive devices for displaying all microforms, as well as of reading and printing digital and analog signals.

EDUCATION

A major goal of the provision of information through the library network is to facilitate learning in its broadest sense. Whether contained in separate informational units or in presentation systems designed to modify behavior in specifically defined ways, information may be provided through cooperative information exchange or networking to meet identified learning needs.

Libraries provide the storage, retrieval, and display systems for information. They should likewise provide a means of identifying and defining a patron's need for information.

In the learning environment, network services should:

1. Provide through bibliographic systems, awareness of the universe of information available to meet the defined needs, listings of the location and modes of access to available information, and methods by which needs for the generation of new informational units or systems can be identified

2. Provide delivery systems, which may be either physical or electronic, interactive or passive, allowing the user to interact with or present the information in a way that will lead to the achievement of the defined learning or behavior goal. (The delivery systems may allow for information movement or interpersonal communication.)

3. Provide formal educational enterprises with systems of (a) instruction, (b) research data and information, and (c) bibliographic data

4. Provide library operatives with continuous input leading to the improvement of library services.

Perhaps an example of network services for a particular field of knowledge will help clarify the true potential of the concept of networking. The field chosen here as an example is *library education*. It might as well have been science education or engineering education, but the Group's choice is designed to emphasize the benefits of and the needs for network services in the field of library education.

The major problems for implementation of library education networks are, like the advantages, shared with higher education generally: (a) accreditation standards, (b) institutional autonomy, (c) financial structures and limitation, (d) difficulty in adapting the institution to the complexities of change, (e) instructional proficiency in both teaching and research, (f) lack of imaginative instructional techniques and utilization of newer media. Moreover, most instructional programs in library science have been hard pressed to find faculty to meet their minimal local commitments.

NETWORK SERVICES FOR LIBRARY EDUCATION AND RESEARCH

A network service for library education itself would differ from most other network services in that it would be an *educational* service as well as an *information* service, i.e., it would serve a demonstration (i.e., instructional) function as well as a research function. The primary user of the instructional function is, of course, the faculty member, who would serve as an intermediary between the network and the students. Faculty, students, and other researchers would use existing and proposed information networks directly.

Ideally, networks could provide and complement the following services to library education and research: (a) instruction, (b) research, (c) bibliography, (d) information generation, and (e) information-sharing. The extent to which these services can be furthered by the use of networking will depend on imaginative development and utilization of new information links among the various library education programs.

A network for library education could provide the links to share existing resources and develop new ones in the following ways: (*a*) *instructional packages, specialized instruction, and evaluation of instruction*, e.g., live lectures by television with two-way voice transmission, access to computer-assisted instruction housed in other institutions, the establishment of telephone ties to coordinate research in teaching through the linking of educational specialists and library instructors; (*b*) *laboratory facilities*, e.g., instructional laboratories in subject areas where hands-on experience is helpful, centralization of laboratories where feasible; (*c*) *bibliographic control of instructional resources*, e.g., bibliographic listing from member institutions and literature clearinghouses, and document transmission, including print and nonprint materials, coordination of collections through cooperative buying in specializations by type-of-library or service or media; (*d*) *documentation on curriculum objectives and implementation, with communication links* to analyze current offerings and innovations and to discuss planned changes in curriculum with personnel in other schools.

CONCLUSIONS AND RECOMMENDATIONS

Network services should provide access to the universe of information for all types of users. To achieve this goal, the following should be done:

1. Establish bibliographic control of all forms of material, at all levels and for all subject areas, based upon the creation of a standard, one-time bibliographic record

2. Provide bibliographic tools, such as union lists, union catalogs, and directories, to make network resources more easily available at the state, regional, national, and international levels (depending on the size and scope of the resource)

3. Provide increased acquisition and accessibility of nonprint materials and data files

4. Develop and make available reference skills appropriate to networking

5. Educate librarians, information producers, and users in the network's operations

6. Provide appropriate communications links, delivery systems, and switching mechanisms at all levels of the network

7. Guarantee availability of information resources appropriate to each functional level

8. Conduct research into user needs, systems evaluation, and the flow of information through the networks

9. Educate and train personnel for the mediation function

10. Promulgate performance standards for personnel engaged in the mediation function.

The Group also developed general comments about the establishment of networks, namely that:

1. Networks should provide for an increase in both the number and kind of access points, including individuals, organizations, institutions, resource centers, and media facilities of all kinds. (They should be *heterogeneous*.)

2. Networks should encompass *existing* information services of all kinds and forms of service. (They should be *evolutionary*.)

3. Feedback mechanisms should be established at every level of the network to monitor performance of equipment, personnel, and services, and to record reaction of staff and users to the operation. (They should be *adaptive*.)

In addition, the Group made specific recommendations for the development of bibliographic control, namely that:

1. The American National Standards Institute Sectional Committee Z39 should be charged with the development of standard content designators for similar items of information across various forms of material. Funding and personnel should be provided by government agencies at national, state, and local levels.

2. The National Commission on Libraries and Information Science should designate or recommend a "national bibliographic center" to coordinate the creation of standard bibliographic records for all forms of material. The record created by any participating organization should fulfill the needs of all users, irrespective of the needs of the creator of the record. While a reduction in duplication of cataloging can be expected to result in reduced nationwide cataloging costs, funding to reimburse participating organizations for more complete

cataloging and to maintain the national center will be required.

3. Appropriate organizations should designate agencies to assign the standard identification numbers for the various forms of material. Such agencies will require the cooperation of a "national bibliographic center" if the broadest coverage is to be attained, or the coordination of standard numbering might be made a function of the national bibliographic center itself.

4. The Council on Library Resources should be requested to begin implementation of a program of Cataloging-in-Publication. Assuming successful initial implementation, an on-going program covering all possible publishers of various forms of materials should be undertaken with funding through regular appropriations. Availability of a standard, if brief, record prior to publication which appears in the published book will go far toward attaining the goal of timeliness as well as promoting acceptance of the standard record by user agencies.

5. The Library of Congress should expand the coverage of its MARC program. Methods of

funding of this expansion should be investigated.

6. The feasibility of an integrated system for recording and accessing information on the location and availability of materials within the network should be studied.

The ultimate success of library communication and information networks will rest largely upon the capacity of qualified personnel to propose, develop, implement, and interpret the services required. One inescapable conclusion of this Conference is the requirement for a new direction in library education in the training and retraining of librarians to function in these networks at all levels.

Thus, it is recommended: (1) the new standards on accreditation should recognize, and indeed, encourage the availability of networks for library education as well as encouraging innovation and diversity in curriculum; (2) professional associations concerned with education for library and information sciences should provide forums for the discussion of the elements of the educational process which could be enhanced by network activities; (3) pilot research projects involving networks for library education should be undertaken. This would provide for experimentation and analysis of potential and existing network services and problems; (4) formal and informal cooperative projects among library education programs based on network concepts should be encouraged to facilitate the urgent need for better communication among the schools.

Bibliographic Services for a National Network

Henriette D. Avram and Josephine S. Pulsifer

INTRODUCTION

Networks may be characterized by the kind of nodes connected, by the information going over the network, and by the type of communication facilities employed. Thus we may discuss a library network with only libraries as nodes, an interlibrary loan network where requests for materials are interchanged among unspecified nodes and a microwave network in which case only the carrier is emphasized but neither the "message" nor the nodes are specified. For any specific information network, however, an explicit assignment must be made of: (1) the operational nodes, (2) the data flowing through the network, and (3) the facilities to be used.

While information networks certainly will exchange other than bibliographic data, we may assume, in the context of this Conference on Interlibrary Communications and Information Networks, that we are chiefly concerned with the interchange of bibliographic references. Text, abstracts, and nonbibliographic reference questions and answers will be transmitted, but these transactions usually will include a bibliographic reference. Much of the traffic through an information network will consist of requests (in the form of a bibliographic reference) for location and loan or copy of a bibliographic item, or for citations on a particular subject.

Rather than postulate the information network in its entirety, we have chosen to concentrate on what we consider to be the foundation of this network — the provision of a standard bibliographic record which will accommodate network transactions. The thesis is that efficient functioning of a network is dependent upon the organization of bibliographic services so that the basic record for each bibliographic item is created once. This record must be minimally capable of serving the needs of libraries, information centers, abstracting and indexing services, and national and trade bibliographies. What is proposed is a centralized National Bibliographic Service, NBS, composed of component institutions functioning as a unified whole.

The authors assume the existence of a national network with appropriate telecommunications. They do not hypothesize: (1) the structure or the communications facilities of the network, (2) the details of organization and funding of the NBS, (3) the mechanics of providing holdings information for a system of union catalogs, (4) the methodology of publication of bibliographic services, or (5) the cost estimates of services proposed. The intent is to demonstrate the need for a centrally

processed bibliographic record, to consider standardization requirements for such a record, and to point up the results of failing to provide this record.

VARIETIES OF BIBLIOGRAPHIC SERVICES

The current complex pattern of bibliographic services consists of a multiplicity of organizations issuing a variety of products. These products vary significantly, depending largely on the uses to be made of them, and reflect the individual requirements of the producers.

It is these "uses" and "requirements" that create one of the fundamental problems in our current attempts to control information. Although the goal of all services is to provide bibliographic information to a user, there are dissimilarities in the principal functions of the agencies involved. Differences in importance given to and treatment of the form and function of elements of the bibliographic record are dependent on the function of the service.

We may characterize certain types of bibliographic services and their functions as follows:

Library catalogs serve to index an individual collection by author, title, subject, and series. To enable the user to find a physical volume rather than merely a bibliographic reference, the catalog also provides a location code, or shelf number. A unique form of entry for each name or topical heading used as an access point is maintained by means of authority files. The Library of Congress, LC, name and subject authority files are frequently the *de facto* authority by virtue of the wide use of LC catalog data. For economic reasons (e.g., filing time, size of catalog) the number of access points often is limited. The various access points serve to bring together works by the same author, works with the same title, and works on the same subject. A unique bibliographic description of each item makes it possible to distinguish between different works with the same title and different editions of the same work. The library catalog, for the most part, is designed to index works as a whole, in contrast to published services which index the contents or parts of composite works, the articles in a journal, or the individual issues of a series.

Union catalogs serve to consolidate location information for library materials within a cooperating group of libraries. Since the catalog does not represent a single library but rather combined catalog entries for several libraries, the various entries are related to each other only incidentally. Apparently identical items are usually merged into a single entry with appropriate location codes, and disparate entries for apparently identical authors may be made uniform. For economic reasons, access is generally limited to main entry. Certainly, multiple access points would enhance the location function of union catalogs.

National bibliographies provide an official record of those items published within a country during a given period of time. By virtue of this time orientation, national bibliographies serve as an awareness service and also may be used as a source of catalog data. They are not themselves catalogs, however, since they are not based on nor limited to any single collection or group of collections. More significantly, because there need be no carry-over from the past, they are not subject to the problems of consistency of entry and description which beset the maintenance of library catalogs.

Trade bibliographies function principally as an awareness service for those publications available through the booktrade. While current announcement services are concerned only with a specified time period, true trade bibliographies are a composite list of all titles in print. While name entries are generally taken directly from the publication, subject entries require updating. Most trade bibliographies contain only the brief information necessary for ordering. Certain announcement services, however, provide essentially complete LC catalog records which serve as a source of catalog data for many libraries.

Abstracting and indexing services are concerned with indexing technical report literature and individual articles from journals and composite works. Because these services generally index more specialized materials and are aimed at the specialist in a particular discipline, in-depth indexing by means of a relatively large number of very specific subject terms is the rule. The tailoring of abstracting and indexing services to a particular clientele or discipline often results in duplication of indexing for the same item in several services since disciplines often are interrelated.

It was the recognition of the different characteristics and functions of the bibliographic services that prompted the research by the American National Standards Institute, ANSI, Z39 Subcommittee 2 (Z39.SC2) in 1967.[1] The study was designed to assist the subcommittee in determining what units of information should be identified in machine-readable bibliographic records. The investigators attempted to identify the elements of bibliographic description of various forms of material and the uses made of the records. The difficulties encountered were many. The subcommittee concluded that the most useful next step would be to draft a format structure which would establish a medium of exchange between various producers and users of information. There would be no attempt to specify data elements to be identified, this being left to the discretion of the user. This effort resulted in a standard format for bibliographic information interchange on magnetic tape. Hindsight indicates that the subcommittee should have extended its efforts and continued work toward standardization of the content of records and the content designators.[2]

An unpublished study performed by Inforonics, Inc., for the Library of Congress in 1969 gave further evidence to the problems of incompatibility due, in part, to functional differences. The purpose of the study was to determine the fea-

sibility of producing a "universe of legends"[3] for bibliographic data. The investigators analyzed machine-form bibliographic records for differences in the content and content designators, and the reasons for the differences.

The results clearly indicated that the distinctions in bibliographic form (book, serial, etc.) alone do not determine the content or content designators of machine records but rather that agreement on standards for machine-readable formats are reached chiefly by those who share common bibliographic practices and who make the same uses of the data bases they create.

The nonuniformity clearly is evident in comparing the bibliographic records of large research libraries and information centers. Without engaging in an evaluation of the merits of one system or the effects of following any one set of conventions, it is sufficient to say that the cumulative consequences of these disparities is costly duplication of producing records for the same item and minimization of the users facility to tap all services as an integrated system.

That bibliographic services have individual functions which differ is not contested. It is the apparent nonrecognition of the urgent necessity for agreement on standards for the identification, representation, and recording of bibliographic and textual data elements which is questioned.

MACHINE-READABLE BIBLIOGRAPHIC SERVICES

Since this article is concerned with bibliographic data services in a network context, it seemed appropriate to examine some of the machine-readable transfer systems that exist today. The aim was to investigate a sufficient number of the systems to arrive at conclusions regarding the state of the art in relation to network services. Bibliographic services for a national network, in an environment using the computer and associated communication and peripheral devices as tools, demand the transmission of machine-readable data.

A considerable number of magnetic tape services are now available, and many problems exist. Both seven- and nine-level tapes are issued. Within each type, a variety of codes are used for the representation of the character set of the producer. In addition to the code variations, tape densities (number of characters per inch recorded on tape) are not standardized.

The structure of the bibliographic record on magnetic tape varies from service to service, as does the degree to which data elements of the record are explicitly identified and the method of identification. For example, names may be identified as personal and corporate, or only as names. In some instances all names are recorded in a single field separated only by a unique character. In other systems names are characterized by their function, e.g., main entry or subject. The same data element may be explicitly identified in two or more systems, but the content designators used to identify the element may be different. Finally, the content of the bibliographic description and the choice and form of access points to that description, e.g., name and subject entries, often are inconsistent.

In summary, the results of this investigation support all prior conclusions as to lack of standardization with one significant exception, i.e., the adoption of the ANSI format as the interchange format by several agencies with operating systems and planned future systems. LC's MARC (*MA*chine-*R*eadable *C*ataloging) Distribution Service, the Federal Clearinghouse for Scientific and Technical Information system; the International Nuclear Information System, INIS; and the British National Bibliography, BNB, MARC system are among those utilizing the ANSI standard. The clearinghouse is one of the many U.S. government agency members of the Committee on Scientific and Technical Information, COSATI, that have adopted this format.

All members of COSATI are in agreement on the content and content designators of the record. The Library of Congress and the British National Bibliography have arrived at almost complete agreement concerning their machine-readable records. The few dissimilarities in content designation that remain again point out the differences in the function of a library as compared to those of a national bibliography. Some of the variations in the form of content reflect lack of uniformity between the North American and British editions of the *Anglo-American Cataloging Rules,* AACR.[4] [5] Other variations stem from the LC "superimposition" policy as contrasted with the complete adoption of the AACR by BNB.

However, little similarity exists in the data elements or the content designators when comparing the formats of either COSATI or INIS with LC and BNB. INIS, like COSATI, principally interested in technical reports, nevertheless has defined different data elements and content designators. It is unfortunate that closer cooperation did not exist between the two systems to ensure compatibility where possible. The Library of Congress, in its MARC system, has defined formats for books, serials, maps, manuscripts, and motion pictures and filmstrips. The correlation of content designators across all forms of material has been an essential part of all design work.

RECOMMENDATIONS FOR A NATIONAL BIBLIOGRAPHIC SERVICE

We may characterize the objectives of bibliographic service as follows: (1) the situation of a bibliographic item for the purpose of establishing its existence, (2) the location of an item, and (3) distribution of a record of the bibliographic item for local use.

Summarizing the present "nonsystem" of services, there is no pattern by which the various pieces fit into a comprehensive whole. Lack of agreement on name and subject entries, and elements of description make identification of different records as belonging to the same bibliographic item often difficult or impossible. Machine-readable services are incompatible in their identification of elements of the record and in the structure of the record. Thus it becomes imperative to begin thinking of an NBS which would assume comprehensiveness and avoid unnecessary duplication in the creation of the bibliographic record. This national service would act as an agency to promote standards; correlate the basic objectives of identification, location, and distribution; and coordinate the variety of bibliographic agencies which should be a part of the national bibliographic picture.

It is indicative of the trend toward centralization through a national bibliographic service to note the recommendations made in the report of the British National Library Committee,[6]

the report of an *Integrated Information System for the National Library of Canada,*[7] as well as the efforts over the past decade to develop a plan for a national information network summarized in a report by the Library of Congress.[8] The LC article characterizes the plans as stemming from those elements of the federal government concerned with science and technology, and having as their principal aim the reduction in the bulk of the accretion of scientific and technological literature through physical means, e.g., microforms and electronic processing, or intellectual means, e.g., abstracting, evaluation, and analysis. This report further points out that reduction in the physical bulk of materials does not achieve a reduction in the number of units that must be handled and controlled in library and information systems, but on the contrary, each surrogate becomes a new, additional information item.

The authors support the views expressed in the report that information is a continuum that cannot be readily fragmented into distinct and nonoverlapping fields; that a national network should not be implemented for science and technology alone, nor among information centers excluding libraries; and that the Library of Congress already stands at the focus of a large national information network.

To quote the opinion of the Library of Congress on the fundamental requirement for success in establishing an effective national information network:

The basic need is to develop a responsive, flexible, communications medium that will serve as the means for moving the information record throughout the system. Solution of the communications problem is more important than administration, or organizational structure, or areas of responsibility for subject coverage or for handling categories of documents. The network problem is an access problem, and the access problem is essentially a file problem. It is a problem, therefore, of what librarians, in their old-fashioned terminology, call bibliographic control — control of the record surrogate for the actual informational piece, the original informational package. For the ultimate national network, which of course must be envisioned as an automated system with fast response time, even real-time capability, there is, then, an overriding need to develop a *standard record* with a full range of appropriate codes, as the 'lingua franca' of the entire system. The standard record should be modular in format, open-ended, multipurpose, highly manipulable and responsive to the need for a wide variety of products and services that the system must be capable of providing.[9]

Building on present LC services, the bibliographic record for all documents published in the United States should be produced within the unified environment of an NBS. The previous statement does not imply that the intellectual analysis required for the entire content of the record is the responsibility of one institution. What is implied is that several agencies operate in unison.

Prompt one-time creation of a bibliographic record and adequate provision of its dissemination of all users would benefit both the producer of secondary services and the ultimate user.

PROGRESS TOWARD A NATIONAL BIBLIOGRAPHIC SERVICE

Several programs undertaken during the past few years by the Library of Congress support the concept of an NBS.

SHARED CATALOGING

Under Title II C of the Higher Education Act of 1965, LC was charged "with (1) acquiring so far as possible, all library materials currently published throughout the world which are of value to scholarship; and (2) providing the catalog information for these materials promptly after receipt...."[10] The Shared Cataloging Division of LC was organized in 1966 to handle the cataloging workload. Wherever available, descriptive cataloging of the national bibliography is used, with modifications of entry when necessary and with the addition of subject headings and classification. Depository sets of cards are distributed to participating libraries. Copies of orders for foreign titles not found in the depository catalog are sent to LC so that the publication may be acquired and cataloged. Thus, in principle, LC already has the authority to be the centralized cataloging agency for the nation.

MARC

The MARC Distribution Service grew out of a pilot project to test the feasibility of centrally producing and distributing machine-readable catalog records.[11] From the First Conference on Machine-Readable Catalog Copy in 1964, attended by representatives of the Library of Congress, universities, research agencies, government agencies, and private industry, the consensus was that early availability of machine-readable catalog copy as a by-product of LC's cataloging operations would be desirable. Since the record would be used for a variety of purposes in many libraries, agreement on data elements to be encoded was desirable, and the design of a machine-readable record by LC was probably the best means of standardization.

The pilot project resulted in: (1) a standard interchange format (ANSI standard), (2) the definition of standard records for several forms of material, and (3) the inception of the MARC Distribution Service beginning with the provision of English-language catalog records in March 1969. Expansion to other languages and other forms of material is planned for the future. While implementation of systems for the utilization of MARC has been slow, no one has suggested that the MARC Distribution Service (or the Card Division Distribution Service) be abandoned in favor of decentralized production of catalog records by many institutions.

RECON

With a MARC format accepted widely by the library profession, libraries throughout the country began to discuss and plan conversion of their retrospective catalog records to machine-readable form. Uncoordinated projects were certain to differ with respect to completeness and uniformity and in addition, would result in duplication of conversion of the same items. Such efforts are not only economically unsound but

threaten the future of a national machine-readable data base of bibliographic information. The Council on Library Resources granted funds to the Library of Congress for a study to determine the feasibility of centralized conversion of retrospective catalog records and their distribution to the entire library community. The RECON (*RE*trospective *CON*version) Working Task Force,[12] which was assigned direct responsibility for the study, recommended that large-scale conversion should be a centralized project under the direction of the Library of Congress, that standards for conversion of retrospective records should be the same as those for current records, and that a pilot project should be undertaken to test empirically what had been hypothesized in the study.

The RECON Project was initiated in August 1969, partially funded by the Council on Library Resources and the U.S. Office of Education. Along with converting approximately 85,000 1968 and 1969 English-language monograph titles, a group of research titles will be selected to test the various conversion techniques for older and non-English titles. Format recognition algorithms are being developed, and the state of the art of input devices monitored. In addition, the RECON Working Task Force was reconvened to study four tasks of national scope. Significant to this discussion are the findings with regard to Task 1 and Task 3.

Task 1 concerned the feasibility of standardizing a level or subset of the MARC II format which would allow a library to input less complex records than LC/MARC but still would permit the library to contribute to a future national data base. A level is defined as: (1) the bibliographic completeness of a record, and (2) the extent to which its contents are explicitly identified for computer manipulation. The study[13] concluded that there are two functions of a national data base: (1) the distribution function, and (2) the National Union Catalog function. Further, it concluded that: The distribution function can best be satisfied by a detailed record in a communications format from which an individual library can extract the subset of data useful in its application, to satisfy the needs of diverse installations and applications, records for general distribution should be in the full MARC II format."[14] This supports the concept that all records needed for distribution purposes are best prepared at a central source.

Task 3 resulted from the awareness of a large number of machine-readable bibliographic records generated through automation projects at individual institutions. The RECON Working Task Force considered it important to explore the feasibility (bibliographic, technical, and economic) of utilizing existing records as part of a national bibliographic service. Requiring investigation was the possibility and associated problems of: (1) comparing records with the MARC/RECON data base and identifying records already in machine-readable form, (2) augmenting records not in MARC/RECON to bring them up to the level of completeness of a MARC II record, (3) changing entries for records not in MARC/RECON to be consistent with entries in the LC Official Catalog, and (4) translating those records not in MARC/RECON into the MARC II format. The first phase of the task was a survey and analysis of existing data bases in machine-readable form. Forty-two libraries, a representative sample of different types of systems, were contacted; thirty-three responded. The study is still under way, and a complete report of findings will be made at a later date. However, within the context of this paper, it is worthwhile to point out that the survey showed that approximately 3 million records are already in machine-readable form in thirty-three libraries in this country, alone. Of this total, 2.5 million are monograph records. The preliminarily analysis performed up to this time indicates that the bibliographic conformity across data bases is practically nonexistent. Considering the resources expended to create the existing data bases, the resultant duplication of titles and the nonuniformity of the machine-readable records, it is urgent to take action.

With the Library of Congress' past history of bibliographic services, it seems desirable, in our view, that LC assume the duties of the NBS. It should again be emphasized that this does not necessarily exclude other organizations from contributing to the NBS. It does place the main responsibility for NBS on LC and in so doing, might result in significant changes in the course of reorganizing LC bibliographic services into an NBS.

In order to create records appropriate to a national service, LC might close off its Official Catalog to achieve greater uniformity in the application of the *Anglo-American Cataloging Rules* (the policy of "superimposition" was adopted by LC in lieu of changing existing entries to conform with AACR) and to make changes in its subject heading system. In this case, libraries using the products of an NBS based on LC cataloging might have to consider closing off their own catalogs to avoid making costly changes. Although the closing of the catalogs would not resolve all problems associated with relating new entries to past records, or making variations in LC records conform with cataloging done locally to expedite the processing of material, it could have the effect of the entire library community following one set of rules and could have impact for the future.

CONSIDERATIONS FOR NATIONAL BIBLIOGRAPHIC SERVICE STANDARDS

The availability from the NBS of records with a standard identification number, a standard bibliographic description, standard rules for entry, greater uniformity in subject analysis, and a standard machine-readable record for each form of material, would enable network members to devote a much larger share of their resources to satisfying the needs of their particular clientele. In some instances, standards already are in being; in others, work has just begun. Standards range in complexity from relatively simple to extremely difficult. They result from the perseverance and the ability of experienced individuals to "endure" the democratic review process and the constant revision while the proposal is eventually transformed to satisfy the majority. Wigington and Wood[15] state:

As the expression of the major significant details in information-transfer system design, standards of representation and practice, agreed to and used by all parties, become the guiding mechanisms which replace unified management. As such they take on an importance in achieving progress in national, and international information-transfer which is beyond the technical importance normally associated with

standards. All parties, however, must be patient with the inevitably slow development and utilization of those standards.

STANDARD IDENTIFICATION NUMBER

Agencies responsible for the assignment of the Standard Serial Number, SSN, and standard numbers for nonbook materials must be designated, as has already been done for the Standard Book Number, SBN. In Great Britain, total book numbering is almost an accomplished fact. The Standard Book Numbering Agency in New York reports a high degree of success in implementing the SBN in this country.

The International Standards Organization, ISO, has recently adopted an international numbering system making the SBN an ISBN.[16] An ANSI Z39 subcommittee is charged with developing an SSN.

STANDARD BIBLIOGRAPHIC DESCRIPTION

A Standard Bibliographic Description, SBD, is being developed by the International Meeting of Cataloging Experts, IMCE, working group of the International Federation of Library Associations, IFLA. "The primary purpose of the SBD is to act as a standard for the making of the descriptive part of the definitive national record of a book....A second purpose of the SBD is to provide a formula to serve as a basis for entries in catalogues, lists, and bibliographies other than the national bibliography."[17] The SBD will consist of a set of recommended elements, a fixed order for their presentation, and a standard system for punctuation. Thus, it would be possible for people to recognize the elements forming part of the bibliographic description, regardless of the language. Catalog records constructed according to the SBD will materially assist the conversion of these records into machine-readable form.

Standard Rules for Entry and Descriptive Cataloging

International agreement on entry and description should be reached so that the content of national bibliographic records from different countries will be uniform. Rules for cataloging scientific and technical reports and monographs should be consistent. Progress in this direction is being made. North,[18] in comparing the AACR and the COSATI *Standard for Descriptive Cataloging of Government Scientific and Technical Reports,*[19] reports that they are more in harmony than the ALA and DDC standards they replace. If libraries and other bibliographic services are to be able to integrate monographs and report literature into one system, further steps in this direction are necessary.

STANDARD APPROACHES TO SUBJECT ANALYSIS

Across-the-board agreement on standard approaches to subject analysis of library materials would be highly desirable but admittedly difficult (if not impossible) to obtain. The vantage point for subject analysis is in the eye of the beholder and this bias, in turn, is reflected in the structure and content of various classification systems and indexing vocabularies. Even an optimum general approach cannot be expected to satisfy the requirements of all special agencies. Thus the most reasonable hope is for the NBS to provide classification numbers that will be acceptable for most general library purposes. Acceptability can be fostered by providing alternative classification numbers when possible.

Efforts should be made also to achieve the greatest possible compatibility and convertibility among major indexing vocabularies. This is no minor task, however. A working group of the U.S. National Libraries Task Force on Automation and Other Cooperative Activities has been making some progress toward the reconciliation of the subject heading lists of the three national libraries, but differences in scope and services of the three collections place formidable problems in the way of development of a single list. The NBS should by its nature make use of an indexing vocabulary that has wide acceptance.

In all of these efforts, consideration should be given to the suitability of specific subject control devices for computer processing. Too little is known about optimum machine searching techniques to assert that a given form of indexing vocabulary is best for this purpose. This problem should be thoroughly investigated without losing sight, however, of the fact that indexing terms almost certainly will have to be displayed in conventional ways for many years to come.

STANDARD INTERCHANGE FORMAT FOR MACHINE READABLE DATA

The adoption of the ANSI format as the proposed ISO format is encouraging. However, progress made toward the use of a standard interchange format structure does not imply agreement on the content or content designators. For an NBS to be most effective and economical to both the producer and user, the data elements and their identification must be coordinated.

CONSIDERATIONS FOR NATIONAL BIBLIOGRAPHIC SERVICE COMPONENTS

The national responsibility for the NBS must be clearly established along with a mechanism that would regularly provide the NBS with advice and guidance from the library and information community. Federal funding will be required, and states might also share in the cost. Services could be sold by subscription. The relationship of the NBS and the book trade, information centers, and organizations responsible for the production of abstracting and indexing services or other bibliographic services must be defined.

Although not formally described as components of an NBS, there is evidence of a trend in this direction.

The Standard Book Numbering Agency, New York, is a collaboration between the American Book Publishers Council, American Educational Publishers Institute, American National Standards Institute Committee Z39, Library of Congress, and R. R. Bowker Company, and includes the U. S. and Canada. NBS component agencies will need to take the responsibility for referring to the SBN agency any items for which no number has been provided by the publisher.

There is a renewal of interest in Cataloging-in-Publication, formerly termed Cataloging-in-Source. Under the proposed plan, the publishers would submit galley proof to the Library of Congress for assignment of main and added author entries, short title, imprint, subject headings, and classification numbers. This information would be input to an incomplete MARC record, and a hard copy of the record returned with the galley proof to the publisher for printing in the book (imprint would not appear in the hard-copy record for the book). If this program can be successfully implemented and extended to the majority of publishers, an official MARC record could be used to produce trade bibliographies, including advance lists. The records would be available to libraries for ordering and for preparation of processing materials in advance of receipt of the book. Timeliness of the bibliographic record will be essential for all segments of the network.

In Great Britain, Whitaker produces the trade bibliography record in a MARC format intended to be used as a temporary record until it is replaced by a full MARC record from BNB. Whitaker also assigns the SBN to those titles furnished to it by BNB which have not had the SBN assigned by the publisher.

It is essential that the abstracting and indexing agencies be integrated into the NBS. The producers of these services — which include the two national libraries, specialized government information centers, scientific and technical societies, and commercial services — could create the standard bibliographic record for all materials within their subject area and publish the abstracting and indexing service for that body of information.

Foreign literature, cataloged by a national bibliography according to standard procedures, would be assigned to the appropriate NBS agency to coordinate names used for entry, convert subject terms, and assign a classification number.

The goal of comprehensive coverage of state and local documents might be best served by assigning the responsibility for cataloging these to the fifty state libraries, with each state responsible for the corporate authority file of its state and local agencies.

The resulting record for either U.S. or foreign publications will become part of the national data base for distribution to subscribers, for use in the creation of a national bibliography, national or regional union catalogs, lists of new serial titles, abstracting and indexing services, periodical indexes, current awareness services, etc.

The national data base might, in fact, be a series of specialized data bases, with a central switching service to permit switching of queries to the appropriate data base. One of the data bases could be the LC name authority records, which are maintained by the Library of Congress and might be shared by those agencies with the responsibility for cataloging certain portions of the literature.

One of the major differences in existing cataloging conventions is in the use of established forms of names. Libraries enter works under the established form of both corporate and personal name. The scientific and technical community and many abstracting and indexing services tend toward establishing corporate names but in most instances, use personal names as they appear on the piece. If a single name authority file could be shared among all producers and each bibliographic *names — established in relation to a single comprehensive authority file — to meet individuality*

record contained both the established form of name and the name as it appeared on the published item, a connecting link would be established. Thus, access could be provided to all works to which a particular person was related. Such a system would increase the serviceability of a bibliographic file to the user.

The suggested system implies more effort in the creation of each record. For the literature of the scientific and technical community and abstracting and indexing services, names would have to be established; for traditional library materials, names as they appear on the piece would have to be included. (The IMCE Working Group for the SBD is recommending that the personal name author statement always be included in the body of the description.) The savings would be in the creation of only one record.

However, the inclusion of the established name and the name as it appears on the piece in each record does not offer a utopian solution. In many instances, if one approaches the file with the author's name as it appears on the piece to determine all works by that author, the result may be all works by many authors. For example, "J. Brown" will be linked to "John Brown" as well as to "James Brown." In addition, new names cannot be established in isolation; they must be established in relation to a single comprehensive authority file to ensure that all of them will meet the same criteria of individuality.

NETWORK SERVICES PROVIDED BY THE NBS

Assuming the existence of a national network, how would the NBS serve the users of this network better than they are served today?

SELECTION

At present, the selection function is accomplished by using a variety of alerting services published in different formats. With a Cataloging-in Publication record available at an early date and an ISBN and/or LC card number to facilitate identification, announcement services could reference reviews, and both could be indexed by classification and subject headings as well as author and title. Such a service also would aid the vendors and users of approval services.

Selection in a network context also implies the ability to determine what need not be purchased by the individual organization if it is available through the network when needed. For this it is necessary to determine with is on order in co-operating agencies, as well as what already exists in their collections. The likelihood of being able to identify orders for the same item by different institutions as being in fact the same item is greatly enhanced by the early existence of a uniform record and the ISBN.

LOCATION

Location of materials for purposes of requesting a loan is fraught with problems in the present system. Communications may speed the process of querying but cannot solve the problem of identification. Examples of conflicting reports submitted to the National Union Catalog, NUC, are cited in the RECON report.[20]

With some imagination and luck, one may locate a name entry in the NUC since names are matched with LC established forms, and added entries and references are included. Working with local or regional union catalogs is much more hazardous since these are often single entry catalogs — the base for coordination is smaller, and less effort and expertise at matching may be contributed.

Efforts to locate materials by subject are even less successful since only titles cataloged by the Library of Congress are indexed in *Library of Congress Catalogs — Books: Subjects,*[21] and most local and regional catalogs do not include a subject index. Access by title is almost nonexistent.

Clearly there is a need for national, regional, and state union catalogs accessible by author, title, and subject (including series). Unless there are uniform entries, produced from a single source, there will be great waste in terms of effort and funds, and also great inefficiency and confusion as one switches from searching local catalogs to searching state, regional, and national union catalogs.

The conversion of the LC retrospective catalog is urgently needed if existing collections of libraries are to be made maximally accessible within a network. There still will remain the problem of disparate entries for titles not in the Library of Congress, but adoption of the RECON record by all libraries as they contribute their holdings information to the NBS would be a giant step toward solving the problem.

The pattern of location files in a national network will be dependent upon the organization and communications pattern of the network, and are immaterial to this discussion. Conceivably, the NUC might list all titles in the national data base under multiple entries but give only the *regions* in which the work is held. Specific locations holding the title could then be ascertained from a machine-readable file at the regional headquarters. Many variations are possible. What is important is that access points, bibliographic description, and identification numbers of the national, regional, and local records be alike. Ultimately, with coordinated bibliographic description and location services, a user should be able to proceed from finding a citation in an index, to calling up an abstract or a critical review, to determining the most accessible location of the item and the current status of that item, and finally, to requesting a loan of the material.

CATALOGING

The benefits of a standard bibliographic record for cataloging have been mentioned throughout this paper. To summarize, this record would be uniform, authoritative, multipurpose, and cover essentially all library materials. In addition, more name and subject approaches would be provided to aid the user, given a national network and economically feasible telecommunications facilities; a variety of improved methods of distribution of catalog data could be implemented.

Direct telecommunication transactions between all libraries and the central NBS for the acquisition of catalog records would not appear to be feasible. Depending upon the organization of the network, regional or state centers might service the cataloging requirements of member libraries as well as maintain the location records for materials within their area. Avram[22] describes a hypothetical network for sharing catalog data in which major regional centers maintain the union catalog for their area and also serve as distribution centers for particular segments of the national data base. The regional center would receive all currently produced records from the national center, but after a stated interval, retain only those records used within its region or pertinent to its national responsibility.

Libraries within the region would report holdings and request machine-readable catalog data or possibly certain catalog products. Depending upon the size and population of the region, state centers may well act as an intermediate level between the regional center and the individual library. In this case, holdings and requests would be reported through the state center. It, in turn, would supply those records already within the state system, report the holdings to the regional centers, and supply the catalog products required by the individual library. It might also maintain a statewide system of union catalogs. The regional union catalog might be in machine-accessible form only or might include only certain locations.

Remote access to the state or regional data base will likely be utilized by some but not necessarily all libraries. At some point in time, the regional data base conceivably may be queried directly by some libraries in lieu of maintaining individual library catalogs.

Processing materials may be produced at the state level, or libraries could contract for cooperative or commercial processing or catalog production services and achieve the same catalog data while only reporting holdings to the network.

Whatever the organization of the network, and the mix of services utilized by libraries and other organizations, the result of the NBS standard record will be a degree of consistency and compatibility that is impossible today. In fact, the proliferation of commercial and cooperative services and of individual automated library systems — each using a different catalog record — will make it more and more difficult to implement a network as time goes on.

OUTLOOK

We now are reaching a time when the discussion of information networks at the conceptual level is generally retreading old ground. Crystal balls should be broken. Further consideration of networks of the far future may be of intellectual interest but offer little to move us ahead. Experience also has shown that results are inadequate where no implementation is begun until research and development has defined the minutest specifications of the design of the total system. This approach fails for large complex systems for two reasons. First, man is unable to comprehend such great complexity. Second, rapidly advancing technology causes technical components to become obsolete during the long period of the total design effort. Therefore, it is imperative that we begin to search for practical means of implementation at the earliest date. The prerequisites seem to be (1) design of one operational module at a time, (2) each module based on operational experience gained from the preceding phase, and (3) recognition of some ambiguity in total

systems comprehension from the beginning. If this approach is accepted, the people involved must recognize the need to constantly revise specifications.

In the final analysis, the time eventually comes when we must face the hard question of how to begin.

Although computers are able to process information more efficiently than humans and telecommunication links are able to make information more rapidly available, it does not necessarily follow that operational large-scale network systems are soon within our grasp.

Our communications link is the common language of bibliographic description, whether the representation of this description is in printed or digital form. Unless we succeed in implementing a national center to coordinate the processing and distribution of standard bibliographic records for multiple uses, networking in our sense will indeed be a fairy tale.

NOTES

1. Ann T. Curran and Henriette D. Avram, *The identification of data elements in bibliographic records;* (Final of the special project on data elements for the Subcommittee on Machine Input Records (SC-2) of the Sectional Committee on Library Work and Documentation (Z39) of the United States of America Standards Institute [Needham, Mass.: The Institute, 1967]), var. p.

2. Content designators are tags, indicators, and subfield codes employed to explicitly identify or characterize information.

3. A legend is a code in the record that identifies the content of the record, i.e., the form of material being described, the data element included, and the content designators used. The legends bring all ANSI format records into a common frame of reference.

4. *Anglo-American cataloging rules.* North American text. (Chicago: ALA, 1967), 400p.

5. *Anglo-American cataloging rules* British text (London: Library Assoc., 1967), 327p.

6. Great Britain. National Libraries Committee, *Report of the National Libraries Committee* (London: Her Majesty's Stationery Office, 1969), 320p.

7. Ottawa, National Library, System Development project, *An integrated information system for the National Library of Canada* vol. 1 (Ottawa: Bureau of Management and Consulting Services, June 1970), 210p.

8. U.S. Library of Congress, "The Library of Congress as the national library: potentialities for service," in D. M. Knight and E. S. Nourse, eds., *Libraries at large....* (New York: Bowker, 1969), p.435-465.

9. Ibid., p.440-441.

10. John M. Dawson, "The Library of Congress: its role in cooperative and centralized cataloging," *Library trends* 16:85-96 (July 1967).

11. U.S. Library of Congress, Information Systems Office, *The MARC pilot project; final report...* (Washington, D.C.: Library of Congress, 1968).

12. RECON Working Task Force. *Conversion of retrospective catalog records to machine-readable form* (Washington, D.C.: Library of Congress, 1969), 230p.

13. Format recognition is a technique that examines data strings for keywords, significant punctuation and other cues in order to assign content designators to the data elements of a bibliographic record. The process will shift some of the burden of editing from the human to the machine and should result in a cost saving in the conversion of bibliographic records to machine-readable form. (U.S. Library of Congress, Information systems office, *Format recognition process for MARC records: a logical design,* Unpublished).

14. RECON Working Task Force, "Levels of machine-readable records," *Journal of Library Automation* 3:124, 126 (June 1970).

15. Ronald L. Wigington and James L. Wood, "Standardization requirements of a national program for information transfer," *Library trends* 18:432-447 (April 1970).

16. Emery Koltay, "International standard book numbering," *The Bowker annual of library and book trade information* (New York: Bowker, 1970), p.71-74.

17. International Meeting of Cataloging Experts, Working Group on the International Standard Bibliographic Description, *Standard bibliographic description (for single volume and multivolume monographs)...*, prepared ... by Michael German (July 1970), [p.2].

18. Jeanne B. North, "A look at the new COSATI standard," *Special libraries* 58:582-584 (Oct. 1969).

19. U.S. Federal Council for Science and Technology, Committee on Scientific and Technical Information, *Standards for descriptive cataloging of government scientific and technical reports, (Rev. no. 1 [Washington, D.C.: Clearinghouse for Federal Scientific and Technical Information, Oct. 1966]), 50p.*

20. RECON Working Task Force. *Conversion of retrospective catalog records....*

21. U.S. Library of Congress. *Library of Congress catalogs--books: subjects* (Washington, D.C.: the Library) quarterly.

22. Henriette D. Avram, "Bibliographic and technical problems in implementing a national library network," *Library trends* 18:487-502 (Apr. 1970).

The Path to Interlibrary Networking for Audiovisual Materials

Gerald R. Brong

PRINT AND NONPRINT MATERIALS AND LIBRARY DEFINED

Before we can explore the relationships of interlibrary communication and information networking as related to nonprint informational units, we must accept the assumption that libraries can no longer consume quantities of energy-making distinctions between the kinds of materials acquisitioned as information storage units — as storage units, books are comparable to films, films to recordings on tape, tape to periodicals.[1] We are considering information. The output of man's activities may be information or knowledge. Knowledge resource centers might be a name for libraries.[2] These knowledge resource centers, KRC, in schools at least, says Clair Eatough, will go a long way toward alleviating today's massive problems of materials logistics — the KRC will provide the patron with needed information in a manner relevant to the patron's need and intended use. The KRC will be a pumphouse for information.[3]

Nonprint materials may generally be defined as those materials not totally dependent on printed words to transmit meaning. These materials are storage devices for information or experiences. These nonprint storage units may take the form of motion pictures on film or magnetic storage devices, audio information on magnetic devices or pressed into vinyl discs, computer-generated graphics or even speech; in each case, the items are not dependent on printed words for the user to extract meaning from the information or experience. As informational storage devices, the nonprint media are the same as any other print item; just the medium of storage is different. One thing all nonprint media have in common is that they require some sort of display device (projector, playback, viewer, etc.) before information may be assessed. Not all print media are free of the display device need, however.

When functionally defining a library, it is in keeping with the information center concept to indicate that it is a collection of informational units organized in a manner allowing for retrieval of the stored information. The library is further organized to function in the process of information transfer between the storage medium and the patron, and the library may become involved in the ultimate use of the information by the patron (this implies much more than just providing information). The content of the library is usually in printed or book form, and reading remains the principle means of information transfer.

Many other storage devices beyond the print are used, however, in this information transfer function.[4] C. Walter Stone stresses the fact that we are experiencing a shift from a material-oriented library operation to an idea information-oriented operation.[5] Stone also indicates that with our new orientation toward the information contained in things and not the storage of things, the library function has become so important that it should not be entrusted solely to librarians or any other single communication group.[6] The information or knowledge resource center (which we shall continue to call a library) will be staffed by catalogers, bibliographers, mediagraphers, administrators, communications specialists, information translators, and audiovisual or media specialists. These librarians will design and operate the functioning components of the library system, which are:

1. Storage systems for the informational units

2. Retrieval systems to bring the items from storage

3. "Bibliographic" systems to inform the seeker of information what he may access to solve his informational need (usually provides indications on how to access the units as well)

4. Display of the informational storage units (Display may be from local or remote informational stores.)

5. Creation of new informational storage units. Libraries are involved in storage of ideas or knowledge. As new ideas are created libraries may be called upon to create the storage unit and to assist in the communication of these ideas.

In *Libraries of the Future* Licklider described types of libraries; he identified the "procognitive" system, the library system we are viewing, as one operating to promote and facilitate the acquisition, organization, and use of knowledge.[7]

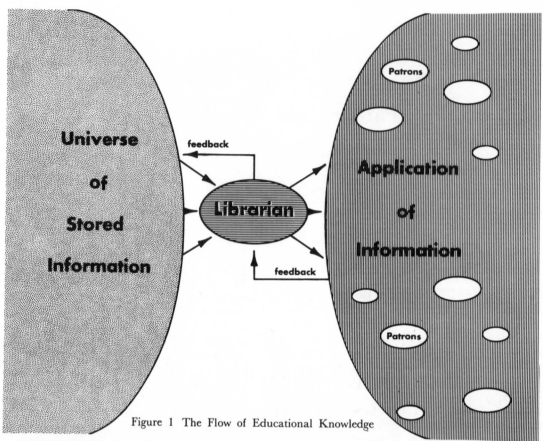

Figure 1 The Flow of Educational Knowledge

Generalizing from the preceding discussion of libraries as organizations which store and provide informational units, we can list the main types of libraries in which nonprint materials are found:

1. *Rental libraries* — these may be commercial or noncommercial. Generally 16mm motion pictures are the rented items. Commercial libraries may circulate the Hollywood variety of entertainment film or the information film. The patron may be charged the rental or in the case with sponsored commercial films, the depositing-sponsoring agency pays the library for each circulation. Noncommercial libraries are generally found at colleges, and their materials are circulated mainly to other educational agencies.

2. *Academic libraries* — frequently a mixed media collection of informational resources is provided through the library. In many cases the audiovisual center is a separate entity within the library with all nonprint materials listed in the master bibliographic file. In a few libraries the audiovisual materials, personnel, and administration are merged into the total resource center program.

3. *Academic nonprint library cooperatives* — a banding together of higher education institutions into a program to provide on a cooperative basis a collection of informational units. These arrangements may be as simple as informal borrowing (since little interlibrary loaning of nonprint materials takes place) or as elaborate as financial arrangements with pooled monies to develop a collection and provide personnel to operate the nonprint system.

4. *Common schools* — a large variety of nonprint resources are used in grades 1 through 12, and many school districts have centralized audiovisual collections which may be supplemented by materials from commercial or noncommercial libraries.

5. *School cooperatives* — operates as the equal to the academic nonprint library cooperative.

6. *Public libraries* — generally the most prominent nonprint resources are recordings of music or dramatic works. Many larger libraries have film and slide collections, and some even provide the patron with equipment he may check out to display the materials. Cooperative programs also have developed to

provide access for libraries to shared collections of films or other materials, nonprint in nature. Public libraries are a most likely contact point with a patron requesting information, and they should be a provider of data on what nonprint resources exist elsewhere and how they can be accessed.

7.   *Industrial and special libraries* — these collections are usually limited to the specific needs of the supporting agency, and most likely the material is available for in-plant use or as promotional material.

8.   *Government agencies* — often, on either the state or federal level, the individual agencies try to distribute nonprint materials to the public. In increasing numbers centralized distribution services are being developed between agencies. These agencies often are sources for considerable recorded history of operations significant to that agency.

9.   *Museums, galleries, historical societies* — nearly the total collections can be classified as nonprint (even old books when considered as a historical object and not the container of information). This is an amorphous combination of things, all valuable and usable.

10. *Private or personal collections* — often of value but most difficult to identify and organize as usable information stores accessible by patrons.

"The record of knowledge is now too extensive to be accommodated in a single library in a single form.[8] What we have described are varieties of libraries which store and provide on demand informational units of a nonprint nature. Identification of potential problems in the exchange of information in nonprint units can be factored into five topics: (1) "bibliographic" control, (2) personnel, (3) administrative, (4) technical, and (5) legal (political). The following sections will explore these five problem areas.

POTENTIAL PROBLEMS — POTENTIAL SOLUTIONS

The promise of the total information access is a most difficult construct for us to grasp. We have an awareness of many conveniences that will be afforded us and our patrons as we operate in information centers and as patrons negotiate for or request information from our stores — we can see operational assistance in cataloging, interlibrary loan, reference, information display; but without a doubt, we can see potential problems. If these problems facing the nonprint realm sound similar to those facing print, this is understandable when the informational unit (not specific storage medium) question is analyzed. Interlibrary communication and information networking will be concerned with stored information.

Bibliographic control, the essential element of organization of all library collections, is highly developed and applied in the print realm. Nonprint libraries (incorrectly called libraries in many cases) often are staffed by nonlibrarian personnel interested in the circulation of a limited-size collection to an identifiable patron group. There are almost as many bibliographic control systems for nonprint collections as there are collections.

Bibliographic control, when the word "bibliographic" is analyzed, is not applicable to nonbook resources. As the term is used for other than books, it is the reference to the construct of information cataloging or control that is being made. Bibliographic control, as it is used here, refers to the processing of information about the information contained in the multitude of storage devices stored ready for access in the library.

For the past few decades we have heard many explanations about why nonprint items could not be cataloged, classified, retrieved, provided to the patron, etc., like print informational units. Since libraries are a procognitive system designed to promote and facilitate the acquisition, organization, and use of knowledge, in each of these functions we are limited by the constraint that when information flows in or out of the library it must pass through people or their system.[9] In the print world there is agreement, generally, on how the bibliographic file representing the content of the collection is to be organized. In the nonprint world this is not quite so.

There are manuals (many manuals — all telling a different story) on how to organize and control nonprint collections. These "reinventions" of the wheel (or attempts to improve on the existing wheel) often are individualized systems that work at one place. Each manual has devotees. Each manual has good points. But they differ from each other in how they call for organizing the information on the library catalog card, or they disagree on the color of the card to represent different physical storage units (blue for slides — some are pink — and green for motion pictures), or they do not use color coding but rather use number coding or no coding. A few manuals base their systems on what is accepted for print. But many nonprint resource specialists, generally not professional librarians, reject the "print approach" — likewise many print librarians reinforce the nonprint person by agreeing that phonodiscs are so different from the printed scores of operas that they cannot be listed in the same "bibliographic" file.

Until a cataloging and/or bibliographic control system that provides the sophistication to meet the indexing, storage, and retrieval needs of information for nonprint informational units is developed, we will have problems. Likewise, as long as the content of print items is treated differently from nonprint, the patron will have difficulty in identifying the total informational store available to him. A unified bibliographic control system presenting information to the patron on the available information (in a wide variety of storage devices, possibly) in a library or system of libraries (or information stores) is an essential ingredient in interlibrary communication and information networking.

The Systems and Standards for the Bibliographic Control of Nonprint Media Institute, funded by the United States Office of Education, brought together library and audiovisual specialists from Canada, Great Britain, and the United States to study and educate themselves about this problem. This group found it difficult to accept the fact that the bibliographic control system for nonprint materials exists — it has been used for years with print materials, and nonprint librarians need to learn to apply it. Retraining of people to use the existing tools and to improve on them is the task that must be tackled.

Professional resistance, found whenever change is being considered, must be analyzed as we develop comprehensive mixed media information stores. In making reference to "book," we will need to learn to think of the generic idea of book with the word "book" representing the concept of informational storage device.[10] In all forms of library operation, except the act of display and physical storage, nonprint materials can be handled as physical objects to be warehoused (allowing for retrieval) and cataloged with retrieval addresses.[11] Ponder for a moment the Library of Congress with the sixty million items (books, serials, maps, photographs, recordings, films, and the like) and the world's largest file which contains 16.5 million records. There are 1,260 different files in use at the Library of Congress.[12] Can a mixed media collection of such magnitude exist? Can the bibliographic data on the informational content of the holdings be merged into a single file?

Within the American Library Association there has been much interest in the bibliographic control of nonprint materials. The Department of Audiovisual Instruction, DAVI (now the Association for Educational Communication and Technology) is extending its activities in the area of applying the principles of library-information science to nonprint resources and information. At the 1970 DAVI Convention, approval was granted to a group of nonprint librarians to form the Media Organization and Control Division. The activities of this division will be in the standardization of bibliographic control systems and the application of library science principles to nonprint resources.

Historically, with the possible exception of the Committees on Cataloging Audiovisual Material and on Information Science, members of the Association for Educational Communication and Technology, AECT, have tended to look on bibliographic organizational processes for nonprint media resources as logistic or high-class clerical tasks. Because of this, professionals concerned with the library and information science skills necessary for the bibliographic organization and control of nonprint media have, by default, turned to professional organizations other than AECT. As recently as 29 June 1970, the Executive Committee of the American Library Association's Cataloging and Classification Section, RTSD, unanimously passed a resolution recommending that the "Canadian Library Association publication, *Non-Book Materials* Preliminary edition), be accepted as an interim guide for the cataloging of nonbook materials, with the proviso that a permanent ALA-CLA committee be established to work on any necessary revision for the final edition and its supplements." Nowhere does the motion even acknowledge the existence of the Association for Educational Communications and Technology by either its present or former name. Space on the program already has been reserved at the 1970 annual meeting of the American Society for Information Science by those interested in forming an ASIS Special Interest Group to deal with problems of nonprint media and the application of information science techniques and technology to its organization and control.

The AECT must become involved with the problems of bibliographic control, as well as the hardware and techniques of educational communications. It is in a position to exert some influence over the numerous, uncoordinated efforts by various services, journals, and other professional organizations to provide information about the availability and utility of nonprint media. It can provide research and statistics concerning the software of educational communications and work with producers and indexers toward standardization of modes of access and user retrieval formats for such materials. It can provide the basis for informed legislation at the local and national levels such as that affecting the Library of Congress's ability to process nonprint materials and to incorporate them into their MARC output. It should work toward a national bibliographic service or system for nonprint media, with a sharp eye toward international implications, which will be able to inform any educator at any time of what is available, to whom, under what peculiar circumstances, and with what results for a specific patron.

Hesitancy to provide full access to nonprint materials available often is justified because, it is rationalized, the nonprint items are more easily damaged than print items, they are costly, and most nonprint items require display devices that may not be readily available. Without a doubt the book is the simplest to use (mechanically) information storage device we have, and it is often the least expensive for amount of information that can be stored. This does not justify excluding from use the more costly items. Today we provide patrons access to expensive print items without much formality — but we might require a deposit or we retain a library card when a patron checks out a sound filmstrip set (the book might cost $20 and the sound filmstrip, $30).

With familiarity through increased use, we will provide access to nonprint materials plus the needed display equipment. Continued technological developments will make the display equipment simpler to operate and more "goof-proof," thus helping prevent damage to the informational unit. Personnel in libraries need to be made aware that these nonprint items are nothing more than information storage devices. The audiovisual specialists need to quit implying how complex, expensive, and difficult to use the nonprint materials are, and the print librarians need to expand their horizons beyond their traditional realm of operation.

Awareness of the holdings in remote collections is as much a problem, if not more, in the realm of nonprint materials as in print. With so many print/nonprint collections existing without a merged holdings information file, the requester of information about a specific subject may receive information only about what is found in a certain storage medium. Union lists of nonprint holdings are a rarity today, but they are being developed as demands for nonprint material increase. In Washington State, for example, one of the groups operating under the State Library as plans for the Washington State Library Network are studied is examining the total nonprint holdings within the state. This group has identified clusters of nonprint materials and grouped these clusters of nonprint stores into a subject arrangement. A task yet to be tackled is the identification of specific items by title and content so that a complete subject-based union listing can be developed. These tasks will be furthered on the way to success when a standardized bibliographic information system is operative, simplifying the origination of bibliographic data and the sharing of this data.

It is interesting that libraries have developed information locating tools in fields where the frequency of demand justifies the production of these tools. Indexes, abstracts, data sheets, etc., exist in areas where society has recognized the urgency of need for information.[13] We are seeing the development of these tools for nonprint resources — the National Information Center for Educational Media listings of 16mm motion pictures, filmstrips, overhead transparencies, and the review services such as *Book Review Digest* or *Landers Film Reviews,* just to name a few. As needs increase, they become evident — as they become evident, they become demands and often are met.

Sources for bibliographic data usable in cataloging and related tasks are increasing. The MARC format now allows for handling certain nonprint items. In time the MARC Distribution System can become a source for bibliographic information on the total of all informational units generated and the MARC records for nonprint accessed and used like the records for print. Copyright procedures offer one means for refining the responsibilities of the creator of an informational unit in providing bibliographic data. It has been discussed by librarians and information specialists that funding for a research project to develop a model of a bibliographic control system for nonprint materials compatible with the existing print systems be sought. The results of this project would be to report to the information field what actually is being done, how it works, how it fits existing systems, and then to offer a heuristic model for bibliographic control of nonprint materials. The system, and model, would be a series of components with each component operating as a usable subsystem that could be part of other systems.

One of the powerful elements that must be considered in the development of a bibliographic control system is the commercial concerns functioning to provide library services. These organizations are affected by decisions on how libraries shall operate, and they influence our decisions. Examine the potential power and value of an operation such as the Xerox Bibliographic Products division in association with the others in the Xerox "family." Bowker produces considerable data essential to the operation of libraries by compiling lists — *Books in Print* and now the publication of the NICEM indexes — and providing information on current production activity in the information field (print now and nonprint in the immediate future). We find Professional Library Service, PLS, operating alongside of Bowker and Library Journal Cards. Combine their functions, let PLS operate as its name implies by providing professional library service in the form of contracted staff for special functions, materials selection, consultants, etc. Add to this the capabilities of Xerox Data Systems and University Microfilms. If we need to retrain staff or provide new skills, Xerox has a behavioral research division that can provide programs to do the training. After it is all said and done, we can

acquire hardware from Xerox to convert stored data into hard copy, duplicate copy, or transmit printed words by facsimile over distances both short and long. Commercial concerns do have a stake in our use of nonprint information.

Bibliographic control — the first gate through which we need to pass if we are to have interlibrary communication about and increased use of nonprint informational units — can be open. Libraries with new technologies can become the mechanisms for identifying what information the patron wants (needs), producing the information in usable form from storage, and providing the patron with freedom of interaction with information.[14]

Personnel with a wide variety of tasks and responsibilities operate our libraries. One of the obstacles to program change is personnel. They may be an obstacle in the implementation of interlibrary communication of information networking programs. A problem to be overcome as a total merging of information in our libraries takes place is the print orientation (rather than information orientation) of most practicing librarians. Librarians working with all media are involved in the process of extending the senses of man, his perceptions, and his total sensorium.[15] Library personnel serve a mediator role between information and user. The librarian in a procognitive library becomes a translator between the patron's perception of his need for information, the identification of the true need, accessing of the information, and then provision of the information in a manner most relevant to meet the specific needs of that specific patron. As a translator the librarian is more than the manager of the information store — he is involved in the use of information.

As Figure 1 implies, the librarian is between the universe of stored information and the application of that information by patrons. The librarian-translator is a feedback link between the user of information and the creator of information or the information store. Translators in our information centers will need to know much about the patron to help identify how he uses information in his cognitive processes, abilities of the patron to communicate an informational need, how to access information, and how to store new information for future access.

Audiovisual specialists have been permeating the information field for many years, and finally, the audiovisual specialist — who was only recently referred to as a gadgeteer — has almost become accepted as a professional peer with colleagues in the classroom.[16] Can we assume that he is being accepted by his library colleagues as a peer? Development of this peer relationship will be the responsibility of the audiovisual specialist. He must learn to apply the principles of library or information science to his operations with nonprint materials. He must make his skills available to librarians, helping them interact with informational stores and meet the needs of the patrons. He must become as competent as his library colleagues if he is to become a librarian.

We find, then, that the present operants in the library field may need retraining. Preservice training for the translators now in translator school (library school) must be modified to help them grasp an understanding of their role in the movement and application of information. They must become familiar with nonprint resources, and they need to know equipment operation so that they can display the nonprint materials. In this age of rapid technical change, as Husen and Boalt in their writings about educational change in Sweden indicate, we need to educate for an increased amount of technical know-how and possibly more important, for flexibility or ability to adapt to change.[17] We will experience a rapid increase in varieties of information storage systems and accessing techniques. The printed word has competition.

The end of the last decade saw man walk on the moon. Long before he had a record of this event in printed-word form, we on earth saw man step on the surface of the moon, the video tape recorders stored the sight and sound of this feat, computers and digital data records stored indication of the astronauts' heart rates, equipment read-outs, etc. The printed word lost the race to record history of man's first lunar step. As our informational glut — especially in the nonprint realm — increases, we must learn to cope with it.

As we develop personnel to serve as translators between a patron's true need for information and the provision of that information, as we develop information-oriented and not think-oriented librarians, and as we become familiar with the non-print information storage systems, we open the second gate between us on the path to information use, interlibrary communication, and information exchange.

The administration of our information center program can be viewed as the enabling activities that allow the library system to exist and meet the informational needs of patrons. Little can be said about the special aspects of library administration that is not as applicable to print as well as nonprint. A thing orientation, not information orientation, in library administration may complicate development of nonprint resource collections since most administrators of libraries, like the libraries themselves, are print- and thing-oriented. As this "thing" orientation is overcome, the administration can see the library acquiring informational units and therefore, provision of support for these units (be they print or nonprint) will follow. The administrative functions are much the same, but the mechanics of performing the functions will differ for print and nonprint.

The administrative gate between total information use and interlibrary communication is an easy one to open if administrators of information centers are sensitive to the needs of the patron group served and the developments within the information field.

Technological developments in the nonprint information field need not be new to have an impact on our information center programs. Within libraries the application of existing technologies represented by motion picture display, video or audio magnetic tape storage and display, photographic storage in color transparencies, closed-circuit television within a library to aid in communication, telephone for "long-distance" reference service, teletype for routine communication between information centers, or community antenna television systems for communication throughout a community have received less than desired attention.

Computers offer many potentials for library operation beyond management and bibliographic control. Computers can provide display of printed or graphic data. Libraries may even provide patrons with access to a local or remote computer via terminals. Employing the CATV system, for example, the patron remote from the library might access stored information or interact with a computer-stored learning program, or the patron might be switched by the local library's computer into an information network which then allows the inquiry to be met by the remote information store applicable. The extent to which the computer will function within the information system will be limited by the defined function of that system.

Storage systems for nonprint materials may take on a variety of forms depending on use of the storage device. Nonprint resources do not lend themselves well to browsing on the shelf; therefore, a closed-stack arrangement with high-density storage may be used. Access may be on a remote electronic basis such as in dial-access information retrieval systems where the patron accesses stored video or audio materials using a switching matrix to address the stored item. Interlibrary networks might carry high-traffic volume in video or audio materials via the electronic interlibrary connections.

Physical items in the nonprint realm are becoming smaller and simpler to store. Audio tape in cartridges or cassettes is more compact and less prone to damage by misuse than either open reel-to-reel tape or audio discs. Motion picture film in 16mm is not difficult to store, but an increasing number of 8mm films, smaller and less costly, are becoming available. In some cases 8mm film is stored in cartridges, further simplifying display and storage.

Display devices are increasing in dependability and becoming simpler to operate. Functions performed by the newly developed devices offer increased capabilities for interaction with stored information or people serving as resources. Telewriters may be interfaced with normal voice telephone lines allowing for the transmission of written documents to either a desk-top receiver or a receiver-projector allowing the remote image creator to draw an image for instant projection to a group of people. Coupled with interactive amplified telephone conversations, information can be exchanged between groups or individuals.

Videophone or two-way television allows for visual contact during communication, but each further allows for the "live" examination of objects. In reference work the questioning-negotiation associated with reference analysis might be expedited if the reference specialist could see the patron and see the materials to which he makes reference — likewise the patron could see the reference person and examine items with potential for solving the informational need. This video communication channel would allow for data transmission or video display as well.

Portable audio playback devices such as cassette players are inexpensive and fairly serviceable. They can be checked out along with the cassettes. Wireless headset units allow a patron in the library to listen to a recording being played while giving the patron freedom of movement throughout the library since he receives the program on a transmitted radio signal over his battery operated radio-headphones. Battery operated video tape recorders and players with monitors, 16mm sound filmstrips, cartridge 8mm sound projectors, video disc players, EVR's (electronic video recorders), etc. could be shown to have implications for libraries.

With telephone service in our information centers, the capability for total information exchange exists. Voice-grade telephone circuits can carry teletype signals or the analog signals of the telewriter devices. These existing circuits can become the distribution system for an audio information system. At Washington State University the decision was made in 1969 to develop a telephone-based dial-access audio system. To avoid the capital investment of wiring the library or city of Pullman, where WSU is located, arrangements were made with General Telephone and Electronics of the Northwest for the installation of a switching matrix allowing an operator to interconnect an incoming telephone line (or combination of lines) with a variety of audio playback sources. Now any telephone anywhere on or off campus can dial the listening library and listen to audio material. The system does not have adequate fidelity for music, but the solution to that problem will be explored in the discussion of CATV system applications. Washington State University pays a normal telephone charge for each phone line coming into the system — the telephone company maintains the system except for the program sources. Services, rates, disconnect orders, or repair are handled like normal telephone service.

Community antenna television systems provide coaxial cable interconnection between homes, schools, businesses, or libraries. The CATV systems generally are associated with the distribution of off-the-air television. The system can function in a much broader application for many forms of video, audio, or data communication. As part of the WSU system, the CATV system (commercially owned) is used to distribute video and/or audio programs from the university library, on demand or by schedule. If large numbers of patrons need to access an audio program or if the fidelity must exceed the telephone's capabilities, the program is carried via FM broadcast to the patron on the CATV system. As CATV systems start interconnecting and as commercial carriers start interconnecting these CATV systems, a network grid begins to develop.

VIDAC, a Westinghouse Learning Corporation development, holds interesting prospects for information storage and use. The VIDAC system is an integrated media system — print or still images, motion, sound — and it is compatible with present telephone or television technology. Information is stored on magnetic video tape in a compressed manner and when accessed, it is provided through a buffer which converts it from its digital storage medium to audiovisual material. The VIDAC system can store seventy-five color visuals on a few cents worth of magnetic tape. A fifteen-minute program can be sent to a remote buffer in three seconds, and the patron views the program in real time. The storage tapes can be duplicated. The buffer can be encoded to selectively receive and store only certain programs. For example, a mass of programs could be distributed over a broadcast TV station before start of the day's programming, and only those desired would be stored by the remote buffer storage system. The only major unique element in the VIDAC system is the buffer. In volume production the buffer might sell for $300 to $400.

Instructional television fixed service and satellites have applications for the distribution of library information. The ITFS systems have the capabilities of interconnecting a group of information centers with medium proximity to one another for the interchange of a wide range of information. Hughes Aircraft has proposed a high-power S band experiment for the ATS-G spacecraft. With this variety of satellite, libraries could, over a continental region, share masses of recorded information. Tech-

nologically, the satellite could serve as a repeater between the earth station which receives the signal from the information library and the receiving earth station that distributes it to the requesting library. The latter could then store the signal in a buffer device for the patron to access at a convenient time.

With satellites we shall pause. Communication technology, from the autothread 8mm sound projector to spacecraft, can carry any message we can design. We need to decide what messages are to be carried and for whom and what information storage units we want to access.

There is one possible caution. People are attracted by hardware, often without rationality, because it has a special appeal or excitement; as new hardware becomes available, there seem to be people who promote its use, promise potentials beyond reason, and apply it with only the weakest of rationales.[18] Another gate has been easily opened with the use of communication and materials display technology.

Legal and political aspects of information generation, storage, and use is the last gate on the path to full employment of nonprint resources in library communication systems. Legal and political aspects start with copyright. What will come out of the present deliberations? Will libraries exist as we know them today under the new copyright law? Will we be able to transmit stored information from the storage device to the patron under the new law? No one knows at this time. This may be a most difficult gate to open, especially when combined with the political-legal implications of funding the interlibrary communication and information network programs.

DEVELOPING IDEAS AND SYSTEMS

In Detroit during the 1970 Department of Audiovisual Instruction Convention, the first and second divisions of that organization were formed (unlike the American Library Association, DAVI had never instituted special interest divisions). The first division was Telecommunications and the second was Media Organization and Control. The Media Organization and Control Division should have a solidifying effect on the nonprint librarians within DAVI, and there might be created a closer working relationship between sections within ALA divisions as problems of common interest are tackled.

At a Joint Council on Educational Telecommunications meeting in March 1970, Clay Whitehead of the White House discussed the concern of the White House in telecommunications policy. At that time, Whitehead indicated that an Office on Telecommunications Policy, with a staff of about thirty, was to be established in the Executive Office of the President. This agency might have involvement with interlibrary networking programs or development of carrier systems employable for library communication.

A further step was taken in April of this year to develop audiovisual equipment performance standards when the ALA Library Technology Program signed an agreement with DAVI to jointly sponsor and finance the drafting of standards for record players, tape recorders and playback units, 16mm motion picture projectors, and filmstrip and combination filmstrip/slide projectors.

In Washington State two developments are worthy of mention. First, the Nonprint Resources Committee working with the

State Library in activities planning for a State Library Network is identifying clusters of nonprint informational resources within the state. All sources, not just formal libraries, are being identified, and techniques are being studied on how to establish a type of union listing of these clusters. Ultimately, specific holdings will be listed and merged into the total informational resources for the state. Second, Washington State University is investigating the possibility of a regional network for total communication. The prime function would be for people-communication via a two-way video system. The system would have additional capabilities for data transfer, and a minilibrary network has been proposed as a demonstration project if the WSU system becomes operational. This mininetwork would undoubtedly involve considerable use of nonprint materials between the involved information centers.

Edgar Dale, one of the pillars in the audiovisual-information field, said that "The good society is above all else a learning society, a society that is growing, moving forward on a rising curve....The good society encourages learning, does not prevent anyone from learning, provides access to learning for all."[19] We librarians have a responsibility to provide access to knowledge. We have an obligation to work with our patrons as they make use of information, regardless of the information's medium of storage.

NOTES

1. Sister M. Claudia Carlen, "Expanding resources: the explosion of the sixties," *Library trends* 18:49 (July 1969).

2. Clair L. Eatough, "What tomorrow's library will look like," *Nation's schools* 77:109 (March 1966).

3. Ibid.

4. T. N. Dupuy, *Ferment in college libraries: the impact of information technology* (Washington, D.C.: Communication Service Corporation, 1968), p.3-4.

5. C. Walter Stone, "The library redefined," *Library trends,* 16:183 (October 1967).

6. Ibid., p.181.

7. J. C. R. Licklider, *Libraries of the future* (Cambridge, Mass.: MIT Pr., 1965), p.21.

8. Ibid., p.21, 28.

9. Sister M. Claudia Carlen, "Expanding resources...," *Library trends,*

10. Sister Helen Sheehan, "The library-college idea: trend of the future," *Library trends* 18:93 (July 1968).

11. Robert S. Taylor, "Technology and libraries," EDUCOM bulletin 4:5 (May 1970).

12. Paul R. Reimers and Henriette D. Avram, "Automation and the Library of Congress: 1970," *Datamation* 16:138 (June 1970).

13. Ralph R. Shaw, "Using advances in technology to make library resources more available," in ALA, *Student use of libraries* (Chicago: ALA, 1964), p.73.

14. Nelson N. Foote, "The new media and our total society," in P. H. Rossi and B. J. Biddle, eds., *The new media and education: their impact on society* (Garden City, N.Y.: Doubleday and Co., Inc., 1967), p.400.

15. Hayden R. Smith, "Media men arise: what if McLuhan is right?" *Educational screen and audiovisual guide* 47:19 (June 1968).

16. James S. Martin, "The audiovisual department comes of age," *American school and university* 40:24 (Feb. 1968).

17. Torsten Husen and Gunnar Boalt, *Educational research and educational change: the case of Sweden* (New York: Wiley, 1967), p.31.

18. Robert M. Gagne, "Educational technology as technique," *Educational technology* 8:11 (15 Nov. 1968).

19. Edgar Dale, "The good society," *The newsletter* 34:1 (May 1969).

Reference Service in the Information Network

Charles A. Bunge

INTRODUCTION

Jesse Shera has defined reference service as the mediation by a librarian between two sets of structures—the need structures of users and the structure of information sources available to satisfy these needs. This paper will discuss such service within the context of the information network. The first section will outline the main phases of the process that has been developed over the years by reference librarians for the performance of reference service. This will be followed by a discussion of the impact that the development of multilibrary systems has had and that future network development might have on the reference process, along with mention of problems to be solved, direction that their solutions might take, and needed research. A brief final section will summarize the paper and offer the author's opinions on research that is most needed.

THE REFERENCE PROCESS

Rees has written that the "inability of questioners to formalize their information needs lies at the heart of the reference process".[1] This is a well-known phenomenon which has been discussed at length in the literature. Such inability is attributable to many factors, most of them as yet not clearly understood. It is very difficult for one to express what he does not know. Also, library users often do not know the extent of the information that can be brought to bear on their questions by the library. Both Taylor and Lancaster point out that patrons frequently will present questions that are overformalized, that is, questions that represent what the users think the system can give them rather than what they really need.[2] [3] Thus, a very early phase of the reference process is the exploration and attempt to improve the congruence between the stated question and the real information need of the patron.

Rees calls this phase the "librarian/questioner dialogue"[4]; Taylor refers to it as "question negotiation";[5] and many writers in traditional reference literature have called it the "reference interview." The appropriate aim of this part of the process seems to be twofold: One is to get a clear, narrative natural language statement of the user's information request;[6] the other is to gather a number of facts and clues to be used to amplify or refine this statement. For example, there are a number of personal characteristics of the questioner that will affect the

kind of information he might find useful. Also, knowledge of the anticipated use of the information requested can help the librarian refine the ultimate search. Lancaster found this latter point to be particularly true for the MEDLARS system.[7] Depending on the nature of the particular reference situation and the information requested, there are other such facts that usefully may be gathered or noted.[8]

The success of this phase of the reference process rests on the knowledge and skill of the reference librarian. A good part of this skill is skill in human communication, including the requisite sensitivity and preceptivity. Also important is his general knowledge of information users and the uses to which information is put. The librarian must have knowledge of the range of information that is available to satisfy the user's needs in order to know the dimensions along which the initial question should be negotiated or explored for clarification. Taylor has found that the subject knowledge of the librarian and the questioner's perception of the librarian's expertise are important to the question negotiation phase.[9]

As this clarification phase is going on, and based on its outcome, another phase of the reference process is taking place. This is what might be called a "translation phase." In this phase the natural language question and the elaborating facts and clues are transformed into a characterization of the information needed in the technical and formal terms of the information system.[10] Having a clear understanding of the information need from the user's point of view, the librarian must translate the request into a characterization of the information from the conceptual and organizational point of view of the librarian and the information system.

This phase also seems to have two components that are interrelated with each other and with the other phases of the reference process. The first of these components is the analysis, classification, or categorization of the question along various dimensions. For example, the question is categorized by subject, by the type of information needed (e.g., brief fact or statistic, synthesized or critical review, methodological discussion, etc.), and perhaps by a potential category of answering documents (e.g., handbook, monographic treatise, etc.), depending on how the librarian knows and views the contents of the system.

The other component of the translation phase of the reference process is that of actually choosing terms from the control and access language of the information system to represent the information need of the patron.[11] Lancaster has characterized this as indexing the question in a manner similar to the indexing that has been done on the documents that mighty eventually answer the question.[12]

The outcome of this phase is what Taylor has called the "compromised" question — that is, a representation of the inquirer's need within the constraints of and in the terms used by the system and its files. It is tempting for the librarian to attempt to combine this phase with the first phase and to help the patron translate his information need directly into the terms of the system. However, Taylor points out that "the compromised question is the information specialist's business...",[13] and Lancaster strongly makes the point that the subject-term list of the system should be used only *after* a clear natural language statement of the question has been obtained.[14]

The success of this phase of the reference process rests on mechanisms provided by the system to assist the librarian, as well as upon his knowledge and skill. Some things as subject-heading lists, cross-reference outlines, and the like can aid this process greatly, as can the availability of bibliographic devices to accommodate preliminarily searching that might be done to assist in translating the question. Also very crucial is the knowledgeability of the librarian concerning the subject indexing languages of the system, the organizational arrangements of the informational store, relationships between the contents of various types of material, etc.

A third phase of the reference process is that of formulating a search strategy to guide the search for the information. The previous phase might be said to constitute a specification of where (conceptually) in some structured body of information the answer to a question resides. This phase represents the design of a plan for getting to that location and for retrieving the information. The nature of this phase is greatly affected by the nature of the specific information system. In some systems the strategy involves devising a search only for citations to potential answering sources. In other systems there is a predominance of strategies where information itself is sought directly, as in a collection of reference books. Finally, the search strategy in some systems includes both the identification of citations to potential answering sources and the retrieval and exploitation of these sources.

In mechanized systems the design of the system places fairly strict constraints on the search strategies to be used for retrieving information. There is a large literature on search strategies, both from the point of view of the system designer and of the searcher. In manual or more traditional systems the formulation of search strategies by reference librarians seems to take place primarily at the subconscious level. The process seems to be one of identifying potential answering document classes, weighing their relative probability of supplying the answer, assessing the procedure necessary for retrieving documents (e.g., use of the library catalog, use of periodical indexes, direct browsing of the shelves, etc.), and deciding on the order in which search steps (at least initial or major ones) will be taken. One standard text says that this is a process of forming a series of hypotheses as to the probable answering source, which are tested in the search.[15]

The next phase of the reference process to be mentioned is the conduct of the search itself. Lancaster distinguishes between "browsing" searches and "one-chance" searches.[16] The former, whether personally conducted by the user himself or delegated to the librarian, is characteristic of the traditional library operation and points up the complex and dynamic relationships among the various phases of the reference process. This type of search often is begun with only a minimal preparation of a formal search strategy, and even that search strategy (as well as the terms into which the question has been translated) is modified and guided by the information found as the search progresses. When the librarian conducts the search, he seems to browse on behalf of the requester, making relevance judgments based on his perception of the user's needs.[17] [18] The "one-chance" search is typical of the noninteractive mechanized system, where a search is formulated and then delegated to the computer to be carried out, with no chance for browsing or changing the search as it progresses. If the completed search is not successful, a modified strategy must be formulated and another search conducted.

If the search produces useful information, the reference process includes the phase of delivering the information to the user, including any interpretation, condensation, integration, or other "repackaging" performed by the librarian. The amount of this latter component that is performed is usually a policy matter of the library. It also depends on how much the user trusts the librarian's ability to do such work. Depending on the library, the answer can be delivered as a simple verbal answer, as a bibliography (with or without annotations or abstracts), in the form of one or more documents known or expected to contain the answer, or as an integrated report based on several sources.

Throughout the reference process, as outlined, relevance predictions and judgments have been made. The final phase of the process to be discussed, then, is that of the assessment of the relevance of information to the requester's needs. In searches where there is little interaction between the librarian and the user during the search, this phase has two fairly distinct components. As the search progresses, the librarian makes judgments concerning the relevance of the information found to the information request negotiated or agreed to by the user and the librarian. Then, at the end of the search, the requester is asked to judge the information produced as to its relevance to his actual information need. Shera and Rees call the former the "evaluation of relevance" and the latter, "evaluation of pertinence." They point out that it is possible for an answer to be entirely relevant to the question put to the system and yet not at all pertinent to the user's real need.[19] In a system where the patron and librarian interact throughout the reference process, these two types of judgment are not so distinct since the librarian's and user's judgment can be made together.

Though not really a part of the reference process, in the narrow sense of the term used here, it is very important that results of the relevance and pertinence judgments be used in the evaluation and improvement of the reference or information system. The reference librarian is a key figure in this feedback process. There is, of course, a very large literature on information system evaluation, and a summary of it here would be inappropriate.

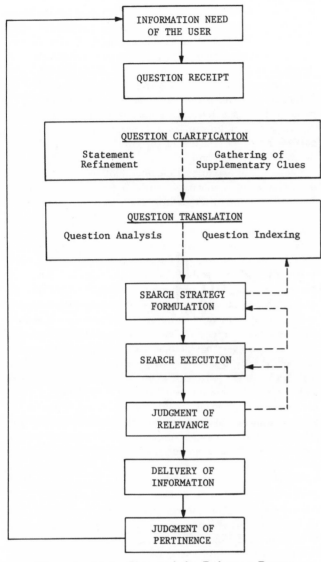

Figure 1   Major Phases of the Reference Process

INTERACTIVE MECHANIZED SYSTEMS

The preceding discussion has been couched in terms of the necessity for human mediation by a reference librarian between the user and the information system. There is currently a great deal of research being done on interactive, question-answering information systems where the functions outlined above are to be handled by man-machine interaction.[20] [21] At the present time, most such systems in existence seem to be experimental or developmental and to be based on relatively small data bases. One operational system that is not fully interactive but which does have a large data base and on-line search formulation dialogue capabilities is the SUNY Biomedical Communications Network.[22]

For a number of reasons, it would seem that the interactive mechanized system will not immediately obviate the need for the reference librarian in the network. For one thing, the network is likely to be composed of a number of subsystems, each containing a different type of information with its own file configuration and indexing language. For example, a study for the Far West Laboratory for Educational Research and Development concluded that organization and operation of a single system which would incorporate all sources of information in education and would use one indexing system is not feasible in view of the present state of the taxonomy of educational information.[23] Thus, even if widespread development of interactive systems based on various data bases were to come about, it would seem that some human mediation would be necessary to help the user choose between appropriate components of the network.

In the SUNY Biomedical Communications Network, the assistance of a reference librarian is frequently sought by users, and it is expected that this will continue to be the case.[24] Project Intrex proposes that in the interim before the ultimate interactive system exists (an interim that Salton sees as a long one),[25] the command "HELP" should connect the user to a human reference librarian.[26] Garfield, Amey, and Rees all argue for the continued necessity of human mediation in mechanized information systems.[27] [28] [29] Thus, it is the contention of this paper that rather than replace the reference librarian on-line interactive systems can be used in the network to support and improve the human reference librarian's performance. Support for this contention will be developed in various paragraphs of the remainder of the paper.

THE EFFECTS OF NETWORK DEVELOPMENT

The development of multiunit library systems has had striking effects on reference service, and future network development will cause further changes. One of the most dramatic effects is the provision of legal access to greatly augmented sources of information at the local level. This has been the major *raison d'etre* of library system development, is its most mature aspect, and undoubtedly will be discussed in detail in various other papers prepared for this Conference. While the major attention in the literature has been given to the various arrangements whereby the collections of other, usually larger or more specialized, libraries and information centers are made accessible to local libraries, another aspect of augmented information availability is likely to assume increasing importance in the future. This is the expansion of resources resulting from the fact that the larger financial base of the network can facilitate acquisition or provision of access to information sources previously too costly for any of the individual units, and that the widened base of user groups that comes with network development can justify provision of information services previously considered uneconomical by individual units (in addition to the fact that sometimes need for or existence of information services were previously unknown to the local units).

An example of the possibilities of this latter aspect of network information ability is access to the increasing amount of information available in machine-readable or machine-manipulatable form. Either as a by-product of the regular publishing process or as specifically converted-for-information system use, very large amounts of document text and raw data in such forms are becoming available for analysis and retrieval. For example, the *New York Times* organization has announced plans to offer mechanized access to a vast amount of information from its files;[30] the availability of such sources as the Chemical Compound Registry, census data, and manufacturers' catalogs in machinable forms is widely known; and Project INTREX plans include experimentation with a computerized handbook based on machinable text.[31] Social sciences data archives, containing largely machine-readable data, are the subject of another paper for this Conference. Certainly expanded financial and user-group bases of networks are going to be necessary for the effective exploitation of these sources.

Of more immediate importance, perhaps, than some of the developmental sources mentioned above are the many sources of bibliographic information presently available in digital form. In addition to the more frequently mentioned examples of organizations offering machine-readable bibliographic records—such as Chemical Abstracts Service, BioSciences Information Service, Engineering Index, Inc., and Institute for Scientific Information—the Committee on Scientific and Technical Information lists as examples some eighteen services by eleven private organizations and seven governmental agencies,[32] and a committee of the ALA has compiled a directory to the data bases of some eighteen organizations.[33] Russell Shank has pointed out that attention must be given to the exploitation of such resources by libraries to avoid excluding potential users who lack extensive financial backing from very important sources of information.[34] Networks would seem to be the natural mechanism for such exploitation, perhaps through the services of such "retail" processing and program development services as are being developed at IIT and the universities of Georgia, Iowa, Louisville, and Pittsburgh.[35 36 37]

Another important type of information source that networks can make more widely available is that of human and institutional resources, i.e., information residing in the minds of people, such as consultants, subject specialists, experts, and agencies. Existing multilibrary systems with extensive reference services have discovered the importance of this type of source.[38] [39] A particularly interesting example of the potential in this area is the Medical Communications Center at the University of Wisconsin Medical Center, through which doctors in the state can dial some 200 brief and up-to-date presentations on problems confronted in day-to-day practice. Also, the center offers regularly scheduled telephone/radio conferences on important and timely topics.[40] It has been pointed out that the present invisible college information exchange system discriminates against those who are isolated, young, not well established in their profession, or simply not aggressive.[41] Efforts by the network to exploit personal sources of information can mitigate such discrimination.

To summarize and to reiterate what has been said repeatedly in the literature, the network can offer the needer of information, through a convenient local outlet, the whole range of information sources that have been developed nationally to serve information needs. The task of network designers, it would seem, is basically to build into the network the ability for each node to put all requesters into effective contact with information appropriate to their needs while encouraging the development of node specialization (so that each node can handle locally the optimum percentage of the needs of its unique user group, whether geographic or subject, and can contribute meaningfully

to overall network strength). This implies, among other things, that the "democratization of information" should not result merely in a leveling of information resources but in the protection and strengthening of major resources while making them readily available.[42]

The mediation between this vastly augmented store of information and the patron with his individual needs will be performed by the reference librarian using the same basic process as that outlined in the early part of this paper. The next part of the paper will discuss the effects on this process that network development might have.

Verner Clapp has argued the desirability of libraries having the qualities of simplicity in their appeal or functions and conspicuity in their availability.[43] Network development might permit this if every one of the many library outlets becomes simply a place to which one can turn when in need of information of any sort. Even the beginnings in this direction made so far mean that the librarian in a given local outlet is confronted with a greatly broadened spectrum of information needs to mediate. On the other hand, it can also mean that the patron has not had to choose on his own among the bewildering variety of different types of libraries, each willing to handle a different narrow range of information needs. Thus, perhaps relatively fewer patrons will come to the reference situation with requests already overformalized by the process of having to make ill-informed judgments as to what various libraries will and will not do. Also, if network development results in a new (more positive) view of the library as a place to go for information service of all kinds, as anticipated by Becker and Hayes,[44] fewer overformalized questions resulting from lack of confidence in the library's and the librarian's ability should be the case.

One of the most complex problems of network design is that of determining at what node levels the various phases of the reference process should be carried out. This is certainly true of the question clarification phase. Amey has pointed out that the Socratic method of perceptive dialogue between human beings is acknowledged universally to be the most effective means for clarifying information requests.[45] However, it will undoubtedly remain the case for some time to come that many library outlets are not staffed with personnel having the knowledge and skill necessary to accomplish this successfully.

There would seem to be three basic approaches to the solution of this problem in the network. One is to use written instructions on a request form to guide the user in formulating a clear statement of his request and in giving other indications of his information need. Lancaster has emphasized the importance of this approach in the MEDLARS system.[46] Another approach is for the network to offer programs of in-service training to help lower-node staff gain the skill necessary to help users clarify their requests. While there is little literature on this subject, the author's experience and conversations with librarians indicate that current practice emphasizes a combination of these two, with attempts being made to improve request forms and to train personnel in their use. Finally, the rapid communications apparatus of the network can be used to put the user into direct contact with a higher node for dialogue with a properly knowledgeable librarian. Gaines suggests this approach in the metropolitan network.[47] While it would seem that this would be the most effective approach, where communication costs permit it, more research on the matter is needed. Lancaster, for example, argues the necessity of a written statement even when a librarian is available for consultation.[48] In any case, the effectiveness of this phase is hampered by our incomplete and imprecise knowledge of the relation between user characteristics and information needs so that it is difficult to know which user characteristics are important to note, either personally or on a written form.

At whatever node question clarification occurs, it requires that the librarian have knowledge of the wide range of information available and the ability to use such knowledge to help the patron clarify his request. Presently, gaps in such knowledge (gaps that are understandable in view of the magnitude of potential sources) inhibit the effectiveness of the reference librarian.[49] It is here that the on-line, interactive feature of components of the network can be of great assistance to the librarian. The librarian can use interaction with the various components to augment his knowledge of network resources and thus enhance the clarification process. For example, knowing quantitatively the amount of material in the store relating to a question as initially stated can have a dramatic effect on its restatement.[50]

The translation phase of the reference process also will be greatly affected by network development. In the single-unit situation, the librarian is fairly familiar with the materials available and tends to translate the question into document classes with answering potential or even into one or more potential documents. In the network, where the information sources are of all types and formats, it would be preferable for the librarian to think in terms of the information needed rather than in terms of formats or documents. This requires, on the part of the librarian, a type of knowledge about information that is not well developed in the profession and which must receive increased attention.

Even in the single library, one of the most important skills required of the reference librarian is the ability to move from one indexing language to another, such as from the library's catalog to various periodical indexes, bibliographies, etc. The importance of such translation skill is increased greatly by the network with its multiplicity of subsystems, each with its own indexing language and system constraints. A number of network capabilities can assist the reference librarian in this area. For those components of the network that have been computerized and with which the librarian can establish on-line contact, he can call up displays of term relationships, language structures, etc. For manual or off-line components, thesauri or subject-heading lists are invaluable. Also, with the increasing prevalence of user-oriented information services for very specific user groups, such as information analysis centers, the translation process can sometimes be one of placing the requester in the appropriate user group and referring his question to one of these services for further processing and answering.

This brings up the matter of the appropriate node at which the translation phase of the reference process should take place. Lower-node staff often lack the broad knowledge of information resources necessary for adequate translation. Also, the bibliographic resources available at local nodes often are quite limited. Thus, if the translation phase is carried out at the lower

network nodes, it often results in the transmission of overly narrow or otherwise inadequate requests to higher levels. On the other hand, higher nodes, which have the requisite bibliographic resources, often lack the manpower necessary to service the inquiries from other nodes.[51] In addition, the staff of libraries at higher levels often lack the familiarity with the needs of special user groups that is necessary for adequate translation of questions from other types of libraries.[52]

In networks, this problem has been attacked from a number of angles. An early solution was to supply referring libraries with bibliographic tools, such as subject bibliographies, union lists and catalogs, and the like. As Clapp points out, this allows the facilities of one library to be extended to the patrons of another without the diversion of the reference manpower of the first.[53] However, this still requires knowledge and skills sometimes not available at the lowest nodes of the network. Another response to the problem has been to have a designated node in the network receive untranslated questions, translate them with the use of skilled staff and bibliographic resources, and transmit the translated requests to appropriate answering nodes. This is typically a function of the state library agency in statewide public library systems.

Still another approach is to have additional staff added to the nodes of the network having substantial resource strength. This staff can include members familiar with the needs of the user groups with which the requests have originated. Since these staff members often not only translate a reference request into a more formalized statement but also formulate search strategies and carry out other phases of the reference process, further discussion of this mechanism will be delayed.

The author's experience and contracts with library system personnel have shown that even the most skilled staff is at a disadvantage in translating the question when at a distance from the patron. Again, the communications capabilities of the network should be used to establish patron-librarian contact so that they may interact through the early phases of the process. On the other hand, it would seem uneconomical for the patron to interact routinely with network nodes at great distances. What will most likely result is regional concentrations of staff skill, bibliographic resources, and communications capabilities. At these regional centers, appropriate portions of the reference process will be performed by the reference librarians in interaction with the user, and the remainder will be performed by the reference librarians on behalf of the user, in interaction with the rest of the system (in those cases where the need cannot be satisfied from local or regional resources).

In any case, translated questions undoubtedly will be transmitted from one node of the network to another. It is important that the language used in such transmission deals with very basic information and user-need categories and concepts rather than with the overly narrow format and document categories presently typical. Unfortunately, our present knowledge of information and its use does not facilitate this approach.

The formulation of the search strategy and conduct of the search for information is a very complex phase of the reference process in the network. It is at this point where the librarian must devise a strategy to exploit the broad range of resources in the network to serve the user's need. One of the most serious inadequacies in present network development is the lack of knowledge on the part of network librarians concerning the resources available in the network and the constraints surrounding their availability.[54] Networks are attempting to solve this problem by instituting directory services. For example, the METRO network in New York City has established the Central Advisory and Referral Service, CARES, which provides member institutions with information about library resources in the metropolitan area. It publishes catalogs and directories, gives information verbally, and assists librarians of member institutions in developing search strategies on behalf of their users.[55] In addition, this center has established liaison with directory and referral services at the national level.[56] Other multiunit systems have established similar services.

As mentioned under question translation, concentrations of resources and staff with the skill to exploit their potential are very important to the formulation and execution of searches in network operations. This can be accomplished in a number of ways. Large or specialized libraries can simply accept the responsibility to serve the needs of users of other libraries and augment their staffs and resources as needed. This seems to be the case with the Indiana Biomedical Information Program, wherein the Indiana University School of Medicine Library is part of a statewide teletype network which enables biomedical requests to be referred to this library from local public libraries.[57] The Countway Medical Library is the locus for intellectual strength in a medical library network in New England.[58] The financial strength offered by network development can be used to compensate these resource centers for the additional staff time and resources required so that service to their primary clientele is not diluted.

Another approach is to have network personnel housed in the resource center so that they may use the resources of the center in an interactive way to formulate and execute searches. For example, in 1964 a Technical Information Center opened at each of four, major public libraries in Tennessee, where qualified librarians handled requests relayed from other libraries.[59] As other examples, the Wayne County Intermediate School District maintains an office in Wayne State University's education library,[60] and the Chicago Public Library houses system staff of a suburban multilibrary system.[61] Finally, specialized regional information centers can be created for the purpose of formulating and conducting searches. Such a center is the Regional Information System of the Michigan-Ohio Regional Educational Laboratory, MOREL.[62] This center does not possess extensive stores of actual information but is composed of searching tools necessary to identify and locate such information on request. This and other such centers have been called "switching centers," a concept which is the subject of another Conference paper.

In present network operations, with their inhibitions and inabilities to fully utilize rapid communications technology, the formulation and execution of the search is typically delegated by the librarian at a lower node to personnel at the resource center or switching center and is often further delegated to a specialized information source for actual search. Thus, for the librarian at the lower node, this search is much like the "one-chance" search of the mechanized system. As is well known, this situation leads to frequent relevance and pertinence problems. There seem to be two interconnected approaches to the solution

of this problem: One is to have the user interact with the system up to a point as late in the total process as possible. Lancaster found that interaction by the user after his having seen the results of a preliminarily or partial search is desirable.[63] The other approach is to move from the delegated, one-chance type search to the browsing type search of upper-level resources by the reference librarian on behalf of the user. With the development of on-line, real-time computerized system for certain components of the network, facsimile transmission of text for other components, and other such uses of communication technology, it should be possible for the librarian to conduct such browsing type searches through a fairly large percentage of the network's resources.[64] This seems to imply, as was outlined previously, a regional center of one sort or another where reference librarians interact with users at lower nodes and with resources at higher nodes (or with other specialized nodes). The design of communications configurations to achieve such a process is a very complex matter and one hopes, a matter to be treated by this Conference.

The expanded financial and user group base offered by networks should affect greatly the delivery of information in answer to user needs. In most current network operations there is a separation (physically, or at least in terms of response time) between the store of information and the bibliographic and directory access devices. This prevents the kind of smooth and fast interaction outlined between the components of the network.[65] Often after having identified a document with a high potential for answering a user's needs, it is a matter of days before the network can deliver it to the user. The delivery service by truck and other surface means that are a common feature of present library systems have cut this to a matter of hours in some instances, but even this frequently is too long.

Technology seems to be developing along several lines that have application to this problem. Various electrical means of transmitting information — some of which may be discussed in other Conference papers — are under development. High priority should be given to testing their applicability to information network problems. Such studies as that for METRO in New York on the possibilities of video information transfer systems for libraries and information centers offer promise;[66] others undoubtedly will be needed.

Also, network development should make it feasible for a great many more local outlets to deliver information that has been interpreted or "repackaged" to meet the needs of specific users and user groups. The distinction between simply disseminating documents and the recasting of information to adapt it to the needs of users, as well as the case for the necessity of the latter, has been well made by the Committee on Scientific and Technical Communication.[67] Most library outlets, because of basic philosophical orientation or because of inadequate staff depth and expertise, have not gone much beyond providing information as it appears in retrieved documents. Some libraries, particularly those serving specialized client groups, do offer such services, and other libraries might do so if the user groups to whom they were relevant were expanded. In addition, institutions intended for such analysis, reviewing, and repackaging (increasingly referred to as information analysis centers) have developed in rather large numbers and probably will continue to increase. The library network can make the products of these libraries and information analysis centers widely available, and can tap the expertise of such institutions for the benefit of local users. The EDUCOM proposal for an agricultural sciences information network outlines the role of the information analysis centers component in the network.[68]

The phase of the reference process characterized as relevance and pertinence evaluation has been dramatically affected by network development. As already mentioned, in present network operations a great deal of the reference process is delegated from user to system and among various nodes of the system. This means that in all too many cases the material ultimately retrieved, after a great deal of system effort and expense, is not pertinent to the user's needs. Frequently, too, the user has waited so long for the material that he is unwilling to initiate another search.

The use of rapid communications capabilities to improve the interactive ability of networks has been mentioned several times. As indicated, this ability will allow the user to make preliminarily pertinence judgments along the way, to have these judgments acted upon by the reference librarian, and to have a quicker response to his evaluation of the ultimate output. As with the single-unit system, it is important that the network have a feedback mechanism whereby such pertinence judgments can be used for the improvement of the network.

The reference process probably always will involve some amount of relevance judgment by the reference librarian on behalf of the user, particularly in the network. Experimental evidence suggests that for both the information system specialist and the nonuser subject specialist, the accuracy of such judgments is far less than 100 percent accurate.[69] There is, of course, a great deal of research currently being done on relevance judgment which might eventually improve this situation. It is the author's belief that our inability to make accurate relevance judgments on behalf of users rests on an inability to characterize user needs and information units effectively, a requisite to predicting relationships between them.

SUMMARY AND CONCLUSION

This paper has attempted to discuss the impact of information network development on the reference process. The reference process typical of a single-unit library was outlined as a process wherein the reference librarian interacts with the user to clarify his information need and then, in turn, searches the resources of the library in a browsing mode, interacting frequently with the user for assessments of pertinence. One of the main limiting factors here has been the relatively small amount of informational material the single library can bring to bear on a reference problem. The development of multilibrary systems has increased greatly the amount of material to which the user has legal access through his local library. This phase of library development has reached some maturity.

To change this legal access to effective access, the user again needs the services of the reference librarian. Unfortunately, these services have been hampered by factors of distance and time that have accompanied multilibrary system development. The librarian having direct contact with the user often lacks the knowledge, skill, and bibliographic resources necessary for adequately receiving and referring the request. The librarian with the requisite skill and proximity to resources is separated from the patron and the pertinence judgments that he can offer. Finally, the materials identified as potentially useful to the requester may take days (or weeks) to reach him. The paper has indicated that the effective use of modern communications technology can allow the reference process in the network to approximate that of the single-unit system (in its interactive, quick-response nature), while helping the user to make effective use of a very wide spectrum of information resources.

However, a problem which has hampered the effectiveness of reference service in the single library also will hamper the development of reference services in the network. This is our lack of basic knowledge concerning information, its users, and the uses to which it is put. At several points in the discussion the inhibiting effect of this situation on one or another phase of the reference process has been mentioned. (Many of the other very serious problems to be solved in network reference services, e.g., compatibility, and hardware and software configurations, have not been mentioned or have been glossed over because they are topics to be treated in other Conference papers.)

Paisley has correctly identified the basic difficulty in this area as a lack of abstract concepts on which fruitful theories and hypotheses can be based.[70] With regard to users of information, we have not been able, as Paisley says, to move beyond the labels such as "basic" versus "applied," "scientist" versus "technologist," and "formal" versus "informal".[71] Concerning information itself, there have not been sufficient typological or taxonomic investigations to move beyond the labels used in reference book lists (handbooks, encyclopedias, dictionaries, etc.) or gross format labels (book, journal, film, etc.). Thus, one wishing to hypothesize regarding the relationships between user characteristics and information use is lacking in concepts and constructs for both the independent and dependent variables.

To paraphrase Paisley again, network designers can incorporate knowledge of information users and uses into network planning in two ways: First, they can be studied after the fact to explain why the system is not working well. Second, such knowledge can become the network's foundation, and the later developmental stages can be tested to see if they rest securely on this foundation. Unfortunately, early and sustained attention to concepts and theories concerning information and its users and uses will be necessary before this second approach can be applied

NOTES

1. Alan M. Rees, "Broadening the spectrum," in W. B. Linderman, ed., *The present status and future prospects of reference/information service* (Chicago: ALA, 1967), p.59.

2. Robert S. Taylor, *Question-negotiation and information-seeking in libraries,* (Studies in the man-system interface in libraries, no. 3, [Bethlehem, Pa.: Lehigh Univ., Center for Information Sciences, 1967]), p.9.

3. F. W. Lancaster, *Evaluation of the MEDLARS demand search service* (Washington, D.C.: U.S. Dept. of Health, Education, and Welfare, Public Health Service, 1968), p.111.

4. Alan M. Rees, "Broadening the spectrum," p.58.

5. Robert S. Taylor, *Question negotiation....*

6. F. W. Lancaster, *Evaluation of the MEDLARS....*

7. Ibid., p.116.

8. Vladimir Slamecka, "Methods of research for design of information networks," *Library trends* 18:13-19 (May-June 1967).

9. Robert S. Taylor, *Question negotiation...*, p.9.

10. Jesse H. Sherra, "The challenging role of the reference librarian," in Texas Library Association, *Reference research and regionalism* (Austin: Texas Library Assoc., 1966), p.29.

11. Ibid., p.29, 32.

12. F.W. Lancaster, *Evaluation of the MEDLARS...*, p.5.

13. Robert A. Taylor, *Question negotiation....*

14. F.W. Lancaster, *Evaluation of MEDLARS...*, p.111-115.

15. Margaret Hutchins, *Introduction to reference work* (Chicago: ALA, 1944), p.30-32.

16. F. W. Lancaster, *Information retrieval systems* (New York: Wiley, 1968), p.181-182.

17. Ibid.

18. Alan M. Rees, "Broadening the spectrum."

19. William J. Paisley, "Information needs and uses," in C. A. Cuadra, ed., *Annual review of information science and technology* (Chicago: Britannica, 1968), p.29.

20. National Academy of Sciences - National Academy of Engineering, Committee on Scientific and Technical Communication, *Scientific and technical communication* (Washington, D.C.: The Academy, 1969), p.228-229.

21. Gerard Salton, *Automatic information organization and retrieval* (New York: McGraw-Hill, 1968), p.7.

22. Wallis E. Bridegam, Jr. and Erick Meyerhoff, "Library participation in a biomedical communications and information network," *Bulletin of the Medical Library Association* 58:103-111 (April 1970).

23. George H. Grimes, *Information services; a survey of the history and present status of the field* (Detroit: Michigan-Ohio Regional Educational Laboratory, 1969), p.28.

24. Wallis E. Bridegam, Jr. and Erick Meyerhoff, "Library participation...," p.106-107.

25. Gerald Salton, *Automatic information organization...*, p.412-413.

26. C. F. J. Overhage and R. Joyce Harmon, *INTREX: report of a planning conference on information transfer experiments* (Cambridge: MIT Pr., 1965), p.98.

27. Eugene Garfield, "The role of the medical librarian in SDI systems," *Bulletin of the Medical Library Association* 57:348-351 (Oct. 1969).

28. Alan M. Rees, "Broadening the spectrum," p.64.

29. Gerald X. Amey, "Channel hierarchies for matching information sources to users' needs," in *Proceedings of the American Society for Information Science, vol. 5,* (New York: Greenwood, 1968), p.13.

30. Stephen E. Furth, "[conference speech]" in North Country Reference and Research Resources Council *New developments in information services* (Summer Conference, Potsdam, N.Y. 12-13 June 1969), p.22-25.

31. C. F. J. Overhage and R. Joyce Harmon, *INTREX:...*, p.59.

32. National Academy of Sciences - National Academy of Engineering, Committee on Scientific and Technical Communication, *Scientific and technical communication,* p.222-224.

33. American Library Association, Reference Services Division, Science and Technology Reference Services Committee, *A guide to a selection of computer-based science and technology reference services in the U.S.A.* (Chicago: The Committee, 1969), 29p.

34. Russell Shank, "Library services to industry: a view from New York City," *Bookmark* 27:269-273 (Apr. 1968).

35. "Information center profile: Chemical Abstracts Service," *Scientific information notes* 2:79-81 (Mar.-Apr. 1970).

36. "Information center profile: Computer Search Center (CSC)," *Scientific information notes* 1:107-110 (May-June 1969).

37. Stella Keenan, "Abstracting and indexing services in science and technology," in C. A. Cuadra, ed., *Annual review of information science and technology* (Chicago: Britannica, 1969), p.273-303.

38. Richard Coenenberg, "Synergizing reference service in the San Francisco Bay region," *ALA bulletin* 62:1379-1384 (Dec. 1968).

39. Nadine Greenup, "System-level reference service: a case study," *California librarian* 30:237-238 (Oct. 1969).

40. William J. Paisley, "Information needs and uses," p.29.

41. *Communication systems and resources in the behavioral sciences* (Publication 1575 [Washington, D.C.: National Academy of Sciences, 1967]), p.14.

42. Joseph Becker and Robert M. Hayes, *A proposed library network for Washington State* (n.p., 1967), p.5.

43. Verner W. Clapp, "Public library systems and the national library networks," in B. Hoyt and L. Dudgeon, eds., *Realities of the public library systems concept in Wisconsin* (Madison: Wisconsin Div. for Library Services, 1968), p.106-107.

44. Joseph Becker and Robert M. Hayes, *A proposed library network...,* p.6.

45. Gerald X. Amey, "Channel hierarchies...," p.13.

46. F. W. Lancaster, "MEDLARS demand search service," p.13.

47. Ervin J. Gaines, "The large municipal library as a network," *Library quarterly* 39:43 (Jan. 1969).

48. F.W. Lancaster, *Evaluation of the MEDLARS...*, p.193.

49. Alan M. Rees, "Broadening the spectrum," p.62.

50. J. C. R. Licklider, "Man-computer interaction in information systems," in M. Rubinoff, ed., *Toward a national information system* (Washington, D.C.: Spartan, 1965), p.68-69.

51. Verner W. Clapp, "Some thoughts on the present status and future prospects of reference work," in W. B. Linderman, ed., *The present status and future prospects of reference/information service* (Chicago: ALA, 1967), p.8.

52. Russell Shank, "Library services to industry...," p.271.

53. Verner W. Clapp, "Some thoughts on the present status...," p.9.

54. Russell Shank, "Library services to industry...," p.270.

55. John Mackenzie Cory, "The network in a major metropolitan center (METRO, New York)" *Library quarterly* 39:90-98 (Jan. 1969).

56. L. Dawn Pohlman, "Special libraries and METRO," *Bookmark* 28:184 (Mar. 1969).

57. Virginia Gillette, et al., "The Indiana biomedical information program," *Bulletin of the Medical Library Association* 58:60-64 (Jan. 1970).

58. T. Mark Hodges, Charles C. Colley, and Harold Bloomquist, "NERMLS: the first year," *Bulletin of the Medical Library Association* 57:331 (Oct. 1969).

59. Nelson Associates, Inc., *Public library systems in the United States* (Chicago: ALA, 1969), p.173.

60. G. Flint Purdy, "Interrelation among public, school, and academic libraries," *Library quarterly* 39:61 (Jan. 1969).

61. "Of note," *American libraries* 1:510 (June 1970).

62. George H. Grimes, "The regional information system in education: its background, structure, development and implementation," in J. B. North, ed., *Proceedings of the American Society for Information Science* (vol. 6 [Westport, Conn.: Greenwood, 1969]), p.387-398.

63. F. W. Lancaster, *Information retrieval systems,* p.189-190.

64. *Ibid.,* p.191.

65. Vladimir Slamecka, "Design of information networks," p.550.

66. L. Dawn Pohlman, "Special libraries and METRO."

67. National Academy of Sciences - National Academy of Engineering, Committee on Scientific and Technical Communication, *Scientific and Technical Communication,* p.43-49.

68. Interuniversity Communications Council (EDUCOM), *Agricultural sciences information network* (Boston: EDUCOM, 1969), p.47-55.

69. H. F. Dammers, "Integrated information processing and the case for a national network," *Information storage and retrieval* 4:115 (June 1968).

70. William J. Paisley, "Information needs and uses," p.24-25.

71. *Ibid.* p. 24.

The Relation of Social Science Data Archives to Libraries and Wider Information Networks

Jack Dennis

This paper concerns some of the organizational requirements for the establishment of a network of interlinked information services. In particular, the analysis concerns the relation of social science data banks to libraries and related organizations. I approach these problems from the standpoint of a director of a social science data archive at a university and as one who has participated in the activities of the national coordinating organization of social data archives. The presentation will be brief and hopefully, to the point. It is divided into three parts: (1) a short description of organizational developments in the archiving of quantitative social science information, (2) a discussion of how local archives could be most efficiently organized, and (3) the relation of social data archives to libraries and thus to any wider network of information services.

THE GROWTH OF SOCIAL DATA ARCHIVES

The past decade in the social sciences has witnessed an exponential growth in the number of active researchers, projects and quantitative data produced. The new store of social data thus provided has expanded greatly our knowledge of society, but it also has brought into being new demands for increased capabilities on the part of institutions that formerly were e-quipped only for the more traditional forms of scholarly activity. A number of social science data archives have been established in response to these demands so that social information of a machine-readable type can be preserved for use by the wider social science community.[1] The founders of these new archives have tried to devise appropriate means for coping with the social information explosion, from the standpoint of maintaining, retrieving, and redistributing valuable project data for further analysis.

As a corollary feature of the creation of these social data archives, an embryonic national and worldwide network of social science information also has begun to appear. Not only such significant service organizations as the Roper Public Opinion Research Center and the Inter-University Consortium for Political Research have been established but also coordinating organizations have appeared — such as the International Social Science Council's Standing Committee on Data Archives and the Council of Social Science Data Archives. The Council of Social Science Data Archives, for example, has attempted to coordinate activities within the emerging A-

merican archive network, particularly in areas of standardization of policies relating to data format and documentation, as well as policies regulating the costs of data distribution and technical developments. Together, the Standing Committee on Data Archives, CSSDA, and the few major archives such as Roper and ICPR, have formed the nucleus for whatever future progress is to be made in developing a broader system of interlinked social science data banks.

What we shall argue, however, that important as these steps have been, the system as a whole is at a crucial turning point in its development — one at which the major attention now needs to be turned to the problem of developing more fully the locally oriented, general-purpose archives. Indeed, only by a greater effort to establish adequate local facilities will the nascent national and international systems reach maturity; without a more pervasive base of local archives, much of the progress made to this point in developing the broader archival networks could well be lost.

In the discussion that follows we will attempt to spell out this argument in more detail — including what we mean more precisely by a locally oriented, general-purpose archive. We will draw especially upon the experience gained in establishing the Social Science Data and Program Library at the University of Wisconsin for our recommendations. One of the most important aspects of the latter experience has been the set of relationships that our organization has had with the emerging national and international archive systems. Let us first focus upon the nature of these archive systems, and subsequently, upon the principles that we would recommend for application in organizing local archives with respect to the broader networks.

AN INTERNATIONAL SYSTEM OF SOCIAL DATA ARCHIVES

The founders and early participants both in the International Social Science Council's Standing Committee and in the Council of Social Science Data Archives no doubt envisioned a future world in which there would be an archive network operating at several levels — international, national, regional, and local. This network would include both the present national data banks, such as ICPR, Roper, Steinmetz, Essex, and Zentralarchiv, and the more limited organizations, such as those at Oslo, Pittsburgh, North Carolina, Iowa, Wisconsin, Northwestern, and Yale. When fully established, this system would have some continuing headquarters and staff, and would help to coordinate policies pertaining to common problems and objectives. It also would serve perhaps in the future as the central point in the telecommunications network in which a data user at one archive could gain access to the holdings of other archives directly by means of a machine-readable index of available data. The user also would be able to analyze the data directly by means of an interactive computing capability.

In the decade of the sixties, some limited progress toward this vision of the future indeed was made. As those who have participated in CSSDA activities know, however, many unsolved practical problems of this ideal system have been carried into the present period. The maintenance of even a small central staff for the CSSDA has proven difficult, given the vagaries of available funding. Nor have even the simpler aspects of interarchival coordination been more than minimally achieved. For example, the inventory of data holdings is not fully operational; nor is it generally available to member organizations. Provision of common data formatting standards and the keeping of an up-to-date inventory of holdings also remain at present as basic but unaccomplished tasks.

This failure to develop fully has been caused in part by difficulties of coordination growing out of disparate experience, organization, subject-matter specialization, and hardware facilities among the various archives. But it is also due, we would guess, to the fact that the various archives have not developed at the same rate. In particular, while the "wholesaler" archives such as ICPR and the Roper Center have experienced marked development in the past decade, their "retailer" counterparts — the local archives — have failed to grow apace. We would strongly emphasize that without substantial growth of these local facilities to make proper use of the resources available from the national archives, the social science information system will probably remain weak and inchoate in the decade of the seventies; the progress made by the more general archives may very well be eroded by rising costs of ICPR or Roper Center services coupled with inadequate use of data at the local university or other local level.

There are, however, some exceptions to this general pattern as far as local archives are concerned. The university-based social data archives at Pittsburgh, Northwestern, and Wisconsin, for example, have attempted to provide facilities which embody some essential principles of organization for the coming decade. Let us turn to what these principles might be.

ORGANIZING LOCAL ARCHIVES

How should local archives be organized in order to ensure that demands for services by users can be met and also that these archives can more effectively become the foundation stones for a general network of quantitative social science information? Our short answer to this question is that new local archives should self-consciously define their functions along the lines provided by the usual university library. What we are saying is that data archives are most usefully thought of as extensions of the traditional information services of a library — a library which serves both faculty and students for purposes of research and instruction.

One of the most important features of this organizational perspective is that, unlike the existing "wholesaler" archives, local archives should be fairly general in the scope of their subject matter. The Inter-University Consortium for Political Research specializes in political data, the Roper Center deals with surveys, the Zentralarchiv concerns itself essentially with the German-related studies, the Essex Social Science Research Council Data Bank focuses upon British materials, etc. All of these "general" archives specialize more than we would suggest should be the case at the local archive level. Rather, the local data bank should include political, historical, sociological, psychological, anthropological, and economic data, at the very least; these data should be both individual and aggregate in character — that is, they should be based upon a variety of data-collection techniques. One might argue further that not simply machine-readable *quantitative* data be included but — as at Northwestern University's Intersocietal Information Center — machine-readable *qualitative* information ought to be built into the archival holdings and services as well. Thus, we would regard the form of local archival organization as being preferably one that is unlike any of the national archives but rather complementary to all of these higher level archives together — the local archive designed to receive data from many different sources and able to service many kinds of users.

At Wisconsin, where the data archive has been organized along these lines since 1966, members of more than thirty different departments of the university have used our services; subject-matter specialties range from political science, sociology, and economics — the major users — to mass communications, social work, home economics, demography, urban and regional planning, and physical education. In this sense, the Data and Program Library Service at Wisconsin acts as a general acquisition, storage, and distribution facility, just as does the university library. As a result of this broad subject-matter emphasis, usage of the data library grew, for example, from 355 visits in academic year 1966-67 to more than 1,300 requests in each of the academic years 1967-68 and 1968-69. Unless there is this broadening of scope of subject matter from early in the the life of the archive, a large and diverse group of potential users necessarily will be excluded.

At the beginning, of course, there are likely to be only a few core disciplines represented — that is, the disciplines in which quantitative social data needs are already paramount and for which the national data archives, such as ICPR, the Roper Center, or the Bureau of Labor Statistics, already provide ready sources of data supply. However, in the second period of development, we would suggest that these services be extended as we have extended ours at Wisconsin.

A second major feature of this form of organization — modeled on the idea of a central, library-like information center at a university — is its considerable emphasis upon servicing users. Were archives at the local levels conceived only as repositories of machine-readable data, then such emphatic user orientation might not be necessary. We conceive the main point of a local archive not to rest upon its "archival" function *per se* — that is, in acquiring, indexing, and preserving these data in some antiquarian spirit for posterity — but rather as the primary means for keeping these data alive — to put them continually, without delay, and at minimal cost into the hands of potential users beyond their originators. By making data easily available, new tests of hypotheses can be made; the considerable effort and expense that goes into producing reliable social information is matched by the increased marginal benefits of use in the wider academic, industrial, or governmental communities.

To be user oriented means also that various other kinds of services will need to be created in order that data requestors, however technically unsophisticated, can make proper use of the evidence provided. In our archive we have found it necessary to provide more than the usual library functions of acquisition, cataloging, indexing, referencing, storing, maintaining, reproducing, and distributing information. We also have discovered that we must edit ("clean") the data, redocument the data in some instances (by updating and editing codebooks), provide computer programs for use in file-handling and statistical analysis, consult on the proper use of the programs, and furnish general information, both to students and faculty, about the existence and proper use of these resources in their scholarly activities. In addition, we maintain a variety of hardware facilities — for example, a remote terminal to access the university's central computer and an array of unit record equipment. Thus, we go far in making a full range of services available in a single location so that the user has a convenient mode of utilizing the data resources of the archive. Each of these functions is important, moreover, given the fact that they are incompletely available elsewhere in the university. Indeed, our program library, for example, is so valuable a part of our services that it has become a coordinate activity with the data library; furthermore, it is the core of a current attempt to extend program library abstracting and indexing services to a range of users beyond Wisconsin.[2]

We thus suggest that a local archive be general in types of information and user oriented in the sense of providing a range of auxiliary services necessary for making efficient use of archival data files. These two features provide together an important means of attracting usage and thus, a means of improving the quality of social research. Scholarship is advanced when local users are able to draw upon data not otherwise efficiently available and when there is an improvement in the cost performance of information-generating activities for the intellectual community as a whole.

Another important and perhaps more basic product of increasing data usage is that a popular base is created for improving the services already established. Once university or foundation administrators begin to see that the archive is a going concern in the sense that many and various types of people are using the facilities — not simply that the archive has acquired a good collection of data files or that it has relatively efficient modes of indexing and processing the data — then, and only then, are they likely to upgrade the facility significantly and put its financing on a more permanent basis. Administrators, after all, are a pragmatic lot, and pragmatists typically want to see what the organization is doing — what services it is, in fact, providing for users rather than simply how comprehensively, or efficiently, organized it is.

As potential data users become acquainted with these services through actual experience, they also are likely to begin to understand the necessity of sharing their own project data with the wider community — once their own projects needs have been met. Short of requiring as a condition of foundation support that researchers deposit their project data in archives, this is perhaps the most effective way of informing members of the social science community of their wider responsibilities. They also are able to see by this method and necessity of proper data documentation, cleaning, formating, and maintenance. Once their own data have been released to an archive, their errors become a matter of visible public record. In this sense, encouraging contributions to archives is a way of maintaining standards of social science evidence, at least at the level of data preparation and documentation.

Perhaps the most important product of building local usage is the acquaintance that clients of these archives gain with the wider social information system. The local archive serves as an essential conduit for building recognition and support for the national archives, for CSSDA, and for other aspects of the emerging international social science information system. As social scientists — particularly those among the current student generation — find these services available and valuable at their present institutions, they are likely to want to build or improve similar resources when they move on to other university settings. Thus, the potential for the worldwide information system will be furthered. The local archive — even if it currently exists only as a means of acquiring and storing political surveys from ICPR — is likely to serve as a stimulus for the development of expanded services of this type.

FURTHER DEVELOPMENTS: ARTICULATION OF SOCIAL DATA ARCHIVE AND LIBRARY

If during the coming decade there is the kind of full-scale effort to develop local social science data archives along the lines that we suggest, what then should be the next steps? Two developments are partially explicit in our discussion thus far: One is the need for more effective growth of interarchival coordination at regional, national, and international levels; the other is the necessity for closer integration of the local archive into existing local university information services — particularly those typically provided by the traditional university library. In that we already have said a good deal about the possibilities for the growth of the national and world archival networks based upon a more comprehensive system of local archives, let us turn our attention at this point to the relation of the social science data archive to the university library.

When we suggested that data archives be organized or reorganized to represent the informational interests of a wide variety of students of society and that these services be user oriented (especially that they be provided at minimal cost to the user), we were saying that the functions and policies of the data archive should be brought into line with the usual operating doctrine of a university library. In an important sense, a library is a university-wide facility servicing all comers on the basis of minimal direct cost to the user. Furthermore, we see the data archive functions of acquiring, documenting, indexing, maintaining, reproducing, and distributing quantitative information as precisely those of the traditional library. Thus, the extension of these library functions to the handling of primary quantitative data is but a very short step. Libraries already go quite beyond simply collecting and making available information that exists in printed form. They store and distribute microfilm and microfiche, for example, and even maps, paintings, and phonograph records. "Libraries," as Ralph Bisco perhaps over optimistically observed, "have been exceptionally responsive to the information needs of their users."[3] While one can argue that data archives have almost in every case originated with social scientist users or data-generating agencies rather than with university libraries, this does not mean that librarians necessarily are unresponsive to these new information needs.

Our own experience — and this has been matched in other instances, for example, at UCLA and Northwestern University — is that the members of the staff of the library are keenly aware of their potential responsibilities in cooperating with social scientists to expand the scope of these services and in coordinating such services with standard bibliographic and other services of the library. Therefore, our suggestion would be that organizers of archives bring the library into organizational planning as soon as possible in much the same spirit that the computing center would be a point of natural coordination from the beginning of archive operations.

Furthermore, after an initial period of cooperation, we would think it feasible to begin building the archive into the library system, itself. Obviously, this further development depends upon how interested the library staff is in moving with the changing informational needs of its social science users. Certainly not every university library will be able — by reasons of shortage of competent staff, appropriate facilities, or financial resources — to enter immediately into this new area. But many libraries will be willing to do so; in our opinion this movement should be encouraged by those concerned with archival development. As more and more aspects of library operations become computerized, library administrators undoubtedly will begin to see the necessity for advancing the computing credentials of their staff and in acquiring appropriate hardware. Then it is mainly a matter of organizational transfer to incorporate social data archives into libraries. The library ought to be given every opportunity to maintain its traditional role as the center of university informational services.

We do not mean to suggest that social scientists and other organizers of data archives should drop from the scene as the archive becomes more integrated with the library. Indeed, to do so would destroy one of the great virtues of present archival activity, namely, the felicitous involvement of social scientists in providing themselves with adequate information storage and retrieval facilities. One needs to work out a new set of relationships in which the archive obtains both library integration and support, and also continues to receive active inputs of administrative energy, fund-raising, and policy participation by social scientists.

The experience we have had in recent years at Wisconsin suggests that there is a considerable potential market for the kinds of data repository services that we have begun to provide. Ready access to machine-readable data collected from a variety of sources improves the quality of research and teaching, and extends the informational services traditionally provided by university libraries. We would urge that these local archives be more extensively organized on a wide subject-matter, user-oriented basis to provide the natural complement of the es-tablished wholesaler archives and to provide a firmer base of organization, nationally and internationally, for social data archives. Our own experience provides a strong impetus toward a library-like facility with a variety of auxiliary services such as a remote access computer terminal, a computer program library, and computational-statistical consulting.

In the future one needs to expand these services in volume and scope at a local level by building in most cases upon the organizational base of the traditional university library — moving the library into new but highly relevant areas of informational service. Thus, in the seventies the benefits of a more comprehensive social information system will be enhanced, and the aggregate costs to the community of scholars of social science data collection will be lowered greatly.

I also would suggest that until these organizational developments have been made, more advanced techniques such as interarchival telecommunications links, while technically feasible, will lack other resources necessary for their maintenance. It would be most uneconomical to install telecommunications equipment in libraries where there is no organization to provide proper data storage and retrieval for local use, where there are few users who have experience and understanding of archival information usage, or where the administrative staff is unable to understand the hardware and software requirements of social science users and lacks an appreciation of the limitations and possibilities of an interarchival network. My argument, therefore, is that we need to expend our greatest, immediate effort in expanding the archival capabilities of local institutions and to establish a set of archive-library linkages which can provide the anchor points for interarchival networks, both technical and organizational.

NOTES

1. For further discussion of this emerging network of data archives, see: R. L. Bisco, "Social science data archives: progress and prospects," *Social science information* 6:39-74 (1967). S. Rokkan., ed., *Data archives for the social sciences* (Paris: Mouton, 1966). D. K. Stewart, *Social implications of social science data archives,* Technical Memorandum 3729/000/00 (Santa Monica, Calif.: System Development Corporation, 7 November 1967). W. A. Glaser and R. L. Bisco, "Plans of the Council of Social Science Data Archives," *Social science information* 5:71-96 (1966). D. Nasatir, "Social science data libraries," Publication A-89 (Berkeley, Calif.: Survey Research Center, Univ. of California, Nov. 1967). R. L. Bisco, "Social science data archives: technical considerations," *Social science information* 4:129-150 (1965).

2. Published descriptions of some of these organizations are available, see: R. L. Bisco, "Social science data archives...." R. L. Merritt and R. E. Lane, "The training functions of a data library," *Social science information* 4:118-126 (1965). S. Rokkan and F. Aarebrot, "The Norwegian archive of historical ecological data: progress report, August 1969," *Social science information* 8:77-84 (Jan. 1969).

3. Under a recent grant from the National Science Foundation, the Social Science Data and Program Library Service at the University of Wisconsin has begun a pilot project on establishing a National Program Library Service--beginning in the initial two-year period to compile a machine-readable inventory of available computer programs of interest to social scientists. The goals of this project will be outlined in a subsequent report in *Social science information.*

Network Services for Interlibrary Loan

Brigitte L. Kenney

Any breakthrough...is likely to come from outside the system. 'Experts' are the most thoroughly familiar with the developed knowledge inside the prescribed boundaries of a given science. Any *new* knowledge must usually come from the outside — not by "expert," but by what someone has defined as an "inpert."

Maxwell Maltz[1]

INTRODUCTION

Interlibrary loan is one of the oldest forms of interlibrary cooperation. Informal networks for borrowing and lending books and other materials existed long before the word "network" crept into the librarian's language. The sharing of library resources probably began when books were first unchained from their desks and began to circulate. Very early, librarians realized that no single library could ever contain all that was wanted or needed; as underfinanced as libraries have always been, they could not attempt to collect all the world's recorded knowledge without spreading themselves too thin. Thus, they borrowed from one another those works which were needed by their patrons and which they did not own. For many years borrowing and lending was governed by *noblesse oblige*— a gracious, voluntary sharing of one's wealth with one's poorer (library) cousin. It was often a one-way street, and sometimes, when abused, detrimental to the richer library's services. Each library could and did set its own rules, and it was difficult — if not impossible — for librarians to know who would lend what, under what conditions, and at what cost.

Thus, we find that there is much precedent, at least in the area of interlibrary loans, for networking of a kind. Before discussing details, it is necessary to set down some definitions. In order to talk about network services for interlibrary loan, we need to clarify some words and concepts which appear frequently in the literature.

"Cooperation" is perhaps the most frequently used term to cover a multitude of ways in which librarians are working together. In the context in which it is used here, it means any venture in which two or more discrete library units work together in some common venture. This may range from the sharing of a bookmobile to school and public librarians discussing teachers' assignments. No formal relationship is implied.

"Library systems" may be thought of as two or more discrete library units tied together by a formal agreement of some sort, which sets forth areas in which these units will work together and means through which administration of the common venture is accomplished, methods of remuneration, if any, and often, if not always, legal restrictions or regulations governing the enterprise. Examples range from centralized processing centers to groups of libraries joining together for total library service to their combined publics.

"Network" may be thought of as either a formal or an informal linkage of discrete library units and other information-dispensing agencies for the purpose of exchanging or transferring recorded information. "Exchanging and transferring" is emphasized, implying two-way communication and some sort of switching mechanism.

Thus, we have three levels of interlibrary relationships, which are, however, not mutually exclusive. An informal cooperative venture might very well include two-way communication and switching while a library system might function as a network, but then again, it may be one-directional in its operation.

"Interlibrary loan" probably need not be defined; however, for the sake of clarity, let it be stated that it is that action which allows transfer of any recorded medium from an agency possessing it to another needing it. Note that we did not say "library" in this statement because the agency may be a commercial information producer, a data analysis center, or another kind of organization providing information in recorded form.

"Transfer of the recorded medium" may be by various means, ranging from messenger and mail service to linked computers. The "recorded medium" may be a book or a PCMI card, a reel of magnetic computer tape or a reel of videotape.

Looking at the interlibrary loan function in its broadest terms, we thus delimit the paper clearly. Excluded are reference and bibliographic transfers not involving full text or facsimiles. We will concentrate here only on document delivery, or to use the broader definition, transfer of recorded media, excluding surrogates.

METHODOLOGY

Rather than presenting a historical review or an inventory of existing services, both of which are the subject of other papers, we will discuss interlibrary loan as part of overall library objectives and in the context of the provisions of the Interlibrary Loan Code. By discussing two examples of networks in some depth, we will attempt to arrive at some conclusions in regard to problems and successes, in terms of people, systems design, legislation, technology, and funding. A final section will present possible directions for the future and needed research.

THE INTERLIBRARY LOAN CODE

We have noted that borrowing and lending of materials among librarians is a time-honored tradition. As collections increased and as library patrons needed more specialized materials for research and other purposes, so did the volume of interlibrary loans increase. It became apparent that there was a necessity for some governing principles and more formal procedures to provide access to the nation's library collections. Thus, in 1917 the first ALA Interlibrary Loan Code was produced and subsequently revised in 1940 and 1952. It provided librarians with several principles, the strongest of which was that:

...Interlibrary loan service is a courtesy and a privilege, not a right, and is dependent upon the cooperation of many libraries.[2]

...Interlibrary loan service *supplements* a library's resources by making available, through direct loans for a *short* period of time, materials located in other libraries and not owned by the borrowing library.[3]

And a third:

The purpose of interlibrary loans is to make available for research and for serious study library materials not in a given library, *with due provisions made by the lending library for the rights of its primary clientele.*[4]

It goes on to spell out in more detail duties and responsibilities of the borrowing library for the safety of the material, accurate verification and screening of would-be users of the service. Photocopying of certain materials is permitted only if permission is first asked of the lending library. Certain classes of materials are excluded from the list of requestable items: current fiction, current issues of periodicals, inexpensive items currently purchasable, books for class use, any large group of materials necessary for a thesis being written, and current books for which there is an anticipated demand. Also excluded are extremely rare books, music to be used in public performance, works difficult and expensive to pack, e.g., newspapers. Whether any item is loaned is entirely up to the discretion of the lending library.

Payment of transportation both ways is the responsibility of the borrowing library, as are any service charges assessed. Further, borrowing libraries are cautioned not to concentrate their requests on any one library to avoid overload. A designation of name and status of applicant are considered desirable but not mandatory. Provision is made for photographic reproduction, with the caveat that if an entire work or issue of a periodical is requested, the ILL request must be accompanied by a written statement from the patron desiring the item that he will comply with copyright provisions.

Wrapping instructions are very specific, requiring corrugated cardboard plus heavy wrapping paper. Use of the standard ALA ILL form is strongly recommended but not required.

In 1968 the code was revised again because of increasing use of photocopies in lieu of original materials.[5] It also reflected some tightening of borrowing privileges; academic libraries were permitted to borrow only such items as were needed for research and thesis work for faculty, staff, and graduate students. For the first time, reference is made to the possibility of absorbing mailing and other small costs rather than keeping an account of postage refunds and photocopies. Photocopying is now permitted for all materials except when specifically forbidden by the lending library. Transmittal of requests can be made either on the standard ALA form or a similar form transmitted by teletype.

Verification requirements are as stringent as ever, and patron name and status are now required on each form. A manual was to accompany the code; it could not be asserted if such a manual was ever published.

In 1969 a further revision presents a Model Interlibrary Loan Code for Regional, State, Local, or Other Special Groups of Libraries. It is a much more formal document, providing for signature by all participants for the first time. It "is intended to promote more liberalized interlibrary loan policy among the libraries adopting it. It is based on the premise that lending among libraries for use of an individual...is in the public interest"[6] and borrowing is no longer restricted to research only.

More emphasis is given to the borrowing library's responsibility to acquire all materials that might be expected to be owned by it; it should not rely on ILL for "ordinary needs." Types of material to be loaned are spelled out carefully; virtually everything is included. Each participating library *is required* to prepare a statement containing its own interlibrary loan policy; this is the first time this requirement is clearly stated. Financing is given more attention — again with the suggestion that negligible costs be absorbed or that clear-cut financial reimbursement arrangements be made. The concept of a "resource library" is introduced in this revision for the first time; these must be "designated" and channels for screening and transmittal of requests clearly spelled out. When telephone requests are accepted, the requirement to follow with a written request may be waived by the lending library, another first in this document. Verification requirements are as stringent as before, but "special agreements" made within the group may waive part or all of these.

In the preface, the statement is made that "matters not spelled out in the model code (for example, screening and routing procedures, charges for photocopying, special contractual agreements, designated resource libraries) should be explicitly stated.[7]

We see here a definite trend; although the basic philosophy governing interlibrary loans has not changed, the code has been made more explicit in many areas and has become more responsive to the changes wrought by photocopying, teletype, systems of libraries banding together, and particularly, to the needs of all types of users. We will discuss the advantages as well as the shortcomings of the ALA code later in the paper when we look at the present status and possible future developments in this field.

OBJECTIVE OF INTERLIBRARY LOAN

As traditionally conceived, interlibrary loan meant the transfer of any recorded medium from one library to another. Its purpose was to make the scholarly record more readily available to all who needed access to it. By transferring materials from one location to another, the library enters into a communications process. It communicates with whatever location is thought to have the desired material. It is true that a library patron requiring material not owned by his library can travel to another location to obtain it, but this is an expensive and time-consuming activity, particularly when the desired items are widely scattered in various locations throughout the country. By means of interlibrary loan, some items, if not all, can be brought to the patron wherever he is — not always quickly but most certainly less expensively than if he had to travel. The implications of this cost savings will be discussed later, and the question raised if the user should, in fact, bear part of the cost of interlibrary loans.

Although librarians have traditionally said: "If we don't have it, we will get it for you," this has often been a somewhat misleading statement. It should probably have been qualified with: "If it is a book or journal," "if we can find it somewhere," or "if it does not take an inordinate amount of staff time to locate it." Certain kinds of printed information have never been part of interlibrary loan activities, for example, preprints of forthcoming articles. If the user simply wishes to know what is currently available and important in the field of high-energy physics, interlibrary loan cannot help.

Thus we find that the objective of interlibrary loan is noble indeed: to provide the user with access to the world's recorded knowledge. However, as we shall see, this objective has not been achieved as yet to any notable degree.

INTERLIBRARY LOAN PROCESS

The ALA Interlibrary Loan Code governs the more general procedures of the process. However, it is useful to look at it in a slightly different way in the context of fitting into a network. As we previously noted the library enters into a communications process when placing a request. In a previous paper we outlined a generalized communications model and showed how traditional interlibrary loan procedures as well as direct access by the user to a data base fit into such a mode.[8] We found that librarians assume a great deal of responsibility when entering into this process; the user merely states his need, and the library takes over all necessary steps until the material is delivered to the user. In contrast, when the user accesses a data base directly, he assumes all responsibility for success or failure to obtain the wanted material, and only occasionally does an intermediate act as an adviser or problem solver. The implications of this are quite far-reaching when considering the future of media delivery via networks. Are librarians going to continue carrying the heavy burden alone, or will we transfer part or all of it to the user, acting mainly as a switching mechanism? Is it feasible to conceive of a system in which librarians merely will monitor and

screen rather than carry out all the present steps? When we speak of access to the scholarly record, do we necessarily mean through libraries? Or are we willing to do whatever is necessary to provide access quickly and efficiently to the user, wherever he may be, by whatever means necessary?

A quick look at some existing facts and procedures will aid in understanding the problem. As mentioned briefly before, one means of speed-up has been the teletypewriter. Interlibrary loan requests are transmitted quickly and accurately, with the advantage of having a written record both at the sending and receiving ends. An alternative means, the telephone, does not provide the library with a written record and is therefore not a preferred means of request transmission unless an emergency situation prevails.

When teletypes were used in a group of medical libraries for the first time, a manual was developed for use by all participants, which required twenty-four-hour turn-around, or answer service, as one condition of participation.[9] Thus, the time for request to receipt of material was drastically cut. We speculated in a previous paper that this twenty-four-hour rule could have been instituted without the machine, but that the banding together in a group and the subsequent formulation of rules now made a firm agreement possible.[10] First-class mail delivery was another agreement reached by participants and again speeded up delivery considerably. Thus, we see that whenever a group of librarians can agree on a formalized procedure, improvement in service is almost always reached. Violators are simply "dropped from the list," a very simple way to ensure that participants adhere to rules.

Why this need for speed-up? What is the picture now and what has it been regarding volume handled by libraries? We find some interesting figures in the literature. Keenan found in 1962 that in ten years the volume of interlibrary lending among medical libraries had increased dramatically, and that the National Library of Medicine, having changed its policies from direct loan to physicians to lending only through libraries, had been called upon far too much by those libraries.[11] New York, Ohio, Pennsylvania, Illinois, and several other library-rich states were its heaviest users, and the journals most frequently requested were those which should have been owned even by small and medium-sized medical libraries. Inconsistencies in ILL policies among the various libraries was blamed for the abuse of NLM; it was far easier to borrow there than to learn all the various rules and regulations prevailing in other libraries.

Pings found a 70 percent increase of interlibrary loans in five years, or a total of 500,000 items, costing $3 million.[12] We stated in a previous paper that:

> Without knowing where to turn for needed materials, what classes of materials can be loaned, copied, have to be paid for, or are free, it is difficult for the borrowing library to provide speedy service, even with maximum effort. It is often very expensive, in terms of manpower, to obtain a needed item if many avenues have to be tried before the desired document is located and delivered.[13]

Agreement is general among medical librarians that a good medical library ought to be able to provide 90 percent of all requests from its own collection. This standard is rarely if ever achieved — not even by some of the largest medical libraries in the country.

Almost all studies suggest that the lack of proper bibliographic tools, such as lists of items *with location indicated,* considerably slows down the ILL process. Union catalogs, union lists, and more recently, machine-stored location information, have increased considerably over the last few years and have aided in the search and verification process. They have, on the other hand, increased volume simply by being available. We found in a recent survey that Indiana special librarians would no longer turn to one of their large state universities for interlibrary loans because it had been swamped with requests since producing its own computer-based serials listing and could not begin to service them in a reasonable time.[14] Thus, many sought their information from much further away, simply because the service was speedier. Interestingly enough, the service from the New York Public Library was considered by one librarian to be quicker than any other source she had found close by, and she now places all her requests there.

Staff training and functioning received considerable attention in a study of public library systems.[15] The investigators found that too often staff did not fully understand or accept the systems concept, attempted to fill requests without proper background or training, and especially did not know when to stop and refer something to a higher level in the hierarchy. This was particularly true in smaller systems with untrained branch personnel. Conversely, the study found that many patrons have access to materials outside their own (sometimes very small or inadequate) library for the first time through belonging to a system and were taking advantage of it.

Restrictions on loans are mentioned by Pings as a very real drawback in a study on Midwest biomedical libraries.[16] He found that slightly less than half the libraries which responded restricted their lending either on a geographic basis to certain types of libraries or by reciprocal agreement only. Only sixteen out of seventy-five loaned current journals, and many did not use the standard interlibrary loan form. Billing procedures varied widely. Pings recommends twenty-four-hour turn-around service, photocopying for journal articles, dropping of fees except for very long articles, and the distribution of serials and other holdings lists to discourage unsuccessful borrowing.

Some of these improvements have been made by the Medical Library Center of New York.[17] Originally conceived as a central storage facility for little-used materials in medical libraries, it developed that services rendered by this center became much more important than the storage capability. Daily delivery of needed items, simplified billing for photocopy by the Medical Library Center rather than from and to individual libraries, and installation of TWX in all participating libraries resulted in faster service for everyone, in spite of vastly increased use of loans.

Some general conclusions may be drawn from the preceding; they will be further detailed later. Turn-around time is probably the largest single factor contributing to the failure or success of any interlibrary loan network or system. It is determined by availability of bibliographic tools, trained staff, photocopy facilities, and most importantly, by the establishment of clear procedures and policy statements by all participants.

We now will examine two existing systems in some depth to see the effect of formalized agreements and streamlined procedures on ongoing operations.

THE NYSILL SYSTEM[18]

The New York State Interlibrary Loan Network, NYSILL, came into being as a "logical extension of developments in library services in the nation and in New York State."[19] In this state, greatly aided by a liberalized library law in 1958 and state-aid somewhat later, public libraries banded together in twenty-two systems, serving 99 percent of the population. The next step was the 3R's system, providing for nine regional resource and referral libraries to backstop the twenty-two systems. At the same time several other cooperative ventures developed, notably the SUNY Biomedical Communications Network, connecting a number of large medical libraries via terminal and offering a computerized data base[20] and the federation of Five Associated University Libraries, FAUL.[21] In New York, METRO[22] had come into being, as well as the New York Medical Library Center.[23] New York also had pioneered by the installation of a statewide facsimile transmission system, FACTS[24] which was later abandoned because of high cost, equipment failure, and insufficient use. Thus the stage was set to formalize interlibrary loans within the state and make them more efficient. NYSILL, begun in 1967, assigns to the State Library the responsibility for switching and screening messages, thus it is, by our definition, an interlibrary loan network. Public library systems and other consortia, as well as academic libraries, are expected to fill as many requests within their own jurisdiction as possible, and no one under the age of eighteen is served by NYSILL. The state provides participation grants to referral libraries, as well as reimbursement of costs for each transaction to subject resource libraries. A tree pattern was conceived as the service moved through its various steps:

1. Readers request materials at their own public, special, or academic library (school libraries are not included because of the age limit).

2. Requests not filled at the local library are searched at systems headquarters; college and special library requests are screened by one of the 3R's participants where feasible.

3. Requests still unfilled are sent to the State Library; it serves as a switching center and clearinghouse as well as a backstop library.

4. If the request is not filled at the State Library, it is referred to one of three major public libraries for backstopping service.

5. If that library could not fill the request, it is referred back to the State Library and from there to one of the eight subject referral libraries, from there to another if the first one cannot fill.

6.   If the request is still unfilled, it is returned to the originating library to be searched through other sources.

Each referral library had a TWX installed to speed communications.

Several revisions in this procedure were made after a six-month trial period. Large academic institutions were allowed to borrow from one another without going through NYSILL, thus speeding up service. Copies of the requests had to be sent to the State Library, however, to ensure reimbursement.

Although the service was heavily used — mostly by academic library patrons whose requests came through public library systems — it was found to be slow and cumbersome. Overall time elapsed from initiation of request to receipt of material averaged twenty-two days. About 46,000 requests were received in Phase I, an eight-month period, of which 55 percent were filled. Of these, the State Library was able to fill 44 percent and referrals were made for 11 percent. More than half of all requests were considered ineligible for referral beyond the State Library. Cost was an average of $15.80 per request filled; this figure includes both the participation grant and the reimbursement per transaction to referral libraries. Academic participation was hesitant; several libraries indicated that they avoided using NYSILL.

Revisions based on these findings included a recommendation for tighter procedures all along the way, particularly regarding improved bibliographic citation, better definition of patron status, standardized TWX format, and more streamlined transmittal procedures, eliminating the requirement of referral back to the State Library.

A second evaluation took place during Phase II of NYSILL. Questions were asked about improved speed and the effects of the new procedures on NYSILL. Volume increase was considered, as was success rate of filled requests. Cost comparisons were made, and an attempt was made to categorize requests by patron status, type of material, and originating agency. A delivery system was considered because of slow mail delivery. Two newly established regional networks in New York State were evaluated as to their role in NYSILL.

Findings were that use of NYSILL was heaviest by public library systems and by academic libraries in Upstate New York. The New York Metropolitan Area relied less heavily on the network but often went directly to another library inside or outside the state known to have the wanted item. In some cases it was found that NYSILL could have filled these requests. Medical and special libraries relied less heavily on the service than other types of libraries, the former having their own regional and national networks and the latter because of a requirement for speed. While at first libraries were expected to go to their area referral library and then to one of the subject resource libraries, it was found to be more expeditious (and therefore became general practice) to approach the subject library directly if that was indeed the best way to obtain material. Most requests were only referred once and were then filled.

Costs were found to have dropped; average cost per referred, filled request was now $10.82 (as compared to $15.80 during Phase I). Of this amount, $6.65 was for unit fees (reimbursement per transaction), and $4.17 was part of a participation grant. Costs per library were often quite high for subject referral libraries if their participation grant was high and their volume of requests handled low.

Time factors had improved somewhat. The average time it took to complete a NYSILL request was now nineteen days as compared to twenty-two before; the range from ten to twenty-eight days. This was attributed partly to the fact that referrals were now direct; the State Library received the request only once, and it was then referred directly from one library to another until filled. Another factor was the institution of a five-day limit on holding and processing a request.

The filling rate improved also — from 44 percent at the State Library during the first phase to 47 percent in the second. The highest rate achieved by referral libraries was 70 percent (for New York Public Library, New York Academy of Medicine, and Cornell), and the overall rate of requests filled was 64 percent.

Volume in NYSILL increased by an overall 29 percent during Phase II to 87,000, with the academic library requests showing the greatest increase (more than 90 percent).

Thus, the four factors by which system performance may be measured had all improved: volume, filling rates, elapsed time, and decrease in costs.

The study recommends a continuation of the service on an operational basis and makes recommendations for improvement. Verification of requests remains a problem, and many librarians indicated that they did not really understand the verification procedures. It was recommended that the source of the citation always be included to facilitate searching for requests which could not be verified locally. Status reports are to be made more promptly so that the patron may know the status of his request as soon as possible. Personnel requested that administrative procedures and the *Operations Manual* be made more explicit, and that assistance with setting up procedures be available from the State Library. In-service training was recommended to alleviate some of the concerns in this area, as well as a revision of the *Manual*.

Delivery time (mail delivery) is still one of the largest chunks of elapsed time between receiving and delivering (seven days). Estimates were made to ascertain if a delivery service operated by the State Library would provide a partial solution. It was found that it would not be economically feasible, even at expected increased levels of volume, because of the large geographic area covered and the problem of sorting and routing thousands of single items for individual libraries. Also, the cost of a state-operated service is no less than first-class mail delivery and would probably be no faster on a statewide basis. Local delivery systems (such as United Parcel Service) were explored and were found to be a possible partial solution for point-to-point delivery of quantities of material, e.g., Albany to New York City. First-class mail for photocopy only was recommended as feasible, while first-class mailing of books was not recommended because of considerably increased costs over the library book rate.

TWX has worked well, not only because of its speed of transmission and the availability of records at both ends but also because the mail room is by-passed completely. Some problems remain with accuracy, largely alleviated by the installation of paper tape on all machines, which allows a typist to proceed slowly and carefully, and then transmit the request at 100 words-per-minute automatically. The paper tape can be kept and retransmitted when a referral becomes necessary; however, this procedure requires additional filing and storage.

The report strongly recommends following a uniform format in TWX requests; some libraries have not done this in the past, and varying formats slow down handling. If a standard format were used, conversion to computer procedures, for which TWX terminals could serve as direct input devices, would be facilitated.

The referral procedure is reviewed, and the report recommends that referral libraries' subject strength be more clearly identified. Too many requests were referred to the wrong place, only to be slowed down by a second referral. An exhaustive listing of subject strengths should be prepared and would substantially enhance the eventual operation of an automated referral service at the State Library.

The report deals with automation next; the anticipated growth of NYSILL volume during the next few years will make automation of the switching function at the State Library mandatory. The State Library must maintain several paper records on each transaction at the present time; an automated system would eliminate all but a single input, the original request, transmitted via TWX. It would require extremely detailed holding information for each referral library so that requests could be referred automatically. In part, a history file for all interlibrary loans would constitute such a listing; based on past response records, a new request entering the system could be referred to the library which has in the past the filled requests in the subject area of the request. The Dewey class number could serve to identify each request, and the computer could monitor success and failure rates.

One of the more startling conclusions reached by the report is that TWX gradually will be phased out. This assumption is based on technological considerations; if an on-line system becomes operational in the State Library, it is likely that the teletypewriter would provide too slow a means of access and would need to be replaced with terminals capable of high-speed transmission.

There is considerable attention to the existence of various networks (some general and some special-purpose) in New York State, and it is recommended that these be interconnected whenever practical and mutually desirable. Intersystem linkage would avoid some duplication and would afford better overall coverage of the state. A warning is issued, however, that an overly complicated network of networks might slow things down rather than improve access to library materials, and that all planning must keep the goal of speedy, successful service in mind.

An extremely interesting section of the report discusses implications for the future of libraries in general in terms of user needs, technology, and the like. The need for subject information, updating of current knowledge, SDI systems, and the like may change the nature of interlibrary loans considerably; dealing with a single document as they do, interlibrary loans cannot provide these functions. Provision of information, rather than documents, may become the pattern, aided by many existing and yet-to-be-developed data bases, informal communications among members of the "invisible college," which might be stored and dispensed via computer, and similar but as yet inaccessible kinds of information.

Finally, some attention is given to political considerations. When NYSILL was established many librarians feared that local development of resources would be handicapped, that centralization would prove to be cumbersome, and that regionalization was to be preferred. NYSILL has been responsive to these fears; the system is, in effect, a decentralized system now, with two regional networks operating harmoniously alongside and within it, and with more direct access provided between origin and destination points. Local resources have not suffered, in part because of the emphasis on service to youth at the local level and also because of the refusal to fill requests for which material should be available locally.

In general, NYSILL is considered to be a success and is, in this writer's opinion, a milestone in library network development.

THE REGIONAL MEDICAL LIBRARY SYSTEM

The development of a regional medical library system in the United States is the culmination of many years of planning on the part of medical librarians at the local, regional, and national levels. It was preceded by several cooperative ventures, some of which have been briefly described.[25] [26] [27] [28] [29] [30] More are reviewed in a previous paper by the author.[31] Better document delivery has long been an important concern of medical librarians, and they have developed some of the most sophisticated techniques to measure performance in existence today.[32] Outstanding among the pioneers in the development of regional services are Pizer and Pings whose operating networks (Pizer's SUNY Biomedical Communications Network and Pings' Detroit Metropolitan Library Network) remain models upon which much of the regional medical library was based.[33] [34] [35] [36]

Regional medical libraries came into being as a result of passage of the Medical Library Assistance Act, which permitted funding for a variety of programs for the benefit of the medical library user's community, only one of which was the concept of a biomedical communications network with regional medical libraries as components. Several studies had been commissioned by the National Library of Medicine or were made previously and virtually all came up with a similar three- or four-level pattern of service, beginning with a local library and culminating with services to be provided by the National Library of Medicine.[37] [38] [39] [40]

Eleven regions have been formed of which ten are presently operational.[41] Each region encompasses several states; consideration was given, in the forming of each region, to existing patterns of interstate relationships. Organizational patterns, services, operating procedures, and regulations vary widely among regions as local conditions may dictate.

For example, while the first of these regions to become operational, New England, has a centralized service operating out of the Francis A. Countway Library of Medicine at Harvard, the Southeast Regional Medical Library is strongly decentralized. While its headquarters is located at Emory in Atlanta, it has designated certain libraries in the region, equally strong, to serve as "designated" or primary libraries for their immediate area of service (most of the time this area is synonymous with a state). Free photocopies are provided to all qualified users who are members of the medical profession, biomedical scientists, and paramedical personnel. Each library is reimbursed on the basis of requests filled, at $2.50 per request. First-class mail is used for delivery exclusively, and quick service is the rule. All regional libraries and designated libraries have now or will soon have TWX equipment.

The Pacific Northwest Regional Medical Library is an example of yet another kind of organizational pattern. It serves five states: Alaska, Idaho, Montana, Oregon, and Washington. As yet, there is no TWX connection with Alaska, but air mail is used to communicate with the Alaska Health Sciences Library, which is a designated library and serves the state. In Idaho, where there is no medical school, the Pacific Northwest Regional Medical Library works with the State Library. The latter has TWX and an internal teletype network among the public libraries in the state through which requests from physicians are transmitted. Montana as yet has no designated agency; attempts are being made to establish a formal relationship with a Veterans Administration hospital or a larger hospital library to serve the state and transmit requests. Direct requests are taken from all unserved areas, as well as from those with designated libraries. However, after filling the request, the patron is informed of his designated library, and it is suggested to him that he channel requests there first. In Washington, requests are taken direct through the State Library and also through the medical school library of which the regional library is apart. Referrals are also made from the Pacific Northwest Bibliographic Center. Searching for material is campuswide in this library, a practice not usual in some regional libraries which require that requests must be in the biomedical area only and available in either their own or another medical collection.

The New England Medical Library has liberalized usual interlibrary loan procedures considerably.[42] [43] For example, verification of requests is not required, only a citation of the

source of the request. This permits small libraries with no access to bibliographic tools to use freely the regional library. Users include "any health science practitioner, investigator, student or educator." A WATS line allows libraries to call in requests regularly; for weekend and holiday use, a Code-A-Phone was installed to permit recording of requests for later servicing. Direct requests are accepted from all qualified users, but as in Washington State, they are informed of their local library's participation in the program and asked to channel requests through it whenever possible.

One of the feared side effects of the establishment of regional medical libraries is that it might decrease the building of strong local collections.[44] The New England library counters this possibility by actively encouraging the building of these collections and aiding with book selection tools, consultation, and similar services as well as in-service training of local librarians. Turn-around time and rate of filled requests for regional medical libraries are truly dramatic. Statistics are available for July through September 1969.

Several interesting observations can be made from the preceding table. The National Library of Medicine, although greatly relieved of some of its interlibrary loan burden, still shows the poorest record in turn-around time. Regional libraries do not allow direct borrowing from NLM in their regions and only send requests there when all resources have been exhausted, including other regional libraries. Although this rule is presently "on the books," it cannot be expected to become truly effective until all regional libraries are fully established.

These libraries have been established for varying lengths of time; thus no firm conclusion can be drawn as yet. Some changes in policy have already taken place as libraries have gained experience. One of the rules in the beginning specified that no library could request any material directly from outside its own region and that all requests had to be channeled through the regional library. This is now changing; if libraries are reasonably sure that the material does not exist in their regions, they may go directly to a source known to them.[46] A list of designated libraries has been prepared for use by regional and other libraries. New York Region is in the process of decentralization; Countway at Harvard is using some large libraries in the region as informal (nondesignated, nonfunded) screening agencies. As previously indicated, that library requires no verification but does expect it from "libraries of substance." Most of the other regional libraries require it and also require that requests be submitted on standard forms whenever possible. The John Crerar Library uses forms which are sent along with rejected requests, stating reasons for rejection.[47] Lack of standard form, lack of verification, nontyped request, request not signed by responsible librarian, multiple requests on one form, only one copy of request submitted, and type of material requested are some of the reasons for rejection. It seems surprising that some regional libraries have very few requirements while others seem overly rigid. Apparently each has a great deal of autonomy in developing its policies and procedures.

As time goes on it will be interesting to see if this embryo national network will coalesce or if each regional library and its region will go its own way. The concept of a Biomedical Communications Network espoused by the National Library of Medicine would suggest that these libraries would form a

TABLE 1. REGIONAL MEDICAL LIBRARY QUARTERLY STATISTICAL REPORT, INTERLIBRARY LOANS, JULY THROUGH SEPTEMBER 1969

REGION	WORKLOAD		AVAILABILITY RATE	THRUPUT TIME	
	Requests Recorded	Requests Accepted	Percent Filled	Filled in 3 days	Filled in 4-5 days
1*	10,142	9,718	85	83	93
3	15,445	15,175	90	99	100
4	10,252	9,854	82	78.2	90
5	12,744	12,481	75	90.1	92.6
7	4,512	4,458	69	91	97.2
10	4,541	4,465	92	84.2	89.1
NLM	25,753	22,373	91	59	83.5

*Regions are: 1, New England; 2, New York (no statistics); 3, Mid-eastern, Philadelphia; 4, Mid-atlantic, National Library of Medicine; 5, East Central, Detroit; 6, Southeastern, Atlanta (no statistics); 7, Midwest, John Crerar, Chicago; 8, Mid-continental, Omaha (no statistics); 9, Southwestern, Dallas (no statistics); 10, Pacific Northwest, Seattle; 11, UCLA Biomedical Library, Los Angeles (no statistics).

cohesive network; as yet this has not happened.[48] There seems to be little direction from NLM and even less contact or work with the Lister Hill Center for Biomedical Communications, which, one would think, would become the capstone of any such network. It remains to be seen whether these relationships will emerge as all regional libraries become more firmly established.

DISCUSSION

What can we learn from the information presented here? We have looked briefly at trends in interlibrary loan objectives and procedures; local applications, and some problems. We have discussed at some length two systems which are operational — one a true network, the other as yet in the beginning stages of network development. Certain conclusions may be drawn:

1. Turn-around time (that is, the time it takes from the placing of a request to receipt of material) is crucial to the success of any interlibrary loan network. The NYSILL network, because of its complexity and slow mail delivery, has not yet been successful in reducing the time factor to satisfactory proportions. The regional medical libraries have been very successful; less volume, strict enforcement of prompt handling agreements, and exclusive use of first-class mail have aided in this. However, it should be remembered that most of the medical requests are for journal articles which can be photocopied, while NYSILL handles many book requests. Also, the NYSILL organization is more complex than that of the RML.

2. TWX has speeded request transmittal greatly. It is used universally for this purpose, wherever a standard format and paper tape transmission are used, it presents very few problems. The cost is modest and well worth the increase in speed.

3. Staff training in the concept of networking has not yet been entirely successful. Entrenched attitudes have given way slowly, and uniformity of procedures are not always observed, resulting in an inevitable showdown. The tradition of maintaining strong autonomy on the local level, of partaking of network services at one's pleasure (in New York), have worked against acceptance of some of the "rules from the outside" which a system must necessarily enforce.

4. We know very little as yet about the value of time versus cost. Is it worthwhile to send all books first-class to ensure speedy delivery?

How great is the need for speed! For whom? Under what conditions?

5. The unfilled requests which appear in all the statistics we have seen make us wonder if this material could not have been obtained somewhere. How far must a library or a system go before it gives up? How much staff time can be devoted to any one request?

6. A liberalized interlibrary loan policy and procedure is a must for any successful library operation. Wherever rules were simplified, as they were at the New England RML and during an experiment connecting two campuses of the California university system via LDX,[49] an immediate speed-up occurred.

CONCLUSIONS AND IMPLICATIONS FOR THE FUTURE

What can we look forward to in network developments for interlibrary loan? Before stating our own thoughts, we wish to call attention to an excellent article by Bregzis, who points out some developments as well as defines areas in which work needs to be done.[50] He expresses his conviction that new patterns of research and information use will emerge as a result of machine-based bibliographic and related services. He says the distinctions between different kinds of libraries blur as users look to the nearest library for all their information needs.

Communications technology looms large in the future; the possibilities of digital-video consols and microteletransmissions screens open up new ways by which documents may be transmitted. Bregzis sees the library as providing information services to the user at work or home rather than requiring him to come to the library. The necessary bibliographic tools to access libraries and other data bases will become more numerous and will be available at different levels in central locations while services will become more decentralized. Access to documents will have to be managed in a different way so that they may always be available when needed.

The necessary work to accomplish some or all of the above includes a different way of organizing library materials to ensure access through the chain of libraries forming a network, as well as providing more and different access points to any given document. Technology must be made to be more responsive to library needs in the areas of large storage capacity as well as man-machine interfaces and data communications links.

To this impressive list, we wish to add some further observations. Any given interlibrary loan system or network is measured by four factors: volume, filling rate, elapsed time, and cost. We have fairly satisfactory ways of measuring these; however, there are some areas in which we have not attempted measurement and which seem to me to be basic for network planning.

Users Librarians have always made certain assumptions about users. Despite studies which have pointed out several disturbing factors, librarians continue to make these same assumptions.

Some of these are: (*a*) a patron will come to the library when he needs something; (*b*) he will be willing to wait for an item for varying amounts of time; (*c*) he knows what he wants. (*d*) he is able to describe it adequately; (*e*) we are able to fulfill most if not all of his needs through traditional interlibrary and other loan procedures; (*f*) the patron expects this service to be free.

Each one of these assumptions has either been shown to be wrong or is highly dubious and has not been proven one way or another.

A patron does not always think of the library as the logical source for his information needs. He often does not know that interlibrary loan is available to him (and it sometimes is not).

He is usually but not always unwilling to wait for material and therefore, does not even bother to come to the library but calls someone and gets what he needs quickly.

He knows approximately what he wants but does not always realize what is available to him in addition to the source, or sources, known to him. Thus, he can miss a wealth of pertinent information through ignorance.

He is not always able to adequately describe his needs, and a skillful interview can reveal that what he really wants is not what he says he wants.

We are certainly not able to fulfill most of his needs; there are whole areas of even the more traditional kinds of library materials which are not easily available to the patron. What small public library knows how and when to obtain government documents free? How many know where the depositories for various technical reports are and how their services may be obtained? How many junior college librarians know how to obtain films? This is not to mention access to videotapes, computer-based data bases, and the like. We simply do not perform as switching agents for information materials.

The patron pays for many services willingly. If he wants a copy made, he pays a dime in a commercial establishment. If this service is provided in the library, librarians often think it is sinful to charge because taxpayers support the library. We feel that if a service can be made truly important to the user, he will be willing to pay part or all of its cost. This would be the cost incurred beyond the minimum service available to all patrons regardless of age. We have long-standing examples for this. The John Crerar Library, although a free public reference library, charges for those costs which go beyond normal use of the library. Industrial information services established in conjunction with libraries almost always charge; if their services are good enough, the customer pays, willingly.

In all these areas we need to institute or refine measurments. Some of these exist; others need to be developed. As yet unsuccessful have been studies of the cost/benefit ratio for libraries; however, efforts are under way in this area.[51] User habits in information gathering have been measured successfully, and it is disappointing that so few libraries have as yet applied the instrument developed for this activity.[52] [53] Studies have shown that certain classes of information users obtain data and text in various ways, and that the library ranks relatively low in the hierarchy.[54] [55] [56] [57] Instruction in the use of the library—that is, in our context here, letting the user know what is available to him in addition to what he knows about — is usually poor and needs to be stepped up considerably in all kinds of libraries. Current awareness services are operated in some libraries; much more needs to be done in this area. Only when the user knows what is available will he be able to utilize the literature. And no one knows what the effect on interlibrary loans will be; we think that we have only seen the top of the iceberg in this area.

Document Delivery We begin with the user once again. We have made the assumption all along that he is either unwilling or unable to supply full bibliographic information for a needed document. This is certainly true in the area of subject requests and also for users not as yet well trained in bibliographic procedure. Thus, we have assumed that librarians must perform all the necessary steps of verification, transmission of requests, and the like to ensure successful completion.

It seems that in some cases, where verification, for example, was eliminated, the success rate was quite high, making the above assumption a doubtful one. We feel that the user should be given much more responsibility for the eventual success of his search; only in exceptional cases should the librarian aid him. He should be able to fill out the top part of a revised ALA form while the lower part would be reserved for internal records among the libraries involved. Typing would no longer be required as long as the request is legible. Telephone requests should be as acceptable as any other kind, thus making the entire interlibrary loan service much more accessible to remote users.

A factor frequently mentioned in the literature on our subject notes unsuccessful first attempts at locating a given document, followed by subsequent referrals. Here again, something may be learned from special libraries. Specializing in a given field as they do, they must not only know their own collections intimately but also must know bibliographic resources elsewhere to obtain needed documents. Why then could not a number of subject specialists be employed by the switching center in a given network (such as the State Library in New York)? It would be their responsibility to be familiar with the subject strengths of libraries in their field of expertise, and we believe that referral could be handled more successfully in this manner. Not every library can have subject specialists in sufficient numbers; thus, another responsibility of these people at the network level would be to hold in-service training workshops in the literature of their field, vastly enhancing the bibliographic competence of library staffs.

Implementing this recommendation would help solve another problem which concerned us as we reviewed the literature. What happens to the unfilled requests which appear in every set of statistics we viewed? Again, we call on our experience as a special librarian; when we say to the user: "If we don't have it, we'll get it for you," we usually mean it. And we leave no stone unturned until the information is located. We know of very few "unfilled requests" in those special libraries where we have worked. Perhaps the employment of subject specialists would bring us closer to filling most requests than we are now; they should know where material can be obtained, both through formal and informal channels.

Finally we wish to devote some attention to technology. Document delivery has been speeded up by first-class mail service or air mail, bus delivery, transmittal of requests via TWX and in some few cases, telefacsimile. There remains the need for a cheap device which would transmit document facsimiles at reasonable speeds and in legible form. Communications links are available, but this author wishes to reiterate her previous recommendation that preferential rates, similar to the library book rate, be sought.[58] Night use of ETV channels should be explored as a fast means of transmission.[59] Computer-to-microfilm devices are a relatively recent development; it may be envisioned that large networks could have storage COM libraries which would transmit, in digital form, full text to the site where it is needed. User-oriented devices are available now for viewing and hard-copy print-out of text, and will increasingly become part of the decentralized service described above.

Administrative Considerations We need to comment on network management a bit. It appears that the network concept is by no means universally understood or accepted. A Conference such as this one is a beginning; it should be followed up by regional workshops, similar to the MARC Institutes, to disseminate findings and recommendations. Librarians must learn to think "network," just as they now think "bookmobile" or "reference service."

Management of networks is an art as yet little understood and for which not many people are trained. The experiences in actual network operation in New York State and elsewhere should offer some valuable suggestions to others as yet untrained. Careful systems design, much advanced planning, and a total immersion program for all participants to fully understand and accept the concept are necessities.

State and federal legislation must be flexible enough to allow network formation in geographic regions, regardless of state lines. This is as yet not true for all the states; much effort should be spent in effecting the necessary changes.

Cost considerations are, of course, important. However, they should be weighed carefully against the actual and potential benefits accruing to the user; how much is his time worth as compared to that spent by the network in speeding his request on the way? If his needs are considered important and if a satisfactory time frame can be achieved, considerable expenditures of money may be justified, part of which should be borne by the user.

Finally, the concept of *economy of scale* should be applied. Is there a minimum, a maximum, an optimum size for a network? What kinds of networks can operate on a smaller scale than others?

Performance standards should be developed for network operations and devices to measure network performance. As noted above, some instruments exist already; others need to be developed. *All should have user feedback built in.* Without user reaction, librarians are prone to base decisions on all the old assumptions previously mentioned.

Finally, we wish to talk about people in general — librarians and users alike. People are what makes any cooperative enterprise work. They may resist innovation but once they understand they accept it. People on all levels of any cooperative venture must be included in planning, from the user to the top administrator. Thus far we see no evidence that this has been done; we feel that this is perhaps the most important of all our recommendations.

NOTES

1. Maxwell Maltz, *Psycho-cybernetics,* (Englewood Cliffs, N.J.: Prentice Hall, 1960)

2. Houston Research Institute, *Facsimile transmittal of technical information* (Presented to National Science Foundation [Houston, Texas, May 1965]) Appendix 2.

3. Ibid.

4. Ibid.

5. "New interlibrary loan code drafted," *ALA bulletin* 62:409-411 (Apr. 1968).

6. "Model interlibrary loan code for regional, state, local or other special groups of libraries," *ALA bulletin* 63:514 (Apr. 1969).

7. Ibid., p.513.

8. Brigitte L. Kenney, *A review of interlibrary communications developments,* (presented at the Conference on Image Storage and Transmission Systems for Libraries, Dec. 1-2, 1969, National Bureau of Standards, Wn., D.C.) (unpublished), 19p.

9. Bell System. *Medical interlibrary communications exchange service (MICES), a pilot project to determine the usefulness of the teletypewriter exchange service for interlibrary communications,* 1965 (unpublished).

10. Warren Bird, "TWX and interlibrary loans," *Bulletin of the Medical Library Association* 57:125-129 (April 1969).

11. A. F. Goodman, *Flow of scientific and technical information: the results of a recent major investigation* (Douglas paper 4516, rev. Sept. 1968 [Huntington Beach, Calif.: McDonnell Douglas Astronautics Co., 1968]).

12. Vern M. Pings, "The interlibrary loan transaction," *Bulletin of the Medical Library Association* 53:204-14 (April 1965).

13. American Psychological Association, *Reports of the American Psychological Association's project on scientific information exchange in psychology* (Washington, D.C.: APA), p.103.

14. Brigitte L. Kenney, *A survey of Indiana special libraries and information centers* (Indianapolis: Indiana State Library, 1970), 44p.

15. Nelson Associates, Inc., *Public library systems in the United States; a survey of multijurisdictional systems* (Chicago: ALA, 1969), 368p.

16. Vern M. Pings, *Study of interlibrary loan policies of midwest biomedical libraries,* rep. no. 15 (Detroit: Wayne State Univ. School of Medicine, Library and Biomedical Information Center, Sept. 1965), 13p.

17. Jacqueline W. Felter, "The Medical Library Center of New York: a progress report," *Bulletin of the Medical Library Association* 56:15-20 (Jan. 1968).

18. Nelson Associates, Inc., *Interlibrary loan in New York State; a report prepared for the division of library development of the New York State Library* (New York: The author, 1969), p.xiv.

19. American Psychological Association, *Reports of the American Psychological Association's project on scientific information...,* p.xiv.

20. Irwin H. Pizer, "A regional medical library network," *Bulletin of the Medical Library Association* 57:101-115 (April 1969).

21. S. Gilbert Prentiss, "The evolution of the library system (New York)," *Library quarterly* 39:78-89 (Jan. 1969).

22. John Mackenzie Cory, "The network in a major metropolitan center (METRO, New York)," *Library quarterly* 39:90-98 (Jan. 1969).

23. Erich Meyerhoff, "Medical Library Center of New York," *Bulletin of the Medical Library Association* 51:501-506 (Oct. 1963).

24. Nelson Associates, Inc., *The New York State Library's pilot program in facsimile transmission of library materials* (New York: The author, June 1968), 85p.

25. "Indiana installs teletype facility," *Bulletin of the Medical Library Association* 55:237-238 (April 1967).

26. Mary E. McNamara, *Establishing a medical library network for the Detroit metropolitan area,* rep. no. 20 (Detroit: Wayne State Univ. School of Medicine, Library and Biomedical Information Center, May 1966).

27. Thomas C. Meyer, "Communications - a supplement to medical library service," *Bulletin of the Medical Library Association* 57:338-342 (Oct. 1969).

28. Elliott H. Morse, "Regional plans for medical library service: medical library cooperation in Philadelphia," *Bulletin of the Medical Library Association* 52:509-513 (July 1964).

29. Irwin H. Pizer, "Medical library network."

30. U.S. Veterans Administration, *Professional services: medical and general reference library staff* (Veterans Administration, Dep. of Medicine and Surgery Manual [Washington, D.C.: Gov. Print. Off., Feb. 1966]), 179p.

31. Brigitte L. Kenney, *Health sciences libraries today* (RM-269 [Boston: EDUCOM, Dec. 1967]), 179p.

32. Richard H. Orr., et al., "Development of methodologic tools for planning and managing library services," *Bulletin of the Medical Library Association* 56:235-267, 380-403 (July 1968).

33. Gwendolyn S. Cruzat and Vern M. Pings, *An evaluation of the interlibrary loan service, Wayne State University Medical Library: III, determination of cost for processing interlibrary loans,* rep. no. 17 (Detroit: Wayne State Univ., Library and Biomedical Information Center, March 1966), 31p.

34. Mary E. McNamara, *Establishing a medical library network....*

35. Irwin H. Pizer, Personal communication, July 8, 1970.

36. Irwin H. Pizer, "A regional medical library network...."

37. "Communication problems in biomedical research; report of a study," *Federation of American Societies for Experimental Biology proceedings* 23:1117-1176 (1964).

38. Herner and Company, *A recommended design for the United States medical library and information system,* vol. 1, 2 (rev. ed.; Washington, D.C.: Herner, 1966).

39. Brigitte L. Kenney, *Health sciences libraries today.*

40. Richard H. Orr and Vern M. Pings, "Document retrieval: the national biomedical library system and interlibrary loans," *Federation of American Societies for Experimental Biology proceedings* 23:1155-1163 (Sept. 1964).

41. Most of the following information was obtained through personal communications: Richard H. Davis, Director, Midwest Regional Library, 6 July 1970; Mary E. Feeney, Director, New England Regional Medical Library Service, 8 June 1970; T. Mark Hodges, Director, Southeastern Regional Medical Library, 3 June 1970; Ann P. Hutchinson, Director, New York Regional Medical Library, 28 May 1970; Dale Middleton, Interlibrary Loan Librarian, Pacific Northwest Regional Medical Library, 7 July 1970; and Irwin H. Pizer, former director, SUNY Biomedical Communications Network, 8 July 1970.

42. T. Mark Hodges, et al., "NERMLS: the first year," *Bulletin of the Medical Library Association* 57:329-337 (Oct. 1969).

43. *NERMLS news* (Jan.-Mar. 1970).

44. Ralph H. Esterquest, "The medical librarians view," *Bulletin of the Medical Library Association* 56:52-55 (Jan. 1968).

45. "Regional medical library quarterly statistical report, interlibrary loans, July-Sept. 1969, *Library networks/MEDLARS technical bulletin* 9:4 (Jan. 1970).

46. T. Mark Hodges, "NERMLS: the first year...."

47. Richard A. Davis, Personal communication.

48. Davis B. McCarn, "Biomedical communications network," *Bulletin of the Medical Library Association* 57:323-328 (Oct. 1969).

49. William D. Schieber and Ralph M. Shoffner, *Telefacsimile in libraries; a report of an experiment in facsimile transmission and an analysis of implications for interlibrary loan service* (Berkeley, Calif.: Institute for Library Research, Feb. 1968), 137p.

50. Ritvars Bregzis, "Library networks of the future," *Drexel library quarterly* 4:261-270 (Dec. 1968).

51. Maryan E. Reynolds, Interview, July 1969.

52. Institute for Advancement of Medical Communications, *Third progress report, Apr.-Aug. 1967.* (Philadelphia; The Institute, 14 Aug. 1967).

53. Richard H. Orr, "Development of methodologic tools...."

54. American Psychological Association, *Project on Scientific Information Exchange.*

55. "Communication problems in biomedical research...."

56. A. F. Goodman, *Flow of scientific and technical information....*

57. Brigitte L. Kenney, *Health sciences today.*

58. ...., *Interlibrary communication developments.*

59. ...., *Interlibrary communications systems.*

Switching Centers for Inquiry Referral

Manfred Kochen

INTRODUCTION

This paper is an extension of "Referential Consulting Networks,"[1] in which we explain the concept of a network of referential consultants each of whom could "field" questions by: (a) answering them on the basis of his own expertise, (b) answering them with the help of library resources at his command, (c) referring the question to a colleague he judges to be more skilled than he in (a), (b), and (c). The querist is part of this network too. He need not, however, know how his request is processed between the time he submits it and the time he gets a response — even if it is only the first pass in a multipass query negotiation "dialogue." If his request leads to extensive but productive library searches or to quality-improving "buckpassing," he will notice this only as increased turn-around time.

The question of primary concern in this paper is the trade-off between turn-around time (response time) and quality of the response. Small response time and high quality of the response both contribute to total benefit — and also to total cost. A key factor determining both response time and quality is the quality of the directories available to the various referential consultants in the organization that services queries. A directory, exemplified by the "yellow pages" or a library catalog, points its user to the optional library resources and colleagues among which he makes choices (b) and (c). It also might jog his own memory in choice (a), but we will ignore that in this paper. The directory serves both to prompt and to teach, but again we confine our study to only the prompting function.

To design a referential consulting network is to: (1) select the number and kinds of referential consultants — each of whom is thus a potential switching point, with the possibility that some units in the organization are exclusively switching centers, (2) specify the directories which characterize each unit, (3) specify the way these units are interconnected. We then ask how the choice of a consulting network affects cost/benefit ratio, and we attempt to search for that organization or its properties which maximize it.

REVIEW OF THE LITERATURE: EVALUATION OF TRENDS

Interest in communication networks as objects of mathematical and experimental study began in 1948[2][3] with Bave-las's work on task-oriented groups. A team of people — paid experimental subjects — were seated at a round table with, say, five radial partitions between them, as shown.

There were slots, such as in mail boxes, into which each subject could drop a message, which would be delivered to one or more specified people according to a particular network scheme. The entire team was given a task which required cooperation and communication. The aim was to investigate the effect of different networks on performance.

Leavitt, in 1951,[4] examined four basic patterns of communication among five people:

He found that leaders emerged in the "fork" and "wheel" structures (positions C and E); also, he found that the wheel is administratively most efficient at information processing. In the chain, A and B were never perceived as leaders.

In 1954 we[5] began a mathematical investigation of such networks, with the aim of relating the flow of information to the performance of the organization. We believed, at the time, as did Rothstein,[6] Brillouin,[7] and Watanabe[8] to mention but a few investigators, that a measure of the "degree of organization," analogous to Shannon's[9] measure of the "amount of information," could perhaps be created and used to prove theorems about the "emergent" properties of *organized* assemblies of *numerous* parts.

It was not until von Neumann[10] introduced the beautiful idea that an assembly of unreliable parts, suitably organized, could in its entirety function like one of the parts but with arbitrarily high reliability, that a major conceptual advance took place. At the same time the economist Marschak began to develop a theory of teams,[11] which led later to profound insights into the economics of information. In 1958 we connected some of these notions.[12] In 1960 Shannon and Moore[13] made a significant advance on how to make a reliable switch with less reliable components, and in 1964 Winograd and Cowan crowned this line of investigation with definitive results about the reliability of networks, analogous to the coding theorems of information theory.[14] In a sense this provided a satisfactory answer to what switching networks can do that could, in principle, not be done without them.

At a less profound level, switching networks have been extensively studied since the days of the first computers.[15] Since at least the pioneering work of McCulloch-Pitts,[16] it was understood that logic could be performed by switching networks. Of course, computers are built of switching networks, and there exists an enormous literature on how to find the cheapest and most effective networks to act as a specified switching function.[17]

At an even more practical level, the proliferation of computers and terminals—more than 50,000 installations exist in the U.S. — telephones, copying machines, etc. — led both "sociological engineers" and computer scientists to concern themselves with "switching networks." The early experiments with time-sharing at MIT and SDC led to the exciting concept of an "on-line intellectual community." IBM began to concern itself with total systems approaches as early as 1956. Farsighted engineers[18] began to investigate computer networks. Experiments like DICO[19] and SASIDS,[20] which extended the notion of SDI to that of a network in which each member acts both as a source of recommended literature and as a recipient of information selectively disseminated to him, showed the value of such exchange nets.

And at a commercial level, airline and hotel reservation systems proved to be extremely cost-effective. Though they required the surmounting of such technological hurdles as the development of a reliable magnetic disc, the conceptual problems were simple, primarily because only a very specialized demand — just two or three stereotyped questions or requests — had to be serviced. The service does, however, require a switching net involving thousands of switching centers, and response time in seconds is as important as up-to-the-minute updating of rather large files

The notion of networks in library and information science arose at several levels. It may well have been inspired by the various attempts to use graph theory in thesaurus design[21] [22] [23] [24] [25]. Interlibrary communication nets are, of course, not new although the use of communication channels, such as the one between New York City and Albany, is fairly recent. Systematic studies gathered momentum at the 1967 EDUCOM conference. A careful study of regional networks was made in 1968 by Meise.[26] In 1969 Duggan[27] analyzed communication networks

of libraries, raising such questions as: How can configurations be evaluated? What is the best type of network configuration? We shall see how the model we present later can help answer these questions.

In "Referential Consulting Networks" we argued for a new, expanded role for the reference librarian[28] as precisely the kind of switching point in a network such as we are discussing here. We noted the work of Grogan,[29] indicating some typical questions that reference librarians are requested to service; the viewpoints of Lorenz,[30] Freiser,[31] and Rees[32] on the division of responsibilities among libraries and information centers in this regard; and such experiments in the use of libraries as community information centers[33] [34]. Aspens[35] has argued that contemporary reference librarians already have a status comparable to that of doctors, engineers, lawyers. Shera and Egan[36] proposed an important revision to the classical definition of librarianship (a collection of books organized for use) by asserting its function to be "to maximize the effective social utilization of the graphics records of civilization." In "Referential Consulting Networks" we proposed a further revision of this to read: "to maximize the greatest potentially attainable effective and efficient social utilization of documented knowledge." And that is where networks come in.

If the literature shows any trends, it is perhaps an increasing concern with the benefits of networks. Professionals at well-endowed, large libraries — and computing centers — are hard-pressed to find uses for communication to or from other institutions if a better network were available. Many investigators and enterpreneurs and managers seem to favor centralized facilities: small, stand-alone facilities (minicomputers, personal or departmental libraries) for those who can afford them and large centers to be shared by all the others.

But this trend may not last. In a series of papers aiming at building a theory of decentralization, K. W. Deutsch and I[37] [38] [39] have shown that historical trends favor decentralization: networks with distributed switching centers. This is primarily due to the increase in the volume of requests to be serviced. For an organization to remain responsive and minimize total cost, the number of dispersed service facilities should increase predominantly as the square root of the load. I believe there will be a trend toward larger centers and satellites organized into a decentralized network, but this trend is not yet evident in practice. This paper is a contribution to develop the theoretical basis.

DIRECTORY DESIGN PARAMETERS

Imagine an organization of $n+1$ active units or potential switching points labeled $0, 1, 2,..., i,..., n$. Interpret 0 to designate the querist. Let D_i designate the directory at i's disposal, for $i = 0, 1,..., n$, and picture D_i to be represented as a table like that of Figure 1. Alternately, picture it as a black box with one of N_i acceptable inputs and as many corresponding outputs. The set of inputs or entries resemble the entries to a library or parts catalog, a classified directory like the yellow pages, or an encyclopedia: They are a mixture of subject headings and proper names, in terms of which any query is to be represented. The output corresponding to each input is a list of surrogates for either documents or colleagues in the organization, or both.

Let M_i be the average number of document-surrogates per entry and let L_i be the number of "colleague"-surrogates per entry. Thus, $M_i + L_i$ is the average total number of surrogates from which the directory user can pick one when he enters the directory with a term that matches. If m_i is the average number of bits per document-surrogate and 1_i that for a colleague-surrogate and b_i is the average number of bits per entry, then the entire directory takes $N_i(b_i + M_im_i + L_i1_i)$ bits to store. If it takes T seconds to check if a given term matches some entry in the directory and the entries are kept in order, it takes approximately $T \log N_i$ seconds to locate a row in the directory if the input term matches some entry. To this should be added the time, T' seconds, it takes the directory user to read the output and make a choice terminating in a new input registered in the system.

Basically, i will have used the directory in response to a query. He must judge, for relevance to the query, document or colleague surrogates which are the outputs of the directory. His relevance judgment can be faulty for two reasons: (1) The surrogate, which is all he has on which to base his judgment, does not accurately reflect the relevance judgment he would have made had he encountered the document or colleague directly; (2) his relevance judgment does not correspond to the requirements of the query.

For example, suppose that *0* requests of *1* the combination to his bank safe, which he lost, giving *1* his name. Now *1* consults his directory, locates *0's* name, and finds listed surrogates of two documents and three colleagues, say, the "List of All Active Savings Accounts" and "*2*, Vice President In Charge of Safe Deposits," etc. *1* should pick the third surrogate. It is possible that *2* does not have in his directory a direct surrogate for the book of combinations either, but only something like, "*3* Officer In Charge of Customer Access." Then *1* should refer the query to *2* who refers it on to *3* who, hopefully, is pointed by his directory to the document containing *0's* combination. Of course, if *0* could see the union of the entries in all the directories of *1*, *2*, and *3*, he could have contacted *3* rather than *1* in the first place. Even better, if *0* had the document of all combinations himself he would not have had to bother anyone.

Let Q be the set of all possible queries — assumed to be characterized by a single term suitable as input for matching a directory entry — with which *0* might ever enter the system. Let $Dom(D_0)$ be the set of entries in his directory. We shall assume, for purposes of analysis, that he does not rely on his own memory at all, only on this directory. Clearly, $N_0 = 1 \mid Dom(D_0) \mid$.

Assumption 1: $N_0 \mid Q \mid$, and if, for some q & Q, q & $Dom(D_0)$, this query is switched to 1.

Assumption 2: $Q \leq \overset{n}{\underset{i=1}{U}} Dom(D_i)$ and if q & $Dom(D_i)$, this query is switched to $i+1$, $i = 1,..., n$.

Theorem 1: Every query in Q will match an entry in some directory, and it will take at most $T \log \overset{n}{\underset{i=1}{\Pi}} N_i$ seconds to effect this match.

Assumption 3: Surrogation is perfect, and i makes no errors in judging relevance, $i = 0, 1, 2,..., n$.

The reason that a directory in which q matches an entry would fail to produce the desired response to 0 for q, even though the output is relevant, is that the output is not yet direct. It may be indirect, pointing correctly to another place where the search can be narrowed down. Will it always be narrowed down, or could it get more diffused? Could it go in nonending cycles?

If i refers a query q to j who has in his directory pointers which lead q back to i, then i has erred in referring to j. If i can neither, through his directory, find an answer to q nor find some j who can either find an answer or find some k who can either..., then the question cannot be answered, and i should so inform 0.

A COMPUTER PROGRAM FOR ANALYZING REFERENTIAL CONSULTING NETS

We present in this section an operational FORTRAN program, created by A. Breveleri, R. Chlopan, W. Everett, and A. Tars for this paper. It can be used by anyone to simulate a great variety of proposed configurations of networks of switching centers with directories. We shall show how to use it and one result of its use. The program resembles simulators like that of Gordon[40] and SIMSCRIPT,[41] but it is not a programming language.

To conform to FORTRAN notation and to simplify exposition, we relabel the following key variables:

LP: Number of people (referential consultants, switching centers), was n

LQ: Number of questions a directory can match, was $N_i = \mid Q \mid$ all i

LD: Total number of documents containing answers.

A particular configuration of switching centers to be analyzed is specified by four input arrays. The first array, called MANS, consists of LP answer-directories, one for each person. Each directory is in the form of an LQ x ADEPTH matrix, in which an entry is any integer from 0, 1, 2...to LD + LP. We denote the people by the integers 1, 2,..., LP and the documents by LP + 1, LP + 2,..., LP + LD. Each row denotes one of the LQ questions; the entry in each row is the set of people or documents each of which is *known* by the directory user to contain the answer. Zeros are used simply to fill out the matrix, the columns denoting nothing. Thus, if there are LQ = 4 questions, LP = 2 people (labeled 1, 2), and LD = 3 documents (labeled 3, 4, 5), an answer-directory for person R_1 may be: D_1 = MANS =

2	4	5
3	0	0
0	0	0
2	3	5

ADEPTH (here = 3) is $\max_i(L_i + M_i)$ in the notation of section three. We read this as: If R_1 gets question 1 (Row1), he can get the answer by asking R_2 or looking in documents four or five. If he gets question 2 (Row 2), he can get the answer *only* from document three. He cannot get an answer to question three at all, and he can get the answer to question four by asking R_2 or looking in documents three or five.

The second array, called MREF, consists of LP "buck-passing" directories, one for each person. Each is given as an LQ x RDEPTH matrix, with entries 0, 1,..., LP. Each row again denotes one of the LQ questions. Posted next to each entry are not more than RDEPTH other people, each of whom the directory user *thinks* can obtain an answer to that question. Thus, for R_1, as above, we might have MREF =

2
0
2
2

with RDEPTH = 1 (it could not be greater here). Here, R_1 thinks that *if* he referred to any questions but 2 (Row 2) to R_2, R_2 could either answer it or refer it more appropriately than could R_1.

The third array, called M A C O S T, consists of LP answering - cost - matrices, one for each person. Each matrix for R_i has LQ rows and LP + LD columns. An entry in row j, column k is any positive real number, representing the cost to R_i of getting the answer to question j from source k. (Recall that k = 1,..., LP is a person, and k = LP + 1,..., LP + LD are documents.)

The last array, called MRCOST, consists of LP reference-cost- matrices each being LQ by LP. An entry in row j, column k of this matrix for R_i denotes the cost of R_i of referring question j to person k.

The four arrays are entered as input parameters. The program consists of five parts, as shown in the rectangular boxes of Figure 2. The top box causes all inputs to be read in, all variables to be set initially. The second part, "Question," reads in a question and the person to whom it is originally directed. This can be input or generated randomly by a program. We can think of the programmer as being the querist who refers his question to one of the persons in the network by his input, or we

can think of the querist as being the first person in the network who is faced with the question. The basic logic of the next part, "Action," is shown in Figure 3. "Action" assumes that a given person cannot be asked the same question twice (in this version of the program), which rules out bureaucratic cycles. The "Pricing" box forms the cost-estimates used in "Action." An adaptive feature is built in which makes the choices converge to the lowest cost per query.

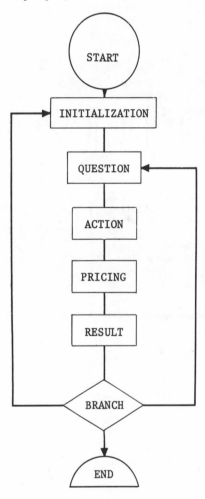

Figure 2

The results printed by the first version of the operating program ("BUCKPASS") are for each input question and starting consultant:

1.   The total cost and

2.   The chain of referential consultants to whom the "buck" was passed, ending with a person or document.

Example: for LP = 5, LQ = 5, LD = 10, ADEPTH = 10, RDEPTH = 15:
Question input: Question 5 to person 1
Output: Cost = $10; chain = 1→2→5→13 (a document).

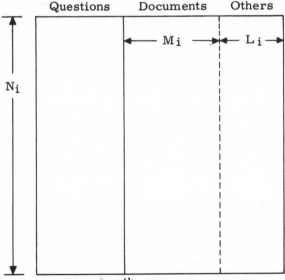

Directory D_i for i^{th} Referential Consultant

Figure 1

It should be emphasized that the last link in the chain is not a referral, even though the last item in the chain might be a person in the network. We distinguished between person i

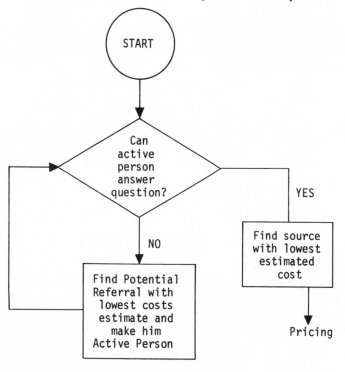

Figure 3

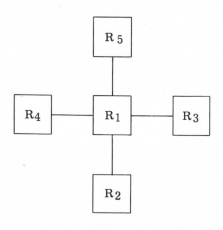

Figure 4

obtaining the answer to a question directly from person j (by use of MANS) and person i referring a question –passing the buck –to person j (by use of MREF).

A variety of refinements in the program are underway. One important improvement is hierarchization of queries. The input question is first classified into gross and high-level categories, with the first consultant receiving it doing the coarse screening and sending it to one of several other generalists, one for each gross category. A second, closely related new feature is the decomposition of the question into parts, and sending, in turn

(or copies, in parallel), to specialists on the parts. Thirdly, as in footnote forty-two, measures of quality are introduced. In place of the MANS matrix, we have:

$p(i,j,k)$ = Probability (i knows k has answer to j and finds it.)

$r(i,j,k)$ = Probability (i judges k relevant to j | k relevant to j.)

$q(i,j,k)$ = Probability (i judges k relevant to j | k irrelevant to j.)

(j,k) = Probability (k is relevant to j and provides correct answer.)

Now the output is:

1. The total cost per query, obtained by adding the consultant costs to the look-up costs

2. The turn-around time, add the times for referral, the times for each question part that is delivered, and the look-up times

3. The quality of a response is the probability that the answer is correct.

This permits us to study a trade-off between quality of responses and turn-around time. We can estimate benefits by the expected utility of a high-quality response. We now can investigate how different configurations and directory designs affect benefit/cost ratio.

	q_1	q_2	q_3	q_4	q_5	q_6	q_7	q_8	q_9	q_{10}
R_1	0	0	0	0	0	0	0	13	14	15
R_2	0	0	0	0	0	0	12	0	0	0
R_3	0	0	0	0	0	11	0	0	0	0
R_4	0	0	0	0	10	0	0	0	0	0
R_5	6	7	8	9	0	0	0	0	0	0

MANS
(ADEPTH = 1)

	q_1	q_2	q_3	q_4	q_5	q_6	q_7	q_8	q_9	q_{10}
R_1	5	5	5	5	4	3	2	0	0	0
R_2	1	1	1	1	1	1	0	1	1	1
R_3	1	1	1	1	1	0	1	1	1	1
R_4	1	1	1	1	0	1	1	1	1	1
R_5	0	0	0	0	1	1	1	1	1	1

MREF
(RDEPTH = 1)

Figure 5

	q_1	q_2	q_3	q_4	q_5	q_6	q_7	q_8	q_9	q_{10}
R_1	5	6	7	8	9	10	11	0	0	0
R_2	1	1	1	1	1	1	0	1	1	1
R_3	1	1	1	1	1	0	1	1	1	1
R_4	1	1	1	1	0	1	1	1	1	1
R_5	0	0	0	0	5	5	5	5	5	5

MRCOST

	q_1	q_2	q_3	q_4	q_5	q_6	q_7	q_8	q_9	q_{10}
R_1	0	0	0	0	0	0	0	2	3	4
R_2	0	0	0	0	0	0	1	0	0	0
R_3	0	0	0	0	0	1	0	0	0	0
R_4	0	0	0	0	1	0	0	0	0	0
R_5	5	4	3	2	0	0	0	0	0	0

MACOST

Figure 6

USE OF *BUCKPASS*

In this section we present an example of the use of BUCK-PASS to analyze a particular network model, a wheel configuration with five persons. Assumptions in this model render the analysis too simplistic for practical use; more realistic assumptions, however, would complicate our illustration and would direct attention to the model rather than to the use of BUCKPASS.

In the wheel (Figure 4) the central person, R_1, can refer questions to any of the persons on the periphery. The peripheral persons, $R_2,...,R_5$, can only refer questions to R_1. We consider ten questions, $q_1, q_2,..., q_{10}$, which can be answered by consulting source documents $s_6, s_7,..., s_{15}$, respectively. (In other models, a person in the network might also be a source of

	q_1	q_2	q_3	q_4	q_5	q_6	q_7	q_8	q_9	q_{10}
R_1	5	5	5	5	7	8	9	0	0	0
R_2	1	1	1	1	1	1	0	1	1	1
R_3	1	1	1	1	1	0	1	1	1	1
R_4	1	1	1	1	0	1	1	1	1	1
R_5	0	0	0	0	5	5	5	5	5	5

MRCOST

Figure 7

answers, e.g., $R_1 = s_1$.) We assume that if one person in the network knows that the answer to q_i can be obtained from s_j, then no other person in the networks knows (assumption of disjoint answer directories). We assume that persons R_2, R_3, and R_4 can answer exactly one question, and R_5 can answer N_5 questions. It follows that R_1 in the center can answer $N_1 = 7\text{-}N_5$ questions. For example, if $N_5 = 4$, we have MANS and MREF in Figure 5.

If we think of ourselves as the querist, we might ask to which person in the network, R_1, R_2, or R_5, we should address our questions. We might also wish to know the effect of N_5 on the average cost of answering a question if the questions are directed randomly to different persons in the network under the following assumptions about costs:

1.   When a person can answer less than two questions, there is no answer directory look-up.

2.   Answer directory look-up proceeds linearly and costs $1 for each item examined.

3.   The cost of obtaining the answer from the source document is $1.

4.   The referral directory is consulted only after failure to match in answer directory; hence, referral cost includes $$N_i$ when $N_i \geq 2$.

5.   Referral directory look-up proceeds linearly and costs $1 for each item examined.

6.   Communication costs $1 for each question referred.

These assumptions determine the costs in MACOST and MRCOST. In Figure 6 these matrices are flattened in the third dimension since there is in this model only one source to answer each question, and referral of an unanswered question is likewise unique. It should be clear that we have optimal directory design under our assumptions (e.g., the fourth item in R_1's referral directory is the first item in R_5's answer directory).

Example: Suppose we direct question q_6 to person R_5:

1. R_5 consults his answer directory and fails to match each of the four items. He does not consult a referral directory since he refers all unanswered questions to R_1. Referral cost is $4+0+1 = 5$.

2. R_1 consults his answer directory and fails to match each of the three items. He consults his referral directory and finds a match after examining the sixth item. Referral cost is $3+6+1 = 10$, and the question is referred to R_3.

3. R_3 does not consult an answer directory since there is only one question he can answer. He

	Network Entry Point			
N_5	R_1	R_2	R_5	Random
7	10.30	10.10	9.20	10.02
6	8.50	8.40	8.60	8.52
5	8.80	8.60	8.80	8.74
4	8.20	8.00	8.60	8.22
3	7.70	7.50	8.40	7.78
2	7.30	7.10	8.20	7.42
1	6.90	6.70	7.00	6.86

Average Cost in Dollars for Model I.

Table 1

	Network Entry Point			
N_5	R_1	R_2	R_5	Random
7	6.40	6.80	7.40	6.90
6	5.50	5.90	7.10	6.12
5	5.00	5.40	7.00	5.70
4	4.60	5.00	6.80	5.34
3	4.40	4.80	6.60	5.14
2	4.40	4.80	6.40	5.10
1	4.50	4.90	5.20	4.94

Average Cost in Dollars for Model II.

Table 2

obtains the answer from source document s_{11}. Answer cost is $0 + 1 = 1$.

4. To obtain the answer to question q_6 by asking R_5, the chain is $5 \rightarrow 1 \rightarrow 3 \rightarrow 11$, and the total cost is \$16.

Table 1 shows the average costs for asking all ten questions of R_1, R_2, and R_5, as well as the average cost for directing questions randomly to any of the five persons in the network. This information is given for each of the values of N_5. For $N_5 = 7$, R_1 acts only as a switching center and can answer no

questions. The case $N_5 = 0$ is of no interest since we would be dealing with a four-person network, with the option of sending a question directly to R_1 or indirectly through a \$1 communication channel R_5. The effect of cost assumption 1 is apparent for $N_5 = 6$. With that exception, the cost decreases as the expertise of R_1 increases. Except when $N_5 = 7$, R_2 is the best entry point to the network under these assumptions.

We can modify our cost assumptions and observe the resulting effect on the cost of the network. If we replace cost assumption 5 by 5′, referral directory look-up is categorical, proceeds linearly, and costs \$1 for each category examined. We have MRCOST as in Figure 7 (with $N_5 = 4$). Questions q_1, q_2, q_3, and q_5 match the first item in R_1's referral directory, that item being the category of questions referred to R_5. In Table 2 we see the results of this model. The reduction in referral costs has made R_1 the optimal entry point to the network. However, if we never use R_5 as an entry point, the minimum cost is obtained when R_1 can answer four or five questions rather than six. This contrasts with the first model in which the lowest cost was obtained when R_1 had maximum expertise.

A more interesting use of BUCKPASS would be to allow referral of any question to any of the other persons in the network and to determine what distribution of question-answering capabilities and what cost assumptions cause the model to converge to a wheel configuration of preferred communication links. In the example previously described, there were no alternative paths and consequently, no opportunity for convergence.

A refinement incorporated in BUCKPASS II allows the user to specify implicit cost functions, eliminating the need to provide the cost matrices as input data. With the additional output statistics mentioned in the preceding section, we have a powerful tool for readily determining cost-benefit ratios of referential consulting networks under different directory designs, distributions of question-answering capability, and cost assumptions.

NOTES

1. Manfred Kochen, "Referential consulting networks," in C. Rawski, ed., *Toward a theory of librarianship* (Cleveland: Case Western Reserve Univ. Pr., 1970)

2. A. Bavelas, "Communication patterns in task-oriented groups," *The journal of the Acoustical Society of America* 22:725-730 (Nov. 1950).

3. ...., "A mathematical model for group structures," *Applied anthropology* 7:16-30 (Dec. 1943).

4. H. J. Leavitt, "Some effects of certain communication patterns upon group performance," *Journal of abnormal social psychology* 46:38-50 (1951).

5. Manfred Kochen, "An information-theoretic model of organization," *Transactions of the Institute for Radio Engineers* 4:67-75 (Sept. 1954).

6. J. Rothstein, "Information, organization and system," *Transactions of the Institute of Radio Engineers* (PGIT-4) 4:64 (Sept. 1954).

7. L. Billouin, "Information theory and most efficient codings for communication or memory devices," *Journal of applied physics* 22:1108-1111 (Sept. 1951).

8. Watanabe, Interview.

9. C. Shannon and W. Weaver, *The mathematical theory of communication* (Urbana: Univ. of Illinois Press, 1949).

10. J. von Neumann, "Probabilistic logics and the synthesis of reliable organisms from unreliable components," *Automata studies*

(Annals of Mathematics Studies, No. 34 [Princeton: Princeton Univ. Pr., 1956]), p.43.

11. J. Marschak, *Elements for a theory of teams* (Chicago: Univ. of Chicago, Cowles Commission for Research in Economics, 1955).

12. Manfred Kochen, "Organized systems with discrete information transfer," *General systems* 2:30-47 (1958).

13. C. E. Shannon and E. F. Moore, "Reliable circuits using less reliable relays," *J. Franklin Institute* 262:191-208 (Sept. 1956), 262:281-297 (Oct. 1956).

14. S. Winograd and J. D. Cowan, *Reliable computation in the presence of noise* (Cambridge, Mass.: MIT Press, 1963).

15. H. Aiken, *Synthesis of electronic computing and control circuits,* Ann. computer laboratory, 27 (Cambridge, Mass.: Harvard Univ. Pr., 1951).

16. W. S. McCulloch and W. Pitts, "A logical calculus of the ideas immanent in nervous activity," *Bulletin of mathematical biophysics* 5:115 (1943).

17. M. Phister, Jr., *Logical design of digital computers* (New York: Wiley, 1958), 408p.

18. J. Griffith and E. M. Boehm, "A method for multiplexing computers," *IBM Memos* parts I-VIII (Dec. 1958-June 1959).

19. Manfred Kochen and E. Wong, "Concerning the possibility of a cooperative information exchange," *IBM Journal of research and development* 6: (April 1962).

20. .... and M. M. Flood, "Some bibliographic and sociological devices to improve maintenance of current awareness about literature," in M. Kochen, ed., *Some problems in information science* (Metuchen, N.J.: Scarecrow, 1965).

21. C. Abraham, "Evaluation of clusters on the basis of random graph theory," *IBM research memo,* Nov. 1962.

22. ...., "Survey of the theory of probabilistic graphs," in M. Kochen, ed., *Some problems in information science* (Metuchen, N.J.: Scarecrow, 1965).

23. L. B. Doyle, "Semantic road maps for literature searches," *Journal of the Association for Computing Machinery* (Oct. 1961).

24. V. E. Giuliano and P. E. Jones, "Linear associative retrieval," *Information handling* (Washington, D.C.: Spartan, 1963), p.30-54.

25. J. C. Olney, "Building a concept network to retrieve information from large libraries," rep. TM634 (Santa Monica, Calif.: Systems Development Corp.),

26. Norman R. Meise, "Conceptual design of an automated national library system" (M.A. thesis, Syracuse University, 1968).

27. Maryann Duggan, "Library network analysis and planning (Lib-NAT)," *Journal of library automation* 2:157-175 (Sept. 1969).

28. B. Vavrek, "The theory of reference service," *College and research libraries* 29:508-510 (Nov. 1968).

29. D. Grogan, *Case studies in reference work* (London: Archon Books, 1967), 166p.

30. John J. Lorenz, "Regional and state systems," in W. B. Linderman, ed., *The present and future prospects of reference/information service* (Chicago: ALA, 1967), p.57-65.

31. L. Freiser, "Reconstruction of library services." in W. B. Linderman, ed., *The present and future...,"* p.48-56.

32. Alan M. Rees, "Broadening the spectrum," p.57-65.

33. Sheffield, England, Libraries, Art Galleries and Museums Committee, *The city libraries of Sheffield 1856-1956* (Sheffield, England: City of Sheffield Printing and Stationery Dept., 1956), p.47-49, 53.

34. A. Kahn, *Neighborhood information centers: a study and some proposals* (New York: Columbia Univ. School of Social Work, 1966).

35. G. Aspens, Librarian for Corgill, Inc., Minneapolis, Minnesota, INTERVIEW, 12 March 1969.

36. M. E. Egan, "Education for librarianship of the future," J. Sherra, et al., eds., *Documentation in action* (New York: Reinhold Publishing Corp., 1956).

37. Manfred Kochen and K. W. Deutsch, "Toward a rational theory of decentralization: some implications of a mathematical approach," *American political science review* 63:734-749 (Sept. 1969).

38. ...., "Decentralization and uneven service loads," *Journal of regional science* 10:153-73 (Aug. 1970).

39. ...., "Decentralization by function and location," (MHRI preprint 267, Univ. of Michigan, April 1970), submitted for publication to *Econometrica*.

40. G. Gordon, "A general purpose systems simulator," *IBM systems journal* (1962).

41. H. M. Markowitz, Bernard Hausner, and H. W. Karr, *SIMSCRIPT: a simulation programming language* (Englewood Cliffs, N.J.: Prentice-Hall, 1963), 138p.

42. Manfred Kochen, "Referential consulting networks..."

Network Services for Library Education and Research

Judith A. Tessier

Librarianship is in a time of critical change. Library education is inadequate.[1] The research and literature of library science does not provide the information we need to plan and implement library services. The National Advisory Commission on Libraries called for interdisciplinary and specialized research, training, and service.

Library education and research are at the center of the change process. They provide the knowledge and training which should influence libraries for the next fifty years. Library educators must identify and integrate the different bodies of knowledge their graduates will need to meet the challenge of the future. Researchers must begin to undertake studies which will lead to the development of a cumulative body of knowledge — studies which will contribute to the development of theory.

Library education and research sorely lack the resources to generate and transmit the required knowledge of librarianship. Lack of qualified library instructors, the inadequacies of library school facilities, inappropriate training programs, and the need for a clearinghouse on library education innovations are major impediments to progress. Needs for specialized training and for personnel from social, behavioral, and applied sciences only increase stress on already scarce resources.

The need for basic theoretical work in library and information science requires a coordination of effort by a variety of researchers from many fields. Research of human and technical variables is required. Yet, there is now no system for communication among researchers in different locations and in different fields; there is no concerted effort in organizing, disseminating, and reviewing the literature in some parts of the field.[2] Moreover, there has been no attempt to ascertain the needs of researchers in library and information sciences, or to describe their information-seeking patterns. Library researchers have been urged to provide insights into the services required by other researchers but are asked to do so without the bibliographic and communications tools posed as necessary for other researchers.

Coordination and sharing of personnel and materials may provide one solution to the scarce resources in library education and research. Making materials and personnel from one institution available to all the institutions in the group is an alternative to competition for scarce resources. The establishment of an information and communication network for library education and research is one means of attempting to deal with the "knowledge explosion."

This paper explores the potential uses of networks in library education and research. The term "network" will include any activities having two elements: (1) formal agreement between two or more library education or research institutions to share stated resources, (2) communication links used to meet the objectives of the agreement. Using this definition, agreement to share library materials and use the mails for interlibrary loan qualifies as a network activity; hiring an instructor from another library school as consultant does not.

After a few qualifications are stated, an ideal network for library education and research is described, and those information requirements that are recognized today are listed. The two-part network definition — formal agreement and communication as a minimum — and the ideal system then can be used as two ends of a continuum to assess current and proposed network activities. An inventory of current networks and of current activities that might become the focus for network service follows. Finally, specific network activities and research are proposed as beginning steps to the establishment of an adequate information network.

Two considerations in planning a network for library education and research are not included in this discussion: costs and technical requirements, and network research. Costs and technical requirements will be major considerations in implementing and recommendations here; however, it was felt that these considerations were secondary to the need for a statement of network objectives and could not be assessed until agreement was reached on needs and priorities for service. The second exclusion, network research, has been subordinated to service networks for researchers. The discussion of facilities for network research is a subtopic here and should be considered in its own right, including the research requirements suggested by this Conference.

Information services for education and research are assumed to be currently inadequate. The coordination and sharing of resource is a necessity. Trends to specialization and interdisciplinary work will continue. The pilot projects recommended in the last part of this paper are based on this last point; the projects are designed to take advantage of specialized curriculum, e.g., computer applications in libraries.

Education and research are treated together in most of this paper. Combining the two is not an attempt to confuse them or to slight the needs of either. Information and communication for both education and research are considered.

A network for library education and research provides unique benefits. It can be a testing ground. The library specialist and sometimes the system manager are also clients of this network. The user role may provide insights that are overlooked from the service side of the desk or that have been unobtainable when relying on user reports. In information retrieval studies, the sample data bases are sometimes files for information retrieval literature, the researcher's own specialty; networks for library researchers and educators follow the same principle and reap the same benefits. Also, the student user may become the system manager, with the benefit of his experience in the client role.

IDEAL NETWORK

The ideal setting for education and research is an environment in which students, instructors, and researchers are no longer limited to their own institutions when seeking information but instead are able to call for and receive information and discussion with people anywhere in the library education and research fields, and those in library service on reasonable need. It is also a setting in which the researcher, instructor, and student can provide information or consulting services to others and can work on joint projects with others in distant places. The ideal setting, in short, is one in which each person acts as a free agent in a pool of materials, facilities, and personnel that make up the intellectual core of librarianship.

An information system in this environment might provide both bibliographies and documents by linking library science and library research collections. It might provide the mechanisms for transmitting videotaped lectures to a school that has no instructor, for example, in special librarianship. Perhaps most intriguing is the possibility of using communications links freely to bring geographically distant people together for consultation or joint projects. A network also might develop facilities which a single institution cannot fund easily, for example, a computer-based laboratory for instruction in information systems or for research on networks.

Generally, library education inadequacies fall into five classes: (1) bibliographic resources; (2) laboratory facilities; (3) instruction, instructional packages, and evaluation of instruction; (4) curriculum content, description, and implementation; (5) library education personnel.[3] These inadequacies have prompted local responses in specific subject areas: collection in international librarianship,[4] laboratories in computer systems (at Syracuse and the University of California, described below), and programmed instruction in cataloging.[5] The needs now are to provide access to what is available in particular schools and to coordinate the development of new resources.

An ideal network for library education would provide the links to share existing resources and to develop new ones in the following ways:

1. *Bibliographic resources:* Bibliographic listings from member institutions and literature

clearinghouses, and document transmission, including nonbook materials; coordination of collections through cooperative buying in specializations by type-of-library, or service, or media

2. *Laboratory facilities:* Instructional laboratories in subject areas where hands-on experience is helpful; centralization of laboratories where feasible, especially for an on-line, computer-based laboratory with programs and data bases typical to library operations and information science research

3. *Instructional packages, specialized instruction, and evaluation of instruction:* Live lectures by television with two-way voice transmission; access to computer-based instruction housed in other institutions, (e.g., computer-assisted instruction in cataloging); and telephone ties to coordinate research in teaching by linking educational specialists and library instructors (for example, for management teachers and experts to compare content, styles, and objectives of management courses and to develop and test packages for a course in management over a set of student groups)

4. *Curriculum information and coordinated innovation:* Documentation on curriculum, objectives, and implementation; access to the documentation by keywords to avoid information lost in course title listings; analysis of current offerings and innovations; a communication link to allow discussion of planned changes in curriculum with personnel in other schools; analysis of network use by schools for data for curriculum change at individual schools

5. *Library education personnel:* Directory assistance and at least telephone to provide easy, informal consultation between instructors, or students and instructors; use of this channel for beginning the coordination of efforts in 1, 2, 3, and 4.

The communication links in such a network would need to allow for a variety of media, including human communications, video tape transmission, document transmission, and digital transmission.

Library research requirements can be divided into three classes: (1) bibliographic resources, (2) computer-based research facilities, (3) communication links between research personnel.

A network could provide the following services:

1. *Bibliographic services:* Control and access to library-related literature, with particular emphasis

on research report literature; an individualized alerting and request service for current literature in areas selected by the researcher

2.   *Computer-based research facilities:* Directory to, and access to, data and programs at two levels: (*a*) to facilitate the researcher's particular projects, as with statistical test programs, data from comparable studies, and supporting data generated elsewhere; (*b*) to provide a central store for coordinated efforts, with input and editing capabilities, for example, in research on computer-based information systems, where descriptive data and test programs are needed. (Testing of computer facilities and network facilities are two areas for coordinated efforts.)

3.   *Research personnel:* Directory to, and access to, research personnel for consultation and coordinated work; equipment for voice, document, and digital transmission would be necessary.

A problem in planning a service network for education and research is to define the appropriate services for both educational and research components and those services appropriate only to parts of the population, and then to provide coordination of the services. The researcher, with his in-depth but specialized knowledge, would benefit from the breadth required of a teacher and from the sometimes perceptive curiosity of the student; they, in turn, can benefit from his mastery of his research area. Combined bibliographic services and personal contact services would reflect both the needs for breadth and for depth of the specialist and the generalist.

The problem of defining appropriate service interrelationships can be indicated by the example of services in the content area of networks. One area of research is information systems and network research; one area of instruction is information systems and networks. Network and computer laboratories are required for both instruction and research, but with dividends in mind.

In this case, the following interactions might occur: Network research may provide the personnel for planning the network services for library education and specifically, for the instructional network laboratory. Research into user requirements, the technologies required, and the appropriate access points will require the skills of network researchers. In turn, library educators will need to cite priorities for the laboratory, and some will be both managers and users of the pilot systems. Instruction, moreover, will use the findings of network and computer research in teaching about networks and computer systems. The research facilities themselves may provide a laboratory for advanced students who may become personnel on research projects. The interaction is first in development when the researcher provides his specialized skills in planning and implementing services. It continues through interaction of personnel and literature by individuals. Formal interaction might

continue when advanced students use research facilities. Network researchers might be involved actively in planning the service network generally; specialized researchers would interact with education personnel primarily in their subject areas.

The interaction of research and instruction activities builds in serious problems for the information network. Some problems are: imbalanced resources, where particularly strong schools or institutes support the weaker ones, e.g., through collections or well-known personnel; overreaching or misuse of facilities by side-stepping basic and less sophisticated resources for more advanced ones, e.g., instructional and research computer files; limiting access to editing and input routines.

These problems can be overcome partially by qualifying access to parts of the network. A series of switches and locks might interrelate research and instructional services at need while protecting both users and resources from inappropriate use or overuse. The following figure suggests a series of combined and separated educational and research network services.

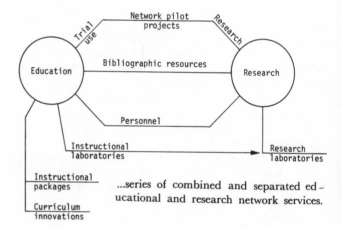

...series of combined and separated educational and research network services.

The ideal system would serve most specialization in librarianship under one umbrella, with some links for specific activities, e.g., research editing capabilities would usually be limited to particular ongoing work. Clustering of activity would be, probably, around areas such as type-of-library- specialization, service areas, or media; the breakdown into five service needs for education and three needs for research cuts across the subject areas and may be applicable in each particular area. The development of the network approaches the interconnection of personnel and resources by subject specialization. The considerations which prompted this are described in the last section.

POTENTIAL NETWORK COMPONENTS IN CURRENT ACTIVITIES

Some attempts have been made to develop new instructional materials, new facilities, and networks to support education and research needs. The projects listed in this section are highlights of current activities and have been chosen because there is potential in each for use by more than one institution. The list was developed by a literature search and personal contact. No doubt some activities were missed; the search for activities yielded surprisingly few innovations. There are two types of service facilities included: Instruction and research facilities which now serve one institution or a few through informal channels; embryonic networks that may provide focus for network activities.

1. *Bibliographic resources:* "There is no one service (or group of related services) to which one can turn to receive reliable coverage on current information."[6] Two new activities are beginning work at controlling parts of library science literature: the ERIC Clearinghouse for Library and Information Sciences, CLIS, operated by the American Society for Information Science, ASIS, indexes and announces research reports and other documents on the operation of libraries and information centers, related technology, and educational research. The clearinghouse lists eventually may be available in machine-readable form through the LEASCO Corporation, under agreement with the Office of Education.[7]

The Discussion Group for Library Science Librarians, a section of the American Library Association Library Education Division, ALA/LED, circulates accessions lists and want and surplus lists for library school library collections. The group is informal and has little financial backing.

2. *Laboratory facilities:* The Library Education Experimental Project, LEEP, Syracuse University School of Library Science, was designed to test the use of MARC records in library education. The MARC I records were used initially, and the IBM Document Processing 360/50 package has been the strongest retrieval program. LEEP personnel are writing an on-line retrieval program for MARC II. The laboratory was conceived as a flexible instructional tool and has been used for assignments in a variety of courses. Students have done research on MARC records and their applications, and on retrieval processes. The Pratt and Drexel library schools are using LEEP through the mails. The Minnowbrook Conference, sponsored by LEEP, highlighted library automation as a focus for cooperation.[8]

AIM Project, University of Wisconsin, attempted to develop programmed instruction for four areas of library instruction: reference, cataloging, library materials, and library management and operations.[11] [12] The cataloging course was completed and will be available through McGraw-Hill. The project lacked the funds and personnel to complete other courses. A controlled experiment to test the cataloging course, using separate campuses and sections in experimental and control conditions, is especially interesting. It is an example of coordinated

research in library instruction. Library educators in other schools worked with AIM in evaluation of the cataloging text.

Other activities of note include the use of closed-circuit television for instruction at the University of Pittsburgh (Phillip Immroth) and radio for extension courses at Wisconsin (Muriel Fuller).

In most cases, developing packages has meant working with educational specialists or computer specialists. Testing has been a costly but critical part of some development projects. Again, costs tend to discourage these efforts and to press for wide use of tested packages.

Of those cited, only LEEP and part of the ILR were originally funded as education projects. High costs in setting up laboratories has limited new projects and the implementation of networks for those now established. The need to share costs across as many users as possible makes this a prime area for networks.

3. *Instructional packages and testing,* aside from LEEP and ILR: Personnel at the University of Michigan School of Library Science have written programmed instruction in reference books and computer-based routines for reference exercises on specific titles; the packages are being tested now.[10]

The Institute for Library Research, ILR, University of California at Los Angeles and Berkeley, is an umbrella institute for library research. Two specific projects show promise for library instruction and network use: the Information Processing Laboratory and File Organization Project. (final reports will be available fall 1970, M. E. Maron, director.) Facilities include: a series of machine-readable files and associate retrieval programs; a computer program called REF Search for reference instruction, including indexed reference tools and routines to test students on each title; a computer-assisted instruction (CAI) program and lab exercise for subject cataloging in the testing stage; and on-line terminals in the laboratory. Interaction between research and instruction has worked successfully at ILR, partially through the crossing of personnel between the school and the institute. The research files are available for doctoral research and for classroom assignment.

The Comparative Systems Laboratory at Case Western Reserve[9] studied the evaluation of information retrieval systems and was the focus of a special course in information retrieval systems.

The pilot Educational Information Network, sponsored by EDUCOM, eventually may provide access to programs and data bases through their directory service to Interuniversity Communications Council, EDUCOM, members.

4. *Curriculum development:* Any school working on curriculum revision must now contact individual schools if comparative information is wanted. School catalogs are the only systematic descriptions currently available. Reports to the Committee on Accreditation

are not public. The result is duplication of survey and development effort. Lack of documentation may result from lack of time, an unwillingness to document problems and doubts, or lack of a clearinghouse.

Informal communication undoubtedly plays a major role in the cross-school discussions on matters of curriculum and faculty. Communications are now served through the Association of American Library Schools, AALS, the Library Education Division and the Library Research Roundtable of ALA, the American Society for Information Science, and regional association meetings and institutes. Students in Upstate New York have generated a mailing list and agreements to share common concerns about library education.

5. *Directories and access to personnel:* The Committee on Institutional Cooperation, Conference Group on Library Schools, includes these universities: Chicago, Illinois, Indiana, Iowa, Michigan, Michigan State, Minnesota, Northwestern, Ohio State, Purdue, and Wisconsin. This cooperative venture started through the parent universities and has percolated down to the library schools. The group has listed its current research for its own uses. It now is proposing a feasibility study of a network for experimentation on network problems. It has exploited the existing links between its institutions and has been able to incorporate the ideas of the potential participants at the beginning of the project. The respective libraries and library schools may act as nodes in the experiments.[13]

The University of Maryland (Paul Wasserman) is preparing a research in progress file to be published fall 1970.

Listings of library educators are maintained by the AALS *Journal of Library Education* directory. The lists are classed by subject areas, schools, and names.

The informal communications that are the foundation of cooperative activity occur through the contacts at conferences. We know little about the effectiveness of these meetings for beginning and maintaining informal contacts.

In summary, library education and research do not encompass many activities that are network activities. Moreover, the service suggested for a service network now are not available. However, there have been developments that could be adapted to networks which suggest areas of strengths that might be most profitably pursued. The information systems laboratory for instructional purposes is one such area of need and strength; the computer-based reference course is another.

A SERVICE NETWORK FOR LIBRARY EDUCATION AND RESEARCH: DEVELOPMENT

A two-part program is needed to begin to develop a service network for library education and research. A research program

should describe current information-seeking patterns of the population such a network would serve. In tandem, a series of pilot networks should be tested; each network should cluster around a subject area of library science and include institutions strong in that area and institutions with recognized needs in that area. A network for research should provide basic communications.

RESEARCH PROGRAM

A research program should be supported to assess the requirements for information and the information-seeking patterns of the proposed client groups. The research sample should include students, library educators, and researchers. This work should begin to answer the questions of user needs and alternative services. What are current information-seeking patterns in library education and research? Can we measure the effectiveness of these? Are these alternative services needed? Can we develop a set of priorities based on the current behaviors and the opinions of proposed clients? This research program has two purposes: It provides information for planning the complex, and the process of assessment may involve a broader base of interested and committed personnel.

Establishment of a communications and information network, for access to personnel, data, and information resources, presupposes a need for such a network. The needs for information systems for education and research have been recognized although not in the network context.[14] Yet we have no data which indicate specific information needs in library education and research. Information seeking in the research process, for example, and the role of communication among researchers cannot be described now with any degree of confidence.

The American Psychological Association's studies on information exchange among psychologists[15] provide a model for describing the complex information system of a profession. Similarly, the concern here is to provide a description of a variety of activities. In this case, the research team should consider the sources of information used by the student, the instructor, and the researcher in library science. The sources then are assessed in terms of ease of access, effectiveness, speed, and cost for the user. The decisions the users make in selecting one source of information over others provide some insights into preferred patterns of access.

Parallel work should be conducted on needs if these differ from uses. Information sought but not found and information found but which the searcher has little confidence in provide some clues. The stated needs of researchers, educators, and students also should be sought.

After this preliminarily work has been done, we will state with more confidence what alternative services are needed, indicate services best met by network activities, and have base measures to test network effectiveness. The research also might provide a set of priorities to use in implementing the complex system.

A second research area has implications in building a national information network for education. The questions center about designing a system that allows for local flexibility in curriculum while using national resources for general services. The scarcity of funding makes this a serious issue. As a network sets priorities, it will be applying resources to particular areas of instruction, perhaps to the consternation of some schools. Another way to ask the questions is: What agreements can be expected locally and what impact will national services have locally? Then, how can the commitments of individual schools be translated into a balanced network?

These two behavioral considerations have been cited as research problems since a proposal of networks for library education and library research is essentially a proposal to change behavior or the effectiveness of some behaviors. This research program will provide part of the base on which we can implement and measure network services.

After the research is completed, feasibility studies, pilot projects, and service implementation will follow more rationally. The particular focus for network activity may be either national information services or critical services to particular subsets of the education and research population. The smaller pilot networks could in turn be combined and built upon toward the ideal network goal. It may be that a combination of imposed national services and locally generated networks will be the result.

PILOT NETWORKS

Because particular areas of library education and research are seriously inadequate now, three specific proposals for pilot education networks and one for research follow. These proposals serve as examples of the locally generated networks that should be encouraged as tests for more ambitious projects and as needed services. By monitoring these, we have contrasts to the information sources available now and can supplement the research previously suggested.

1. *Computer-based laboratory:* Library students need instruction in computer applications in libraries. The need is for a flexible, graded laboratory experience, closely simulating computer systems in libraries. Laboratory instruction should include explanatory materials where these are not available locally. Exercises should include decisionmaking, use of management data gathering programs, and evaluation of student results. One laboratory with a computer could provide the necessary technology, data bases, and programs for retrieval, workspace maintenance, file generation, and input and output for a set of schools. The facility would need ongoing instructional evaluation for planning and revision. A network of not less than five schools, with heterogeneous orientations, might provide the pilot setting.

2. *Education for service to the disadvantaged:* Personnel are probably the critical resource in training for service to the disadvantaged. Both instructors and students need theoretical understanding and practical experience. Short-term placements for students and telelectures from qualified instructors may be one solution. A small set of schools, including those with coursework or research in service for the disadvantaged, would provide the testing ground for telephone and sometimes, television access to personnel on other campuses. Cooperation in such a sensitive and current need area might also provide the skepticism needed for quality control — that is, by working with other schools, those now beginning specialized programs would be challenged to defend their programs and to weigh alternative programs.

3. *International librarianship:* Cooperation in the form of training, placement abroad, and shared monitoring and returnee debriefing would provide a service needed in library education but which no one school can support. Other areas for networks might center around schools that already have developed instructional packages, or around media programs or type-of-library-specializations. A series of such networks, each centered about one area of curriculum, creates as many problems as it solves. This developmental process, however, provides a basic ingredient to continued networks: Each network focuses on an area of need; membership is on the basis of commitment to the need, and thus, provides the momentum so far lacking in library school cooperation. Volunteer activity takes into account the library schools' needs for flexibility and autonomy. It can be suggested that beginning networks in one area of curriculum will lead to coordinated efforts by the same schools in the other areas of the curriculum.

4. *Research network:* Informal communication among researchers is probably inadequate now. This proposal is interim and is suggested in part to provide comparative data. During the planning phases of particular research projects, the researcher should be provided with means of discussing ideas with colleagues not necessarily in his own institution. A free telephone line might be all that is required. A more formal way of encouraging coordinated efforts is through institutes and traveling fellowships; these, however, are not potential network activities or ongoing services.

SUMMARY

Requirements for information services in library education and research suggest that a national network is necessary.

Planning such a network, however, requires information we do not yet have; nor do we now have projects that can provide models for proposed services. Library education has not shown leadership particularly in cooperative ventures. Local considerations may continue to remain most important to library schools.

Balanced against these impediments to network implementation are the serious inadequacies that have not been solved locally. With increasing specialization and interdisciplinary work, the interconnection of researchers, educators, and students will become even more necessary. Benefits unique to network services for library education and research include the dual user-manager role and student recruitment into network specialization. More important, our ability to service national information needs will in part depend upon the effectiveness of our own information system.

The development of a national library education and research network is an evolutionary process. Bibliographic services might be imposed from the national level. Other services — generated on a lower level in subject areas of librarianship — might be combined with national services and eventually provide a balanced access to the knowledge of librarianship.

Information-seeking patterns in education and research should be described and needs assessed. A series of priorities for national service should be stated. In tandem, pilot projects for education and research should be encouraged to provide services needed now. These pilot projects should be studied for their implications to a national network. Systems evaluation and instructional evaluation should be given major emphasis in planning and funding pilot projects. Communication, basic to the implementation of a network through pilot projects, must be improved to link specialists conveniently and at minimal cost.

Notes

1. The problems posed here are cited in the report of the National Advisory Commission on Libraries. D. M. Knight and E. S. Nourse, eds., *Libraries at large....* (New York: Bowker, 1969), p.515-519.

2. The American Society for Information Science is the exception. Through their information services and evaluation program, the Society provides some information services to the librarians represented.

3. Douglas M. Knight and E. Shepley Nourse, eds., *Libraries at large....* (New York: Bowker, 1969), p.495-521.

4. Beverly J. Brewster, "International library school programs," *Journal of education for librarianship* 9:138-143 (Fall 1968).

5. Margaret E. Monroe, "Core course at Wisconsin," *Journal of education for librarianship* 9:116-122 (Fall 1968).

6. Conference on the bibliographic control of library science Literature. *Short summary of papers and proceedings* (Albany: State Univ. of New York, 19-20 April 1968), manuscript.

7. "ERIC files," *Journal of library automation technical communications* 1:6 (May 1970).

8. Pauline Atherton and Judith Tessier, "Teaching with MARC tapes," *Journal of library automation* 3:23-25 (March 1970).

9. Tefko Saracevic, "Linking research and teaching," *American documentation* 19:398-403 (Oct. 1968).

10. Thomas P. Slavens, *The development and testing of materials for computer-assisted instruction in the education of reference librarians,* final report, project no. 8-0560, OEC-5-9-320560-0043 (Washington, D.C.: U.S. Office of Education, Bureau of Research, 1970), 178p.

11. Margaret E. Monroe, "AIM: an independent study program in library science," *Journal of education for librarianship* 6:95-102 (Fall 1965).

12. ...., "Core course at Wisconsin...,"

13. Miles Libbey, Director, Research Center for Library and Information Science, Indiana University, Interview.

14. "ASIS information program developments," *Newsletter of the American Society for Information Science* 9:1, 6 (Jan.-Feb. 1970).

15. Thomas J. Allen, "Information needs and uses," in C. A. Cuadra, ed., *Annual review of information science and technology* (Chicago: Britannica, 1969), p.4-29.

Network Technology

Working Group Summary On

Network Technology

Aim: To explore the capabilities of communications and computer technology to meet library and information network requirements.

After reviewing the commissioned state-of-the-art papers on various aspects of computer and communications technology, the Working Group on Network Technology proceeded to identify, discuss, and debate relevant technology considered essential for building telecommunications networks. The group especially concentrated on the technology required to link the user of a network with the network.

Among the many questions explored were the following: What is the best method for establishing a telecommunications network of libraries and information centers? What new technological advancements will be needed? What adjunct technology will aid the development of library telecommunications networks? In what sequence should telecommunications be phased into other library automation plans involving technology? What alternative telecommunications configurations are possible now and will be in the future? How should the user interface with the network?

To answer these questions and to provide a sound rationale for subsequent technical deliberations, the group made several assumptions:

1. That library and information networks can effectively satisfy unmet needs for information

2. That networks would be technically compatible at each interface level

3. That networks would be linked directly to the individual as well as to the institution

Working Group Leader: John W. Meaney, Notre Dame University, Notre Dame, Indiana 46556
Associate Leader: Edwin B. Parker, Institute for Communication Research, Cypress Hall, Stanford University, Stanford, California

4. That networks would embrace all media

5. That networks would use the most advanced technologies

6. That networks would evolve rapidly, and that the group, therefore, should restrict its projections to a five-year time frame.

DESCRIPTION OF A HYPOTHETICAL NETWORK

On the basis of these assumptions, it was possible to postulate a general description of a probable future network: Its scope will be national, regional, and local; it will include all types of libraries, data and information analysis centers, instructional media centers, and educational facilities; it will facilitate the exchange of bibliographic data, mediation of reference inquiries, and the distribution of library and audiovisual instructional materials; it will have no geographic constraints; it will make maximum use of computer and communications technology; it will provide timely access and response rates consistent with the urgency of a user's need for information; it will adopt a standard format for bibliographic interchange and establish other protocols and common practices; it will supply incentives and evolve a financial structure to stimulate network use; it will consist of a formal set of major nodes at the national and regional level, and individual access points within a ten-mile radius of local nodes; it will incorporate switching stations for request and response referrals; and it will enable users connected to one node to have access to any other node.

TELECOMMUNICATIONS

The group believed that existing commercial telecommunications services were already available to accommodate most of the communications services required by a library and information network and that these could be introduced at a reasonable cost. In examining data-rate requirements, for example, it was found that teletype speed or lower was all that would probably be required from the user to his local access node for some time to come. This requirement can be met by a voiceband line within which several user-to-node channels can be provided. However, the data rate from node-to-user was expected to be greater and require a full voiceband line. Node-to-user network services, nevertheless, are not expected to require more than a full TV channel of bandwidth, and this service will soon be available locally through the United States at costs within easy reach of most libraries and information centers. On the other hand, the cost of long-distance wideband service direct to individual users will probably continue to be expensive for some time to come.

Because many long-distance interlibrary services can be provided over voiceband lines, it will be possible to rely on the commercially available dial-up telephone network for low-usage services. The dial-up network's advantages include the capability of switching a user at any node in the library and information network directly to any other node. Automatic computer-controlled dialing through existing voice telephone systems can thus give any network user access to the data he needs at a node other than the one to which he is normally connected. When sufficiently heavy traffic develops between nodes, cost savings can be achieved by using dedicated private lines (switched by network computers at the nodes) between them. All major national and regional nodes undoubtedly will be interconnected initially by broadband channels since heavy traffic can be expected between these nodes as soon as connections are established.

An important benefit of this type of network configuration is the fact that it can evolve over a period of time without requiring any capital investment by libraries in either communication lines or switching equipment. As traffic increases, additional channels can simply be leased as needed. However, the use of the commercial dial-up network for data transmission is not without problems. Whereas line quality may be adequate for voice transmission, it is unreliable for data transmission. It would be extremely helpful, therefore, to have a minimum amount of standard data service that could be specified and paid for on the dial-up network, but this communications service offering does not yet exist. While dial-up switched service is available from the telephone carriers, private line services, both at voiceband and broader band transmission rates, also can be provided by special-service common carriers, library-owned microwave systems (possibly shared with other users), or possibly through future new carriers using proposed domestic satellite systems.

Assuming an evolutionary increase in both machine-readable bibliographic information and full text, the network should also be capable of serving interactive terminals located at user points such as local libraries, schools, businesses, research organizations, and so forth. These terminals will incorporate available technology including keyboard input and cathode ray tube (CRT) or hard-copy displays, using digital or analog technology in various combinations, depending upon the purpose of the terminals. Except in unusual circumstances, terminals will be connected with the voiceband network previously described. Bibliographic and surrogate text searches will be conducted through digital transmission in both directions. Full text, including graphs and pictures will of necessity be received in analog form at speeds consistent with voiceband transmission facilities, on screens of at least 1,000-line vertical resolution, with consistent horizontal resolution, using local storage in the form of magnetic disc, long-persistence phosphor CRT or hard-copy facsimile equipment.

CABLE TELEVISION

A potential future alternative to the telephone system for many node-to-user systems is cable television. Of particular interest to a library and information network is the possibility of using a burst-broadband technique to transmit still pictures or pages of text from a library to a user on a time-shared basis, thus allowing many users to share one television channel. Such systems require no switching because the user can be reached at his residence or office through a party-line cable network, which digitally addresses his terminal when a picture is destined for him. Switched cable systems providing separate channels to individual users are also possible but at substantially higher costs than part-line systems. While the cost of cable TV systems are expected to be competitive with the telephone system, their precise tariffs are not yet known.

Eventually, the extension of library and information network terminals directly into the home will probably take the form of touch-tone telephone inquiry, with response via cable TV. Bibliographic searches could, for example, be directed by a computer program which would lead the user through a series of multiple-choice inquiries controlled by his own touch-tone responses. Digital-to-video conversion at the computer would condition responses for reception and display on modified home television receivers equipped with coding and storage accessories for individual frame (picture) storage. Since a conventional TV channel provides 1800 frames per minute, response time within such a time-shared system would not be limited by the characteristics of the communications system.

To ensure that the information benefits of cable TV are realized, the Group felt it imperative that appropriate steps be taken now by the library and information science community. Cable TV companies are currently negotiating franchises with local communities for the right to build systems. These companies are under pressure from the FCC to offer new and different services, and to originate programming on some of their channels. Local authorities are usually in a position to draft service specifications under which they are willing to receive competitive bids for franchises. In the face of such pressures and requirements, cable companies are often willing to reserve up to 20 percent of their channel capacity for free educational and public use.

COMPUTER TECHNOLOGY AND STANDARDIZATION

In focusing its attention on the computer area, the working group expressed great concern about the problem of standardization. It believed that a major first step toward a library and information network would be to secure agreement among all concerned parties on strict compliance with American National Standards Institute standards for all computer components of the network. For example, common adoption of the American Standard Code for Information Interchange, ASCII code, of flowcharting and documentation procedures, of bibliographic record formats, and of communications protocols was considered to be an absolutely essential prerequisite.

As part of its concern with standards, the Group also recognized the value of building a comprehensive and complete bibliographic data base for meeting a variety of operating and service needs in a library and information network. To this end, it suggested extending and consolidating Machine Readable Cataloging, MARC; Retrospective Conversion, RECON; and similar projects aimed at stockpiling machine-readable bibliographic records for community use. In connection with MARC, the group specifically recommended increased funding in order to expand the size of the bibliographic data base available for network use.

Because conversion of printed bibliographic data to machine-readable form constitutes a staggering input requirement for a library and information network, the working group spent considerable time reviewing the current state of the art of optical character recognition machines, OCR. Development of a machine capable of reading intermixed type fonts and logically processing format instructions was considered desirable, particularly if it could provide throughput processing that took less human effort and cost less than keyboard methods. In this regard some suggestions were made for research and development. These included the development of local input mechanisms (e.g., slow speed, a maximum of fifty characters per second), such as a fiber-optics wand ("pencil") to capture lines of text directly, remote OCR equipment for input and recognition of hand-printed material, and design of a general-purpose high-resolution scanner to permit full input from either microfilm or textual and graphic hard copy.

Another area of computer technology that received the group's attention was the user terminal. Although user terminals are available which can perform many network functions, immediate improvement was deemed necessary in a number of areas to satisfy the new requirements which a library and information network are likely to generate. The following examples represent the new features which the group believed would improve existing user terminals:

Accommodation of character sets of at least 128 characters per alphabet and provision for a reasonable number of such alphabets in order to accommodate the principal non-Roman character sets

Operationally simple methods of shifting between various alphabets

Provision of print-on-paper-like contrast and precision insertion on display devices in order to eliminate eye fatigue and to achieve unambiguous definition of the smallest elements in any of the alphabets

Refinement of split-screen features for controlled handling of record excerpts

Provision for hard-copy generation directly from soft-copy display systems

Increased reliability of user terminals for continuous operation and public use (and abuse)

Cost reduction to approximately that of a home TV set

Data collection capability to read from the spine or outside cover of the book and from bar and optical character-encoded identification cards

In addition, research and development was suggested as follows: development of split-screen zoom features for (*a*) focusing on a given position of the screen and (*b*) direct hard-copy or microform output from that position. And, hard-copy generation from terminal output that is instantly available, permanent, and with multicopy facility at less than one cent out-of-pocket cost per copy.

Another area singled out for research and development concerned the requirement for a very large-capacity direct-access memory to store the vast amount of machine-readable bibliographic data that will form the heart of a national library and information network.

CONCLUSIONS AND RECOMMENDED ACTION

1. Urge Congress to continue and increase funding for the Library of Congress's MARC program

2. Urge the Library of Congress to:

   a. Expand retrospective bibliographic data conversion with the aim of producing 2,000,000 machine-readable records, as well as adding to the existing MARC tapes within the next two years

   b. Expand the production of machine-readable records of current materials to include the entire intake of national library acquisitions, including foreign languages and nonprint materials, within the next eighteen months

   c. Expand retrospective record conversion activities to encompass all three national libraries within the next two years

3. Encourage development of user-library networks using telephone or cable TV systems to provide interconnection; in order to simplify terminal design and lower terminal costs, encourage carriers and cable operators to provide lines with definitely specified and guaranteed performance characteristics

4. Encourage libraries to enter into local, cable TV franchise negotiations in order to reserve channels and ensure access to such systems by libraries during the next few years; also, local libraries should seek the use of public channels on a common carrier basis

5.   Encourage private-line communication channels with a wide variety of bandwidths and as few restrictions on sharing and band subdivision as are appropriate for technical reasons, in order to provide low-cost interlibrary interconnection; also, support development of competition in the provision of these services in order to increase diversity of services offerings and to reduce costs

6.   Request the Corporation for Public Broadcasting, through the U.S. Office of Education, to consider including digital-header frames in all educational TV movies and video programs

7.   Apply scientific planning tools and techniques, such as network modeling, simulation, and testbed and pilot operations, before making large-scale investment commitments to network operations

8.   Support research and development through development of multifont character sets, including non-Roman alphabets, and format recognition:

a.   Specifications for keyboard-CRT user terminals specifically designed for input and retrieval of bibliographic and surrogate information

b.   Page-turning devices and page presentation procedures to facilitate automatic reading by optical scanning equipment

c.   An ultra-high-speed scanner with very high resolution to use for input of text or microimage materials into storage, OCR logic, or for facsimile transmissions

9.   Replicate machine-readable bibliographic data bases and arrange for their physical security as insurance against fire, damage or loss.

In Information Networking

Morton W. Bachrach

SCOPE OF PAPER

Electronic communications will play an ever-increasing role in the vital process of information dissemination and exchange. As I am sure many of the papers for this Conference will attest, the conventional library system is inefficient and will not meet tomorrow's needs. The constraints upon moving from a conventional library system to a more automated, rapid, and convenient information system include technological, economical, inertial, and legal. This paper will concern itself with the legal constraints and will concentrate upon the copyright problems involved, particularly as they relate to cable antenna television, CATV, sometimes referred to as community antenna television. CATV systems, which have a unique capability for mass information dissemination and exchange because of their broadband, multichannel characteristic, are likely to be the links in the information networks of tomorrow. However, CATV also presents some unique legal problems, primarily because of the diverse interest groups involved.

These groups include the TV industry (the networks and independent VHF, UHF, STV [subscription TV stations]), radio, copyright owners, newspaper, common carrier, and the CATV industry, itself. One could include also the users and potential users, and the federal government agencies looking after the user's interests, the Federal Communication Commission, FCC, the Department of Justice, and Congress.

It should be borne in mind that the initially conceived function of CATV was to bring to those homes within a community, television signals which, because of the topography of the land or because of some other interference, could not be received. Over the years CATV has grown very rapidly and has demonstrated its profit-making ability. Because of its growth in size and in technical capabilities, CATV has potential for becoming a universal system, and its capabilities in the information areas, as well as in the entertainment areas, are far-reaching.[1] For example, the initial CATV system was a three- to five- channel arrangement. As technology improved the capacity increased to twelve channels; now twenty channels or more are possible.[2] It is the excess channels—those not needed

for entertainment fulfillment—which hold enchantment for the information industry. This is so because the CATV system has the capability to originate its own programs as well as to retransmit off-the-air TV broadcasts.

Most of the problems to date and most of the discussion have involved conventional TV broadcast and CATV retransmission, thereof. Although the legal aspects of program initiation are quite different from those of retransmission, the latter will be discussed first so as to establish an understanding of the concepts involved and as a means for distinguishing the two concepts, from a legal standpoint.

COPYRIGHTS OF CATV IN ITS CONVENTIONAL ROLE OF PROGRAM RETRANSMITTER

The current copyright statute was enacted in 1909 and has changed very little to date.[3] It is now codified as Title 17 of the U.S. Code. Congress, in enacting the 1909 law, did not contemplate problems concerning CATV because such systems were not then in existence. What has happened of course is that the law has not kept pace with the advances in technology. That has been recognized for a long time, and there has been a continuing effort to revise the copyright statute over the past fifteen years, with no substantial success to date.[4] In 1967 a copyright revision bill was passed by the House of Representatives (H.R. 2512) but the companion Senate bill (S. 597) was not passed. A similar bill was introduced in the Ninety-first Congress (S.543) but as yet has not come up for full Senate consideration.

Although federal laws are enacted by Congress and must be revised by Congress, the law can change, or at least be extended, without congressional action. One way is by court interpretation.[5] Another is by action of a quasi-legislative body such as the FCC. That is what has happened in the fields of radio and television. The courts ruled on many copyright cases in those areas and frequently found that copyright infringement had occurred. The courts reasoned that the intent of Congress was to promote the progress of sciences and useful arts (U.S. Constitution, Article 1, Section 8, Clause 8) by protecting the rights of persons in their intellectual creations. That is what Judge Herlands attempted in the landmark case of *United Artists Television, Inc.* versus *Fortnightly Corporation*, 23 May 1966. Judge Herlands ruled that the defendant CATV systems had infringed

The views expressed herein are those of the author only and do not necessarily represent the policy or position of the U.S. Office of Education.

the plaintiff's copyrights in motion pictures which had been broadcast under license by three distant TV stations, picked off-the-air by the defendant's antennas without permission, and retransmitted by cable to the defendant's subscribers. The Fortnightly case held that what the defendant had done constituted an unauthorized "performance" in violation of Section 1 (d) of Title 17.

However, the Fortnightly case was appealed and although Judge Herlands was affirmed by the court of appeals for the second U.S. Circuit on 22 May 1967, he was overruled by the U.S. Supreme Court.[6] The Supreme Court said, in effect, that it would not impute to Congress an intention which it could not possibly have had, i.e., to legislate on the copyright aspects of CATV. The Supreme Court decided to defer to Congress its proper role in so far as CATV legislation is concerned.

An analysis of the Supreme Court decision in the Fortnightly case will show that the Court found itself on the horns of a dilemma.[7] It will show, I think, that the result was prompted as much by economical and perhaps, by social considerations as by legal principles. If the Supreme Court had affirmed the decisions of the lower courts, it would have thrown the entire CATV industry into turmoil. In effect, the CATV industry would have had to cease to operate unless it could come to terms with the TV broadcasters, including the networks and the copyright owners.[8] That could well give the TV industry a strangle hold on the CATV industry and perhaps, destroy it or force it to sell out to the powerful TV networks, despite the assurances by the TV industry that it would be reasonable with regard to granting copyright licenses to the CATV systems.[9] In addition, an undetermined amount of retroactive royalty payments would have had to be made, of which the financial effect upon the infant CATV industry could not be predicted. The Supreme Court obviously did not desire to destroy the CATV industry because of its immense potential for social benefits, and it obviously did not wish to make the industry a pawn of the powerful TV networks which could then either stifle its development or eliminate the desired competition between those two media.[10]

A matter of equity also was involved. As long as the CATV systems did no more than retransmit broadcasts of local TV stations, neither the TV broadcasters nor the other copyright owners were hurt. The CATV systems did no more than to fill in the holes, i.e., extend the reception to those homes which, for one reason or another, were unable to receive a signal which perhaps a neighbor was able to receive. The copyright owners believe that they should be entitled to a portion of any revenues, including CATV subscription proceeds, which result from the use of copyrighted materials. However, the likelihood is high that the copyright owners, even under Judge Herlands ruling, would still benefit from CATV operations limited to the retransmission of local TV broadcasts to local subscribers.[11] And there is some question whether the copyright holders should receive an additional royalty in this circumstance. Some argue that the CATV subscriber would be paying a double royalty—once indirectly when he buys the advertiser's product and once directly when the CATV operator passes onto him the royalty in the form of higher subscription fees.

The situation was even more complex because the CATV systems wished to make their offerings more attractive to po-

tential subscribers, first by bringing into the community broadcasts from distant stations and second by originating their own programs. Both of these operations would tend to dilute the audience of the local TV station and consequently, reduce the advertising revenue and also the copyright royalties from local advertisers, which are customarily tied to advertising revenues.[12]

A possible solution would be to take the stance that the retransmission of local programs would not constitute an infringement of the copyrighted materials whereas the retransmission of distant programs would. (The matter of CATV program initiation was not an issue before the courts in the Fortnightly case.)[13]

Neither the district court nor the court of appeals considered such a divided result. The courts treated the issue simply on a precedent basis, i.e., whether the retransmission of copyrighted materials constituted a "performance" within the meaning of the copyright statute. They applied legal precedents, particularly the Jewell-La Salle Case,[14] and came to the conclusion that such retransmission does constitute a "performance;" accordingly, the courts held that such action constituted copyright infringement.

The Supreme Court, on the other hand, considered but rejected the possibility of holding that retransmission of copyrighted materials from local stations would not constitute infringement whereas retransmission of distant signals would. That proposal was advanced before the Court by the Solicitor General of the United States in an amicus curiae brief.[15] However, the Court decided that retransmission did not constitute a "performance" within the meaning of the copyright statute,[16] rejected the Jewell-La Salle concept,[17] reversed the lower courts, and let the CATV industry go "Scot-free."

The Supreme Court rejection of Jewell-La Salle is questionable. It grounded its rejection on the fact that the original broadcast in Fortnightly was authorized whereas the original broadcast in Jewell-La Salle was not. However, as pointed out by Mr. Justice Fortas in his dissent, whether or not an original transmission is authorized does not affect whether the retransmission is a "performance" in a copyright sense.[18] Accordingly, since the holding was based upon the "performance" concept, it is difficult to rationalize the Court's holding. Unfortunately, the Court did not respond to this key point made by Mr. Justice Fortas. It must be assumed then, I think, that the Court was "forcing" the removal of this stumbling block—the main precedent relied upon by the lower courts—in order to reach a result which it believed to be proper.

But this still does not explain why the Supreme Court was unwilling to treat the retransmission of distant signals differently from the retransmission of local signals insofar as copyright infringement is concerned. The Court does not say. Most likely it was a reluctance to legislate. Mr. Justice Fortas merely remarks that "I do not believe it is open to us, in construing the Copyright Act, to accept the Solicitor General's proposal.[19] The Court could have found legal justification for taking the divided approach. It stated, as a ground for holding that retransmission did not constitute a "performance" that "CATV equipment is powerful and sophisticated, but the basic function the equipment serves is little different from that served by the equipment generally furnished by a television viewer."[20]

Whereas that statement may be true insofar as the reception of local signals is concerned, it is obvious that a viewer must provide more than a roof antenna to receive broadcasts from stations beyond the reach of the most sophisticated roof or even community (in the original sense) antenna.[21]

Nevertheless, the Court preferred to defer the matter to Congress,[22] even though it was aware that the likelihood of immediate and comprehensive action by that body was unlikely.[23] Of course, the Court was aware of the legislative problems because of the difficulties already encountered with the copyright revision bills at the time the Court was deliberating on the Fortnightly case.

THE RESPONSIBILITY OF CONGRESS TO LEGISLATE

Congress would appear to be the most appropriate agency to take action in this matter and fill the vacuum left by the Supreme Court decision in the Fortnightly case. That body had been biding its time awaiting the outcome of the Fortnightly litigation. When the Supreme Court left the situation unchanged, the focus of attention was redirected toward Congress. However, congress is a broad, diverse body and is quite sensitive to pressure groups. Its record in the field of copyright legislation is not very creditable. Congress has been trying to enact needed copyright reform for the past fifteen years, without success. Miss Ringer reflected a measure of frustration in 1967 when she remarked:

Two years ago our most significant problems came from jukebox performances and educational copying, today they come from uses by computers and community antenna television systems, and two years from now there may well be whole new industries whose future will be directly affected by the copyright law.[24]

Miss Ringer tells use that when Subcommittee No. 3 on Patents, Trademarks, and Copyrights of the House Judiciary Committee held hearings on the copyright revision bill in 1965, a "total of 163 witnesses, representing an extraordinarily wide range of public and private interests," testified. The record of those hearings comprised nearly 2,000 pages of printed text.

The CATV problems were so severe in 1967 that in order for the House of Representatives to pass H.R. 2512, it was necessary to delete the CATV provisions.[25] The history of the copyright revision legislative attempts — from the time bills were introduced in both the Senate and the House of Representatives in 1965, and even before that, up to the present time — is a story in itself and is beyond the scope of this paper. However, that story is set forth in detail in Miss Ringer's paper. Suffice it to say that knowledge slayings has been enacted and its prospects, particularly the CATV provisions, are none too encouraging.

In the meantime, the CATV industry has continued to grow, to improve, and to attach its roots more firmly into the communications terrain. As the industry grew, its impact upon the TV industry and the public increased. The problems became so severe that the FCC decided to assume certain authority over the CATV industry in 1965.[26] That jurisdiction continued to expand as the recognized problems have become more complex.[27]

THE ROLE OF CATV IN INFORMATION SYSTEMS

Perhaps the potential for CATV to satisfy social needs is not fully appreciated. As has been stated before, it is the multichannel capacity of the CATV systems which holds tremendous potential for satisfying these needs. The President's Task Force on Communication Policy, speaking about the television industry, which includes for these purposes the CATV industry, has stated:

The structure of the industry should make it possible to cater to as wide a variety of tastes as possible, the tastes of small audiences and mass audiences, of cultural minorities and of cultural majorities. Ours is a pluralistic society, in culture as well as in the ethnic origins and the life styles of its people. A medium of expression as pervasive as television should reflect and enrich the cultural pluralism.

Television should serve as varied as possible an array of social functions, not only entertainment and advertising, important as they are, but also information, education, business, culture, and political expression.[28]

It goes without saying that TV has had a tremendous impact upon our society. However, as presently constituted, the industry cannot fulfill the stated needs.[29] One reason is the relative lack of competition among the media.[30] More important, however, is the natural limitation upon the available over-the-air frequency spectrum.[31] Even so, because of interference between adjacent stations, the FCC has had to limit any one locality to just a few channels.[32]

It is true that the UHF channels are not so severely limited although they are limited in other respects.[33] The UHF segment of the industry has operated at a disadvantage vis-a-vis the VHF segment and has not made a significant impact. The reasons are numerous. In the first place the VHF segment was established first and in a sense, monopolized the potential viewing audience. It has operated and continues to operate from a position of strength, buttressed by the very strong network arrangements. It has been an up-hill battle for the UHF stations, virtually all independents, and including the noncommercial so-called educational stations. In the early days of the TV industry, very few TV sets were equipped to receive UHF. Equipping a receiver with a UHF adapter was expensive, and not many viewers were willing to undertake the expense. In 1964 Congress enacted legislation requiring the manufacture of all TV sets with UHF receivers.[34] However, by that time TV viewing habits were well established. In addition, it was inconvenient to tune into a UHF broadcast because the receivers were not equipped with a "click" type of selector. Furthermore, the marginal nature of the UHF business was discouraged was many UHF owners from providing the power necessary to assure uniformly clear pictures for the viewing public.

CATV appears to be the answer insofar as the provision of the multichannel capacity is concerned. It can retransmit many of the existing TV frequencies clearly, including UHF frequencies, which it can reduce to VHF frequencies for ease of transmission and convenience of selection on the home receivers.[35] And there will still remain a large number of channels for CATV program initiation and for lease to others for the provision of various services.

But CATV does have drawbacks. First, a subscription fee is required.[36] Although that fee is deemed to be reasonable in the light of the services received, it is recognized that the requirement of the fee will make the service prohibitive for some viewers. Accordingly, there is a strong desire to encourage the continuance of free over-the-air broadcasts, including UHF availability. Second, it is uneconomical to bring CATV into sparsely settled rural areas.[37] Accordingly, there is a strong desire to encourage the servicing of such areas by over-the-air TV directly from either satellite or repeater stations.

The foregoing should serve to give the reader insight into the magnitude of the problems currently confronting the FCC. There are delicate balances which must be struck or preserved by the FCC in its regulatory role.[38] The point to be remembered is that for CATV to prosper, conventional TV must prosper. And for CATV to provide facilities for information delivery and exchange, the CATV systems must be permitted to grow and mature. They will only do so by offering to the subscriber what he wants. Right now the subscriber wants a choice of high-quality entertainment. When that need is satisfied he will gradually come to want, and then demand, those other services which are as yet beyond the horizon.

In 1968 cable systems served some three million subscribers out of some fifty-eight million homes equipped with television.[39] Obviously, cable systems must become more universal before networking — entertainment, information, or otherwise — will become feasible. Cable systems are growing rapidly, and that growth is sure to accelerate if subscribers are given what they want (several channels of entertainment, supplemented by CATV initiated programs and services) at a reasonable charge.

A CATV system which functions in the conventional sense, as a result of the Supreme Court decision in the Fortnightly case, need not concern itself with copyright problems. It uses all copyright materials with impunity.

Of course, Congress could enact legislation and change the status quo. Bill S. 543 which would impose copyright liability in other than retransmission of local programs already has made some progress in the Ninety-first Congress; it has been reported out of the subcommittee. Even if the Senate should act, there still must be action in the House of Representatives and a resolution of any differences. As time passes with little progress, the chances for enactment, at least during the Ninety-first Congress, become less promising.

THE EVER-INCREASING ROLE OF THE FCC

In the meantime the FCC is moving in to fill the vacuum. Certainly the FCC cannot impose copyright liability; only the Congress can do that.[40] However, it can regulate, or attempt to regulate, in a manner which will be equitable to all interests. What the copyright owners could not obtain directly through Congress or the courts, they could perhaps obtain indirectly through the FCC. For example, should the FCC follow through on its proposal to require CATV systems to substitute local TV advertisement, particularly UHF TV advertisement, for the advertisement associated with the distant signals which it would retransmit,[41] the copyright royalties from local programs would increase because they are tied by agreement to advertisement revenues.

Such action could relieve some of the pressure on Congress which would like very much to enact copyright revision. If it could eliminate from consideration some of the more controversial provisions, such as CATV, it would obviously have a better chance of passing the legislation. Thus, the possibility of Congress eliminating the CATV provisions and in effect, relegating the matter to the FCC must be recognized.

COPYRIGHT LIABILITY FOR CATV INITIATED SERVICES

But whatever happens in this regard, the furnishing of self-initiated information services by CATV systems will not be affected. Such information and data will not be transmissible, if copyrighted, without obtaining licenses, individual or blanket, from the copyright owners. The copyright shelter afforded by the Fortnightly case is not available to the CATV industry for the programs it originates. That was alluded to by the Supreme Court in the Fortnightly case. It was specifically so held by the district court in *Walt Disney Productions* versus *Alaska Television Network, Inc., et.al.*[42] In this situation the CATV system is a broadcaster rather than a retransmitter and as such, stands in the same position vis-a-vis the copyright holders as does the conventional TV broadcasters.[43]

The immediate reaction of some, to the last point made, is that copyright liability will make it impossible to construct an effective information network system because it will be difficult to obtain copyright licenses. Of course, that is the same problem that is currently facing the information industry in regard to computer storage and retrieval systems.[44] Actually, the computer problem and the transmission problem might be considered companion problems in so far as the copyright aspects are concerned because it is likely that the information to be transmitted will frequently originate from a computer storage and retrieval system. The latter is deemed to be such a complex problem that it is not addressed directly by S. 543. Instead, Title II of that bill would establish a commission to study the matter and make recommendations for future legislation. It is likely that the transmission problems will be studied along with the companion computer problems in the event the copyright reform bill is enacted into law and the commission is established pursuant thereto.

As of now, no CATV systems are deemed to constitute common carriers within the meaning of the Communications Act of 1934.[45] There is a possibility that such systems will be treated as common carriers if one or more channels are utilized for the transmission of data as a conduit for an information system.[46] Although common carriers are immune from copyright liability, that arrangement cannot be utilized to avoid the copyright problems. In such an event, the offense merely is shifted from the transmitter to the originator; Copyright licenses would still be a prerequisite to information delivery and exchange.

NEED TO RECOGNIZE COPYRIGHT INCENTIVES

The current situation with regard to potential copyright liability should not be used as an excuse for not pursuing with vigor the establishment of information networks and the provision of other information services. After all, a great deal of information is already in the public domain and available for unhampered use. Licenses for other materials may be easily obtainable at a reasonable cost. Those materials which are beyond reach insofar as the obtainment of licenses is concerned will have to be eliminated from the systems, at least until such time as those materials do become available for licensing. That could happen through legislation, industry agreements, or changed economic circumstances.

It is a view among some, particularly in the educational community, that copyright licenses and royalties should not be required when the purpose of the system in which copyrighted materials will be utilized is educational.[45] Those who take a strong stand in this regard often overlook the fact that, except for the incentives the copyright system provides, much of the materials they would dispense royalty free would not then be available for use in the first place. Education, even in its narrower context, constitutes a huge market for copyrighted materials. Remove that market from the copyright incentive system, and you destroy that market.

Some say that authors would continue to write even without the royalty incentive.[46] That may be true to some extent. However, such writing would devolve into a part-time activity. After all, an author must sustain himself and his family. If he must depend upon other sources for his income, then the main focus of his activities will not be on his writing. He will not likely have the time to write books as contrasted with articles. Books normally constitute the in-depth treatment of a subject whereas articles often provide a much shallower treatment. What we need then is to increase the incentives rather than to decrease them.[8] Society cannot afford to lose one potential masterpiece for the lack of providing an adequate incentive.

Accordingly, let us pay for copyright property the same as we pay for other necessary educational expenses, such as buildings, electricity, teachers' salaries, and in the the information business, transmitters, wires, computers, etc. Let us not despair because copyright appears to be an obstacle but rather persevere to establish effective systems by working to overcome obstacles within — not without — the incentive systems which have contributed so much to the rich heritage we all enjoy today.

It is possible that Congress will act to ease the copyright impact insofar as educational TV broadcasting is concerned. That could have an impact upon CATV retransmissions. However, it is clear that any relief will be severely limited. Congress does not want to kill the goose which lays the golden egg. Information network planners should not be deluded into believing that any such easing will supply much relief insofar as information systems are concerned in the foreseeable future. Again, such planners are urged to recognize that copyright is with us and will stay. They should embrace copyright, live with it, and succeed in their endeavors despite of and because of it.

CONCLUSION

It can be expected that CATV systems will serve as conduits for tomorrow's information networks. CATV holds promise for fulfilling this need because of its broadband multichannel capability. However, CATV cannot be dealt with in one capacity alone. It must be considered at one time in its many capacities inasmuch as they are interdependent. In order for CATV to successfully serve in its information network role, it must be successful in its many other roles. Unless that happens, CATV will not be a universal system; its ability to serve information users will be limited.

CATV can be thought of as having two basic function, i.e., retransmitting TV programs and initiating its own programs and services. With regard to the former, whether retransmitting local or distant signals there is currently no copyright liability. Pending legislation would impose copyright liability on the retransmission of distant signals, at least.

The role of the FCC is increasing. If it can regulate in a way as to satisfy all concerned, it is likely that Congress will not legislate. However, the FCC will find it difficult to balance all the interests, e.g., the UHF and the VHF, the networks and the independents, and the CATV and the broadcasters, and other copyright owners. One thing the FCC is determined to do is to assure an adequate choice of free over-the-air broadcasts. Another thing it is determined to do is to give CATV an opportunity to mature and provide the services for which it only is capable.

Regardless of the CATV role as a retransmitter, insofar as self-initiated services are concerned, it is in no better position than any other broadcaster from a copyright standpoint. Accordingly, the information industry must learn to live with the copyright system if it is going to supply copyrighted material by CATV. It would behoove the industry to work within the system; to try to fight it at this point would be useless and not availing.

NOTES

1. Some of the potential uses of CATV are set forth on page 5 of the FCC *Notice of proposed rule making and inquiry*, Docket No. 18397, released 13 December 1968: "...could be utilized to provide a variety of new communications services to homes and businesses within a community, in addition to services now commonly offered such as time, weather, news, stock exchange ticker, etc. "...some of the predicted services include: facsimile reproduction of newspapers, magazines, documents, etc., electronic mail delivery; merchandizing; business concern links to branch offices, primary customers or suppliers; access to computers, e.g., man to computer communications in the nature of inquiry and response (credit checks, airline reservations, branch banking, etc..) information retrieval (library and other reference material, etc..), and computer to computer communications; the furtherance of various governmental programs on a Federal, State and municipal level, e.g., employment services and manpower utilization, special communications systems to reach particular neighborhoods or ethnic groups within a community, and for municipal surveillance of public areas for protection against crime, fire detection, control of air pollution and traffic; various educational and training programs, e.g., job and literacy training, pre-school programs in the nature of "Project Headstart," and to enable professional groups such as doctors to keep abreast of

developments in their fields; and the provision of a low cost outlet for political candidates, advertisers, amateur expression (e.g. community or university drama groups) and for other moderately funded organizations or persons desiring access to the community or a particular segment of the community."

2. *Final report*, President's Task Force on Communications Policy, (Washington, D.C.: Gov. Print. Off., 7 Dec. 1968) Chap. 7, p.36.

3. Barbara A. Ringer, "Copyright law revision: history and prospects" in *Automated information systems and copyright law, a symposium of the American University*, (Reprint from the *Congressional record*, 11-14 June 1968), vol.114, no.102 p.2.

4. Ibid.

5. "While statute should not be stretched to apply to new situations not fairly within their scope, they should not be so narrowly construed as to permit their evasion because of changing habits due to new inventions and discoveries", *Jerome H. Remick & Co., v. American Automobile Accessories Co.*, 5 F. 2d 411.

6. Fortnightly Corp, v. United Artists Television Inc., 392 U.S. 390 (17 June 1968).

7. Mr. Justice Fortas, dissenting at ibid., p.402: "This case calls not for the judgement of Solomon but for the dexterity of Houdini." Again at p.403: "Applying the normal jurisprudential tools--the words of the Act, legislative history, and precedent to the facts of the case is like trying to repair a television set with a mallet."

8. *Harvard law revue* 1514-1537 (1967) p.1528: "Blanket extension of copyright liability to CATV, as was done in *United Artists,* could foster increased concentration of control of the communications industry. It would give major copyright holders not just a means of preserving their exclusive marketing arrangements, but a powerful weapon to gain control of the CATV industry itself. Most of the material which is used in the broadcasting industry is controlled by a very small group."

9. Statement of Ernest W. Jennes, on behalf of the Association of Maximum Service Telecasters, Inc., hearings before the Subcommittee on Patents, Trademarks, and Copyrights of the Committee on the Judiciary, United States Senate, 89th Congress, 2d Session, on S.1006, 2, 3, 4 and 25 August 1966, at p.125: "...I am unaware of any situation of the CATV system which is performing this function which has asked program producers for licenses either at a wholly nominal figure or indeed for permission to retransmit without paying anything and heard of such a request being turned down"

10. Fortnightly Corp. v. United Artists Television, op. cit. p.40, Mr. Justice Fortas dissent: "On the one hand, it is darkly predicted that the imposition of full liability upon all CATV operations could result in the demise of this new, important instrument of mass communications; or in its becoming a tool of the powerful networks which hold a substantial number of copyrights on materials used in the television industry."

11. Ibid. p.881: "...defendant offered to prove at trial that the royalties paid to plaintiff by the original broadcasting stations took into account or could have taken into account the reception of the broadcasts by defendant's subscribers as well as by other members of the stations audiences. "...Since this offer of proof was rejected, we shall assume its accuracy although it seems debatable, at least so far as the royalties were based upon revenues from local advertisers, who might well have had little or no interest in reaching Clarksburg and Fairmont viewers...or even from national advertisers who wish to advertise in Clarksburg and Fairmont through other stations or media."

12. Ibid. p.1523, 1524: "One can confidently say that the copyright owner benefits when the audiences reached by CATV are in areas that do not have their own local stations. When, however, CATV begins to carry distant stations into another station's market, the copyright holders argue that, regardless of the effect CATV has on their revenues derived from distant stations, CATV has destroyed the penetrated areas as a market for future licensing of their programs since the local stations will not want to pay royalties and advertisers will be reluctant to sponsor a program which has already had a substantial showing in the area."

13. Ibid., p.392.

14. Ibid., footnote 18, p.396: "The Court formulated and applied this test in the light of this Court's decision in Buck v. Jewell-La Salle Realty Co. 283 U.S. 191.... But in Jewell-La Salle, a hotel recieved on a master radio set an unauthorized broadcast of a copyrighted work and transmitted that broadcast to all public and private rooms of the hotel by means of speakers installed by the hotel each room. The Court held the hotel liable for infringement but noted that the result might have differed if, as in this case, the original broadcast had been authorized by the copyright holder. 283 US at 199, n.5. The Jewell-La Salle decision must be understood as limited to its own facts."

15. Ibid., footnote 32, p.401: "The Solicitor General would have us hold that CATV systems do perform the programs they carry, but he would have us 'imply' a license for the CATV 'performances'. This 'implied in law' license would not cover all CATV activity but only those instances which a CATV system operates within the 'Grade B Contour' of the broadcasting station whose signal it carries. The Grade B contour is a theoretical FCC concept defined as the outer line along which reception of acceptable quality can be expected at least 90 of the time at the best 50 of locations. *Sixth report and order,* Fed. Reg. 3905, 3915. Since we hold that the petitioner's systems did not perform copyrighted works, we do not reach the question of implied license."

16. Ibid., p.395: "At the outset it is clear that petitioner's systems did not 'perform' the respondent's coptrighted works in any conventional sense of that term, or in any manner envisaged by the Congress that enacted the law in 1909."

17. Ibid., footnote 30, p.401: "It is said in dissent that, Our major object...should be to do as little damage as possible to traditional principles and to business relationships, until the Congress legislates.... But existing 'business relationships' would hardly be preserved by extending a questionable 35-year-old decision that in actual practice has not been applied outside its own factual context...so as retroactively to impose copyright liability where it has never been acknowledged to exist before."

18. Ibid., Mr. Justice Fortas dissent at footnote 5. p.406-7: The majority attempts to diminish the compelling authority of *Buck* v. *Jewell-La Salle,* by referring to a vague footnote in that opinion to the effect that the Court might not have found a 'performance' if the original broadcast, which was picked up by the hotel and brought to its various rooms, had been authorized by the copyright holder--as it was not. I cannot understand the point. Whatever might be the case in a contributory infringement action (which this is not), the interpretation of the 'perform' cannot logically turn on the question whether the material that is used is licensed or not licensed."

19. Ibid., Mr. Justice Fortas dissent at footnote 2, p.404: "The Solicitor General, in his brief on the merits, recommends that we adopt a compromise approach--finding a license implied in law with respect to some CATV operations, but not with respect to others. Regardless of the advisability of such an approach from the standpoint of communications, antitrust, and other relevant policies, I do not believe it is open to us, in construing the Copyright Act, to accept the Solicitor General's proposal."

20. Ibid., p.399. The Court stated that: "Essentially, a CATV system does no more than enhances the viewer's capacity to receive the broadcaster's signals; it provides a well-located antenna with an efficient connection to the viewer's television set. It is true that a CATV system plays an 'active' role in making reception possible in a given area, but so do ordinary television sets and antennas."

21. Ibid., Mr. Justice Fortas dissent at p.407: "It may be, indeed that insofar as CATV operations are limited to the geographical area which the licensed broadcaster (whose signals the CATV has picked up and carried) has the power to cover, a CATV is little more than a 'cooperative antenna' employed in order to ameliorate the image on

television screens at home or to bring the image to homes which, because of obstacles other than mere distance, could not receive them. But such a description will not suffice for the case in which a CATV has picked up the signals of a licensed broadcaster and carried them beyond the area--however that area be defined--which the broadcaster normally serves. In such a case the CATV *is* performing a function different from a simple antenna for, by hypothesis, the antenna could not pick up the signals of the licensed broadcaster and enable CATV patrons to receive them in their homes."

22. An explanation of the Court's stance may be gleaned from Justice Brandeis dissent in *International News Service* v. *Associated Press*, 248 US 215 (1918) wherein at p.267 he states: "Courts would be powerless to prescribe the detailed regulations essential to full enjoyment of the rights conferred or to introduce the machinery required for enforcement of such regulations. Considerations such as these should lead us to decline to establish a new rule of law in an effort to redress a newly disclosed wrong, although the propriety of some remedy appears to be clear."

23. *Fortnightly Corp. v. United Artists Television*, p.404: "An important legal issue is involved. Important economic values are at stake, and it would be hazardous to assume that Congress will act promptly, comprehensively, and retroactively."

24. Barbara A. Ringer, "Copyright law revision...," *Automated information systems....*

25. Ibid.

26. Federal Communications Commission, *Public notice, regulation of CATV systems, 6 Pike & Fischer Radio Reg. 2d 1637* (15 February 1966), followed by *Second report and order*, 6 ed. p.1717 (8 March 1966).

27. Harvard law revue, p.1532: "In the fast-changing field involves many considerations besides protecting copyright property, it would appear wiser to continue to rely on FCC regulations which can be changed as needs require rather than impose judicially a rigid rule of general CATV liability."

28. President's task force on communications policy, op. cit.

29. Ibid., p.5: "The television industry has not yet achieved a diversity and variety in programming comparable to that of book or magazine publishing, radio, or movies. The situation is roughly analogous to that of the movie industry prior to the 1950's. Before that time, four or five large studios provided most of the films, and generally aimed at the largest possible national and international audiences for each film. Their policies have been altered by the growth of independent film makers and distributors who cater to specialized tastes and interests and, in many instances to much smaller markets."

30. Ibid., p.10: "Cable systems now serve some three million subscribers, out of some 58 million homes equipped with television."

31. Ibid., p.13, 14: "A television channel requires more bandwidth (or spectrum space) than a radio channel."

32. Ibid., p.14.

33. Ibid., p.15.

34. Ibid., p.15.

35. 75 *Harvard law revue* 366 (1965), p.366, 367: "The system theoretically can relay signals of up to thirty-five stations both ultrahigh frequency (UHF) and very high frequency (VHF)--to subscribers, and the operator can place the signals on whatever cable channel he chooses."

36. Fortnightly Corp. v. United Artists Television, Inc., op. cit., footnote 7, p.393: "The monthly rate ranged from $3.75 to $5, and customers were also charged an installation fee. Increased charges were levied for additional television sets and for commercial establishments."

37. Harvard law revue, op. cit., footnote 54. p.1524: "Since CATV cable costs average $3500 to $4000 per mile, CATV can be profitably operated only in areas where residences are in close proximity to each other. This means that CATV cannot expand its operation far beyond the confines of towns and cities. Consequently it cannot reach those persons in outlying areas who can receive their programming 'off the air'..."

38. Ibid., p.1531: "CATV copyright liability should be evaluated in the light of the efforts of the FCC to deal with CATV by direct regulation. In recognition of the varied impact which CATV has on its objectives, the FCC, after initially declining jurisdiction, has begun to regulate CATV by the promulgation of a series of station carriage rules for CATV systems. In order to minimize the audience drawn away from local stations, CATV must carry on request, the signals of any stations within whose 'B contours' it operates, and it must 'black out' from its transmission of distant stations, any programming carried on the same day by the local stations, In an effort to promote the development of independent and educational television stations in areas which may have a sufficient population to support them the FCC has laid down a general prohibition against the carriage of outside station signals into the 100 most important television markets, where the development of independence seems most likely. Subject to these restrictions, the FCC is allowing CATV to continue and expand operations in order to help fill the gaps in existing service and provide more varied programming service."

39. President's task force on communications policy, p.10.

40. Federal Communications Commission, *Second further notice of proposed rule making*, Docket No. 18397-A: "11. There is also the issue of fairness to the copyright owners. This, however, is not a matter which can be resolved by this Commission. Only the Congress can impose what it believes to be fair compensation in the circumstances. Our concern here is therefore the narrow issue whether the proposal is defective in that the copyright owner cannot be treated fairly thereunder. We have studied the question in that light, and have tentatively concluded that there is no bar in this respect."

41. Ibid.

42. D.C.W.D. Washington, N. Div., 164 USPQ (Decided Nov. 17, 1969) Headnote:

"Defendant made video tape of Washington television station's broadcast of copyrighted motion pictures, transported tape to Alaska and, about a week after broadcast, disseminated pictures by use of tape over defendant's coaxial cable to subscribers who viewed pictures on their television receiving sets; preparation of tape infringed upon copyright owner's right under 17 U.S.C. 1 (d); dissemination over cable system also constituted infringement; whether dissemination constitutes a 'performance' is immaterial."

43. Ibid., p.213: "The 'recording' system used by the defendants captured the impulses and put them in such form that they were capable of being perceived, with proper equipment, innumerable times, and after the passage of time, subject only to the limitations imposed by the characteristics of the plastic tape upon which the iron particles were mounted."

44. Melville B. Nimmer, "Project new technology and the law of copyright: reprography and computers," *UCLA law review*, (April 1969).

45. Doris M. Timpano, "Copyright legislation and you," NEA Journal (April 1969).

46. "The copyright law revision and ETV: an alternative to the wasteland?" *Rutgers law review* 1:112-113 (Fall 1968): "The possibility exists, however, that 'community welfare' may, in fact, be adversely affected by the grant of an exception to ETV (Educational Television). Hypothetucally, ETV's use of copyrighted materials could affect the incomes of authors so drastically that they may be discouraged from continuing their work. That the incomes of authors (as distinguished from copyright proprietors) could be substantially affected seems an unlikely event if ETV's free use of copyrighted materials is reasonably controlled.... That creative individuals will lose the urge to write, for example, seems even less likely. If any result can be predicted at this time, it is that more individuals will achieve the level of literacy needed to produce or consume copyrighted materials because of ETV's influence,"

Telecommunications Costs

Donald L. Dittberner

INTRODUCTION

The primary focus of this paper is the interrelationship of those parameters which affect the costs associated with various forms of telecommunications services. The basic limitation in the scope of this paper is that costs will be examined primarily in a relative sense rather than on an absolute basis. We feel that a summarization of actual dollar costs for alternative forms of telecommunication services or a detailed explanation of existing common carrier rate structures would only serve to confuse the issue or result in an oversimplification of the cost problem. This paper will only refer to specific costs for the purpose of illustrating specific points or general trends.

TELECOMMUNICATIONS PARAMETERS

Telecommunication costs are a function of distance, amount of usage, and channel capacity. In addition, the form of the transmitted information and the inherent characteristics of the transmission media affect telecommunication costs. For example, a page of information in the form of an analog video signal would represent approximately 630,000 bits of information when digitally encoded while the same amount of information could be represented by about 24,000 bits if encoded in a digital data form. Telecommunications costs will be highly dependent on the media chosen for storage of the information prior to transmission

DISTANCE

Transmission distance is a fundamental parameter affecting telecommunication costs. Telecommunication rate structures are such that total cost increases with distance while cost per unit either decreases or remains constant with increasing distance.

AMOUNT OF USAGE

Telecommunications usage has a direct effect on cost. Existing common carrier tariffs allow the user to select either full-period or shared telecommunications services. One example of a shared service is the DDD network. Charges for this service are directly related to the length of time the service is used. On the other hand, full-period service charges are fixed since the user has the transmission facility dedicated to his sole use 100 percent of the time. If a user does not utilize the facility all of the time, the cost-per-unit time utilized increases.

CHANNEL CAPACITY

Channel capacity refers to the maximum limitations on information transfer imposed by the particular nature of the telecommunications facilities being utilized. Capacity is measured generally in terms of bandwidth (hertz or cycles/second) or data rate (bits/second). It should be noted that there is not necessarily a one-to-one correlation between the two measures for a particular communication facility.

The relationship between channel capacity and telecommunication costs is not easily definable. It is highly dependent upon the nature of the material being transmitted, the mode of transmission, and the types of available terminal equipment. Also, there is a definite trade-off between channel capacity and utilization time; however, this is only true in those situations where real-time communications is not a fixed requirement. Voice communication, Picture-phone, and live television channel capacities are dictated by signal quality considerations.

EXISTING TELECOMMUNICATION SERVICES

Existing telecommunication services, as exemplified by the tariffed offerings of AT&T, encompass a broad range of channel capacities and pricing arrangements. The voice-grade channel with a nominal bandwidth of 3 kilohertz is the basic building block of virtually all telecommunication service offerings. Table 1 shows the hierarchy of telecommunication channels. The groupings illustrated are not arbitrary but reflect the manner in which common carriers historically have combined channels in a physical sense.

In making some basic comparisons about the costs associated with existing telecommunications services, one can divide these services into three categories. Narrowband services include those services which are classically referred to as telegraph, utilize digital transmission rather than analog, and operate at speeds of

150 bits per second and below. Mediumband services are those which are classically referred to as voice grade, utilize analog transmission rates up to 9600 bits per second. Wideband services are those which are classically called group and super-group bandwidths and are greater than voice grade. Wideband facilities will handle data rates in excess of 9600 bits per second, with maximum data rates determined by the specific type of facility being used.

TABLE 1. HIERARCHY OF TELECOMMUNICATION CHANNELS

CHANNEL DESIGNATION	NOMINAL BANDWIDTH	EQUIVALENT VOICE CHANNELS	APPROXIMATE COST RATIO
Telegraph channel	75 kHz	1/18	1/2
Voice channel	3 kHz	1	1
Group	48 kHz	12	10
Super group	240 kHz	60	30
Sub-Master Group no. 2	960 kHz	240	85
Sub-Master Group no. 1	1440 kHz	360	Not tariffed
Master group	2400 kHz	600	Not tariffed

COSTS OF EXISTING SERVICES

When one examines the cost structure associated with existing services, several facts immediately become clear. Cost comparisons between narrowband and mediumband services indicate that, except in special situations where very low volumes of data transmission are involved, mediumband or voice-grade facilities are the more cost-effective choice. For example, at a distance of 1,000 miles, a full-period telegraph facilities, with a maximum speed of 150 bits per second, are available at approximately $800 per month while full-period voice-grade facilities which can handle much faster data rates are available for a basic price of $1,100 per month. Again, at the same distance on a switched basis, narrowband TWX charges are $.50 per minute whereas direct-dial voice-grade charges are $1.15 for the initial three-minute period. Even at the present time, there are serious questions with respect to the cost-effectiveness of narrowband, telegraph-type facilities and services.

With respect to trade-offs in the cost of both mediumband and wideband services, there is little that can be said that would be meaningful because the particular type of service which would represent an economic choice is highly dependent upon the actual or projected traffic characteristics of the system in question. The general relationship between cost of mediumband and wideband services is that the basic wideband service (a group equivalent to twelve voice channels) is approximately ten times more costly than a single, mediumband voice-grade channel. This is true for both switched and full-period private line services. The actual channel capacity available to users of mediumband and wideband services is dependent upon the terminal equipment which is utilized. For example, on mediumband services there are modems commercially available to handle transmission speeds from approximately 75 bits per second up to 9600 bits per second.

Table 2 illustrates the cost per megabit transmitted for some of the commonly available telecommunications services. The costs shown are minimum rather than average and are based on 100 percent operating efficiency. The basic conclusion to be drawn from the existing structure of telecommunication costs is that peak information volume is a highly critical factor affecting not only total telecommunications costs but the per-unit volume cost as well.

TABLE 2. TRANSMISSION COSTS (1000 Mile Distance)

FACILITY	BANDWIDTH	SPEED	$/MEGABIT (APPROX.)
**Telpak C	240 kHz	250 kbps	.05
**Series 8000	48 kHz	50 kbps	.09
*Data Phone 50	48 kHz	50 kbps	1.20
**Series 3000	3 kHz	9.6 kbps	.08
*DDD	3 kHz	2.4 kbps	2.70

* Terminal charges not included
**Assumes twenty-four hours, seven days a week utilization

TRENDS AFFECTING FUTURE TELECOMMUNICATIONS

Certain trends now evident are expected to have a dramatic effect on telecommunications costs over the next two decades. This section identifies those trends and discusses the likely effect on telecommunication costs. Most cost reductions in the future will be the result of developments in two areas, technology and regulatory policy. The primary areas which we will examine are the following: (1) digital transmission systems, (2) Picturephone, (3) data compression techniques, (4) special-service common carriers, (5) competitive forces.

DIGITAL TRANSMISSION

The existing telecommunications network utilizes both analog and digital transmission systems. Analog systems are by far the most common at the present time, but digital carrier systems are being installed at a rapid rate. The primary difference between these systems is the manner in which information is represented. Digital systems transmit information as discrete signals while analog systems encode information into continuous signals.

On a cost basis, digital transmission systems will be approximately equivalent to analog transmission systems of equal voice channel capacity. The primary advantage with digital transmission systems is their ability to intermix various types of signals and achieve more efficient transmission of signals other than voice. An example of the efficiency of digital systems can be seen by comparing the equivalent bit rates on digital and analog voice-grade channels. On analog systems, 9600 bits per second appears to be the highest practicable bit rate that can be obtained now, and because of certain constraints in much of the telecommunications network, this is much more likely to be 4800 bits per second. On a digital transmission system one voice channel is equivalent to 56,000 bits per second.

PICTUREPHONE

Another example of the efficiency of digital transmission is Picturephone. Although the Picturephone set produces an analog signal, it is possible to sample and encode the signal for digital transmission. Picturephone signals transmitted on an analog system displace either 300 or 400 voice channels (depending on whether the transmission medium is microwave or coaxial cable radio relay). Picturephone signals transmitted on a digital system displace ninety-six voice channels. As a further example, one can obtain 250 kilobits-per-second transmission today on the equivalent of sixty voice channels on an analog super group whereas the Bell System T-2 carrier, which is scheduled to be installed initially this year, is a digital system that will provide 6.3 megabits per second on the equivalent of ninety-six voice channels.

There are other, more advanced digital transmission systems under development which will have data transmission capabilities far in excess of the input/output data rates that present-day computers can handle. For example, the T-5 carrier system, which is a high-capacity long-haul carrier scheduled for initial installation around 1975, has a per-channel data rate in excess of 5000 megabits per second. Millimeter wave transmission systems utilizing wave guides and optical systems using lasers are expected to be placed into service in the late 1970s or early 1980s. These systems are expected to have data transmission capacities in the neighborhood of 25,000 megabits per second. We expect, because of these advances, that data transmission costs are likely to drop by a factor of two by 1974 and very likely by a factor of five by 1980.

Initially, digital transmission facilities only will be used for common carrier interoffice transmission. However, by the mid-70s digital transmission capability will be extended to user premises.

DATA COMPRESSION

Advances in data compression techniques will affect the cost of transmitting analog and digital signals. These techniques are expected to be particularly effective in reducing the cost of transmitting such analog information as facsimile or video. This will be done by digitally encoding the analog signal prior to transmission in such a manner that a large percentage of the redundancy is eliminated. Bell Labs has indicated that they may be able to substantially reduce the equivalent voice channel transmission requirements for Picturephone using techniques of this type. Similar techniques can be applied easily to encoding the transmission of analog images stored on microfilm, video tape, or by facsimile.

Data compression encoding techniques also are applicable to digital data. One such technique in use at the present time eliminates excess transmission of repetitive blanks or zeros. There are also highly efficient variable-length codes available for alphabetic information which take advantage of the frequency of occurrence of the letters of the alphabet in the English language.

SPECIAL-SERVICE COMMON CARRIERS

With the MCI decision the Federal Communications Commission gave the go-ahead for the establishment of special-service common carriers who will offer private line communication facilities for both analog and digital transmission in competition with the telephone carriers. These carriers are proposing price schedules that are substantially below those currently provided by the established common carriers. We expect that approval eventually will be granted for the establishment of these special-service common carrier networks although it will be approximately three to five years before these services will be universally available. Although these carriers are proposing to provide telecommunications services at costs substantially lower than the Bell System, it remains to be seen whether these price schedules are realistic and whether the proposed rates are actually compensatory.

COMPETITIVE FORCES

With the advent of the special-service common carriers, we are beginning to see the development of competitive forces within the telecommunication industry with respect to the offering of common carrier services. It is likely that the existence of the special-service common carriers, or even the threat of their existence, will cause some radical departures from past practices on the part of the Bell System and other telephone companies in the manner in which they determine their rates. The Bell System has stated that if the MCI-type carriers are allowed to compete with them on their high-usage routes that Bell very likely will have to drop its previous policy of national averaging when establishing rates. The alternative approach which they will likely develop is to base rates between cities on the actual cost of the facilities installed. The experimental tariff for Series 11000 channels, now in effect, does in fact constitute a step in this direction. The overall effect of such a change in rate-making philosophy will substantially increase telecommunication costs for rural and less heavily populated areas in the country.

CONCLUSIONS

Telecommunications costs are highly dependent on the volume of information transfer, system response time requirements, and the form of information storage media utilized. Existing trends point toward technological developments which are expected to reduce radically the cost of transmitting digital data; however, no equivalent reduction in the cost of analog information transmission is expected.

Typical data communications costs on a per-megabit basis have a variation of almost two orders of magnitude. Full-time utilization is the key to achieving maximum economies in information transfer. Long-term telecommunications economies only can be achieved when the network design process allows for the technological advances which are likely to affect the telecommunications cost structure. Failure to anticipate these technological strides will result in networks which may be nowhere near optimum in even as short a period as five years. In addition, a lack of anticipation may result in the selection of information storage media which results in an extremely expensive conversion at some future date.

Principles of Telecommunications Planning

D. A. Dunn

INTRODUCTION

The objective of this paper is to present a general framework for telecommunication system planning into which specific information on cost and performance of individual components can be put. The viewpoint taken is that of a decisionmaker responsible for deciding on the form of a telecommunication system to provide access to remote information for a user community such as a university, a city, or a professional user class such as lawyers or nuclear physicists. Such a decisionmaker must normally decide among alternatives that can be produced from existing technology or from minor modifications of existing technology, such that precise performance characteristics, delivery time, and price information is available. However, in some cases where there is adequate lead time, it may be feasible to consider alternatives that involve some amount of technological development. In these cases the output of the development program will be to some extent uncertain, and it will be important for the decisionmaker to be able to estimate the degree of uncertainty and to provide for this aspect of the decision problem in his plans. There are well-developed systematic techniques for dealing with uncertainty[1][2] that can be applied to this problem, and these techniques are described briefly herein.

The basic framework for telecommunication planning that is presented here is built around the decision model of Figure 1.[3] This model is important to an understanding of the decision process because it allows us to separate any decision problem into a number of clearly defined elements. We may or may not be able to give a precise form to each element of Figure 1, but by attempting to do so, we can become aware of the precise nature of the information that may be lacking and decide whether to attempt to acquire the missing information.

In Figure 1 there are two types of variables: (1) decision variables, which are variables under the control of the decisionmaker, such as the system performance specifications; and (2) state variables, which are variables not under the control of the decisionmaker. For a library administrator decisionmaker, an example of a state variable might be the regulatory policy adopted by the FCC with respect to interconnection of private networks with the public switched network. For the FCC as decisionmaker, this variable would be a decision variable. A decisionmaker is normally confronted with a limited set of alternatives. An alternative consists of a complete set of decision variable "settings" in a particular decision problem. For example, in the present context an alternative might be a specific, complete system design.

Outcomes are the results associated with each particular choice of a system alternative in the context in which the alternative is to be implemented. The interaction model is whatever model we may have to predict outcomes, and it may be only a very simple verbal model or it may be a mathematical or computer model. Outcomes can be specified in various degrees of detail and at various levels. For example, we will almost certainly be interested in the outcome that the system perform according to its specifications, and be delivered and in operation on time at the cost specified. The cost and technical performance can be viewed as outcomes; in most cases these dimensions of the outcome will be predictable with a high degree of certainty. We would normally also be interested in outcomes related to the use of the system after it is installed. For example, the extent of its usage, by whom it would be used, what time cycle of usage might occur, and the opinions of the users would all be important outcomes.

Finally, the decisionmaker must be able to provide some kind of value model in order for him to decide among competing alternatives with different outcomes. At the very minimum, the decisionmaker will be required to choose among alternatives with different costs and different technical performance characteristics. He will have to be able to specify his trade-offs between performance characteristics and cost in order to state which alternative he prefers. If he considers probable behavioral outcomes such as usage, he will have to consider trade-offs at this level as well.

In the following sections of this paper, a typical telecommunication system is described in terms of its basic functions, its components, and its performance characteristics. Alternative system configurations are considered in terms of costs and in terms of a set of performance dimensions such as data rate of access messages, daily usage in hours, etc. Then a typical hypothetical decision problem is considered that hinges on the trade-off between terminal costs and communication line costs. An example of an uncertain outcome is considered as a part of this example. Finally, consideration is given to a value problem in which a decisionmaker must decide between alternatives that differ in the form in which the cost information is available. For one alternative the cost is given as a fixed dollar amount; for the other, the cost may be either of two values and the probability for each cost value is given.

DESCRIPTION OF A TELECOMMUNICATION SYSTEM

A telecommunication system normally can be analyzed in terms of the costs and performance of three major hardware components: (1) user terminals, (2) communication lines, and (3) the central computer and data storage system.[4][5] In addition, a substantial cost in most systems is associated with the software that enables the user to operate the system simply and efficiently. Maintenance and operating costs either can be associated with each of the above subsystems or lumped as a single separate item.

The functioning of a telecommunication system designed to provide a library-type service also can be described in terms of a sequence of steps that constitutes a single transaction, as follows:

1.　　User indication of desire to use the system

2.　　System indication that it is available or not

3.　　User indication of data sought to be accessed in terms that can be accepted by the system

4.　　System indication that data sought is or is not available

5.　　System provision of data sought to user

6.　　Recording of usage made of system for charges or other use

7.　　System indication that transaction is complete and its availability for another transaction.

In the above sequence of steps, Steps 1, 2, 4, 6, and 7 are usually referred to as signaling functions analogous to the dial tone and ringing or busy signal of the telephone system and of course, may in fact involve these telephone signaling functions. Step 3 is a low data rate (usually less than 300 bits per second) operation that may take the form of a voice conversation, a teletyped statement to a computer, or a conversation with a computer programmed to ask the user a set of questions that can be answered in various simple ways like a multiple-choice test using a teletypewriter or a Touchtone pad.

Step 5 is the key step in the operation as far as system design is concerned, and a number of alternatives are open to the designer at this point. A cathode ray tube, CRT, display of the data is typical, with some separate provision for making a hard copy being necessary if desired. A critical distinction must be made at this point between systems designed to transmit only certain, prespecified characters and systems designed to send arbitrary patterns of data such as photographs of persons or scenes. One page of ordinary written text, when viewed in terms of characters (characters require about six bits per character to store or transmit), represents about 10,000 bits of information. The same page of text or a page with a diagram or a photograph, when viewed simply as an arbitrary page of bits that can have an arbitrary pattern, represents about 1,000,000 to 10,000,000 bits of information. A critical feature of this distinction insofar as the cost of a telecommunications link between the user and the central file is the data rate needed to transmit the message. If the message consists only of standard characters, it is possible to transmit such a message about as rapidly as it can be read or skimmed by a human over a voiceband line. If the message is a sequence of unrelated diagrams or photographs, a much greater data rate is necessary; a television signal is capable of transmitting data at a rate sufficient for this purpose. In most cases, however, the user will wish to examine a series of pages of text, diagrams, or photographs with substantial viewing periods per page (up to minutes per page). In this case a much lower average data rate is required to transmit the necessary information than is the case if there is a rapid sequence of arbitrary patterns. In order to take advantage of this possibility for lowering the cost of data transmission, however, the user terminals must have data storage capability, which increases their cost. A basic system design trade-off thus exists between local storage costs and data transmission costs.

A variety of options also exist in the design of the central data storage and retrieval system. For example, data may be stored magnetically in core, on discs, or on tape with different resultant access times. Data also may be stored in microfilm and read out by stopping the film for viewing by a user. However, the cost of tying up the full system may be very high if this is done. Therefore, some type of buffer system may be appropriate to provide temporary data storage and to allow the main microfilm system to be used by other users in more rapid sequence. Such choices depend on the number of users sharing the system and their habits in terms of the average length of usage period and frequency of usage. Readout system options also include the question raised earlier of whether data is to be read out in the form of characters which can be economically coded for low-cost transmission at moderate data rates or in the form of a scanned system like TV or xerography which can handle either pictures or text but which requires far higher data rates than a character transmission system.

System performance characteristics of interest to the designer include those mentioned plus a number of others that relate more to how the system is to be used, such as average usage in hours per user per day. A number of these performance characteristics are listed below, along with a summary of those suggested above:

1.　　Data rate of user transmission of description of data sought (typical: 100 bps)

2.　　Data rate of transmission of data to user (typical: 1000 bps)

3.　　Mode of display of data to use (typical: CRT display)

4.   Total amount of data displayed to user at one time and duration of display (typical: one page of text displayed for as long as user wishes)

5.   Capability of system to provide a hard copy to user

6.   Degree of privacy offered to users

7.   Total amount of data in central file

8.   Classification system used to access data

9.   Form in which data stored—access time

10.   Sharing capability of central file — buffering

11.   Pattern of usage — hours per day per user, number of users, probability of more than n users seeking to use the system simultaneously, etc.

EXAMPLE OF ALTERNATIVE SYSTEM CONFIGURATIONS

As an example of the choice that might be offered to a decisionmaker, a specific set of alternatives is presented next that emphasizes the trade-off in system design between telecommunications line data rate and terminal complexity.

Let us first consider a system with a central data file subsystem that stores only written text in the form of uniform, standardized characters and that is capable of transmitting characters in the form of a standard code with, say, six bits per character. With an average of five characters per word at a rate of 2000 words per minute, such a system can transmit faster than a human can normally read and at a rate sufficient to allow quick scans of the material without much waiting time. The corresponding data rate is 2000 x 5 x 6 x 1/60 or 1000 bits per second (one kilobit per second). The average telephone line can transmit 2000 bits per second so this system easily falls into the category that can use such a line.

If the central data system stores ordinary text in the form of microfilmed pages, this system requires a high-speed character recognition and scan system to encode this data, character by character, and convert it to electrical impulses. Such an encoding system would be feasible, although costly, and an alternative would be a much simpler TV raster type of scan system that would, however, require a much greater data rate in order to transmit the signal to the user. A typical value might be of the order of a thousand times the value obtained with efficient coding or 1 megabit per second rather than 1 kilobit per second. Consequently, the line costs would be much greater for such a raster-type system. The raster-type system, however, has other advantages. At 1 kbps, we noted that the "paint-on" speed or the speed at which a picture would appear was about 2000 words per minute, which is a moderate scanning speed for a human. At 1 Mbps, on the other hand, the page would appear essentially instantaneously.

Another related trade-off in this system occurs at the user terminal where a raster-type display turns out to be a very simple and low-cost approach. TV sets already are available in every home so if the system were for home use, this fact would be very important and would favor the use of a raster display. The length of time the information needs to be displayed to the user is a critical performance dimension here. Normally, a user wishes to be able to look at the information as long as he wishes, up to minutes at a time. If this capability is to be provided, either the information must be stored locally or it must be continually retransmitted from the central data file until the user is through, as in the case of the usual raster display. The consequence of this approach is that a full TV bandwidth is consumed in simply retransmitting old information with its associated high line cost. The basic alternative is a user terminal with sufficient local storage to remember the contents of one page.

One solution is, of course, to make a hard copy. This solution provides both long- and short-term storage and frees the central data file for other tasks as soon as the information is sent once. However, it is difficult, noisy, and costly to produce hard copy at the speed suggested at the beginning of this discussion using present technology, such as line printers. There are two other major alternatives for the user terminal with storage. The first involves conventional magnetic core storage to store the received information for each character using an ordinary computer memory. The present cost of this type of storage for a full page of text (about 10 kilobits in the form of characters) is of the order of $1,000 or more. The other alternative would use a magnetic disc to record the information in one TV frame (about 1 to 10 megabits in the form of an arbitrary pattern). Such a technique would allow the use of a TV raster system but would require the signal to be sent only once. It would then be repeated by the magnetic disc as long as the user wished to view it. Such a system could equally well be used to store pictures of other non-character information. It would allow a burst of information to be sent using the full TV bandwidth for one-thirtieth second (the time of one full frame), and it would retain this information locally until the user asked for a new frame. Obviously such a system would have the advantage of freeing both the central data file and the wideband channel used to send the information to serve other users on a time-shared basis. Such a system can be imagined as a service offered to homes via cable television during the next few years.[6]

We are now in a position to formulate several basically different system alternatives that, if this were a real problem, could be costed out in detail. Here we will assign some hypothetical cost figures to each alternative in order to pose the problem for analysis in a specific form. In all cases we will assume that the central data file is the same, except for the presence of the character reader and encoder which we will use for some systems in place of the TV camera that will be used for the raster-type system alternatives. A list of the components available for this hypothetical system is given in Table 1 and illustrated in Figure 2.

Alternatives now can be described simply by the letters associated with the components in Table 1, and three system alternatives are shown in Figure 3. In addition, we must specify the number of users to determine total system costs. We will consider two cases, a system with 1,000 users and one with 10,000 users; it is assumed that the central data file is adequate to serve the larger number of users. It is convenient to express all costs on a per-user per-year basis, which requires that hardware costs be converted from initial total values to annual values. The maintenance costs, life, and interest rate are assumed to be such that the conversion is on a four to one basis, i.e., the initial costs in Table 1 are four times the annual costs. We also assume that maintenance costs for the three types of communication lines considered in Figure 2 are included in the costs listed in Table 1 which are already on a per-user per-year basis. (The simplest way to think of this annual cost is that this is the price that the decisionmaker would have to pay to lease rather than buy, because it includes all the factors of cost, including maintenance and capital costs. If we take the position of the owner of the equipment who wishes to lease the equipment to the decisionmaker, we can calculate our total annual cost as follows:[7]

Assume: life $=$ N years
interest rate $=$ i percent per annum
maintenance $=$ m percent per annum

$$
\text{Annual cost} = [\text{First cost}]\left[\frac{m}{100} + \frac{i/100}{1 - \dfrac{1}{(1 + i/100)^N}}\right]
$$

For example: $N = 10$
$i = 8$
$m = 10$
Annual cost $=$ [First cost] [0.25]

Which is the ratio used in the example here.)

TABLE 1. COMPONENTS AND COSTS FOR
HYPOTHETICAL LIBRARY SYSTEMS

COMPONENT	HYPOTHETICAL COST
A. Central data file	$1,000,000
B. Character reader and encoder	$ 100,000
C. TV camera setup	$ 10,000
D. 5 MHz line for TV raster transmission	$ 600*
E. 2000 bps line for character transmission	$ 60*
F. 5 MHz line on time-shared basis	$ 200*
G. TV-raster user terminal without storage	$ 300
H. User terminal with local character storage using magnetic core	$ 1,500
I. User terminal with local storage of raster using magnetic disc	Uncertain. Probability 0.2 that can be produced for $600. Probability 0.8 that cost will be $1,000.

*These are hypothetical costs expressed on a per-user per-year basis, assuming an average user-to-central data file distance and an average usage that is independent of the number of users.

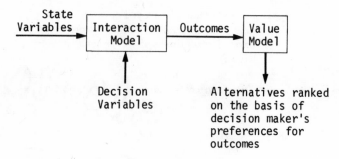

Figure 1   Model of the Decision Process

Alternative System 1
Character coding, transmission using 2 kbps line
Components A, B, E, H

$C_{1000} =$ $710 per user (including $60 line costs)

$C_{1000} =$ $462 per user (including $60 line costs)[8]

Alternative System 2
TV raster, transmission using 5 MHz line
Components A, C, D, G

$C_{1000} =$ $928 per user (including $600 line costs)

$C_{10000} =$ $700 per user (including $600 line costs)

Alternative System 3
TV raster, transmission using 2 kbps line and local storage
Components A, C, F, I

$C_{1000} =$ $602 per user, with probability 0.2 (including $200 line costs)

$=$ $700 per user, with probability 0.8 (including $200 line costs)

$C_{1000} =$ $375 per user, with probability 0.2 (including $200 line costs)

$=$ $475 per user, with probability 0.8 (including $200 line costs)

Note that the terminal costs for System 2 are much less than those for System 1, but the total cost for System 1 is lower. If we regard both systems as having the same performance, the choice is clear as between these two systems. However, System 2 has a potential performance that could be more useful than System 1 if it were later desired to convert the central data file to one that stored diagrams and photographs or pages of printed text with different type sizes and styles. In order to simplify the comparison, it was assumed here that all data was printed text stored in characters of the same size and style. If this were not the case but if the data were still only printed text, it would still be possible to make a system comparison; however, the character reader and coder would be much more expensive, and it is possible that in this case System 2 would be the lower cost system.

System 3 is the lowest cost system for 1,000 users, without regard to which terminal design ultimately is developed. If the decisionmaker does not have to share in the development costs and can delay purchase of his system until System 3 is available it is a clear choice for a 1,000-user system. If the system must serve 10,000 users, the problem is more complex. Only if the lowest cost terminal is the result of the development program will this system be lower cost than System 1. If the higher cost terminal is the one that proves feasible, System 1 is lower cost than System 3. How should the decisionmaker choose between Systems 1 and 3, assuming that he must make up his mind before the terminal development program is complete?

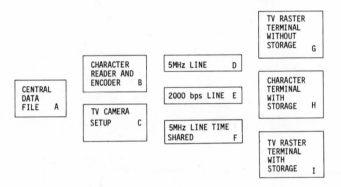

Figure 2   System Components for Library Systems

A VALUE PROBLEM

It is helpful in visualizing problems involving probabilistic outcomes to make use of a "decision tree" illustrated in Figure 4. The cross is a "decision node" at which the decision between Systems 1 and 3 is made. The circle is a "chance node" at which the outcome can be either of the costs shown, $375 or $475 per user, each with the probability indicated. These probability estimates are those of the decisionmaker in the light of all the information that he has available. The solution of such problems is the purpose of decision analysis.[9] [10]

There are two basic steps necessary to the solution of such a problem. First, the decisionmaker must make probability assessments like those expressed in Figure 4. Second, he must provide a fairly precise indication of how he values the various possible outcomes. The way this is most conveniently done in general is in the form of a utility function. If there were many dimensions to the outcome, he would have to give us his utility when confronted with trade-offs among all of these dimensions. In the present problem, all that is involved is the single dimension of dollars of cost. But there is still an issue as to how highly the decisionmaker values dollars in various quantities. What is needed is a curve of utility (in arbitrary units) as a function of dollars.

Figure 5 shows two such curves. The meaning of these curves can be made more clear if we interpret them in terms of "lotteries." A lottery is a situation like that of Figure 4 in which

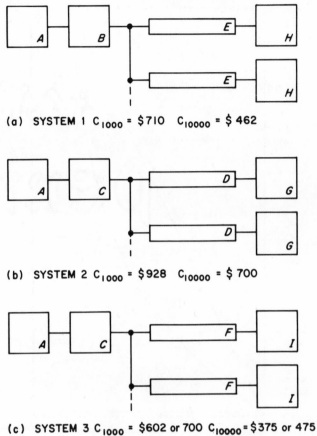

(a) SYSTEM 1 C_{1000} = $710 C_{10000} = $ 462

(b) SYSTEM 2 C_{1000} = $928 C_{10000} = $ 700

(c) SYSTEM 3 C_{1000} = $602 or 700 C_{10000} = $375 or 475

Figure 3   Three Hypothetical Library Systems Annual Cost of Leasing Equipment Alternative System 1, Alternative System 2, Alternative System 3

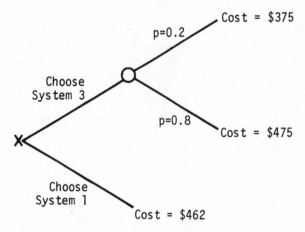

Figure 4   A Decision Tree Describing the Decision Between the Alternatives of Systems 1 and 3

the decisionmaker selects System 3. He then obtains the lottery: With probability 0.2 his cost will be $375; with probability 0.8 his cost will be $475. An important thing about a lottery is its certain equivalent, i.e., the amount that the decisionmaker would be willing to pay for sure and be indifferent as to whether he paid this amount or the amount determined from the lottery. If this certain equivalent in our example turns out to be less than

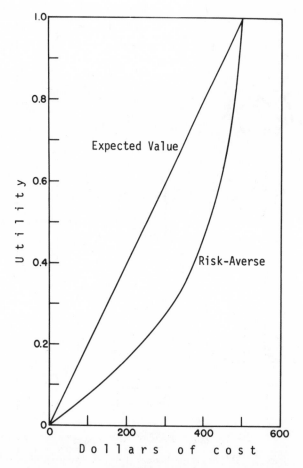

Figure 5   Utility as a Function of Dollars of Cost for Two Types of Decision Makers

$$u(c) \;=\; p(a)u(a) \;+\; p(b)u(b) \qquad\qquad \text{where}$$

u(c) = utility of the certain equivalent of the lottery in which a is received with probability p(a) and b is received with probability p(b). (p(b) = 1-p(a))

u(a) = utility of receiving a with certainty

u(b) = utility of receiving b with certainty

In our problem, for the expected-value decisionmaker in Figure 5

u(a)	= 0.95	p(b)	= 0.2
p(a)	= 0.8	u(c)	= 0.91
u(b)	= 0.75	c	= $455

so he would prefer System 3. The risk-averse decisionmaker on the other hand has

u(a)	= 0.77	p(b)	= 0.2
p(a)	= 0.8	u(c)	= 0.70
u(b)	= 0.4	c	= $462

This certain equivalent is just equal to the cost of System 1 so he would be indifferent between Systems 1 and 3. Thus, the risk-averse decisionmaker would pay slightly more than the expected-value decisionmaker to avoid the lottery associated with System 3, but in this case he would be unable to decide between the two systems on this basis alone. In such a case he might reexamine his probability assessments and also reexamine the assumption that the two systems would have identical performance. As noted previously, System 3 seems to have more potential for the future if there were any likelihood that the system might be used for diagrams and photographs at a later date. Another variable in this decision problem was the number of user terminals, assumed here to be known with certainty. In an actual problem the number of user terminals would be a function of predicted demand. It would be known only probabilistically, and as we have seen, it clearly affects the decision.

In this and in almost every decision problem, there is at least one variable that can only be known within broad limits. In such cases the issue arises as to whether more information should be gathered. More information always comes with a price tag, and so we must have some measure of the value of information if we are to make a logical choice as to whether to gather it. Decision analysis can give a very precise answer to such questions by tracing through the effect that having more information would have on the decision. This process can be carried out by assuming that perfect information is available and examining the cost savings that might result in the best possible case, thus establishing an upper bound on how much it would make sense to pay for perfect information. Of course, we cannot normally

$462, then the decisionmaker should choose System 3. If it is greater than $462, he should choose System 1.

In the curves of Figure 5 the interpretation that may be made in terms of lotteries is as follows. We can assign an arbitrary value of utility to a cost of $500, such as 1.0. Now we ask what is the maximum amount that the decisionmaker would pay to avoid a lottery in which a fair coin would be flipped and he pay $500 if it came up heads and $0 if it came up tails. The expected-value[11] decisionmaker would pay exactly $250 to avoid this lottery while the risk-averse decisionmaker in Figure 5 would pay more than this amount. The expected-value decisionmaker is indifferent to risk. The risk-averse decisionmaker is less inclined to take fair gambles as the stakes become large in comparison with his total resources. Thus, we all might be willing to match pennies, but only a few of us enjoy matching $100 bills even though the game is fair. The risk-averse decisionmaker in Figure 5 is pictured as a person or organization that is quite sensitive to cost in the vicinity of $400 per user. He is not willing to gamble very much in the hope of getting the cost per user down to $375, as long as there is a risk he may have to pay $475 if things turn out badly.

Once we know the decisionmaker's utility curve, we can insert his utility for each outcome and the probability of this outcome occurring in the following equation.[12]

get perfect information so we also may need to know the value of imperfective information. A typical example is the kind of information obtained by sampling opinion or testing quality by random sampling of a large lot of some manufactured good. In the references cited problems of this type are examined in detail.[13] [14]

CONCLUSION

In decisions involving large sums of money, such as the decision of whether to invest in an interactive library system and if so, which kind of system, it is worth carrying out an extensive analysis of the alternatives. In this paper it has only been possible to introduce the decision analysis methodology that I believe is well suited to this type of problem. Extensive work has been done in this field, however, and the references cited can lead the reader to more comprehensive presentations. As a rough rule of thumb it is probably worth investing about 1 percent of the amount of money at stake in analyzing the decision. Thus, a $1 million decision is worth examining to the extent of around $10 thousand, which is about the threshold at with a meaningful decision analysis can be carried out.

We have seen that the choice of alternatives to be examined is a critical feature of the analysis. It is extremely important in a real analysis, as distinguished from the hypothetical problem described here, that the technical alternatives be very carefully delineated in such a way that the systems being compared have their performance and costs described in the same way. It probably would not be possible to compare system alternatives with the same performance, as was done here. If the alternatives have different performance, we must get into a much more extensive discussion with the decisionmaker about his preferences than was the case here. Again, the methodology exists for dealing with such problems,[15] [16] but a further investment of time is required to carry out the analysis in such cases. In particular the problem becomes much more complex when different alternatives are likely to lead to different behavioral responses by the users. In this case it is, at the very least, unwise to rely on purely technical advice to determine the probable outcomes associated with each alternative.

Another element of a real decision problem that was only hinted at here has to do with the time dimension. Technology is always changing, and the costs that are estimated today are likely to be wrong a year from now. This especially is a problem when we are seeking to compare changing technologies. Technology changes in steps, not in a continuous manner. Therefore, if we compare three quite different technologies in Systems 1, 2, and 3, we are almost certainly comparing yesterday's technology in System 1 with today's technology in System 2 with tomorrow's technology in System 3. Consequently, about the time we install System 3, an improved version of System 1 is likely to be along which is a jump ahead of System 3. The only answer to this issue and to other technical problems of this type that I am aware of is to get the best possible technical advice, both from advocates of particular technologies and from independent sources, and to do a careful planning job that includes as much of this information as possible within the planning budget that is available.

In summary, a good job of planning requires a combination of three functions: (1) decision analysis, (2) technical analysis, and (3) behavioral analysis. Decision analysis provides the analytical framework; technical analysis provides the alternatives and describes the technical outcomes; behavioral analysis describes the behavioral outcomes. Finally, direct interaction with the decisionmaker, both early in the planning process and at the time of the decision, seems to be essential to a good decision.

NOTES

1. R. A. Howard, "Value of information lotteries," *IEEE transactions, systems science and cybernetics* SSC-3:54-60 (June 1967).

2. H. Raiffa and R. Schlaifer, *Applied statistical decision theory* (Cambridge, Mass.: Harvard Press, 1961).

3. R. A. Howard, "Value of information lotteries."

4. D. H. Hamsher, ed., *Communication system engineering handbook* (New York: McGraw Hill, 1967).

5. James Martin, *Teleprocessing network organization* (New Jersey: Prentice-Hall, 1970).

6. Edwin B. Parker, "Technological change and the mass media," in *Conference on Information Utilities and Social Choice* (Chicago: Univ. of Chicago, 1969).

7. E. L. Grant and W. G. Ireson, *Principles of engineering economy* (5th ed.; New York: Ronald Press, 1970).

8. C_{1000} = annual cost for case of 1,000 users, C_{10000} = annual cost for case of 10,000 users.

9. R. A. Howard, "Value of information lotteries..."

10. H. Raiffa and R. Schlaifer, *Applied statistical decision theory.*

11. The expected value of an uncertain reward...

12. W. North, "A tutorial introduction to decision theory," *IEEE transactions, systems science and cybernetics* SSC-4:200-210 (Sept. 1968).

13. R. A. Howard, "Bayesian decision models for system engineering," *IEEE transactions systems science and cybernetics* SSC-1:36-40 (Nov. 1965).

14. R. A. Howard, "Value of information lotteries..."

15. P. C. Fishburn, "Additivity in utility theory with denumerable product sets," *Econometria* 34:500-503 (1964).

16. H. Raiffa, *Preferences for multi-attributed alternatives*, RM5868-DOT/RC. (Santa Monica, Calif.: Rand Corp., 1969). (Santa Monica, Calif.: Rand Corp., 1969), RM5868-DOT/RC.

Narrow Bandwidth Telecommunications

William J. Kessler and Michael J. Wilhelm

INTRODUCTION

Narrow bandwidth telecommunications systems are perhaps more familiar to the layman than any other kind. Ordinary telephone and teletypewriter systems are common examples.

Before treating the subject matter in any detail, it might be well to specify precisely what is meant by the key words in the title. That is, what kind of systems are we talking about? What do we mean by telecommunications? And most important, how narrow is a narrow bandwidth? For that matter, what is bandwidth in the present context?

It is the objective of this paper to provide useful answers to the above basic questions and to discuss possible application of such systems to interlibrary communications requirements and other information networks.

A *system* may be defined as an assemblage of elements or objects arranged in a coordinated manner to achieve a stated objective. In this instance, the objective is to transfer in-

The term *telecommunications* is a relatively new one in common use. Consequently, there is no universal agreement at this time on the precise meaning of the term. For the purposes of this paper, telecommunications is defined as the electronic transmission of any information that can be translated into electrical signals.

Bandwidth is one of the most significant characteristics of an electronic transmission medium and may be defined as the frequency interval expressed in hertz (cycles per second in the earlier terminology), which represents the frequency range between the lowest frequency and the highest frequency of electronics signals which can be successfully transported along a given transmission medium. The term *narrow bandwidth* is of course a relative one. The Western Union Company, which requires a bandwidth of only a few cycles per second (or hertz) to provide teleprinter communications services, regard telephone circuits which employ a bandwidth of from 300 to 3000 hertz as "broadband." On the other hand, the transmission of

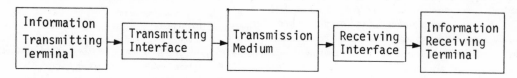

Figure 1 Basic Elements of An Electronic Transmission System

formation translated into electronic form from one point to another. The information transmission and reception points are frequently referred to as the terminals of the system. These terminals are interconnected by means of a suitable transmission medium through terminal-to-medium interface units. The basic elements of such *telecommunications* systems are illustrated in Figure 1.

The transmission medium is the electronic interconnection between the terminals and in the general case, may consist of a pair of ordinary wires, coaxial cable, or a radio microwave system. The interface units provide the necessary compatibility between the requirements of the transmission medium and the characteristics of the terminal devices. The terminal devices are always some form of transducer which converts sound or light variations into desired forms of electrical variations or vice-versa. In the case of an ordinary telephone system, the terminal device would consist of the telephone handset.

standard television signals requires a bandwidth extending up to four million hertz. Clearly, the teletype circuit is regarded as narrowband in comparison with telephone requirements, and telephone circuits are regarded as narrowband in comparison with television requirements. Furthermore, television circuits may be regarded as narrowband in comparison with high-speed data links requiring bandwidths up to twenty or thirty megahertz. For purposes of this paper, a narrow bandwidth is considered to be the bandwidth of any electronic transmission medium encompassing a frequency range of about 3000 hertz or less. A transmission bandwidth of 2700 hertz is conveniently economically available as a standard voice-grade telephone line, which extends from a lower frequency of 300 hertz to an upper frequency of about 3000 hertz.

Although narrow bandwidth telecommunications circuits are normally used for voice transmissions, it is one of the cardinal points of this paper that high resolution graphics can be ex-

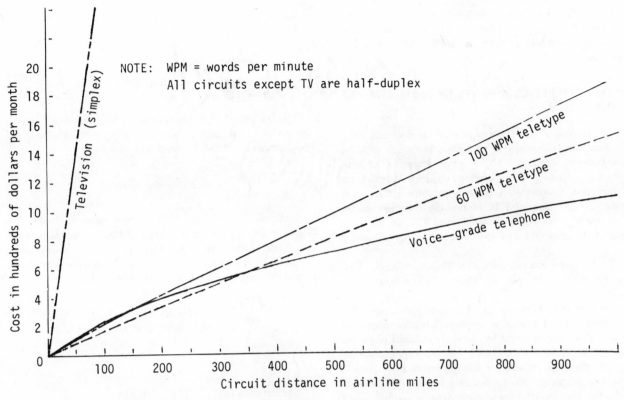

Figure 2   Comparison of Wide Band and Narrow Band Transmission Costs

changed between libraries over low-cost voice-grade circuits by exchanging transmission time for bandwidth, and hence cost, as shown in a subsequent section.

THE ECONOMICS OF TRANSMISSION CIRCUITS

One of the important nontechnical characteristics of transmission circuits is that bandwidth costs money. That is, the greater the bandwidth requirement, the greater the cost. Furthermore, the cost is proportional not only to bandwidth but to the distance between the information terminals and the period of time over which the circuit is used.

The emphasis on narrow bandwidth telecommunications for interlibrary use is based on the simple fact that narrowband circuits are far less expensive than broadband circuits and that such circuits are identical to ordinary telephone circuits and are thus universally available. Figure 2 is a graphical comparison of the approximate costs of leased full-period dedicated transmission circuits ranging from a teletypewriter circuit to a wideband television circuit. One of the most striking conclusions that can be drawn through an examination of Figure 2 is that wideband (four million hertz) video transmission service is very expensive compared to narrowband teletype and voice-grade service. Another striking conclusion is that dedicated teletype interconnections are not the bargains compared to voice-grade circuits one would logically expect when it is recognized that such circuits should require far less bandwidth than voice-grade circuits. This exception to the general cost-bandwidth rule is probably due to the fact that voice-grade lines are actually used

for the teletype service. Furthermore, it is noted that due to the graduated mileage rate of the voice-grade circuit, the monthly cost for distance in excess of 360 statute miles is actually less than the teletype circuits. When the virtually universal applications of the voice-grade circuits for interlibrary use are considered in comparison with the applications of the teletype circuits, the voice-grade circuits are clearly the most attractive.

The comparative economies of leased dedicated lines versus "dial-up" lines can be illustrated by examining a typical hypothetical system. The assumptions for the system are that high-resolution facsimile transmission is required between Jacksonville and Miami, Florida, and that the "standard" information to be transmitted is on an 8 1/2 by 11-inch document which requires a transmission time of four minutes. The station-to-station toll rate for a four-minute call between the two cities is $1.45. The per-month cost of a dedicated half-duplex (two-way) line between the two cities is $533.10. Figure 3 shows the cost-per-document relationship for the two systems under comparison. Examination of this figure reveals that to justify the cost of a leased dedicated line, the user must transmit at least 367 documents per month.

The reader should be cautioned against applying the information presented in Figures 2 and 3 to a specific requirement in a specific geographical area. The costs of transmission circuits provided by the common carriers are regulated by federal (interstate) and state (intrastate) agencies, and in some states, by municipal agencies. The filed rate structures commonly referred to as tariffs are very complex. Therefore, it is usually necessary to contact the sales office of the common carriers in a specific area to establish the exact charges for the transmission services required.

BANDWIDTH, TIME, AND IMAGE-RESOLUTION TRADE-OFFS

One of the major cornerstones of modern electrical communications theory is the well-established trade-offs that are possible between bandwidth requirements, transmission time, and information for a given transmission channel. Although the basic principles of information theory were suspected by early scientists such as Samuel F.B. Morse, the complete mathematical theory was not formulated until Claude Shannon enunciated the principles now known as the Hartley-Shannon Law.[1]

One of the major contributions of the Hartley-Shannon Law was a mathematically precise, objective definition of information.

A satisfactory definition and useful measure for "information" posted a problem to communication engineers not unlike the problem faced by the early classical physicists attempting to define work. Work—or the expenditure of energy—is, and was, regarded as a subjective or physiological concept, i.e., people get tired when they expend energy or do work. During the development of classical physics, it was found desirable to ascribe a nonphysiological meaning to work which would lend itself to a purely physical definition, would be applicable to machines and could be assigned useful units and measured. The result was the well-known physical definition: WORK = FORCE X DISTANCE, or in symbols, W = F x D. Thus, work, so defined, is measured in foot-pounds with F in pounds and D in feet through which the mechanical force F acts, and as such, is purely physical and is therefore not a physiological concept.

The problems facing the formulators of modern communication theory were similar in that they were faced with the problem of defining information in precise mathematical terms so that it could be related to the known measurable parameters of a transmission system. A "message" contains no useful information unless it is unpredictable at the message destination point. Obviously, that which is predictable, calculable, or known is not news. In other words, news or information is something previously unknown, unexpected, or unpredictable. This simple fact introduces the element of probability into the definition.

In striving for a precise definition and a useful unit of measurement, the communication engineer must eliminate the personal or subjective characteristics of information and stress its statistical properties. Therefore, he starts with the following relationship:
INFORMATION (I) = Logarithm to the base 2 of the probability (P).
In symbols, Equation 1:

$$I = LOG_2 P$$

where the probability P is defined as equal to 1 if the event is certain to occur and equal to 0 if it is certain not to occur.

The remaining known important parameters of a communications system are:

T = Transmission time measured in seconds
B = Frequency range or bandwidth in hertz
C = The communication carrier level in watts
N = The noise power level in watts.

Through logical mathematical steps, Shannon combined the above parameters to form the following expression known as the Hartley-Shannon Law, Equation 2:

$$I = BT \ LOG_2 \ (1+C/N)$$

For purposes of this presentation, the terms in bracket of Equation 2 $(1+C/N)$ may be regarded as a constant K if the magnitude of the communicating carrier level C is maintained at some fixed level above the noise power level represented by N. Equation 2 may then be simplified to Equation 3:

$$I = BT \ log_2 K$$
$$where \ K = (1+C/N)$$

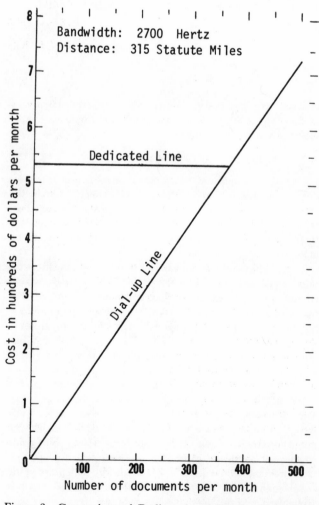

Figure 3   Comparison of Dedicated and Dial-Up Line Costs

Equation 3 states simply that the maximum information that may be transmitted is directly proportional to the bandwidth, or frequency range, of the transmission system and the time available to make the transmission. The variable B (bandwidth in Hz) and T (time in seconds) have been defined previously. However, the definition of I (information) requires some elaboration.

Using the most elementary signaling system (a well-known example: "One if by land, two if by sea"), we can arbitrarily establish two distinct signal levels, such as any finite level or zero level, i.e., the presence of a given signal or the absence of that signal. These two distinct levels or magnitudes are known as binary digits, either 1 or 0, YES or NO, a Mark or Space, "On" or "Off," etc. Coining a term by taking the first letter of binary and the last three letters of digits, gives BITS, which is universally accepted as the fundamental measure of information, in Equations 1, 2, and 3: Equation 4:

$$I = BITS = BT \log_2 K$$

Thus, information is measured in BITS and is simply –i n a communication theory sense –t he absence or presence of a binary signal. The implication of this definition –w hether by design or accident –f or machine-to-machine communication or communication between digital computers and man through appropriate coding procedures is evident. The interpretations and extensions of the Hartley-Shannon Law are numerous. For our present purposes, the most important consequence is the conclusion that the communication engineer can exchange or "trade off" one parameter for another.

This fact becomes more evident through the use of a specialized form of the Hartley-Shannon Law applicable to the transmission of visual signals in which I, the information in BITS, is replaced by the RESOLUTION of the reproduced images. Such becomes equation 5:

$$\text{Image Resolution} = K(B/N)T$$

where K is a constant depending on the type of transmission system involved, N is the number of complete images transmitted, B is the frequency bandwidth in hertz, and T is the transmission time in seconds. A dramatic example of the bandwidth-time trade-offs which are possible in an image transmission system can be given by considering the requirements for an ordinary television signal. Standard television, which is capable of providing the illusion of smooth motion in the reproduced image, utilizes a frequency range or bandwidth of approximately four-million cycles per second (or Hz) to transmit thirty complete pictures per second at an average resolution of approximately 400 lines over the entire picture. The relationship between resolution, the rate at which images are reproduced, and the bandwidth or required spectrum space required on the transmission channel can be summarized by a minor variation of Equation 5, as follows in Equation 6:

$$\text{Image Resolution} = K(B/M)$$

where K and B are as defined above and M is now the number of complete pictures transmitted per second.

It can be readily seen that bandwidth B can be scaled down by the same factor that the number of complete pictures per second M is scaled down, without affecting the magnitude and ratio and hence, image resolution. Applying this principle of "trade-offs" to electronic transmission systems reveals that if the picture transmission rate is reduced from thirty per second to one per minute (a factor of 1800), the bandwidth requirement can be reduced from four million hertz to a mere 2200 hertz. This bandwidth requirement is well within the range of an ordinary 2700 hertz voice-grade telephone line.

Thus, a series of sixty still pictures such as slides, film strips, charts, pages of a book or periodical, etc., could be transmitted over an ordinary narrow bandwidth voice-grade telephone line at a rate of one document per minute with a resolution comparable to that of television. If higher resolution is required, the transmission time could be increased to two hours for the sixty documents to achieve a line resolution in the reproduced image twice that of conventional television.

COMMONLY AVAILABLE TYPES OF TRANSMISSION CIRCUITS

Transmission circuits to interconnect the terminal equipment discussed in the previous section are available to the telecommunications user in the following ways:

1.   Privately owned

2.   Leased.

A comparison of the cost of privately owned circuits versus leased circuits is too complex to discuss in this presentation. The final choice is usually based on the types of funds available, i.e., capital or operating, and the period of time over which the transmission circuits are required.

Leased transmission circuits may be further categorized as "dial-up" (direct distance dial) or leased (dedicated). The transmission bandwidths are generally similar for both circuits, but other characteristics may differ appreciably depending upon whether analog or digital signals are to be carried. In the simplest terms, analog signals are continuously variable electrical signals which are directly proportional to some characteristics of the information to be transmitted. Voice signals are good examples of analog signals. Digital signals, on the other hand, generally exhibit only two magnitudes –zero and the maximum permissible. The information to be converted to digital signals must almost always be encoded in some manner. Ordinary Morse code and teletypewriter signals are familiar examples of encoded digital signals.

Transmission circuits also may be categorized as simplex, half-duplex, and full-duplex. These classifications refer to the simultaneous or nonsimultaneous directions of operation as illustrated in Figure 4. It is worthwhile to note that the transmission characteristics of the opposite-direction channels of an intercity duplex circuit may be completely independent. Accordingly, it is practical to tailor the transmission bandwidth to the actual requirements in each direction. Obviously, if the transmitting and receiving terminal equipments are identical

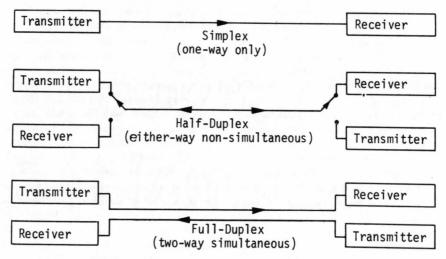

Figure 4 Types of Common Transmission Circuits

(such as they are in a full-duplex telephone circuit), the requirements of the transmission circuits would be identical.

TERMINAL EQUIPMENT COMMONLY AVAILABLE FOR GRAPHICS TRANSMISSION AND RECEPTION

There are many options open to the user who wishes to transmit graphic information from one point to another electronically. The following paragraphs constitute a brief discussion of the more important devices.

THE TELEPRINTER

One of the oldest and still the most common devices in use is the teleprinter, most commonly called a teletype machine. Although "teletype" refers to the equipment manufactured by the Teletype Corporation, they are by no means the only teleprinter manufacturer.

Teleprinters are useful primarily for message transmission since it is necessary to "type" information to be transmitted on the teleprinter keyboard at the sending end. Once typed, the information can be stored for future retransmission. The most common storage medium is punched paper tape although magnetic tape also may be used.

One form of message which does not have to be "typed" on the teleprinter keyboard is the output of a computer, and teleprinters are widely used as remote computer output terminals.

Teleprinters, of course, produce hard copy, and many teleprinters are equipped with an integral paper tape punch and reader. The punch permits preparation of copy in advance of transmission and even allows error correction in that the tape can be corrected by striking over errors and retyping a misspelled word or ungrammatical sentence. The punched tape can be saved for future retransmission of a message. The paper tape punch also can be used on the receiving end of a teleprinter system. This permits the "recording" of an incoming message so that multiple copies may be prepared.

When teleprinters are used with dial-up circuits, "real-time" operation of the machines is somewhat wasteful since the operator cannot type at the 60- or 100-wpm transmission rate capability of the circuits. Savings in line costs can result if the message is typed in advance of transmission at normal typing speed and "recorded" on punched paper tape. When the message is completed and checked for correctness, connection with the receiving teleprinter can then be established and the message "played back" on the tape reader at the full 60- or 100-wpm capability of the circuit.

Most teleprinters are used in conjunction with the worldwide TWX or TELEX public networks. Any subscriber on these networks can reach any other subscriber on a dial-up basis and either "converse" with the other party or send a "one-way" message to an unattended machine. Many private teleprinter networks also are used by industry, such as airlines, and by law-enforcement agencies and the military. Recently developed teleprinters even allow reception of teleprinter messages by mobile radio telephone systems in vehicles.

Teleprinters need not be two-way devices. A print-only device without a keyboard may be installed at those locations where only message reception is desired.

Teleprinters may be characterized as "medium-speed" devices. Those in message service operate at a maximum speed of from 60 to 100 words per minute, somewhat beyond the capabilities of an average typist.

In general, teleprinters are limited to the transmission of printed text materials. Elementary graphs and charts can be produced, however, by "drawing" lines made up of periods, Xs, or other characters. Some ambitious teleprinter operators have even produced crude pictures using various letters and numbers to approximate halftones. However, these pictures are very time-consuming to produce and are really only novelties.

The teleprinter uses a digital code for each letter, number, and symbol on the keyboard, and transmits the code as a series of on-off pulses, or in some systems, as a series of tones. If one were to connect a speaker across a teleprinter line, the signals would sound very much like Morse code.

The on-off pulses are arranged in seven-unit or "seven-bit" digital code. The letter "A," for example, is sent as a seven-bit sequence: off-on-on-off-off-off-on. The word "CAT" is the rather tedious sequence:

Off-off-on-on-on-off-on

Off-on-on-off-off-off-on

Off-off-off-off-off-on-on.

While this on-off code is certainly an awkward method of communication in human terms, it is ideal for machines and digital computers in particular. The teleprinter code can be transmitted over very narrow bandwidth channels. For example, up to fifteen separate 100-wpm teleprinter channels can be accommodated in the 300 to 3000 hertz bandwidth, which is required for a single telephone conversation. The teleprinter code is also highly immune to noise or "static" and has a very low transmission error rate even on a noisy transmission circuit.

The on-off transmission code is, of course, ideal for communication with computers since the on-off digital code is the basic internal language of all digital computers.

There are three basic types of teleprinter mechanisms. The most common type is the impact printer in which a typing bar or element strikes a typewriter ribbon in contact with paper, just as in a conventional typewriter.

An electrostatic printer places a wire matrix in contact with paper which darkens when an electric current is applied.

A recent and unique printer is the "Inktronic" printer introduced by the Teletype Corporation. The characters on this printer are formed by a thin stream of fast-drying ink, which is "squirted" onto the paper while being electrostatically deflected to form the desired character.

Within the past three years there has been a proliferation of new teleprinters due to the demands of the computer industry for these devices. The newer teleprinters are more compact than previous devices, and in general, more economical.

Many companies are producing adaptors which convert standard office typewriters into teleprinters. The most popular adaptation makes use of the IBM "Selectric" typewriter which is capable of higher-speed operation than conventional machines.

TELEFACSIMILE

The most significant differences between telefacsimile and teleprinter systems is that the user need not type out the material on a keyboard — the entire document can be transmitted merely by placing it in the machine. Another important difference is that the facsimile machine can transmit line drawings and continuous-tone material such as photographs, as well as printed text. In fact, one of the common uses of facsimile is the transmission of newspaper photographs. When used for this purpose, facsimile is referred to as "wire-photo" or "radio-photo" transmission.

The document intended for transmission on a facsimile system must be placed on a rotating drum, or on some of the more elaborate machines, on a flat bed. This requirement imposes some serious limitations for library use of facsimile since bound documents generally cannot be placed in the machine. The usual expedient is to make an intermediate copy of the desired material on a copier, such as a Xerox machine, and to feed the intermediate copy into the facsimile machine for transmission. This procedure is not only expensive and time-consuming but even worse, results in very poor resolution and gray-scale rendition in the reproduced copies at the receiving terminal due to the degradation introduced by the intermediate copy. This limitation on facsimile transmission can be readily solved by redesign of the facsimile transmitter. However, demand for transmission of bound materials has apparently not been sufficiently great to persuade manufacturers to produce suitable machines.

Once the copy has been placed on the drum of the facsimile transmitter, the drum begins rotating and the copy is scanned by a photocell moving along the length of the drum. The copy is scanned from left to right in a helical pattern resembling the threads on a bolt. The photocell responds to changes in the lightness and darkness of the copy on the drum and converts these changes into proportional changes in electrical voltage. The voltage, in turn, is made to vary the pitch of a tone, which is transmitted as the facsimile signal. If one were to listen to a facsimile line, a signal would be heard which sounds like a rapidly varying whistle.

Recall that the signal from a teleprinter sounds like Morse code — a series of on-off tone pulses which constitutes a digital signal. The facsimile signal on the other hand is an analog signal and for this reason, is more difficult to transmit than teleprinter signals. Analog signals may be considered more "fragile" than the system "on-off" digital teleprinter signals. Therefore, the transmission of facsimile signals over a low-quality transmission system may cause severe distortion of the received copy. The bandwidth required for facsimile transmission is greater than that required for teleprinter transmission and like teleprinter transmission, the bandwidth required is a function of the speed of transmission.

At the receiving end of a facsimile system there is another rotating drum, revolving at exactly the same speed as the drum on the facsimile transmitter. To accomplish this, a synchronizing signal accompanies the facsimile information to insure that the two drums remain locked to one another. A scanning head on the facsimile receiver follows exactly the same spiral path as the photocell in the transmitter. In most facsimile receivers, the scanning head contains a small wire stylus which contacts a special paper attached to the drum. This treated paper darkens when current is applied from the stylus, and the degree of darkness is a function of the strength of the applied current. Since the current applied to the stylus is proportional to the lightness or darkness of the copy as seen by the photocell on the transmitter, the stylus produces a faithful copy of the original material.

There are variations on the facsimile process just described. Some facsimile machines intended for high-quality photographic reproduction use light-sensitive photographic paper at the facsimile receiver. Although the quality is significantly better with this process, the photographic paper must be chemically processed in a photographic darkroom. Some facsimile receivers, generally the more expensive ones, use an alternate scanning system, abandoning the drum for a linear scan system which produces copy on a long roll of sensitized paper. These machines require less effort on the part of the operator at the receiving system since he is not required to place a new sheet of paper on a drum for each new document received. These roll-fed receivers are thus suitable for unattended operation.

Numerous variations of and accessories for the facsimile machine are available. Machines are available for the transmission of microfilm and microfiche cards, some machines permit enlargement or reduction of copy size, and there are machines capable of transmission of full-color facsimile.

SLOW SCAN TELEVISION

The electromechanical facsimile process has an all-electronic counterpart in slow-scan television. However, a slow-scan television is similar to facsimile only in its basic principles of operation, which involve the scanning process.

Although true slow-scan television is not commonly used, it is the most readily understood system and therefore, merits discussion here since it is the basis for the more sophisticated "sampling" system.

In conventional television, a rapidly moving beam traverses the screen, and because of the physiological characteristic of persistence of vision, the moving beam or "dot" is perceived as a line. The beam traces 525 lines to form a complete television picture and forms one picture or "field" every thirtieth of a second. As the dot traverses or "scans" the TV receiver screen, it varies in brightness in proportion to the darkness or lightness of the picture being reproduced.

In conventional television, information is transmitted at an exceptionally rapid rate—thirty separate pictures per second, 15,750 individual lines per second. The price for such rapid transmission rates is bandwidth, and the conventional television system uses a bandwidth of four million hertz — enough to accommodate 1,000 simultaneous telephone conversations or 20,000 separate teleprinter channels. Because of the cost/bandwidth relationship in transmission systems previously discussed, conventional television transmission systems are very expensive.

Economical transmission of television-type signals can be achieved by slowing down the scanning process to achieve a practical trade-off between bandwidth and time. For example, in conventional television the beam moves across the screen in 63.5 millionths of a second (63.5 microseconds). If the scanning speed is reduced by a factor of 1800 as in the earlier example, one scanning line will occupy a period of 63.5×1800 microseconds. Therefore, a complete 525-line picture will occupy a period of 60 seconds. The bandwidth requirements also are reduced by a factor of 1800 so that the signal is accommodated in 2200 hertz which is the bandwidth of an ordinary voice-grade channel.

The "soft-copy" display at the receiving terminal is displayed on a special slow-scan monitor. The display tube in the slow-scan monitor is equipped with a high persistence screen which continues to glow a short time after the beam has passed. This high persistence screen replaces persistence of vision which is effective only with the high-speed visual stimuli of conventional television.

Unfortunately, reproduced pictures on true slow-scan TV are generally unsatisfactory compared to conventional television. The screen will be uneven in brightness from top to bottom due to the decay characteristics of the high persistence tube, and the color of the image will be either green or blue since white phosphors with high persistence are not available. Any motion in the original picture will result in a blurred image because of the long "exposure time." The cause and effect of the blurred image are the same as that which occurs in conventional photography when one attempts to photograph a moving scene using a slow shutter speed.

Because of these limitations, a true slow-scan TV is seldom used. Instead, a scan conversion process is employed which permits the use of standard TV cameras at the transmitting terminal and conventional TV sets or monitors at the receiving terminal. In such systems the interface components shown in Figure 1 would include the necessary scan converters. In such systems, the reproduced display at the receiving terminal looks almost identical to a stationary television image. Each time new material is transmitted, the new picture "wipes" across the screen from left to right, displacing the old picture in the process.

The terminal hardware for transmission of graphics via slow-scan TV can be exceptionally simple—an inexpensive TV camera, some lighting equipment, and a slow-scan converter at the transmitting end and a receiving slow-scan converter and an ordinary TV monitor at the receiving end. Recording the slow-scan signal for future viewing or retransmission can be accomplished with an ordinary audio tape recorder. If a stereo recorder is used, one channel can be used for the picture information and the second channel for an accompanying audio commentary.

Slow-scan television can be used to accomplish the same function as a facsimile machine where a hard copy is not required. Transmission of copy from books is somewhat easier than with facsimile since the camera can be focused on a page, or portion of a page, without the need to mount the book page on the rotating drum or copy bed, as is required with facsimile.

Slow-scan TV is ideal for the transmission of a sequence of still pictures, such as film strips, 35mm slides, overhead transparencies, and the like. Group viewing is possible and the number of viewers limited only by the number of available television receivers. Large-group viewing is possible with a single large-screen television projector for use in auditoriums.

The picture can be accompanied by a sound-track transmitted—or recorded and played back—on a separate audio circuit.

STYLUS WRITER

Stylus writers may be called remote "electronic slates." At the stylus-writer transmitter, the sender writes or sketches on a special surface and at the receiver, a pen duplicates the writing by following exactly the movements of the sender's pen or stylus to produce a hard copy. Like the teleprinter, the stylus writer is a message-type device, that is, it is not suitable for the reproduction of existing documents such as those transmitted by facsimile or slow-scan TV. Unlike the teleprinters which require typing skill, the stylus writer requires only that the sender be able to write legibly. Normally, the stylus writer "receiver" is used by only one person at a time; however, an accessory device does make group viewing possible. This accessory device is a

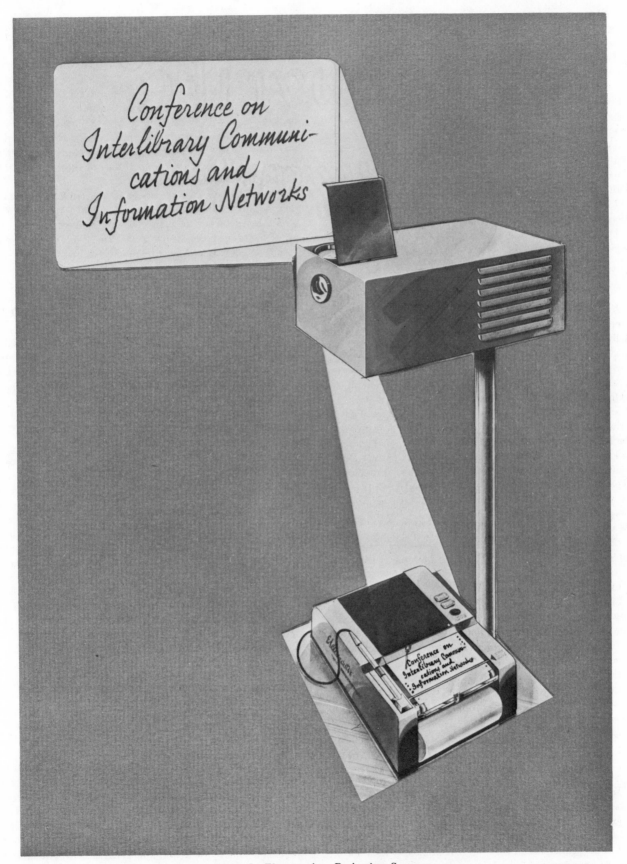

Figure 5 Electrowriter Projection System

special overhead projector which projects the "screen" of the receiving stylus writer on to a standard projection screen as shown in Figure 5.

The stylus writer is also a narrow bandwidth device which operates satisfactorily over ordinary voice-grade circuits. Its operational principles are quite simple. The transmitter senses the movement of the stylus in the X and Y axes — that is, it senses both the up and down and left and right movement of the stylus. Two separate signals are transmitted as varying tones, one signal for the X-axis and one for the Y-axis. At the receiving end of the system, the control tones operate separate X-axis and Y-axis motors which cause the receiver's pen to follow the position of the stylus at the transmitter.

The signals of the stylus writer also can be recorded for delayed transmission on an ordinary audio tape recorder.

The stylus writer, because of its simplicity of use, has become popular as a form of "written-intercom" system.

Blackboard by Wire

A close relative to the stylus writer is the Blackboard-by-Wire sytem which "marries" the stylus writer with television. Basically, the Blackboard-by-Wire system replaces the stylus writer hard-copy receiver with a conventional television receiver which provides a soft-copy display. This permits large-group viewing of the stylus-writer messages and ready distribution of the material over existing television distribution systems.

The Blackboard-by-Wire system is almost identical to the stylus writer at the sending end. At the receiving end, however, the X-axis and Y-axis signals go to an electro-optical converter which produces a standard television signal at its output. On the television receiver screen, the written or sketched material can appear as black writing on a white background or white writing on a black background. The moving dot which produces the image on the TV screen follows, or is "slaved," to the point of the stylus at the transmitting end.

Like every good blackboard, the Blackboard-by-Wire comes equipped with an eraser, simply a pushbutton at the transmitting end, which blanks out the TV screen to provide a fresh writing surface.

Like the stylus writer, the Blackboard-by-Wire is useful for message transmission — the video intercom idea. It is also a valuable instructional tool and when used for instruction purposes, it is almost always accompanied by an audio channel. Group viewing is easily accomplished by using multiple television monitors or receivers or a large-screen television projector. The Blackboard-by-Wire signals also can be recorded on an audio tape recorder, and if a stereo recorder is used, the accompanying audio track can be recorded on the second channel.

Machine Readable Data

To this point, narrowband devices which involve person-to-person communication have been treated. Today there is also a requirement for person-to-machine communication and vice-versa.

The teleprinter discussed earlier is a common terminal for use with a computer, and many conversational computer languages such as BASIC, FOCAL, and APL permit "interactive dialogue" between the user and the machine. The teleprinter provides a hard copy of both ends of such a conversation. When a hard copy of the conversation is not required, a device called a cathode ray tube terminal, or simply "CRT terminal," is used. This device is similar to a teleprinter, except that the printed text appears on a television-type screen instead of being typed on a sheet of paper. This is the only basic difference in the two devices. The keyboards of the teleprinter and CRT terminal are identical, and the CRT terminal is "plug-compatible" with the teleprinter — that is, the terminal may be directly substituted electronically for the teleprinter.

When it is necessary to receive graphs, sketches, and other such nonprint data from the computer, it is necessary to use a sophisticated version of the stylus writer called a plotter. The principles of operation of the plotter are identical to the stylus writer, except that greater accuracy is required and the signals are generated by the computer rather than by a user tracing a sketch or writing with a stylus. In addition, the data is presented to the plotter in digital rather than analog form.

The computer readily accepts data from a teleprinter or CRT terminal since the output of these devices are digital code signals in the internal code language of the computer. Another medium suitable for feeding data into the computer is the ubiquitous computer card. The most common version is the punched card which is produced on a card punch with a keyboard similar to that on a teleprinter. A unique hole pattern is punched into the card columns for each letter, number, and symbol on the key order. The letter, number, or symbol is simultaneously printed at the top of the card.

The information on the card is transmitted to the computer by a card reader which reads the hole patterns in the card, converting them into tone-coded signals suitable for transmission on a voice-grade telephone line. As with the other media we have examined, the required bandwidth is a function of the speed of transmission. Over a voice-grade line, the maximum number of eighty-column cards which can be transmitted is approximately twelve per minute. Cards need not be punched to be transmitted. The so-called "mark-sense" card also can be used. The mark-sense card is coded by filling in boxes on the card with a pencil. Generally, the mark-sense card is laid out in a "multiple-choice" format. For example, if the card is used to indicate a selection of books by title and quantity, each of the titles would be printed on the card followed by a box after the title. The user would darken the boxes following the desired title with a lead pencil. Once completed, the card is fed into the reader, which recognizes the marked boxes and transmits the information to the computer in the form of a digital code.

Devices also are available which permit direct transmission of typed or hand-printed documents to the computer. These devices, called OCR equipment for "optical character recognition," scan typed or hand-printed copy, identify the discrete letters or numbers, and derive from them a unique digital code for each character. Obviously, the OCR equipment greatly improves the man/machine interface; however, as usual, there is a price. In this instance the price paid is a high error rate, compared to other devices, and high cost of the OCR equipment. Due to these limitations, use of OCR equipment is not yet widespread.

MAGNETIC TAPE

Magnetic tape has been the classic storage medium for computers and almost every computer center has at least one row of high-speed and high-cost tape drives. For narrowband telecommunications, these high-speed devices are not necessary, and information may be stored on small, inexpensive slow-speed recorders which utilize 1/4- or 1/8-inch tape of the quality generally used for audio recording. Several manufacturers provide recorders using cassettes, which are convenient to use and store. The available magnetic tape drives are also suitable for digital data recording and are thus compatible with teleprinters, punched paper tape, punched and mark-sense cards, and OCR equipment. The drives can be used to accumulate data which is stored and then forwarded to a computer. They are also valuable for storing files of frequently used data and "canned" computer programs.

Magnetic tape also is suitable for the storage of analog signals such as those from facsimile machines, stylus writers, and Blackboard-by-Wire equipment. As mentioned previously, these signals may be recorded on a high-quality audio recorder. The recorders used for this application should have precise speed control since speed variations which would be almost unnoticeable in the reproduction of sound can cause serious distortion in the reproduction of facsimile and other "picture" devices. Some devices are more sensitive to speed irregularities than others, and for some of these devices, high-quality reproduction requires recorders with servomechanism speed control.

THE INTERCONNECTION OF NARROWBAND TERMINAL DEVICES

Prior to June 1968 connection of graphics equipment to a dial-up line had to be accomplished through the use of special equipment owned and installed by the telephone company since the telephone subscriber was prohibited by the telephone tariff regulations from attaching "foreign equipment" to the telephone lines. Thus, graphics and data handling equipment were connected to the dial-up lines through a special device provided by the telephone company known as a DATA-PHONE or data set. Such devices were ordinary telephone instruments with an interface built into the base of the telephone for use with a particular terminal device. Furthermore, the telephone company provided a *separate* DATA-PHONE or data set for each type of terminal device. As if to add insult to injury, use of the DATA-PHONE incorporating a particular interface was necessary even though the terminal equipment owned by the subscriber included the same interface device. Obviously, the use of different types of graphics and data transmission terminal equipments by a particular subscriber such as a large library presented a ludicrous situation.

On 28 June 1969 the Federal Communications Commission ruled that the telephone tariff regulations were unreasonable and unduly discriminatory. In deciding the Carterphone case which was primarily concerned with the connection of mobile radiotelephone equipment to the dial-up network, the commission said:

> We hold that the tariff is unreasonable in that it prohibits the use of interconnecting devices which do not adversely affect the telephone system.[2]

As a result of the Carterphone decision, telephone subscribers using graphics equipment now have the option of using a telephone company-supplied data set, or supplying their own interface equipment and interconnecting with the telephone system in one of two ways:

1. Appropriate interface equipment can be physically connected or "hard wired" to the telephone lines via a Data Access Arrangement (DAA) supplied by the telephone company. The DAA is a common telephone instrument equipped with a simple switch to connect or disconnect the graphics equipment from the telephone line. When establishing a connection with the DAA, the subscriber uses the DAA as a conventional telephone and can converse on the telephone handset. When it is desired to activate the graphics devices, the subscriber depresses a pushbutton on the DAA which disconnects the handset and connects the graphics equipment to the line. A $2 per month surcharge is made by the telephone company for providing the DAA feature. This surcharge is in addition to the usual service charge for the telephone instrument and line.

2. The terminal equipment and appropriate interface can be "attached" to any common telephone instrument via an acoustic coupler. No direct "hard-wired" connection is made to the telephone lines, and no special telephone company-supplied equipment is required. With an acoustic coupler, the telephone handset is placed in a holder on the acoustic coupling device so that the telephone handset receiver and transmitter are in contact with a small speaker and microphone in the acoustic coupler. The tone-coded information from the interface is fed to the speaker and coupled into the telephone handset transmitter. The received tone-coded information appearing at the telephone handset receiver is coupled into the microphone in the acoustic coupler unit, and the amplified signal fed into the receiver interface for "decoding" The acoustic coupler is widely used with portable graphics terminals since it permits connection of the terminal to any telephone instrument by simply placing the handset into the coupler.

SIGNIFICANT PROBLEMS

Problems in the utilization graphics of transmission systems fall into two general categories — technical problems and people problems. Technical problems can be subdivided further into equipment malfunctions, transmission impairments, and problems associated with exceeding the capabilities of the hardware.

Equipment malfunctions are inevitable in the best of hardware "families." They can be reduced by the application of scheduled routine maintenance procedures. Equipment down time, once a malfunction has occurred, will depend on whether the equipment is maintained by your own staff or by an outside agency.

If the equipment is to be maintained by the company which installs it, the quality of their service and their "call-out" time should be a factor in deciding with which company to deal. In many instances this factor is as, or more, important than the type of equipment supplied or its cost.

Transmission impairments are a frequent problem in graphics transmission. Seldom does the telephone line go completely dead; however, its frequency response, distortion, and noise characteristics can change without warning.

The effect of these abnormalities will depend on the type of equipment being used and on the importance an error or distortion will have to the user. For example, a transmission impairment which results in a misspelled word in the text of a teleprinter message may be inconsequential when the teleprinter is being used in message service since the correct spelling of the word may be evident to the party receiving the message. When the teleprinter is used to communicate with a computer, however, the correct spelling — or worse, the transmission of an incorrect number — will not always be evident to a machine, and erroneous output will result.

The dedicated telephone line will generally provide better and more reliable service than dial-up lines; however, when a bad dial-up line appears, the user can usually obtain a satisfactory line by replacing the call.

The degree of transmission impairment difficulty encountered also will depend on the geographical area in which your facilities are located. Certain areas of the country have notoriously poor telephone service. In such instances, the dial-up lines often are not even satisfactory for normal voice communication, let alone adequate graphics transmission. In these areas a dedicated line is almost mandatory, even for intracity graphics transmission.

The performance and reliability of the telephone service is a factor outside of the direct control of the user. A certain indirect control can be exercised, however, by frequent and vocal comment to appropriate telephone company officials when things do go awry, and if necessary, the filing of formal complaints with the appropriate regulatory agencies.

Occasionally, poor performance in a system is a result of attempting to transmit information which is beyond the capabilities of the equipment. This problem arises when one tries to transmit extremely small print on a facsimile system, for example. The average facsimile system has a maximum resolution capability of approximately eighty lines per inch, which, as a practical matter, means that printed letters less than a sixteenth of an inch high will be "fuzzy" and indistinct. A similar difficulty arises when one tries to transmit pictures with subtle gray-scale values over slow-scan television since slow-scan television is limited to the reproduction of a maximum of ten shades of gray, at best.

These problems can be prevented best by carefully defining the required performance of the graphics system before the equipment is chosen and installed.

It is to be expected, however, that there will be occasional instances wherein equipment is taxed beyond its limitations. This just seems to be part of human nature. In these instances it is only possible to advise the user that the reproduction quality will be less than ideal and hope for the best.

The "people problems" affecting narrowband graphics transmission equipment are most difficult to analyze and treat. In general, both the disseminators and users of graphic information have set patterns in their information-seeking habits that are not easily changed. The proponent of graphics transmission systems must have an almost evangelical zeal to stir even mild interest in the the use of his system. He must contend with such criticisms as: "Why did we purchase that when my department needs (a new adding machine, broom, candlestick, doorknob, eraser, and most important, higher staff salaries)." When an equipment failure occurs, there can be almost a Greek chorus of "I told you so's." And an employee who is asked to operate a teleprinter in addition to his regular duties is liable to react as if you just asked him to scrub the entire exterior of the building with a toothbrush.

The impact of these various people problems can be minimized by careful systems planning and the introduction of new hardware on a gradual, scheduled basis. A small-scale pilot program is often valuable as a means for testing assumptions regarding need and utilization patterns without the investment required for a full-scale system. The pilot program also permits the staff to become familiar with the new services on a gradual basis.

FUTURE POSSIBILITIES

One of the most critical needs in the general field of narrow bandwidth graphics transmission systems is the introduction of low-cost reliable terminal equipment. Briefly, during the past few decades, we have witnessed numerous technological breakthroughs. The decade of the seventies now is ready for a significant economic breakthrough. Such economic breakthroughs will occur only when engineers apply their talents to cost reduction and volume production, and enlightened consumers actively promote large-scale acceptance and utilization of such equipment. Virtually all of the terminal equipment discussed in this paper is less complex, technically, than the ordinary television receiver but has a price tag ten to twenty times the cost of a TV receiver. Volume production and competition between manufacturers will serve to equalize this price difference. The introduction of large-scale integration, LSI, microcircuits will serve to further reduce costs, but this circuitry, too, is only feasible when high-volume production is involved.

Some future cost reductions may be expected in the transmission media for narrow bandwidth equipment. It is technically possible now to utilize the Subsidiary Communications Authorization, SCA, subcarriers on FM broadcast stations for the transmission of narrow bandwidth graphics signals. Utilization of SCA will permit simplex transmission to an unlimited number of receivers in the coverage area of an FM station.

In the past years the FCC has broken the telephone company monopoly on common carrier data transmission systems, and has granted licenses to several special-service common carriers to establish "public" data communications systems. With this competition there is a possibility that we will also see reduced rates for dedicated leased lines and other related services in the near future. It is also possible that transmission quality on the data-transmission lines will be somewhat better than that provided by the telephone company since the data-transmission lines will be optimized for data rather than voice.

SUMMARY AND CONCLUDING COMMENTS

Frequently when the application of new technology is considered in any area of interest, there is an inclination to consider a given new device as an end in and of itself. The new device is installed — the staff made aware of its fantastic capabilities and commanded to use it. After a few months of experience, it is "concluded" that the new device provided a solution for a problem which never really existed. Therefore, the device is generally relegated to the nearest dark closet. The moral, of course, is that technology itself has no inherent properties of magic. For reasonable expectations of success in the introduction of technology into an existing system, there appear to be at least three prerequisites:

1. The technology must meet a realistic need which has been clearly defined.

2. It must be integrated into the system gradually to permit user training and acceptance.

3. It must be supported. Funds must be made available for operating personnel, service personnel, and supplies and maintenance.

It is inappropriate for the telecommunications engineer — regardless of his qualifications — to attempt to define the needs of libraries for graphics hardware. These needs are best defined by the innovative librarian. The most valuable service the engineer can render is to provide accurate information on the capabilities and limitations of existing hardware which, incidentally, has been one of the objectives of this paper. The capabilities of the hardware discussed to this point can be summarized as follows:

1. Teleprinters—hard-copy message-handling device; economical of bandwidth — excellent man/machine interface with computers; limited to transmission of the printed word; storage possible on paper or magnetic tape

2. CRT terminal—soft-copy version of the teleprinter

3. Facsimile—hard-copy device which reproduces the original document; suitable for transmission of printed word, line copy, or continuous-tone copy; storage possible on magnetic tape

4. Slow-scan television—soft-copy" device which reproduces original document or scene viewed by the television camera; large-group viewing possible; readily accompanied by audio commentary; storage possible on magnetic tape

5. Stylus writer—hard-copy message-handling device which transmits handwriting or drawing to a remote location in real time; storage possible on magnetic tape

6. Blackboard-by-Wire—soft-copy version of the stylus writer with display on TV screen; group-viewing possible; storage possible on magnetic tape

7. Machine input equipment:

    a. Punched and mark-sense cards

    b. Magnetic tape drives

    c. Optical character recognition devices.

The only intrinsic limitation of any of the above narrowband devices is the limitation on transmission speed and hence, an inability to reproduce motion. Their application to interlibrary graphics transmission is limited only by the creativity of the user. The most obvious advantage of narrowband graphics technology is its ability to extend the resources of a library beyond the actual physical plant, to other libraries, schools, or industry.

The common denominator to all of the narrowband devices is the communications line which may consist of either a dedicated or dial-up telephone line.

Funding support must be provided beyond the initial cost of the equipment to provide for supplies, maintenance and spare parts, and staff salaries for those who will operate the equipment. Considerable resistance to the introduction of new equipment and services can result when responsibility for the new equipment is given to employees who regard this responsibility as an unreasonable addition to their workload.

Frequently, the introduction of new technology is made possible by a federal grant which supports the project for only a limited time, usually one year. The record for continuation of these projects beyond the federally funded period has not been encouraging. The reasons for noncontinuation of these projects are various, but the most frequent reason is that little thought was given to the continued funding support for the project until the federal support was discontinued.

If a library has identified a well-defined application for narrowband graphics transmission equipment, the engineer can assist in the design of an appropriate system and the choice of optimum equipment. The design of an optimum system is best accomplished by an engineer possessed of an "open mind" with respect to the comparative merits of the various equipments available on the market. There is available "systems planning" and "engineering assistance" from equipment manufacturers, but the persons providing this service are often, and understandably, oriented toward the products of their employers.

The integration of technology into an existing system requires a good deal of thought and preplanning. A trial or "debugging" period is often desirable to minimize the traumatic effect that equipment malfunction may have on an existing system. Often the success of technology is enhanced when the staff personnel who will be utilizing the equipment participate in the planning and procurement stage and are given careful and complete training in the operation and care of the equipment.

NOTES

1. Claude Shannon, "A mathematical theory of communication," *Bell System technical journal* (July, Oct. 1948).

2. Federal Communications Commission "In the matter of use of the Carterphone device in message toll telephone service" 13 FCC 2nd. 423.

The Implications of a Mixed Media Network
For Information Interchange

John W. Meaney

INTRODUCTION

A mixed media network for information interchange is not something for which we will have to look far into the future. It is what we have now –or potentially have –and it is what man has had experience with all through his history. It includes or has included at one time or another the media of mail, messenger service, print, pneumatic tube, carrier pigeon, clay tablets, and a nearly endless series of other devices.

Our experience with mixed media development has shown that its elements are constantly subject to recombinations, mutations, revitalization, and unexpected proliferation with hybrid vigor. Even among our own modern media we see 2x2 slides appearing now with magnetic sound additions, 8mm film appearing in cartridges with sound or in super-8 form, 1/4-inch audio tape appearing in cartridges and cassettes, and video tape, also beginning to appear in cassette form. In addition to these reappearances of old media in new forms there are constant appearances of radically new media –holograms, for instance.

In view of our past history, we may suspect that our choice is not between a mixed media network and an unmixed one. We may safely assume that we will always have a somewhat mixed system, try as we will to come to some common denominator. Our choice seems to relate more to the question of how gracefully or efficiently we are prepared to live within the mixed media system. There are things we can do –standardization, for instance –that will considerably relieve the difficulties of mixed media operation. There may also be steps that we must take to reduce the confusion in such a system and to keep the mix within manageable bounds. Like Lewis Carrol's Alice, we have to run as hard as we can just to stay in the same place.

THE FLOW QUESTION

One of the questions constantly posed by a mixed media system is the flow question. How do we get from here to there? How do we transfer a store of information from one medium into another storage medium? How do we transmit retrieved information from a given storage deposit to a user in a remote location? The latter question frequently becomes a matter of electronic bandwidth in which we juggle the variables of resolution or fidelity, time, and money, much as the electric power grids juggle voltage and amperage. In other words, thirty frames of television pictures per second requires a broad capacity transmission whereas a single frame every ten seconds allows us to achieve the transmission with a much narrower band.

This double flow of information, between storage systems and between a given storage medium and the user, seems to divide the media logically into those used primarily for storage and those used primarily for distribution of information. Modern storage media include: (audio) phonograph records and magnetic tapes; (video) print and graphics, photographs, slides, film, video tape, facsimile, electron beam recordings, holographs; (digitalized data) computers using disc, tape, drum, or core memories. The distribution media include the mail, AM and FM radio, telephone, teletype, Picture-phone, TV microwave, TV cable, TV broadcast, satellites, slow-scan TV, and lasers.

Apart from the daily operational flow among and between these various media there seems to be present, as well, a kind of design flow or trend toward reaching at least two common denominators: electronic and digital. These meeting points of so many media are to be seen particularly in the frequency with which their display or terminus turns ought to be the standard television set or the computer's cathode ray tube. At times there is even an occasional hint that these terminus points may eventually be combined or consolidated into a single instrument.

The trend toward TV display is to be seen even in the area of still pictures. There recently has been introduced a slow-scan visual delivery system enabling us to send slides over FM radio –with audio accompaniment and with student feedback options. The obvious economies of such a system are being stressed by its marketers, Educasting Systems, Inc.[1]

Audio also advances toward the TV terminus: The dial access audio system originally introduced by Ampex at the Oak Park-River Forest High School in Illinois is now being extended to a dial access video capability in which still pictures are retrieved on TV sets either independently or along with the audio. This system is based on a master loop or "bin" storage system using 1-inch magnetic tape with 32 tracks for audio and on a video master storage which uses the magnetic disc recorder coupled with disc "buffers" for dubbing off the program selections for individual display.[2] This "Pyramid" system also is paralleled partially in the same company with a "Videofile" system for document storage and retrieval.[3] In Videofile, which has found applications with regard to railroad waybills, insurance records, law enforcement records, and in other areas, the documents are magnetically recorded and coded on 2-inch video tape, then searched by a computer and reproduced for examination by means of a magnetic disc buffer and a television screen. Hard-copy print-out is available through an electrofax process whenever the image on the screen needs to be fixed in such form.

These Ampex systems, again, clearly have the standard television screen as their common denominator, and they should offer no great problems of compatibility with other systems which meet them at this same point of delivery.

Westinghouse Learning Corporation, for instance, has another system which does much the same job as the Ampex "Pyramid" but in a somewhat different way. It delivers dial access audio and still pictures, but it bases its rapid delivery not on high speed dubbing as Ampex but rather on an audio compression process which permits many segments of audio to be recorded on 1-inch video tape. Like the Ampex system, the Westinghouse system uses a magnetic disc buffer for individual program delivery to the TV sets.

These Ampex and Westinghouse systems also may be pointing the way around the fiasco of the helical scan im-compatibility. The hodge-podge of competing standards in the 1/2-inch and 1-inch video tape recorders long has been a horrible object lesson in how a mixed system becomes a mixed-up system. Now perhaps the way is opening not so much for salvage of the medium as for a by-pass around the mess. This new hope is represented by the magnetic disc buffer. We used to assume that vast libraries of tapes in a given format ideally ought to be available for making dubs to be used in the same format –although such media libraries as that in Great Plains have long since found ways of living within the helical scan jungle by equipping themselves with a great many different brands of machines and thus, offering dubs onto the customer's tapes from almost any format to almost any format. Now with the possibility that the dubs onto magnetic discs will be remotely accessible via cable TV or other networks and thus, recordable into whatever format one has locally, the way around the basic equipment incompatibility appears to be simply to relegate local recorders to holding and scheduling functions. The intercampus microwave network also has found a similar solution: The same basic lecture going down the backbone of the system may be tapped off and held in any combination of formats at the local institutions, provided those institutions do not expect also to use their recorders to input into the system. In other words, the "off-brand" equipment reduces its buyers to a receive-only capability. To an objective observer, that may not appear to be a crucially significant limitation, but it sometimes turns out to be such in fact when the faculty at the local institution makes clear its staunch adherence to the Christian concept that it is more blessed to give than to receive –at least where television is concerned.

Another hopeful sign in the Ampex and Westinghouse systems is the fact that they do not rule out the possibility that the same TV set which is their display device for still pictures may at other times be used for display of live television or conventional television program recordings from magnetic tape or film or newer processes such as Electronic Video Recording or SelectaVision. We might call this a kind of compatibility – tandem compatibility, perhaps. If we cannot play EVR into the Pyramid system or vice versa, at least they can come out at the same place on the standard TV set, alternately.

The Electronic Video Recording system of CBS Laboratories uses a special thin film, 8.75mm in width, for electron beam recording of programs originally produced either in standard film or TV formats.[4] The player of the sprocketless and automatically threaded film feeds directly into a standard TV set. The player is made and marketed by Motorola for less than $800, and the programs –billed as the video long-playing record –are to be made in the CBS labs for less than $18 apiece when ordered in batches of as many as 200 (of thirty-minute length). Each of the 7-inch diameter EVR cartridge reels represents a picture potential of 187,200 frames, and the company is reported to have under development a Reference EVR adaptation which will offer page storage with random access retrieval. Special publication in the medium so as to use the TV screen for the reading of enlarged type is possible even earlier.[5]

Recently RCA has announced its SelectaVision system which incorporates holographic video recording and laser beam reproduction in a player designed to sell for less than $400.[6] It uses a very cheap, clear plastic film for its transfer dubs of film and TV materials, and promises a library of selections that will retail for about $10 per half hour of color program. Again, practically the only point on which it reaches compatibility with the EVR system lies in the fact that it will play into the same standard TV set.

One is reminded of an earlier competition between CBS and RCA –that of the long-playing audio disc recording: the battle of the big-hole 45 rpm records with the little-hole 33 1/3 rpm units. We may hope that our public welfare and patience will not be so ill served again. Destructive competition by great industries should be headed off by a strengthened process of standard-setting in the public interest whenever possible, and even the federal antitrust authorities should be encouraged to promote cooperative standard-setting by industries whenever this would be more largely in the public interest than would the generally unrestrained competition. Just as some areas of trade might need to be built up by judicious exceptions or relaxations of the general antitrust rulings, so the areas in which the evolution of cooperative standards would be likely to benefit the general public ought also to be marked out by the antitrust authorities for favorable treatment.

However, if CBS and RCA can find no larger interface between EVR and SelectaVision than the standard TV set, it is possible that a further common denominator already may have appeared from outside these companies in the color VTR cartridge machines recently demonstrated by Sony and Panasonic.[7] There is no assurance, as yet, that these Japanese companies will achieve compatibility between their own developments although both have gone to some length to insure compatibility with certain European manufacturers. There also has been evident, of late, a very salutary government pressure toward compatibility in Japan. With the basic units of almost all video tape recorders now being manufactured in Japan, we may find eventually that the compatibility which our native American industry has found so hard to achieve will arrive here with the label: "Made in Japan." At any rate, the Sony and Panasonic units are rumored to be aiming at a price range, per unit, as low as SelectaVision, with a half hour of color recording made possible on a 1/2-inch (at least with Panasonic) tape cartridge giving single-copy economy much lower than either EVR or SelectaVision.

Traditional photographic processes also have found ways of adapting to the age of data storage and retrieval—for example, the Eastman Kodak Company's "Miracode" system, using 16mm cartridges in 100-foot lengths with 2,400 frames each, machine accessible.[8] Index data is interspersed in optically coded frames using a binary system of clear and opaque bits of space so that a retrieval station may punch up and run the cartridge to the required frame within ten seconds. The reading machines can be equipped to provide hard-copy print-out of entire pages within a very few seconds. Both color and black-and-white visuals may be included in the system. From such storage the first distribution medium that has traditionally suggested itself has been the mail, but it is also clear that the system would be easily adaptable to access by television projectors or flying spot scanners. The binary system of coding suggests, also, that some interface with computerized indexes should not be too difficult to achieve.

In the computer field there has been a long succession of developments offering easy file conversion from punched cards to paper tape to magnetic tape to magnetic cores, drums, and discs. Now there is report of a breakthrough in the offing that will use an erasable hologram memory or polarized light for storage of digitalized information and thereby, achieve a capacity of 100 million bits per square inch. However, until computers arrive at a far greater and more economical storage capacity than they have at the present time, it seems likely that bulk storage of documents themselves –as differentiated from abstracts and indexes –will have to make use of various forms of graphic or magnetic storage, including photographic, electron beam, video recording, or holographic. Indexes and abstracts, along with control functions, are well within the capability of present generation computers. It is therefore of great importance to make provision for adequate interfaces from each of the storage systems into the digital computer.

A number of two-way audio developments recently have given us other examples of media acquiring further impetus and life from new applications and combinations of old services. An instructional FM radio service at Stanford University sought and obtained FCC approval for a classroom radio feedback link to the originating studio.[9]

Meanwhile, the development of two-way amplifiers for CATV installations has opened up the possibility that interactive television may be available for home use in the near future. Such a development is being encouraged and hastened by recent FCC rulings which offer the opportunity for massive cable TV expansion at the price of new service explorations and payment of a 5 percent gross receipts royalty for subsidy of public television.[10] Viewer responses from individual sets could, with computer coding and access to data banks, turn a television system alternately into a device for programmed instruction or a town meeting or shopper's guide or a library console.

The leadership of the Corporation for Public Broadcasting, CPB, and other educational agencies (National Educational Television, National Association of Educational Broadcasters, National Education Association, and the Joint Council on Educational Telecommunications) in securing the pioneer use of domestic satellites for educators also has extended the potential of audio response from ground cable to satellites. In fact, CPB has even more recently requested the reservation of Instructional Television Fixed Service frequencies for satellite communication; the audio response development which we already have noted in ground-based radio may ride along automatically now in the satellite application.

Facsimile services are among the oldest media beginning to take on new impetus at this time. An early facsimile system had appeared in the mid-nineteenth century, only to be stunted by the competition of the telegraph. After World War II, a facsimile system using FM radio was born only to be blighted by the age of television.[11] Now new applications for facsimile are appearing because it seems to offer an easy interface between graphic information and digital transmission, plus the fact that it is adaptable to radio, television, and even satellite transmission. A newspaper in Japan is sending its pages via radio facsimile from Tokyo to Hokkaido and is running tests on the reception of the *New York Times* via satellite facsimile.[12] RCA in New York has successfully demonstrated a method of transmitting facsimile-printed matter over a standard broadcast TV channel without interference with the regular programs.

THE MIXED MEDIA SYSTEM

Such intersecting and cross-pollinating media are the prospective components of a mixed media system that is at once richer, more redundant, more wasteful, more surprising and confusing, and more inevitable than any unmixed system could be. Everything seems to be pointing toward the enormous potential today of linking such media together into a flexible mixed media system for information interchange, a system that would explore many of the untapped potentials of such media: The design flow is right for such a move; the availability of distribution media is prospectively enormous; the national policy is encouraging. The implications of this type of system for information interchange may be grouped generally under economic and administrative headings.

The economic implications are far more than monetary — for they include that basic economy of means which is a key principle in the attainment of efficiency and quality of performance. A mixed media system necessarily implies by the very survival of the mixture that each element has a certain irreducible advantage to offer. Even before we reach complicated questions of transfer and cross-media reinforcement, or the possibilities of contrapuntal media utilization in instruction, for example, there is the simple and obvious fact that if each medium is used precisely in the area of its greatest specific advantage there will result an overall efficiency of operation which should produce the highest quality result at the lowest cost in effort and money.

From another point of view, this matter of efficiency and economy of operations in mixed media systems might be said to imply a principle of subsidiarity: In general, using the simplest means available for a given end and thus, avoiding situations in which relatively simple material is transmitted over relatively complex media merely because such media are available. The classic example of the thing to be avoided is the instructional television lecture in which the fundamental requirement of the material is for a verbal statement in which an audio transmission would be adequate.

A mixed media system also clearly implies a relatively miscellaneous set of equipment at local institutions. It requires us to forego the utopian dream of the single black box that can do everything. It means that our libraries will need more kinds of listening stations, more viewing and display devices for tapes, microforms, slides, 8mm cartridges, EVR or SelectaVision cartridges, video tapes, etc. It means that our libraries will continue to expand their functions as sound and picture as well as book depositories –or at least, access points for these.

Having this great mass of media continuing to exist and function side by side will also mean a greater degree of redundancy among them. The same still pictures in color may be available in both photographic and magnetic devices, the same motion pictures in both film and EVR cartridges. However, such overlapping of media also may lead to more highly individualized uses and greater flexibility and creativeness in user adaptation.

On the administrative side, such a mixed media network will present more persistent problems of access, indexing, and control at the local level, but at the same time, it will have the advantages of greater autonomy and decentralization. If it is valid to draw a parallel between the electric power grid and the information network of the future, we may conclude that a somewhat greater total reliability is to be anticipated in the relatively decentralized structure.

The fact that the mixed system will not depend on any startling breakthroughs but will include many of the present media with which we are familiar is also a fairly good assurance that the mixed system will offer an easier introduction for its users, a more tranquil evolution, and possibly a more extensive pattern of utilization. While it is true that media will not be used unless they are made available, it is unfortunately not so certainly true that making media available will necessarily lead to their effective utilization. Mass transit authorities often have found that merely providing a cheap, efficient, and fast transport system is no guarantee that people will use it in sufficient numbers to make it pay. In the media field, we have seen broadband telecommunication networks linking campuses together over wide areas for years assuring scholars of their availability for library facsimile transmissions, and yet they go on transmitting television lectures almost exclusively. Obviously, even the most modern media do not escape the elementary facts of human inertia and habit. However, the mere convenience implied in making more means available to more people at the local level should lead to a greater total utilization.

The kinds of utilization also will change. New and unforeseen uses must be expected to emerge. The mixed media network will not simply lead to the accomplishment of the same old tasks in new and betters ways; it will lead to the discovery and addition of new goals on top of the old ones because the new ones suddenly appear to be possible.

A mixed media situation offers its administrators a relatively complicated bibliographical indexing and control process. They will have to know where the pictures, films, and tapes are; how to get at them; what is in them; how to index them. Something very radical is implied in all of this. We know how to index books, but how does one index pictures? By a verbal description of what they contain, by a truly pictorial representation, or by some combination of the two? Along with the technological interface between media we need to develop what we might call "trans-media" analogs. And here we are up against the ancient problems of synesthesia. The ears and the eyes of men represent two senses with certain areas of radical and perhaps, irreducible difference, even though we reduce them physiologically to similarly transmitted impulses in our nerves. There are interesting experiments with television grids projected onto the skins of blind men in order to enable them to feel a kind of vision, and yet the sound and the picture fringes of our libraries continue to present us with enormous problems of day-to-day bibliographic integration. There is no advantage in delivering the typewritten card by means of facsimile print-out a hundred miles away if the necessary visual indexing is not on the card to begin with.

RECOMMENDATIONS

The prospect of living indefinitely with a mixed media system should bring us to face certain needs which are inherent in such a situation, needs which include standards, new research, depositories, and demonstrations. These four areas of need lead to the following recommendations:

COMPREHENSIVE STUDY

There should be launched a comprehensive study leading to the design of improved standard-setting procedures for the U.S. Something is radically wrong with present procedures which have allowed us to enter the helical scan morass and apparently to be unable to extricate ourselves from it unless it be by default to foreign systems. We need to pinpoint the reasons for our difficulties and the steps needed to take us out of them, and to prevent their recurrence in future developments. Granted that we want to protect the great advantages of the free enterprise system and the proliferation of competing devices; we also may need to give more direct protection to our common good. We are finding this to be true in other areas –environmental pollution, for instance. There it seems that a great many competing industries operating in our free enterprise system have somehow failed to take adequate account of our common good. Where so many are so intent on their private profit, it may be that the common good does not automatically accrue without someone to speak for it. We are likely to find that fact to be equally true in the field of technical standards.

We need this study to probe very carefully into our recent history in the matter of standards. How could the long-playing record war have been avoided? Is it true that the American electronics industry simply has shown insufficient interest in arriving at standards for helical scan recorders — each industry giant naively confident that its system would win out in the end or at least box off a large enough segment of the market to be profitable, regardless of the inconvenience and limitations for their customers? Is it true that fear of the federal antitrust authorities inhibited many industries having conversations with others about standards? Have the American National Standards Institute and such standards generating agencies as the Society of Motion Picture and Television Engineers been crippled by inadequate funds to get the job done?[13] If it is true that our standards necessarily are industry generated, is it not still possible to achieve a stimulus role for government, something less arbitrary and indirect than the present buying power of the Department of Defense? If we can evolve a revision of our copyright law more in harmony with the international scene, can we not harmonize our standard-setting procedure with the international practice? The study of such questions ought to call upon the expertise of many agencies –the Standards Institute, Society of Motion Picture and Television Engineers, Department of Justice, Department of Commerce, National Bureau of Standards, Library of Congress, American Library Association, National Commission on Libraries and Information Science, Corporation for Public Broadcasting, National Institutes of Health, National Institutes of Education,

U.S. Office of Education, Department of Defense, Electronic Industries Association, and many others. The study might be undertaken on contract by almost any of these –or by others, such as The Rand Corporation; the dimensions of the problem require a funding of at least $300 to $500 thousand.

RESEARCH AGENCY

When it becomes apparent that competitive industry has allowed an interface gap to develop in some area, there ought to be an agency in a position to research, design, partially subsidize new interface devices. For instance, in spite of our great present trend toward TV distribution, where is the projector that can be used to input 8mm cartridge films into TV systems? Or, can the Reference EVR reader be designed so as to accommodate Miracode cartridges, as well? (There are reports of a Broadcast EVR version in 16mm; if this comes out, and if Reference EVR were compatible with it, would there also be a chance for compatibility with other 16mm systems?)

We also need additional research to develop designs and recommended practices for catalogs and machine-readable indexes of media materials. Before we can have the logical starting tools for networking, we need to design the tools. These should be developed as compatible extensions of standard bibliographic tools, thus insuring integration with central catalogs rather than isolation as special mediatory sources.

There already is beginning what is certain to be a most interesting pilot prototype for a national information network: the Picture phone development.[14] Here are many of the parallel problems and techniques to be mastered: TV-computer interface, alternate CRT and TV use for a picture tube, two-way interaction, switching, directory publication, standardization, evolution through processes of consumer experience, and demand. Information utilities may be born as a spin-off. All of this experience needs to be studied and applied through the persistent review of a national agency. Perhaps the new National Commission on Libraries and Information Science is the proper agency to undertake such research, subsidy, and review functions.

We recently have seen in the space program a striking demonstration of what industries can accomplish when they are given adequately defined goals: film, radio, and TV technology combined to do what would have been regarded as impossible until very recently — putting high resolution pictures of the moon and Mars into digitalized form, transmitting them over narrow bandwidths for very long distances, and then reconverting them to pictorial form; transmitting live color television pictures from the surface of the moon with low-power, compact devices of small weight. After such achievements, it appears that all the library networking problem requires is adequate specification and definition –along with an operating authority backed by adequate appropriations to get the job done. A national network of libraries might be quite efficiently set up and run by an organization equivalent to NASA. The only problem with this is that libraries are far closer to the sensitive nerve of our nation than is the surface of the moon. A national library network operated by a government agency would surely raise fears of thought control, and this fact clearly has been taken into account by Congress in setting up the new national commission as an independent agency rather than an arm of HEW. The actual operation of network services is better left to decentralized and regional units.

REGIONAL NETWORK DEPOSITORIES

We need stimulation and subsidy for comprehensive and interconnected regional network depositories. The original conception of the regional educational laboratories and the operational experience of the ERIC centers would be pertinent parallels here. Not only would geographical regions be served by the decentralized units, but ideally these should be committed to dividing the total task into specific areas of specialization. Thus, each regional unit would be the national depository in specific subject areas, and the nation at large would be flexibly served by the interconnections between all regional units.

SUBSIDY PROGRAM

We need a subsidy program for selected mixed media publication and for demonstrations and pilot operations using mixed media—with a built-in provision for disseminating information about these ventures. The fact that we are now poised for a great expansion of cable television is one auspicious factor involved here. Another is the fact that traditional publishing of textbooks is encountering difficulties at the present time and seeking new solutions.[15] The surest long-range solution to the input problem in library networking is to gain the cooperation of the original publishers –insuring a dual form of publication, one traditional and one machine readable.

NOTES

1. Jones, Stacy V. "Illustrated lessons sent by an FM System," New York times (20 June 1970).

2. Kuljian, Maynard J. "A random-access audio-picture retrieval system," Journal of the Society of Motion Picture and Television Engineers (Oct. 1969).

3. Steinberg, Charles A. "Information storage and retrieval system," Information display (Feb. 1970).

4. National Cable Television Association. Membership bulletin II:32 (19 Aug. 1969).

5. Gould, Jack. "Books reproduced on TV cartridges," New York times (14 April 1970).

6. "RCA achieves major technological breakthrough in development of color-TV tape player employing lasers and holography," RCA news release (30 Sept. 1969).

7. "Panasonic announcement," Training in business and industry 7:47 (Feb. 1970).

8. Miller, R. K. "Quick access to land documents via 16mm microfilm file system," Electrical world (4 Aug. 1969).

9. Morris, Albert J. "University-industry television, radio and telephone links," Educational broadcasting review 4:44- (Feb. 1970).

10. New York Times (26 June 1970), p. 71, (27 June 1970), p. 45.

11. Axner, David H. "The facts about facsimile," Data processing magazine 10:42 (May 1968).

12. New York Times (8 April 1970), p. 7, (30 June 1970), p.3.

13. "Symposium on video-tape recording standardization," Journal of the Society of Motion Picture and Television Engineers (July 1968).

14. Janson, Donald. "Picture-telephone service is started in Pittsburgh," New York times (1 July 1970).

15. Raymont, Henry. "Publishers report a decline in sales of textbooks," New York times (14 May 1970).

Potential Interrelationships between Library and Other Mass Media Systems

Edwin B. Parker

FUNCTIONS OF A LIBRARY

In examining the relationship between libraries and other communication media and institutions, it is helpful to postulate the social functions of libraries. A list of functions should aid in distinguishing functions of libraries from other media and institutions. The following list assumes that a library is a social institution intended to serve at least part of the information needs of a community of people, whether in a company, a university, a school, a town, or some other kind of community. All of the detailed functions can be subsumed under the more general statement that the function of libraries is to make it easy for people to obtain information from other people or environments that may be distant in space, time, or imagination.

To Store Information in Whatever Media Seem Efficient

The kind and quantity of information stored depends in part on the size and interests of the community being served. Libraries must not only store information to meet current needs but also must anticipate future needs. The extent to which they should be concerned with future needs is a joint function of two factors: (1) the probability that currently available items of information will be needed later, and (2) the difference in cost between acquiring and storing it now, and acquiring it later. Historically, the storage medium has been print although microfilm and microfiche copies of print have been commonly stored. Some libraries have performed better than others in storing information in other media: films; records; audio and video tapes and cassettes; computer cards, tapes, or discs; etc. Sometimes other institutions or agencies (audiovisual centers, film libraries, computation centers, museums, art galleries) have provided information in other media for the print library's community. In other cases information most appropriately stored in nonprint media have not been adequately stored because libraries were slow to respond to changes in information storage technology. We are postulating that it is the library's function to store needed information in all media unless there has been a division of labor such that some other institution is meeting part of the need. This function requires effective communication with other institutions if the library is not attempting to store information in all media. It also requires that libraries have extremely good communication with their communities in order to determine their information needs. Methods for obtaining such communication from users were discussed by Paisley and Parker in 1966.[1]

To Facilitate Retrieval of Information from Storage

Storage without adequate means of access would make it impossible for libraries to meet the information needs of their communities. Traditionally, the means of access has been the local card or book catalog, supplemented by a variety of guides and indexes (usually printed and sold to more than one library). With changes in technology of storage and increases in the size of collections, the complexity of retrieval problems has increased. Changes in the technology of access and retrieval (principally computer systems) are creating new challenges and new opportunities, but the function of providing retrieval from storage to meet the requests of the library's community remains unchanged. Retrieval service may be requested on a one-time basis and on a standing request basis (e.g., selective dissemination of information services). Retrieval services may be requested for reference retrieval only (to get the right book for the client) for specific content information (e.g., library reference services). Libraries failing to provide a sufficiently broad range of retrieval services to meet the needs of their communities are failing just as much as libraries that do not store information needed by their communities. An appropriate acronym for systems that emphasize storage without adequate retrieval would be SNARL (Storage Now and Retrieval Later).

To Teach People To Use the Media of Storage and Retrieval and To Inform Them about the Library's Services

Examples of traditional library services intended to enhance the efficiency or enjoyment to use the library's services are: children's story hours designed to teach children the enjoyment of books, instruction in how to use the catalog and other bibliographic tools, and newsletters announcing planned events or new acquisitions. This function requires libraries to assume the role of communicator, sending informative and instructional messages to their communities. A variety of media may be used for such communication, including interpersonal communication with individuals or groups, cheaply duplicated instructions, expensive newsletters, book review or story hour programs on radio or television, physical displays of books, documentary or instructional films, and computer-aided instruction. Programs of instruction to improve reading skills or to provide literacy training for functional illiterates sometimes have been included as a function of libraries. Such tasks are appropriate for libraries whenever other institutions, such as the schools, have not adequately performed them. As new media for storage and retrieval come into increasingly common use, instruction in the use of such media may become more needed, particularly if schools do not teach it (as they do for print).

To FACILITATE LEARNING

This function is redundant with the previous three in that storage, retrieval, and provision of information and instruction about how to retrieve information do facilitate learning. The point in listing it separately is to emphasize the role of the library as an educational institution. The establishment and maintenance of public libraries were justified on the basis of the adult education function they performed. The university library was formerly thought of as the heart of the university although that view has been in decline recently, particularly in the sciences. The library provides education not as a teaching institution with scheduled courses and curricula (except possibly for the limited function discussed above). Rather, it serves as a continuing education center or people's university in which people are assisted in learning what they want to learn when they want to learn it. The storage and retrieval functions can provide much of the assistance to individualized learning, but careful analysis of what is needed to facilitate individualized learning by the library's community may indicate additional services not available elsewhere that the library may be best equipped to provide. Availability of programmed instruction materials, teaching machines, facility for playing and recording audio materials (to facilitate language learning, for example), and computer-aided instruction programs are examples of services that might be included. Current educational philosophy is turning toward concepts that emphasize individualized learning and a student choice of subject matter and time of learning. The concept of a library as a place of learning is an ancient one into which new life can be breathed by recent and impending changes in the technology of individualized learning.

To PROVIDE AN INFORMATION SWITCHING AND REFERRAL CENTER

No institution can provide all things for all people; nevertheless, there is a need for an information center or service where people can go to find out where they can turn to find information they are seeking. Many library reference services and specialized information centers provide such services, at least in the subject matter of their special expertise. As society becomes more complex and more specialized, information services become available; as interconnection becomes more feasible technically, there is likely to be increasing demand for referral and switching services so that individuals can use their local library as a one-stop information service, with confidence of being referred to the appropriate place when the desired information is not available locally.

DIFFERENCES IN USE OF MEDIA BY LIBRARIES AND OTHER INSTITUTIONS

It is helpful to emphasize the obvious distinction between communication media (books, magazines, films, television, telephones) on the one hand and on the other hand, institutions that produce media content, manage media channels, store media content, or utilize media. Schools, libraries, bookstores, publishing houses, and broadcasting companies are examples of institutions involved in the production, management, storage, or use of media.

In contrasting and interrelating the functions of different communication institutions, it is helpful to contrast different kinds of media. Communication media in general perform the function of making possible communication between people who are distant in space or time such that face-to-face interpersonal communication is not possible. Communication through time requires a storage medium (stone tablets, papyrus, books, films, magnetic tape, etc.). A storage medium may be used for communicating with oneself through time (shopping lists, private diaries, etc.), for private person-to-person communication (letters sent through the mails), or for communication to larger selected or public audiences. If the contents of a storage medium are to be available in more than one place at the same time, then there must be a duplication medium (printing press, Xerox machine, microfiche printer, etc.) to provide multiple copies. It is useful to further subdivide duplication media into single-copy duplication or multiple-copy duplication. Xeroxing a copy of an article for a library client is obviously single-copy duplication, duplication printing a newsletter for distribution to many clients is multiple-copy duplication. A single copy of a book held by a library, although once duplicated, is not a duplication medium because it cannot be available at more than one place at the same time without further duplication.

If a storage medium (duplicated or unduplicated) is used to communicate through space as well as time, then the medium itself must be transported (usually by means used for people or other goods: trucks, planes, trains, bicycles, etc.) or transformed into a form suitable for a transmission medium (as in the transmission of a film via television or a taped message by telephone).

Some communication media are transmission media only, requiring some other medium for storage. Transmission media can be subdivided usefully into point-to-point (as in the telephone) and broadcast transmission (as in radio and television). Transmission media are of little use for libraries or library networks unless they are combined with a duplication medium. The combination of a transmission and duplication medium may be point-to-point (as in telegraph or teletype systems or point-to-point facsimile) or broadcast (as in broadcast facsimile or broadcasts recorded on audio or video tape at the reception end of the transmission).

To date, libraries have been concerned with transportable and nontransportable (noncirculating) storage media, occasionally with single-copy duplication, but rarely with point-to-point transmission and duplication. Multiple-copy duplication is usually thought of as a publishing function rather than as a library function. Broadcast transmission (whether duplicated or unduplicated) is quite remote from library functions because broadcast transmission does not permit users to retrieve information on demand.

Unlike schools operating under compulsory attendance laws, libraries typically do not have a captive audience and do not have prescribed curricula that some agency has decided their clients must learn. The library is a client-centered institution serving a community of receivers of information (See Paisley and Parker[2] for a discussion of information retrieval as a receiver-controlled communication system.) Other institutions (schools, advertising agencies, publishers, broadcasters, etc.) serve the senders in the process of social communication. The library has the unique function of being the general agent for the receiver in the communication process.

As a consequence of this emphasis, libraries primarily are concerned with media for storage of information rather than media for transmission of information. Libraries may use transmission media such as telephones or radio or television, but it would be out of keeping with the function of libraries to operate communication media that do not have storage properties or provide connections to storage. Storage is an essential ingredient if the information is to be made available to the receiver at a time of his choosing rather than at a time of the sender's choosing.

Similarly, libraries are not concerned with the original production of communication media or communication messages, with the exception of tools for access to previously existing messages. Libraries may be centers where scholars engage in original creative work, but the primary function of libraries is to provide the information needed by such users. The intellectual task of providing tools for access to information is a significant and challenging one — one that becomes increasingly important as the volume of primary information increases — but it is a special case of research needed to improve the library's functioning.

Libraries differ from bookstores in a significant and ironic way. The key difference is the basis of economic support. The bookstore (or that now almost extinct species, the profit-seeking lending library) is concerned with serving those information needs for which the clients can pay sufficient money that it is profitable to provide them. The source of income for a bookstore provides a close communication link with its clients. Either it continues to meet the information needs of the clients, or it goes out of business. Clients influence what is available by their economic transactions. The bookstore management usually has the option of choosing to serve one group of clients instead of others or meet one particular kind of information need rather than others, depending on what services and clients are likely to prove profitable. The library typically receives its financial support not from the individual clients but from an institutional surrogate for the clients, such as a governmental unit representing taxpayers or a university or school management. This lack of a direct economic link with the clients makes it more difficult to serve as an agent for the receivers of communication. The feedback information from the clients is much slower and

less reliable when it is filtered through some other bureaucracy before reaching the library. The library is not motivated by profit, but it must remain economically viable. In the short run, this can be accomplished by pleasing the funding agency, but because the funding agency is likely in the long run to be responsive to its source of support, usually the taxpayers, then the library is more likely to survive if it has adequate feedback from its clients and can demonstrate to the funding agency that it is meeting their information needs. The community it serves is usually defined for the library by the outside funding agency rather than open to free choice (like the bookstore) although libraries often end up serving only a fraction of the potential audience because there are inadequate mechanisms for the others to communicate their needs. Libraries are thus in need of special communication links to their communities to compensate for the fact that they have a responsibility to serve a particular audience not chosen by them and the fact that usual economic feedback links are absent. "Free" library service has the advantage of redistributing funds so that poor and rich alike can obtain access to needed information, but the lack of economic feedback mechanisms may make it less responsive to the needs of its community than it might otherwise be.

FUNCTIONAL AND PHYSICAL NETWORKS FOR LIBRARIES

We can think of a communication network as a transmission medium with switching capability to interconnect different nodes (points in the network) at different times. The interconnection between nodes may sometimes provide for only one-way communication, but more typically two-way communication is required so that the roles of sender and receiver can be reversed. Some networks permit broadcast communication in which the same messages are received at multiple nodes, but frequently, only a single receiver is associated with a single message (as in the telephone network). Some networks do not provide duplication or storage capability, while others (e.g., facsimile transmission) require that the message be duplicated at the receiving end in some medium other than the transmission medium. Before discussing the physical means of providing library networks, it is helpful to discuss the functions that the network is intended to serve. We should first ask what are the nodes that should be connected together, what kinds of messages are to be transmitted, who controls the choice of messages, and what duplication of messages into a storage medium at the receiving end is required.

There are three basic types of library networks to consider. One is the network connecting a library to each of its clients. Unlike the telephone network that permits any client to be connected to any other client, this kind of library network provides the option of connecting any client to the information centrally stored by the library. The second network is that connecting different libraries to each other. There are a large number of network configurations possible. Each library can be connected to each other in the network; each branch library can be connected to a main library but not to each other; a hierarchy can be established in which each branch library is connected to a regional library, which is in turn connected to a central library (e.g., the Library of Congress). Mixed modes can be established in which main libraries are all interconnected, but branch libraries are connected only to their main library. The third network is a combination of the first two: the network for connecting the clients of one library to a different library. There are two basic forms of this network. One is for the original library to serve its client by using a library-to-library network to obtain for him what he needs. The other is for the original library to switch the client directly to the appropriate other library so that the client can be served directly by the other library.

All three types of networks exist already, using technology that has been available for many years. Interlibrary loan agreements that depend on mail or messenger service constitute one way to implement the second and third type with current technology. By taking out a library card and coming to the library to borrow a book, a client becomes part of the library-client network. It is thus helpful to distinguish between two kinds of network questions: (1) the administrative agreements by which different libraries enter network arrangements or by which clients are entitled to obtain library service, and (2) the technical means by which the network agreements are implemented.

There are a variety of technical means by which networks can be implemented. Detailed comparisons of the technical choices are provided in other papers prepared for this Conference. For our purposes we can distinguish three types: traditional, dedicated electronic, and shared electronic. Traditional means include interpersonal communication and transportation, use of messengers, mail, etc. Dedicated communication lines can be used for computer interconnection, facsimile transmission, etc. Cheaper than dedicated lines, unless the transmission volume is very great, are shared communication networks, such as telephone or teletype networks. Another possibility is to share communication networks developed for computer or cable television interconnection. A key property of electronic networks for library systems, whether dedicated or shared, is that the message must be duplicated so that it still exists at the sending end after it has been received. Traditional networks may or may not have this property — original copies of books are sometimes transported without duplication.

SOCIAL TRENDS AFFECTING MEDIA AND LIBRARY NETWORKS

Continuation of several present social trends is likely to create additional demand for library services and library networks. Increases in the average level of education and of reading skill will continue. Library circulation has continued on an upward path even during the introduction of paperback books and television. Even though competition from other media resulted in lower utilization than would otherwise have been the case, demand for library services has been increasing steadily. See, for example, the Parker (1963) study of the effects of television on library circulation.[3] As our society becomes more complex, both organizationally and technically, an increasingly higher proportion of human energy must be spent on information processing. Two propositions from system theory are particularly relevant: (1) "As the complexity of a system increases, a disproportionate increase in information processing components is required;" (2) "Up to a maximum higher than usually attained, the greater the percentage of energy consumed in information processing relative to other functions, the more likely the system is to survive."[4]

Increased geographic mobility and increased interest in the boundaries between subject fields both contribute to the growing demand for diversity in information and the difficulty of any one library in providing all of the information required. The increase in scientific interest in interdisciplinary areas provides one example of demand for interconnectability — it is becoming harder to compartmentalize information requirements on either a geographic or subject-matter basis because people who are primarily working in one geographic or subject area often are interested in information from other areas and are on the boundaries of whatever division of information was established. The range of variation in information requested is likely to increase faster than any "average" information demand. As people become more geographically and physically mobile, the range of information needs will increase. The implication for libraries is that there will be increased need to back up local library holdings with information resources in other libraries if the information needs of library clients are to be met.

Social trends in education are likely to increase the importance of and requirements for libraries and library networks. According to Dr. Thomas F. Green, director of the Educational Policy Research Center at Syracuse University in recent congressional testimony: "The growth of education outside the formal system has probably been the most significant change in education over the years just past. In the current year, more people will be receiving instruction of a formal sort outside the formal education system than within it."[5] Demands for informal education also are increasing. For some years now we have been paying lip service to the concept of life-long learning. The need for continuing education to compensate for the fact that what is learned in school no longer provides sufficient information or skill to last a lifetime. In most occupations it is not possible to take a sabbatical in order to go back to school. In many occupations it is not possible or convenient to engage in regularly scheduled continuing education of the night school or summer school variety. The library provides the major means for self-study programs. As the technology of individualized instruction changes to permit individual learning from computer-aided instruction and audiovisual media, libraries are challenged with the option of continuing to perform that traditional function of catering to individualized learning or giving it up to other institutions by default. Student demands for more "relevant" education and for more flexible curricula with a wider range of choice are moving education (at least higher education) in the direction of providing the education that the student chooses. The movement for "relevant" education is essentially a movement toward a student-controlled curriculum in which the learner is instructed in what he wants to learn. Psychological studies have long demonstrated that learning is more effective when the learner is motivated to learn. These trends toward individualized instruction in subjects chosen by the learner are trends toward exactly the kind of educational service libraries have long been providing. Both the need and the opportunity are evident: it is possible to build "living libraries" or "education delivery systems" that are responsive to the educational needs of their clients by providing individualized instruction in a variety of media, including computer-aided instruction. In order to provide such a service, it will be necessary to have a communication network connecting the library to its clients.

If the library is to maintain its present functions as the society places new demands and the technology provides new opportunities, this is the direction libraries must develop. Since individualized instruction in nonprint media is likely to be expensive to provide and since people are willing to pay for such service, it may be necessary to charge for some library services instead of providing all services free. In order to maintain the beneficial distribution of wealth function that is one of the advantages of a free library system, it may be desirable to provide public education subsidies to the consumer in the form of "information stamps" that can be spent at the library or other educational institutions. This way favorable distribution effects can be maintained while gaining the advantages of letting people with the financial resources pay for additional service and providing an economic feedback to ensure that the library is responsive to the information needs of its clients.

TECHNOLOGICAL TRENDS IN MEDIA AFFECTING LIBRARY NETWORKS

Three technological trends in communication media will be taking place during the first half of the 1970s. All three should be followed carefully because of their implications for libraries and library networks. One is the video cassette for home display of audiovisual materials. The second is development of computer systems for library automation, information retrieval, and computer-aided instruction. The third is rapid expansion of cable television.

Within the next two years both CBS and RCA are planning to market video cassette systems that will permit people to watch movies, plays, instructional lectures and demonstrations, or other audiovisual material over their home television set at times of their own choosing, just as people now play records on their home record players. The video cassette player attaches to the antenna leads of the television set. The recorded information and entertainment is in cassette form, making the system as easy or easier to operate than a record player. One merely has to drop the cassette into the appropriate slot and push a start button. By providing an economical and simple to use audiovideo storage and duplication medium, much information now available only for transmission media can be available in stored form, just as books are stored.

This development in media has two implications for library networks. One is that there will be a great public demand to be able to borrow cassettes, just as now there is a great demand for borrowing books from libraries. Library acquisition policies and interlibrary loan policies will have to be developed to respond to the opportunity and the demand. Public libraries may have an excellent opportunity to broaden their base of public support by providing on loan video cassettes for all segments of the population, including those who seldom borrow books from the library. It is quite possible that communities will be willing to increase the amount of taxes allocated for library services if services can be expanded to include video cassette loan services.

Cassettes are not as easily damaged as phonograph records so libraries may be more willing to circulate cassettes than records. Cassettes, like books, are a transportable storage medium. A cassette lending service would constitute almost the least possible change in type of library service.

The second implication of video cassette systems for library networks is that it is likely to increase public demand for library to client networks. Assuming that libraries do respond to the need and provide loan copies of the kind of information and entertainment now provided by transmission media (i.e., television), people are more likely to articulate the already present but latent demand for communication networks to deliver both print and audiovisual information to their homes on demand. This is speculation, of course, but it seems reasonable that the fact of receiving video information from libraries on demand when they formerly received it (and concurrently receive it) by a transmission medium (television) will increase the articulated demand for on-demand transmission of information. On-demand video service is unlikely to be economically possible in the next ten years unless AT&T increases the resolution quality of its Picture-phone service. What may be economically possible in ten years is point-to-point transmission and duplication network connecting libraries and clients for transmission of print information (possibly using telephone or cable television channels).

There are two main classes of use of computers for library automation: on-line, in which librarians or library clerks interact conversationally with the computer system from a visual display or typewriter-type computer terminal; and batch processing, in which jobs are submitted to the computer to be run at a later time, with the results obtained some hours later or the next day. When we think of library networks, we tend to think of on-line systems, but batch systems for library automation also have implications for library networks. Implementation of computer systems permits standardization and centralization of services that can bring about significant economies in operation. Use of MARC tapes from the Library of Congress, for example, connects libraries in a network with the Library of Congress, as does use of LC cards, even when the tapes or cards are distributed by mail.

On-line library automation projects lead more naturally to transmission networks (as distinguished from transportation networks for delivery of cards, tapes, or books). On-line systems within a single library provide a simple kind of network within the library, connecting to a central file all librarians and clerks who have access to terminals. Such a network, with a central "in-process file" for acquisition and cataloging functions can be particularly useful in decentralized branch library systems that have centralized ordering and processing. Branch librarians can perform their functions better if they have access to current status information on all orders by their own and other branches, just as computer airline reservation networks make the work of airline reservation clerks much simpler. Since the costs of on-line systems are still very great, it is possible that a system developed for one library system will be used by others, or that such systems will be developed by outside organizations with the intention of selling services to several libraries. At present, the cost of on-line storage for large catalogs is still high, but costs are coming down and demand is likely to go up. Some such systems already exist. The SUNY Biomedical Communication Network in New York has provided a union catalog of bibliographic information from several medical libraries which can be searched by computer terminals in each of the libraries.[6] The Bell Telephone Laboratories' Library has activated an on-line circulation system.[7] That system includes the catalogs of three libraries several miles distant from each other.

On-line systems for library automation link libraries and librarians together into networks. Once such systems are developed it is logical to permit library users to have access (particularly to catalog or circulation files). At this point the distinction between on-line library automation and on-line information retrieval systems becomes blurred. The on-line library automation system is an information retrieval system. Whatever other functions it also serves internally for libraries, the on-line information retrieval system available to library clients is a network linking clients to libraries. Two examples of such systems are the INTREX system at M.I.T.[8] and the SPIRES/BALLOTS system at Stanford.[9] The Stanford Public Information REtrieval System, SPIRES, has been used for on-line searches of physics preprint files at the Stanford Linear Accelerator Center since spring 1969 and is being developed in conjunction with the Stanford Library's Project BALLOTS (Bibliographic Automation of Large Library Operations using a Time-sharing System), which will provide on-line technical processing service for the Stanford libraries.[10]

Library-client networks using computer systems are developing first in universities and research laboratories, not surprisingly, indicating the beginning of a general trend for the future. Once libraries are connected to their clients by computer networks, then many other possible services should be considered. The most significant service, in addition to information retrieval, is computer-aided instruction. There are two reasons why libraries should be following closely developments in computer-aided instruction as well as computer information retrieval. One is simply that if they are providing programmed instruction textbooks on loan (a typical library service), then why shouldn't they offer the same kind of programmed instruction when it is available by computer instead of between printed pages? The other reason is that information retrieval and computer-aided instruction systems are developing on converging paths. As information retrieval systems develop, more complex facilities will be added, including retrieval of text material as well as references to text, and fact-retrieval or other processing of textual information. At the same time, as computer-aided instruction systems progress beyond drill and practice programs, they will begin to look more like complex information retrieval systems. At some point it may be both hard and irrelevant to distinguish whether a set of computer programs and associated data base for a college-level history course is an information retrieval system or a computer-aided instruction system. In any event, the present implication is clear: Those concerned with future development of library-to-client networks should follow developments in computer-aided instruction as well as computer information retrieval.

The third technological trend that should be followed carefully is the growth of cable television. The cable television industry is predicting that nearly 50 percent of U. S. homes will be connected to cable television systems by 1975, and that 85 percent will be connected by 1980.[11] The technology of cable television is developing more rapidly than many observers had earlier expected. Some systems are being introduced with forty-two-channel capacity and return communication capability. A June 1970 Federal Communications Commission proposed rule-making specified the FCC's intention to impose a rule requiring the availability of two-way communication capability. The 24 June Notice of Proposed Rule Making released by the FCC 1 July 1970 stated:

"We intend that future cable systems should be installed in such a manner that...each subscriber may be afforded a means for directly communicating with a local program origination point. This return communication capability should provide at least the capacity equivalent to a single 4 kHz message channel and may be shared with a limited number of other subscribers so that cuing problems are avoided."[12]

The implication of cable television developments is that two-way cable television channels will provide libraries with the opportunity for broadband communication network access to the homes of many of their clients. All over the country local governments are issuing cable television franchises, many of them for periods as long as twenty years or more. Librarians in any community in which cable television franchise decisions are pending should look into the terms of the franchise agreements that are proposed. Many franchise agreements include requirements for civic channels to be available to the franchising municipality. Libraries should consider urging the reservation of channels that could be used for transmission of library services and should encourage requirements for early implementation of two-way channels.

KEY ISSUES IN NETWORK DECISIONS

Viewed from the perspective of interrelationships with mass media and communication institutions, there are six key issues to consider in library network decisions. The issues cannot adequately be examined separately since they are closely interrelated. The six issues are: (1) Who is to be connected by the network? (2) What general type of network is intended? (3) What information will be available in the network? (4) Will the network be dedicated or shared? (5) What distribution of power does the network require? (6) Should the network be centralized or decentralized?

WHO IS TO BE CONNECTED BY WHAT TYPE OF NETWORK?

Both library-client and library-library networks will be needed. The meaningful question is what priority should be placed on these alternatives. In order to answer this question it is necessary to consider what changes in the type of network for each of the two major alternatives will be the most useful in carrying out the functions of libraries. Present library networks, whether library-client or library-library networks, depend primarily on physical transportation of the storage medium (i.e., the book is borrowed). There are essentially two ways to improve these networks. One is to interpose a duplication medium so that multiple users may be served from the original copy. (This kind of a single-copy or on-demand duplication should be distinguished from the multiple-copy duplication that we now know as publishing.) The other is to improve the transmission link.

Until there are improved transmission links in the library-client network, it is premature to concentrate on technical improvement of the library-library transmission link. Instead, the priorities should be to work on improved duplication for both networks and improved transmission for the library-client network. Primarily because of copyright problems, there are serious administrative difficulties as well as technical difficulties to be resolved in creating duplication networks. The potential gain both for the library and the client is so great that it is worth investing major effort in solving this problem. Transmission without duplication cannot help libraries to perform their functions because storage is an essential part of the mission of libraries. Whether duplication is made by Xerox copies, photoduplication, distribution of disposable microfiche from which hard copies can be made, facsimile, or some other means, the library would always have a copy of all of its information available for all users without users queuing for the same material or being inconvenienced by theft or loss of the original. The borrower would be able to keep the copy he receives without needing to return it for other borrowers.

The reason for putting library-library transmission networks at the lowest priority level is simple: Duplication rather than transmission is the bottleneck in interlibrary transactions. Libraries may be reluctant to enter into interlibrary loan agreements if their information is out of circulation for their own clients when on loan elsewhere. Electronic transmission plus duplication is likely to be much more expensive than duplication plus transmission through present channels (such as the U.S. Postal Service) for some time to come, particularly if microfiche rather than hard copy is used. See, for example, the February 1968 report, "Telefacsimile in Libraries" by William Schieber and Ralph Shoffner.[13] The advantage of electronic transmission is the greatly increased speed of transmission (although queuing problems may prevent some of that advantage from being realized). That advantage may be almost completely nullified if there is no electronic link to the client and he must depend on traditional transmission channels. Until the transmission links extend from the library to the clients, the expense of library-library transmission links will be largely wasted if the link to the client depends on traditional transportation. Therefore, the priorities should be clear: Give highest priority to solution of problems associated with duplication, second priority to library-client transmission networks, and lowest priority to library-library transmission networks.

What Information Will Be Available?

Present library networks that include transmission capability provide only status or surrogate information such as catalog (or augmented catalog) information or circulation status information. Actual content (with the minor exceptions of the Project INTREX text-access experiment and occasional fac-simile experiments) is transferred by the traditional transportation mechanisms of interlibrary or library loan systems. Network characteristics and cost considerations will be quite different depending on which of four general classes of information are available. Reference retrieval, text access, data or fact retrieval, and processing capability (including computer-aided instruction) constitute the four general classes. Retrieval of the text of a book or article is not the end process in information access. There will be a continuing demand for access to particular facts, data, or information contained in storage media, whether in books or in machine-readable data archives. Social scientists examining census data, for example, are no longer satisfied with data reported in published census volumes. Instead, they often want to study particular data tables or cross-tabulations that may not be contained in the printed census reports. With access to basic data, or to the one in ten thousand sample of census data, the desired table can be constructed. In other words, he needs both data retrieval and processing capability to find the information he is seeking. Computer-aided instruction is another example of the combination of retrieval and processing capability. Demand will be strong for all four classes of information. Which can be provided soonest will be more a function of technical possibility and economic factors than of demand factors. All four classes should be considered in the course of network planning.

Will the Network Be Dedicated or Shared?

Telephone and telex networks are often the most economical for many purposes, especially when the traffic volume is light, because costs are shared with a large number of other users. Even when volume is sufficiently large to justify a dedicated line, it often is economical to lease it from AT&T. Even though use is dedicated to a single user during the term of the lease, the term of the lease may be for less than the life of the equipment, which is shared with other users at different times (measured in months or years). Sharing of conduit space or maintenance costs also may be economical. The comparisons to be made are the technical and economic ones to which other papers in this Conference are devoted.

A key question of sharing arises in library-client networks, particularly in considering networks connecting public libraries to homes. It is unlikely that a dedicated network could ever be justified for library-client communication, but both telephone and cable television links into the home provide an opportunity for libraries to share networks. Depending on how costs are billed, communication charges could be low in both networks. When local telephone calls are billed at a flat monthly rate instead of unit time charges, client communication charges may be "free" although there would be additional equipment costs at each node in the network. With cable television operators looking for additional services that they can offer their subscribers as inducements to pay a flat monthly rate for the cable connection, that broadband channel may also be free except for terminal equipment costs. Thus network planning should not overlook the possibility of obtaining transmission links at a small or zero marginal cost by sharing with another network instead of developing dedicated links. The economies of shared networks are likely to be considerable.

WHAT POWER DISTRIBUTION IS REQUIRED?

When a single library develops an internal network among its branches or within the single library, or between the library and its clients, then little change in the distribution of power is required or to be expected. On the other hand, when library-library networks are developed, some redistribution of power may be required or may be expected to follow. Suppose that two or more libraries when joined together in a network can produce a cost savings through joint operation or division of labor without reducing service, or that improved service can be provided without increase in cost. It would seem logical to implement the network connecting such libraries. However, in order to accomplish the savings or improved service, it is necessary for each library to give up some of its autonomy. Joint standards have to be adopted, and each library no longer has full authority over all of the operations for which it has responsibility. As an experienced administrator can point out, separation of authority and responsibility can lead to serious administrative difficulties. A director of libraries who has the responsibility to provide service to his community but who has lost his authority to provide that service can find himself in serious difficulty. It is for this reason that library directors involved in library automation would prefer to have the computer staff under their direction rather than reporting to someone else (such as a computation center director). The computation center director (or the administrative officer of any other node in a network to whom authority has been transferred) may not understand the local library's problems as well as its own director does. Consequently, what is optimal for the entire network or system may not be optimal for a given local library. If the network involves other media and institutions besides the library (computation centers, cable television systems, etc.), the danger of administrative difficulty is more severe than if only libraries are involved. If the directors of all the institutions involved in the network report to a common higher authority (as branch librarians report to the director of the library system), then questions of authority and responsibility can be resolved. When there is no such administrative mechanism, it may be dangerous for a library to give up some of its authority in the interests of larger efficiency because its own local operations may suffer. Explicit analysis of potential effects on power relations should consequently be part of any network analysis.

SHOULD NETWORKS BE CENTRALIZED OR DECENTRALIZED?

In addition to the administrative organization questions raised in the preceding paragraph, the basic question of technical reliability must be asked. The question can be posed as one of soundness of the ecology. The typical arrangements in electrical power networks are such that each node in the network is completely dependent on the network for power, with the exception of particularly critical nodes such as hospitals which may have emergency power generators. This can lead to serious difficulty and inconvenience as serious power blackouts on the eastern coast of the United States and elsewhere demonstrate. The vulnerability to technical failure or to deliberate sabotage is much greater in a centralized network. Although it would be more expensive, a decentralized system with local power generation and dependence on the network for auxiliary service would be based on sounder ecological principles. This decentralized network principle is typically practiced by library clients. They will buy books most frequently needed, whether or not the library has them, in order to be as independent of the library as possible. In the case of library networks, it may be more economical than in power networks to provide a given level of decentralization, using the network facilities as backup rather than as primary sources of essential service. Given the speed of the past and projected future change in computer technology, computer systems are unlikely to be as stable as power systems for some time to come. Therefore, reliability considerations should be carefully weighed in making network decisions. It is likely that reliability considerations would push an otherwise close decision in the direction of decentralization.

NOTES

1. W. J. Paisley and E. B. Parker, "Research for psychologists at the interface of the scientist and his information system," *American psychologist* 21:1061-1071 (1966).

2. Ibid.

3. Edwin B. Parker, "The effects of television on public library circulation," *Public opinion quarterly* 27:578-589 (1963).

4. James G. Miller, "Living systems" *Behavioral science* 10:193-411 (1965).

5. Thomas F. Green, *Education and schooling in post-industrial America: some direction for policy.* Presented before the Committee on Science and Astronautics, U.S. House of Representatives at its 11th meeting with the panel on science and technology, Jan. 27-29, 1970, Washington, D.C.

6. Irwin H. Pizer, "A regional medical library network," *Bulletin of the Medical Library Association* 57:101-15 (April 1969).

7. R. A. Kennedy, "Bell Laboratories' library real-time loan system (BELLREL)," *Journal of library automation* 1:128-146 (1968).

8. C. F. J. Overhage and R. J. Harmon, eds., *INTREX* (Cambridge, Mass.: MIT Pr., 1965).

9. Massachusetts Institute of Technology, Project INTREX Staff, *Semiannual activity report* (15 March, 15 Sept. 1966-1970).

10. Stanford University, Institute for Communication Research, *SPIRES annual report; a report of the Stanford Public Information REtrieval System,* (Stanford: Univ. of Stanford, 1970).

11. For example: Robert A. Dunlop, *The emerging technology of information utilities,* paper presented at the Conference on Information Utility and Social Choice, University of Chicago, (Dec. 1969).

12. Federal Communications Commission, *Notice of proposed rule making,* Docket number: 18894 (24 June 1970).

13. William D. Schieber and Ralph M. Shoffner, Telefacsimile in libraries; a report of an experiment in facsimile transmission and an analysis of implications for interlibrary loan systems (Berkeley, Calif.: University of California, Institute of Library Research, 1968).

Broad Bandwidth Telecommunications Systems

John Sodolski

BROADBAND DEFINITION

In recent years the term "broadband communications" has come into popular usage. As used by lay people, the term has become curiously inaccurate and limited, and "broadband" usually refers to CATV (community or cable television) distribution systems, or other similar cable arrangements. Also, although most of these systems are at present one-way, use of the term "broadband" usually implies a two-way system.

It is important to note that this lay definition of broadband focuses on a developing technology, and other types of broadband transmission systems such as microwave, cable, and recently, satellites, have been and are available.

As to what is "broad" and what is "narrow," recently it was jokingly observed that if a "narrowband" system (such as the telephone) is compared to a garden hose, then a broadband system is like Niagara Falls. Indeed, so substantial is the increase in capacity of broadband systems that their development may well portend a true revolution in communications.

"Broad bandwidth," as a terminology, in the past has not been defined uniquely but generally has been used to mean portions of the frequency spectrum which are at least several, and certainly more than one, conventional four kilohertz (kHz) voice channels in width. The designation of channels was originally in terms of the service they were designed to render, for example, in Table 1

TABLE 1. BANDWIDTH OF SOME COMMON SERVICES

SERVICE	REQUIRED BANDWIDTH ÷ 1,000 FOR MHz
Telegraph (hand)	0.030 kHz
Teletype	0.170 kHz
Voice (telephone)	4.0 kHz
Facsimile (6 minutes)	4.0 kHz
Facsimile (6 seconds)	240.0 kHz
Television	4,500 kHz (one TV channel)

AVAILABLE SYSTEMS AND SERVICES

In the process of long-distance transmission of these various bandwidth requirements, it became apparent that it was a matter of good economy on high-density, long-haul transmission trunk lines to collect a large quantity of signals and transmit them together over a broad bandwidth facility rather than by individual circuits for each. One plan for doing this was to use "frequency division multiplex," whereby a specific band in the frequency spectrum was assigned to a specific subscriber's signals. Since this frequency division multiplex scheme originally was devised for the transmission of telephone channels, the spectrum was divided into voice channel equivalent 4 kHz segments as shown in Table 2.

TABLE 2. FREQUENCY DIVISION MULTIPLEX

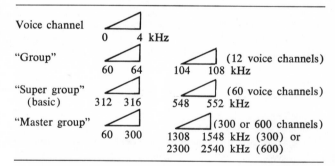

While it is possible by suitable modulation and demodulation techniques to assemble anywhere from 12 to 1,800 voice channels in this manner for transmission over broadband microwave or cable circuits, it also is possible to enter the multiplex system on a wideband basis. The "group," "supergroup," and "master group" bandwidths shown in Table 2 have evolved from telephone practice into the normally available "broad bandwidth" telecommunications channels and are the *de facto* standards around which broadband terminals are designed for use by the subscribers.

Recently another form of multiplex, designed initially for use on cable, has been introduced into the various telephone systems in the United States. This new multiplex is called "time division" because it shares segments of time between specific subscribers instead of bands of frequency. It also builds up into a hierarchy of multiple channels, as shown in Table 3, and is very important since it is the planned way of the future for the transmission of data and video telephone over existing telephone plant cable and long-haul facilities, and hence may establish new *de facto* terminal standards.

TABLE 3. TIME DIVISION (DIGITAL) MULTIPLEX

VOICE CHANNEL	64 KILOBITS TRANSMISSION RATE SEC.
T1	1,544 K_b (24 channels)
T2	6,312 K_b (96 channels)
T4	281,000 K_b (approximately 4,000)
T5	562,000 K_b (approximately 8,000)

When the concept of multiplexing a number of voice channels over a broadband transmission facility was first developed, it was purely a matter of optimizing the use of the cable transmission plant investment dollars, and the "broad bandwidth" ports into the transmission system were not made available to the ordinary subscriber. After World War II, "broad bandwidth" microwave transmission licenses were made available by the Federal Communications Commission, FCC, for private communication systems users as well as common carriers. When this happened, it became desirable for the common carriers to make available competing broad bandwidth services in their tariffed offerings. The most widely used of these new tariffs was called "TELPAK" by the Bell System and was simply an offer to let subscribers purchase large blocks of transmission spectrum directly into the multiplex equipment ports at the "group," "supergroup," and "master group" levels. These were called respectively TELPAK A, C, and D and were the first widely used common carrier "broad bandwidth" subscriber services.

Special broad bandwidth services in larger sizes than TELPAK D have been made available, especially for the government and the military, but in general, the next largest widely used wideband service is 4500 kHz for the transmission of TV quality video signals primarily for network TV program distribution (although various entrepreneurs have offered point-to-point TV conference services based upon the purchase of video channels from AT&T long lines facilities).

Let us review, then, the more popular, presently available, broad bandwidth service offerings created from common carrier practices so that we can proceed toward new and different concepts. Table 4 shows the name, the designated service, the equivalent voice channels, and the rating for data transmission (voice included for comparison).

TABLE 4. SOME POPULAR BROAD-BANDWIDTH SERVICE OFFERINGS

NAME OF OFFERING	INTENDED SERVICE	EQUIVALENT 4 kHz CHANNELS	EQUIVALENT DATA RATE b.p.s.	EXPLANATORY NOTES
Dial up	Voice	1	1,200 to 9,600	Usable data rate limited by noise, most systems 1,200 or less.
Private	Voice	1	to 9,600	Usable data rate depends on conditioning, *most* systems 2,400 or less.
Telpak A (group)	Voice or data	12	48,000	(Up to)
Telpak B (two groups)	Voice or data	24	96,000	(Up to)
Telpak C (super group)	Voice or data	60	240,000	(Up to)
Telpak D (master group	Voice or data	240	960,000	(Up to)
Video	TV	1,125	4,500	—
T1	Voice or data	24	500	In service, cable plus developmental microwave T1WG1 = 8 x 64 Kb T1WB2 = 2 x 250 Kb T1WM1 = 1 x 500 Kb
T2	Voice or data	96	2,000	In test, cable only carries one picture phone
T4	Voice or data	Approximately 4,000	90,000	In laboratory only
T5	Voice or data	Approximately 8,000	180,000	In laboratory only

A comparison of Table 3 with Table 4 indicates that in the "T" systems shown, the digital transmission rate is about three times the data handling rate while the analog systems (2) versus (4) have data rates which are equal (or greater if multilevel modulation is used) to the bandwidth they occupy.

LIMITATIONS OF PRESENT TRANSMISSION SYSTEMS

The result of this relationship is that where bandwidth is costly or the bandwidth is limited by considerations of available spectrum or interference, it is the general practice to use the more tightly packed analog systems. Microwave, satellites, and buried coaxial cable usually follow this practice. On the other hand, where bandwidth is cheap and repeater sites readily available, for example, in a 200-pair telephone cable trunking between exchanges, the digital T systems offer a simpler, less costly approach.

Now that we have examined the conventional ways in which conventional transmission facilities are carved up into useful pieces of broad bandwidth spectrum, let us examine what constraints mitigate against extensive wideband services expansion of these systems. Table 5 shows the more useful frequency bands commonly used by microwave systems.

TABLE 5. FREQUENCY BANDS COMMONLY USED BY MICROWAVE SYSTEMS

BAND GHz	WIDTH SPACING, MHz	SERVICE	TOTAL CHANNELS (TV)
3.7 to 4.2	500/20	Common carrier	25
5.9 to 6.4	500/30	Common carrier	16
6.5 to 6.8	300/10	PSIT (Public Safety, Industrial, and Transportation)	—
7.1 to 8.4	1300/30	Government	43
10.7 to 11.7	1000/30	Common carrier	33
12.2 to 12.7	500/20	PSIT	25
			142

If one examines the ratio of the width to the channel spacing, each of the bands can be host to only a relatively small number of channels as shown in the last column, and each channel, in general, can carry only one one-way video signal, i.e., for a TV quality videophone transmission, full duplex, two channels would be required. If we took the full microwave spectrum from 2.0 GHz to 12.7 GHz, we would have 10,700 MHz of bandwidth divided by 20 MHz (x 2 for duplex) per subscriber yields only 267 simultaneous video conversations. While this basic figure can be much enlarged upon by consideration of actual traffic patterns, one MHz bandwidth video telephone, and reuse of the same frequencies, it still is obvious that in large metropolitan areas a system likely would be several orders of magnitude below being able either to provide the necessary entrance links or the local transmission for a full videophone service.

Extension upward into the spectrum beyond 12 GHz offers some hope of temporary relief, but metropolitan multipath propagation problems appear to threaten this escape valve also, and the "broad bandwidth subscriber drop" seems to be gradually but inexorably moved toward that old reliable connection medium, the copper wire — in this case, a coaxial cable.

Coaxial cable is the usual transmission medium in CATV systems. It also is used very widely in other broadband communication installments, and it is likely that much more will be used in the future.

The cable attenuates the signals; therefore, amplifiers and equalizers have to be spaced out regularly along the cable if the level of the signals is to be maintained. Since each repeater degrades the signals slightly, there is a limit to the number which can be cascaded, and a corresponding limit to the length of the spur, depending on the quality of the cable. With existing CATV equipment, the limit is about fifteen miles for a system carrying twelve TV channels, but trends in the technology will certainly extend both the distance and the bandwidth in years ahead.

EVOLUTIONARY DEVELOPMENT OF CABLE SERVICE

The coaxial cable, as a local distribution medium, has a permanent advantage over any form of radio frequency propagation; its inherently broader bandwidth of 300 or more megahertz can be used and reused, even on the same poles or in the same ducts, as often as the economies of the service dictate, by simply laying in another cable.

In visualizing a "wired city" concept of the future, there have been a myriad of service concepts generated on the tacit assumption that the "excess capacity of CATV systems" held the key to untold benefits for everyone. If any reasonable person stops to think about it, he can generate largely from his own experience a list of the differences between today's CATV systems and a true transmission system capable of supplying a full-service "broadband-drop" to a high-density subscriber area. For example:

1. The broadband communications network (BCN) must be two-way. The CATV distribution network (CATV DN) currently is one-way. It is technically feasible to make it two-way by directional filters at increased cost and sacrifice of some part of the one-way bandwidth, or simply by putting in two cables and repeater amplifiers.

2. The BCN will require better noise and distortion characteristics than the present CATV DN if interconnection to distant points through high-quality transmission trunks (e.g., TD-3 microwave, L-4 cable, or domestic satellite) is to be satisfactory. This is technically feasible and requires improved (and more expensive) line amplifiers or shorter runs of cable between amplifiers.

3. For switching purposes, many feel the BCN will have to be configured like a star rather

than a tree (as is the CATV DN because even with 300 megahertz of bandwidth, true interconnection with a large number of subscribers in a high-density area will require a hierarchy switching at nodal points just like the telephone exchanges because there simply are not enough (twenty?) video channels to serve all, even in the relatively pregnant 300 megahertz cable system.

A switched service (or system) is one in which messages originated by a sender are sent only to designated addresses. A switched service may be circuit switched where a direct transmission path is established between sender and receiver or message switched where messages are relayed to the receiver by switching centers in a store and forward manner. Multiple address is available with most switched services. However, multiple address is considerably more common with message-switched services than with circuit-switched services.

In nonswitched services, the communications channel remains unchanged, and all messages are sent to all receiving stations, as in a CATV DN. However, messages can contain addresses so that the receivers can select (i.e., display and/or print-out, etc.) desired messages.

4. It is generally assumed by communications engineers that the BCN must be designed to a much higher reliability than the CATV DN. Many BCN services once offered can be expected to become just as vital to the population as telephone service. Telephone service is highly reliable, battery powered, with gasoline generator emergency charger backup so that even a 60 hertz power "blackout" does not interrupt service. CATV DN is powered by the 60 hertz service. Besides power source reliability, standards for circuits, components, and lighting protection also must be established.

There are many other things which keep the CATV DN from being the transmission quality network which is required ultimately to fulfill the needs of the BCN.

Should we then at this point concede defeat and start all over again? No. CATV DN can be said to have somewhat the same relationship to the BCN that the telephone networks of the early 1900s had to the telephone systems of today. CATV DN can grow into a satisfactory BCN through evolutionary processes similar to the genesis of the telephone system. An immediate task is to guide the evolutionary process by planned experiments designed to hasten the optimization processes which will lead to BCN. In the meantime, care must be exercised not to create restrictive, inhibiting legislation in eagerness to hasten matters.

Let us then examine some compromises and adjustments which may allow us, for the time being, to evade the consequences of the four "sticking points," CATV DN versus BCN, which previously were enumerated.

1. *Two-way requirement:* For initial experiments, the outbound subscriber traffic will be limited to voice or keyboard entry/request capable of being sent over his existing telephone line. The CATV DN could dedicate certain of its channels to the same end, with video response, however.

2. *Reduced noise and distortion:* CATV DN has a unique characteristic in that its network can be broken into small "communities of common interest;" it may be desirable to do so, especially in the light of local origination requirements. Ethnic/sociological area pattern needs are likely to at least result in the short-cable runs conducive to reduced noise and distortion properties in the network.

3. *Star versus tree switching:* BCNs generally would be designed for distribution of information from one source to many receiving locations. The network is like a "tree," a main trunk and many branches. Separate "trees" could economically serve separate communities of as few as 1,000 homes. Separate "trees" could build neighborhood communities within massive urban centers. The several trees could be coupled to some common distribution channels and also could choose to tap into separate specialty program sources or interactive meetings, or games such as each community might desire. By starting with basically small "trees," we can obtain the most flexibility in providing services that are of utility to a few local communities of interest or to the whole nation.

Also for purposes of establishing demand, any experimental service can be kept local in character initially to avoid the need for the degree of quality to sustain long-distance interconnection.

Some feel the "community-of-interest" network and local origination will cause the system to be rather more nodal than dendritic. Switching, if required, can for purposes of an experiment be kept very simple, if automatic, or even be limited to manual patching. However, even if the system were dendritic, by using presently available digital technology, flexibility in addressing can be provided so that each receiver can be given an individual (discrete) address. The sender can then select the desired receiver(s) by sending proper address information with messages. Multiple addressing can be accomplished by sending each discrete address of each receiver or by establishing and sending a code that designates a class of subscribers.

4. *Higher reliability:* Let the CATV DN be used in the experiment and as these experiments grow more sophisticated and frequent, the

reliability requirement, unsummoned, will make its presence known.

The previous four points indicate it is possible to utilize developing CATV transmission technology to supplement and augment existing systems. At least it is a beginning.

EXPERIMENTATION ON CABLE

An approach to library services utilizing broadband communications was described in a recent filing to the Federal Communications Commission.[1] The service described was called the *electronic home library service* (designated BCNL). With such a service available, a reader could request a book or periodical from a central library using a narrowband channel to the library (a phone circuit or the BCN, itself). The desired book is then "transmitted" from microfiche, microfilm, or video tape, page by page, and received via the BCN network on a dedicated wideband channel.

Several modes of operation are possible. In one, the entire book or selected article is transmitted at the maximum reception speed of the user's facsimile recorder. Several hundred simultaneous transmissions in time-division multiplex are possible with 6-MHz BCN channels and reasonable recorder speed.

As an alternative, a soft-copy display can be used. Each page is transmitted and stored at the receiver for reading. When the reader has finished one page, he signals for the next page, and this is transmitted in a small fraction of a second with no perceptible delay. This is another form of time-sharing of the broadband channel.

In its early stages a library service would undoubtedly be limited in quality of the recorded images. The goals of graphic arts quality, color reproduction, and other refinements gradually will be attained as technology advances and as public demand develops. BCN offers a favorable transmission medium in bandwidth and propagation characteristics for such growth in image quality.

In addition to public access to libraries, the BCN could operate at the "wholesale" level between libraries. Rare volumes at remote locations would be readily available. Earliest applications might be expected in rather specialized uses, such as medical or law libraries. For any of these services, the terminal equipments and bandwidth requirements would be about the same.

When thinking about terminals, one should remember just what are the human senses and sensory responses. Existing and yet-to-be-developed terminals are extensions of these human capacities, extended to a distance utilizing broadband transmission techniques. It is perfectly obvious that these extended senses will expand greatly and enhance the capability of an operator to perform difficult and complex tasks.

As broadband techniques evolve and as local systems are interconnected with one another, the user/subscriber could have a telephone, a high-speed printer, a video screen, and a facsimile machine all available at his console. The interaction of these terminals with computers, other terminals, and among themselves offers a flexibility of such great proportions that it is now only dimly recognized by even those closest to these developments.

INDUSTRY ORGANIZATION

When most people think of the telecommunications industry, they think of the phone company. While this assumption generally is a valid one, there are in fact a number of phone companies, many of them independent. Some substantial areas of the U.S. are within the purview of non-AT&T companies. Also, there are other common carriers — some well known such as Western Union and others, like ARINC, known only within the airline industry it services.

Most broadband services and facilities are procured from common carriers. Many users who have large bandwidth requirements lease "dedicated" facilities from a carrier.

Since World War II, there has been a substantial growth in private microwave systems. This has been particularly true in the case of right-of-way companies such as railroads or gas transmission pipelines where ownership of right-of-way makes installation of microwave equipments considerably more economical than it otherwise would have been.

Lately, there has been a new development likely to affect the provision of broadband services. The Federal Communications Commission has received a number of applications from so-called "special common carriers." These special carriers propose to provide unique services which differ from the traditional offerings of existing carriers. In some cases the offerings are digital for use with data; in other cases the offerings are simply broad bandwidth in nature; and in still other cases, the customer is offered an option of various services between two cities such as Chicago and St. Louis. All the returns are not yet in on the special "common-carrier" question. One such system has been authorized by the FCC, but many more are pending.

With regard to the growing CATV distribution system — and the BCN — it is likely that a number of locally franchised companies will wire cities. If the FCC sets proper standards early enough, all of these then can be interconnected. This interconnection can be accomplished via an existing common carrier, via satellite, or via "special" common carriers. If such interconnection is accomplished and should the network evolve with significant switching capabilities, the final network could look very much like the current telephone system.

No discussion of broadband communications or any other type would be complete without mentioning the regulatory environment. Indeed, there are those who maintain that the only limitation on the productive use of burgeoning communications technology is regulatory in nature. Be that as it may, to quote from the previously mentioned IED/EIA response to the FCC:

> The broadband communication facility would tend to have public monopoly characteristics and thereby should be regulated, but only to the extent necessary (1) to insure equitable access to all desiring to offer a communication service, and (2) to protect the right of attachment of associated terminal equipment, and (3) to insure competitive purchase of necessary hardware. These communication services and associated terminals should not be regulated anymore than other information media are regulated — such as newspapers, magazines, books, movies, etc. This situation is similar to the Carterfone case where the clear distinction was drawn be-

tween the terminal equipment and the common carrier facility. This decision has and will continue to encourage the application of new technological resources from potential new suppliers to help solve the numerous communications problems. And:

The public interest can best be served currently, in the immediate future, and the long run by preservation of free, open, and effective competition for the communication services that are and will become economically feasible where broadband capable systems are installed. To insure this development, there should be a clear distinction between the communication service (CATV, video telephone, mail, and data communications, etc.) being offered the public and the transmission medium (broad-band cable system) which carries the communication service.

These paragraphs represent a consensus among many knowledgeable observers in the electronics and communications industries. It would be well for every interested party to recognize the implications of the decisions regulatory agencies must make, and to watch closely the regulatory as well as the technical development of broadband systems. Hopefully, with a high degree of vigilance and understanding, we may be able to avoid some of the mistakes of the past.

There are a myriad of services which may be provided by utilizing broadband communications. The list of potential services is endless, and in many cases, the viability of the service is dependent on sharing facilities with other users and services. Early planning and experimentation to determine which services lend themselves particularly to broadband techniques and to identify opportunities — and perhaps problems — involved with the sharing of facilities should be encouraged.

How and by whom the interconnection of local distribution systems is accomplished can have a tremendous effect on the system's flexibility and its ultimate utility to the user. Not only are there competing technologies for the interconnection task, but also competing entities. Some hard choices will have to be made. You should be involved in those choices.

As with the potential and promise of broadband transmission systems, the difficulty of the problems involved and the decisions to be reached are only beginning to be recognized outside the communications fraternity. The Federal Communications Commission, in particular, must address a number of knotty problems which will affect the composition and structure of the BCN. Interlarded with the FCC's interest are the ambiguous and often contradictory regulatory policies of some state and local governments. For example, unwise local franchising policies may stifle or misdirect CATV and BCN growth, and prolong the period we must wait for the promised benefits of broadband systems. As a matter of fact, franchising agreements already have become a political question in at least one major city.

Probably more than at any time in the past, it is essential that "interested publics" keep a watchful eye on telecommunications policy to ensure that broadband systems develop in a competitive, innovative, and orderly manner. Of prime importance — experimentation should be encouraged in order to exploit maximum benefit from broadband communication technology.

SUMMARY

Broad bandwidth transmission systems have been around for years. They include microwave, assorted cable systems, and recently, satellites. With the exception of some privately owned systems, broadband services have been furnished by the common carriers.

Recently, a new element has been added — CATV distribution systems. The "excess" channels available in CATV systems are seen as an answer for the demand for capacity to transmit large amounts of information.

There are some difficulties in utilizing CATV systems as currently configured for two-way communications, but the difficulties seem small when compared to the tremendous benefits which can and should accrue from the interaction of broadband communications and advanced terminal developments.

"Interested publics" should watch closely telecommunications developments — particularly regulatory developments — to attempt to escape mistakes of the past and to ensure close coupling between communications innovations and their beneficial use.

NOTES

1. Electronic Industries Association, Industrial Electronics Division, *The future of broadband communications.* In response to FCC Docket 18397, Part v, 29 October 1969.

Compatibility Problems of Network Interfacing

Mary Elizabeth Stevens

INTRODUCTION

In the early 1960s, the National Bureau of Standards, with the support of the National Science Foundation, prepared and issued a special literature review on *Cooperation, Compatibility, and Convertibility Among Information Systems*.[1] Of these "three Cs," the greatest was and is still *cooperation,* which has had a long and healthy history in the library community.

From the standpoint of information network technology, however, there is a necessary emphasis upon compatibility requirements which, in turn, will be met at least in part by various techniques of achieving convertibility — between machine and machine, between man and machine, and between man and man. It may be hoped that improved compatibilities between machines and between men and machines will lead to more effective man-to-man communications.

In general, the compatibility problems in network planning and implementation are precisely those of interface and interchange. If we take the long view, then certainly these problems are not new. If we define an *information management system*[2] as emphasizing not only listing or retrieval by category but also the explicit identification of the individual record (including information on its location and availability) and as providing individual record retrievability, then, again, the interfacing problems are not new.

However, at least two major factors are new under the sun of the 1970s. These are, first, the formalization of information exchange networks[3] and secondly, the emergence of teleprocessing technology, the "marriage"[4] of computers and communications.

THE STATE OF THE ART

The new technologies are literally forcing a new look at our problems of compatibility. At the same time, these technologies offer new opportunities and new aids for the solution of some of the problems. Among the obvious requirements for compatibility are questions of compliance with applicable standards — the development of mutually acceptable conventions of description, documentation, access, and accounting, and the adoption of preferred common practices.

The compatibility problems at the many points and the many levels of interfacing are manifold, and many of them are unprecedented. In particular, the types of interface to be encountered in the teleprocessing situation present special problems, ranging from the technological (the possible use of adaptive modems) to the sociopolitical and the economic (differential tariffs for intrastate versus interstate communications).

Nevertheless, the literature pertinent to compatibility requirements in network is surprisingly extensive and highly diversified. The 1966 study on cooperation, compatibility, and convertibility cited 600 references, and a bibliography of 469 references is included in a report to the National Library of Medicine. The topics range from standardization (including published standards) through communications (e.g., the FCC Inquiry on Computers and Communications) and descriptive cataloging (the MARC II format) to management control requirements (e.g., charging and pricing policies).

However, very little of this literature is directly addressed to compatibility problems in *network interfacing*. Notable exceptions of course include some of the available standards themselves (ASCII code, MARC II, microfiche, and signaling speeds, in particular), the EDUNET studies,[5] the emphasis on the interface message processor (IMP) in the ARPA network,[6] the Auerbach studies for the National Agricultural Library,[7] and the 1968 paper by Little and Mooers,[8] among others. In a few cases, the state of the practice in specific situations has been described — for example, some of the solutions to incompatibility in the MEDLARS system for magnetic tape interchange.[9]

Becker and Olsen, reviewing the 1967 literature, state that: "Much was written on the virtues of connecting smaller information networks to larger ones, but no blueprint is yet available that outlines how compatibility is to be achieved."[10]

These authors emphasize the following problem areas:

1.   Critical questions of standardization

2.   Copyright requirements

Contribution of the National Bureau of Standards, based upon a study of standardization, compatibility, and convertibility requirements in network planning, conducted for the Lister Hill National Center for Biomedical Communications.

3.   Privacy safeguards

4.   Costs and economic justifications

5.   Social acceptance

6.   Present or potential regulatory policies and
      practices

7.   International implications.

In general, the problems of information are so new and so complex that a state-of-the-art assessment of compatibility requirements for interfacing is not yet possible. Nevertheless, compliance with established standards, rules, codes, conventions, and protocols for each and every interface situation in any real or prospective network is the first prerequisite for good management planning and effective management control. A second prerequisite is that of developing appropriate compromises (technological, managerial, and sociopolitical) in the design of network processes, procedures, and most importantly, policies. The third and most significant prerequisite is that of adequate responsiveness to the challenges (both implicit and explicit) in the "marriage" of computers and communication systems to the development of truly efficacious "networks for knowledge."

STANDARDIZATION

The first compatibility requirement to be considered is that of compliance with current standards. These are mostly of a voluntary nature, whether promulgated at the national level (e.g., the American National Standards Institute, ANSI[11]) or the international (the Internations Standards Organization, ISO), by professional societies such as the American Library Association or by special interest organizations such as the Council on Scientific and Technical Information, COSATI. However, the emergence of the Federal Information Processing Standards, FIPS, program especially is to be noted.

It is to be emphasized that "a 'standard' is a mutually agreed upon method for referring to or describing the essential aspects of some object or some action of common interest,"[12] and that a standard is an agreement "by which the design, performance, and other characteristics of products, processes, services and systems are described"[13] rather than an arbitrary rule or constraint. It is to be recognized further that standardization of the many and varied types of data elements, formats, languages, and procedures that already exist is generally impossible and probably undesirable so that current standardization efforts emphasize description, interchange, and the problems of effective interfacing.

In general, standards are voluntary standards, arrived at cooperatively. For the federal community, however, mandatory information processing standards are authorized under the Brooks Bill (P.L.18-306) of 1966. Some ten or more Federal Information Processing Standards have been issued as of the date of this Conference. The FIPS are binding, with the exception of the meeting of appropriate waiver requirements,

upon all federal agencies and importantly, upon contractors and grantees supported by federal agency funds. Thus, for informationmanagement networks that will have U.S. government participation or federally sponsored participants, supported in whole or in part by such funds, these standardization requirements must be faced.

Most of the FIPS that have been promulgated to date have to do with standard representations of data elements such as calendar date, counties of the United States, and the like. Three, however, directly affect network interfacing requirements. These three involve the Code for Information Interchange, ASCII, and its representation on perforated tapes and on magnetic tapes. These FIPS adopt the corresponding ANSI voluntary standards (X3.4-1967, X3.4-1968, X3.6-1965, and X3.22-1967).

Although these FIPS requirements are binding only upon federal agencies and upon federally supported potential contributors to and participants in an information-management network, it is to be stressed particularly that the standards are directed specifically to *interface* and information *interchange* — leaving considerable latitude for local procedures and practices to continue as they now are or to be adapted as necessary. For example: "This standard will be prescribed for the interchange of formatted machine sensible coded data between and among agencies. Use within agency systems is encouraged when such use contributes to operational benefits, efficiency or economy."

Additional FIPS currently under development and likely to affect compatibility requirements at network interfaces include the following (the corresponding American National Standards designation are given as appropriate):

1.   Signaling speeds for data transmission (X3.1-1962)

2.   Parallel signaling speeds for data transmission
      (X3.13-1966)

3.   Specifications for general purpose paper cards for
      information processing (X3.11-1966)

4.   Time-sharing and remote console considerations

5.   Hardware interfaces

6.   Recorded magnetic tape for information
      interchange (X3.14-1969)

7.   Bit sequencing of the ASCII in serial-by-bit data
      transmission (X3.15-1966)

8.   Signal quality at interface between data processing
      terminal equipment and synchronous data
      communication equipment for serial data
      transmission (X3.24-1966).

It will be noted that with the sole exception of the area of time-sharing and remote consoles, the standardization considerations are strictly directed to the interfaces between machine and machine. Similar emphasis is to be found in the work of many of the sectional committees of ANSI: X3, Computers and Information Processing; X4, Office Machines; PH5, Photocopying; and PH7, Photographic Audio-Visual Standards.

Both man-machine and man-man interfaces are involved, however, in the work of ANSI's Section Committee Z39, Library Work and Documentation and Related Publishing Practices. Current voluntary standards developed by this committee are:

1.   Z39.1-1967, Periodicals (corresponds to the international standard ISO R8)

2.   Z39.4-1968, Basic Criteria for Indexes

3.   Z39.5-1963, Periodical Title Abbreviations

4.   Z39.6-1965, Specifications for Trade Catalogs

5.   Z39.7-1968, Compiling Library Statistics

6.   Z39.8-1968, Compiling Book Statistics.

Most important from the standpoint of compatibility requirements in information center and library networks, however, is the current work on the adoption as a voluntary national standard of the format for bibliographic information interchange on magnetic tape. The draft of the proposed American National Standard contains as an appendix: "Preliminarily Guidelines for the Library of Congress, National Library of Medicine, and National Agricultural Library Implementation of the Proposed American Standard for a Format for Bibliographic Information Interchange on Magnetic Tape as Applied to Records Representing Monographic Materials in Textual Printed Form (Books)." This, of course, the implementation of the MARC (*MA*chine-*R*eadable *C*ataloging) II format.

The following points are to be noted:

1.   If adopted, the proposed ANSI standard will undoubtedly be considered for adoption as a Federal Information Processing Standard and thus, would become mandatory for federal components of an information network.

2.   By mutual agreement, the proposed ANSI standard in the MARC II implementation is being followed by the three national libraries in exchange of monograph information amongst themselves.

3.   The MARC II implementation is in use by the Library of Congress for the weekly distribution service of LC cataloging on magnetic tapes. The RECON (*RE*trospective *CON*version) Pilot Project provides for the

conversion of retrospective cataloging records to this format.

4.   A second implementation of the proposed standard has been developed for the technical report literature by Panel 1, COSATI.

5.   As stated in the American National Standards Institute draft, Z39.2-1968: "This standard defines a format which is intended for the *interchange* of bibliographic records on magnetic tape. It has not been designed as a record format for retention within the files of any specific organization. Nor has it been the intent of the subcommittee to define the content of individual records. Rather it has attempted to describe a generalized structure which can be used to transmit between systems, records describing all forms of material capable of bibliographic descriptions as well as related records such as authority records for authors and subject headings." Thus, the adoption of this standard need not require feasibility modification of in-house programs and procedures, provided that general conversion programs (from and to the standard format) can be developed, that adequate documentation of deviations or specialized usages are made available for the use of others.

6.   The proposed standard is highly flexible and character oriented and therefore, machine- or program-language independent.

The four major intended characteristics of the format are, in the words of its principal developer, as follows:

1.   "It establishes the means by which bibliographic information may be transmitted between libraries."

2.   "It describes the rigorous rules by which bibliographic information, available in human-readable form, may be converted to machine-readable form."

3.   "It suggests that if the same format is used for the exchange of information by all libraries, programs and procedures may be exchanged and automation costs reduced."

4.   "It follows the...[ANSI] Code for Information Interchange (ASCII), the Standard Recorded Magnetic Tape for Information Interchange, and the proposed Standard for Magnetic Tape Labels and File Structure."[14]

A wide variety of other standards have been developed at various levels such as the international (UNISIST, the Joint ICSO-UNESCO feasibility study looking toward a worldwide system for the handling of scientific information; various standards of the International Standards Organization including ISO R9-1955, International System for the Transliteration of Cyrillic Characters; the International Electrotechnical Commission; the NATO Automated Data Handling Working Party and the F.I.D., for example) or the institutional (Council on Library Resources, American Library Association, National Microfilm Association, COSATI, and the Conference on Data System Languages, CODASYL, among many others).

In general, compliance with standards as appropriate to an information network, where "more than two participants are engaged in a common pattern of information exchange through communications for some functional purpose,"[15] poses a wide variety of compatibility requirements; on the other hand, compliance with standards offers considerable promise for the resolution of interfacing problems.

MACHINE-MACHINE COMPATIBILITY PROBLEMS

From a technological standpoint, the machine-machine type of interface is, of course, the most tractable. There are, equally obviously, many severe compatibility problems with respect to communication links, the communication systems as such, data access arrangements, buffering requirements, internal processing, programming languages, multiprocessing, multiplexing, physical materials, and media. The broad areas of requirements for compatibility or convertibility between machines involve:

1. Data transmission, with emphasis upon information interchange but also including major considerations of differential speeds and costs

2. Input/output equipment

3. Reprography, specifically including microform technologies

4. Other information storage equipments and media, including magnetic tapes, magnetic disks, and video tapes

5. Machine interaction, including problems of scheduling and routing, resources allocation and reallocation, queue management, programming languages and program documentation, and especially, linkages between processors of different types.

Considering the terminology "through communications" as essential in the Becker and Olsen definition of information networks previously given, we begin with the data transmission area. Compatibility problems arise with respect to both common carrier and non-common carrier services and practices, with respect to reformatting and transformation requirements, and with respect to interface message processing and network buffering, among other factors.

Compatibility problems are likely to arise in network interfacing with regard to such communication questions as the following:

1. What facilities and services (such as the public switched network, leased lines, closed circuit TV, facsimile transmission, microwave communication links, satellite services) are available at *each* node of the network? For example, to what extent could present or expanded educational TV networks be included in the system?

2. What are the applicable tariffs and regulatory provisions for each data link or communication service between nodes, and what are the comparative costs, performance factors, and reliabilities for each type of link or service for each connection requirement?

3. What stand-by and emergency links and services are required? To the extent required, will they be available freely or must they be planned and paid for in advance of actual use?

4. What are the switching facilities and requirements at local nodes, for clusters of nodes, and throughout the network?

5. What *differential* transmission rates, signaling speeds, line conditioning provisions, interface devices, and similar factors are likely to be involved?

From the standpoint of many of these technical considerations it is to be emphasized that:

The important characteristics of data transmission are: the speed of transmission, the transmission method used (whether synchronous or asynchronous), the character coding, the order of transmission of bits for each character, and the usage of control characters and procedures. Conditions now exist that point to a need for uniform standards.

1. "The increasing proliferation of data transmission equipment and need for compatibility"

2. "The tendency of the federal government towards a unified set of data processing standards."

3. "The projected future growth of EDP in...[national systems] and the need to integrate with other systems, local or statewide."[16]

It is to be noted particularly that compatibility problems are at the heart of the "foreign attachment" controversies. First came the significant FCC decision reversing the Bell Telephone Company's previous arbitrary exclusion of customer-provided interface equipment from being interconnected with the public network[17] and requiring that the burden of proof of *in*compatibility should rest with the carrier rather than with the client. More recently there have been questions of the compatibility or lack of compatibility of intrastate and interstate tariffs, especially for "information service access lines."[18]

The most recent development in the foreign attachments area is the establishment of a National Academy of Sciences panel to hold hearings, to arrange informal conferences for interested parties, and to prepare recommendations for FCC decision. Among the issues to be considered are problems of network control signal equipment, interface requirements, transmission quality, and protection mechanisms.

With respect to tariffs and regulatory provisions affecting compatibility problems in information network interfacing generally, it is to be noted that "the success of the planning of the three national libraries in the area of networking depends upon the careful revision of the Federal regulatory policy."[19] Further, the FCC Inquiry on the Interdependence of Computer and Communication Services and Facilities raised the following questions: "(1) the extent of regulation if any, of the computer industry, including questions as to whether carrier and computer entities should provide service in each other's area; (2) the adequacy of carrier services and facilities, including possible new bases for charges; and (3) the protection of privacy and security of data, while stored in computer memory and during transmission over common carrier facilities."[20]

Among the responses to the inquiry, as analyzed by a study team at Stanford Research Institute, some that are pertinent to compatibility requirements for information networks are as follows:

1. "A need for data on error performance and circuit characteristics with respect to amplitude and delay...A need for standards with respect to circuit reliability and transmission quality...A need for reduction in the variability of transmission performance in the public switched networks..."

2. "Interconnection of users' computer interface equipment, communications links and systems with carriers' systems should be permitted, subject only to well-defined technical standards to protect the integrity of carriers' systems."

3. "Data on system error performance should be published so that the data processing industry can develop appropriate error protection systems."

4. "The variability of data transmission performance on the public switched network should be reduced."

5. "The variability of intrastate tariffs and services among the states should be reduced."[21]

Compatibility requirements for the communications system or systems for an information network considered as a whole are first directed to questions of organizational structure: centralized, partially centralized, or distributed. In the fully centralized case, compatibility problems of interfacing are usually amenable to relatively straightforward resolution.

A partially centralized network is exemplified by a system of interconnected regional centers, each serving a number of separate nodes. The partially centralized system is typically a multipoint network, raising serious questions of optimizing the many possible configurations.[22] Regional centralization techniques may extend down to the "cluster" concept.[23]

The organizational principle of distribution may affect either the physical structure of the network or the routing of message traffic or both. Thus, "by a distributed implementation of an information service system we mean that the data processing activity is carried out by several or many installations....The data base is now distributed among the installations making up the information network....The distributed information network should offer considerable advantage in reducing the cost of terminal communications by permitting installations to be located near concentrations of terminals."[24] It is further claimed that: "The concept of distributed data bases and distributed access to the data is one of the most powerful and useful applications of the [ARPA] network."[25]

For highly distributed systems the compatibility problems obviously include the questions of the types of processing to be performed at stations at each given level and of the accounting and reporting to be required at successively higher levels.

Other compatibility problems in linking computers and communications systems in an information network involve questions of circuit switching as against message switching; synchronous and parallel modes of transmission; simplex, half-duplex, or full-duplex lines and data sets. It may be assumed that an information network for the handling of recorded knowledge will require both analog (voice, facsimile) and digital data transmission.

A proper balancing of cost, speed, and distance considerations in the choice of specific communication facilities (narrowband, voiceband, broadband, and other services) must be achieved. Nevertheless, "it must be noted that not all of the various kinds of channels and methods of transmission are available to the data customer on an off-the-shelf basis. Not all bandwidths are available in every part of the country."[26]

Since the information network undoubtedly will involve participation and cooperation by individuals, systems, and institutions in other countries, compatibility difficulties with respect to international communications standards and procedures must be considered. Thus: "To change analog signals into digital form, European Countries, for example, follow a different coding law than the U.S. and Japan. As things stand now, the prospects for agreement have to be rated as poor. Moreover, the English handle 24 voice channels on a single line as do the Americans and Japanese, but the Europeans bundle 30 together. And some countries code analog samples into seven binary digits, others into eight."[27]

Compatibility problems with respect to communications format occur at at least three levels: that of character set, e.g., ASCII; that of composition format, "concerned with the arrangement of the data and is the space allotted to them within the message";[28] and that of physical format involving the physical structure of the information signals.

In particular:

Wherever there is an interface between equipments collecting information and those transmitting it, between two types of transmitting equipment, or among transmitting equipments and receptors, a facet of the formatting problem occurs. The formats chosen have a strong effect upon the design and interfacing equipments and therefore upon the capabilities of the information handling system, and the delays incurred in passing through it. Thus, the solution of...format problems will have far from negligible effects upon the economics of providing an information handling system, its capabilities, and its response times."[29]

Compatibility or convertibility at various communication interfaces (originators, distributors, receivers) will be required for some or all of the following:

1.   Conversions, as to and from analog and digital or serial and parallel

2.   Message blocking and message segmentation, particularly in terms of standardized packets

3.   Message elements, including headings, ID information, information separators, function effectors (e.g., control characters)

4.   Escape coding and privacy transformations

5.   Error detection and correction requirements, including procedures for the recovery of missing or garbled messages.

The control procedures as such require standardization or at least, established rules or conventions governing network-wide usage. In a proposed ANSI standard for data control procedures using ASCII for information interchange, a number of categories of control procedures are defined. Functions presently covered include polling of the different stations, identification, contention, selection, framing of messages and transmission blocks, replies to messages or blocks, invalid or no reply situations, termination, and mandatory disconnection. Also to be considered are preemption, interrupt, and abort functions; handling of "transparent mode" messages, and system timing and synchronization requirements.

Convertibility as a solution to reformatting, retransmission, and error checking problems may be achieved both by the adoption of appropriate protocols and by combined software-hardware techniques, as in interface message processors. Some examples of protocol considerations are as follows:

1.   "Communications protocol here refers to the uniform agreed-upon manner of exchanging messages....This includes data link control, acknowledgments and error recovery procedures. It may also include message buffering and routing techniques....A single standard procedure may not be practical because of varying needs of different systems and discrepancies in their hardware/software characteristics. Operation could be synchronous or asynchronous, full duplex or half duplex, point-to-point or multipoint, centralized or decentralized, and over private line, switched network, or a general network environment employing store-and-forward routing techniques. In many of the above cases, the protocol needs would differ, and hence the procedures adopted would vary."[30]

2.   "It is proposed that there would be an agreed-upon standard control signal which will cause any cooperating automated system to go into the standard mode. This stratagem will allow local parochial control methods to live side-by-side in more or less harmony with whatever standard control methods that may be established. Each automated system can then be receptive to the basic command "go into standard mode" with a minimal burden upon the rest of its operation."[31]

3.   "It would appear that it should be an EDUCOM responsibility to standardize on-line communications up to the interface with the members, and that the members should have the responsibility of meeting these standards through acceptance of them or through local translators into alternative local systems."[32]

4.   "...The establishment by the network controlling body of universal standards to which all nodes must conform. Thus a message arriving at or leaving any node would appear identical, requiring two (or more) routines (unless the local standard was the universal standard) at each node to convert between the standard local. There would probably have to be more than one standard (e.g., ASCII for messages, a standard for boundary conditions to routines, and a standard for requesting of execution and storage facilities on other nodes)."[33]

5.   "...The establishment of a message protocol, by which we mean a uniform agreed-upon manner of exchanging messages between two computers in the network."[34]

6. "For a large-scale party-line (multidrop) network, provisions should be made to maintain a network discipline that will ensure increased system efficiency as well as dependable service."[35]

Other compatibility problems related to protocols and network discipline include the following:

1. Compatible entry and access controls must be provided, including the identification and authentication of authorized terminals, authorized users, and authorized destinees.

2. Buffering requirements at sender, relay, receiver, and processors stations. For example, at receiver terminals or other sinks, the necessary refresh-rate controls, reformatting capabilities, and code conversion facilities must be considered.

3. Routing requirements also must be considered, including types of routing, addressing schemes, and provisions for traffic control.

Typically, such compatibility requirements demand the use of some degree of interface message processing. For example, differential signaling speeds and rates of information transfer usually require the use of speed-change mechanisms.

Solution of compatibility problems for network interface buffering generally will provide:

1. Intermediary message processing capabilities (in particular, the transliteration or transformation of encodings, or formats, or modes of interchange such as analog/digital, or rates of data transfer) to meet specific requirements of immediate interchange, retransmission, or local use

2. Retransmission without substantive change other than, for example, signal amplification or error correction to one or more next-addresses

3. Determination of best or next-best routings under normal, overload, and emergency-priority conditions

4. Collection and recording of management accounting and control information

5. Substantive modifications to the contents of messages or files

6. Management of feedback information.

Specific buffering requirements arise in the clustering of local stations or consoles and in displaying processing at remote terminals. Further, "there is a growing awareness that display buffers should, in fact, be small general purpose computers, which opens up a whole new spectrum of possibilities in properly assigning tasks within the overall system."[36]

Logical design considerations with respect to terminal compatibility in network interfacing relate to character sets and information transfer rates, to control functions and control codes and keys, and to data and format convertibility. Engineering design considerations range from questions of ambient lighting and design of keyboards (including the use of overlays which may be of particular interest in terms of specialized local usage) to those of interfacing with the communication system, with local processor facilities, and with other processors.

It is to be noted that different terminals for output and display that are available commercially are not usually compatible with one another. Often a CRT display terminal is not compatible with teletype transmission requirements either; yet, many potential patrons of the network services will be dependent upon teletype rather than more sophisticated and more costly output and display equipment.

The spectrum of terminal equipment to be expected at network interfaces will include:

1. Keyboard entry devices, single-stroke and multiple-stroke

2. Keyboard devices with subsequent conversion by means of optical character recognition or stenotype decoding

3. Hand-entry devices such as light pens

4. Display consoles for alphanumeric and graphic information, with or without hard-copy or microform print-out options

5. Printers, both on-line and off-line, with or without typographic quality capabilities

6. Direct computer-output-to-microform (COM).

In the case of graphic display equipment, some of the questions of compatibility concern are the X-Y plotting capabilities, the image-manipulation facilities (including rotation, translation, change of scale, blow-ups, contrast enhancement, perspective projection, shading), and the availability of hard-copy options, among other factors.

In the case of microforms, there are questions of the number of page images to be placed on a microfiche or an ultrafiche, of reduction ratios, and of reproducibility (i.e., how many copy-generations can be produced with adequate readability and contrast). For ultrafiche, in particular, the technological factors requiring standardization or compatibility considerations include the effects of size, contrast, handling of media, and resolution on the control of access and retrieval, and on the usefulness of the microcopy, especially at very high reduction ratios.

In general, *mixtures* of output modalities will pose serious compatibility problems in planning for network interfacing. Mayeda points out that, with the exception of some military applications, most information processing systems have been "single path," but that the newly emerging network requirements will demand "the mixing of normally incompatible media into one information transfer system."[37]

MAN-MACHINE COMPATIBILITY PROBLEMS

While the general compatibility problems between and amongst machines are reasonably tractable and are beginning to yield both to hardware and software developments for more effective convertibility in interfacing and also to standardization efforts, the interfaces between man and machine present both more fundamental and also more difficult challenges. The man-machine compatibility problems occur at three major levels:

1. The individual and the specific machine component of the network

2. The individual and the network system

3. The community or communities of users and the system.

Consideration of the compatibility problems of man-machine interaction obviously should begin (and always return to) the ultimate interface — that between the *user* and the network services provided to him. Thus, there is first the thorny question of user requirements. Shall we ever be able to assess objectively what our users (or patrons, or clients) really want and what they really need? (A basic difficulty in terms of resolving this problem is, of course, that "wanting" and "needing" often have no correlation.) From a technological point of view, we can obviously leave some of the more severe problems actually involved at the user interface to others (including users themselves).

The compatibility problems of network users begin first, of course, with the problems of accessibility — from physical access to ease of use of system facilities and resources, and ease of *learning* to use them.

Who requires direct physical access, *when, where,* and *for what purposes* to terminals, microform viewers, hard copy of books, documents, and records? Is the computer room at a major processing node accessible only to "authorized personnel"? How often are requested items off the shelves? What happens when all the lines are busy or a massive power failure occurs?

Next we may consider the user's physical interaction. Here the areas of compatibility involve on the one hand his interests, habits, attitudes, and expectancies, and on the other hand, the physiological constraints such as flicker-rate acceptability, reaction time, reading time. "How clumsy are light pens or pointers to use? Are they heavy or difficult to aim? Should light-pen inputs be displayed a little to the left or to the right of the actual light-pen location so that the active part of the input is not blocked from view by the moving light-pen itself? ....For graphic input and display should the input surface be flat, upright, or slanted?"[38]

What are the compatibility problems for the individual user in actual use of various types of terminals at various nodes of the teleprocessing network? Standard mode of access and use procedures are required to tackle such problems as programmable format control, switching from one character set to another, and a minimum set of logical control functions, mutually agreed-upon, which will in turn influence keyboard layouts. The user needs to know whether he is actually connected and how he is to query or otherwise use the system.

Motivational factors in man-machine compatibility involve the acceptability of the equipment itself[39] and the acceptability of system performance including quality and legibility of outputs and displays and particularly, speed of response.

Scherr has emphasized that "the response time of the system to a line of input from the user is an important parameter of a time-shared system. In fact it is one of the few, well-defined, measurable performance parameters available. This response time determines the basic rate at which the user can operate."[40] Further, a major distinction must be made between *actually* adequate and *apparently* adequate response times.[41]

Finally, with respect to individual interaction with system components and subsystems, there are problems of the languages. "It has been estimated that the number of time-sharing installations is roughly equal to the number of languages offered among them."[42]

At the level of individual interaction with the network as a whole, it is necessary to know for each and every contributing node:

1. Precise and accurate identification of its capabilities

2. Precise and complete descriptions of the nature, format, scope, etc., of its holdings and other resources

3. Full and complete documentation of procedures, programs, etc., as necessary for interactive use

4. Specifications of applicable local arrangements, protocols, and requirements.

It is necessary for the user to comply with system protocols, information interchange requirements, and management and control policies (including priorities, resource allocation, pricing, accounting, audit trail, and performance evaluation requirements). Requirements for the identification and authentication of legitimate users and legitimate usages of network resources are obvious.

Some specific compatibility questions are as follows:

1. How do we guarantee authorized, but only authorized, access to privileged files and privileged information?

2.   How do we resolve priority and scheduling conflicts?

3.   How do we handle abuses or misuses, inadvertent or otherwise, of network resources and services?

It is necessary for the network management to know who the users are, to gather usage statistics, to monitor user performance, and to provide training and retraining facilities as required. There is apparently an appalling dearth of systematic, empirical data with respect to user *effectiveness*.[43]

1.   How is user performance to be monitored and appraised?

2.   What are the initial training requirements? (The "riding-circuit" procedures of the North Carolina Educational Computing Service may be of interest here.)[44]

3.   What retraining facilities could be made available to member nodes where user inefficiencies can be observed?

Man-machine compatibility requirements at the level of community interactions with the system involve, primarily, the diversity of clienteles to be served and the variety of services to be provided, recognizing that:

"The information needs of scientists, engineers, and practitioners vary markedly with the nature of their numerous types and combinations of responsibilities, such as design, development, teaching, basic research, administration, and marketing."[45]

A special challenge is posed to the information science community itself:

"Individuals across the many disciplines that contribute to information science must cooperate in the development and use of common data forms and procedures, despite the requirements of their special interests. Also, effective logistics must be developed for the distribution of data to core centers and the transmission of data to core centers and the transmission of data from centers to satellites.[46]

CONCLUSIONS

Compatibility problems at the machine-machine and man-machine interfaces are indeed critical and urgent, especially in the context of teleprocessing networks, but the frequently neglected issues of man-to-man interface present the most significant, difficult, and challenging problems of all.

The challenges of man-man communications (including the new possibilities of interchange between any one machine-as-sisted-man with another) lie principally in the areas of; direct human intercommunication; improved utilization of recorded information, especially with respect to the scientific and technical literature; requirements for natural language text processing, and inevitably, the problems of knowing, of knowledge itself.

From the technological standpoint, however, we may conclude that the new technologies are literally forcing a new look at our problems of compatibility — at the same time these technologies offer new opportunities and new aids for the solution of some of the problems.

Resolution of man-communications-processor interface problems will range from the sociopolitical or economic problems of the "computer utility" and "of copyrights and patents" to the actual design of improved modems.

Four current trends are to be noted. The first is that of the *conspicuity* of the compatibility problems as such. It was said of the COSATI microfiche standards that: "For the first time the federal government is on a standard before too many non-compatible systems get started."[47] A second trend is toward increasing *compromise*.

Compromise necessarily involves both systems and society. What are the specific needs for interface message processing and for normalization and standardization in information interchange? What, on the other hand, are the real requirements for the protection of the individual, in general, from the individual, in particular? More specifically, compromise involves:

1.   Emphasis upon interchange

2.   Emphasis upon versatile "black boxes" at interfaces

3.   Agreement upon standardized descriptions

4.   Agreement upon standardized documentation requirements

5.   Agreement upon protocols of interface and interchange, and for overall network management, control, and evaluation.

In general, "A network must impose a series of constraints in order to operate, but it also allows for the flexibility that a rigidly structured system cannot accommodate. A network also fosters a sense of competition in which each community must ever strive to reorient itself in order to survive and progress in its changing environment. In addition, each must become sensitive to the changes in the other communities in order that it may react, re-evaluate and adapt to the new set of goals that are inevitable."[48]

A third current trend is that of increasing *commitment* to the use of machines as aids, or even as alternatives, to man in problem-solving, decisionmaking, and the maintenance of appropriate checks and balances in social, economic, and political areas (medical data interpretation and diagnosis, novelty searching in the case of patent applications, relief of the creative artist or engineer of innumerable tedious tasks of routine design, air traffic control, and the like).

Fourth, but not least, is the continuing trend toward increasing *cooperation*. There remain a number of unresolved problems and difficulties. For example:

1. How is greater collaboration and cooperation to be achieved? By fiat? By charging-policy advantages and penalties? By salesmanship? (And if so, how?)

2. What can we do about convertibility for the "underprivileged" or the "disadvantaged" or the "underdeveloped"?

Nevertheless, the solution of tractable compatibility problems in network interfacing should promote the more effective collaboration and cooperation throughout the computer science, information science, and library communities. We may conclude that "the little that has been done to this time is only the earnest of what is yet to come"[49]

NOTES

1. Madeline M. Henderson, et al., *Cooperation, compatibility and convertibility among information systems,* (Washington, D.C.: National Bureau of Standards, 1966).

2. The information management system in contrast to "management information systems," which are designed to provide managerial, accounting, and statistical data for a variety of policy, planning, auditing, billing, and evaluation purposes.

3. P. J. Paulson, "Networks, automation and technical services: experience and experiments in New York State," *Library resources & technical services* 13:516 (Fall 1969) and Saul Herner, "The place of the small library in the national network," *Journal of chemical documentation* 6:171 (Jan. 1966).

4. Joseph Becker, "How library automation will influence new building plans," in S. R. Salmon, ed., *Library automation - a state of the arts review* (Chicago: ALA, 1969). p.30.

5. G. W. Brown, et al., *EDUNET - report of the summer study on information networks* (New York, Wiley, 1967).

6. C. S. Carr, et al., "HOST - HOST communication protocol in the ARPA network," L. G. Roberts and B. D. Wessler, "Computer network development to achieve resource sharing," in *AFIPS proceedings Spring Joint Computer Conference, vol. 36* (Montvale, N.J.: AFIPS Pr., 1970), p.589-97, 543-49.

7. G. Cadwallader, et al., *Formal compatibility and conversion among bibliographic data bases* (Technical report no. 1582-100-TR-7 [Philadelphia: Auerbach Corp., 1969]) and H. B. Landau, "Research study into the effective utilization of machine-readable bibliographic data bases," in J. B. North, ed., *Proceedings of American Society for Information Science 32nd annual meeting, vol. 6* (Westport, Conn.: Greenwood Pub. Corp., 1969), p.101-04.

8. J. L. Little and Calvin N. Mooers, "Standards for user procedures and data formats in automated information systems and networks," in *AFIPS proceedings Spring Joint Computer Conference vol. 32* (Washington, D.C.: Thompson Book Co., 1968), p.89-94.

9. C. J. Austin, *MEDLARS 1963-1967* (Washington, D.C.: Gov. Print. Off., 1968).

10. Joseph Becker and Wallace C. Olsen, "Information Networks," in C. A. Cuadra, ed., *Annual review of information science, vol. 3* (Chicago: Britannica, 1968), p.318.

11. Formerly the United States of America Standards Institute and before that, the American Standards Association.

12. Calvin N. Mooers, *Standards for user procedures and data formats in automated information systems and networks, part 1, The need for standardization and the manner in which standardization can be accomplished* (unpublished report, 5 July 1967), p.1.

13. C. J. Rothwell, "The performance concept: a basis for standards development," reprint from *ASTME vectors* 2:1 (1969).

14. Henriette D. Avram, "Using computer technology - frustrations abound," in *AFIPS proceedings Spring Joint Computer Conference, vol. 34* (Montvale, N.J.: AFIPS Pr., 1969), p.43.

15. Joseph Becker and Wallace C. Olsen, "Information networks," p.289.

16. M. S. Colah and R. W. Strunk, *Civil defense communication studies: data transmission standards* (Menlo Park, Calif.: Stanford Research Institute, 1969), p.v.

17. K. A. Cox, "Carterfone and the computer utility," *Law and computer technology* 2:3 (April 1969).

18. *Datamation* 16:165 (Jan. 1970).

19. L. G. Livingston, "Computer utilities and the three national libraries" (preprint of paper prepared for the *Symposium on the computer utility - implications for higher education,* Manchester, N.H. 5-7 May 1969), p.2.

20. K. A. Cox, "Carterfone and the computer utility," p.4.

21. D. A. Dunn, *Policy issues presented by the interdependence of computer and communications services (Report no. 7379B-1 [Menlo Park, Calif.: Stanford Research Institute, 1969]), p.47.*

22. L. I. Krause, *Analysis of policy issues in the responses to the FCC computer inquiry* (Report no. 7379B-2 [Menlo Park, Calif.: Stanford Research Institute, 1969]), p.53 and L. R. Esau and K. C. Williams, "On teleprocessing system design, part II - a method for approximating the optimal network," *IBM systems journal* 5:144 (1966).

23. R. L. Simms, Jr., "Trends in computer/communication systems," *Computers & automation* 17:23 (May 1968).

24. J. B. Dennis, "A position paper on computing and communications," *Communications of the ACM* 11:37 (May 1968).

25. L. G. Roberts and B. D. Wessler, "Computer network development to achieve resource sharing," in *AFIPS proceedings Spring Joint Computer Conference, vol. 36* (Montvale, N.J.: AFIPS Pr., 1970), p.548.

26. H. J. McMains and G. L. Bromleigh, Jr., "Telephony and the library," paper prepared for the *Conference on Image Storage and Transmission Systems for Libraries,* Gaithersburg, Md., 1-2 Dec. 1969, p.4. (unpublished)

27. W. Bucci, "PCM: a global scramble for systems compatibility," *Electronics* 42:94 (23 June 1969).

28. D. C. Friedman, *Global information handling system - aspects of the formatting problems* (unpublished report, National Bureau of Standards, Nov. 1963), p.3.

29. *Ibid.,* p.1.

30. A. K. Bhushan and R. H. Stotz, "Procedures and standards for inter-computer communications," in *AFIPS proceedings Spring Joint Computer Conference, vol. 32,* p.102.

31. J. L. Little and C. N. Mooers, *Standards for user procedures...,* p.9-10.

32. G. W. Brown, et al., *EDUNET...,* p.172-173.

33. Ibid., p.251.

34. T. Marill and L. G. Roberts, "Toward a cooperative network of time-shared computers," in *AFIPS proceedings Fall Joint Computer Conference, vol. 29* (Washington, D.C.: Spartan Books 1966), p.428.

35. H. Liu and D. W. Holmes, "Teleprocessing systems software for a large corporate information system," in *AFIPS proceedings Spring Joint Computer Conference, vol. 36,* p.2.

36. J. E. Ward, "Systems engineering problems in computer-driven CRT displays," *IEEE transaction systems science & cybernetics* SSC-3:49 (June 1967).

37. T. Mayeda, "Methodology in presentation - a new objective: the multi-media network" (Draft of lecture delivered to the Washington, D.C. Chapter, The Institute of Management Sciences, 1 Nov. 1967), p.4.

38. M. E. Stevens, *Research and development in the computer and information sciences, vol. 3, Overall system design considerations - a selective literature review* (National Bureau of Standards monograph 113, vol. 3 [Washington, D.C.: Gov. Print. Off., 1970], p.10.

39. D. J. Dantine, "Communications needs of the user for management information systems," in p.406. computer conference, vol. 29, p.406.

40. A. L. Scherr, "An analysis of time-shared computer systems," Ph.D. dissertation Rep. no.MAC-TR-18 (Cambridge, Mass.: MIT Pr., 1965), p.19.

41. J. D. Aron, "Real-time systems in perspective," *IBM systems journal* 6:53 (1967).

42. T. Marill and L. G. Roberts, "Toward a cooperative network of time-shared computers," p.426.

43. H. Sackman, "Current methodological research," in *Proceedings 23rd national conference, ACM* (Princeton, N.J.: Brandon/Systems Pr., 1968), p.367.

44. M. S. Davis, "Economics - point of view of designer and operator" (preprints of papers), *Interdisciplinary Conference on Multiple Access Computer Networks,* Austin, Texas, 20-22 April 1970, p.4-1-3.

45. *Scientific and technical communication: a pressing national problem and recommendations for its solution* (a synopsis of the report of the Committee on Scientific and Technical Communication of the National Academy of Sciences - National Academy of Engineering) (Washington, D.C.: The Academy, 1969), p.10.

46. H. D. Avram, "Using computer technology - frustrations abound," p.86.

47. C. P. Yerkes, "Microfiche, a new information media," in H. P. Luhn, ed., *Automation and scientific communication, short papers* (Washington, D.C.: Am. Doc. Inst., 1963), p.129.

48. P. Vlannes, "Requirements for information retrieval networks," in B. F. Cheydleur, ed., *Colloquium on Technical Preconditions for Retrieval Center Operations* (Washington, D.C.: Spartan, 1965), p.4.

49. *Proceedings of the librarians' convention* (New York, 15-17 Sept. 1853) reprinted for W. H. Murray (Cedar Rapids, Iowa: The Torch Pr., 1915), p.55.

Network Organization

Working Group Summary On Network Organization

Aim: to determine how all echelons of the library enterprise will be affected by the network concept.

The paramount concern of the Working Group on Network Organization was for the public good. The group believed that networks are intended to serve all, and that in their construction, they should be general purpose so far as is possible. Group deliberations adopted the premise that information is a public asset and that network organization should therefore serve the public interest.

A distinction was made between libraries and information centers that serve a general class of users, (e.g., public and academic libraries) and those that serve a specialized class of users (e.g., those in the fields of medicine and law).

A general-purpose national library and information network was thus defined to be: "A formalized structure which interrelates existing and future libraries and information centers, involving the organization of these units at the local, state, regional, and national levels. The major purpose of this network is to mobilize all appropriate resources to provide service to any user no matter where he accesses the system." And a special-purpose network was defined as: "A formalized arrangement which interrelates existing and future libraries and information centers that have unique characteristics, that are mission-oriented, and that serve special client groups." These specialized information networks may interconnect with general-purpose networks at all appropriate levels but do not necessarily coincide with them. Although elements of a national library and information network already exist, general and special networks have been formalized yet. However, the group believed that a sophisticated information network will not develop unless immediate steps are taken toward mobilization and organization of existing library and information agencies into a formal structure.

Questions pertaining to legal, fiscal, political, jurisdictional, staffing, and social problems of networks were deliberated; the group concluded that networks will bring drastic changes to administrative relationships among existing institutions and that new agencies are likely to be created to meet the pressures of networking potential and capabilities.

If the information needs of a user cannot be met satisfactorily at his local level, then a network should provide him with appropriate channels of communication to other organizational levels of response. Four levels of network organization were identified to serve this purpose in a hierarchy proceeding upward from the local level (within a state), to the state level, to the regional or multistate level, and finally to the national level. This kind of network organizational hierarchy should be designed with sufficient flexibility to enable a user in any particular geographical area to contact the network with full assurance of operational compatibility.

A coordinating agency to tie together the resources of each of the four levels was considered to be an essential element of the network hierarchy. Specifically, the group felt that such a coordinating agency will be the heart of network organization and that its role will be vital to network development. A coordinating agency will be created at each hierarchical level with appropriate authority and responsibilities as follows:

1.   It will be the main switching center for the level, providing referral and coordinating functions for satisfying information requests emanating from any point in the network.

2.   It will perform services of concern to all levels by offering collection development advice, centralized technical processing services, consulting assistance, and management and administrative support.

3.   It will be the channel used for transmitting information to a user through a variety of electronic and other delivery systems.

The functions at each level of the hierarchy are expected to be:

1.   *Local level*

Ensuring maximum access to and use of area resources (private and public), and minimizing the

---

Working Group Leader: Robert Heinich, A-V Center, Indiana University, Bloomington, Indiana 47401

Associate Leader: Richard Dougherty, Syracuse University, School of Library Science, 119 Euclid Avenue, Syracuse, New York duplication of existing and anticipated resources and services

Providing for the sharing of available resources and services within the area

Adding new services as appropriate to the needs of the constituencies served

Establishing a local agency to coordinate the evolution of network functions at the local level

Funding the coordinating agency from state and federal sources as well as securing financial commitments and contracts from network members. (State and federal legislation may have to be passed to allow local coordinating agencies to be established, to receive operating funds from any and all sources, and to use such funds with only the customary restrictions on public accountability. At present, some state laws limit such flexibility.

2.   *State level*

Integrating special information sources in various state agencies, such as the state historical association, state museums, state law library, into the network as integral components

Initiating, planning, and designing network services to meet the information requirements of all the people in the state

Receiving and disbursing all federal and state funds available for network use throughout the state

Providing consulting services to local coordinating agencies and network members

Initiating public information programs to secure public and legislative support

Developing and operating centralized technical services

Programming continuing education courses for the public as well as network personnel

Securing legislative and fiscal support

Providing evaluation services for local, regional, and national agencies

Directing the planning and execution of statewide bibliographic services, and coordinating resource development at the state and area levels, including the administration of grants to strengthen state or multistate collections in subject areas of major concern to the state

Promoting area and statewide technological and communications programs.

3.   *Regional level*

The regional level will consist of a combination of state networks, special-purpose networks, and subsets of national information networks. Each regional group also will have its own coordinating agency. Many special-purpose networks would start at the regional level, interfacing with other local, state, and national networks.

State and federal legislation will be required to permit establishment of regional coordinating agencies with full authority to receive funds and provide services to members and other parts of networks outside the region's jurisdiction.

Regional coordinating agencies should be financed by: state funds contributed under contract, federal funds, foundation grants, and user and membership fees where appropriate. The federal government should take the initative in establishing the regional agencies.

The functions performed at the state level also will be carried out at the regional level.

4.   *National level*

National information resources — the Library of Congress, the National Library of Medicine, the National Agricultural Library, the federal library community, the science and technology specialized information centers, and others — represent tremendous sources of information on which a national network should be able to draw. A coordinating agency will be needed, however, to ensure that there is a smooth interface between the national level and the regions and the states, and between the national level and international information networks. A single contact and coordinating point for this purpose is considered essential. Federal legislation will be needed to create this coordinating agency and empower it with sufficient authority and funding to carry out its mission.

The proposed structure is a conceptual model which is technologically adaptable. It focuses on the user and the area within which the user is to be served. As new technological devices are introduced into the structure, it undoubtedly will change.

A national general-purpose network should not be a monolithic structure but instead, a series of networks organized to meet local information needs. The group expects the national network to be equipped with adequate communications that will smoothly interconnect the state, regional, special, and national networks on behalf of the local user and at points most convenient to him. This concept, however, demands a high degree of systems compatibility.

Special-purpose networks pose other problems, such as questions of privacy, industrial security, and commercial protection, which would not exist in a general-purpose network.

The group recommends Harold Hacker's paper on "Implementing Network Plans" to anyone desiring to become conversant with the many problems confronting general- and special-purpose network organizers. It also contains an excellent summary of legislative experience in New York State, and Hacker's personal observations of the reasons for the successes and failures of the New York program.

CONCLUSIONS AND RECOMMENDED ACTION

1.   Library and information networks should be
          regarded as a public utility; an appropriate

regulatory agency should allocate resources, monitor operations, and evaluate performance in order to ensure that networks are developed and used for the public good.

2.   Federal information programs should be coordinated effectively in order to ensure that their combined resources will support a national library and information network in optimum fashion.

3.   The National Library Task Force on Automation should strive to integrate the automation programs of the three national libraries as soon as possible. The automation programs of the Library of Congress, the National Library of Medicine, and the National Agricultural Library are of paramount importance in achieving a unified national library and information network development program.

4.   The individual's need for information is vital to his cultural development, to his ability to work, and to his meaningful involvement with society. Emerging network organizations should pay special attention to the self-enrichment needs of the disadvantaged such as minority groups, the handicapped, and the mentally retarded. Lay and business groups, through voluntary action, should be enlisted by network organizations to help interpret library and information resources for the disadvantaged.

5.   Enabling legislation at state and federal levels is needed to permit local agencies to participate freely in networks and to authorize establishment of local-level coordinating agencies.

6.   Studies should be initiated at state and national levels to examine existing legislation in order to identify laws that inhibit network progress and to determine what new legislation is needed to accelerate implementation of the network concept.

7.   The Council of State Governments should be made acquainted with information network aims and objectives, and urged to sponsor legislation encouraging interstate agreements and contracts that would facilitate network development.

8.   New funding formulas are required to encourage cost-sharing between the federal government and the states in the interest of establishing, operating, and maintaining library and information networks. (An example is the interstate highway network –which is funded by 90 percent federal and 10 percent state contributions.)

9.   Increased attention should be given to the ways and means by which special-purpose networks can be integrated with general-purpose networks. It is a national responsibility to ensure that access to specialized information is made available at each level of the network hierarchy.

10. There is need for a radically different educational approach to library and information science continuing education utilizing the new technologies. A new national program must make available to any librarian or information scientist at any time and at any place the resources and expertise he needs in order to provide effective services in a network environment. Network staffing will demand new skills, new positions, and a new philosophical base; hence, an aggressive national educational program must be launched for education and reeducation at all levels.

11. Research is needed to ensure optimum effectiveness in network operations, e.g., development of evaluation models to measure effectiveness at all organizational levels; development of organizational models that are adaptable to the needs of different localities; and development of network funding models that can facilitate network implementation.

12. A broad program for public and professional education is needed to advance the network concept and to motivate people to support changes in information methods, practices, and organization.

13. The merits of a national library and information network program should be made known to legislators at every political level. These advantages are:

a. Information networks eliminate duplication of effort while at the same time equalizing access to information.

b. Information networks serve all citizens; people of all ages, in all walks of life, and at any geographic location can obtain whatever information they need for their own economic survival or personal enrichment.

c. Information networks are an extension of education; they can improve literacy, increase local employment, and further local business.

d. Information networks are cost-effective because they reduce local capital investments by amortizing the installation of modern technology over a wider geographic base.

Legal and Contractual Aspects of Interlibrary and Information Service Operations

Maryann Duggan

The first purpose of this paper is to review legal and contractual aspects of interlibrary and information services operations from the viewpoint of a practitioner in the field. The second purpose is to identify specific operational areas needing legal clarification or codification.

It should be emphasized that the author in no way claims this paper to be a "legal brief" on interlibrary operations. Furthermore, the author assumes no legal responsibilities for any interpretation or actions resulting from the information presented herein. This paper is simply a presentation of "legal" problems encountered in developing and/or operating networks in the Southwest.

The complex matrix of local, state, and federal laws applicable to network activities is an uncharted labyrinth of contradictions, confusion, and legal jargon. This paper will attempt to outline the legal aspects of:

1. Establishing interlibrary activities or network services as a legal entity

2. Operating networks and providing services from the viewpoints of participants, information base, and network development or extension.

Copyright law, Federal Communication Commission regulations, or laws influencing telecommunication hardware were omitted from consideration.

THE LEGAL BASIS FOR NETWORK ESTABLISHMENT

Using the rationale that an interlibrary network is a combination of individual "nodes" or a linkage of separate organizational parts, let us start our analysis with each node. Each library participating in the network, whether public or private, has been legally established. Public libraries operate within the city charter or ordinances and are therefore subject to the restraints and operational policies so stated. State libraries are established by state law and are subject to the operational policies as interpreted by the state attorney general. It also is evident that federal libraries are legally authorized to operate on the basis of enabling federal legislation or federal code.

Private libraries in industry operate within the restraints specified by corporate policy and laws of incorporation of the parent firm.

The varying basis of legal establishment and operational policies results in a virtual hierarchy of legal constraints individually affecting each library or library system. The author did not find a concise review of the existing laws pertaining to each type or level of library or "node." From actual experience, however, it is believed that the restraining influence imposed on each network member, as a result of the varying legal base for existence, is a real factor in establishing networks during the process of putting together existing components into an organizational structure. For example, a review[1] of various state laws pertinent to interstate networks or library consortia among six state libraries revealed legal barriers which would seem to inhibit interstate network development. The most prevalent state laws enabling state libraries to engage in interstate networks are those concerned with interstate library compacts, joint exercise of powers, and interlocal cooperation. Analysis of these laws (and an attorney general's ruling) indicates several constraints, namely:

1. Inability for a state with an interstate library compact to enter into an agreement with a state not having this law

2. Statutory limitations restricting a state to agreements with adjoining states only

3. Incompatibility of state laws negating any general agreements.

Another method for developing networks is via the creation of a new agency, i.e., a "network corporate body" which may or may not be chartered or incorporated. This body then contracts with participants or members to provide certain services or perform certain duties. Academic library consortia are an example of this type of network organization. Each participant agrees to certain objectives or to a role in the consortium with the funding grant being administered by a core agency acting in behalf of the other members.

Apparently the source of funds for establishing the network determines which of the two organizational structures will develop, i.e., interlocking of existing "nodes" or establishment of a "central agency." If we limit our consideration of networks to only those organizations using telecommunication devices, the formation and establishment of library networks primarily has been motivated by four federal laws:

1.   Library Services and Construction Act, Title III

2.   Higher Education Act, Title II

3.   State Technical Services Act

4.   Medical Library Assistance Act.

Each of these laws may be interpreted as "enabling legislation" in that funds are provided to develop networks to achieve some purpose or objective as outlined in each law. Apparently the federal laws take precedent over state or local laws, in these cases. For example, although many states do not have an interstate compact law, they are participating in one or more networks involving the crossing of state lines for library services. By accepting federal funds, the state agencies apparently give precedent to the federal laws in cases of conflict. Most of the cases reviewed involve contracts or service agreements of individual state agencies or institutions with a "central agency" created by federal grant, e.g, the regional medical library programs. The attorney general of one state has ruled that the state library cannot participate in interstate activity, and yet another state agency in that same state is very much involved in interstate library activity under one of the mentioned federal programs.

Apparently federal laws provide enabling legislation and funding permitting the establishment of various types of networks. The guidelines pertaining to these laws provide interpretation and procedural instructions which—in essence—become part of the law. Each participating state then reviews the federal program and in some manner, adjusts state rulings to permit the implementation of the intent of the federal law. Each state usually prepares a state plan which must be reviewed and approved by the federal agency administering the program. Theoretically, the state plan serves as a "legal framework" for implementing the program within the state. Unfortunately, most state plans are extremely vague and leave many policy and procedural questions unanswered.

It is impossible to discuss legal and contractual aspects of establishing a network without also discussing funding and regulations pertaining to use of federal and state funds. Apparently many conflicts exist between United States Bureau of Budget circulars and state fiscal regulations. Such interpretations as encumbrance policy, fiscal year, matching funds criteria, and redistribution of budget line items present a confusing array of conflicting regulations. Interpretation of indirect cost calculations continue to be an exercise in "one-up-manship." The network administrator is treading on thin ice if legal connotations are seriously considered and fiscal integrity is attempted.

This situation is complicated further by federal programs that oscillate between "grants" in one year and "contracts" in a following year. The legal implications of these two methods of establishing networks need clarification.

The relationship of the network agency to the "host institution" is also a source of legal confusion. Apparently most existing networks are legally and fiscally appended to some previously existing institution. The question then arises as to which fiscal and legal codes are to be adopted by the network, i.e., the "host institution" or the "funding agency." Based on interviews with several network directors and my personal experience with two networks (one in a private university and one in a state university), establishment contracts should clarify these important policies. If the regulations and laws of the "host institution" are restrictive, the network will continue to be hampered in operations and development. The most successful networks reviewed seem to be those that transcend inhibiting regulations of the host institution or that operate as a separate legal entity. The network administrator is caught between the federal regulations defining qualified agencies eligible for network development funds—thus inheriting the restrictive regulations of the host institution—and the desire to enjoy freedom of action in developing its own policies. Contracts imply commitment. The importance of the establishment contract with the host institution (and the implied commitment) cannot be overemphasized. Too often the network is pushed to one side within the host institution after the establishing contract is signed and the federal funding assured.

Thus, in summary, existing networks are an ephemeral quasi-official organization with questionable legal identity and powers resulting from a long series of contracts generally following this pattern and subject to legal interpretation of the following:

1.   Enabling federal law

2.   U.S. Bureau of Budget rules

3.   Guidelines to the federal law

4.   State agency rules and grant agreement between federal and state agency

5.   State plans for that particular law

6.   Qualifying host institution's contract with state agency (or federal agency)

7.   Host institution regulations

8.   Agreement between network administrator and host institution.

One legal counsel suggested the following interpretation and "modus operandi" for network administrators, namely:[2]

Don't look for laws enabling you to perform certain functions; assume you have the right until you are confronted with a law that says you cannot. Network operations require an extra-legal attitude and operating policy in the current jungle of levels of laws.

It thus appears that clarification of the local, state, and federal laws regulating the establishment of library networks is needed.

THE LEGAL BASIS FOR NETWORK OPERATION

Networks do get established in spite of the contradictory legal interpretations. However, the uncertainty of their legal origin and jurisdiction does adversely affect operational capabilities. Three operational areas of concern in this paper are:

1.   Participant's role

2.   Information banks

3.   Network interfacing.

With regard to participants, a variety of relationships are possible. In the case of networks established by interlocking agreements, the establishment instruments usually determine and clarify the participant's role and expectations. In the case of networks developed around a "central agency," participants usually contract for certain services at a predetermined fee. Examination of some of these contracts reveals a great diversity. Apparently, a "standard contract" has not been developed. A review of contract components shows that some or all of the following have been included:

1.   Definition of participating parties and individuals authorized to request services

2.   Time period covered by the contract

3.   Work to be performed or services to be provided and responsibilities of each party

4.   Fees (or costs), discount rates, method of billing (i.e., reciprocity or exchange versus cash payments), and method of conveying funds

5.   Eligible users or authorized method of use, with constraints on "rebroadcasting"

6.   Liability disclaimer or other limits of legal responsibilities, i.e., patents and copyrights

7.   Contract cancellation rights and procedures

8.   Penalties for nonconformity or noncompliance

9.   Legal process for contesting disputes.

This author reviewed the "membership agreements" or "participants contracts" being used by seventeen networks operating within or in one state. No two networks had a similar instrument, and the lack of standardization was obvious even within the boundaries of *one* state.

One legal counsel questions the legality and binding nature of these contracts. To avoid this issue, some networks simply call these contracts a "membership agreement." There is considerable question concerning the legal right for a network to enter into contracts—depending on its founding charter, its state of incorporation, its tax status, etc. One network was advised by legal counsel that the state law required the collection of state sales tax for photocopy charges or fees charged for search reports. In networks involving industry members, the legal implications of antitrust laws and "restraint of trade" laws are an impeding factor. The question of liability for inaccurate or incomplete services to network users also has been raised in two networks serving industry. Although the "membership a-greement" contained a disclaimer relieving the network from any such responsibility, legal counsel felt that such disclaimer would not hold up in a court test. It must be reemphasized, however, that formal, written agreements of some type are believed to be essential in operating a successful network. Again, contracts imply commitment—and networks cannot operate without full commitment by participants.

With regard to the information bank provided by the network, several factors seem evident. The question of ownership of the information bank has been raised in several networks. For example, a computer-based catalog of serial holdings prepared by a network and housed in a participant's facility is subject to questions of ownership. Who has the legal right to access this information bank, and for whom and for what purpose? If the information bank is compiled for the network under contract by an outside agency, differences of opinion can occur on the ownership of this product if these factors are not clarified at the time the contract is first let.

Another very real question pertains to the procurement of an information bank by a network from a commercial or sem-icommercial agency. For example, suppose a library network desired to procure and make available to its members a commercially available information bank of current journal ci-tations (by subject, author, etc.). Does the network contract with the supplier as a "franchise agent," as a "retail outlet," or as a "distributor"? The terms of access/use of this information bank become entangled in the pricing structure, the "guaranteed return," and the fair and equitable distribution of costs among network members.

In the case of "information banks" provided by federal programs, i.e., GPO depositories, the legality of fees for services rendered to network members from these depositories has been questioned. When the library agrees to become a federal de-pository, is it legally committed to provide gratis service from this "information bank"?

Another type of "law" influencing network development and the information bank is the accreditation standards for colleges and universities. These standards reflect the library collection requirements of a totally self-sufficient institution. The conflict between this "law" and the changing patterns of access to collections via networks needs to be resolved. This recodification is particularly important in the case of newly founded academic institutions seeking accreditation and desirous of enriching collections through network access rather than through building large collections of research materials.

With regard to network interfacing, the legal aspects become even more complex. Incompatibility of operational policies, fee structures, user's access, funding base, etc., becomes evident when two or more networks attempt to interface. At the national level, considerable negotiating is usually required to develop an interface between a network operating under one federal program with a network operating under a different federal program. The legality of federal money provided to one network being conveyed to another federally funded network creates considerable concern to program administrators.

If a "national network" is to be developed, it seems that a recodifying of the pertinent laws will be essential. Both the National Advisory Commission on Libraries and the SAT-COM Committee studies identified the need for a national library policy and improved planning, coordination, and leadership at the national level. Certainly, those responsible for national planning and policy formulation should be cognizant of the legal and contractual implications on network activity at the practicing level.

Thinking of the future and visualizing an idealistic concept, perhaps a public network of all libraries might be a solution. This might take the form of a "library utility" owning all library resources and providing services by contract—similar to an electric or gas utility. To some, this system might be utopia; to others, a nightmare of loss of autonomy and private control. Certainly, a nationally operated "library utility" would simplify the legal and contractual aspects of networks.

RECOMMENDATIONS

Based on this author's experience and findings,[5] the legal and contractual aspects of network establishment and operation are somewhat unclear. Networks are a relatively new type of "social organization" which do not fit into our existing laws; yet, networks are very much in evidence and very much operational. If laws are a codification of social behavior, it seems that the following actions are needed:

1. A legal review of existing local, state, and federal laws pertaining to network establishment and operation

2. A legal opinion on the legal nature of networks and their right to enter into contracts, receive funds, convey funds, collect taxes, etc.

3. A standardization of contract forms and elements

4. A national networking law applicable to all federally funded networks to codify current and future practices and legal bases for establishment and operation.

NOTES

1. Katherine McMurrey and Ralph Funk, "Legal, organizational and financial aspects of interlibrary cooperation in the southwest," presented 17 Sept 1970 at SWLA Working Conference, Arlington, Texas.

2. Dr. Roy M. Merskey, Director, Law Library, University of Texas, Austin, Interview.

3. Douglas M. Knight and E. Shepley Nourse, *Libraries at large...*(New York: Bowker, 1969), 664p.

4. National Academy of Sciences - National Academy of Committee on Scientific and Technical Communication, *Scientific and technical communication* (Washington, D.C.: The Academy, 1969) 322p.

5. A preliminary literature review did not find any published material on this specific topic, per se. The paper presented by Mrs. McMurrey and Mr. Funk to the SWLA Working Conference on Interstate, Interlibrary Cooperation is the only semipublished material located by the author on the assigned topic. A variety of publications mention various implications of laws on network activity, but none really confront the problems identified herein. The various topics covered in this paper were reviewed with knowledgeable people in the field and with a corporation attorney, an attorney for a private university, and with an attorney of considerable note in the field of law bibliography. Thus, the author feels reasonably certain that these problems are real and that the recommendations are valid.

Implementing Network Plans in New York State: Jurisdictional Considerations in the Design of Library Networks

Harold S. Hacker

TABLE OF ABBREVIATIONS

ANYLTS
 Association of New York Libraries for Technical Services

B&ECPL
 Buffalo and Erie County Public Library

CCLD
 Commissioner's Committee on Library Development

DLD
 Division of Library Development, State Library, State Education Development

ECPL
 Erie County Public Library

ESEA
 Elementary and Secondary Education Act (federal)

LSCA
 Library Services and Construction Act (federal)

LTF
 Library Trustees Foundation of New York State

MCLS
 Monroe County Library System

METRO
 New York Metropolitan Reference and Research Library Agency

NYLA
 New York Library Association

NYPL
 New York Public Library

NYSILL
 New York State Inter-Library Loan Network

OCLS
 Ontario Cooperative Library System

PLS
 Pioneer Library System

RRRLC
 Rochester Regional Research Library Council

SED
 State Education Department

3R's
 Reference and Research Library Resources (state and regional programs)

INTRODUCTION

New York State is covered by two types of regional library networks: public library systems, twenty-two of which serve the state's sixty-two counties; and reference and research library systems, nine of which cover the same territory. In very recent years some regional school library networks have begun to develop, thanks to ESEA Title III funding. At the state level there is one operating special-purpose network, the New York State Inter-Library Loan Network, NYSILL. A second special-purpose state network is in the early stages of implementation. It is the Association of New York Libraries for Technical Services, ANYLTS, formed by the twenty-two public library systems. The New York State Education Department, through its Division of Library Development, its State Library, and its Bureau of School Libraries, has been very much involved in the planning, implementation, and operations of these library networks.

For my own part, I have spent the greater part of my professional career in network planning and implementation — both in my several library posts and as a volunteer at state and regional levels. I have served as a member of all five state study committees and have participated actively in most of our twenty annual efforts to persuade the governors and legislatures to enact library network legislation and/or to increase library funding at the state level. In two cases of regional network funding — Erie and Monroe counties — I have participated at every stage of the planning and implementation except for the political caucuses. I have benefited greatly from on-the-job experiences in the planning, implementation, and operations of these New York State networks: the Buffalo and Erie County Public Library, B&ECPL, and the Pioneer Library System, PLS (the former, a single-county public library system and the latter, a five-county system); the Rochester Regional Research Library Council, RRRLC, comprising university, college, public, and special libraries in a five-county area; and the state's NYSILL Network in which our Rochester libraries serve as an area resource center. Finally, during many years of service as secretary and treasurer to the Library Trustees Foundation of New York State, I had the opportunity to work with network regional planning groups throughout the state.

It was for these reasons that I hoped that in a very short time I could prepare a paper on network implementation for this Conference. I was asked to discuss the problems that networks encounter when they operate within the jurisdiction of several layers of government and when several types of libraries undertake a common network activity. I also was asked to suggest some solutions to those problems. This I have tried to do.

Since New York State is famous for its library systems, I often will be using the word "system." The words "system" and "network" have a common meaning throughout this paper.

PLANNING: THE DEVELOPMENT OF THE IDEA FOR THE NETWORK

The first stage of network implementation is that of planning the network. New York State owes much of its library network progress to sound studies and planning. Techniques have varied substantially among the nine major planning efforts which I will mention in this chapter: four dealing with public library networks, one with reference and research library networks, two with both of the above, and two with special-purpose state networks. Of the nine studies, three were conducted by committees representing the varied library interests of the state, aided by paid staff; two were conducted by committees without staff; two were conducted by the Research Division of the State Education Department, SED, one with and one without an advisory committee from the field; and two were conducted by an educational consultant firm under contract with SED.

Because other papers for this Conference will deal extensively with network planning, I will limit this section to identifying the nine studies and reporting in capsule form their purposes, scope, major recommendations, and results. The results of these studies — legislation and network implementation — will be treated more fully in subsequent sections.

NEW YORK STATE EDUCATION DEPARTMENT — RESEARCH DIVISION

Report title and date: *Development of Library Services in New York State, 1949*[1]

Study period: 1945-1947

Committee: Four-member advisory committee, appointed by the New York Library Association

Purpose: To respond to request of NYLA for SED to conduct study to determine state's role in the improvement of public library service

Scope: SED Research Division staff conducted statewide study of public libraries

Major recommendations: Fourteen state-operated regional library service centers financed by state, plus state-aid payments direct to three New York City libraries, in lieu of centers; regional centers to provide "wholesale" services to public libraries; creation of county and regional advisory boards; cost to state — $7 million

Results: SED Board of Regents recommended operation of one experimental regional center for a three-year period; Watertown Region was selected and began operations in 1948 on annual $100,000 state budget.

GOVERNOR DEWEY'S COMMITTEE ON LIBRARY AID

Report title and date: *Library Service for All, 1951*[2]

Study period: 1949

Committee: Fifteen-member study committee, appointed by Governor Thomas E. Dewey

Purpose: To determine the state's financial role in support of public libraries

Scope: Committee "blue-skied" without benefit to staff

Major recommendations: Supported library systems formed at least on a countywide basis as eligible for state-aid; accented local initative and responsibility; stressed value of system services; encouraged multicounty development of systems; established first state-aid formula in legislative format; cost to state — $3,650,000

Results: Passage in 1950 of first state-aid law with $1 million appropriation for which six public library systems serving eight counties immediately were eligible. Shortly after, two additional systems serving three counties were established.

COMMISSIONER'S COMMITTEE ON PUBLIC LIBRARY SERVICE

Report title and date: *Report on the Commissioner of Education's Committee on Public Library Service, 1958*[3]

Study period: 1956-1957

Committee: Twenty-one-member study committee, appointed by Commissioner James E. Allen, Jr.

Purpose: To review the progress of public library systems since 1950 and to make recommendations to improve the state-aid law since only thirty of sixty-two counties were served by eight library systems

Scope: Staff study of system operations in thirteen counties; case studies of system planning to determine obstacles to system implementation; comparative study of system and nonsystem libraries

Major recommendations: Reaffirmed system concept, state-aid, and local initative and responsibility; new flexibility through cooperative library system structure; accented multicounty system and importance of central library (defined as requiring 100,000 volume nonfiction collection); expressed principle of gradualism permitting systems five years to meet some standards; dealt with specific problems of New York Public Library's Research Libraries, Watertown Regional Library Service Center, and the State Library; recommended separate study of research library needs; revised state-aid formula; cost to state — $10.3 million, plus central library book aid

Results: Passage of new state-aid law in 1958 with reduced formula; full formula enacted 1960; within four years, remainder of state organized so that by 1962 twenty-two library systems served the sixty-two counties.

COMMISSIONER'S COMMITTEE ON REFERENCE AND RESEARCH LIBRARY RESOURCES

Report title and date: *Report of the Commissioner's Committee on Reference and Research Library Resources, December 1961*

Study period: 1960-1961

Committee: Twenty-member study committee, appointed by Commissioner James E. Allen, Jr.

Purpose: To study problems of library information service and research library facilities, and their ability to meet needs; to review technological developments and administrative and fiscal devices that may contribute to solution of the problems

Scope: Staff study of growth of research activities and college population; information explosion and automation in libraries reviewed by committee; comparative data on college university and special libraries collected; use of various libraries by college students examined; devising of new hypothetical system by committee

Major recommendations: Creation of state reference and research library board and special staff; designation of major state subject centers; creation of state-wide interlibrary loan and communications network; establishment of five to six regional research library systems, including all but school libraries; state-aid formula; cost to state — $8 million

Results: Legislative proposals were never enacted — no formula; five straight years of legislative defeat until 1966 when appropriation was made; since 1966 nine regional systems have been established, plus statewide interlibrary loan network, NYSILL.

GOVERNOR ROCKEFELLER'S COMMITTEE ON LIBRARIES

This study requires a bit of explanation. It took several years of effort to persuade Governor Nelson A. Rockefeller to call the first Governor's Conference on Libraries. Early in 1965 he appointed an advisory committee to plan the conference for June. The same people were reappointed to make legislative and budgetary proposals to him late in 1965. There was a published report of the proceedings of the conference, but no published report of the Governor's Committee on Libraries.

Governor's Conference

Report title and date: *Proceedings of the First Governor's Library Conference, June 24-25, 1965, n.d.*[5]

Committee: Seventeen-member advisory committee, appointed by Governor Nelson A. Rockefeller to plan the conference

Purpose: To focus public attention on library needs in New York State

Scope: Librarians and scientists presented papers on research library problems and solutions during two-day conference

Result: Delegates to conference unanimously voted to request the governor to extend the life of the advisory committee so that it could make recommendations to him to improve library service in the state.

Governor's Committee on Libraries

No report

Study period: 1965

Committee: Same as advisory committee

Purpose: To recommend library legislative and budgetary programs to the governor

Scope: Committee meeting, without staff, fall 1965, to propose revisions in the public library state-aid formula and appropriation levels to launch reference and research library, 3R's, program in the state

Major recommendations: Increase basic state-aid formula for public libraries by about 33 percent and add a new section providing state-aid to improve central libraries — total added cost of $3.8 million; and appropriations of $1.2 million to launch state and regional 3R's programs

Results: Legislature and governor approved state-aid formula revision and appropriation of $13.3 million for public libraries; and $700,000 was appropriated for 3R's programs.

STATE EDUCATION DEPARTMENT –EVALUATION DIVISION

Report title and date: *Emerging Library Systems: the 1963-66 Evaluation of the New York State Public Library Systems, 1967*[6]

Study period: 1963-1966

Committee: None

Purpose: To evaluate the effectiveness of the public library systems' programs, last reviewed in 1957

Scope: Intensive analysis by Evaluation Division staff and consultants of systems' services, resources, organization, management, and finances; study of accessibility of library service and of library users; review of the role of the state and of the special problems of the New York City public libraries.

Major recommendations: Coordinate library services of all types at all levels; modify public library programs to meet student needs; new approach to public library financing — equalization, county support, and state-aid as a stimulant; strengthen central libraries; intermediate level service; clarify roles of SED's Division of Library Development and public library systems; develop intersystem cooperation; initiate State Library building construction fund; involvement in systems affairs by trustees and librarians; and appointment of an advisory committee by the Commissioner of Education to review report and recommend next steps

Results: Commissioner's Committee on Library Development was appointed in 1967.

COMMISSIONER'S COMMITTEE ON LIBRARY DEVELOPMENT

Report title and date: (Uncertain at time paper was written) probably, *Report of the Commissioner's Committee on Library Development*

Study period: 1967-1970

Committee: Twelve-member study committee, appointed by Commissioner James E. Allen, Jr.

Purpose: To review *Emerging Library Systems* and the state of the 3R's program, and to recommend next steps to the commissioner

Scope: Development of user-oriented philosophy by committee with aid of staff; review of eighty recommendations in *Emerging Library Systems;* Preparation and commissioning of numerous reports; study of status of 3R's program

Major Recommendations: In such fields as access; services to children, students, and residents of institutions; government of libraries; manpower; library materials; library buildings; research and development; and many areas of library finances

Results: The report was transmitted to the commissioner and the board of regents in June 1970; it will serve as the prime source of the New York State Education Department's 1971 legislative and budgetary program for libraries.

SPECIAL PURPOSE STATE NETWORKS STUDIES

The New York State Education Department's Division of Library Development contracted with Nelson Associates for two studies of statewide significance. The first dealt with centralized processing activities of the twenty-two public library systems. The second evaluated SED's pilot statewide interlibrary loan and communications network, NYSILL. Here are brief summaries of the two studies:

Report title and date: *Implementing Centralized Processing for the Public Libraries of New York State, 1966*[7]

Study period: 1965-1966

Committee: Fifteen-member advisory committee appointed by SED's Division of Library Development

Purpose: To evaluate the system service to public libraries and to recommend improved methods

Scope: Analysis of operations and costs of most systems and special EDP studies by Theodere Stein Company

Major recommendations: Establishment of statewide computer and cataloging center; and several regional processing centers to handle acquisitions, cataloging, and preparation workload for all public libraries

Results: Association of New York Libraries for Technical Services, ANYLTS was formed; ANYLTS continues planning with high-priority federal LSCA funds; staff is assembled and production timetable i set.

Report title and date: *An Evaluation of the New York State Library's NYSILL Pilot Program, 1968*

Study period: 1967-1968

Committee: None

Purpose: To evaluate the NYSILL experimental program

Scope: Study of NYSILL operations at all key points: State Library, area resource centers, and subject resource centers; analysis of service to public

Major recommendations: Retention of NYSILL with improvements

Results: NYSILL is now in its fourth year — much improved.

FINANCING THE NETWORK PLAN: THE LEGISLATION AND APPROPRIATION ROUTES

After the planning is finished and agreement is reached on the goals to be achieved, the hard work begins; the difficult task of persuasion follows. The network planners must win support for their program from librarians, trustees, state education department officials (in the case of New York), members of the executive department (the governor and his staff), and members of the state legislature (particularly the leadership).

THE LEGISLATION VERSUS THE APPROPRIATION ROUTE

One of the first decisions on implementation strategy that must be made is whether to select the legislation rather than the appropriation route to achieve network funding goals. In some states the legislation route will be required if the state does not have a legal base for library networking. But most states do have the necessary enabling legislation.

The legislation route will be preferred if the planners seek assurance for continuity of state funding through a legislated formula, e.g., New York State's public library network. On the

TABLE 1. NEW YORK STATE LOG OF MAJOR STATE LEGISLATION & APPROPRIATION EFFORTS

YEAR	LEGIS-LATION SOUGHT	APPRO-PRIATION SOUGHT	PUB-LIC LIBS.	3R'S LIBS.	WON	LOST	LIBRARY PROGRAM AND COMMENTS
1947	X		X			X	NYLA* bill: state aid to public libraries
1948		X	X		X		$100,000—SED* budget approved for Watertown Regional Library Service Center experiment
	X		X			X	NYLA bill: state aid to county library systems
1949	X		X			X	(Same as above)
1950	X		X		X		Governor's Committee on Library Aid Bill: state aid to county library systems—$3.65 million maximum
1951	X		X			X	SED-NYLA bill: to amend state-aid law—refinement
1952	X		X			X	(Same as above)
1953	X		X		X		Refinement amendment to state-aid law passed
1958	X		X		X		SED's Commissioner's committee on Public Library Service Bill: major changes in state-aid law: proposed new state-aid formula compromise approved
1959	X		X			X	SED bill to implement full state-aid formula
1960	X		X		X		(Same as above)—$10.3 million maximum, formula approved
1961	X			X		X	SED bill: state-aid formula for Reference and Research Library Program (3R's)*
1962	X			X		X	(Same as above)
1963	X			X		X	NYLA bill: (Same as above)
		X		X		X	SED request: $100,000 appropriation for 3R's pilot project
1964	X			X		X	SED bill: state-aid formula for 3R's program ($75,000 regional pilot amendment passed by legislature, but vetoed by governor)
1965	X			X		X	SED bill: state-aid formula for 3R's program (bill with $275,000 appropriation passed by legislature, but vetoed by governor)
1966	X		X			X	Governor's Committee on Libraries bill: state aid to public library systems amendments—$13.3 million maximum (new central library aid included)
		X		X	X		SED request: $1.2 million 3R's appropriation sought; $700,000 appropriation approved by legislature and governor
1967	X		X			X	Bill to provide state aid for library building construction
1968	X		X			X	(Same as above)
	X		X			X	SED bill: to amend public library state-aid formula, increasing central library aid
		X		X		X	SED request: to increase 3R's appropriation by over $1,000,000
1969	X		X			X	SED bill: to increase central library state-aid formulas and add $1 million to NYPL* aid
	X		X			X	Bill to provide state aid for library building construction
		X		X		X	SED request: to increase 3R's appropriation by over $3,000,000
1970	X		X			X	SED bill: to increase state aid to public library systems, central library aid, and NYPL aid
	X		X			X	Bill to provide state aid for library building construction
		X		X		X	SED request: to increase 3R's appropriation by $680,000

*Abbreviations: NYLA = New York Library Association
NYPL = New York Public Library
SED = State Education Department
3R's = Reference and Research Library Program

other hand, the planners may seek the appropriation route to achieve an earlier start of the program, e.g., New York State's reference and research library network.

If the legislation route is selected, the planners must be as precise as possible in drafting the bill to be submitted to the legislature, including such elements as the purpose of the program, its administration at the state level, the types of network organizations eligible for state-aid, the standards for eligibility of networks, and state-aid formula factors. Of key importance to state officials will be the maximum state cost of the formula and the appropriation level for the first year of operation. The network legislative bill then must be explained to and understood by those in state government who make the decisions on all "money bills." No affirmative action on network financing will be achieved unless the bill is specifically approved by the legislature and the governor, either as submitted or in amended form.

If the appropriation route is selected, the course is an easier one. Usually the appropriation will be a small part of a much larger agency budget (the State Education Department's budget, in New York's case). In many instances, only the approval of the state budget agency is needed to assure network funding if the appropriation level is not a substantial one, compared with other new and expanding programs in all of the state agencies. If the appropriation is incorporated in the governor's budget, the prospects for approval by the legislature are substantially greater than they are if the appropriation is sought in special library network legislation.

NEW YORK STATE'S LEGISLATION AND APPROPRIATION EFFORTS

Library network planners in New York State have been seeking network funding by legislation or appropriation for twenty-three years. The log in Table 1 records efforts in twenty of those years.

There were twenty-three efforts to win approval for network legislation and five successes; there were six efforts to seek substantial appropriation gains and two successes. There have been three types of major state-aid network legislation during that period: public library systems, reference and research library systems, and library building construction. The state-aid legislation for public library systems has been introduced in various years at the request of the governor, or the State Education Department, SED, or the New York Library Association, NYLA. The state-aid legislation for 3R's systems has been introduced at the request of SED or NYLA. The library building construction legislation has been introduced by two legislators with the informal backing of SED and NYLA.

Table 1a is a summary of the legislation and appropriation efforts for each of the three programs, as itemized in Table 1.

The most successful of the twenty annual campaigns were:

1. 1950: First public library system state-aid law was passed.

2. 1958 and 1960: First public library system state-aid law was revised substantially.

3. 1966: Second major formula revision was enacted for public libraries, and the first appropriation for the 3R's program was approved.

Substantial gains in appropriation levels have been recorded by public library systems since the first appropriation in 1950, but the 3R's appropriation gains have not been very great because the program is so new. Following are the comparative figures:

1. Public library networks: 1950-51 appropriation ... $1,000,000

2. Including aid for central libraries and the research libraries of New York Public Library: 1970-71 appropriation ... $15,500,000

3. 3R's state and regional networks: 1966-67 appropriation ... $700,000

4. Including some increase for the nine regional networks and some state activities: 1970-71 appropriation ... $900,000

TABLE 1a. SUMMARY OF LEGISLATION AND APPROPRIATION EFFORTS

| PROGRAM | LEGISLATION | | MAJOR APPROPRIATIONS | |
	INTRODUCED	APPROVED	REQUESTED	GRANTED
Public library systems	14	5	1	1
3R's systems	5	0	5	1
Library building construction	4	0	0	0
Total	23	5	6	2

EXPLANATION OF NEW YORK'S LEGISLATIVE SUCCESSES

While New York State's library legislation and appropriations batting averages have not been sensational (legislation,.228, and appropriations,.333), the final product for 1970-71 indicates a fair measure of success compared with other states. Following are some of the reasons for the success of the New York State Library legislative strategy over the years:

1. *Work partnerships:* There have been two important partnerships throughout our legislative campaigns. The first features members of various state study committees: the State Education Department and the board of regents; members of the executive and legislative branches of the state government; leaders of the New York Library Association

and leaders of the Library Trustees Foundation of New York State. I cannot overemphasize the effectiveness of this partnership throughout the last twenty-three years. The second partnership is particularly significant in New York State. It included at all times the active cooperation of library leaders in New York City and "up-state" (the other fifty-seven counties). The rivalry between the legislative factions representing these two important segments of our state is notorious. Fortunately, we have been able to prevent such a negative impact upon library legislation, thanks to statesman-like positions taken by librarians and trustees on many occasions. This latter partnership resulted in the inclusion of annual earmarked state-aid for the unique research libraries of the New York Public Library in the public library state-aid law.

2. *Effective state studies:* The various library studies described earlier were important not only for the end products of the studies, usually library legislation, but also for providing the opportunity during each study for the leadership among the library interests in New York State to arrive at a consensus and for the involvement of key personnel from the executive and legislative branches of the state government. This latter group provided effective spokesmen within the executive and legislative branches on behalf of improved library service in New York State.

3. *Knowledge of the legislative process:* Another factor in our success was the knowledge gained over the years of how the legislative process *really* works. We gradually learned how decisions on major legislation were reached and by whom the decisions really were made. Thus, we identified the key leadership of the state government. We focused much of our attention on those leaders during our legislative campaigns.

4. *The art of lobbying:* Throughout our twenty years of active legislative campaigns, our efforts were marked with these characteristics:

a. An early appreciation of the importance of some of the key leadership personalities in the state: our governors (particularly Governor Dewey and Governor Rockefeller), our lieutenant governors (particularly Frank Moore and Malcolm Wilson), other key executive officers who advised governors (particularly Chief Counsel Charles Breitel and Secretary William Roana); the legislative leaders and their staffs; the commissioners of education (particularly former Commissioner James Allen, Jr., and current Commissioner Ewald Nyquist, both of whom had experience on library study committees); deputy commissioners of education, who coordinate the State Education Department's legislative programs; and members of the board of regents, the state's educational policy-making body.

b. We have had both paid and volunteer lobbyists. While the latter group worked on a part-time basis and lacked personal knowledge of the legislative process as they began their work, it was really the amateurs who achieved the greatest success in dealing with state leaders and in informing library interests throughout the state of the kind of action needed when it was needed. Among those who served as volunteer and unpaid lobbyists were Francis St. John, Edward Freehafer, Joseph Eisner, and currently, John Frantz and myself.

c. Over the years we have been fortunate in having the right person in the right place at the right time. This was particularly true of the leadership of the Library Trustees Foundation of New York State. I cite particularly Mrs. Frank Moore, Thomas McKaig, Anthony Cerrato, and Richard Lawrence. Each of these trustees established a link with key state leadership at the very time when it was most needed for library legislative success.

d. Our lobbying tactics over the years were marked both by dignity and honesty. No high pressure was employed, nor did we spend any significant amount of money on lobbying efforts. Our low-key approach was much appreciated by state leaders who customarily dealt with either very suave lobbyists or those who used pressure and threats.

e. We learned from each of our failures (particularly in 1952), thanks to continuous vigilance. It was important to learn the nature of legislative opposition and the reasons for such opposition.

f. New York State's politics often are bitter and very partisan. Somehow we won bipartisan support for all of our legislative efforts.

g. We realized early in the game the importance of effectively answering questions about proposed library legislation. Our representatives in the field and within the State Education Department kept good liaison with each other, had quick access to facts, and were able to interpret the impact of legislation on the regions — usually of great interest to legislators.

5. *Patience and persistence:* As you will note when studying Table 1, the library leadership in New York State had to possess both patience and persistence. Failures far outnumbered successes. We suffered some real heartbreaks: notably in 1951 (when we won a $653,000 library appropriation, only to lose on the legislation required to permit us to spend it), in 1952 (when we discovered active opposition among the leaders of the legislature without knowing why until it was too late), in 1963 (when we thought that we had won our first victory for the 3R's program, only to lose it all because of a revolt of the legislature against the governor), and in 1964 and 1965 (when we won minor victories in the legislature only to lose both times due to vetoes by the governor).

6. *Adjustability:* That is another word for "compromise." On a number of important occasions, we decided to accept "half a loaf" in the interest of progress. Thus, in 1949 we drafted the first state-aid formula after being told that the state would provide in 1950 $1 million for such a formula. It required that we had to tailor-make the long-range formula so that its first year cost would not exceed $1 million. In 1958 we accepted a compromise in a state-aid formula and had to work two more years before the original formula was adopted. In 1966, we revised the state-aid formula, making parts of it effective in 1966 and other parts in 1967 because the legislative leaders said that was all the state could afford in 1966. In 1966 we were happy to settle for a $700,000 first appropriation for the 3R's program — despite the Governor's Committee on Libraries' recommendation of $1.2 million.

7. *Good timing and good luck:* It is important to note that neither libraries nor any other government service can expect to make big legislative and appropriation gains each year. The New York Library legislative successes seem to run in eight-year cycles: 1950, 1958, and 1966 mark the years of our major

victories. We hope that it doesn't mean that we have to wait until 1974 for our next success. One lesson that we learned — but never could apply to our satisfaction — was to build in a growth factor in the various formulas that we proposed. The best that we could do was to tie the formulas to population growth, but that has not kept up with the the inflationary spiral. It always appeared that state leaders wanted a maximum price tag figure and were unwilling to accept some open-end formula that could increase automatically during periods of inflation. It is difficult to explain how often good luck was on our side, and since there is no way to plan for good luck, I won't dwell on that point.

8. *Visibility factor:* Jean Connor, Director of SED's Division of Library Development, has stressed the importance of the visibility of a program to demonstrate its value at the time we sought funding for it. Thus, in 1950 when we first sought state-aid for county library systems, we could point with pride to the recently established and operating Erie County Public Library, Schenectady County Public Library, and the Chemung County financing of the Steele Memorial Library of Elmira. In 1968 when new legislation was introduced to amend the formula and to encourage multicounty library systems, we could point to the Monroe-Livingston-Wayne Tri-County Library System and the Clinton-Essex integrated two-county library system. In 1966 when we finally won our first 3R's appropriation, we could point to METRO, the first regional 3R's system to be formed in the state.

THE FUNDING MIX STATE, FEDERAL, AND LOCAL

The importance of fiscal flexibility in financing library networks is very great. New York State's funding mix is illustrated in Table 2.

Since the enactment of the 1958 public library system state-aid formula, the percentage of state-aid income of total public library operating expenditures has more than doubled. In 1957 state-aid income amounted to 7.7 percent of total public library expenditures; in 1968 it comprised 16.3 percent of the total. As Table 3 demonstrates, state-aid receipts rose 533 percent in the eleven-year period; per capita state-aid rose from 15 cents to 82 cents.

ACTIVATING THE NETWORK
IMPLEMENTATION: PERSUADING PEOPLE TO
WORK AT STATE AND REGIONAL LEVELS

Following successful network legislation or appropriation efforts, the next step is to persuade people to work at state and

TABLE 2. MAJOR FUNDING SOURCES: NEW YORK LIBRARY
NETWORK SERVICES

NETWORKS	STATE SOURCES	FEDERAL SOURCES	COUNTY SOURCES
Public library systems	State aid—systems	LSCA Title I & II	Erie County 100 percent; varying amounts elsewhere
Central libraries	State aid—central libraries	LSCA Title I & II	Erie, Monroe, Chemung, Tompkins, Schenectady 100 percent
NYPL research libraries	State aid—NYPL	None	None
3R's program			
State level	SED appropriation for 3R's	None	None
Regional level	SED appropriation for 3R's	None	None
NYSILL	SED appropriation for 3R's	LSCA Title III token amount	None
ANYLTS	None	LSCA Title I	None

TABLE 3. FINANCIAL DATA ON PUBLIC LIBRARIES IN NEW YORK STATE
1957 AND 1968

POPULATION DATA AND RECEIPT AND EXPENDITURE CATEGORIES	1957	1968	PERCENT INCREASE
Population	14,830,192	17,652,161	+ 19
Selected receipt sources:			
Local public funds	$23,718,188.00	$ 59,711,480.00	+151
Per capita	$1.60	$3.38	—
State aid	$ 2,282,174.00	$ 14,456,385.00	+533
Per capita	$ .15	$ .82	—
Major expense categories:			
Salaries and benefits	$21,445,155.00	$ 60,175,640.00	+180
Library materials	$ 4,869,241.00	$ 14,648,996.00	+201
Per capita	$ .36	$ .83	—
Other operating	$ 3,308,627.00	$ 15,820,394.00	+378
Total operating expenditures	$29,623,023.00	$ 88,735,891.00*	+200
Per capita	$2.19	$5.05	—
Capital expenditures	$ 2,794,533.00	$ 12,095,788.00	+333
Total expenditures	$32,417,556.00	$100,451,928.00*	+219
Per capita	$2.40	$5.72	—

*Adjusted totals, due to dual reporting of some contractual expenses.
Source: State Education Department, Division of Library Development

regional levels for the activation of the networks. Once again, a good partnership is needed between state library agency personnel and professional and lay leaders in the field. New York State was fortunate to achieve and retain this fine working partnership throughout the course of our library network history. Here are some of the highlights in the implementation of the various networks in our state.

PUBLIC LIBRARY NETWORKS

In comparing tactics for encouraging the establishment of larger units of governmental services, we have learned that the success in system library development is due to an active leadership role by professionals and lay people at the regional level. While state leadership is extremely important in any such project, it cannot take the place of regional leadership when informed professional and lay people who live in the region work for implementation of the network concept on a regular and continuing basis.

The years from 1945 through 1962 mark the period of intensive work by trustees and librarians seeking to establish county or regional public library systems. Leadership and coordination for these planning activities came from three state sources: the Library Trustees Foundation of New York State, LTF; the New York Library Association; and the Library Extension Division of the State Library, LED, forerunner of the Division of Library Development. LTF prepared and distributed county library planning kits to trustees throughout the state. LTF appointed a state committee of trustees to work on library system implementation. That committee, together with a similar NYLA committee, staged a workshop on system planning at Syracuse University to assure the availability of informed trustees and librarians for leadership at county and regional levels. LED staff provided help and advice to planners at every opportunity and assisted in distributing LTF planning kits and in sponsoring the workshop.

As a result of this leadership at the state level, many county and regional planning committees worked hard throughout the seventeen-year period. Most of the committees began their efforts with general information meetings at which trustees and librarians from existing library systems told about network implementation in their own areas. These "missionary" speakers brought a great impetus to the public library system movement in New York State. Most of the planning committees had no funds for planning purposes so LTF offered to supply speakers at no cost and to provide modest grants of money to planning committees for promotional expenses.

The Erie County Library Association was formed by library trustees from towns outside of the city of Buffalo. The trustees could see the advantages of a county library system and wanted to organize so they could have a voice in future planning of such a system. In 1947 the Erie County Republican leadership expressed an interest in establishing a county library system which would make possible the transfer of financial responsibilities for the two Buffalo libraries, Buffalo Public Library and Grosvenor Library, from the city of Buffalo to Erie County. The decision was made in 1947 to establish the Erie County Public Library which formed the first major federated public library system in the country by contracting with the two city public libraries and libraries in the towns of the county. The county supplied the funds for the operating budgets of all member libraries. The Erie County Library Association leaders played an active role in advocating the establishment of the county library and in influencing political decisions on the appointment of able trustees to that organization.

With the formation of the Erie County Public Library, trustees and librarians in Monroe County began their work toward the establishment of a similar federated county library system. They formed the Monroe County Library Association and worked for five years before persuading the Monroe County Board of Supervisors to establish the Monroe County Library System in 1952.

After the formation of the Monroe County Library System, trustees and librarians in adjoining Wayne and Livingston counties intensified their own planning efforts and succeeded in forming county library systems in 1955. As part of their planning they sought an alliance with the Monroe County Library System so that the people and libraries in those two rural counties could have access to the collections and services of the Rochester Public Library, the central library of the Monroe County Library System. Following the formation of the Wayne County Library System and the Livingston County Public Library in 1955, the trustees of those two systems entered into contractual agreements with the Monroe County Library System to form a three-county federation.

All three county library systems — Monroe, Wayne, and Livingston — were established by their boards of supervisors as federated library systems. The availability of state-aid was the deciding factor in the decisions by the board of supervisors. Each system board then negotiated contracts with the city, town, village, school district, and association libraries.

During the next several years, trustees and librarians from Ontario and Wyoming counties worked on planning committees seeking to establish their county library systems. Neither planning committee was successful in persuading its county board of supervisors to establish a federated library system. However, after the passage of the 1958 State-Aid Law, the planners were able to take advantage of a new option to form cooperative library systems, which were established by the participating libraries rather than by boards of supervisors. Upon the formation of Ontario Cooperative Library System and the Wyoming County Library System in 1959, the trustees of these two systems petitioned to join with Monroe, Wayne, and Livingston counties to form a five-county federation. This was achieved, and the federation was named the Pioneer Library System, PLS, since this was the first substantial example of a metropolitan county (Monroe) joining forces with rural counties to form a major library system. Five system boards and fifty-nine member library boards comprise PLS.

While the above activities were taking place in the Buffalo and Rochester regions, similar developments were brewing throughout the state. When the Commissioner's Committee on Public Library Service was in the process of drafting its 1958 proposed legislation, there were only eight library systems serving thirteen of the state's sixty-two counties in operation and receiving state-aid as a result of the passage of the 1950 State-Aid Law. Three of those systems were located in New York City (serving five counties), and the remaining five were centered in Buffalo, Elmira, Rochester, Schenectady, and Plattsburgh. With the passage of the 1958 State-Aid Law, a new element of flexibility in system planning was introduced — he cooperative library system. As previously indicated, the cooperative library system is formed by the member libraries rather than by a government legislative body. Upon the formation of such a system, the participating libraries elected a board of trustees which, in turn, petitioned the board of regents for a charter, thereby achieving corporate status. Such systems were eligible for state-aid funds in the same manner as federated or consolidated library systems.

The cooperative library system concept swept the state. Many of the county and regional planning committees that had been at work for some years had run into frustrating roadblocks because either their county boards of supervisors refused to

TABLE 4. DEVELOPMENT OF PUBLIC LIBRARY SYSTEMS IN NEW YORK STATE

CATEGORY	1957	1968	PERCENT INCREASE OR DECREASE
Population of New York State	14,830,192	17,652,161	+ 19
Population served by systems and nonsystem libraries	13,530,985	17,544,121	+ 30
Percent of population served	90%	99%	—
Number of systems	8	22	+175
Number of libraries in systems	89	702	+688
Number of nonsystem libraries	554	17	— 97
Total number of libraries	643	719	+ 12
Percent of libraries in systems	14%	98%	—
Counties wholly served by systems	13	61	+369
Counties partially served by systems	0	1	—
Counties unserved by systems	49	0	—

establish a system or in cases where multicounty library systems were being planned, not all of the boards of supervisors were agreeable to forming a library system. So, these planning groups recommended the formation of cooperative library systems in their regions and met with early and remarkable success. In 1958 immediately after the passage of the new law in April, five cooperative library systems were established. In 1959 another five were started. In 1960 another four were chartered. The remaining two systems were established in 1961 and 1962. That accounted for twenty-four library systems in the state, but Chemung County entered into a contract with the the the Southern Tier Library System, and Schenectady County entered into a contract with the Mohawk Valley Library System so the ultimate number of library systems in New York State was reduced to twenty-two. In the five-year period from 1958 through 1962, sixteen new cooperative library systems were established serving forty-six of the state's sixty-two counties. During the same period, three other counties joined the older eight systems. Thus, when the Onondaga Library System (based in Syracuse) was established in 1962, it became the twenty-second public library system, and all sixty-two counties of the state were served by a library system. The only system growth to occur since 1962 has been the slow but steady growth in the number of public libraries that belong to systems as boards of trustees of independent libraries reversed their earlier decisions against system membership. By the end of 1968, only 17 of the state's 719 public and association libraries were not affiliated with library systems.

Table 4 illustrates the dramatic development of library systems in New York State from 1957 to 1968 — a period that was probably the most dramatic and briefest reorganization of a government service at the state level in the history of New York State.

REFERENCE AND RESEARCH LIBRARY SYSTEMS

When the State Education Department received its first appropriation for the 3R's program in 1966-67, the establishment of the nine regional 3R's systems followed almost immediately. There were two reasons for this phenomenon: The need for regional 3R's systems had been suggested in 1961 (so there had been plenty of lead time for planning regional systems), and secondly, funding for a pilot regional program had come close to reality in several of the previous years, forcing regional planners with ambition to move very fast so that their region might be selected for the pilot project. However, the pilot funding never came off because the governor vetoed both proposals by the legislature.

The greatest stimulation to the establishment of regional 3R's systems came from the work of the Commissioner's Committee on Reference and Research Library Resources, which had issued reports in 1960 and 1961, and gave great emphasis to the formation of regional 3R's systems. Following the final report of the committee, its recommendations were discussed at regional meetings of public, college, and special librarians in many sections of the state. In 1964 librarians in New York City area formed the New York Metropolitan Reference and Research Library Agency, METRO, as the first of the regional 3R's systems in New York State.

SED's Division of Library Development contributed greatly to the organization of regional 3R's systems, both by the staff efforts of its newly formed Bureau of Academic and Research Library and by funding the initial study by Nelson Associates in 1962 for purposes of developing a model regional plan for the Rochester area. When the report was published, librarians throughout the state had one more working tool for applying the potential benefits of the 3R's program to their respective regions. Other regions followed suit by commissioning similar types of studies by Nelson Associates and by some librarians. Reports were published for New York City, Brooklyn, Mid-Hudson Valley, Buffalo-Niagara region, and the North Country.

In the Rochester region, for example, the following developments led to the formation of the Rochester Regional Research Library Council in 1966:

1. In 1960 Nelson Associates conducted a study for a group of Rochester area colleges on the possible advantages of interinstitutional cooperation. One of the recommendations was the formation of a Council of College Librarians. This council was formed shortly after the completion of the study.

2. The Rochester Area Council of College Librarians held regular meetings in the years following its formation and spent much time discussing potential cooperative programs. On some

occasions, public librarians and special librarians were invited to join in the discussions.

3.   It was this group that served as the prime sounding board to Nelson Associates when they conducted the 1961-62 study of the potential 3R's service plan for the Rochester region.

4.   When it became apparent that funding for 3R's was likely to be achieved in 1966, the Council of College Librarians voted to take the lead in establishing a regional 3R's system in the Rochester area. The group voted to invite representatives of the boards of trustees of the Rochester area colleges and public library systems to attend an information meeting for the purpose of considering whether a regional 3R's system should be formed. The meeting was held in December 1965, and an ad hoc planning committee was established to appoint a nominating committee and to call a formal organizational meeting of delegates of the institutions in Rochester region eligible to form a 3R's system. These were the nonprofit institutions that provided research library services. The formal organizational meeting was held in April 1966; the delegates voted to establish the Rochester Regional Research Library Council, and it elected its first board of trustees of fourteen individuals recommended by the nominating committee. The newly elected trustees (all lay people) then requested a charter from the board of regents to give the organization corporate status. Upon the chartering of RRRLC in June 1966, the organization became eligible for an establishment grant of $25,000 that allowed it to begin planning and to seek its executive director.

Most of the regional 3R's systems were established within a twelve-month period. This startling progress was accomplished because the DLD staff kept the planning groups in touch with one another and made it possible for them to share their planning and incorporation documents.

STATE SPECIAL PURPOSE NETWORKS

The implementation of the two current state statewide special-purpose networks was somewhat different from the establishment of the regional library networks. The two are: New York State Inter-Library Loan Network and the Association of New York Libraries for Technical Services.

In the case of NYSILL, the Commissioner's Committee on Reference and Research Library Resources had recommended

the early establishment of a statewide interlibrary loan network to extend beyond the resources of the State Library, at which point the then current public library interlibrary loan network would stop. As soon as 1966-67 appropriations for 3R's were a fact, DLD staff began to work with the Regents' Library Advisory Council, a nine-member library advisory committee to the State Education Department, DLD quickly contracted for a special study of interlibrary loan costs in some libraries and library systems in the state.[9] Armed with cost information and with ideas for a four-level network operation, the DLD staff, with the help and advice of the Regents' Library Advisory Council, worked out the NYSILL details. DLD staff were able to secure agreements from the participating service libraries to activate the network early in 1967. Three public library systems agreed to participate as area resource centers, and a group of university and special libraries (the latter concentrated in the New York City area) agreed to participate as subject resource centers.

In the case of ANYLTS, the focal point for its inception was the report by Nelson Associates, *Implementing Centralized Processing for the Public Libraries in New York State.* This report was presented to the public library leadership in the state at the 1966 annual Public Library System's Conference in Niagara Falls. Each library system was given an opportunity to decide whether it wished to participate in the formation of a corporation to determine the feasibility of a single computer center for acquiring and cataloging materials for all the public libraries in the state. The other charge to the new corporation would be to activate such an operation if it was found to be feasible. Because centralized processing was the most expensive system service and because Nelson Associates pointed out the potential savings through a centralized statewide operation, the boards of trustees of the twenty-two public library systems soon voted to participate in the formation of the new corporation. ANYLTS was created in 1966 by the representatives of the twenty-two systems, on which occasion a nine member board of trustees was elected. The board of trustees since has decided that a statewide processing operation is feasible. It has engaged its own director and staff, adopted an implementation timetable, and secured sufficient pledges from library systems to serve as customers that it may become a reality in the early seventies if sufficient venture capital is made available to it.

NETWORK ORGANIZATION AND PROGRAMS IN NEW YORK STATE

This section will deal with the structure of library networks in New York State at the state and regional levels. It also will describe the intergovernmental and interlibrary relationships that have been achieved by the formation of such networks with the aid of contracts and will summarize in checklist form the major network programs offered by public library systems and regional 3R's systems in New York State.

LIBRARY NETWORKS IN NEW YORK STATE

The two regional library network programs in New York State have been discussed at great length in this paper to this

TABLE 5. COUNTIES SERVED BY PUBLIC LIBRARY AND 3R'S NETWORKS
IN NEW YORK STATE

| PUBLIC LIBRARY SYSTEMS | | | 3R'S SYSTEMS | | |
COUNTIES SERVED	NUMBER OF SYSTEMS	NAMES OF SYSTEMS	COUNTIES SERVED	NUMBER OF SYSTEMS	NAMES OF SYSTEMS
1	7	Brooklyn, Buffalo and Erie, Nassau, Onondaga, Queens Borough, Suffolk, Westchester	2	1	Long Island
			4	1	Central New York
			5	1	Rochester
2	2	Chautauqua-Cattaraugus, Upper-Hudson	6	2	METRO, Western New York
3	4	Clinton-Essex-Franklin, Mid-York, Nioga, New York	7	1	North Country
			8	1	Southeastern
3.5	1	Ramapo-Catskill	10	1	Capital District
4	4	Four-County, Mohawk Valley, North Country, Southern Adirondack	14	1	South Central
4.5	1	Mid-Hudson			
5	3	Chemung-Southern Tier, Finger Lakes, Pioneer			

point. New York has sixty-two counties, and there is variation among the number of counties served by the public library systems as a result of the informal and long-term development. Other factors determining the county "mix" of these systems were intercounty rivalries, desire of some metropolitan counties to go it alone, and the jig-saw pattern of unorganized counties that were left after the early stage of system development had taken place.

The story of the territorial development of the regional 3R's networks was totally different. These had the advantage of studying the public library system development, and because existing patterns of regional delivery and interlibrary loan service had already been established by public library systems, SED established a regulation that required the regional 3R's systems to include entire territories of public library systems when affiliation occurred.

For a better understanding of New York State's geography and of the service territories of the public library and 3R's networks, the reader is referred to: Map 1, Location of Public Library Systems in New York State, and Map 2, Reference and Research Library Resources Systems. Both maps were prepared by SED's Division of Library Development.

Each of the two statewide special-purpose networks, NYSILL and ANYLTS, is structured differently. The NYSILL network is held together by a series of contracts between SED and the participating area resource centers and subject resource centers. The coordinating and communications center for NYSILL is the State Library in Albany, a unit of SED. The remaining parts of the network are the public library systems and the regional 3R's systems, and occasionally, individual members of

those networks with their own teletype facilities. All requests for materials through NYSILL are transmitted by teletype from regional points to the State Library where, if not filled by the State Library and if eligible for NYSILL, they are forwarded to the appropriate area resource center. If the area resource center is unable to supply the material, it forwards the request to the appropriate subject resource center. Each of the participating area and subject resource centers are reimbursed by SED for their search and supply services under an annual contract. NYSILL is financed from state 3R's appropriations and federal LSCA Title III funds.

ANYLTS, on the other hand, is an educational corporation established by the twenty-two public library systems and managed by a board of trustees elected by the participating library systems. To date, ANYLTS has no contractual relationships with library systems, but it is anticipated that it will have annual contracts with customer systems when it becomes operative. At the present time, the operating costs of ANYLTS are provided largely by SED from LSCA Title I funds, which are augmented by rather token annual system dues.

NETWORK CHARACTERISTICS

The library networks in New York State have a number of differences which demonstrate the flexibility of network planning in the state. Following are some of the areas in which networks differ:

1.   State controlled versus locally controlled

2.   Publicly controlled versus privately controlled

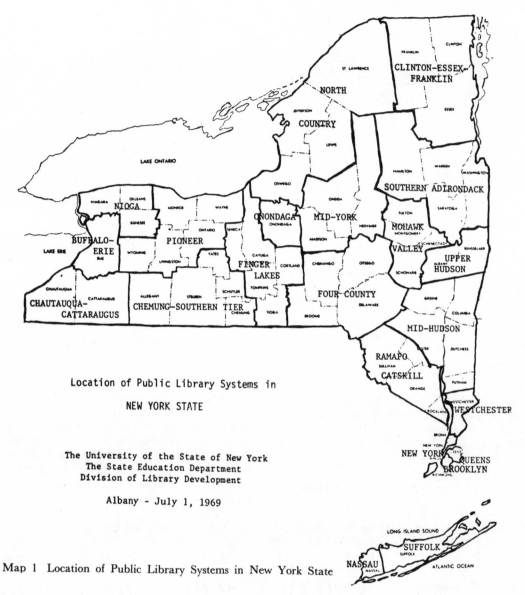

Location of Public Library Systems in

NEW YORK STATE

The University of the State of New York
The State Education Department
Division of Library Development

Albany - July 1, 1969

Map 1 Location of Public Library Systems in New York State

3.   Consolidated versus federated versus cooperative

4.   Primarily locally funded versus regionally funded.

An example of a state-controlled network is NYSILL, which is controlled and operated by the State Library, with contractual agreements with other participants. The other statewide network, ANYLTS, on the other hand, was established by the public library systems and is operated by trustees elected by the systems. Another illustration: the Watertown Regional Library Service Center was controlled and operated by the state until it was succeeded by the North Country Library System, which is controlled and operated by a regional board of trustees.

Illustrations of publicly controlled and privately controlled networks are: the Monroe County Library System, established by the county board of supervisors which also appointed its trustees, making MCLS a publicly controlled network; and the Rochester Regional Research Library Council, established by a group of nonprofit educational institutions (both public and private) which also elected its trustees, making RRRLC a privately controlled network. Both the MCLS and RRRLC boards of trustees received incorporation charters from the New York State Board of Regents, which has power to charter both public and private educational agencies.

The public library systems in New York State demonstrate the differences among three network organizational forms: consolidated, federated, and cooperative. Following are the major differences with illustrations:

1.   Consolidated: New York Public Library is a consolidated library system serving three counties in New York City. It is consolidated because it has *one* policy-making board and *one* administration *controlling* all libraries in the NYPL system.

MAP OF REFERENCE AND RESEARCH LIBRARY RESOURCES SYSTEMS

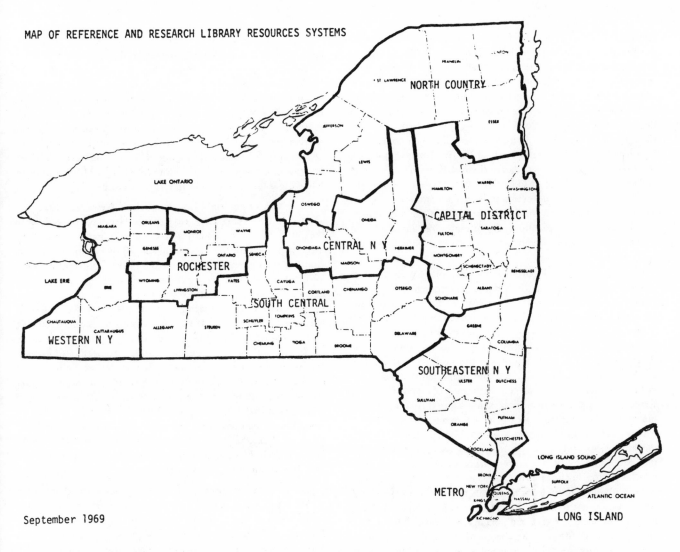

September 1969

Map 2   Reference and Research Library Resources Systems

2.   Federated: Monroe County Library System is a federated library system. The MCLS Board of Trustees is *appointed* by the county *legislature*. It does *not control* the libraries in the county, but it has a *contract* with them, thereby creating a federation.

3.   Cooperative: Ontario Cooperative Library System is a cooperative library system. The OCLS Board of Trustees is *elected* by its *member libraries*. It does *not control* the libraries in the county, but it has a *contract* with them, thereby creating a cooperative.

Please note the italicized words. Consolidated systems *control* all libraries with *one* board and administration; federated library systems are bound together with *contracts* between each library and the system's board of trustees, which is *appointed* by a public body — the county *legislature;* and cooperative library systems are similar to federated systems, except that their boards are *elected* by their *member libraries*. The Pioneer Library System, described earlier, is a federation of five systems, three of which are federated (Monroe, Wayne, and Livingston) and to two of which are cooperative (Ontario and Wyoming).

The other difference among systems is the chief local funding source. Buffalo and Erie County Public Library, B&ECPL, and Monroe County Library System both are federated library systems, but B&ECPL is a regionally funded federation whereas MCLS is a locally funded federation. The operating expenses of B&ECPL and all its member libraries are borne by Erie County; the operating expenses of MCLS and its member libraries are borne by a variety of local governments.

INTERGOVERNMENTAL RELATIONS: PUBLIC LIBRARIES

The fantastic growth of public library systems in New York State has involved every level of government in the state. The fact that almost 700 boards of trustees in communities throughout the state made major policy decisions to join library systems is evidence that more than a ripple was created in the pool of intergovernmental relations throughout the state. While the library boards rather than local government legislative bodies approved the contractual system agreements, most community library boards had the good sense to explain their actions to their local governments. Thus, city councils, town boards, village boards, and the voters in school districts learned that their libraries were seeking to broaden their services through membership in cooperative or federated library systems. While the public library system movement in New York State preceded by some years the current growing interest of local governments in regionalism and cooperation, the climate was favorable for library participation in regional programs in the late fifties and early sixties.

What happened in Monroe County is in many ways a mirror of the events in each county. The first governmental impact on library service was from the state offer of financial aid if the libraries would reorganize into a network. Library trustees and librarians from a variety of communities spent several years convincing the county's board of supervisors to establish the system. One of the key factors was the position of the city of Rochester which had established and supported the Rochester Public Library, the logical central library of a county library system. The city administration, being assured that some state funds would come from RPL via the system, advised RPL's trustees that it could support a county library system. Finally, the supervisors and the county manager gave the green light for the establishment of a county library system in 1952. The trustees of the libraries in the towns and villages then went to work explaining to their local officials that membership in the system would not hamper local library development, nor would it lessen the need for local support of the libraries. But it took county officials fifteen years before they voted to contribute substantial support. That decision was made by the county legislature (which replaced the board of supervisors) in 1967 when it voted 28 to 1 to provide substantial county financing for the central services of RPL in the interests of fiscal equity and furthering the city-county partnership. During the sixteen years that I have worked in Monroe County, the library system has had dealings with city and county officials, with every one of the nineteen town boards, and with most of the village mayors and village boards. It has been my staunch claim that our federated library system has done more to bring about goodwill and cooperation among the various levels of government than any other government agency or program in our county. One of the major factors for this achievement, in my judgment, has been the active participation of lay people as trustees and policy makers in the nineteen MCLS member libraries.

One of government's major roles in library development is financing, and I foresee a new trend in intergovernmental relations in the years ahead. At the present time, the state of New York, although providing less than 20 percent of the total income of public libraries, has achieved a revolution in library service through its state-aid program. The great bulk of public tax support for public libraries, however, continues to come from cities, towns, villages, and school districts. The dream of the 1949 planners on the Governor's Committee on Library Aid

was that the *county* would become the dominant financing agency since it is the largest unit of local government with tax levying authority. That dream has not yet materialized although it was given substantial impetus by Erie County in 1947 when it financed the operating costs of all the public libraries through its newly established Erie County Public Library. But in recent years, county governments have shown some signs of awakening, and there have been a number of major developments in county financing of library services. To demonstrate the complexity of county financing of library service, following is the 1970 picture in New York State.

Since five of the sixty-two counties in New York State are located in New York City, we will concern ourselves only with the other fifty-seven counties. During 1970 twenty-four of the fifty-seven counties are providing no funds for library service. Another six are making annual token grants of $6,000 or less – mostly less. Another twelve counties are making larger annual appropriations for library systems serving their area. Of the twelve: Six are appropriating between $10,000 to $25,000; four between $25,000 and $57,000; one is appropriating $100,000; and another $285,000. The largest two appropriations are being made by Suffolk and Nassau counties, respectively, to their county library systems on Long Island. Three counties are making substantial appropriations to their own county library systems (including their central libraries) which are part of larger federated multicounty systems. These three counties — Tompkins, Chemung, and Schenectady — have appropriated $247,000, $329,000, and $764,000, respectively, in 1970. Tompkins also includes small amounts for the multicounty system and for other community libraries in the county.

One of the most substantial of the financing trends has been in Monroe County which in 1970 appropriated $1,277,000 to support the central library services of the Rochester Public Library and another $44,500 to augment the budget of the Monroe County Library System. This move to provide funds primarily to the city library is unique in the state at this time. As indicated earlier, however, by far the most substantial recognition of the importance of library service by a county government is in Erie County, which in 1970 is appropriating $6,289,630 to finance the operating costs of the entire library system, including the central library and all member libraries.

Many New York State public library systems are multicounty, and some county governments find it hard to justify contributing substantial sums to a library system without assurance of similarly scaled contributions by the other participating county governments. As a result there has been a recent trend among some counties to appropriate money primarily for the community libraries within their counties that also are members of a larger multicounty system. Three counties are providing relatively small appropriations (between $13,000 and $20,000 annually), primarily for member libraries of the systems located within their county boundaries, with a small fraction for the systems too. There are another seven counties that make appropriations only for the community libraries within their borders, ignoring the needs of the library system entirely. One of these appropriates under $10,000 annually; two between $10,000 and $25,000; two between $25,000 and $50,000; and two between $50,000 and $60,000.

While these figures on county appropriations are not very startling, in some cases they constitute the beginnings of what may become an important trend in governmental relations affecting libraries.

INTERLIBRARY RELATIONS

The development of public library systems required interaction among all of the 700 participating library boards, administrations, and staff. But the newly formed regional 3R's systems have achieved a striking record for cooperation among libraries — regardless of type. In the nine regions that form 3R's systems, a refreshingly new partnership has developed among university and college librarians, public librarians, and special librarians. Only the school librarians have been left out to date. In most of the regions the librarians work together to form the system and comprise the great majority of the trustees in the nine regional systems. Only the Rochester Regional Research Library Council has an all lay board but that board has established an advisory committee of librarians which reviews every major policy proposed for action. Not only have these varied groups of librarians worked together to plan and organize regional systems (including the tedious jobs of preparing charter applications, bylaws, and annual operating budgets), but they have worked together to activate the programs of service. To top it off, they have been participating together in a great variety of continuing education programs, proving that librarians have far more in common than the isolationists of our breed imagine. The voting institutional members of the 3R's systems are the nonprofit educational institutions that operate research library service. These institutions usually are the universities, colleges,

special libraries in nonprofit institutions, e.g., museums and hospitals, and the public library systems and some of their central libraries. Nonvoting, but important, members or affiliates are the special libraries of profit-making institutions. These are excluded from voting membership because of the public tax funds administered by the 3R's systems.

THE IMPORTANCE OF CONTRACTS IN SYSTEMS

Eighteen of New York State's twenty-two public library systems are either federated or cooperative. These systems and their members are bound together through a series of contracts, some reviewed annually and some automatically renewed each year. Because systems vary in what services they supply directly and what they supply through contract with their central libraries, no two system contracts are identical.

Table 6 is a checklist of the major contract provisions within the Pioneer Library System which demonstrates the flexibility of our three basic contracts.

MAJOR SERVICE PROGRAMS OF NYS NETWORKS

The major functions of library networks in New York are: leadership, planning, coordination, consultative, fiscal, public relations, and liaison (on behalf of members with other library and governmental agencies). These functions are discharged through a variety of programs and activities. The SED report, *Emerging Library Systems,* listed the following 1965 major programs and activities for the twenty-seven reporting systems (the twenty-two usual systems, plus five smaller systems federated

TABLE 6. MAJOR CONTRACT PROVISIONS—PIONEER LIBRARY SYSTEM

NUMBER	MONROE COUNTY LIBRARY SYSTEM AND MEMBER LIBRARY CONTRACT PROVISIONS (1958 AGREEMENT)	PIONEER LIBRARY SYSTEM INTER-SYSTEM CONTRACT: LIBRARIES IN OTHER FOUR COUNTIES (1960)	ROCHESTER PUBLIC LIBRARY CENTRAL LIBRARY CONTRACT WITH MCLS (1960)
1.	Member: provides free access and loan privileges to all PLS residents	Same for PLS	Same for RPL
2.	Member: agrees to lend via interlibrary loan to all PLS residents.	Same for PLS, but PLS agrees to share cost of MCLS staff performing service in central library	Same, but PLS agrees to reimburse at $.20 per loan
3A.	MCLS: agrees to provide centralized book processing services (ordering, cataloging, preparation for use) and supplies free of charge to member libraries (purchased from RPL)	MCLS: agrees to extend these services to PLS for which PLS will pay →	MCLS: agrees to pay RPL $63,000 to process its own materials and to pay $.50 for each $1 worth of materials processed for MCLS and PLS and their member libraries
3B.	Further recentralized processing: Member: guaranteed free choice in selection MCLS: selects vendors Member: guarantees to pay vendors when billed	Same provisions for PLS members	Not applicable: RPL, as provider of service for MCLS, acts for MCLS

Number	Monroe County Library System and Member Library Contract Provisions (1958 Agreement)	Pioneer Library System Inter-System Contract: Libraries in Other Four Counties (1960)	Rochester Public Library Central Library Contract with MCLS (1960)
	Member: has option to process own materials Member: agrees to use MCLS order forms MCLS: makes decisions on cataloging and classification systems and materials used MCLS: sets monthly book repair quotas		
4.	MCLS: provides free delivery service to members (purchased from RPL)	PLS: provides delivery service to their members	MCLS: agrees to pay RPL 100 percent of cost of delivery to its branches and other MCLS members
5.	Members: agree to comply with regulations of board of regents	Not applicable (PLS have same provisions in contracts with their members)	Same for RPL
6.	Members: agree to keep records and make reports as requested by MCLS	Not applicable	Same for RPL
7.	MCLS: agrees to submit plan of service to commissioner of education for his approval and to supply reports and information that he requests	Same for PLS	Same in RPL contract
8.	MCLS: to advise and counsel member libraries	Not applicable	MCLS: ditto to RPL
9.	MCLS: agrees to share cash grants of $.15 per county capita among member libraries, based upon material expenditure percent of previous year	Not applicable	MCLS includes RPL
10.	MCLS: agrees to conduct six program meetings per year for member libraries	Not applicable	Not included
11.	(See RPL)	Not applicable	MCLS agrees to pay RPL 50 percent of poster and display and multilith services to extend to other MCLS members
12.	(See PLS and RPL)	PLS: agrees to pay MCLS for RPL—$500 per county in lieu of nonresident fee	MCLS: agrees to pay RPL the $500 per county from PLS
13.	Contract is automatically renewed unless terminated by either party at least sixty days prior to 31 December renewal date	Same provision	Same provision

into larger units). The numbers indicate the statewide scope of the services.

1. Coordination:

    a. Direct borrowing access   24

        1) Return of materials anywhere   19

        2) Bookmobile service   17

        3) Station service   12

        (Note: Six Western New York library systems have formed a Reciprocal Borrowing Cooperative, extending access via single library card to nineteen counties.)

    b. Interlibrary loan and photocopy service   27

    c. Centralized processing

of materials   27

    d. Library materials selection aides   27

        1) Book discussion meetings   23

    e. Library materials programs

        1) Rotating collections and bulk loans   27

        2) Pool collections   19

        3) Book grants to members   17

        4) 16mm film collections   26

        5) Phonorecord and tape collections   23

    f. Delivery service   27

2. Leadership and consultative:

    a. Consultant service –general   27

        1) Adult service   10

        2) Young adult service   9

        3) Children's service   15

        4) Audiovisual service   9

    b. Workshops and in-service training

        1) For professional staffs   24

        2) For trustees   17

        3) For clerical staffs   14

        4) Program meetings   21

3. Public relations:

    a. Publicity (posters, bookmarks, booklists, news releases)   27

        1) Public relations directors   14

        2) Display artists   17

        3) Exhibits   23

        4) Radio programs and spots   21

        5) Television programs and spots   10

    b. Bulletins and newsletters   25

4. Fiscal: cash grants to members   19

In terms of dollar costs, these were the most expensive system services in 1965:

1. Centralized processing

2. Grants (cash, materials, travel)

3. Consultant service

4. Deposits and rotating collections

5. Bookmobile service

6. Interlibrary loan service

7. Delivery service

8. Public relations services and materials

9. Audiovisual services and materials.

The regional 3R's systems do not yet have the financial resources of public library systems so their list of programs is not as extensive. They have been concentrating their efforts on planning and on programs concerned with: interlibrary loan, delivery service, consultant service, workshops and continuing education, publicity, and bulletins and newsletters.

NETWORK TRENDS IN NEW YORK STATE

The library network history in New York State has been an exciting one. Substantial changes have taken place at the state and regional levels during the twenty-three years of network developments and undoubtedly, there will be further substantial changes in years to come.

At the risk of oversimplification, I will borrow from the computer language and state that we are now in our second generation of network trends at the state and regional levels, and are preparing to embark on our third generation of trends, beginning in 1971.

REGIONAL TRENDS

At the regional level, the first generation included a series of steps that transformed the public library pattern from 650 isolated, independent, and usually, inadequate public library units into twenty-two systems or networks. These networks afforded their individual members great opportunities to extend and improve their services through a great variety of cooperative programs. Some of the twenty-two networks have further joined forces for specific purposes. Examples are three LSCA-funded recruitment projects — based in Rochester, Syracuse, and New York City — established to aid most of the public libraries in the state to meet their long-range professional recruitment needs. Another example of a multisystem program is the Western New York Reciprocal Borrowing Cooperative, through which five library systems serving fourteen counties have a single borrower's card, issued by any of the 200-plus participating libraries, which permits patrons to use public libraries free of charge from the Niagara Frontier to Syracuse and from Lake Ontario to the Pennsylvania border. Culminating this first-generation network development was the formation of ANYLTS in 1966 — the corporation founded to centralize processing of library systems materials at one point in the state of New York.

The second generation of regional networking in the state began with the formation of the nine regional 3R's systems that include public, college, university, and special libraries sharing their resources to better serve their publics. The 3R's development has not only broken down geographical barriers but also the psychological and institutional barriers that have long existed among various types of libraries. This second generation regional movement culminated in a series of statewide programs, the most notable being NYSILL, the communications and interlibrary loan network linking public library systems and 3R's systems with the State Library and with the area and subject resource centers via teletype communications.

Now, as a result of three years of study and work by the Commissioner's Committee on Library Development, we are looking forward to and planning the third generation of regional library networks. CCLD, in its report to the Commissioner of Education, has reaffirmed its faith in the network concept. It stated in its preamble the right of all residents of New York State to free access via their local libraries (whether they be public, school, college, university, or special libraries) to a statewide network. CCLD envisions statewide coverage by special-purpose library networks that are cooperatively planned, jointly financed, and state coordinated, which give all library users access to all library resources and programs through local access. Every library of any type should be eligible for participation in the network. Access to the network services

should not be restricted by age. New regional networks serving the special needs of school libraries should be established, and strong programs of coordination should be implemented to guarantee that the three regional networks, public libraries, 3R's, and school libraries, be coordinated to the greatest degree possible. CCLD envisions that these networks should have access to strong nonbook materials collections now lacking in so many sections of the state. It recommends that planning be undertaken to establish relatively strong intermediate libraries in those sections where access to strong central libraries is negated because of great distances. It urges the strengthening of the NYSILL Network and the linking of that network to other strong out-of-state resources. At the community level CCLD looks forward to the day when there may be established a single media agency (library) to serve the general public and students where the community also has benefited from integration of some educational, cultural, health, or social services through physical grouping and functional consolidation. Also at the community level, CCLD urges public libraries and school libraries to examine carefully the potential benefits of concentrating in the elementary school media center the responsibility for meeting all the library needs of all elementary school-age children. CCLD also recommends that a statewide library system to serve the residents of health, welfare, and correctional institutions be established as a single network to bring long overdue quality to institutional library service. It looks forward to the implementation of the ANYLTS statewide processing center and to its expansion or adaptation to provide similar services to all types of libraries in our state.

STATE TRENDS

At the state level we have seen our state library agency move in the first generation from serving inadequately the individual, isolated public and school libraries to developing new methods for dealing with public library systems and some emerging regional school library systems. The second generation of statewide networking began with the addition of the Bureau of Academic and Research Libraries to the Division of Library Development to form a new partnership with the regional 3R's systems. For the first time this allowed the state agency to provide service to college and special libraries. In that same generation the State Library initiated the NYSILL network and experimented briefly with facsimile transmission, only to find that we were ahead of our time.

During the third generation of statewide networks, CCLD looks forward to further coordination and strengthening of the library agencies within the State Education Department, bringing together those responsible for all types of library and audiovisual services. It has urged that there be representation in the Commissioner of Education's cabinet by a SED official responsible for and directly involved with library development in our state. CCLD has recommended the establishment of an intradepartmental Council of Education Media and Resources, chaired by the commissioner of libraries, to work toward integration of library planning at the state level. It recommends that the Regents' Advisory Council on Libraries be strengthened and made as representative as possible to maintain a strong partnership between the state agency and those in the field. CCLD expects that the state agency personnel will concentrate much of their efforts on their role as coordinator of statewide and regional library network activities so that maximum benefits from networks will be achieved with minimum duplication or unnecessary effort. CCLD hopes and expects that present and emerging technology will be utilized by state library personnel not only for centralized processing and communications but also to improve public service through new devices such as cable television and developing film and video tape cartridges that promise to revolutionize communications.

The third generation of library networks in New York State, both at regional and state levels, affords librarians and lay library leadership an opportunity for progress in service that should eclipse the achievements of the first two generations of library networks in New York State.

KEY PROBLEMS AND SUGGESTED SOLUTIONS: NETWORK FINANCING, IMPLEMENTATION AND ORGANIZATION

This last section attempts to summarize the key problems that have confronted librarians during network implementation in New York State — in the past and the present. Many of the solutions suggested for today's problems have been devised by the Commissioner's Committee on Library Development in its June 1970 report to Commissioner Ewald Nyquist.

NETWORK FINANCING

1. *Problem:* The current status of library finance is deficient; why seek network funds? Examples: library appropriations are low; local government's property tax and college's tuition income are too narrow bases; most state agencies are underbudgeted.

    Suggested solution: The establishment of networks makes sense to government and education policy makers. Regionalism is a growing trend. Networks can help members demonstrate fiscal needs and seek greater share of state and federal funds not now available — both of which overcome narrow-base problem.

2. *Problem:* How can libraries succeed in gaining network funding?

    Suggested solution: Libraries can succeed by careful studies and planning; by strong legislative campaigns; by hard work and learning from other areas and states; by establishing priorities for the use of state and federal funds.

3. Equity issues

    a. *Problem:* Central libraries of public library systems give far more than they get and are supported by only a small fraction of the systems' population; the same is likely to be true of research network central libraries.

    Suggested solution: The long-range CCLD solution is total library funding by the state. Short-range solutions include: (1) Ear-marked state-aid for central libraries, (2) broader tax base for central libraries, e.g., county or region, (3) special research library collection development fund, (4) require fair payment for services rendered via contact.

    b. *Problem:* Some communities or institutions support library service well; others support poorly and benefit greatly; some districts do not support library service at all, but residents benefit.

    Suggested solution: Set minimal network standards and prevent entry by substandard libraries; admit them provisionally and have the network aid them in order to upgrade themselves; or provide matching state and network funds as an incentive and as a reward for effort.

4. *Problem:* State-aid formulas fail to provide for future increased funding requirements due to inflationary costs, population growth, and increased network service demands.

    Suggested solution: Some solutions include: (*a*) Include inflationary escalation clause in formula if possible, (*b*) key formula to per capita aid so it will grow with population, (*c*) make some services optional, to be financed by libraries requesting service, (*d*) maintain accurate cost records, seek regular reviews of formula, and justify increases needed.

5. *Problem:* State-aid formulas fail to take into account economic variations: varying ability to pay in some regions and higher costs to serve sparsely settled areas and areas with disadvantaged populations.

    Suggested solution: Some solutions include: (*a*) Seek as broad a tax base as possible to limit need for equalization, (*b*) include an equalization and/or sparsity factor in the formula, (*c*) include special formula provision for extra aid to disadvantaged areas (CCLD).

6. *Problem:* There is great fear that libraries that join state or federally financed networks will suffer compensatory losses in local income.

    Suggested solution: It certainly has not happened in New York State in twenty years. ALA national systems study also proved this fear to be unfounded.

7.   *Problem:* How do states secure funding for special-purposes statewide networks, e.g., NYSILL and ANYLTS?

Suggested solution: First they must have high state priority in planning and funding. Other points include: giving priority in planning to use of federal and state funds; including percent factor in state-aid formula to finance such networks serving all systems; seeking compensation from user libraries for all or part of services rendered.

ACTIVATING NETWORK IPLEMENTATION

1.   *Problem:* Lack of understanding potential value of networks by librarians, policy makers, and by the public.

Suggested solution: Planning leaders must undertake a vigorous educational program.

2.   *Problem:* Lack of lay and professional leadership in the regions to spark implementation process.

Suggested solution: State planning leadership (state library association and state agency staff) should seek out potential leadership personnel in the regions. They should utilize individual and group training methods to prepare them for leadership roles.

3.   *Problem:* Two additional liabilities: complete satisfaction with the status quo by trustees and librarians and a fear of loss of autonomy if their library joins the network.

Suggested solution: The first attitude, smugness, is most difficult to overcome without offense to the person. Try to involve the individual in the planning process through appeal for his "leadership"; he may learn en route. Response to fear of loss of autonomy is to invite participants in other networks to speak from experience.

4.   *Problem:* Personality problems: mistrust, jealousy, and desire for power or leadership.

Suggested solution: Try to involve these people in every step of the regional planning and activation process. They will know what is going on and thus, will have less reason to imagine the worst or to misjudge the abilities of others.

5.   *Problem:* Attitude of "isolationism" from other types of libraries: conviction that there is no common interest ground, feeling of superiority, exaggerated concern to protect the interests of their immediate clientele.

Suggested solution: Cite examples of operating networks that include various types of libraries, e.g., New York State's 3R's. Point out use of different area libraries by high school and college students who ignore artificial interlibrary barriers.

6.   *Problem:* Fear of imbalance in use by network patrons: that their libraries will be asked to provide a disproportionate share of loans and service; concern for inequity of use; desire to restrict network access to select groups, excluding students.

Suggested solution: There are several possible solutions: (*a*) Incorporate in regional or state plan an equitable compensation program so that libraries used most heavily are reimbursed, (*b*) institute access service on a pilot or gradual basis to determine facts in access patterns, (*c*) cite experiences of similar libraries that participate in other networks, (*d*) start interlibrary loan service before access service to minimize direct access impact.

7.   Problems with central libraries of networks:

a. *Problem:* Key central library is "luke warm" about accepting responsibility to serve as hub of network.

Suggested solution: A network must provide benefits to the strong, as well as the weak. These benefits usually are cash. Build into network financial plan special aid to strong libraries, e.g., New York State central library aid and adequate compensation for services rendered.

b. *Problem:* No qualified central library exists in the region.

Suggested solution: This is a tough problem. Reexamine the region and seek to enlarge it; or contract with nearest strong library in another network; or build into state and regional formulas special grants to strengthen weak central libraries, e.g., New York State central library book-aid grants.

c. *Problem:* Central library's building is inadequate for new role.

Suggested solution: Seek top priority for central library buildings in any state or federal construction grants, e.g., LSCA Title II grants.

8. *Problem:* Opposition to some potential network services because of fear of their inadequacy, e.g., centralized processing; or desire to share in only limited number of services e.g., interlibrary loans.

Suggested solution: Build flexibility into the network plan, giving members option to select services desired, provided that they meet minimum membership qualifications.

NETWORK ORGANIZATION AND SERVICES

1. *Problem:* Tendency to design networks for single type of libraries, e.g., public libraries or school libraries, to the exclusion of all other types.

Suggested solution: This may be necessary and even desirable at times, but first consideration should be given to a library network in which every type of library is eligible. If single-type library networks are needed, build coordination at regional and state levels, as CCLD recommends. Some services, e.g., delivery and interlibrary loan, are naturals for a multitype library system.

2. *Problem:* Tendency to design inflexible network structures, e.g., New York State 1950 law envisioned only two types of public library systems: consolidated and federated.

Suggested solution: Devise flexible network legislation to permit the greatest variety of network structures, e.g., New York State cooperative public library systems and regional 3R's systems. Add flexibility by permitting regional networks to contract with each other for some services.

3. *Problem:* Danger of planning regional networks that are too small in area, population, or members which will lack the funds necessary to provide a full range of services to its members and the public.

Suggested solution: Some possible solutions include: (*a*) Establish minimum criteria for network eligibility, e.g., New York State public library state-aid law; (*b*) encourage small systems to contract with larger systems for

some services by increasing aid for that purpose or giving priority in granting federal funds; (*c*) encourage networks to band together for some services, e.g., New York State ANYLTS.

4. *Problem:* The temptation for small groups of libraries to form exclusive local, regional, or special-purpose networks.

Suggested solution: While some of these may serve useful purposes for their members, try to limit the number. CCLD recommends that such networks be ineligible for state or federal funding unless they are compatible with overall plan and really serve state purposes.

5. *Problem:* The possibility that network planners may overlook their responsibilities to the public.

Suggested solution: Encourage active participation in the evaluation of the networks by students, faculty, research personnel, and the general public through advisory committees, lay network boards of trustees, and evaluation of network performance at regular intervals.

6. *Problem:* The possible failure of regional and state network administrators to involve their member libraries in the policy-making process, resulting in unsatisfactory network relations.

Suggested solution: CCLD makes several recommendations here: (*a*) that networks be required to demonstrate to the state agency that they afford opportunities for member library participation in the network decisionmaking process, (*b*) that the Regents' Advisory Council on Libraries (statewide advisory body) be strengthened and made as representative as possible by solicitation of nominations from he field and limiting the terms of office, (*c*) that the Regents' Advisory Council on Libraries conduct annual spring hearings on library finances and network problems in which library interests could participate.

7. *Problem:* Clarification of the role of the state library agency in network planning, operations, and coordination.

Suggested solution: CCLD makes a number of recommendations on this point: (*a*) Primary responsibility of the state is to insure comprehensive statewide library service network by planning, financial support, and provision of state-level services and facilities; (*b*) state leadership, funds, and expert assistance are required to achieve interstate network linkage; (*c*) state library network responsibilities include: service as unit or center of statewide networks, service as switching center, and coordinating information agency re: acquisitions of major libraries and for insuring state-level adequate bibliographic control of all media; (*d*) the primary consulting role of SED should be to provide leadership and assistance, mainly through specialist consultants, to library networks of all types; (*e*) SED library units should have sufficient staff, properly classified, to carry out CCLD recommendations.

8.   *Problem:* Problems of personnel shortages and lack of network-oriented professional staff.

Suggested solution: Some suggested solutions include: (*a*) State agencies should conduct in-service training and continuing education programs dealing with network problems and programs; (*b*) networks, by centralizing some services, reduce the need for some specialists; (*c*) by working together in networks, libraries best can solve their manpower problems, e.g., recruitment, in-service training, and continuing education in many fields; (*d*) CCLD has made many specific recommendations regarding library manpower through its state study.

9.   Some major library service problems re: inadequate materials that networks may or may not solve

a. *Problem:* Lack of nonprint materials

Suggested solution: There should be unified media programs in all libraries at all levels, including strong central audiovisual collections and provisions for special nonprint funding programs from State and Federal sources.

b. *Problem:* Duplication of evaluation efforts

Suggested solution: Establishment of a statewide evaluation center.

c. *Problem:* Inability of librarians to examine materials personally

Suggested solution: Establishment of statewide network of materials examination centers.

d. *Problem:* Unnecessary duplication of materials.

Suggested solution: Establishment of coordinated acquisitions programs at regional, state, and interstate levels.

10.   *Problem:* Network services, e.g., centralized processing and interlibrary loan, are too slow, inefficient, or costly.

Suggested solution: A working partnership of the state agency and the networks can tackle these tough programs through study, evaluation, and sharing of experiences and methods. Examples in New York State: formation of ANYLTS and great improvement in NYSILL due to evaluation studies and input from networks at regional hearings.

11.   *Problem:* The need for a more speedy and effective network communications system and for utilization of modern technology by libraries.

Suggested solution: Here again partnership between the state agency and the networks promises the only solution. CCLD recommends that the state should provide leadership and expertise in exploiting technology for all aspects of library development. Special competencies should be added to SED staff, and reports on important developments should be made regularly to the field. New York State examples: the statewide teletype network, exploration of thruway state delivery service, facsimile transmission experiment, ANYLTS, and state computer program for NYSILL and serials bank.

12.   *Problem:* Some of the handicaps of networks inherent in their cooperative nature: slow decision progress, lack of "muscle," least used by the poorest members.

Suggested solution: You do not overcome them, but you can minimize them. If networks are to share policy-making responsibility with members and make services available on optional bases, they cannot at the same time operate in autocratic style. But maybe this is not so bad in the long run. Members are more apt to implement policies which were adopted with their help than those imposed upon them. No one can make a librarian an effective person if he is unwilling.

13.   *Problem:* How do you meet the need of evaluation of network performance?

Suggested solution: That is the responsibility of the state agency. In New York State, there have been three major reviews of the public library system, plus evaluation of NYSILL, the facsimile transmission system, and centralized processing. CCLD recommends for New York State: that SED should seek assistance of a public administration-oriented agency with appropriate experience to design a system for evaluation of library service in the state.

NOTES

1. Charles M. Armstrong, *Development of library services in New York State* (Albany, N.Y.: Univ. of the State of New York, 1949), p.

2. New York (State) Governor's Committee on Library Aid, *Library service for all,* report 1950 (Albany, N.Y.: State of New York, 1951), 103p.

3. New York (State) University, *Report of the Commission of Education's committee on public library service, 1957* (Albany, N.Y.: State Education Dept., 1958), 43p.

4. Commissioner's Committee on Reference and Research Library Resources. *Report* (Albany, N.Y.: N.Y. State Library, 1961), 43p.

5. New York (State), Governor's Library Conference, *Proceedings of the first governor's library conference, June 24-25, 1965.* (Albany, N.Y.:), [n.p.] 67p.

6. New York (State) University Office of Research and Evaluation, *Emerging library systems; the 1963-66 evaluation of the New York state public library systems* (Albany, N.Y.: State Education Dept., 1967), 291p.

7. Nelson Associates, Inc. *Implementing centralized processing for the public libraries of New York state ([New York]: the author, 1967), 35p.*

8. ...., *An evaluation of the New York State Library's NYSILL pilot program* (Albany, N.Y.: the author, 1968), 150p.

9. ...., *Interlibrary loan in New York State* (New York: the author, 1969), 1v. (loose-leaf) tables.

Financial Formulas for Library Networks

Phoebe F. Hayes

LIBRARY SERVICES: A BACKGROUND OF SUPPORT PROBLEMS

The hard core of the financial problem of network development differs only in degree from the present fiscal concerns of libraries.

Libraries and existing networks already are preoccupied with the ever-growing demands of identifiable users and are increasingly aware of the dimensions of needed service to non-users; however, this group may be described and categorized. Financial projections for network support realistically and as nearly accurately as possible, must assume that among the advantages of a truly national network will be that of more easily and effectively reaching the former while participating in any efforts to reach the latter.

Present library users for the most part pay taxes somewhere or at least, find that some portion of their annual tax payments, directly or indirectly, go to library support. This generalization could include the funding of the many contract research and development adjuncts of the federal government. The dilemmas of providing access to library services for all are far from simple in solution. We need not go into any extensive treatment of those nonserved, disadvantaged areas: population-poor rural areas, students, racial minorities, the aged, the disabled, the institutionalized. We are very conscious of the need for great improvement in the support of state library agencies, the lack of tax base for many local communities where demands may outrun ability to pay or to raise tax revenues. The multiplicity of local government taxing units, with cumbersome fiscal practices, is a further barrier to service. In some places it is impossible (or officials are unwilling) to accept federal- or state-aid. The public library, relying as it does on local tax sources to satisfy program demands, faces a struggle for status quo support in many communities as it competes for funds.

Public libraries depend heavily on local government appropriations; in 1965 these sources provided 84 percent of public library revenues. The remainder, 16 percent, came from state and federal transfer funds, with added income from endowments, gifts, fines, and other miscellany.[1] In 1962, when these percentage figures were substantially identical, these funds totaled $359.3 million from reporting libraries, of which $26.4 million came from state grants and $301.5 million from local appropriations.[2]

Corporate support of libraries for the benefit of specialty-users can be charged off in the price structure applied to the end product, and therefore, ultimately paid for by the consumer. Nongovernmental, nonprofit agencies supporting library services for a usually highly defined group frequently can trace their funding to the advantages enjoyed by tax-deductible contributions of the erstwhile taxpayer.

Financing patterns in themselves are complex. Federal contributions are lumped in with state subsidies in percentage figures so that it is difficult if not impossible to separate local support. Joint costs of services do not provide distinguishable segments within governmental units and institutions.[3] There is, financially, lack of uniform accounting. The end result: It is most difficult to determine what really are the precise costs of library/information services.[4]

Access to reliable library statistics containing fiscal information is uncertain and behind the times. The National Advisory Commission on Libraries found it impossible to ascertain the total amount of national library expenditures and to estimate the costs required to fully support *present* library services, much less future ones.[5] Statistical standards are woefully lacking. Current statistical reporting programs are erratic; subsequent publication lags do not help. Currently available statistics are years behind the times. For example: The latest figures for colleges and universities published by the U.S. Office of Education cover Fiscal 1967-68. Some selected statistics exist for certain liberal arts colleges and for members of the Association of Research Libraries for Fiscal 1966-67. Purdue University has published an interesting projection to 1980 for research libraries. Public library statistics for libraries in cities with more than 25,000 in population exist for Fiscal 1967-68, with a 1968-69 survey underway.

There never has been a comprehensive collection of statistics for special libraries. A survey of special libraries serving state government gives figures for 1963-64; a similar study of these libraries serving federal government agencies exists for 1965-66. Some specialized groups have fared better; more recent studies have been conducted for health science and law libraries. No figures for corporate libraries are available; there are no plans to update or make more inclusive overall statistics for this important group. A new survey of school libraries is being planned in 1970; the only presently existing statistics are for Fiscal 1962-63. This group is eliminated entirely from a current census of libraries in the United States.[6] Present library costs are not only greater than has been recognized, but cost per unit of output may have been increasing. Manpower costs, population growth, and evolutionary inflation contribute to a rate of cost increase which is uncertain;[7] what is less uncertain is that the fiscal needs of libraries are moving faster than the present slow growth of the economy.

Library costs appear to vary in rough approximation to acquisitions costs. It is safe to predict that an increase in library budgets and salaries will have to move at the rate of 10 percent per year. Book prices, subscription costs, communications and equipment costs are all increasing; in some instances, services essential to the average library are being priced out of the library market. No thorough evaluation of the costs to the user of secondary services exists, e.g., NASA, DOD, and ERIC are examples. In the federal executive branch alone, information programs were budgeted at $380 million in 1966.[8] A single directory of services is now in the publishing phase; a multiplicity of distribution channels confuses the user. Restraints on use provide an added hazard. The regional technical report centers were discontinued in part due to alleged limited use. What the user does not, or is not, able to use cannot be effectively costed. Quality standards for existing services also are needed.

There is little need to dwell on cost justification for library support in this paper. Justification was stated expertly and succinctly in one of the studies commissioned by the National Advisory Commission on Libraries, which concluded that national productivity and technology might well be adversely affected if library research did not contribute; furthermore, one necessary condition for assuring a rising per capita income is the existence of libraries. The commission recognized that any increase in library costs would mean a negligible percentage of national income growth, and if not allowed, a foolish economy.[9]

Whether the cost justification of a national network is not as a salable commodity may be dependent upon the amount and success of the library homework that remains to be done. Somehow we will have to establish the record on present programs.[10] In discussing the New York State Inter-Library Loan Network, NYSILL, S. Gilbert Prentiss raises the question of value judgments versus absolute cost as well as relative cost of New York's network effort, suggesting that a one-to-one charge from lender to borrower might be the simpler, less costly method of handling interlibrary loan business.[11] We will have to produce the correct answers to the embarrassing questions of cost versus social objective, of maximum practicable access, of optimum service areas and units,[12] and of network costs involving expensive technology.[13]

The national commission reminds use that even to approach ALA standards, we would need (as of 1968) $1.6 billion of funds for school libraries and $9.9 billion for academic libraries. It concludes that very large increases in federal support of libraries will be not only necessary but actually inevitable.[14] The report criticizes weaknesses in the present support programs: a diffusion of legislation; overlapping, uncoordinated programs; no supporting program, nationally, for research libraries *per se*; very little support for library manpower and for planning at the state library level. Its recommendations, hopefully, would help to remedy these lacks.

CURRENT NETWORKS AND THEIR SUPPORT: SOME EXAMPLES

Certain current programs which engage in one or more facets of networking can be described to illustrate the variety of funding sources. No attempt has been made to assure complete inclusiveness; however, the types of organizations alluded to, and their financing patterns, can be viewed as reasonable examples of what is occurring today. Reference will be made to the specific funding pattern employed in each. A most extensive study of interlibrary cooperative services which has been conducted by Dr. Edwin E. Olson of the School of Library and Information Services, University of Maryland, when published, should reveal much more about present financial patterns, their uses and abuses, weaknesses and strengths. From preliminarily presentations of his findings at the ALA midwinter meeting in Chicago and during the ALA conference in Detroit, there is, in my judgment, no reason to expect a startling disagreement with the author's tentative conclusions as presented in this paper.

Funding of such groups of data banks, consortia, information centers, bibliographical centers, or union catalogs; courier services, corporate networks, and the many illustrations of state or intrastate networks is dependent to a considerable degree upon federal and/or state grants, the latter often merely transferral devices for passing on federal monies. Initial grants have come from these sources; initial grants also have come from the private sector. Via charter, contract, or very informal agreement, additional funds come from membership or use of services. These user fees are based on variations in formulas and yield unpredictable incomes. Many of these groups could not exist without some indirect subsidy; usually this includes cost absorption of rent-free quarters, maintenance, and other overhead by a host institution. Varying amounts of additional income are derived from other sources: gifts and supplemental foundation support, subcontracts for services performed, royalties or other revenue from publications, dividends or interest on savings and investments, use of accumulated surplus. In the case of certain simple cooperatives, e.g., local federations of public libraries, income for basic activities is provided from the several local tax sources affected, with special project monies frequently granted from state and federal transfer funds.

STATE/FEDERAL GRANTS

This paper need not describe the many federally funded authorizations for programs which can be carried on under the Library Services and Construction Act titles, the Higher Education Act, the Elementary and Secondary Education Act, and other legislation. These are currently listed and described elsewhere.[15] The National Library of Medicine's support of biomedical networks is well known, as is the National Science Foundation's support of mission- and discipline-oriented information systems. The type of grant: establishment, demonstration, or a special project; the requirements for use: contractual, informal, or special purpose also are amply described.

MEMBERSHIP OR ACCESS FEES

Membership or access fees, when assessed, open the doors to users under limitations stipulated by the institution levying them. Some are entrance fees only; actual service is provided by payment of additional fees. Some are self-inclusive and allow access to all services tendered. The basis of the fee may be population, enrollment in academic institutions, a percentage of operating or book budgets of affiliators; or volume of interlibrary loan.

User Fees

User fees are charged for services in a more particularized fashion. They may be arrived at by a simple division: cost of the service divided by use. Few of them have been determined as the result of any truly comprehensive cost analysis, and in fact, this represents one of the real dilemmas of developing formulas. User fees can be many things: a search fee; a current-awareness charge; a transaction fee for processing an interlibrary loan; or a charge for the performance of a service or combination of services.

Data Banks

Data bank charges have not been explored for this paper. Data banks are frequent by-products of one-to-one relationships of research and development organizations to federal government agencies funding them. These banks are available to defense contractors, to the general public on proof of need, or may be sold as a service by subcontractors (e.g., a NASA data bank that is tapped for specific searches or for current awareness on demand of the customers is available on contract from the Technology Application Center, University of New Mexico). This center has a price structure, presumably bearing some relationship to the cost of searching the several data banks at its disposal since its services offer access to a large number of additional data sources other than NASA.

Information Banks—Information Centers

The Library Reference Service, Federal Aid in Fish and Wildlife Restoration (U.S. Department of the Interior, Bureau of Sport Fisheries and Wildlife) is an indexing and reference service funded under two programs of this agency, with quarters furnished by the Denver Public Library. Its services — bibliographic, photocopy, reference, and computer search — are free to state and federal personnel allied with the programs or to serious researchers sponsored by them; so-called noncooperators pay specified service charges.[16]

Southern Methodist University's Industrial Information Service is one of the most successful, if not the most successful, information center outlasting the demise of State Technical Services Act funding. These technical information centers originally matched 50 percent grants from federal funds via state-assigned disbursing agencies, with equal amounts contributed from sponsoring institutions and/or membership and service fees. IIS has established an access fee for various member categories, based on dollar volume use of its services in a previous twelve-month period. Its service fees establish charges for the loan of materials, photocopy, bibliographic verification, ready reference, literature searches or search guidance, location of material outside of the Dallas-Fort Worth area, referral to

information/data sources; and for delivery service. This schedule was designed after a cost study and concurrently with renewal of agreement for assumption of overhead costs by Southern Methodist University. Presumably its viability will continue to reflect a realistic cost appraisal as well as an aggressive service promotion effort.[17]

A very similar set of charges is in effect at the Regional Information and Communication Exchange, RICE, at Rice University, Houston, and at the Colorado Technical Reference Center, housed at and otherwise supported by the University of Colorado.[18]

Consortia

A recent study of academic consortia presents some interesting facts on library participation in these groups. Of a total of 1,017 reporting institutions, 5.4 percent indicated some library activity. Most of them (971) said that the consortium was supported financially although only a third of these reported a separate budget. Most of them receive no present federal or state funding although responses on planned new consortia show signs of an increased reliance on federal funding, using the Higher Education Act and other legislation presently available. Other funding comes from the private sector (gifts and grants) or from the participating institutions. Some consortia activities require little or no funding; however, clear fiscal and administrative agreements are not always present, as perhaps they should be, if only to justify the advantages of joint use and support of facilities otherwise unaffordable.[19]

Courier Services

Courier or delivery services often are arrangements within arrangements, parts of larger cooperative efforts such as resource centers, processing centers, or information services. The service administered by the Colorado State University is linked with the Colorado Academic Libraries Processing Center but available for other uses such as interlibrary loan and message transfer. The expense of this particular service, after experiment with an earlier, weighted formula, now is costed simply by dividing salary and mileage by the number of items delivered to each participant member.[20]

Center for Research Libraries

As is well known, membership in the Chicago-based Center for Research Libraries originally was confined to major academic institutions in the Midwest carrying on research programs, and with specific requirements for library volume and expenditures for books and materials. Now open to membership without geographic restriction, it offers also a second class of membership to associates based on the same formula but with lesser requirements. The center also is able to support extensive materials acquisition programs by agreement of the participants, securing added funds from federal sources.[21]

METRO: An Example of an Intrastate Network

METRO (New York Metropolitan Reference and Research Library Agency), as a representative of the well-known 3R's structure in New York State, received an establishment grant under the program in 1967 and since, has received added funds. Chartered in 1964 it had received in 1966 a one-year operating grant from the Council on Library Resources. Within the regulations of the State Education Department, METRO membership is available to any system of libraries, library of a college, university, or other nonprofit educational institution; business corporation; or any other organization interested in the improvement of reference and research libraries in the metropolitan area. For METRO purposes the metropolitan area includes the five boroughs of New York City, Westchester County, and contiguous areas of Connecticut and New Jersey.

Each of the nine 3R's agencies in the state currently receive equal grants of $55,000. A recommended state-aid formula which has not yet been funded would provide per capita annual grants based on student enrollment in institutions of higher education and on census-reported professional persons living in the area.

A dues structure was adopted in 1967. This sets forth several classes of library memberships, each paying in a dues scale according to amount of annual library budget; the maximum is one-tenth of one percent. State-aid via basic formulas and special project grants amounted to $100,000 for Fiscal 1968-69; foundation grants have added approximately half that much annually. The New York Public Library originally subsidized space, utilities, staff services, and some staff salary but now receives payment for overhead expenses.

UNION CATALOGS BIBLIOGRAPHICAL CENTERS

The experiences of three of the union catalogs — bibliographical centers which have endured since the mid-1930s provide pertinent case histories and demonstrate endurance on limited means. Some examination of their various fiscal programs is in order. From original funding by the Carnegie Corporation, each has for many years relied upon membership goodwill or lack of it, upon largess from host institutions for quarters and sometimes, for staff and supporting services. Two of the regional centers within recent years have benefited from statewide network development programs. Discussion of their fee structure is confined to the primary services rendered by these centers — that of bibliographic assistance, location, and interlibrary loan and referral. Each institution has had added income from projects or other sources, usually marginal in amount.

UNION LIBRARY CATALOG OF PENNSYLVANIA

This catalog-bibliographical center originally limited its services to the Philadelphia metropolitan area, in which are located many academic libraries and small special libraries. Subscription (membership) fees for academic libraries and related nonprofit institutions are low, based on library income, and at a maximum are a fifth of one percent of total income, with certain exceptions for libraries making small use of the catalog. Subscription fees for industry range from $50 to $500 per year. In addition, the catalog charges nominal per inquiry fees.[24][25][26]

For the past seven years the catalog has been a part of the Pennsylvania statewide reference service program, receiving an amount of money for services rendered to the entire state. In 1968 a statewide arrangement was inaugurated with the New Jersey State Library.

PACIFIC NORTHWEST BIBLIOGRAPHIC CENTER

Lura Currier's just-completed study of this center, undertaken subsequent to the Becker-Hayes working paper on the proposed Washington state network, explicitly details the problems of a voluntary organization to which no public funds are directly appropriated. Low dues, a fluctuating membership, income which lags behind need, an inability to plan because of fund uncertainties caused by an undisciplined membership; and a lack of firm policy, directed by short-term officers with varying interest in or commitment to the organization: All these are disadvantages if one seeks a successful network operation.

The formula implementing this state of affairs has been in effect since 1951 and calls for a maximum membership payment of $1,000 based on (1) a fourth of one percent of annual library expenditures for academic institutions or others without buildings and grounds costs, provided income is in excess of $25,000; or (2) for public libraries, a fee of a fourth of one percent of an amount equal to 80 percent of income. Small libraries pay very small amounts; very small libraries are not required, but are encouraged, to make token payments. Mrs. Currier's recommendation for adequate support proposes a shift of PNBC support to the states on a pro rata population base, each state contributing in ratio to total population of all the states served. Her recommendations are under current discussion. She proposes a budget which would be presumed to be based on income from application of the pro rata fee.[27]

BIBLIOGRAPHICAL CENTER FOR RESEARCH ROCKY MOUNTAIN REGION INC.

This regional center provides a record of the most extensive experimentation with membership and use fees. For many years it accumulated funds from voluntary contributions. In 1951 it set a pattern of low basic membership fees based on academic enrollment, and for public libraries, population. There was a geographic price differential as between Colorado and the remaining states in the region. To supplement this base, a percentage service charge was to be made once the center's budget was adopted. The difference between the total amount of money collected from basic membership fees and the amount of money needed (budgeted) was to be prorated among the members according to each members' percentage of total requests processed in the center in the year preceding. There was no basic fee established for other types of libraries.[28]

A new fee schedule was effected in 1962. This arbitrarily set minimum membership fees for all types of libraries, including state library agencies. The fees were nominal; added to them was a unit, per item charge, based on a moving average of use over an immediately prior two years (a parity feature). During this period the center, aware of the precedent set with the Pennsylvania State Library by the Philadelphia Union Catalogue, began thinking about the possibility of contractual arrangements with state libraries in its area. It successfully concluded such arrangements in three states in the period 1965 to 1968.[29]

A revised schedule, adopted to go into effect in 1969,[30] put this policy into the fee structure. It called for two plans of membership: A *statewide support plan* was negotiated in accordance with services rendered to a group of libraries designated by a state library agency and funded by the state, usually from LSCA Title I monies; some Title III money was used; and in the case of one state, state grants-in-aid were available. *Direct* support plan memberships were charged at a fourth of one percent of current annual operating budget. Nonmember use fees also were stipulated. Intended as a transitional schedule, with provision for compromise and negotiation, this schedule brought a demand for a cost study of the center. The study was made,[31] and a resultant fee schedule was placed in effect in 1970.[32] This schedule continues to incorporate the state plan approach, and in fact, is designed deliberately to encourage this pattern. It sets mandatory fees for state agencies, based on population figures. For those libraries remaining outside a statewide program, i.e., either the states in which they are located are not willing, for a variety of reasons, to negotiate, arrange, and pay for the program; or the libraries are in a peripheral geographic location with the potential of state linkage deemed unrealistic, there remained the alternative of individual payments of access fees. Based on the rationale of the preference for the state plan, individual libraries can pay access fees on the basis of *total* interlibrary loan borrowings, plus a transaction fee, into which was built a quality factor. Libraries or state agencies are requested to define the kind of service desired in terms of location of materials, bibliographic verification, and priority service. Nonmember charges are set to exceed any combination of these factors. The schedule has resulted in new and renewed state contracts, with some accommodations to within-state facts of life which retain an element of local responsibility for transaction fee payments.

The Present Programs Advantages and Disadvantages

Some of these programs represent substantial steps in or contributions toward networking. That some of them are precariously financed is obvious. Projects inherently necessary to ongoing functions and essential for important new undertakings remain static or dormant due to want of funds. Clearly, support policies and support levels not only demonstrate fiscal weaknesses and misdirections but more importantly, are creatures of lack of administrative and political planning. Thus it is the want of design — and perhaps the want of commitment — which may be responsible for fiscal impoverishment. The present programs include some viable features and where based on long-term, large-scale development programs or the elements thereof, they appear to have these common denominators: a grant program, with extensive filtering down of federal funds; a measure of local and user responsibility for payment; certain other evidences of subsidy (within-house support, absorption of overhead, etc.). Present programs clearly suggest that there must be a sound financial structure for networks.

PROPOSED PROGRAMS FOR NETWORK DEVELOPMENT

There are several significant proposals for network development. With the pursuit of the charges given to the newly established National Commission on Libraries and Information Science,[33] this body may provide some cohesiveness to network planning.

There already has been planning and pro and con argument for some time around the activities of the Committee on Scientific and Technical Information, COSATI.[34] The National Academy of Sciences, National Engineering Committee on Scientific and Technical Communication, SATCOM, has a Joint Commission on Scientific Communication working with COSATI in initiating and carrying out analyses and exploration of network components under a properly funded program.

In reaction to the original COSATI proposals, the Ad Hoc Joint Committee on National Library/Information Systems, CONLIS, proposed an integrated national information system with local, self-supporting outlets. It anticipated building on existing structure after thorough investigation of its inadequacies. CONLIS expected support and use of private as well as public agencies. The nationalization envisaged would be expected to contract with others or operate itself the essential national bibliographic services, and to negotiate with other agencies for supplemental services at the local level once the measures of need were established.[35]

The SATCOM report shows particular concern for the need to study cost and value factors, cost-effectiveness ratios, input costs of information, the pricing of services to the user, especially of the basic access services of document availability—bibliographic control, abstracting, and indexing. It also is preoccupied with the form of continued federal support, overlaps and gaps in coverage. It suggests topics for study: An evaluation of potential support for academic and research libraries; equation of library revenues with costs of required services, possibly on a cost-reimbursable basis; how to obtain effective local access to current technical literature; improvement in the flexibility of access to information systems. It wants cost studies on different methods of storage and transmission of information, on optimums of information centers, the location of these centers in relation to the question of centralization versus decentralization.[36]

Downs, in proposing a regional library authority for the Kansas City Regional Council of Higher Education, advocated LSCA support in recognition of the services supplied by such an authority. The enumerated services were to be directed toward bibliographic access, acquisition, cooperative storage, processing, and advisory service to the college libraries participating. His study proposed National Science Foundation support to the Linda Hall Library as an adjunct resource; the solicitation of area business and industry support; application to foundations for special projects; and annual assessments for some equitable formula.[37]

Among the organizational considerations discussed in *EDUNET: Report of the Summer Study on Information Networks,* conducted in 1967 by EDUCOM in Boulder, Colorado, were various financial proposals. Fiscal problems of the proposed networks were explored in terms of fund sources and allocations, external versus participant support, cost distribution as related to local responsibility and local use. Brainstorming produced detailed suggestions for pricing mechanisms, internal accounting, billing of users, costs of data bank acquisition, royalty and copyright payments. Recognized were the burdens placed upon participant institutions; and the need to resolve inequities via payment schedules, contractual arrangements, and other reimbursement features. User fees were generally proposed although it was suggested that ability to pay might not be the sole criteria of access. To finance this extensive educational network, federal funds are to be sought for a demonstration period, possibly from a combination of agencies. The developmental plan would employ such subsidies, to which would be added membership dues and private subsidy, plus indirect and direct subsidy from participating institutions. These monies would be intended as the backing for the planning activities of EDUCOM, the next stages of operational testing and development, and the ultimate full operational status.

Alternatives in communications layouts were outlined. Cost estimates for network development and for the communications proposals were stated.[38]

In a working paper for a statewide library network, Becker and Hayes projected costs of such a network for the state of Washington but supplied no budget or fiscal formula; nevertheless, the considerations incidental to the next steps in the planning of this network are important and resulted in the Currier study mentioned previously. Further studies are in process.[39]

As a basic document for a symposium on an agricultural sciences information network held this year, EDUCOM's plan for this network provides some cost elements, particularly for the telecommunications.[40]

A modest project on a regional level is that currently seeking letters of intent from a group of academic libraries. It suggests a credit arrangement with billings for filled and unfilled interlibrary loan requests administered by a clearinghouse to be designated by the signators. The costs would be absorbed by the libraries participating, billed to patrons, or financed by a special grant proposal.[41]

Intended for application in the biomedical community, a Rand Corporation paper looks at some of the inherent economic considerations in directing the choice of communications systems and advises against a single technology. The costs are illustrative.[42]

Another discussion of technology and the decisions required of research libraries in such matters as machine-readable catalogs, the impact on library building requirements of advanced communications devices for data and information transmission such as facsimile, the picturescope, or optical scanners, is to be found in the published volume on the work of the National Advisory Commission on Libraries. In further consideration of technological impact in this work, Cuadra recommends a program of action contemplating five projects, leading to a fully integrated national library system, and indicates that cost appraisals would be required. It is assumed that massive support would be an absolute; that identification of all potential sources of support would be a necessity; but that most of the funding would come from the federal sector.[43] If such is the judgment, it is highly likely that federal funding will impose controls in order to obtain the desired cooperative action.[44]

Other thinking about what states can do to finance network activity is to be found in Connor's recommendation that each state should seek funds to set up its own version of the LSCA Title III program, supplementing that source of funding.[45] In Swank's California study, he recognizes cost elements and proposes federal and state grants, along traditional lines, to meet the need of reimbursement to resource libraries.[46] Cost data are wanting.[47]

FUTURE SUPPORT OF NETWORKS

There is near-unanimous expectation that Washington — the federal government — must be the source of major library funding, at least initially. So pervasive is the belief in this as a justified expenditure that it is reflected in the consistent conclusions in the literature whenever support of networks is discussed. While the National Advisory Commission on Libraries echoes this, it did not consider it within its province to offer a dollars-and-cents formula.[48] The National Academy of Sciences study considered a number of possibilities: (1) a system so centralized, federally operated, that it resembled the Soviet pattern, (2) initial or developmental subsidies of limited duration, (3) input cost charges to authors and output costs to be borne by users, (4) direct subsidies for input costs only and output costs to be met by marketing the service.[49]

Cost Elements

Any formula for network support requires consideration of cost elements, and these are embedded in the structural and operational decisions of network construction. The questions of what kind of network, the projected stages of development, and who pays for what must be answered before a viable formula can be advanced; otherwise, we would be prescribing a fiscal remedy without benefit of diagnosis. Communication costs must be specified in terms of equipment, routing, channels, volume, and outlets.[50] Alternatives may lead to alternative formulas. Indirect costs may vary, as between simple and complex networks. Contractual relationships may provide reimbursements from one political level to another which requires subsidy, such as federal or state support to the research library providing for the use of its collection. Use of expensive data banks or information analyses centers may require cost reimbursement or service fees from the network. The formula will have to have a built-in schematic not only for raising money but for paying it out.

Cost design as related to formula will demand prediction of use and must provide flexible alternatives and adaptations based upon a series of variables. Use of program budgeting by libraries is just beginning. Cost justification should be founded on this kind of planning and budgeting. Functional costing, along with the imperative of cost-effective programming, must be accompanied by standards.

While there is this acceptance of reliance upon federal funds, the question of the fair share of federal versus state versus local support is interjected in several current writings. Knight and Nourse suggest more research is in order to arrive at a fair-share formula to replace present speculative or assumptive acceptances. These authors note that Joeckel suggested a formula of this kind in reporting to the President's Advisory Commission on Education in 1938; Joeckel and Amy Winslow later spelled this out in percentages: 60 percent local, 25 percent state, 15 percent federal funds. At an Allerton Park Institute in 1961, Hannis Smith is reported to have supported these shares as 40 percent local, 40 percent state, 20 percent federal.[51] *Actual* support of public libraries, as we have noted previously in this paper, does not approach this optimum, if such it is. If this is a generally accepted ratio, its application has been directed to public libraries only; the issue has not been faced for school, academic, or state libraries. Frantz makes the point that "...we need to nail down the generally emerging but still vague concept of the continuing federal share...."[52] He looks at the dogma of matching funds with some question since it appears that matching may be more in myth than in reality.

In looking at program goals for public libraries for this decade, Drennan's projection of possible funding trends considers three levels of funding into which he has built sharing formulas. Noting that in 1965 local governments received 30 percent of their revenues (for *all* purposes) from nonlocal sources, supplying 70 percent themselves, he compares this ratio and the more usually advocated 60-25-15 to speculate on what could happen to library funds under three conditions: a prevailing status quo economy, a projective trend based on the experience of the 1960s, and the optimum of meeting present ALA standards.[53]

Whether formula construction for network application can pursue as simple an approach even if the ratios were a matter of firm acceptance is highly questionable. Very possibly networks may require an inverse ratio, e.g., 20 percent local, 20 percent state or regional, 60 percent federal. What is not at all to be questioned is that network planners are forced to look at the politico-economic debate on revenue-sharing which preoccupied economists, fiscal experts, and politicians and which is implicit in all tax-reform measures before Congress. A most valuable compendium[54] of historical review, current concerns, and authoritative position papers should not be overlooked by library-information specialists, nor should the tax reform measures which have so far come out of Congress or remain in debate. The bibliography appended to this paper calls attention to the contributions in the three volumes of the compendium of special pertinence to a consideration of a network formula. This paper attempts to synthesize relevancies rather than to extend itself to a lengthy and specific consideration of the contents. Therefore, concentration of interest for our purposes in this Conference is indicated and some conclusions drawn:

1.   The arguments over conditional/categorical versus block/unconditional grants represent positions which require political resolution. While some movement may be made toward block and unconditional grants (such as favored by the Commission on Intergovernmental Relations and given to librarians by Colman),[55] the traditional use of categorical or functional grants (not without some

amalgamation of these) will continue. These are grants to which librarians are accustomed.

2.   Equalization formulas, such as built into the Hill-Burton Act and other health measures (and which have been applied in part to LSCA), will continue to be employed and in fact, expanded since this factor is missing from many present revenue-sharing measures. It may be applied even if unconditional grants are accepted in the United States. (Another area of equalization might be compensatory payments to specialized data bases, mission-oriented networks, copyright owners.)

3.   Even conservative fiscal experts predict more federal sharing. This may be accompanied by such features as open-ended grants, with built-in controls, perhaps a lessening of distinction as between capital versus operating grants. There will, however, be:

4.   Emphasis on what is termed efficiency is germane. This warrants subdefinition. It implies a cost/benefit analysis requirement, an evaluation of social investment, a systems approach to formula building, and an evaluation of what is called "spillover." This term is directed to a special consideration of cost/benefit. It suggests the determination of internal versus external benefits of any program. In library consonance, this would appear to have application to the economy of larger units of service, to support from the taxpayers living within the core unit, e.g., a metropolitan area serving persons outside of the boundaries of the corporation. A cost spillover might *not* warrant grant support; a *benefit* spillover might. The cautionary advice — plan accordingly. By extension, this should engage the attention of the network planner and should include a further requirement: a *correct analysis of demand.*

5.   The cost/benefit, systems approach is linked in several challenging proposals to suggestions that a *regional* approach to federal grants may be used increasingly. It is used now in the funding of the Appalachia programs, in the Public Works and Economic Development Act of 1965 in which the Secretary of Commerce is directed to encourage multistate regional planning commissions; the several educational planning commissions in New England, the South, and West are other examples of regionally coordinated planning. The

political arrangements could vary, as could the contractual. Interstate compacts are one approach. The funding from federal sources might emerge as more generalized, permissive, and generous, provided this comprehensive approach.

Finally, there is a recognition of the need to collect much more data on expenditure, on the geographic distribution of expenditure, with computerized models to identify the direction for the best use of funds. These appear to be ideal considerations for network construction at a time when the federal-state-local-private sector participations may be readjusted under presently insufficient guidelines and the need for new formula development.

With all of this as, indeed, cautionary, there remains to the contributor of this paper only the most generalized conclusions for building a formula suitable to network planning. Since no expertise as fiscal expert or mathematician can be claimed, it would be presumptuous to suggest otherwise. What is suggested in this context is (1) an exhaustive examination of present funding formulas and their applications; (2) the correlation of these formulas to the formulas suggested in such exercises as EDUNET; (3) any result should be based on a consistency of financial support, politically acceptable to ALA, to other library groups, and to the presently fragmented fundgivers in both the private and public sectors.

Such a formula should take into consideration the elements of demand, cost/benefit, and other planning approaches for long- and short-term application to network application, including projection of fixed and variable costs, the cost of interlinkage among networks (a near-impossibility at present), and the costs of inputting the great multiplicity of present and proposed information sources and data banks. Priorities must be stated. Models should be constructed and tested; prototypes should emerge. "Everyman" presumably waits for information; a truly national network will discover the marketplace and plan accordingly.

NOTES

1. Henry T. Drennan, "Public library program goals in the decade of the 1970's," in *The Bowker annual of library and book trade information, 1969* (New York: Bowker, 1969), p.16.

2. Douglas M. Knight and E. Shepley Nourse, eds., "The costs of library and informational services," in *Libraries at large: tradition, innovation and the national interest: the resource book based on the National Advisory Commission on Libraries* (New York: Bowker, 1969), p.214.

3. Ibid., p.171.

4. E. Shepley Nourse, "Areas of inadequacy in serving multiple needs," *ibid.*, p.163-164.

5. Douglas M. Knight and E. Shepley Nourse, eds., "The costs...," *ibid.*, p.170.

6. Frank L. Schick, "A century of U. S. library statistics of national scope," in *The Bowker annual of library and book trade information, 1970* (New York: Bowker, 1970), p.7-8.

7. Douglas M. Knight and E. Shepley Nourse, eds. "The costs...," *ibid.*, p.193.

8. William T. Knox, "Toward national information networks: 1. The government makes plans," *Physics today* 19:44 (Jan. 1966).

9. D. M. Knight and E. S. Nourse, eds., "The costs...," *ibid.*, p.206-07.

10. Foster Mohrhardt, "A challenge to habit: some views on library systems, in *Libraries and automation, proceedings* (Washington, D.C.: Gov. Print. Off., 1964), p.246.

11. S. Gilbert Prentiss, "The evolution of the library system (New York)," *Library quarterly* 39:85 (Jan. 1969).

12. G. Flint Purdy, "Interrelations among public, school and academic libraries," *Library quarterly* 39:62 (Jan. 1969).

13. National Academy of Sciences - National Academy of Engineering, Committee on Scientific and Technical Communication, *Scientific and technical communication; a pressing national problem and recommendations for its solution* (Washington, D.C.: The Academy, 1969), p.170-172. This report has an excellent section on prices and price differentials of secondary services, on forms of support for aids to literature access, including federally operated or supported aids; and describes the obstacles to and the procedures for procuring publications from federal scientific and technical agencies.

14. U. S. National Advisory Commission on Libraries, "Library services for the nation's needs: the report of the National Advisory Commission on Libraries," in D. M. Knight and E. S. Nourse, eds., *Libraries at large...*, p.503.

15. "Legislation and grants," *The Bowker annual...,1970* p.77-147.

16. "Service fee now in effect," *Newsletter* [Library Reference Service, Federal Aid in Fish and Wildlife Restoration] 11:1 (June 1970).

17. "New IIS fee schedules," *IIS industrial information service, Southern Methodist University newsletter* 4:2 (28 July 1970).

18. "A comparison of fees charged by the Colorado Technical Reference Center and by centers in other states," *CTRC newletter* 2:3 (Nov.-Dec. 1969).

19. U. S. Department of Health, Education and Welfare, Office of Education, *Consortiums in American higher education: 1965-66; report of an exploratory study* (Washington, D.C.: Gov. Print. Off., 1968), 47p.

20. Richard D. Hershcopf, Colorado State University. Letter to interlibrary loan courier members, 6 July 1970.

21. "Circulation policy," *Newsletter* [Center for Research Libraries]. 109:6 (Jan. 1969).

22. John Mackenzie Cory, "The network in a major metropolitan center (METRO, New York)," *Library quarterly* 39:90-98 (Jan. 1969).

23. New York Metropolitan Reference and Research Library Agency, *METRO: what it is and what it does* [New York, 1968?] folder.

24. Henry C. Longenecker, "Financial support of the Union Library Catalogue," (Union Library Catalogue of Pennsylvania) *Newsletter* 85:[8-11] (Feb. 1962).

25. Union Library Catalogue of Pennsylvania, *Contract for service* (Philadelphia: The Catalogue, n.d.).

26. ...., *Schedule of subscriptions for academic and related non-profit institutions voluntary support of the Catalogue* (Philadelphia: The Catalogue, 1966).

27. Lura Gibbons Currier, *Sharing the resources in the Pacific Northwest; a study of PNBC and interlibrary loan* (Olympia: Washington State Library, 1969), 188, [72]p.

28. Bibliographical Center for Research, Rocky Mountain Region, Inc., *The basis for the support of the Bibliographic Center* (Denver: The Center, 1951), 2p.

29. ...., *Membership fee schedule* (Denver: The Center, 1961 and 1963), 1p.

30. ...., *Revised fee schedule* (Denver: The center, 1968). (Adopted by the Board of Trustees 27 June 1968) 2p.

31. Joan M. Maier, *The Bibliographical Center for Research, Rocky Mountain Region: a cost study of the Center's present operations* (Denver: The center, 1969).

32. Bibliographical Center for Research, Rocky Mountain Region, Inc., *1970 fee schedule* (Denver: The Center, 1969). 3p.

33. "National Commission on Libraries and Information Science," *LC information bulletin* 29:374-377 (30 July 1970).

34. William T. Knox, "Toward national information network," p.39-44.

35. Ad Hoc Joint Committee on National Library/Information Systems (CONLIS), *Improving access to information; a recommendation for a national library/information program* (Chicago: ALA, 1967).

36. National Academy of Sciences - National Academy of Engineering, Committee on Scientific and Technical Communication, *Scientific and technical communication...*

37. Robert B. Downs, *A survey of cooperating libraries for the Kansas City Regional Council of Higher Education* (Kansas City, Mo.: Kansas Regional Council, 1964), 60p.

38. George W. Brown et al., *EDUNET: report of the summer study on information networks* (New York: Wiley, 1967), 440p. on information networks [conducted by the Interuniversity Communications Council (EDUCOM)] (New York: Wiley, 1967), 440p.

39. Joseph Becker and Robert M. Hayes, *A proposed library network for Washington State, working paper for the Washington State Library* [n.p.], 1967), 50p.

40. Interuniversity Communications Council (EDUCOM), *Agricultural sciences information network development plan,* Research Report 169 (Boston: EDUCOM, 1969), 94p.

41. Regional Information Network Group, (Denver) *Academic library teletype experiment; letter of intent* (Denver: The Group, 1970). 2p.

42. J. A. Farquhar and J. A. Dei Rossi. *Alternative technologies for information networks,* p-4272 (Santa Monica, Calif.: Rand Corp., 1969), 8p.

43. Douglas M. Knight and E. Shepley Nourse, "Some problems and potentials," in their *Libraries at large...,* p.279-288.

44. Orin F. Nolting, *Mobilizing total library resources for effective service* (Chicago: ALA, 1969), 20p.

45. Jean L. Connor, "Stages in and fields for interlibrary cooperation," *Bookmark* 13:18 (Oct. 1967).

46. Raynard C. Swank, *Interlibrary cooperation under Title III of the Library Services and Construction Act: a preliminary study for the California State Library* ([Sacramento: California State Library], 1967), 78p.

47. Virginia L. Ross, "Review of: Interlibrary cooperation under Title III of the Library Services and Construction Act., by Raynard C. Swank," *News notes of California libraries, Suppl.* 65:367-375 (Winter, 1970).

48. E. Shepley Nourse, "Areas of inadequacy...," in D. M. Knight and E. S. Nourse, eds., in *Libraries at large...,* p.163-164.

49. National Academy of Sciences - National Academy of Engineering, Committee on Scientific and Technical Communication, *Scientific and technical communications.*

50. J. W. Emling et al., "Library communications," in *Libraries and automation, proceedings* p.203-219.

51. Douglas M. Knight and E. Shepley Nourse, eds., "The role of local-state-regional cooperation," in *Libraries at large...,* p. 408.

52. Jack C. Frantz, "Big city libraries: strategy and tactics for change," *Library journal* 93:1968 (15 May 1968).

53. Henry T. Drennan, "Public library program goals in the decade of the 1970's," in *The Bowker annual...1969,* p.14-18.

54. U. S. Congress, Joint Economic Committee, Subcommittee on Fiscal Policy, *Revenue sharing and its alternatives: what future for fiscal federalism?* (90th Cong., 1st sess. Joint Committee Print [Washington, D.C.: Gov. Print. Off., 1967]) 3v.

55. William G. Colman, "Federal and state financial interest in the performance and promise of library networks," *Library quarterly* 39:99-108 (Jan. 1969).

Some Social Considerations of Networking

Robert Heinich

Anticipating McLuhan by a number of years, Franklin Delano Roosevelt asserted the difference between electrical and mechanical energy in terms of organizational influence on society at the World Power Conference of 1936:

Now we have electric energy which can be and often is produced in places away from where fabrication of usable goods is carried on. But by habit we continue to carry this flexible energy in great blocks into the same great factories, and continue to carry on production there. Sheer inertia has caused us to neglect formulating a public policy that would promote opportunity for people to take advantage of the flexibility of electric energy; that would send it out wherever and whenever wanted at the lowest possible cost. We are continuing the forms of overcentralization of industry caused by the characteristics of the steam engine, long after we have had technically available a form of energy which should promote decentralization of industry.[1]

Under government auspices, the area served by TVA to some extent reflected FDR's position, but on the other hand, the mechanical and electrical energy of Hoover Dam combined to allow Los Angles to defy geography and become the largest city on the West Coast. Nor is Los Angles itself the model of the centralizing influence of mechanical energy that FDR hinted at and McLuhan later proclaimed. The automobile dominates Los Angles, and the city is as anarchic as the device it is dependent upon. The irony of the late President's statement is that the very flexibility of electrical energy *permits* further centralization if this is what we want and that is the way our political and social structure push us. Bruner's famous geography lesson where he gives students a map showing natural resources and physical characteristics of the land and then asks them to locate major cities is fifty years out of date. Modern technology can destroy geography — unfortunately in the literal as well as the figurative sense. The point is that our hopes for a new form of energy often are confused with the dynamics of the innovation in interaction with the existing social structure and human wants. Electric energy *has* transformed the United States but in the direction that Innis first, and then McLuhan, have indicated rather than the physical decentralization for which Roosevelt (more likely his planners) hoped.

We are in this situation in regard to networks. Energy is information — and electronics is not only literal information but interactive as well. It is the responsiveness, the interactiveness, added to the all-at-onceness of electricity that creates the powerful energy system of information networking, with the consequent capability of transforming society. However, in attempting to identify possible transformations, we tend to extend into the future present trends within our own institutional frameworks. In addition, what seems important to us in this new capability, may not be important to someone ten or twenty years in the future. It is tempting to substitute in the Roosevelt quote the words "electronic information" for "electric energy" and all other means of information handling for "steam locomotive." Then, if we substitute "libraries" for "factories" and rewrite the paragraph accordingly, we have one forecast of an institutional change that would startle many of us. (The revised paragraph is more likely to be verified by the future than the original!)

This Conference is concerned not only with the technology of information exchange but also with the organizational and social structures of present and future networks. The "blue sky" of the papers dealing with the technology of information handling clouds over somewhat when future social implications of networks are discussed. For example, we tend to assume that libraries will be the focal points of networks. This is not at all certain. Other networks exist such as the telephone, cable television, etc., and others will. The structure that may evolve may be a thorough mix of several or all of them. Cable television, in private hands, could become the dominant network, in terms of the public, with library network nodes as ancillary suppliers. At the other end of the transmission spectrum, satellite systems may become the meta-network, subsuming many earth-bound networks. If I may mix metaphors, McLuhan's global village is on the horizon. Becker and Olsen[2] in defining a network presuppose the existence of units waiting to be interconnected. This no doubt is true now, but the dynamics of information handling will generate the units to be joined. Drucker[3] sees knowledge as one of the major growth industries of the future; if he is right, private enterprise will likely move in to dominate this aspect of networking. The patterns are by no means as set as a reader of the papers at this Conference would infer. (The text and context of the rest of my paper may refer to and imply "libraries," but the reader should keep the warning of this sentence in mind.)

Eras of scientific development have been characterized by dominant and overarching metaphors which determine the pattern of model analysis during the period. The era of scientific conceptualization that started phasing out at the beginning of the twentieth century has been characterized by the dominant metaphor of mechanism.[4] The models that were used reflected the dominant metaphor, with some variation of the clock favored because it so clearly represented sequential, dependent actions and was absolutely predictable. Adherents of a particular mechanical model often criticized users of other mechanical models, as when Lashley derided Freud for developing "psychohydraulics."[5]

The present era of scientific conceptualization has been characterized as organicism. The whole is treated rather than its units.[6] Bertalanffy, the originator of general systems theory, claims that the era of mechanism was concerned primarily with analysis while the present era of organicism is occupied with synthesis, with putting the world back together. During the prior period the sciences were individuated, but now the more fruitful investigations are carried out by merging several fields. The emerging science of ecology is an elegant expression of the metaphor of organicism. According to Herbert Simon, the same phenomenon is occurring in the social sciences:

> The social sciences...weakened by a half-century of schisms among economists, political scientists, sociologists, anthropologists, and social psychologists...are undergoing at present a very rapid process of reintegration. This development is so rapid, and so obvious from even a casual survey of the journals and new books in these fields, that it hardly requires documentation.[7]

In applied sciences, our concern with thinking in terms of "systems" is a manifestation of the same metaphor. Networking is inherently a systems concept.

It should come as no surprise, therefore, that the device most often used as a symbol of organicism is the computer. McCollough, the late mathematician, once described the computer, in its more sophisticated uses, by using the Greek-derived word "anastomotic," where inputs can be treated both as individual entities and as woven wholes.[8] The models of organicism are parallel rather than linear in operation and tend to result in probabilities rather than certainty. Bertalanffy specifically rejects vitalism in biology and Oppenheimer has rejected teleology in physics:

> From this follow all the well-known features: the ineluctable element of chance in atomic physics based, not on our laziness, but on the laws of physics; the end of the Newtonian paradigm of the certain predictions of the future from the knowledge of the present.[9]

I believe that networks as expressions of organicism will reflect these characteristics in their process of becoming.

The distinction made by FDR was really between the two metaphors. Couching one facet of this distinction in modern terminology, the statement may be made that the territoriality of electronics is distinctly different from that of mechanics. By territoriality, I mean where decision points are located, who makes them under what kinds of restraints and constraints, who

goes to whom for what purposes, and what kinds of structural relationships are appropriate.

I will illustrate this point with an example from education. The territoriality of the teacher, on whom we rely in education and in whom we have invested pretty complete authority, is the classroom and the school. When we started to consider ways in which enriched educational programs could be offered to more students, we automatically put two compatible territorialities together to solve the problem: the school bus (mechanics) and the school. In other words, we transport the child to the territory of the teacher. The consequent journeys have become so time-consuming in certain areas that, ironically, the all-at-onceness characteristic of electronics, in the form of radio and television, is used to instruct the child while he travels to his teacher's territory, where his "real" education takes place. What makes the territoriality of electronics the servant of the territoriality of the teacher is the authority we have invested in the latter. Remove the authority, and the rules of the game change. Electronics is putting the pressure on to do just that. When Marshall McLuhan read the report of the Commission on Instructional Technology, he promptly sent a letter to Sydney Tickton of the Academy for Educational Development, the agency with the grant that financed the commission. Because the letter is so pertinent to this point (and by extension libraries reflect the same problem) I will quote it in its entirety:

Dear Mr. Tickton:

You may have noted that with Xerox the publishing industry has been put into the hands of the reading public. *The Report by the Commission on Instructional Technology* belongs to the age of mechanical industry and, indeed, of the horse collar, as witness page 7 where it speaks of "harnessing technology to the work of schools and colleges."

The first motor cars had buggy-whip holders and that is the stage which your report has achieved. The meaning of the electric age is the switch from "hardware" to "software." It means that all instrumentation is to be taken from the hands of the instructors and put into the hands of the students for programming. All electric technology is basically as decentralist as the telephone. The computer means the return to the "cottage economy," i.e. run your factories from your cottage. The age of bricks and mortar, schools and colleges, is as finished as the Paramount Studios in relation to the movie industry, and for the same reason — speed-up. The environment itself has become a teaching machine. Education is now by immersion. All things are now learned as our native tongue, by immersion. Subjects and specialties are over as we move into the new Stone Age of the hunter — the man who plays the total field — the Cyclops.

I do not endorse or desire any of these changes. They have already taken place. The U.S.A. is the one country in the world that began its existence on the Gutenberg basis. This fact puts it in the worst possible position in the age of electric circuitry. It has more to lose and more to change than anybody.

Marshall McLuhan,
Director

Centre for Culture and Technology
University of Toronto[10]

The parallels between schools and libraries as similar kinds of public institutions may be instructive. The printing press established the territoriality of the library. Networks as an expression of the new technology of information handling will, in all probability, generate a territoriality quite different from that of the book. At present we tend to look in the rear-view mirror of our new technology and fit it, like the buggy whip, into the old technology. The second generation of the new technology will start breaking the old territoriality apart, when and if incompatibility surfaces. When television and language laboratories were first introduced into schools, educators forced both into the old patterns by treating them as electronic classrooms. The second generation of each, in the form of random access and other communications systems, with the aid of computer-administered instruction, is breaking the classroom apart.

Some critics of education maintain that education is still a cottage industry in industrial parlance and a craft industry in relation to technology. If so, education could leapfrog from preindustrial cottage to past-industrial cottage. Peter Drucker in conversation with Robert Snider of NEA referred to education as a *pre*craft culture, then warned that chaos could result from injecting sophisticated technology into that primitive a society. The libraries are in somewhat the same situation, except that the introduction of sophisticated technology will not represent as direct a job threat as it does to teachers. In the first place, there is likely to be little direct challenge to establish decisionmaking except perhaps to the head librarian, but even here decisions and authority retained by the local center will be of a different order than those made at nodes. But more importantly, networks will represent primarily expanded service opportunities of a different order, which, as I mentioned before, may not always function within established libraries. Much more interesting is the relatively sudden advent of a hierarchy of positions within the field, itself. More of this later.

The vast majority of the papers at this Conference are preoccupied with what Rupert Hall[11] refers to as the technical act, which can be briefly described as the combination of technological process and the resultant products of the process. By technological process I mean the ability to analyze and subdivide tasks into their component parts and devise *replicable* solutions. By technological products (or just products) I mean the instruments created by the technological process that permit replicability. Devising a computer program is an example of technological process; the program itself is the product. We need to keep in mind that software as well as hardware are technological products.

It is clear that we are becoming highly proficient at the technical act and designing extremely sophisticated technical products all along the line of network development. However, an essential condition for a successfully implemented, universal technology is the existence of a facilitating environmental structure that welcomes and encourages technological change of a fundamental nature. Encouragement must occur at the developmental stages, implementation stages, and among the professional community concerned.

The developmental stages are reasonably financed now when we consider the many inputs into the research and development system. Private as well as public money is busy developing the various technologies necessary although no doubt much more is needed and much more is likely to be allocated. The importance of development money is easily seen by federal agencies and by Congress because the nation has a history of stepping in to help finance large-scale research and development operations when the price is too high for industry. Atomic energy, satellites, and the supersonic transport are examples of acceptance of governmental responsibility for research and development in enterprises too large for private investment. The post-World War II alliance of government, industry, and university (or nonprofit research institute) has paid off handsomely in terms of scientific and technological development. It is reasonable to expect the same helping hands to continue to develop network technology.

As a result, research and development in general have become so closely related and so systematically treated that the time span between discovery and implementation has been reduced dramatically. For example, while it took sixty-five years for the electric motor to be applied to practical tasks, and the vacuum tube thirty-three years, the transistor was in use just three years after its discovery. The laser experience parallels that of the transistor.[12] We can expect the same rapid rate of development in network technology.

Creating a facilitating environment for implementation is a more difficult problem, particularly when dealing with public institutions. The private sector of our society generally finds our economic and political structure encouraging to technological innovations. I am referring primarily to laws and regulations that either encourage or discourage the introduction of new techniques. High on the list of discouraging factors are codes and restrictions imposed by unions. The most cited examples being the building codes. On the other hand, straight wage demands increase the pressure to develop more productive techniques. However, by and large our political and economic structure is friendly to technology.

Sometimes it is too encouraging:

The Army recently denied permission for a private dredging-and-filling operation in navigable waters of Florida, responding to the argument of health and conservation agencies that the project would injure fish and wildlife. A Federal court overturned the decision on the ground that the law makes interference with navigation the only basis for refusing permission to dredge and fill.[13]

One of our obvious problems today is that we have too encouraging an environment for technological growth in the private sector. The federal government has sponsored several studies to study how new technological innovations may be assessed for long-term effects. However, the public sector faces a different situation.

The metaphors of clock and computer are not restricted to scientific eras. As Dewey once pointed out, metaphors have a way of becoming all pervasive so that the social and philosophical rubrics of society exhibit the same evolution. The quest for certainty in philosophy lost dominance during the same period that saw the beginning of the end of Newtonian mechanics. The arts are our "distant early warning systems" that alert us to emerging reorientations of our societal patterns.

We should expect then that the political and social institutions that evolved during one era may not be appropriate in another. This is easily seen and acceded to in minor laws and regulations, or when someone else's vested interest is involved. But sweeping, fundamental disjointedness and threats to security, identity, and power are not readily seen or accepted. For example, one of the most serious questions that has been raised is whether the Constitution of the United States is appropriate to changing demands placed on it. But a movement to adopt a new constitution, such as the one proposed by the Center for the Study of Democratic Institutions, will understandably have hard, if not impossible, going. The issues here are not of this magnitude, but some are equally difficult to effect. But a formal, systematic examination of the political, economic, and social structures that may not facilitate networking needs to be undertaken. At present a piecemeal approach is being used — from copyright to local tax structures.

Public institutions operate under heavier restraints than do private ones. The rigidity and extent of the laws and regulations vary from state to state. They also vary with the kind of institution governed. For example, the schools are no doubt more tightly locked in than public libraries. Fundamental changes in education are difficult to effect. Many innovative programs exist because of federal money, but withdrawal of that support would see the end of the programs. Title III of the Elementary and Secondary Education Act sponsored many large-scale innovations, but the mortality rate after federal funds stopped has been high, partly because state and local structures did not permit institutionalization of the programs. Libraries may be facing this same problem in regard to networking.

Maryann Duggan has commented to me that in the preparation of her paper she discovered that interstate networking may be illegal in some situations. If so, it is best to challenge the law if necessary to get a change. This reminded me of the early days of community television services by way of translators. While the Federal Communications Commission was trying to make up its mind about their legality, the late Senator Edwin C. Johnson of Colorado simply ordered them installed in his home town. It was years before the FCC finally gave the go-ahead.

Territoriality is protected by men and institutions operating within the superstructure that evolved out of certain fundamental relationships and forces. Not only laws and regulations but also prerogatives based on a tradition contribute to the superstructure. An interesting example of how the direction of network services will be pushed by the dynamics of territoriality is provided by a brief report on the Association for Graduate Engineering and Research of North Texas, TAGER, a television network.[14]

First, the purposes of TAGER:

The TAGER system was set up for two different but related reasons. First, it was intended to enable the co-operating institutions to share teaching, for use on their own campuses. Second, it was designed to extend the scope and raise the quality of engineering teaching at graduate level in North Texas. The engineering teaching on the network is aimed at graduate engineers, who have gone into industry with a bachelor's degree and now want to take a master's or a doctorate. The Southern Methodist University Institute of Technology is thus using technology in order to extend its functions in continuing education.

Then, the experience:

The TAGER network has been used very much less for exchanging teaching internally between its members. But three of the ways in which it *is* being used seem of major importance. First, it has enabled the SMU Institute of Technology to avoid establishing one department on its campus. The Institute has no aerospace department, but there is one at the South-West Center for Advanced Studies (SCAS), a research institute run on university lines. Instead of creating his own department, Dean Martin has therefore arranged for the aerospace staff at SCAS to hold associate membership of the staff of the Institute of Technology and to teach his students principally over the TAGER network.

An inference of the report is that the continuing education of engineers already in the profession has nowhere near the territoriality strength of training for *entry* into the profession by each institution. (This is related to a point made later in the section on personnel.) If the reader will think along these lines for a moment, he will understand why offices of correspondence instruction (or continuing education) have had virtually no influence on the instructional program of the universities which house them.

One other observation. Dean Martin of SMU made his operation more cost-effective by using the resources of other institutions rather than duplicating them. But his decision would have been extremely difficult to make if he had had even one staff member as an aerospace department. Territory would have been established. If a department had been established before TAGER started, it is not likely to have voted itself out of existence or voted for transfers to other institutions regardless of cost/benefit possibilities. Decisions of that kind have to be made at administrative levels. Very frequently when we discuss diffusion and adoption we do not make adequate distinctions between levels of decisionmaking. We often waste a lot of time trying to get the wrong level to adopt an innovation.

CENTRALIZATION AND DECENTRALIZATION

McLuhan maintains that electronics is decentralizing. He is right if he is referring to the ability to be and go everywhere, and to the uniform distribution of culture. However, there is an element of centralization in terms of control and planning—enough to make many people leary of the implied power.

Actually two characteristics of systems based on organismic models help keep a balance between centralization and decentralization: more inclusive representation in initial planning stages, and shared power and decisionmaking all along the line.

As a system becomes more comprehensive and technologically oriented, more far-reaching decisions have to be made by more people earlier in the planning stages. When decisions are made, parallel rather than linear operations are carried out. In a mechanistic model, decisions are sequential and discrete — the problem is passed along step by step. In an organismic model, a much more representative group from up and down the line participates in planning and decisionmaking right from the start, and operations are carried out in parallel.

This leads to the second characteristic which is shared power during the operational stages. By shared power I mean that units tend not to carve out exclusive territories and operate them arbitrarily. Because they are dependent upon each other, they tend to share decisionmaking. I believe, for example, the nodes of an existing network would confirm this position.

In general, contrary to generally held opinion, large-scale technology allows the individual to exercise greater responsibility and increases the possibilities of public control.[15]

NETWORKS AND INSTRUCTION

I tend to agree with Dan Lacy in *Social Change and the Library, 1945-1980*[16] that the most widely discussed use of computer — retrieval, as the term is generally used — may be least significant with respect to the general public. Minor, or incidental, intelligence, which I suppose is the public's major storage and retrieval need, is now taken care of quite nicely by a telephone call to a reference librarian. If the network removes the librarian and fails to hook into my phone, my modest demands are going to be much harder for me to satisfy. It very well may be worth paying the telephone company for the service.

On a larger scale and with more specialized audiences, ERIC clearinghouses are supposed to make documents readily available, but the complications and hardships of *use* result in all storage and no retrieval. There is a parallel to our transportation system here. Information flashes from center to center at an incredible rate, but it has a hard time with the final leg of the journey. It is quite possible that formal (with accreditation) and informal instruction may become the most important aspect of networks to the general public. Advances in instructional technology, diversity of instructional demands by very disparate groups, and the inability of the present educational system to adjust to demands are some of the more important pressures that may change drastically the institutional framework of future instruction.

I mentioned earlier that the territoriality of the classroom teacher is incompatible with that of electronics. The development of electronic distribution systems, the computer, and advances in techniques of organization of instruction, particularly programmed instruction, combine to allow us to instruct successfully by separating teacher and student in distance and in time. Disregarding the social function of the school

(which we cannot), very little of what the student learns *cannot* be taught by instruction incorporated into electronic systems. Some of you, not familiar with developments in computer-administered instruction, CAI, which combines the power of electronics with response-oriented programmed instruction, may believe that only low-level cognitive skills may be taught in this fashion. Not at all. CAI is being used very successfully in instructional situations requiring problem-solving, decisionmaking, and other complex skills. At present, this instruction is very expensive, but amortization over a large number of students can reduce the cost to very acceptable figures. Networking is an obvious way of reaching the optimal number of students. The same point can be made about cost-effectiveness in regard to television — another network. So far, neither has been able to penetrate school districts, or colleges for that matter, to any appreciable extent. As mentioned earlier, TAGER is one operating network that *has* started to make inroads into traditional territories with some savings in instructional costs. A few places, such as Pennsylvania State University and Dade County, Florida, have increased instructional productivity with television, but to the vast majority of educational institutions, this form of instruction falls into the luxury category — very nice to have if you can afford it and if the latest bargaining session with the teachers' group didn't squeeze it out of the budget.

Rupert Hall, in commenting on the problems of introducing advanced technology into underdeveloped countries, postulates that to be successful there must be "an industrial framework within which the kinds of changes that may be effected by science are not only useful but acceptable." He goes on to say that:

> Scientific knowledge is of little material value if the object of technological proficiency is the manufacture of objects of luxury; hence in backward contemporary societies the arbitrary installation of a few modern industrial plants, without modification of the basic economy, has little more result than to allow the rich to adopt Cadillacs and television in place of more barbarous means of ostentation.[17]

Drucker claims that information will be a growth industry of the future but indicates that increased productivity in education must occur first:

> Learning and teaching are going to be more deeply affected by the new availability of information than any other area of human life. There is great need for a new approach, new methods and new tools in teaching, man's oldest and most reactionary craft. There is great need for a rapid increase in learning. There is, above all, great need for methods that will make the teacher effective and multiply his or her efforts and competence. Teaching is, in fact, the only traditional craft in which we have not yet fashioned the tools that make an ordinary person capable of superior performance.[18]

The new technologies of instruction are the obvious means of achieving the goal of "multiplying" a teacher's efforts through network distribution, thereby securing favorable cost-effectiveness figures mentioned before.

But the "basic economy" of education tends to prevent the introduction of sophisticated technology, and without revision, technology will remain peripheral to the enterprise. "Basic economy" in education should be translated into the base of education — the fundamental premises on which it is structured and in whom authority is vested. The laws, regulations, and policies that form the superstructure of education are designed to reinforce and support the base. The elaboration of a superstructure over a period of time was necessary to assure quality education *within the accepted framework*. But it is a superstructure that does not encourage or facilitate technological solutions to problems.

Due to a number of pressures, such as taxpayer resistance and teacher militancy, cracks may start appearing in the superstructure.[19] Just a few of the basic edifices need to be removed to set in motion forces that could radically alter the institutional relationships in education. For example, if accreditation were based solely on student performance regardless of where he receives instruction, the door would be wide open for other agencies to get into the business of instruction. If, at the same time, state-aid formulas were changed so that money would be distributed solely on the basis of students or if the voucher system really became a reality, profit-making groups as well would start offering a wide range of instruction. This is not as far-fetched as it may seem. The courts are deciding a case that may presage a series of decisions that could fundamentally alter education. Marjorie Webster Junior College, a profit-making institution, is suing the Middle States Association of Secondary Schools and Colleges, a regional accrediting agency, because the association refused to evaluate the institution for accreditation. So far the courts have ruled in favor of the junior college, throwing out the association's claim that its charter prevents it from accrediting profit-making institutions. The court held the association was acting in restraint of trade. Marjorie Webster is a resident junior college, but the reasoning of the court could easily extend to nonresident instruction as well. If it does, and someone is sure to enter a test case, a major step will have been taken to create an environment encouraging to instructional technology.

Instruction will be available wherever the terminal is, and where the terminal will be located depends on the responses of the institutions involved. Special courses leading to specific jobs, courses designed to prepare people for the next rung on their career ladders, and courses simply to maintain competencies are examples of the kinds of instruction that eventually will be handled by some sort of networking operation. In addition, because of the foregoing argument, courses which we now associate strictly with formal schooling will be incorporated in the resources of some form of network courses that will apply toward degrees and various forms of certification. The "open university" idea in England would fit easily into this same framework. These are some of the reasons why I believe that instruction will be one of the main functions of networks. The question is — where will the terminals be located?

The public library is one logical choice. If the schools prove to be unresponsive, the public library system is the other main public institution that is widely distributed and can provide the necessary atmosphere, both social and academic. The phenomenon of store-front schools may spread rapidly. So far these efforts have been tentative and relatively poorly financed. However, the right program with adequate financial backing, and given the encouragement mentioned above, could make a success of a chain of such stores hooked together in a network (McLuhan's cottage industries). And we must not forget cable television. CATV centers are being installed that are capable of handling forty-some channels. The FCC has forced the CATV industry to view their capabilities in a much broader framework by imposing public service obligations. This reorientation plus the increased capability will put the CATV companies in an excellent position to capitalize eventually on the information industry.

Let us speculate on the possibilities. Suppose a national curriculum group such as the Biological Sciences Curriculum Study, BSCS, were to design a course that by using an interrelated series of films and programmed instruction permits self-study by individuals or small groups. The films would be available over cable television and students would view them in small groups (or individually). The related programmed instruction would be available at the end of a terminal in a public library (or other institutional setting). Finally, assessment of student achievement and accreditation would be turned over to Educational Testing Service or American College Testing, and carried out over those same terminals. Tuition would be collected by credit card, naturally. Revisions of the course would be a periodic responsibility of BSCS while proposals for additional courses in biology would be entertained constantly. The reader will see other ways of arranging the components, but the point is that we are able to build an instructional system of great power and flexibility by networking. This is simply an up-dating of a concept of the late James D. Finn.[20]

SOME PERSONNEL CONSIDERATIONS

One of the characteristics of advanced technology is that the majority of jobs it creates require higher-than-average education. In fact, as our society has incorporated more sophisticated technology into the industrial and service sectors, the character of the whole work force has changed. Galbraith describes the manpower change in a particularly graphic way:

In the early stages of industrialization, the educational requirement for industrial manpower was in the shape of a very squat pyramid. A few men of varying qualifications — managers, engineers, bookkeepers, timekeepers and clerks — were needed in the office. The wide base reflected the large requirement for repetitive labor power for which even literacy was something of a luxury. To this pyramid the educational system conformed. Elementary education was provided for the masses at minimum cost. Those who wanted more had to pay for it or to forgo income while getting it. This insured that it would be sought only by a minority. To this day the school systems of the older industrial communities in West Virginia, central and western Pennsylvania, northern New Jersey and upstate New York still manifest their ancient inferiority. It is assumed that an old mill town will have bad schools.

By contrast the manpower requirements of the industrial system are in the shape of a tall urn. It widens out below the top to reflect the need of the technostructure for administrative, coordinating and planning talent, for scientists and engineers, for sales executives, salesmen, those learned in the other arts of persuasion and for those who program and command the computers. It widens further to reflect the need for white-collar talent. And it curves in sharply toward the base to reflect the more limited demand for those who are qualified only for muscular and repetitive tasks and who are readily replaced by machines.[21]

We can certainly expect that an industry such as information handling will exaggerate an already dramatic situation. The proportion of jobs created that will fall into the category of high educational requirements will be much greater than the average.[22] Characterizing our society as a "knowledge society" shows that within the swelling educated class the greatest growth is taking place in the areas dealing specifically with knowledge. We can expect recruitment problems in the future. We may find, too, that more and more graduate students will look with favor on the field, particularly if our very recent experience of a shrinking job market for Ph.D's continues. Many graduate students who would never have considered librarianship would be attracted to information sciences.

Perhaps the happiest aspect of the enlarging job market is that these added positions will not eliminate many other jobs. However, two serious problems may emerge, if they have not already. The first concerns the possibility of creating class distinctions within the field, and the other pertains to the necessity of providing upward mobility. The second can help solve the first.

If we consider the whole field of information handling, the new positions that will result will tend to require higher skills than the old. To the people in information sciences, traditional library functions may seem like paraprofessional activities. (I wonder if some of the traditional library schools will require them to take Card Catalog 104?) Galbraith believes that the trend toward differentiation on the basis of education is creating a new class distinction:

Much may be learned of the character of any society from its social conflicts and passions. When capital was the key to economic success, social conflict was between the rich and the poor. Money made the difference; possession or nonpossession justified contempt for, or resentment of, those oppositely situated. Sociology, economics, political science and fiction celebrated the war between the two sides of the tracks and the relation of the mansion on the hill to the tenement below.

In recent times education has become the difference that divides. All who have educational advantage, as with the moneyed of an earlier day, are reminded of their *noblesse oblige* and also of the advantages of reticence. They should help those who are less fortunate; they must avoid reflecting aloud on their advantage in knowledge. But this doesn't serve to paper over the conflict. It is visible in almost every community.[23]

I may be setting up a straw man, but based on experiences in other fields (including my own), this issue may become a very sore spot. Smooth functioning of network establishment and operation may be interfered with considerably in the process. Some of you may reply that the two groups will probably be separated by distance and therefore, fix is not likely to occur. But this very situation is what could cause the most serious kinks in operational activities.

Implied in all the above is the likelihood of the establishment of a career ladder, and it should be encouraged. Far better to look at it this way and facilitate—rather than inhibit—upward mobility. It would be unfortunate if the newer members of the field regard themselves as an elite and set up artificial obstacles to career mobility. Although we are discussing a higher order mobility problem than the problem that the Harvard study addresses in the following quote, the problems may be quite similar:

Whatever the nature of the social choices that will be made to help minimize the disruptive effects of technological change and to maintain mobility and fluidity in the occupational structure, technological change in industry has resulted in the blocking of certain older paths of mobility. In industry, because of "the need for managerial personnel to have a broad educational and technological background,...a moat (has been established) between the workers and their foremen and all other supervisory personnel. It is increasingly rare for a working man to advance more than one step up the managerial ladder. He can become a foreman, but that is all." Mobility in office work appears to be similarly blocked as "the middle step in the old promotion ladder" — positions requiring experience and seniority, but beneath the managerial level — appears to be growing smaller with the introduction of automation. And among managerial and supervisory personnel in industry, "a 'gap' is forming between lower and higher levels of management... Yet in the wide number of areas where promotional paths are being modified the extent to which modified job and work environments call for the (technical) degree is not clearly established. There is a clear tendency to overestimate its relevance. In addition, where higher level skills are indicated, the development potential of existing company personnel is frequently overlooked."

Such inability to move up within the hierarchy of an employing organization has been a source of frustration to many workers; and since the blockage often results from exaggerated notion of the importance of formal education, there is an underutilization of existing talents. In many instances on-the-job training has been used quite effectively to permit the existing work force to assume the new roles and responsibilities. Furthermore, in the face of rapid technological change, even recent college graduates suffer from the problem of knowledge obsolescence.[24]

One of the major obstacles to vertical career mobility in the professions is the requirement that full training precede entry into the profession. Even after the individual is admitted into the profession, he may not find it easy to advance. What we need are programs that prepare people for "new careers" as well as programs for midcareer changes.

Keeping in mind that we are looking only for analogs here rather than assuming situations that are the same, the Harvard study continues:

The "new careers" concept thus focuses on those occupations in which on-the-job training could replace advance preparation. It departs also from the observation that societies need as much health, education, and welfare services as they can afford. There is room for expansion of existing careers in these service areas. Many more people could become qualified teachers, for example, if a process of moving up from the position of teacher's aide through a series of steps allowed them to become certified teachers. In addition, various social service "activities not currently performed by anyone, but for which there is a readily acknowledged need and which can also be satisfactorily accomplished by the unskilled worker" could be developed. The attempt to design new types of career's is thus also responsive to the problem of providing meaningful work for the increasing numbers of workers who will not be able to find gainful employment in the labor force of the future.[25]

We need a program of continuing education available to the interested individual just about anywhere that would prepare him for whatever rung on the ladder he is capable of reaching. *If professionals in information sciences fail to use for this purpose the networks they are creating, it will be a classic high-level case of the shoemaker's children.* The problem of mobility is not simply the concern of the schools of information science, it is a problem of the profession.

In my own field, the Association for Educational Communications and Technology has sponsored a proposal to the U. S. Office of Education to establish a national continuing education program in instructional technology to permit complete career mobility. There is no intention to replace the professional schools. The program will, if funded, provide advancement opportunities to those people unable to go the more direct route. I think this is a proposal of great vision, and I would urge this group to do the same.

CONCLUSION

...we possess, in absolute terms, far greater physical power and technical capability than ever before. It is not necessary to claim that atomic energy represented a greater change than gunpowder to realize that the atomic bomb is more powerful than TNT. Printing might easily have induced a greater social shock than the computer — it upset the educational monopoly of the Church, for one thing — yet the fact remains that the computer can deal with far more information almost infinitely faster than printing can. In absolute terms, we have far more power than anybody.[26]

Our new technologies of information handling are going to produce fundamental changes in the social structure. If we accept the statement that the book "upset the educational monopoly of the Church," we inevitably wonder what monopolies may tumble in the electronic wake of the computer. We are not dealing with a simple difference of degree but rather one of kind. It is always tempting to try to gain reassurance by pointing out similarities between an innovation and our accustomed way of doing things, and of course, there are always similarities because all ideas derive from *some* historical context. But it is false reassurance when we are faced with a change in kind and still act as though we were in complete continuity with the past.

The major contribution to the history and philosophy of science made in the last ten years is that science is *not* an unbroken, steady accumulation of knowledge that continuously adds to our understanding of natural phenomena. Thomas Kuhn has advanced the idea that the kind of fundamental discovery that establishes a new research tradition, such as Copernican astronomy or relativity theory, is a break with the past and cannot be accounted for by simple extension of prior knowledge.[27] His theory has gained widespread support among scientific historians.

We are faced with the same kind of disjuncture with the past. We will be far better off by concentrating on the differences between the capabilities we now have and those of a prior tradition. Networking is not just a more sophisticated way of handling information — it is a radical departure.

NOTES

1. James W. Carey and John J. Quirk, "The mythos of the electronic revolution" *The American scholar* 39:219-241, 395-425 (Spring, Summer 1970).

2. Joseph Becker and Wallace C. Olsen. "Information networks" in C.A. Cuadro, ed., *Annual review of information science and technology, vol. 3* (Chicago: Britannica, 1968) p.289-327.

3. Peter Drucker, *The age of discontinuity; guidelines to our changing society* (New York: Harper and Row, 1968), 402p.

4. Paul Meadows, "Models, systems and science" *American sociological review.* 22:3-9 (1957).

5. Karl W, Deutsch, "On communication models in information *Public opinion quarterly* 16:355-380 (Fall 1952).

6. Ludwig von Bertalanffy. "General systems theory" *General systems, vol. 1, Yearbook of the Society for General Systems Research.* (Ann Arbor: Braun-Brumfield, 1956). (Ann Arbor: Braun-Brumfield, 1956) pp.

7. Herbert A. Simon. "Some strategic considerations in the construction of social science models," in P. Lazerow, ed., *Mathematical thinking in the social sciences.* (New York: Free Press, 1954).

8. National Film Board of Canada, *The living machine* (Motion picture) 60 min. sd., b&w., 16mm.

9. Robert Oppenheimer, "Physics and mans understanding" in P. H. Oehser ed., *Knowledge among men.* (New York: Simon and Schuster, 1966), p.143-155.

10. *Communications review,* 18:307 (Fall 1970).

11. Rupert A. Hall, "The changing technical act," in C. Stover ed., *The technological order* (Detroit: Wayne St. Univ. Pr., 1963) 280p.

12. William O. Baker, "The dynamism of science and technology," in E. Ginzberg, ed., *Technology and social change* (New York: Columbia Univ. Pr.), p.82-107.

13. Harvey Brooks and Raymond Bowers, "The assessment of technology," *Scientific American* 222:13-20 (Feb. 1970).

14. H. D. Perraton, D.A.L. Wade, and V.W.R. Fox, *Linking universities by technology.* (Cambridge, England: National Extension College, 1969.

15. Emmanuel G. Mesthene, *Technological change: its impact on man and society* (Cambridge, Mass.: Harvard Univ. Pr., 1970) 127p.

16. Dan Lacy, "Social change and the library: 1945-1980" in D. M. Knight and E. S. Nourse, ed., *Libraries at large...* (New York: Bowker, 1969) p.3-21.

17. Rupert A. Hall, "The changing technical act...."

18. Peter Drucker, *The age of discontinuity.*

19. For a more elaborate discussion, see Robert Heinich, *Technology and the management of instruction* (Washington, D.C.: Assoc. for Educational Communications and Technology, 1970), 198p.

20. James D. Finn, "Technology and the instructional process," *AV communication review* 41:371-378 (June 1960).

21. John Kenneth Galbraith. *The new industrial State* (Boston: Houghton Mifflin, 1967),427p.

22. Daniel Bell. "The measurement of knowledge and technology" in E. B. Sheldon and W. E. Moore, eds., *Indicators of social change* (New York: Russell Sage Foundation, 1968).

23. John Kenneth Galbraith, *The new industrial state...*[direct quote -]

24. Harvard University, Program on Technology and Society, *Technology and work* (Research Review No. 2 [Cambridge, Mass.: Harvard Univ. Pr., 1969]).

25. Ibid.

26. Emmanuel G. Mesthene. "Educational realities," (an address delivered at The American Management Association's Second International Conference and Exhibit, Aug. 1966, New York).

27. Thomas S. Kuhn, *The structure of scientific revolution* (Chicago: Univ. of Chicago Pr., 1962), 172p.

Network Organization—A Case Study Of
The Five Associated University Libraries (FAUL)

Ron Miller

INTRODUCTION

Unless it deals with some mental or physical abnormality with which we can secretly identify, a case study is more often than not a recitation of historical events, important and unimportant, all jumbled together. Somehow enough truth, enough similarity to future events, is supposed to be hiding amid the jumble that discovery helps us avoid others' past mistakes.

Anyone who has been foolhardy enough to participate in a library network or consortium must have realized, surely, that what the organization says it is in its official documents, compared to what the leaders really want it to be, compared to what the lower echelons think it is, is a little like the parable of the blind men and the elephant. Becker and Olsen[1] have characterized an information network as having a formal organization, communications circuits, bidirectionality, a directory, and switching capability. Generally, such a definition implies some kind of electronic component. At the very least, a self-respecting network should have plans for computerization even though it can sanguinely call itself a network if a delivery system or regional interlibrary loan arrangement has been agreed upon. FAUL is an example of a network which is not yet really a network in its own right: It is a free-loader on components of *other* networks, e.g., NYSILL, national interlibrary loan codes, TWX, telephone, United Parcel Service, U.S. Post Office, and the like. In fact, the organization could wake up one day and find all of its objectives met by other means; its last cooperative act would be to vote itself out of existence.

Indeed, some members would define FAUL as an unincorporated group of people bound together by a constitution, bylaws, and prior investment; and some have an uneasy feeling that money and time devoted to the enterprise could be spent better at home.

In short, it is faith which holds the organization together—faith that somehow it will all fall into place, that someone will throw a switch and like Christmas, all the lights will go on.

Which leads this writer to assert unequivocally that "objective" observations, editorial comments, and the selection of material included in this paper are purely his own doing, reflecting the idiosyncrasies of his own brand of truth. To be more truly a case study, someone who is not himself a part of the case should be making these observations.

COUNTERPOINT

In a recent book review in *Life* magazine, the reviewer observes that every man contains his own generation gap. Part of him, the anonymous reviewer continues, is attracted to the future, to change, while another part is drawn toward the past, toward the maintenance of continuity. The same dichotomy, the same schizoid quality, exists in organizations as large as nations, as small as families, and certainly exists in library consortia. In general, if the voices of these opposites can carry on serious dialogue, new forces can be built. Indeed, such is one face of progress.

During the past six to ten years, libraries have been forming groups at a great rate, many of them for contradictory purposes: to foster change — to prevent unwanted change; to defend an entrenched position — to absorb others; to increase local resources by gaining access to others — to keep hold of resources which local libraries already own. For every force toward change, a restraining counterforce opposes it, which, like the Ying-Yang principle in Chinese dualistic philosophy, may be characterized more by indifference and passivity than by clear forceful expression. The movement forward is bogged down in a swamp of tradition and distrust; therein lies frustration.

Yet it can seldom be any other way. Men and institutions resist a loss of control and autonomy, and some loss of autonomy seems to be necessary if useful cooperation is to occur. The very fact that member libraries divert local funds to the new institution (the consortium) means that some local leverage is sacrificed — fewer books can be purchased, a new staff member cannot be hired, a new machine cannot be rented. If something is lost something else must be gained, or logic asks: Why voluntarily give it up at all? It is within this counterpoint of heady expectation and hard-nosed reality which the Five Associated University Libraries, FAUL, as a consortium is discussed here.

A NEW INSTITUTION

On 10 August 1970 FAUL was three years old, as dated from the adoption of its constitution in 1967. For its birthday celebration the organization began an intensive self-evaluation which will not end until late November when screening of various reports by key library staff members is completed.

FAUL is composed of the libraries of the five largest universities in Upstate New York: SUNY-Binghamton, SUNY-Buffalo, Cornell University, Syracuse University, and the University of Rochester. Collectively, there are more than eight million volumes administered by about 1,135 staff members, more than 385 of which are professionals of one kind or another. The total library expenditures were more than $13.2 million during Fiscal 1969 — about $1 million less than Harvard expects to spend for its libraries in 1976. Another measurment reveals that about 5.7 million transactions per year occur in the various circulation control systems which include interlibrary loan reserve room activities and the normal check-out/in transactions. This works out to about 16,000 transactions per workday for all five libraries.

Some ranges within the group are indicated by Cornell's volume count of 3.5 million compared with SUNY-Binghamton's 420,000. Other measures place the libraries in different sequences. For instance, in terms of "degree of automation," SUNY-Binghamton would be considered the most advanced in implemented systems, but Syracuse might be the furthest along in terms of integrated automation planning. SUNY-Buffalo, historically in the forefront in computer applications because of its early commitment to local shelf-list conversion, has suspended most of its efforts except for the implementation of an interesting but as yet undocumented on-line circulation system in one of its branches, the Health Science Library. The University of Rochester Library has produced short-title lists of serials and monographs by computer. And Cornell operates a widely known, complex monographic acquisitions system. So far, none of the above efforts has yielded very much to cooperative effort with the exception of circulation systems automation, a case study by itself. This experience is described in more detail later in this report.

GEOGRAPHIC ORIENTATION

The main campuses of the five universities are in western New York State and are distributed along two axes in the rough shape of the character "L." The New York Thruway forms the major east-west axis and Interstate Route 81, the north-south axis (see Figure 1). The longest distance in both mileage and driving time is between SUNY-Buffalo and SUNY-Binghamton, two hundred miles or four and a half hours. The shortest distance and driving time is two-way tie: Syracuse-Cornell, Binghamton-Cornell (see Figure 2).

Some other campuses of these private universities are located in New York City, Utica, Poughkeepsie, Rome (New York), the Caribbean and Europe. FAUL has not attempted to involve these centers in its activities so far.

FINANCE

To date, all financial support has been provided by the member libraries. Currently, each member pays base dues of $13,000, which provide central office staff salaries, travel, equipment, space rental, consultants, and the like. In addition, small research and development projects are supported from these monies. If the board approves short-term projects which require supplemental support, additional funds are assessed on a prorated basis, depending upon the character of the project. Several proposals have been sent to the U.S. Office of Education, the Council on Library Resources, and the National Endowment for the Humanities. None has been funded so far. FAUL is ineligible for New York State funds directly since it is not incorporated.

Since August 1967 the cumulative monetary investment through June 1969 is $153,300, an average of $10,000 per library per year.

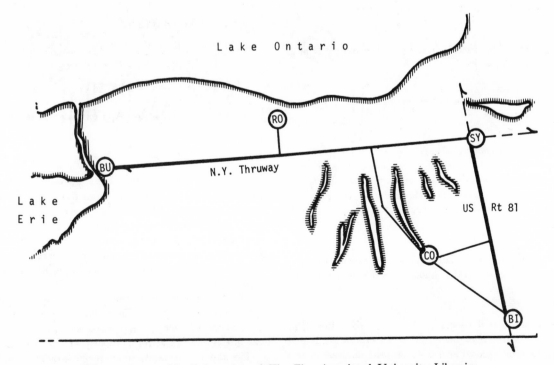

Figure 1 Geographic Orientation of The Five Associated University Libraries

BACKGROUND OF FAUL

To determine the genesis of an organization can be a fruitless voyage into mythology, but to begin, late in 1966 the librarians of the three private universities with some senior staff members composed a series of "talk papers" relating to different aspects of cooperative development. These papers explored computer applications, delivery systems, compact storage, budget, and coordinated acquisitions. This exercise attracted interest from the two University Centers in the State University of New York, SUNY; the result of these early efforts to find areas of common exploration was the present group — the Five Associated University Libraries.

The reasons for the coming together are many and subtle, but there appear to have been four primary forces: (1) the astonishingly rapid growth of SUNY and the New York State Library, (2) the bandwagon growth of library consortia across the country, (3) the promise of federal and private funding of library consortia — especially the "Networks for Knowledge" Title IX of the Higher Education Act — and, (4) a genuine and deeply felt belief by the chief librarians that the problems of academic research libraries are unique in the spectrum of library types but are fairly similar in scale and kind among themselves.

Whatever the reasons of the founders, the official objectives of the organization are fairly typical of many consortia and can be characterized by a few articles of faith: (1) that five libraries can do some things in common at less than five times the cost of doing them separately; and (2) that a synergistic effect is possible whereby the whole could be greater than the sum of its parts.

ORGANIZATIONAL OBJECTIVES AND STRUCTURE

The purposes of the association are stated in Article II of its constitution as follows:

Improve and develop cooperation among the Five Associated University Libraries.

Work towards a *coordinated policy for long-range library growth* and development with *coordinated acquisitions policies, shared resources,* and *development of compatible machine systems,* provision of *easy and rapid communications systems* among the membership, the provision of *shared storage facilities,* and exploration of *other areas of cooperation.*

After enumerating these fairly specific objectives, the document describes the general methods by which they might be attained:

The Association will cooperate with other educational, library and research institutions and organizations inside and outside the geographical area to further the purposes of this Association.

In pursuit of its purpose, this organization shall initiate, promote and support research studies and projects and operational systems and projects which may lead to a knowledge of available resources and services and provide the means for increased interlibrary cooperative plans and services among five member institutions.

ORGANIZATIONAL STRUCTURE

A glance at Figure 3. FAUL Organizational Structure shows that the consortium has been organized into eleven functional units or committees of varying degrees of activity. Each of these groups has a specific charge which is periodically reviewed by the Executive Council. The last review, made in April 1970, resulted in a few important changes in committee structure, names, participants, and charge. Most changes occurred in three groups: the Executive Council, the Technical Services Committee, and the User Services Committee. In the following each committee, its charge and current status is named and described.

Bi		Bi						
Bu	200	4.5	Bu					
Co	46	1.2	150	3.0	Co			
Ro	150	3.5	75	1.5	90	2.5	Ro	
Sy	78	1.5	150	3.5	60	1.2	90	2.2
	D	T	D	T	D	T	D	T

Bi = SUNY-Binghamton

Bu = SUNY-Buffalo
Co = Cornell University
Ro = University of Rochester
Sy = Syracuse University

Figure 2   Table of Approximate Distances (D) and Driving Times (T)

BOARD OF DIRECTORS

The chief librarian and the academic vice-president (ex officio) from each member institution form this governing group of the consortium. Each member library has one institutional vote, three-fifths being a quorum, and each personal representative may designate one or more representatives. The group therefore contains a minimum of ten members who serve continuously during the tenure of their positions at the member institution.

The board's charge is conceptually simple: It has the responsibility of managing and controlling the affairs of the association and is empowered to take any appropriate actions. It can hire employees, acquire property, and make contracts.

The above is explicitly stated in the group's constitution and bylaws.

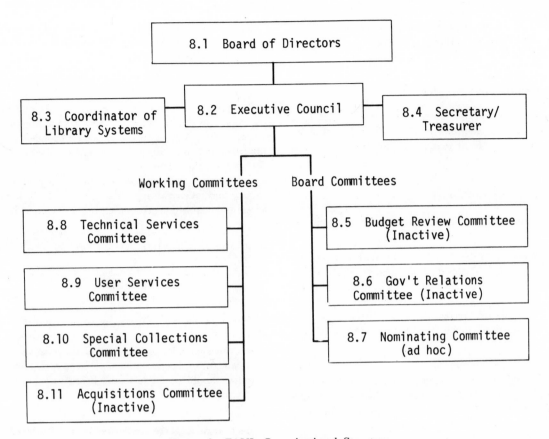

Figure 3 FAUL Organizational Structure

The board annually elects a chairman and a vice-chairman from its membership. Traditionally, the administrative assistant to the coordinator of library systems has served as an appointed secretary/treasurer.

This group meets at least four times each year, usually inviting committee chairmen to attend and report as well.

EXECUTIVE COUNCIL

This group is composed of the chairman and vice-chairman of the board, a third chief librarian on a monthly rotating basis, and the coordinator of library systems. It meets monthly except during the summer, monitoring the day-to-day operations of the organization more closely than the full board is able. The board frequently delegates much of its decisionmaking to this group in an effort to involve more intimately those chief librarians not holding elected offices in the organization.

COORDINATOR OF LIBRARY SYSTEMS

An employee of the board, his role is not defined very clearly. He and his staff form an information switching center, secretariat, proposal writer, investigator, contract signer, committee hound, and gadfly. His true role is that of integrator. That work which members of committees performed in the consortium's early days as overload has very often been delegated to his office. This act alone has reduced the involvement of a few key individuals who participated heavily in the early months of the organization.

SECRETARY/TREASURER

These functions are vested in the person of the coordinator's administrative assistant. Accounting, however, is done by Syracuse University under contract to FAUL.

BUDGET REVIEW COMMITTEE (INACTIVE)

Usually composed of a vice-president and a chief librarian, this group has been a subset of the board reviewing budget proposals prepared by the coordinator before the full board approves them. This committee is inactive at present, its functions having been taken over the Executive Council. It probably will not be revived.

GOVERNMENT RELATIONS COMMITTEE (INACTIVE)

Without a chairman for more than a year, this group is formally charged as follows:

To inform the Board and the coordinator about the pertinent local, state and federal legislation pertinent to library funding. Of primary interest are SUNY and other N. Y. State government sponsored library activities. Written and/or oral reports of activities and recommendations for action should be made to the Board at the request of the Chairman.

In general, this function is performed informally by all board members. Historically, all that the group has done is send a letter to the state regents requesting them to involve FAUL in building a centralized bibliographic data base. No discernable effect resulted.

NOMINATING COMMITTEE (AD HOC)

This committee is self-explanatory. Elections are held in June for chairman and vice-chairman who serve from July through June, the consortium's fiscal year. Office-holders may succeed themselves.

TECHNICAL SERVICES COMMITTEE

The charge and procedure for this committee reads as follows:

To work closely with the FAUL Central staff to determine areas of cooperation in acquiring, organizing and processing materials for optimal use. The Committee may appoint *ad hoc* task groups to study specific problems. Written and/or oral reports of activities and recommendations for action will be made to the Board of Directors at the request of the Chairman.

This group is composed of the Head of Technical Services from each library but has not yet convened since its formation in June 1970. It is a direct outgrowth of a predecessor Systems Committee which had a broad mandate to investigate the application of technology to cooperative problems. The extensive work of that group is reviewed under Inventory of Activities.

USER SERVICES COMMITTEE

To study, develop and recommend procedures for increasing the ease of access to FAUL collections and information services by its user populations. Investigations should emphasize cooperative activities in circulation control, intra-FAUL loans, intra-FAUL information channels, reference services and other public service activities. *Ad hoc* task groups may be appointed to study specific problems. Written and/or oral reports of activities and recommendations for action will be made to the Board of Directors at the request of the Chairman.

The members of this committee are generally from the assistant or associate director echelon. Its predecessor was the Access Committee which contained a mixture of branch and circulation librarians, and one assistant director. The new committee, formed in June 1970, represents equivalent echelons from each library. The broad activities of the Access Committee also are described below.

SPECIAL COLLECTIONS COMMITTEE

To determine areas, procedures, and projects for cooperation among FAUL members in special collections (e.g. rare books archives, manuscripts, etc.). The Committee may appoint *ad*

hoc task groups to study specific problems. Written and/or oral reports of committee activities and recommendations for action should be made to the Board at the request of the Chairman.

In general, rare book librarians, archivists, and manuscript curators form this group. Since there is great unevenness in the scope, quality, and quantity of special collections among the five libraries, and differing specialties among the committee representatives, this group has many weaknesses inherent in it. It has, however, produced two editions of a joint manuscripts catalog and taken group positions on several policies relating to access and acquisition procedures. See the next section.

ACQUISITIONS COMMITTEE (INACTIVE)

This group produced a joint acquisitions policy survey and then disbanded in April 1969. Its charge was:

To determine areas of cooperation in acquisitions activities among FAUL members, and to study and recommend plans and procedures for promoting these cooperative efforts. Written and/or oral reports of activities and recommendations for action should be made to the Board at the request of the Chairman.

Since April 1969 the Executive Council approved a contract with an outside expert for an intensive evaluation of joint acquisitions possibilities in FAUL. This report will be submitted to the board for action in October.

An official historical record of work done by the several committees is maintained by minutes and monthly status reports. Bidirectional communication is kept open through a bimonthly newsletter which alternates with an internal bimonthly status report of projects.

INVENTORY OF ACTIVITIES

A judgment of the adequacy of the structure described to fulfill the objectives of the organization can be made with greater certainty if a rapid inventory of accomplishment and failure is presented. This inventory of FAUL activities follows.

As the italicized phrases in the excerpt from the FAUL Constitution indicate, seven areas of exploration were specifically mandated as organizational objectives:

1. To develop coordinated acquisitions policies

2. To develop means for sharing resources

3. To develop shared storage facilities

4. To develop easy and rapid communications systems among the membership

5. To develop compatible machine systems

6.   To explore and develop other areas of cooperation

7.   To develop a coordinated policy for long-range growth.

Each of these objectives is discussed below in terms of the effort FAUL has made to attain them during these past twenty-six months.

To Develop Coordinate Acquisitions Policies

The Acquisitions Committee was given this area of investigation in its charge as stated above. After a year's work the committee submitted its report to the board in April 1969 entitled: "Joint Acquisitions Policy: Subject List Arranged by the Library of Congress Classification Scheme (Draft)."[2] The report contained a list of Library of Congress subject categories adjacent to which each library had indicated its current "level of collecting intensity." No subsequent record has been kept of local acquisitions policy changes resulting from this exercise; therefore, no measure of its effectiveness can be reported.

A proposal to test a machine-based book ordering procedure whereby machine-readable data would be supplied by vendors to the member libraries was forwarded to the committee for consideration. Because of the "selection" orientation of the group (as opposed to "technical" orientation) and other events noted below, the proposal was not considered by the committee and remains dormant. The committee was disbanded in April 1969 because the problem of coordinated acquisitions development appeared to the board to be too time-consuming and too closely tied to the vagaries of curricular changes and research programs at each institution. It is interesting to note that since that date all members of the Acquisitions Committee have left their respective institutions, except one, SUNY-Binghamton. No cause-effect relationship is intended.

Incidental to this activity was the implementation of an arrangement to transport all Public Law 480 materials in Arabic from Syracuse to SUNY-Binghamton for cataloging and housing because of the latter's strength and the former's weakness in academic programming in this area. The arrangement probably would have occurred whether or not FAUL had existed.

Two events have occurred, however, which are directly attributable to FAUL effort. First, a two-month contract to review acquisitions activity in FAUL libraries was signed with an outside acquisitions expert. The contract will result in a report which will recommend a plan for coordinating resource development in FAUL. This contract will be completed by the end of September 1970.

Second, the University of Rochester library has responded quickly to an idea which SUNY-Binghamton originated. Rochester has offered to share with each of the other FAUL libraries the costs of purchasing particularly expensive items with no conditions placed upon the location. All Rochester requires in return is a unit catalog card and the right to request the items on interlibrary loan. The precedent should contribute to further developments, but no formal procedures have yet been agreed upon. It is interesting to note here that one member of the group

eagerly seized upon a variation of an idea initiated by another — kind of idea sharing which should be nourished in all consortia.

In any event, interest in sharing expensive acquisitions for the purpose of reducing costs of duplication seems to be awakening. It has been the experience so far, however, that good ideas die quickly if they are not taken seriously by at least two libraries in the membership.

To Develop Means for Sharing Resources

In this context the word "resources" is defined to include people's ideas, the work they do, as well as the materials and facilities which they use.

Useful experiences and ideas are shared among member libraries during mutual visits and meetings, and FAUL has indeed committed itself to maximize these opportunities. Since April 1968 more than 3,300 man-hours have been devoted to meetings by library staff members; this figure does not include preparation time or other informal visits. The time spent is the equivalent of more than one and a half man-years in a little more than two calendar years. Very little has been done to measure either the efficiency of the meetings or their effect within the member libraries. Presumably, a series of small changes are continually occurring, which in the long run do make the member libraries "fit" together better. In general, the assumption operating here has been "the more people with similar professional interests communicate, the greater the chances for stimulating and infusing good ideas and practices among them." By corollary, the chances for maintaining poor practices are thereby decreased. A counterassumption could be that a mutual defense pact *against* change would develop. There is in FAUL a tendency for both assumptions to work under varying conditions.

The most interesting example of resource-sharing as previously defined has been the FAUL Staff Visitation Program. Over a span of six months, each library has invited staff members from its sister libraries to spend one and a half days examining the facilities and procedures, and talking with their counterparts about common problems. The final visitation in this current series occurred in June 1970. The series dealt mainly with the transfer of experience and comparison of circulation services procedures. A report was made to the Access Committee which indicates that this activity has been of great personal value to the participants, and there is strong feeling that the technique should be continued and expanded into a full-blown continuing education program for other groups within the organization.

There are three other activities which also give support to the attainment of this objective. The first is the publication of the *Directory of Personnel of the Five Associated University Libraries and Computing Centers*.[3] This directory lists about eighty-five professionals from FAUL universities, indicates titles, addresses telephone numbers, and states if they participate in FAUL committees or projects. A proposal before the board, developed by the Access Committee, recommends the expansion of this directory to include language and special subject competencies of library staff members, thereby widening the potential application of rare and unusual skills through the association.

In order to increase the ease of access by faculty and students to each member library, two agreements were made relating to In-Person-Borrowing Privileges, IPBP. In April 1968, IPBP were offered to faculty members. This agreement meant that any faculty member could borrow circulatable items from any FAUL library merely by showing his ID card in person. As a measure of use by FAUL borrowers of Cornell resources, exclusive of interlibrary loan, 158 faculty members and 360 students borrowed 2,400 items during fiscal 1968-69.

In January 1970 similar privileges were announced for doctoral candidates. Authorization cards are issued by the user's home library after clearance by a designated staff member. Monthly reports are made to the Access Committee, and problems are cleared up handily. Recent figures suggest the following summary statement, projected over one year at current activity rates: All FAUL libraries will issue about (275 IPBP) cards this year to students who would not have received permission before. The principal flow has been from Syracuse to Cornell (76 percent); Cornell has not been asked by students to issue any cards so far this year.

A series of policy statements relating to future expansion of the borrowing privilege was adopted by the Access Committee. In general, the committee strongly recommended that this trend should be continued. Monitoring and implementation of this kind of policy decision could be more easily accomplished if compatible computer-based circulation control systems were operating in FAUL.

In early summer 1969 the Access Committee began assembling data to compile the *FAUL Handbook.*[4] The publication provides basic information to aid the faculties and students of the five universities to use each other's libraries fully and efficiently. It includes such information as transportation, lodging, locations, and important telephone numbers. It was published in June 1970.

The Access Committee adopted the following agreement about photocopies on 16 December 1969:

No charges will be made among FAUL libraries, including branches, for photocopies and associated charges relating to interlibrary loans. All interlibrary loan requests sent to Cornell which are eligible for NYSILL will continue to be so coded.

Since extensive resource-sharing requires a knowledge of items owned, three projects were undertaken.

First, in spring 1969 a request for matching funds was submitted to the National Endowment for the Humanities. The request totaled $10,000, which would have allowed production of a monograph entitled, "Notable Research Collections in Upstate New York: Critical Descriptions." It was to have been a one-year project, but the NEH did not support the request, saying that it was of limited national value. No further action has been taken.

Second, two editions of a publication entitled, *Manuscripts for Research*[5] have been published. The first was distributed in February 1969; the second in October. More than 700 manuscript collections are listed. Cornell assumed compilation, editorial, and printing responsibility for the second edition; and

FAUL Central paid out-of-pocket expenses. This series appears to have been well received by the academic community; more than 7,000 copies have been mailed. The responsibility for the series resides with the Special Collections Committee. Entries were composed on an IBM Magnetic Tape/Selectric Typewriter so the cost of a third edition should be minimal.

Third, the organization is well along in the compilation of a "Short Title Catalog of 18th Century British Imprints." About 20,000 citations from the member libraries have been assembled in card form at Cornell. After editing they will be converted to machine-readable form, indexed, and printed. An added bonus will be the magnetic tape containing the citations. Citations in this form can be used by literary researchers for quantitative analysis of printers (for instance), as well as for minimizing the effort of updating the file. FAUL is working with the National Committee on an Eighteenth Century Short Title Catalog to produce this product, which relies heavily upon FAUL's experience in the computer manipulation of text. See MASFILE.

To Develop Shared Storage Facilities

A major way to share book resources is to share storage costs of seldom-used materials and transport the materials on demand. A talk paper on shared storage was written in March 1967: "Organizing a Compact Storage Collection of Library Material." The paper was a thoughtful beginning of a pilot project which was not carried out for two basic reasons: (1) Syracuse, Rochester, and Buffalo each had local off-campus storage facilities; (2) Cornell, Rochester, and Buffalo became members of the Center for Research Libraries. Syracuse also supports some of the center's projects.

In the intervening months the picture has changed somewhat. In spring 1970 the University of Rochester opened a new and spacious library; Syracuse will open new facilities in less than two years; Buffalo is opening up other facilities but still maintains a large off-campus warehouse; Cornell is beginning to plan for additional library space needed earlier than anticipated; and Binghamton has moved more than 40,000 volumes to the local county library because of space pressure. All libraries have uncataloged backlogs which are increasing.

Shared storage facilities can take two basic forms: a single centralized facility or a series of specialized facilities tied together by rapid delivery services. The first configuration does not yet exist in FAUL since the Center for Research Libraries is designed to serve that need and some FAUL libraries substantially support that institution. The second configuration already exists by historical accident. Special collections in poetry, Arabic, railroad archives, and Southeast Asia materials, for example, have developed almost by whim and opportunity but are completely unplanned. Where these specialized collections overlap and/or supplement each other, there appears to be fruitful grounds for single-building storage and processing services.

A recent study by an operations research team explicated the economic advantages of centralized compact storage for FAUL libraries as it might relate to the Center for Research Libraries acting as an intermediate node in a national repository system.[6] The barriers to establishing such a center appear to be more psychological than economic.

To Develop Easy and Rapid Communications Systems among the Membership

Communication theory tells us that a message, a sender, a channel, and a receiver are the basic components of any communication system. The direction is reversible, and some monitoring component must be included in order to maintain system operation. In FAUL the major effort has been under the control of the Access Committee and has been directed mainly to the transport of (1) documents, (2) people, and (3) messages from one library to another.

In line with the results of the study of telefacsimile devices made for the New York State Library by Nelson Associates,[7] the FAUL Central Staff also concluded that the process would be not only too expensive for ILL document transfer but also for administrative communications between the coordinator's office and a FAUL Systems Group at SUNY-Buffalo. Until equipment and procedures are developed which will allow books and microimages to be transmitted legibly and at reasonable speed and cost, FAUL has elected not to investigate this technology further. It should be noted that Syracuse University Library does use such a system successfully between its main building and a warehouse about two miles from campus.

All FAUL libraries have TWX facilities as a result of their participation in NYSILL and the 3R's programs. (These are described in other Conference papers.) Therefore, the following resolution was adopted in December 1969:

That teletype machines be used for reference services as well as for interlibrary loan queries among FAUL libraries.

Since the committee structure of FAUL was changed during summer 1970, follow-up on this resolution and other cooperative reference services has been deferred until the reference librarians have an opportunity to study the problem within the User Services Committee.

As part of its study of interinstitutional transportation, the Access Committee also looked at bussing faculty and students between the campuses. An ad hoc test from Binghamton to Cornell, a relatively heavy-use corridor, revealed paradoxically that little demand for bus service existed. This test was not preceded by publicity, nor was Cornell or the coordinator aware of it until it was concluded. A recommendation by the committee that a similar test be run between SUNY-Buffalo and Rochester has not been implemented.

The major activity concerned with the attainment of the above objective is the FAUL Library Delivery Service Pilot study. The board instituted a two-phase study designed to discover the most appropriate way to move books and other materials between the member libraries. The first phase consisted of identifying nine modes of transport, ranging from helicopter service through a FAUL stationwagon fleet and common carriers. The second phase resulted in a test of United Parcel Service while simultaneously gathering data on times, loads, and costs of such transport compared with alternate modes. Preliminarily observations indicate that speed of transport is not of very much concern, either to librarians or to users; that most of the delay occurs *within* the libraries — not between them; that U. S. mail service, though unpredictable, is the cheapest mode considering the low volume of materials now moving between FAUL members.

To Develop Compatible Machine Systems

Responsibility for pursuing this objective has rested largely with the FAUL Systems Committee, the predecessor of the Technical Services Committee. Since there has been resistance to adopting particular machine systems for any purpose in more than one library, standardization of a "FAUL system design" has not been accomplished in any significant way. There has been, however, one area which the Systems Committee has developed to some degree: the development of a central file of bibliographic records in machine-readable form. This effort is called the MASFILE Project. The principle working group has been the MASFILE Input Group, MIG, a task group of catalogers monitored by the Systems Committee.

The MASFILE Project is conceived as a long-range series of experiments designed to produce a centralized data base composed of records selected from each library and from MARC tapes. So far two phases have been completed. MASFILE-I resulted in a final report,[8] a report of an on-line editing experiment,[9] and a 365-page bound print-out of a bibliographic file arranged alphabetically by author, indexed by LC class number, LC card number, and title.[10] The records were selected from each library and centrally converted to machine-readable form. The print-out also was produced in microfiche on a KOM-90 Computer-Output Microfilm machine. Most of the computer work was done by subcontract, and the on-line experiment was completed and reported by the Research and Planning Group at Syracuse University Library.

The next phase, MASFILE-II, was built upon the first and is not yet completed. A print-out has been produced as specified in both paper and computer output microfiche. The greatest problem in this phase was the bankruptcy of the contractor and a consequent delay of seven months. A report will be issued together with a microfiche set containing the second expanded experimental catalog. The cost of both phases of this effort in contract expenses has been about $22,000, including that part of the experiment conducted by the Syracuse University Library—on-line editing of the data base located at SUNY-Buffalo using the IBM Administrative Terminal System, ATS.

Members of the board and the Systems Committee have been raising questions about the utility of the MASFILE series. In order to alleviate the uncertainty, a rather elaborate set of questions relating to long- and short-range planning were processed through each FAUL committee in a series of "rounds" built upon a procedure described by Olaf Helmer in *Social Technology* known as the "Delphi Technique." In general, the weighted consensus favored the development of a method to query the holdings of each library for interlibrary loan and cataloging purposes. These and other conclusions are articulated in the MASFILE-II report to be published in fall 1970. Building upon that consensus, the library staffs now are evaluating a proposal to trade main entry catalog cards for items which are cataloged locally.

The MARC tapes distributed weekly by the Library of Congress have been processed since June 1968. Software has been written, debugged, and implemented which converts the incoming tape codes to IBM 360 coding (USASCII to EBCDIC), merges new records with those already in the file, produces LC card number indexes, and duplicates tapes. This action was accomplished by the Technical Information Dissemination Bureau, TIDB, at SUNY-Buffalo under contract to FAUL. Originally, the weekly tapes were processed monthly and distributed to each member library. After noting that no library had plans for using them (despite early assertions to the contrary), the secondary distribution was terminated. With the deactivation of the TIDB, the processing center was moved to Syracuse and is now on the local IBM Service Bureau machine.

The MARC tapes have been used in the MASFILE experiments to extract selected records and merge them with other records in the MASFILE data base. It is expected that the MARC Processing Center and the MASFILE-III project will merge under a new contractor, but a contractor has yet to be selected and the work yet to be defined by the Technical Services Committee.

As referred to previously, the following "micro" case study of an attempt to cooperate in circulation system development reveals problems typical of noncentralized automation projects. In spring 1969 the time was propitious, and many FAUL libraries sought ways to either upgrade their current mechanized circulation control systems or began studies to implement a first one. Accordingly, Cornell invited all FAUL libraries to participate in a systems study of local circulation procedures. At first no one responded, then Rochester joined, and finally, Buffalo sent an observer. Binghamton and Syracuse did not participate because the former was busily upgrading its IBM 357 system to an IBM 1030 system, and Syracuse wanted to experiment with a variation of the Binghamton system.

With this uncertainty, one assumption was made by the coordinator and the Access Committee: that at least three libraries would eventually adopt a 1030-like system (Binghamton, Syracuse, and Buffalo), whether or not such a system would be the best one to implement. The first level of compatibility with which the committee could grapple seemed to be standardized codes for user ID cards since no agreement seemed possible on book cards. Accordingly, a twelve-digit code was adopted for Hollerith punching into plastic ID cards. Syracuse immediately began to implement use of that code, but as of this date, no one else has done so. The outcome of the Cornell-Rochester feasibility study is not yet known, but the Cornell administration does not favor the Hollerith coding scheme for ID cards. Now Syracuse is pretty well committed to a Colorado Instruments system, Cornell wants bar-coding, Rochester wants the Colorado Instruments data collection system, and Buffalo has just installed an on-line ATS-based system in one of its branches which requires no book cards or ID cards at all. The libraries are somewhat closer together than before with respect to circulation system compatibility, but one major block appears to be the frequent lack of library control over computer operations at the local institution. And the potential "clout" apparent in the composition of the board has not been effectively mobilized.

A final activity directed toward machine compatibility is the development of a "FAUL Systems Team." In October 1969 the directors of the five computing centers met with the FAUL Board of Directors and Joseph Becker. A major recommendation emerging from that meeting was that FAUL should establish a central group of library systems analysts of the highest quality. Originally, the group was to have been five persons under one roof at FAUL Central. As it turned out, it became two full-time equivalent staff located in Buffalo in a group which was in the process of disintegration. Generous supporting funds were allocated by the board; most of it carried forward into the next fiscal year. But of the full-time equivalent staff available, only one could be called a library systems analyst, and he was half time or less for the three months he was assigned to the team.

The mission of the team was to analyze the technical processing activities in each of the five libraries at a fairly high level of generality. So far five reports have been drafted, but the team has disbanded, with staff members accepting other job offers. The main reason for the diaspora was the lack of firm long-term commitment by the board to maintain such a team. When the team members realized this, they naturally looked elsewhere.

On 17 August 1970 a contract was awarded to Upstate Medical Center to begin the development of an on-line serials control system for three member libraries, continuing the "contract" orientation of the group.

Several lessons have been learned in the process of working toward compatible machine systems: (1) An outside national authority or standard helps members to agree — MARC for example; (2) libraries which are relatively more highly mechanized are least willing to change their systems very much; (3) at least three member libraries consider themselves prima donnas, asserting that they can do most machine projects better than any of the other members; (4) the prima donnas are essentially competitive with each other; and (5) few, if any, members really want centralized systems planning anyway, particularly if, as a result, money flows away from local computer centers.

To Explore and Develop Other Areas of Cooperation

Other areas of investigation can be quickly listed: (1) joint support of four research fellowships at funding agencies for review, (2) another proposal involving FAUL and the library schools at SUNY-Buffalo and Syracuse to build a pilot set of microfiche packets, machine-readable tapes, and an evaluation of current reserve room activities is still in the works.

An inventory of publications produced by FAUL libraries has been completed. The User Services Committee must take the next steps here.

Five short documents relating to special collections policies were distributed to library directors. They are a broadside attempt to produce a consistent set of policies. The titles of these documents are: *Establishing Legal Title to Gifts Made to Members of the Five Associated University Libraries, Statement of Recommended Policy Regarding Appraisals in the Five Associated University Libraries, Policy Affecting Accessibility of Manuscript Materials in the Five Associated University Libraries, Policy Affecting Photocopying of Manuscript Materials in the Five Associated University Libraries, Policy Affecting Provenance and Integrity of Manuscripts in the Five Associated University Libraries.*

As of this date only two libraries have endorsed them. When they are approved, they will be so publicized.

To Develop a Coordinated Policy for Long Range Growth

The "traditional" method for planning in FAUL has been for a position paper to be written about a particular subject and then counter papers written to modify it. This process can take an exceedingly long time. The papers are intended to bring to light salient factors relating to particular interests of FAUL members and have usually been written by individual board members. A recent talk paper entitled "Talk Paper on FAUL Program and Budget Projections" was distributed to the library directors for comment; only one responded. The respondent was very much in favor of this paper, but no one else picked up the lead. Clearly this technique has limited use, particularly if decisions are to be made quickly. The interim conclusion reached by the Executive Council (which originated the paper) was that few board members can or want to grapple with the future five to fifteen years away.

FAUL faces a quandry. The question is often asked: "Why don't we pick just one thing and do that?" The unsatisfying response is always: "which one thing?" As the reader can readily see, the board has no real planning mechanism; FAUL has relatively low priority in most members' minds, and it is guilt more than anything else which produces any action at all. A comparatively simple act such as incorporation — accomplished so easily within the 3R's councils to which each library belongs — still has not been resolved in FAUL after eighteen months of effort. By not acting the organization has cut itself off from state funds, and the group is viewed with some reservations by granting agencies because long-term commitment is not assured.

To promote such planning the move to restructure some committees as described in *Organizational Structure* was made. The Systems Committee and the Access Committee were renamed and reconstituted as the Technical Services Committee and User Services Committee, respectively. But these changes probably will not get at the root of the quandry.

SUMMARY AND SOME OBSERVATIONS

About thirty-five projects or activities have been mentioned in this report. Two have been completed, three tabled, and three dropped. The remaining twenty-seven are either continuous or in various stages of completion. Six of them are in the proposal stage, either before committees, the board, or funding agencies. This load may appear heavy, but relatively few library staff members are engaged in any of them at any one time and they can probably be continued without much strain on staff.

The acquisition of a central facility for storage, centralized computer processing, or message switching seems further off now than a year ago. Tight money, lack of coordinated commitment. increasingly deeper entrenchment in local computer systems, and a competitive rather than a cooperative spirit inhibit its development.

Cooperative acts which are dependent upon the agreement of counterparts within each library are crippled by lack of counterparts. This situation is particularly acute in special collections

activities where SUNY-Binghamton, SUNY-Buffalo, and to some degree, Rochester have been weak. In such situations committee work tends to be dominated by the larger institutions. The cycle of unauthorized representatives rechecking with the decisionmakers is an endless exercise in futility. A radical solution (but a cooperative one) would be to combine departments of libraries under a single strong head, effectively creating a branch department of one library at a second FAUL library. To assert that member libraries can afford to become more independent than they are now is reactionary and counter to a major reason for FAUL's existence: sharing resources.

Fiscal 1970-71 will be decisive. Since its nativity the organization has been groping for an identity, and it will continue to do so. Embedded in this process has been a continual testing of the limits cooperation can reach and a concomitant gradual delineation of what each library's objectives are in joining together. But very soon it must decide as a group which future FAUL will choose to become three to ten years from now. Otherwise the grope, the vague discontent, will continue and no one will be satisfied.

FAUL will continue to be embedded in several networks and consortia, itself. One member library, for instance, can count at least fifteen other cooperative agreements which it is trying to honor. New York State, one of the most advanced in cooperative library development, is fortunate in having excellent leadership at the state and regional levels. The coordinator and other persons related to FAUL sit on a large number of advisory boards of regional and national library networks. This kind of cross-pollination insures some form of liaison and parallel development. A key question for all consortia which see themselves in FAUL's model is how such groups can interface both conceptually and technologically. This question should form a basic area of concern for attendees at this Conference.

The reader can readily observe that this case study of a young library consortium has been unrestrained in its reportage. Glossing over the struggles and rough edges would have been strategically wise perhaps, but the gut issues of network building must be raised during this Conference, or its value to the consortium movement could be lessened. It should be clearly understood that FAUL and other consortia will be successful in the long run only if they face honestly the problems raised by this and other papers, and determine to resolve them.

In conclusion, the words of S. Gilbert Prentiss are appropriate here:

> It is my deep conviction that over and above the problems and techniques of network establishment and operation which we have touched on, there is an overriding urgency to try to understand what it is that we would accomplish with our networks and to make our own evaluation of whether this is the best thing we can do as librarians for the society in which we live or to the particular community of users we serve.[11]

NOTES

1. Joseph Becker and Wallace C. Olsen. "Information networks" in C.A. Cuadra, ed., *Annual review of information science and technology, vol. 3.* (Chicago: Britannica, 1968), p.290.

2. Five Associated University Libraries, Acquisitions Committee, *Joint acquisitions policy: subject list arranged by the Library of Congress classification scheme* (Draft).

3. ...., *Directory of personnel in the Five Associated University Libraries and computing centers* (Syracuse, N.Y.: FAUL, July 1970).

4. ...., *FAUL handbook* (Syracuse, N.Y.: FAUL, May 1970).

5. ...., Special Collections Committee, *Manuscripts for research.* (1969).

6. Unpublished.

7. Nelson Associates, Inc. *The New York State Library's pilot program in the facsimile transmission of library materials: a summary report.* (Albany: State Dept. of Education, 1968). 85p.

8. Five Associated University Libraries, Systems Committee and Masfile Input Group, *Masfile-I pilot project. Final report.* (Syracuse, N.Y.: FAUL, April 1969).

9. Linda Webb and James Turner, *Searching and editing bibliographic records using the IBM Administrative Terminal System (ATS)* (FAUL Technical Memorandum 70-1, May 1970).

10. Five Associated University Libraries, Systems Committee and Masfile Input Group, *An experimental holdings list of selected research monographs in the Five Associated University Libraries. Book trade and library science* (Syracuse, N.Y.: FAUL, Jan. 1969).

11. S Gilbert Prentiss, "Evolution of the library system (New York)" in L. Carnovsky, ed., *Library networks—promise and performance.* (Chicago: Univ. of Chicago Pr., 1969), p.88.

Authority and Responsibilities of a Network Director

Maryan E. Reynolds

INTRODUCTION

A comprehensive but fruitless literature search was undertaken to learn what concepts had been advanced on the topic "Responsibility and Authority of a Network Director" as well as what experiences had been reported by individuals having held such positions. The initial reaction was incredulity that among the endless flow of information on how to contain and retrieve the endless flood of information, not one (well, hardly one) word appeared on the management. Apparently all this change is to occur through the efforts of disembodied beings.

The thought came to me that as far as the management aspects were concerned, all of the discussions were like a bikini: What they reveal is interesting, but what they conceal is vital.

One problem became evident: "Network" is a term that means everything, anything, or nothing. Total confusion exists, such confusion no doubt having some bearing on the lack of discussion of managing the beast. It therefore will be necessary to define what kind of a network the hypothetical director (the subject of this paper) is supposed to manage.

More reading and thinking made a statement by Henriette Avram seem more and more applicable. "The parts, functions and attributes of a library network are so inextricably related that the examination of any element must impinge on the other elements." While every effort has been made to avoid impingement, the objective proved impossible to achieve. It is impossible to discuss the responsibility and authority of a director without *some* overlapping into areas assigned to others.

A tentative premise has become a conviction in the process of developing this paper –an information network, within the definition postulated, cannot be separated from an institution or from the participating institutions. To separate management of the network from the agencies forming the network will, in this writer's opinion, doom its success. We are on the threshold of an entirely changed method and structure for meeting the information needs of society.

Peter Drucker takes the position that knowledge has become the central economic resource in today's world. He also postulates that continuing education is essential and that access to information throughout life is vital. In discussing this, he says:

Information is energy for mind work. This is indeed the first era when energy for mind work has been available. Information through the ages has been all but completely lacking. At best it has been expensive, late, and quite unreliable. Most people in responsible positions today, whether in government, in hospitals, in research labs, or in business, spend most of their time scratching to get a little incorrect and unreliable information on what happened yesterday.

The impact of cheap, reliable, fast, and universally available information will easily be as great as was the impact of electricity. Certainly young people, a few years hence, will use information systems as their normal tools, much as they now use the typewriter or the telephone. Yet the telephone eighty years ago evoked somewhat the same panic the computer now does. In another generation, it is safe to predict, people will have learned that the computer is their tool and not their master, and that it enables them to do the mind work they want to do and are unable to do today for want of cheap, reliable, and fast information.[1]

To assume we can "superimpose" a network is to fail in developing the information resources Mr. Drucker envisions. Institutional change into network components is what is required.

DEFINITION

As used here, "network" means a statewide system encompassing on a formal basis all types of information agencies meeting specified criteria, tied together with a communication system having bidirectional capacity, including a look-up system and providing switching capabilities for optimum routes. The network also provides the capability for communicating with information networks at the regional and national levels.

Such a network will utilize all print and nonprint information resources, most probably will develop original information files, and will make possible an enlarged concept of information service.

If (to quote one interested person) "this network is to be just beefed-up interlibrary loan," we can never justify the costs.

CHARACTERISTICS OF A NETWORK DIRECTOR

A network director should be an individual who: is visionary yet practical; possesses understanding of the human animal; has good interpersonal relationships; is committed to the user not the institution; is knowledgeable in regard to the various types of participating institutions; recognizes the network must be built strength on strength; is a skillful change agent; comprehends the need for research and development before implementation; recognizes the role of management improvement; recognizes the need for retraining; has the ability to generate fiscal support; utilizes various disciplines; understands the place of law; and is knowledgeable and effective politically.

At the risk of being redundant, each characteristic will be examined in greater detail as to *why* it is important.

VISIONARY YET PRACTICAL

What now seems improbable will one day be ordinary; consequently, in developing information networks the goal should be based on potential, working back to where we are today. In this manner steps toward the improbable future will be realistic in terms of achievement. The director must have an understanding of the potential of computer and communications technology as well as present limitations. While there are many questions which must be answered before the future is the present, progress has been made on solutions to these tough technical and professional tasks.

AN UNDERSTANDING OF HUMANS

Such an understanding is needed by everyone, of course, but to comprehend insofar as is possible how humans behave and react is a quality so valuable and desirable it is in a special category. Apparently, an individual endowed with this capacity has sensory antennae which convey important signals alerting him to such things as: The person is not saying what he thinks; he is not hearing what is said; policies will be "interpreted" to suit the individual's personal convictions on the subject; warning of potential personality clashes; etc.

Many theories of management completely ignore how people really work (which explains their failure). It is essential that the person in charge of a highly complex operation be able to assess management theories in order to accept elements that will be successful and reject those that will not. Special recognition must be given to acknowledging that one method does not work equally well with everyone. This capacity cannot be acquired by people without it but can be improved and developed by the person endowed with it.

One speaker, an expert on management, was expounding on the subject and told about the astounding discovery he had finally made after years of advocating sensitivity training, courses in how to relate, etc., that "you can't make an insensitive person into a sensitive one."

In the early days of aviation, especially good pilots talked about flying "by the seat of their pants." Even in today's highly technical instrument flying, a pilot having this "feel" for interaction among individuals and reaction of an individual can make the difference between success and failure.

CONCERN FOR THE USER

We need to have a marketing approach that looks upon the network from the viewpoint of its ultimate purpose and justification—that is, from the point of view of the users. What do we really know about users (and potential users), their expectations, values and behavior, and especially, how do people seek information now? What studies there are challenge our current approach to meeting "needs" by revealing that most people do not now turn to libraries and information centers first in seeking answers. These findings could be used to justify nonaction on network development on the basis that the "need" does not exist. This argument was used in regard to the telephone when first invented. New technology needs new markets which were not even conceivable until the new technology created new demands. We believe that in the future, information network usage will be as great and as much a part of daily life as the telephone today.

KNOWLEDGE OF THE VARIOUS TYPES OF PARTICIPATING AGENCIES

Librarians of each institutional type are convinced their problems are special and that only a member of "their" community can understand and help solve. Actually, the problems vary more in scope than in kind. However, there are some deeply rooted philosophies of how the various communities of users should be served that differ sharply and must be understood. Not all librarians in each category subscribe to the philosophy of the majority of their colleagues, a point also very important to understand. To successfully bring these traditionally separate institutions into an organization which achieves more than interlibrary loan, a working knowledge of the present situation within each institutional type is needed.

STRENGTH ON STRENGTH

Not all components of a network will have *equal* strength, but each participant should be able to be a contributor as well as a user (institutional). Criteria for participation are essential. Not even the largest institution can acquire "everything," yet there should be a basic structure of strength of resources before turning to others, regardless of the type of library. How this basic structure is organized may vary from area to area, state to state, region to region, and even conceivably, nation to nation.

CHANGE AGENT

No institution and no individual staff member within the institution participating in the development, implementation, and operation of a network will ever be the same again – if the network is to become a successful reality. No everyone likes change. No one likes all changes. In developing such a concept, a zest for change is essential but should be modified by a clear recognition that not all change is necessarily desirable or essential. To be able to enlist people in an enthusiastic drive to discover desirable and effective changes is a quality much needed in a network director.

RESEARCH AND DEVELOPMENT

Skill in utilizing business and industry methods and techniques to measure information values is a must. The inability of those of us in information services to adequately utilize research as a means for planning development may well be one reason for the slowness of development as well as for the failure of some programs.

The rate of technological change is said to be determined by:

1. Amount of resources invested in research

2. Number of persons understanding the problem and having sufficient knowledge to tackle it

3. Amount of effort put in to make improvements that lean heavily on practical experience (This is usually done by a succession of minor improvements.)

4. Market structure

5. Legal strictions

6. Attitudes toward change

7. Timing

8. Willingness to take risks.

We need to be able to measure the effectiveness of information as well as the efficiency of the information services. It is acknowledged that it is difficult to measure the value of information, but is it possible?

The problem was once put very succinctly by Dr. Robert D. Leigh: "It is easy to arouse the public to the financial and social costs of an epidemic of smallpox, but how do we arouse them to the terrible costs of an epidemic of ignorance?"[2]

MANAGEMENT IMPROVEMENT

Anyone working toward an operating information network as herein defined must understand that *before* final programming and implementation, a searching system analysis of all phases of present operations must be made and changes in manual procedures incorporated. Why provide a speedy means of forwarding requests and delivering the material by facsimile *if* the library receiving the requests only handles them once a week? As of today significant improvements can be made by improving our internal operations as well as our attitudes. In the process of working with this aspect, the enthusiasm for and understanding

of the need of further change can be developed within the participating institutions.

The potential for generating management information not now available is almost limitless; consequently, careful analysis must be made as to the kinds of continuing data which may be utilized by all participants to plan for improved service. Clearly, an opportunity for more precise *collection* management is basic in network operation. To capitalize upon the opportunity will require changes in attitudes and goals.

RETRAINING

Hand in hand with "retooling" of operations goes retraining of personnel. Its importance cannot be overemphasized. Leadership in generating recognition of the need and desire to participate in programs of continuing education, along with implementation of effective programs, is definitely within the scope of the management area of networking.

SKILL IN GENERATING FISCAL SUPPORT

This hardly needs elaboration.

UTILIZATION OF VARIOUS DISCIPLINES

We could say that this is like funding — so obvious it needs no elaboration — but as yet, we as a profession have shown no great inclination to bring into our ongoing planning, development, and operation the noninformation science oriented expertise. We *contract* for technical help but have been slow to add such skills on our own staffs where the specific knowledge of day-to-day operations and exchange between disciplines, *all* with an understanding of what the problem is, will bring solutions which can be successfully implemented and maintained. New and different demands upon the executive mean new and different opportunities. All the skills needed must be brought together to solve the problems and to build a viable operation.

LEGAL

The network director must possess a clear understanding of the need for statutory authority drafted in such a way as to provide the necessary legal base, yet allow for flexibility in operation and development. Knowing how to handle this aspect in relation to existing situations and in regard to administrative and legal attitudes about how to interpret laws can be especially critical in helping to avoid future need for changes in statutory language.

KNOWLEDGEABLE AND EFFECTIVE POLITICALLY

Perhaps "politics" needs to be defined. There are many kinds of politics although the basic elements in all remain the same whether in business, family, organizations, or government. In this instance we are referring to the politics of government regardless of partisanship. Actually, knowledge and effectiveness are not the same for a person can have technical knowledge of the entire political process and be totally ineffective. However, to be effective one must be knowledgeable. Being able to work with the political process in such a way as to achieve the backing, both financially and philosophically, for the program objectives is essential to the successful development of such a complex conception as the information network.

ANALYSIS OF RESPONSIBILITY

As we review these "characteristics," it becomes clear that in performance these become *responsibilities*. No one individual will ever be able to handle all of these responsibilities equally well. Perhaps then the most important responsibilities of a network director are to assess personal weaknesses and attract top-flight personnel with strengths in the needed areas. Having succeeded in this, the next responsibility would be to assign personnel where they can operate most effectively for the benefit of the network and the individual. Thus organized, provision will have been made for all aspects of known and potential responsibilities.

Possibly we need two organizations, the innovative and the managerial. The innovative organization would be responsible for blue-skying, research, and pilot development. The managerial organization would be responsible for the actual operating network. If this approach appears to be the most productive, the director has the responsibility to interweave the approaches so that as the innovations are ready for testing, the home institution is ready to become the pilot project. At this point we are impinging on structure, which is not the topic we were assigned.

When all is said and done, network needs will be met if they are regarded as *opportunities* and *not* responsibilities.

AUTHORITY

Apparently no one has wanted to face up to what authority would be required to achieve massive institutional change in how information is produced, organized, stored, and retrieved.

Society cannot afford to duplicate the present storehouses, but there is nothing to prevent new organizations arising to serve as producers, organizers, storers, and retrievers of all future information, resulting in the present institutions becoming "vestigial remains" of previous eras.

In most discussions of effective organizations, the statement is made that "authority" is needed to get the job done, yet rarely is the *scope* of the authority needed defined. Inasmuch as we have addressed ourselves to a network largely composed of public agencies, it can be assumed that the political decisions (choice between values) will not be easily achieved. Sources of funding also will have much to do with the assignment of authority.

Perhaps we can only say that real authority will have to be given to the administrator, no matter how, and some authority will have to be relinquished on the part of the participating institutions.

In the introduction we stated that institutions will be changed. This change will come about gradually, and no doubt, the placement of authority will change gradually as experience and increased understanding of networking indicate.

CONCLUSIONS

The task of managing library networks involving a variety of types of institutions is an uncharted area. From what we know now, the task is so complex no one individual will have the necessary skills to properly discharge the responsibility; therefore, networks will bring about new organization structure and methods of management. The amount and kind of authority will develop somewhat gradually as the concept takes form and levels of development are put into operation.

NOTES

1. Peter F. Drucker, *The age of discontinuity; guidelines to our changing society* (New York: Harper and Row, 1968).

Network Planning

Working Group Summary On Network Planning

Aim: To explore the prospects and implications of planning a national network of libraries and information centers.

The Working Group on Network Planning developed one fundamental recommendation:

That the National Commission on Libraries and Information Science devise a comprehensive national plan to facilitate the coordinated development of the nation's libraries, information centers, and other knowledge resources.

This summary does not purport to be the recommended plan for a national network of libraries and information centers. Rather, it indicates why a national planning effort is needed, what the conception of a library-information network is, what problems and issues will need to be resolved, and how the required planning effort might be undertaken.

There was sharp dissent within the Group on many points, including the final recommendation. Some participants regarded it as much too strong; others, as distressingly weak. It was necessary to identify, explore, and report such differences because they are part of the context in which network planning — national or otherwise — must take place.

The United States today is a society in which the capability for developing, organizing, and using information effectively is a major factor in our social, political, scientific, and technological progress. Most of the serious problems of the seventies are interdisciplinary in character, and their solutions must be based on data from many different fields.

The need for improved sharing of our knowledge resources is recognized at many levels in our society. A number of individual information systems and information networks[1] have been and are being developed. Some are at local, state, and regional levels; others, such as those in professional societies, are discipline- wide and recognize no geographic boundaries. All information systems and networks will continue to develop. But it is vital to consider how these networks — and others as yet unplanned — can evolve to become a part of a coordinated set of interconnecting knowledge centers available to all disciplines at all levels of society and in every geographic region.

If our nation is to achieve the most effective use of national information resources and the largest return for funds invested, clear guidelines are needed now for the coordinated development of information facilities. Unless a nationally coordinated development is established, expenditures and effort will be duplicated, and interconnection will become increasingly difficult as local systems develop without the benefit of common standards and protocols.

CHALLENGES IN NETWORK PLANNING

As a concept, planning is fairly well understood. Planning has to do with anticipating some aspects of the future, considering and weighing alternative courses of action, and choosing a particular sequence of actions. It also has to do with the allocation of vital resources — e.g., space, money, machines, labor, information, and time — for some predetermined purposes. Even in view of the crucial importance of planning in all human activities, this function is still often viewed by some as unnecessary. Why? There are perhaps three major reasons. The first is that planning and the results of planning — that is, plans — act as constraints on our actions. That, in reality, is what planning is intended to do: to tell the users of the plans what they should or should not do and when they must do or not do something. This limitation on freedom of action accounts, in part, for some negative reactions to planning. For example, the reluctance of administrators of libraries or other information facilities to enter into mutual compacts — cooperatives, consortia, and networks — reflects, in part, this kind of concern.

A second reason for reservations about planning is that long-range plans and planning compete for resources that might otherwise be allocated to on-going activities. No matter how potentially important or valuable a plan may be, it cannot be described, demonstrated, or justified as readily as can a tangible operation. Yet no one, surely, can advocate an extensive action without prior planning. Few, if any, successful systems are, in fact, unplanned. A third reason is that evidence of poor planning abounds in many aspects of life. Planning often is begun by

Working Group Leader: Carlos A. Cuadra, System Development Corporation, 2500 Colorado Avenue, Santa Monica, California 90406

Associate Leader: Calvin N. Mooers, Rockford Research 140 1/2 Mt. Auburn Street, Cambridge, Massachusetts people who are ill equipped to do it and implemented without adequate supporting information. However, this is really an objection only to bad planning. Good planning is admittedly difficult.

In order to eliminate these reservations, any national planning effort for library and information networks should ensure that:

> Goals and purposes are clear.
>
> The planning effort has, or can develop, the cooperation, commitment, and early involvement of intended users of the network.
>
> The scope of the planning effort is consistent with available resources in terms of time, money, experienced planners, and adequate supporting information.

Planning for information transfer networks, particularly large-scale or national networks, requires careful attention to the potential effect of network operations on *individual* libraries and other information facilities and on *their* ability to serve local needs. Exacting care should be taken in the planning process to protect the on-going valuable services provided at the local level.

CONCEPT OF A NATIONAL LIBRARY AND INFORMATION NETWORK

A viable library-information network is viewed not as a rigid, monolithic structure but rather as a flexible, continually changing and evolving interrelation of resources. The major elements of such a network are its nodes, links, information, and protocol. An essential part of the planning effort is to specify the nodes, links, information, and protocol that are to be the major elements of a nationwide information network.[2]

1.   *Nodes* are loci of information input, output storage, processing, organization, control, and use. They may include organizations and individuals, manual processing and computers, document files and digital data banks as well as films, recordings, and other nonprint media. A node may be a library, editorial office, indexing and abstracting service, information analysis and evaluation center, or any other organization that makes extensive use of information services. It also is likely that some of the most active nodes in the future may be multiaccess computers used as "thinking tools" to facilitate manipulation and retrieval of information for any user.

2.   *Links* are the channels of communication that bridge all nodes and through which information (used herein the broadest sense) may pass from node to node. They make possible the physical sharing and transfer of resources throughout the network and thereby, increase the availability of information to any one user. In the broadest sense, "links" include all communications channels, including the U.S. postal service. However, electrical and electromagnetic telecommunication links have the greatest potential for providing rapid information interchange among the nodes of a national information network.

3.   *Information* includes documents, data, and other forms of recorded knowledge. Although cost considerations probably will limit the initial flow of information over telecommunication links to machine-readable bibliographic data and high-priority facsimile documents, there is promise and capacity for a much greater flow of information through the network as it grows, including "metainformation" pertaining to the use of the network itself.

4.   *Protocol* includes the rules, conventions, agreements, contract rights, and fee schedules relating to use of the network. These are needed to equalize the workload among the nodes, inhibit irresponsible demand, compensate nodes for services rendered, and at the same time, ensure the access rights of all network members. Control of access is essential to orderly networking, but not at the price of subjugating local initative to central authority or letting "bureaucratic rigidity" come in through the cable.

It is implicit in the foregoing that the nodes of the network will occupy various levels in an approximately hierarchical system. Actually, the interconnection pattern is likely to be richer than a pure, tree-structured hierarchy. It will more nearly approximate a nervous system, with networks within nodes as well as nodes within netted works. In any case, the interrelationships among network elements will not be static. Some networks may, in fact, undergo partial or complete coalescence at the initiation of their users. For example, some users may use the services of several networks. As these users communicate with users of other networks, they may help to bring the networks closer together, with administrative action providing the final step in the coalescence. Another possibility is that entrepreneurs may set up clearinghouses, drawing from various network services and distributing information to their clientele. Thus, the neat administrative relationships that are envisaged in a hierarchical network may not persist but are likely to give way to evolutionary changes in the relationships among network participants.

It is tempting to become more specific about the nodes, links, and other elements of the general network concept outlined above. There are, in fact, a number of existing institutions, systems, and networks that may be considered to have "obvious" roles in any proposed national information network. However, it is important to resist this temptation. The issues involved are very complex, and it is premature to speculate about a particular network configuration. Before reaching this stage, it is essential first to:

> Identify and specifically define the objectives of the proposed national network
>
> Identify and evaluate resources — physical, human, financial, and other — that are potentially available to meet these objectives
>
> Identify and evaluate the constraints — technical, financial, and administrative — within which network development and system improvement programs must take place
>
> Identify and evaluate alternative means for meeting network objectives, within the resources and constraints already identified
>
> Select and propose a desirable course of action (i.e., a network development plan) and an appropriate schedule, consistent with available resources and known and foreseeable constraints.

It is to accomplish these necessary tasks that the Working Group on Network Planning recommends a concerted national network planning effort. The various issues, problems, and desiderata outlined by the other Conference Working Groups all need to be considered and examined in detail within the framework of that planning effort.

FOCUS OF NATIONAL RESPONSIBILITY

Since the National Commission on Libraries and Information Science has been authorized by congressional and Presidential action and is about to be appointed and undertake its charge — that of developing the nation's libraries and information systems to their full potential — the commission should play a major role in initiating, devising, and encouraging the recommended national planning effort. The U.S. Office of Education, which has demonstrated long-standing interest and vital support in the development of the nation's libraries, also should play a major role.

It is assumed that the commission will receive qualified technical support from the government and private sectors, and that the network planners it selects will be well qualified in administration and management, computer and information science, telecommunications, librarianship, political science, economics, law, and other related areas. Also, it is essential that the users of information, the distributors of information, and the repositors of information be continuously and creatively involved from the very start. These persons can assist in resolving or developing a consensus on many of the economic, technological, and policy matters that are certain to arise.

ISSUES IN THE PLANNING EFFORT

At the present time, there is by no means unanimous agreement in the library and information science community on questions of cooperation, networks, and planning. A number of critical issues must be resolved or accommodated before either large-scale network planning or network implementation can be successful. Among the issues discussed and debated by the Network Planning Group were the following:

1. *The need for a national information plan:* There is some concern that a national plan might be premature, limiting, confining, and/or wasteful of scarce funds needed for action. There was also concern that the very initiation of a national planning effort might forestall needed local action. One alternative to a national planning effort is a standardization effort to facilitate the exchange of information. Networks could then develop from the bottom up in response to local needs. Special emphasis should be given to the compatible development of emerging state plans.

2. *The definition of the proposed network:* Will the proposed network be for conventional libraries or will it include library-like institutions that may not now exist? Some people talk of "library networks," others of networks that include both libraries and other information processors and "data banks." Should the national planning effort attempt to encompass the full range of information facilities or only a limited set? What set?

3. *The purpose of the national network:* Some believe that saving money or improving services without incurring additional costs should be the primary purpose of the network. They argue that the consequence of national network planning is likely to be increased local costs (e.g., for changes necessary to meet standards) and that if an institution is unable to pay for additional services, no amount of such services is compensatory. Others view the primary purpose of the national network to be increased intellectual power and accelerated social and economic progress. They take more of a cost/benefit viewpoint toward the changes required for network participation. For them it is sufficient that (1) the changes do not involve costly modification of the existing systems, and (2) network participation does not increase the cost of existing services without compensatory benefits.

4. *The time frame for a national plan:* Is the proposed plan to be implemented immediately, or should it be viewed only as the foundation

of a network that will be cost-effective in some future period? Some members of the Group believed that there are some steps that are so obvious and so urgent that one can hardly wait for the commission to take action. Others prefer to take a more deliberate approach and are not prepared to support any recommendation for immediate implementation until the objectives and framework for a national network plan have been more clearly defined.

5. *The range of applicable network technology:* Some see a national network embracing all methods by which information is communicated while others restrict the techniques to high-speed machines, connected by wires or microwaves, and sophisticated interactive terminals. Some foresee, very soon, the distribution of documents from microform collections through electrical channels to library substations or even directly to users. To others, this kind of development appears so remote as to be of questionable value in any consideration of a national network planning.

6. *The need for hierarchy:* In a network many users will take the shortest route to needed information, and the path of the request will not always be the same as the path of delivery of the answer. This will result in by-passing a hierarchical arrangement and may overload certain nodes. Are there special advantages to a rigid arrangement? Should an unordered network be designed? Or can the proposed national network embody hierarchy but with the freedom to by-pass higher nodes through switching points?

7. *Sources of funding:* It was generally agreed that funds for planning are not likely to be available in significant amounts from potential network users and that the federal government would be the most likely source for such funds. It was not clear, however, which agencies should be involved nor whether one might expect that new funds (i.e., over and above what these agencies normally provide in support to library/information systems work) would be available.

8. *Priorities:* What comes first in implementing networks — hardware, software, communication channels, media, or content? Should one concentrate on the needs of individual users, on special subject networks, or on institutions? Which is more critical — network planning and development for the long term or supporting and improving the existing tools and methods for the short term? Those in favor of the latter argue that the existing tools and methods are the basis for our present and future information and educational systems.

9. *How to plan:* Can we plan effectively without undertaking experiments on prototype systems? Such pilot tests can sometimes be more expensive than conceptual work, but the empirical evidence they provide may be vital to the validation of a particular plan. The question is: How much of what kind of experimentation needs to be done during the planning process?

10. *The role of the federal government:* How strong should the role of the federal government be in coordinating the development of the nation's knowledge resources? Some members of the group immediately equate "national" with "federal" and "national planning" with "federal intervention." Others feel that there will never be widespread cooperation and information interchange unless the federal government takes a very active role in fostering and facilitating coordinated development. If we are, in fact, dealing with a "national" "problem — a problem beyond the concern of individual information facilities and individual information networks — is there any effective alternative to active federal involvement?

The diversity of viewpoints reflected in the issues briefly stated here attests to the complexity of national network problems. But this diversity also illustrates one of the great values of interdisciplinary discussions — the surfacing of conceptual differences, differences in nomenclature, and differences in value systems which, if unrecognized, can surely disrupt and weaken the potential value of any planning effort. If either network planning or network implementation is to be successful, mechanisms must be found for identifying and resolving or accommodating the differences expressed above.

PLANNING PRIORITIES

One cannot, of course, attend to all areas and issues at once; nor can one carry out all the planning steps in parallel fashion. However, the Group believed that priority attention should be given to identifying means for overcoming the major impediments to cooperation between and among libraries and networks. Two major classes of impediments were identified: technical incompatibility and administrative incompatibility. Technical incompatibilities in networking have to do, for example, with character codes and signaling modes, log-in protocol, communications network control methods, data formats, file structures, and referral protocol. Network planning should determine, in a systematic manner, where the most critical technical incompatibilities exist and how best to develop and encourage the use of compatible, convertible, or standardized data formats and procedures. Adherence to such standards and specifications will be a precursor to widespread interlibrary and internetwork cooperation.

Administrative incompatibilities have to do, for example, with jurisdictional issues, resources to be obligated in cooperative activities, range and cost of services provided, eligibility of user classes, provision for data privacy, copyright and property rights, and reporting requirements. Administrative incompatibilities must be resolved by agreement among the organizations concerned, in some cases through the legislative extensions of jurisdictional authority. The planning effort can contribute by identifying the major kinds of administrative incompatibilities and proposing means for resolving or reducing the impact of such incompatibilities. Existing cooperative arrangements (e.g., in academic library consortia) can, of course, contribute much valuable information to the planning group on the methods that have proved successful in coping with administrative barriers to cooperation.

A well-conceived and clearly described methodology for network planning at the national level will facilitate the development of individual networks as well as the interconnection of these networks at the local level. The description of network objectives, requirements, and constraints in a common conceptual framework will enable the planners and administrators of existing, emerging, and proposed networks to determine whether there is real, potential, or only illusory compatibility with other networks.

The methodology required for effective national network planning needs to provide more emphasis on goals and objectives than is provided by most system design approaches. The goals and objectives of information networks are derived from a multiplicity of desires and intentions of information users and the institutions that serve them, balanced against known and foreseeable constraints. A good methodology for network planning should be sufficiently flexible to allow for the different goals and objectives of individual networks and network elements. It should help the users of the methodology to differentiate between ultimate goals, long-range goals, midrange goals, and short-range goals in order to avoid confusion about the various possible time frames for planning.

The ultimate objective of a national network planning effort is to see that all who can benefit from access to information, wherever they may be located, have ready access to all of the information they need. This objective must, in the planning process, be translated into a number of shorter-range goals that are technologically and financially achievable and that have the widespread support of the community that the networks are intended to serve. Accomplishing this translation should be a priority item in the national planning effort.

THE URGENCY FOR NATIONAL PLANNING

How urgent is the need for national-level planning of networks? Some of the problems and challenges in information

transfer outlined above, and discussed at the Conference, have existed for many years. Many are of more recent vintage. Some of the problems have been and are being ameliorated by innovative uses of technology; others, by innovative organizational (i.e., cooperative) arrangements. Some are largely unsolved, but because of the adaptability and/or resignation of many information users, are not yet recognized as requiring urgent action or even urgent planning.

On the other hand, there are some aspects of the information-transfer problem that urgently require attention. For example, there are in the offing[3] major policy decisions on telecommunications that will greatly affect the feasibility and cost of modern information communication for many years to come. Also, our nation is witnessing a period of rapidly escalating conventional library costs. The various cooperative efforts and networks under development to cope with this problem, although designed to help the local, state, or regional participants in those arrangements, may indeed increase some of the problems of coordinating nationwide internetwork sharing as time goes on and the number of these localized systems increases. The large investments in localized network facilities and procedures may, in many instances, act as a serious deterrent to internetwork sharing.

The Network Planning Group believes that there is a great need for continued development of cooperation among existing libraries and other information facilities. There is also an urgent need to develop a national planning framework that will facilitate and help to coordinate this development. It is both possible and desirable to advance on *both* fronts.

Libraries and other information facilities will certainly need to continue to give primary attention and primary support to near-term operations. However, in the interest of long-term viability and effectiveness, they also need support in planning for the future. Planned action for better management of our nation's information resources, if taken promptly, should bring about increased use of these resources; improvements in the level, quality, and availability of education; higher standards of local planning; and increased local use of our national information resources and services.

The group believes that networks will play a very important role in the future of all knowledge resource centers. The development of a comprehensive national plan for their coordinated development will help to provide that needed support.

NOTES

1. The term *information system* is used in this report in a very broad sense; it encompasses the operations of libraries, information centers, abstracting and indexing services, information retrieval and dissemination facilities, and other institutions concerned primarily with the flow of recorded information. The term *information network* is also used in a very broad sense; it includes conventional as well as electrical and electromagnetic linkages between the participants, and encompasses both cooperative information-interchange arrangements and arrangements imposed by higher authority.

2. It is recognized that attention must be given in the planning effort to international as well as national information transfer.

3. As indicated by the recent hearings of the Federal Communications Commission and the current development of a U.S. position for the World Administrative Radio Conference.

Network Prospects for the Legal Profession

Earl C. Borgeson and Peter Freeman

THE LITERATURE AND LIBRARIES OF THE LAW

The importance of precedent to the Anglo-American legal system has made the law a literature-dependent profession. Throughout the nation's history lawyers have demanded speedy publication of controlling authorities and research aids providing multiavenue access (e.g., by jurisdiction, names of parties, legal principles, fact situations, citations). That demand has been met by commercial law publishers, who now distribute all but a minor portion of the American primary authorities (case and statute law) of all jurisdictions and at all levels of government and excepting the academic law reviews, almost all of the secondary sources (e.g., treatises, encyclopedias, loose-leaf services, journals). It is the commercial law publishers who have provided access devices for current and retrospective legal data, for historical inquiry, or for updating; and manipulative devices for comparison and coordination of data (e.g., the digests, encyclopedias, loose-leaf services, indexes, and citators). Their publications have given the legal profession better bibliographic organization than that of other disciplines and have served as models for some of the more recent efforts in the sciences. The much-cited "Weinberg Report" emphasized the advanced quality of legal bibliography by including in its introductory statement these words:

> The Panel wishes to call the attention of the technical community to a promising new method of access to the literature called the citation index: a cumulative list of articles that, subsequent to the appearance of an original article, refer to that article.[1]

Skill in the use of these publications always has been considered basic to successful lawyering. Instruction in legal bibliography and legal research was incorporated long ago into American law school curricula, in varying doses between formal courses required in the first year and self-instruction necessary to the completion of seminar papers, moot appellate briefs, and other legal analysis and writing assignments.

The various branches of the legal profession require special collections, which may be developed and supported by individuals, lawyers' associations, law schools, or governmental agencies. Lawyer-users frequently double as librarians for the smaller collections; in all cases, they show unique concern for the administration of their libraries.

The purchase and upkeep of a law library is an expected major overhead expense for even the sole practitioner. How much it expands with a growing practice (he can pass the cost on to his clients) and enlargement of the firm depends on whether it is convenient to share the support of a cooperative collection or to use a public law library capable of supporting his research needs. The practitioner is looking for the immediate solution to his problem. His library will reflect the activities of his clients, and he often needs, beyond his local jurisdiction, only the materials for neighboring states and for the federal jurisdiction. His interest in the immediate answer helps to account for the popularity of the loose-leaf service, a combination "current awareness" and encyclopedic tool which, through its currency and capacity for collecting all relevant matter on a particular subject, has become an essential part of the lawyer's world. The specialties in his practice will be reflected in his collection of loose-leaf services and other secondary materials.

The judge's use of legal materials will be similar to that of the practitioners appearing before him. He will not have the pressure of immediacy but normally will be able to depend on research of counsel. In most appellate courts and in some trial courts, a judge will have the assistance of a law clerk for in-depth research.

The corporation lawyer differs from the general practitioner in having only one client although the client's interests may be many, extending over many jurisdictions including those of foreign nations. The jurisdictional coverage of the corporation lawyer's collection responds accordingly, and his library is likely also to contain materials from nonlegal subject areas.

Within specialties, the collections of corporations and those of large big-city law firms usually are deeper and more current than the corresponding coverage in the larger county or association law libraries; often their special coverage is better than that of the best academic collections.

The Association of American Law Schools, AALS, and the American Bar Association demand law school collection development beyond core jurisdictional coverage[2] and use their accreditation powers to enforce the demand. Law school library collections, like other academic research collection, have grown beyond the requirements of accrediting associations, in degree according to the research and curricular interests, the energies and influence of their faculties, and the strength of their finances. Whatever the size of his collection, the academic researcher, unlike the practitioner, usually is not interested in the law of the jurisdiction; he is interested in comparisons among jurisdictions. More and more law school collections begin to reflect the need to spread those comparisons beyond the jurisdictional limits of the United States. Some international law materials are available in all law school libraries, and an increasing number contain materials from selected foreign jurisdictions; only four or five of the nation's larger law school libraries have extensive foreign coverage, and none approaches completeness. Responding to the interdisciplinary nature of today's social and legal problems, the academician expects his law school library to provide nonlegal information, either by additions to the law school collection or by resorting to other libraries.

CHANGING PATTERNS

Lawyers have been slow to place network planning on their listings of necessary or fruitful endeavors, just as they have been slow to demand computer-assisted access to their literature. Only now are they beginning to approach that stage of discontent which is essential to the coordinated search for improved methods and an efficient pooling of resources.

Existing retrieval systems enabled them to keep the lid on the information explosion longer than their scientific colleagues. Now, they are deluged by the outpouring of printed pages which must be read for competence in dealing with daily matters. An estimated 30,000 judicial decisions are added to the existing two and a half million each year; an estimated 10,000 legislative enactments are added annually;[3] we know of no inventory of foreign legal materials from proliferating jurisdictions or of the papers produced by federal, state, and local administrative agencies and legislative bodies. When each lawyer conducts research on a particular problem, moreover, he adds to that load. Even if he by-passes his books in the initial search and consults a colleague,[4] he will have authority cited to him; that will lead him to other authority, and the probability that he will stir more citations into the total information system is very great.

Much as the lawyer's hitherto satisfactory access to the literature has been disturbed by sheer increase in bulk, greater impetus to networking probably will come from the increasing recognition throughout society that many of today's problems are interdisciplinary. One of the lawyer's necessary skills always has been to absorb knowledge about and to relate to the nonlegal background of his clients. But rapidly developing social change has affected the law's traditional conservatism, and lawyers are beginning to approach interdisciplinary problems for the purpose of effecting law reform or the improvement of social and political institutions rather than waiting for the stimulus provided by problems of specific clients. A growing interest in empirical research is developing, especially among the academicians. Our use of that term must include students as well as faculty; the kind of student who joins "Nader's Raiders," who is serious about the study of the ill-defined area known as "poverty law," places great pressures on the resources of the conventional law school library. Lawyer habit demands the citation of published authority, regardless of the subject area

under investigation, and lawyers expect the materials they need, legal or nonlegal, to be available to them. The demand for information from other disciplines may have done more than the proliferation of legal publications to bring the patrons of law libraries to the realization that library self-sufficiency is not possible today.

The increasing cost of maintaining independent and duplicative collections cannot be ignored. Law books are expensive and in the cumulative nature of their supplementation, carry a built-in annual cost increase considerably sharper than the general cost-index curve. *A Basic Working Law Collection for the U.S. Lawyer,*[5] compiled in 1969 and intended to inventory the kinds of materials which would serve a cooperative collection in a city or county library without relieving the individual practitioner of the cost of secondary materials in his specialty, projected an initial purchase price barely under $64,000, with an annual encumbrance (at 1969 prices) of more than $8,000.

The standards of the Association of American Law Schools advise member schools to spend $40,000 annually on their collection upkeep and development. That is a bare-bones figure, however, sufficient to support only a minimum collection. The average reported 1969 book budget for 134 of the nation's law schools was closer to $60,000, even including 36 schools (25 of them AALS members) not meeting the AALS standard[6] in that year.

In competition with the costs of acquisition and continuation of collections, library housing costs seem increasingly burdensome to lawyers. It ought to be noted that the greater bulk of the lawyer's searching in case law is retrospective, unlike that of other professionals who may be concerned primarily with currency; the decisions of courts are published, for the most part, in chronological order, and reliance on precedent gives potential value to every decision which has not been overruled or discredited by later authority. The lawyer's inability to separate the "leading" and the potentially valuable cases from the mass has prohibited the discard of older volumes from the "self-sufficient" collection. For those who maintain law libraries, the cost of stack space is a problem of extreme urgency.

AVAILABILITY OF RESOURCES, USERS' ACCESS

If we can assume that realistic network planning will take advantage of existing resources rather than bulldozing and building anew, stock-taking becomes an essential preliminarily step to legal network discussion. Strong statistical information about law libraries in general is not available.[7] Several ad hoc "countings" indicate that there are about 995 law libraries with collections of 5,000 or more volumes, employing 1,414 librarians.[8]

TABLE 1. LAW LIBRARY STATISTICS

TYPE OF LIBRARY	LIBRARIES	LIBRARIANS
County	353	363
Law school	162	449
Law office	130	125
Court	113	134
Government	88	118
Company	76	87
Bar association	37	75
State	36	64

Geographical distribution places the largest number of "countable" law libraries in New York (130), California (118), Ohio (83), Pennsylvania (72), District of Columbia (59), and Illinois (47), with the smallest number in New Hampshire (1), North and South Dakota (2 each), Rhode Island (2), Hawaii (2), and Vermont, West Virginia, and Wyoming (3 each).[9]

It is known that distribution of library resources is uneven, with concentration of strong collections, like those of other kinds of research libraries, in the urban areas. It is known that no serious attempts yet have been made to promote a sharing of resources.

William R. Roalfe's 1953 survey of practicing lawyers' and judges' libraries[10] found among some of them the most common forms of library cooperation (i.e., informal exchange of information and services, interlibrary loans, reciprocal use and coordination of collection development). He concluded, however, that "when the field is considered as a whole, cooperation is not as widespread as it is between some other types of libraries."[11] This he attributed to the fact that law libraries are highly specialized, that they are created to serve limited groups of users, that their basic collections must be kept intact at all times, that there is institutional jealousy, that the many law libraries are widely separated, and most important, that law libraries are staffed "by persons who, however desirable their qualifications, may otherwise have no awareness of, or interest in law library service as a profession."[12]

A survey of the literature since that date finds isolated examples of cooperation,[13] but aside from certain regional programs (e.g., the union list of foreign legal periodicals of the Southwestern Library Association, the union catalog of the Chicago Association of Law Libraries, the union lists of legislative histories of the Law Librarians' Society of Washington, D. C., etc.), most of the arrangements are informal ones among two or more neighbors, little publicized and little known to law librarians at large. The American Association of Law Libraries has been responsible for the first coordinated national programs of significance (e.g., publication of the *Index to Legal Periodicals,* the *Index to Foreign Legal Periodicals, Current Publication in Legal and Related Fields*) and the Association of American Law Schools more recently compiled and published (with the aid of a Council on Library Resources grant) the useful advisory *Law Books Recommended for Libraries* (1967-).

These identifiable forms of cooperation among law libraries and law librarians have been designed to improve access to the literature by library users, leaving quite untouched the equally pressing problem of users' access to libraries.

Lawyers' association libraries, and in some states county law libraries supported by statutory filing fees, vary in the strength of their collections according to the size and affluence of citizen and lawyer population. The more meager the collection, the greater the users' need for interlibrary loans and the less likely · the presence of a professional law librarian to initiate them. On the other hand, neophyte lawyers in the large cities often are hard pressed to pay for access to extensive association libraries, while those in rural areas may receive more help from neighboring law schools than they could expect to receive from the overtaxed law school libraries of the great urban centers. The practitioners' access to law libraries beyond their office collections thus varies wildly, ranging from the privilege of direct

mailings from good collections to no supplementary access at all. Overall, practitioners may be the least well served of all the users of legal information.

The layman should not be neglected in any discussion of access to legal materials; his right and his need to become acquainted with the law which governs him cannot be ignored. Presently, if he is an unskilled layman bent on satisfying his curiosity, on "helping" his attorney, or even on do-it-yourself lawyering, he may rely on the public library system, which ought to provide the statutes and case law of the jurisdiction as well as secondary materials written for laymen. He presently has access to the public law libraries which are supported by court filing fees, but it is less likely that he will be allowed to consult materials in an urban law school library (even one supported by the state) or in a lawyers' association library. If he is a serious researcher, however, he may be allowed not only access to the collection in every type of law library but also may expect to receive whatever reference assistance the staff is equipped to give.

Legislators present a special problem. The legislator, lawyer or layman, needs to have noncompetitive access to the statutes of his own jurisdiction as well as speedy access to statutes of other jurisdictions which might serve as models for proposed legislation. He needs nonlegal materials as background for legislation he proposes or studies. He relies heavily on legislative reference collections as well as on state law libraries, and because of his sense of urgency and emphasis on statute law over case law, he has provided the early market for computerization of legal information retrieval.

FUTURE NEEDS AND SUGGESTED NEXT STEPS

The foregoing has been directed toward a description of existing legal information resources and user habits. We turn now to speculation about future needs and suggested next steps for the legal profession. That speculation is based on the assumption that the best prospect for successful national networking lies in a linking of existing library and special subject information networks, of which a special legal network will be one. We believe that organization of the legal network channels should not wait upon computerized control of legal literature or perfection of the communication technology; we believe that organizational planning must begin now, that it must be coordinated with national planning, and that we can depend upon future technological development to meet identified needs.

Lawyers will expect the network plan to promise them bibliographic help (i.e., identification and location of pertinent material, legal and nonlegal) as well as computerized information retrieval with the capacity for delivery in full text.

The first objective, so nearly achieved under the present legal information system, should be the first focus of the network planners. It is the second objective, however, which will supply the stimulus for profession-wide cooperation in the planning so essential to universal acceptance of the resulting network structure.

Several prerequisites to successful networking can be identified in the existing system:

1.   The literature of the law already is under superior bibliographic control, and the users of legal

information are well trained in existing research methods.

2.   The legal profession understands the need to standardize bibliographic form. That understanding might have evolved unassisted through the cross-citing demanded by reliance on precedent or through the publishers' now customary insertion of citation form instructions in their publications. It has been greatly assisted by academic leadership, through required study by law students of the law school review-sponsored *Uniform System of Citation*.[14]

A newer but perhaps more important development is the almost complete abandonment by law librarians of "home-made" systems of cataloging library materials. While some libraries which could serve as major resources produce original cataloging without waiting for L.C. hard copy and none is yet dependent on MARC II, only those units too small to support trained personnel seem unconcerned about standardization.

3.   The number of dedicated and professionally trained law librarians has increased greatly since Roalfe[15] described the disinterested lawyers who presided over many of the bench and bar libraries. The administrators of law school libraries recognized long ago the need for librarianship as well as legal training for their librarians,[16] and the stronger libraries of the profession have followed. Consequently, those libraries best able to serve as state, regional, or national resources are staffed by specialists who value the concept of organized resource-sharing and understand the futility of attempted self-sufficiency.

4.   The core collections are clearly defined. While the unique importance of jurisdiction to practitioners controls the shape of office collections and ensures state-by-state differences among them, certain *types* of materials are basic to research in every jurisdiction, all lawyers know what they are, how to cite and use them, and usually they know which nearby collections can serve their out-of-jurisdiction needs.

For access to library materials beyond the core collections, a union catalog is highly desirable. We think it would be impractical, however, to delay a legal information network until that is achieved. Agreement among law libraries establishing hierarchical channels for forwarding interlibrary loan requests, using existing means of communication (in law libraries, this generally means mail, with the use of telephone increasing) could bring immediate benefits. Now the assurance that an unsatisfied request will bounce back instead of bouncing forward along network channels often prompts requesting libraries to start at the top of the resource hierarchy. The bulk of the nation's requests for copies or loans of research materials now go to the Harvard Law Library or to the Law Library of Congress.

5.   The users of legal information have not yet made great investment in incompatible programs for processing computer-readable materials. Generally satisfied with their commercially produced and controlled literature, they have been slow to demand computerized storage and retrieval systems, even largely unwilling to accept microform substitutes for the printed book. Recent imaginative excursions into computer manipulation of legal literature (e.g., Mead Data Central, Inc.'s OBAR System, Law Research Services, the University of Pittsburgh Health Law Center System, Project LITE) now must be considered, however, as well as suggested[17] systems not yet demonstrated. If the national network planners are to give high priority to bibliographic and technological standards, the legal profession's foot-dragging may yet prove a good thing.

6.   The staggering investment in law libraries, on the other hand, grows more burdensome annually and creates fear in those of the profession who must raise and allocate funds. They want something cheaper. Part of the appeal of automation is the possibility of avoiding some of the present costs. The new costs may be greater, of course, but the promise of increased productivity and the saving of duplicative effort should make such costs easier to justify.

The effort to achieve a legal information network will not be spared problems which stand in the way of cooperative efforts in general or of networking efforts in particular. The nature of the existing system and the habits of its users seem to us to emphasize certain problems, however, and we need to comment on some of them while disclaiming their uniqueness or that the inventory is complete:

1.   Who will exercise the initial leadership? We assume that creation and operation of network machinery should be attempted only

after careful planning, coordinated with national effort, and that new management will be essential to its success. We assume that the network, once established, would be administered through a central agency empowered by the contracting members to negotiate, educate, innovate, and enforce protocol.

We cannot assume that all segments of the legal profession can be led soon into coordinated network planning, much less agreement on details of a plan or on siting a central administrative agency. Beyond the common reluctance of information users and librarians to give up any degree of autonomy in advance of the benefits having been demonstrated, lawyers cling to a special tradition of independence. The constitutional doctrine of separation of powers insulates the judiciary, academic freedom finds its strongest supporters in law educators, and the bar's responsibility for its own affairs extends state by state to controlling admission to the practice and standards of ethical conduct. No one group or agency controls or even much influences the others or their libraries. Federal court librarians answer to their individual judges, are funded through the Administrative Office of the Courts, and may some day be influenced by studies coming out of the Federal Judicial Center. The state court libraries at all levels and the lawyers' association libraries are controlled by local judges and practitioners. Some of the more influential belong to the American Judicature Society, a powerful educational force for improvement of the nation's court system, but neither practitioners nor judges respond collectively to national leadership. Law school libraries fall under the influence of the American Bar Association, a voluntary association which many lawyers never have joined but which, nevertheless, is the principal accrediting agency, and of the Association of American Law Schools, an organization of schools meeting higher standards than those required for ABA accreditation. The AALS deserves special credit for having forced the spread of collections adequate to serve as intermediate resources in a legal network, but its philosophy, like that of the ABA, has emphasized library autonomy and self-sufficiency over cooperation.

Only the American Association of Law Libraries views as its concern the problems of all kinds of law libraries and all classes of legal information users. Its mission has been an educational one, and because its members are professionally dedicated to the kinds of benefits networking may produce, it seems the logical candidate to organize the planning effort. Cooperation with ABA, AALS, and the American Judicature Society is necessary and expected, but the initial push must come from those whose interest and expertise is greatest.

2. Funding is not a problem special to a proposed legal information network, nor one we undertake to solve here. Public support will be necessary for full network development, and the libraries of the legal profession have existed in the past largely unblessed by federal funding. Justification for changing

that pattern begins to appear in the awakening realization by the public that a strong legal system is essential to the national welfare and by the profession, itself, that equal access to legal information is essential to equal justice.

3. The copyright problem looms large for a profession whose literature has been produced commercially. The official texts of primary authorities are not copyrightable, but annotations or indexing and abstracting headings and paragraphs are so intermingled with primary authority that for all practical purposes, the commercial publishers "own" our most important retrospective legal literature as well as the existing means of retrieving it. The problem must be solved if the legal information network is to develop capacity for electronic communication, even for the more immediate increased sharing of resources through xerography.

The publishers will not watch their market disappear, nor will lawyers continue to support old arrangements if more productive means of distributing information can be found. It is absolutely essential that the commercial law publishers, besides being involved in network planning, meet with representatives of their lawyer users in a serious planning conference; rumors can be clarified, and some area of agreement may be reached. Without such a conference, the breach can only widen.[18]

4. The availability of personnel to institute a sophisticated electronic network would pose a greater problem to lawyers than to their counterparts in any of the sciences. Few law libraries house computer experiments; few law librarians have been trained in technology, and the trained minority has had little opportunity to gain experience. The schools of librarianship now are beginning to meet their responsibilities for training in the manipulation and use of machine-readable records, and we expect law librarians to take advantage of growing opportunities for continuing their education. We need greater effort by the legal profession to recruit personnel who are skilled in computer technology as well as in law and librarianship. The usefulness of traditional skills will not fade away, of course, but it is certain that a new requirement must be introduced into law library personnel requirements.

NOTES

1. *A Report of the President's Science Advisory Committee, Science Government, and Information: the responsibilities of the technical community and the government*

in the transfer of information (1963). (The long and successful existence of the Shepard system received recognition at another less prominent part of the report.)

2. The standards are specific, naming titles as well as classes of materials. They are published annually in the A.A.L.S. *Proceedings.* American Bar Association, Section of Legal Education and Admissions to the Bar, "Standards of the A.B.A. for legal education; factors bearing on the approval of law schools by the A.B.A.," (1969).

3. Morris Cohen, *Legal bibliography briefed* (1968) p.1-2.

4. On the weakness of "human indexes," see Miles O. Price, "The Anglo-American law," *Library trends* 15:624 (1967).

5. Jacquelyn Jurkins, "Development of the county law library," *Law library journal* 62:140-152 (May 1969).

6. Alfred J. Lewis, "1969 statistical survey of law school libraries and librarians," *Law library journal* 63:267-272 (1970) summarizing statistics in the annual series conducted by the American Bar Association's Council of the Section of Legal Education and Admissions to the Bar. The 1969 survey collected additional data requested by the American Association of Law Libraries, and promises to introduce an era of better information about law libraries.

7. Frank L. Schick, "The century gap of law library statistics," *Law library journal* 61:1-6 (1968). But cf.: The recently established Statistics Committee of the A.A.L.L., working under a grant from the Council on Library Resources, plans to close the gap; as a preliminary step, aided by the accrediting clout of the A.B.A., they have published basic statistics of law school libraries. Alfred J. Lewis, "1969 statistical survey of law school libraries and librarians," *Law library journal* 63:267-272 (1970).

8. Roy M. Merskey, "Progress in law librarianship," *The Bowker annual of library and book trade information 1970,* (New York: Bowker, 1970) p.278. There are hundreds more of the 5,000 volumes-plus law libraries than the "counting" shows, of course; many of the law firm collections are organized and run by the lawyers themselves, the court collections by the judges or their bailiffs, the bar and court collections by lawyer committees, secretaries to county agencies, etc. To them, the completion of directory questionnaires hardly equates with opportunity.

9. American Association of Law Libraries, *Recruitment checklist 1969,* p. 36-38.

10. William R. Roalfe, *The libraries of the legal profession* (St. Paul, Minn.: West, 1953), p.356-357.

11. Ibid., p.352.

12. Ibid., p.354.

13. "Cooperation in law library service - a panel," *Law library journal* 49:413-436 (1956). "Cooperation among law libraries - a panel," *Law library journal* 52:418-434 (1959); Margaret E. Coonan, "The opportunities law librarians are missing," *Law library journal* 54:218-222 (Aug. 1961); Myrtle Moody, "Opportunities for library Cooperation," *Law library journal* 54:223-226 (Aug. 1961); Helen A. Snook, "Cooperative effort in cataloguing," *Law library journal* 53:115-117 (May 1960); Joseph T. Vambery, "The new scope and content of cooperative cataloguing for law libraries," *Law library journal* 60:244- (Aug. 1967).

14. *Uniform system of citation.* (11th ed., Cambridge, Mass.: Harvard Law Review Assoc., 1967), 117p.

15. William R. Roalfe, *The libraries of the legal profession*

16. That standard was not written into the A.A.L.S. Regulations until 1968. Association of American Law Schools. Executive Committee Regulations 8.3 - published annually in the *Proceedings* of the A.A.L.S.

17. Stephen M. Marx, "Citation networks in the law," *Jurimetrics journal* 10:121-137 (June 1970).

18. Relations between publishers and their principal consumers generally have been good. Recent noticeable ripples are marked by the Federal Trade Commission's industrywide investigation to determine whether law publishers are engaging in unfair or deceptive practices violative of Section 5 of the Federal Trade Commission Act. See B.N.A. *Antitrust* (11 Nov. 1969). The action was stimulated by an irate state court librarian: Raymond Taylor, "Law book consumers need protection," *American Bar Association journal* 55:553 (1969). For a more sympathetic view of the publishers' distribution practices by a law school librarian, see Julius Marke, "The gentle art of making enemies or law book publishing revisited," *Law library journal* 63:3-13 (Feb. 1970).

The National Biomedical Communications
Network as a Developing Structure

Ruth M. Davis

INTRODUCTION

HISTORICAL BACKGROUND

The development of a National Biomedical Communications Network can be considered the culmination of a long series of actions beginning some twelve years ago with the "Baker Report," named after Dr. William O. Baker of the Bell Telephone Laboratory. This report to the President on a study led by Dr. Baker was the first of a series of such reports having national information networks as their theme.

These studies continued into the decade of the 1960s and wound up recently with a set of recommendations in the two presidential task forces concerned with National Telecommunications Policy and with the Network for Knowledge. The first of these was headed by Eugene Rostow, and its report was transmitted to the President in November 1968; the second was headed by Donald Hornig. The Biomedical Communications Network is a relevant model of the national networks considered and recommended during these last ten years.

The theme of all these studies is that national networks or information systems are proving to be increasingly necessary for the proper application of science and technology, and the orderly development of research and development applied to the social problems of today.

Indeed society, itself, has become mission oriented. The medical community, both as customers for and suppliers of information and education services, occupies a privileged position. The medical community has traditionally espoused continuing medical education. At present, its active interest exceeds that of any other equivalent profession or community of interest. This education, aimed at preventing technical and professional obsolescence, can be considered as any process by which an individual having been brought abreast of current knowledge in his chosen medical specialty through traditional college, medical school, and postgraduate curricula continues to keep his knowledge up-to-date as new developments occur in his specialty.

The medical community also has actively supported medical libraries. The Medical Library Assistance Act of 1965 is the only legislation directed toward improvement of the libraries of a single discipline or profession. There are only two national

libraries specifically charged with serving single professions — the National Library of Medicine and the National Agricultural Library.

National political leaders and leading scientists have recognized the overriding importance to each individual citizen of health information. The timeliness, accuracy, and intelligibility of health information permit measurement in terms of human lives. Everyone has a personal interest in reducing his own medical illiteracy both through information and education. As a result, it is not surprising that the first national scientific and technical information system directed by the President upon the advice of his Scientific Advisory Committee was the Toxicological Information System.

The aggregate of these somewhat unique characteristics of the medical community and of health information led to the demand in 1965 and 1966 for the establishment of a biomedical communications network. Members of Congress, of the executive branch, and spokesmen for the medical community all separately endorsed the concept.

In the period since 1965, the Biomedical Communications Network, BCN, has taken shape. It consists for planning purposes of four service-oriented components and one supporting component as follows:

1.   The Library Services Component

2.   The Specialized Educational Services Component

3.   The Specialized Information Services Component

4.   The Audio and Audiovisual Services Component

5.   The Data Processing and Transmission Facilities
        Component.

With its definable community of customers, its substantive importance to every individual, its supporting community of medical professionals dedicated to services and to self-improvement through continuing medical education, the Biomedical Communications Network is a natural prototype for a national information network.

Rationale for National Network Development in the Medical Community

From the viewpoint of the responsible organization, a network development offers the opportunity for limited experimentation with accompanying organized and continual evaluation. It provides the structure for local or regional experimental developments while simultaneously allowing large or national-scale testing. Thus, it avoids the possibility of "failing" many times at the same experiment in different locations throughout the country. It also allows, for the same reasons, the rapid spreading of "success" in innovations from the single point of origin to all desirous customers. Scarce resources can as a result be spread further in meeting customer needs.

For example, there appears to be little need for four or five local institutions to expend developmental funds on setting up experimental models of electrocardiogram transmission via facsimile or for designing experimental dial-up access systems for computer-provided data bases. Coordination by a group with wider geographical or national interests would allow the national group to "sit down" with regional or local groups and determine the best allocation of a planned set of experimental developments among the interested regional or local representatives. In this way unnecessary redundancy will be reduced, and local centers of excellence can develop.

The Biomedical Communications Network is viewed as a prototype or a model which as it evolves will adjust to individual consumer needs and to social and technological changes. The construction of a network implies the adding of links connecting various centers of activity and individual customers, the moving of links as customers or activities move, and the deletion of links as centers or resources are no longer needed. A network stands for orderly change and structure: It obviates the need for unrealistic deterministic planning. In the case of the BCN, it allows the interests of the Department of Health, Education, and Welfare to be pursued without demanding a long-term commitment to a rigid predetermined structure.

There is an excellent radio advertisement by AT&T which illustrates quite effectively one of the major advantages of a network. The actors in the little drama discuss the fact that the telephone instrument is identical in France and in the United States, and yet the service is so much better here in the United States. The AT&T proponent concludes by stating that it "isn't the telephone that makes the difference; it is the network." It is indeed the network which provides the interconnections, the control, the structure, the reliability, and the cost economy.

It is such an understanding of the advantages of networks which has caused the studies of the last decade concerned with information, education, libraries, and communications to increasingly emphasize the need for national networks.

National networks, as their name implies, assume responsibility that differs from regional and local networks. It is their objective to provide equal opportunities and equal capabilities everywhere in the nation constrained only by local needs and local traditions. History has shown that this can be done best through encouraging individual initiative wherever it can be found and providing assistance to those regions and groups with the need and motivation but without the capabilities or resources. When done properly the whole can be made greater than the sum of its parts.

One of the strengths of a national Biomedical Communications Network lies in its symbiotic relationships with the individual institutions and programs which are springing up throughout the country to improve biomedical communications. No national network can be created out of whole cloth. It must be constituted from vigorous, lively, and progressive systems, networks, programs, and institutions. The State University of New York's, (SUNY) Biomedical Communication Network, the Computer Center at the University of Missouri, and the University of Wisconsin's "Dial Access" system epitomize these kinds of regional endeavors. Such regional projects should never be lost in the structure of any larger national networks. They should be highly visible entities surviving and viable because of the local freedom of initiative responsible for their very creation.

One might question the reason for a national Biomedical Communications Network at all. What are the advantages for the medical community of having such a network, and why does one need a network to obtain these advantages?

One reason is that networks are required for point-to-point communications among members of a community. Specifically, this means that networks are demanded by the existence of individuals or individual institutions needing selective information, documents, or educational resources which are available from geographically dispersed locations. In short, the medical community possesses special information or data collections, or other communicable resources, located at a single institution but useful to an audience which is geographically dispersed. Such information sources require a network in order to disperse information.

From the local users' point of view, inadequacy of local data banks underlies a second reason for networks. A network can provide access to information collections in other areas to meet the needs of a specific area in a complementary fashion.

The third reason for networking is a combination of the first two: A variety of unique data collections or information sources spread throughout a geographical area through interlinking can provide complementary reinforcing services to a variety of users who are also geographically dispersed.

The fourth major reason for network development is that economy and improved use of technical competence can be achieved through the centralization of programming services, processing capabilities, and scientific resources which can still be made available to geographically dispersed users.

The fifth reason for network development is the simple need of interpersonal (including intergroup) direct communications, such as teleconferencing and educational activities. A sixth class of justifications for network development includes economic, privacy, or professional reasons for distributing responsibility or workload among a variety of organizations or geographic regions.

Most of these abstract justifications for network development have immediate and obvious application to biomedical information requirements; i.e., medical libraries are each in a way unique and a composite network has substantially greater holdings than does any one individual library as is shown for example by a recent study of New York medical libraries.

The problem of biomedical communications is assuming increased urgency because of both the "technology push" and the "need pull." The fact that technology now offers new hope for solutions to old problems already has been stated. There also seems to be some evidence that the need is becoming more urgent, particularly in medical libraries.

These then are the reasons advanced for considering a network for biomedical communications. But is a network feasible? We believe the answer is yes. A network is a complicated development. It represents the application of technology to complex processes which are heavily dependent upon communication, control, and feedback, where each of the many components within the process may have varying functions. Yet, a network is possible today.

COMPONENTS OF A NATIONAL BIOMEDICAL COMMUNICATIONS NETWORK

A network designed to assist in the transfer of biomedical information is more encompassing than communications for the medical community. It includes the dissemination of medical information to nonmedical audiences. It also includes the transfer of information from the allied health professions which number more than one million in this country.

In this paper, however, the network under consideration is a network for the medical community. The transfer of information or communications within the medical community includes more than the dissemination of research results, journals and books, or the formal and informal communications associated with conferences. It includes:

1. *Communications about patients' health status:* These might be patient records. They might be more dynamic in nature such as the outputs of body sensors. Patient monitoring involves real-time communications. Patient records, on the other hand, are historical except when used as a part of a clinical diagnosis. Then, they too become real-time in nature.

2. *Communications about patients' health services:* These are generally administrative records used for health insurance or other health payment services. The advent of MEDICARE and MEDICAID have highlighted the need for these records. These programs also have highlighted the present lack of good record-keeping capabilities and the direct translation of poor record-keeping into excessive costs for the country as a whole.

3. *Communications about doctors:* Doctors are intermediaries between medicine and patients. The professional services they provide relate directly to their training and education. The medical community has long maintained records about doctors listing their location, their specialties, their continuing education, and their experiences. Recently, a number of states have set up requirements for relicensure of physicians, based on completion of a minimum number of continuing education courses. Relicensure regulations necessitate more record-keeping about doctors.

4. *Communications about medical facilities:* The medical community monitors or accredits its medical facilities. These are principally hospitals and medical schools. It keeps its own records and furnishes selected statistics in its own publications. It assesses the capabilities of its facilities itself. These records are of prime importance in determining means of increasing health manpower, of providing health care, and of costing health services.

5. *Communications about procedures and products:* Exchange of information on the effects of various drug dosages or medical procedures used is essential to good medical practice. Regular and standardized record-keeping is a prerequisite to this exchange which presently occurs too infrequently. The transfer of information about new industrial products or drugs is much better organized. It is done principally by industrial salesmen or drug detail men.

6. *Communications in support of continuing medical education:* The Report of the President's Commission on Heart Disease, Cancer and Stroke of December 1964, stated that:

Most of the physicians practicing today received their education in the 1930's and 1940's. The fact that they are practicing two or three decades later would have been unimportant in earlier, quieter centuries. Today, it poses a critical obstacle to the delivery of up-to-date health care. Therefore, a systematic, nationwide program of continuing education for physicians is a categorical imperative of contemporary medicine....the imaginative use of new communications media offers the best hope for necessary breakthroughs in continuing education.

7. *Communications in support of undergraduate and graduate medical education:* In the United States all members of the medical profession graduate from one of ninety-nine four-year medical schools or five two-year medical schools. Presently, at any given time, there are approximately 35,000 students enrolled in these schools which graduate 8,000 per year. In medical schools, as in all universities, communications form the basis for the transfer of knowledge and skills.

8. *Communications to support the physician (dentist) in practice:* The physician (dentist) in practice

needs a continuous stream of information. He needs journal articles and books to inform him of research underway, of meetings, of events of interest, of available courses and educational material, of new developments, etc. He needs specialized information packaged to meet his individualized needs covering topics he has selected. Information analysis centers, specialized information services, or audiovisual repositories have been established for this purpose. In practice, many other sources are more commonly used.

9. *Communications to support the medical researcher:* The research worker generally needs highly specialized information in areas relevant to his research or he needs the ability to browse as a means of intellectual stimulation. Both these needs are commonly met through library resources available to the medical community.

It has been found possible to satisfy these needs by designing a network separated into components distinguished by broad type of services provided, by information media or carrier characteristics, and by supporting technology.

The Biomedical Communications Network is thus an interrelated complex of four service components and one network support component.

The Library Component or Document Handling Component, the most advanced of present biomedical communications forms, has as its primary functions the acquisition, indexing, cataloging, and classifying of reports of new medical scientific knowledge wherever recorded; the storage of this knowledge for use in both present and future time; bibliographic access to and retrieval of this knowledge; and the dissemination of books, reports, journals, containing knowledge as well as the bibliographic tools for access to them. The component will be a flexible netting of a large number of medical libraries and other repositories of scientific information. In its entirety, the library component will serve to provide access to medicine's scientific and professional knowledge. This component is essential to and ultimately relates to all biomedical communications facilities.

The Specialized Information Services Component, like the library component, is an organizer and a disseminator of medical scientific knowledge; however, this component operates only in relatively narrow, well-defined fields and in response to queries, provides specific information bearing on a subject. Unlike the library component, the specialized information services component provides information rather than the bibliographic services and books normally associated with a library. This component will be a sophisticated meeting of existing facilities, e.g., DHEW biomedical information analysis centers, other federal information analysis centers, and new systems, e.g., a toxicology information system, now being developed. The component will make use of computer processing, data communications, electronic displays, and a wide range of advanced information handling technology.

The Specialized Education Services Component provides the basic communication services and facilities required for the continuing education of medical professionals, for undergraduate and graduate medical education, and for the delivery of basic health information to the medically uninformed. With regard to medical professionals, the component is oriented to providing that information which is necessary to improve the overall quality of medical services. In addition to providing purely health-oriented information and transmitting the results of ongoing research, this component will keep the health professionals informed about relevant, new technologies that are potentially exploitable for the advancement of medicine. A major portion of the specialized education services component will be directed toward the undergraduate and graduate programs of medical schools. With regard to the medically uninformed, the component will make available the facilities for transmitting basic health science information services aimed at increasing health awareness of the public.

The Audio and Audiovisual Component is responsible for the acquisition, creation, maintenance, and distribution of audio and audiovisual materials for the Biomedical Communications Network. These materials complement the information and other educational materials provided by other network components. The audio and audiovisual component will create materials where necessary to satisfy user requirements; it also will arrange to acquire such materials from other agencies or to have another agency produce such materials for use in the Biomedical Communications Network. The component may well provide a variety of other services such as serving as a national referral center for biomedical films, and providing a network of audio lecture materials.

The Data Processing and Data Transmission Component is a support component comprising all the data processing and communications facilities of the Biomedical Communications Network; in effect, it is the bond which holds all the other biomedical communications components together in a disciplined network. In the areas of library component and specialized information services component, this component will provide the computer processing and communications facilities to receive requests, search and retrieve responses, and transmit the answer back to the requestor. In the case of specialized education services, this component will provide the communications facilities for transmitting alphanumeric educational materials of various kinds to locations wherever medical educational activities are conducted.

An example of a computer-based service recently initiated within the library component of the Biomedical Communications Network is the AIM-TWX service providing rapid, responsive searching of the medical literature. The bibliographic information for the last five years on more than one-hundred journals in clinical medicine is stored in a large, time-sharing computer in Santa Monica, California, run by System Development Corporation. The journals covered include those in the new *Abridged Index Medicus.* This computer can be called from either TWX terminals or teletype terminals connected to the telephone network. After placing a call to the computer and signing in with his number, the terminal user will have instructions provided to him from the computer explaining how to search the bibliographic information in the computer in a simple, conversational way. The user will be able to search the vocabulary to find appropriate search terms or directly enter subjects, subheadings, dates, authors' names, language, or other search terms. The computer will respond by informing him of the number of documents for each term. He will be able to combine terms using "or," "and," and "not" to pinpoint his interest. And finally, he will be able to print out his bibliography at his terminal or have the print-out mailed to him from the computer center. This service is offered from 8:00 A.M. to 12:00 noon pacific time (or 11:00 A.M. to 3:00 P.M. eastern time), Monday through Friday, and started in June 1970. The computer costs for this service are being paid by the Lister Hill Center; the costs of terminals and toll calls will have to be paid for by the users. Most users of the system would start with available terminals for which there would be no additional cost. Communication costs would run from twenty cents to sixty cents per minute for TWX and from local call costs to forty-five cents per minute for phone-system teletypes. An average search runs nearly fifteen minutes and may cost up to $9 to the user.

FUNDAMENTALS OF NETWORK DESIGN INHERENT IN A NATIONAL BIOMEDICAL COMMUNICATIONS NETWORK[1]

BASIC NETWORK ELEMENTS

A connection set. Networks have inherent to them a set of *connections* between isolated points or separated locations. The separation distance is widely variable. "Intercom" networks connect staff members of the same organization located in the same building. Intelsat uses satellites for communications between the west cost of the United States and the mainland of Asia. The NASA communications network now allows men on earth to talk to men on the moon.

Network structure. Networks also have inherent to them the notation of *structure.* When a communications network is constructed, someone has in mind an organization of channels, connections, terminals, telephone lines, or routes by which a user in one location can talk to a user in another location. The element of chance is generally ruled out through network structure. When a highway network is designed, it is intended to interconnect a predetermined number of locations by a minimum set of road miles. It may be required that the roads be so constructed as to permit vehicle speeds of N miles/hour.

Network control. Networks also have inherent in them the concept of *control.* The existence of a structure to serve a process, say, in the case of communications, necessitates control over the location of users, the numbers of users, the equipment used in the network, the kinds of allowable communications, allowable traffic loads, and the like. Most of these types of control are accepted without question and really, without thought. It is apparent that one cannot talk via phone to someone in Africa if there are no phone lines in that region of Africa; it also is obvious that both users need phones and that equipment is needed at intermediate locations to route the call and maintain a "hearable" signal. Control over traffic loads is tolerated rather than understood by the average customer. He realizes that if a large number of new phones were added to an existing tel-

ephone exchange, busy signals would be common and many users would have to share lines. Therefore, he is easy to convince that additional phone service must wait for additional lines and exchanges.

The main element of network control is generally connoted as switching logic. In its most simple manifestation, it allows one to pick up a telephone, get a dial tone, dial and cause a phone at another location to ring. It is the switching function that allows the network to exist in a continually varying set of states. These states are characterized by the combination of terminals interconnected via any given allowable combination of connections (or channels or routes). The change from one allowable network state to another is governed by switching logic.

In the field of transportation, switching logic allows the control of trains to be performed with safety and dispatch. Aircraft control is accomplished by a manual switching process commonly referred to as air traffic control. Here the logical switching device is the human controller who receives the necessary inputs and produces the necessary output with the assistance of a radar scope or modern variations of radar scopes.

Presently, the switching logic of electronic digital computers represents the peak of modern switching theory. These computers operating at high rates with pulse frequencies measured in megahertz have made it necessary to develop new types of switching circuits and to introduce more complex switching logic. Other facets of network control involve availability of network access, monitoring of network status, network diagnosis, control of the network process (e.g., of the information disseminated through the network), and maintaining records of network status and usage.

Terminals. Finally, networks must consist of a set of terminals. These terminals may be any kind of physical devices whose interconnection is essential to network operation. There are often more than one type of terminal, particularly in networks of hierarchical structure. For example, a television network has local TV stations with their receivers and transmitters as terminal devices. The homeowner's TV set is also a terminal of a television network. In a railroad network one type of terminal is the local railroad yard. Another type of terminal device is the telegraph by means of which operators transmit messages on the location and content of railway cars. In a banking network, terminal devices may include facsimile machines for check transmittals, input keyboards for transmitting fiscal information, and telephones for checking bank account status.

It is apparent that terminal devices may serve the specific function or purpose of the network itself or they may serve the control function. The railroad yard as a terminal serves the specific function of the railroad network, i.e., the movement of freight or passengers via railroad car: The telegraph serves the control function of the network.

A network as a physical entity. A network as described in the previous paragraphs is a physical entity intended to function as a unit. The physical elements which comprise a network have been cited as: (1) a set of connections, (2) a structure, (3) a control system, (4) a set of terminals. A network can be depicted pictorially as in Figure 1.

In Figure 1, the T_{F_i} are the terminals serving the specific function of the network in question. The T_{G_j} are the terminals serving the control system of the network.

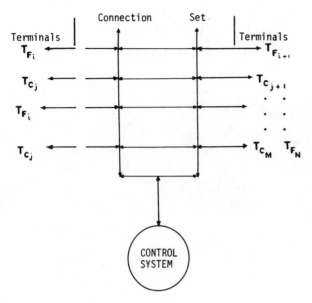

Figure 1   Network Structure

Performance Goals

Networks usually are designed with some performance goals in mind. The goal may be the transfer of a given volume of traffic in a given time period. It may be the servicing of a given number of customers in a given time period. Often, in computer-centered networks, the goal is to keep the customer wait-time less than a prescribed maximum.

Whatever the performance goal is, it generally impacts upon all the basic network elements. It affects the number of interconnections and the type of interconnections through demands on speed of transfer and on numbers of parallel or duplicative interconnections between terminals.

It affects the network structure by requirements of redundancy of terminals and by demands on types and means of access to terminals. Performance goals markedly influence network control. The sophistication of the queuing required, the allocation of requests around the network, and the control over transactions underway throughout the network is dependent upon the performance goals prescribed.

The privacy afforded to requests and to the content of network traffic can escalate rapidly the numbers of controls needed for network transactions.

Performance goals are most clearly visible to network customers in their impact upon network terminals. The type of terminal, e.g., keyboard or CRT, reflects the demands for speed and customer interaction in certain kinds of communications net works. High-speed printer terminals generally signify batch-processing computer networks designed against traffic volume goals.

As might be expected, an explicit statement of goals is essential to network design. Cost of network implementation increases as understanding of network goals lessens. The typical "user need" study must be translated into performance goals before these needs can be reflected in network design. Indeed, questions asked of potential users should be so formulated as to

result in explicit performance goals and to allow differentiation between the several possible types of performance goals.

Time

Throughout all discussions of networks and contained in each general network element is the important ingredient of time. The switching logic used for networks cannot be described completely by logical algebra. Combinatorial logic most often is used as the basis of switching logic but it does not take into account the sequential nature of switching. Generally, the same combinatorial logic operators can be used for switching logic, but one must add another operator which can be called the delay operator. Then most network structures can be defined adequately. The algebra that evolves has been termed by some engineering groups as sequential logical algebra. The introduction of the delay operator and the delay line permits the essential transfer between spatial and temporal distribution of networks.

The dependency on time is often the determining factor in the set of interconnections of a network. It determines whether slow-speed 4 kilohertz lines can be used or whether 9600 baud lines are demanded. The feasibility of interconnection of slow- and high-speed lines in turn determines the kinds of control logic and of terminals that must be introduced.

The timeliness (or time element) demanded in availability of network product at the terminals of the network can impose requirements on the interconnections, the control system, and the types of terminal devices themselves. The monitoring of network performance deemed necessary dictates the complexity of control logic, the numbers and types of monitoring devices, and consequently, has a profound effect on network cost.

There is probably no more important pervading factor in network structure, cost, and control than the critical element of time. It is probably safe to surmise that no structure which is static, i.e., in which the processes carried out are time-independent, can be called a network.

Examples of Network Structure

The totally decentralized network, N_D. The simplest form of a network is one in which every terminal T_i is directly connected to all other terminals via bidirectional links or crosspoints. This is pictured in Figure 2.

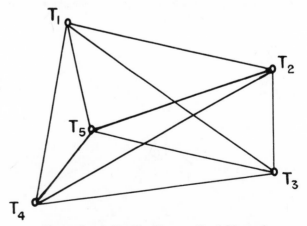

Figure 2   A Totally Decentralized Network

In this network structure, each of the five terminals requires four crosspoints or links to reach the other four terminals, yielding a total of twenty links. Utilizing two-way crosspoints reduces the number to ten as in Figure 2. For N terminals, however, a total of $N(N-1)/2$ links is needed. As an example of the inappropriateness of this structure, consider the 200-odd computers in the hospitals in the United States. Linking them together with bidirectional communications in the structure of Figure 2 would require $200(199)/2 = 199 \times 10^2$ or 19,900 links. This structure represents total decentralization and such a network will be denoted as N_D.

The totally centralized network, N_C. Another very common network structure can be called the totally centralized structure. There are two distinct types of terminals, T_1 and T_i ($i = 2,...,N$). To dramatize T_1 on the network graph of Figure 3, the label $T_1 = T_C$ will be used. Again the crosspoints will be bidirectional. The number of two-way crosspoints or links in N_C is $N-1$, a reduction of

$$\left[\frac{N(N-1)-(N-1)}{2}\right] \text{or} \left[\frac{N^2-3n+2}{2}\right] \text{or} \frac{(N-1)(N-2)}{2}$$

from the totally decentralized networks. Here it takes two links for any T_i to reach any other ($i = 2,...,N$) where each link is connected to any other at the node T_C. This network structure is that of the NASA tracking network where all stations or terminals report in to the central terminal. It is also typical of most time sharing systems, such as is exemplified by Project MAC at MIT.

The structure N_C is thus typical of what is frequently referred to as a computer network, which is a single computer center having a multiplicity of remote terminals. In this case T_C is the computer center and the T_i ($i \geq 2$) are the remote terminals. In the case of N_C being a computer network, one immediate implication is that the entire control and information bank functions for the network are performed at the central installation T_C.

Organizational networks that connect the main office of an organization to its many branch offices also often utilize the centralized network structure N_C. Local law enforcement is generally centralized with each patrol car reporting in to a central dispatcher and receiving its orders from the central dispatcher, as depicted in Figure 3. A final example of a totally

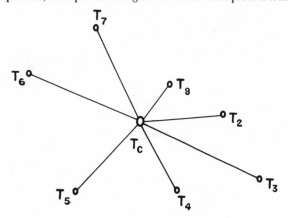

Figure 3   A Totally Centralized Network: N_C

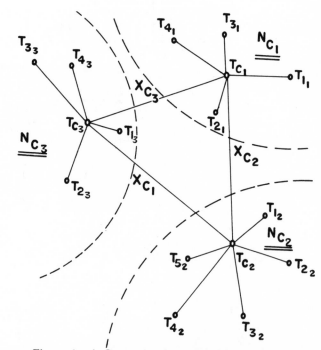

Figure 4   A Composite Centralized Network

centralized network is the automated airline reservation system. Terminals of the type T_j ($j \geq 2$) are located at ticket agencies and airline desks in airports. They communicate directly and only with one central computer terminal T_C. Actually, most information networks now in existence are of the type N_C.

One could surmise with some validity that the totally centralized network N_C is the most easily controlled network structure.

The composite-centralized network, N_{CC}. A simple extension of the totally centralized network structure N_C is depicted in Figure 4. It is constructed by taking several centralized networks N_{C_1}, N_{C_2}, ... N_{C_k} and joining the terminals $T_{C_1}, T_{C_2}, ... T_{C_k}$ by crosspoints X_{C_1}, $X_{C_2}, ... X_{C_k}$. This is the most simple extension in that for K networks N_{C_k}, $K(K-1)/2$ bidirectional links or crosspoints are used to connect the centralized networks N_{C_k}. No hierarchical or ranking order is imposed on the resultant network N_{CC}. Each centralized constituent network N_{C_k} retains its original status and no constituent network is given precedence over the others. Integration of the centralized networks is minimal, and each can operate as a separate entity merely by severing the $K(K-1)/2$ crosspoints. In Figure 4 with $K = 3$, these are X_{C_1}, X_{C_2} and X_{C_3}. Such a network will be termed the composite-centralized network N_{CC}.

The control system for a composite-centralized network N_{CC} normally controls only the operation of the crosspoints X_{C_k}. In addition, it often is a passive receiver of information from the control systems of the constituent networks N_{C_k}. Traffic in the network N_{CC} is usually the sum of the traffic of the N_{C_k} augmented by the traffic over the crosspoints X_{C_k}.

The composite-centralized network structure N_{CC} has been that most frequently advanced by those realistically attempting to set up national or communitywide networks such as National Scientific and Technical Information, STINFO, Networks. For example, it permits the NASA-sponsored STINFO Networks N_{C_1} to be linked to the Biomedical Communications Network N_{C_2} of the Department of Health, Education, and Welfare. Both of these, in turn, could be linked to the AEC-sponsored STINFO Network N_{C_3}, etc.

No ranking is required. All constituent networks have equality of status. Control of the resultant national network N_{CC} can be equated to standardization and compatibility requirements imposed on the traffic passing over the crosspoints X_{C_1}, X_{C_2},...X_{C_k}. Accordingly, no new terminal representing a control terminal or central organization is added to the constituent networks when the composite-centralized national network N_{CC} is formed.

Probably the most significant feature of such a network N_{CC} is that in forming it from a set of totally centralized networks N_{C_k} no new terminal is added and therefore, no senior control system terminal exists.

Hierarchical Networks, N_H. The totally decentralized network, N_D, is, of course, very inefficient in its use of crosspoints (or links or channels). As was noted in the discussion of these networks $N(N-1)/2$ bidirectional links are needed. Even if all N terminals were in use simultaneously only $1/N$ of the channels would be busy, or $[N(N-1)/2]/N = (N-1)/2$ unidirectional links. The only way to reduce the number of links (crosspoints) and maintain the same amount of connectibility is to add switching to the network. The addition of switching is equivalent to adding terminals to the network whose function is to interconnect the original set of network terminals. The original set of terminals is designated customer or user terminals T_{U_j}. The new switching terminals set is designated T_{S_q}. The addition of T_{S_q} causes a decrease in the number of needed crosspoints X_i to effect the same amount of network connectibility.

One method of introducing switching is to go to the totally centralized network N_C of Figure 3. Here one central switching terminal T_S ($\equiv T_C$) is added. Each customer terminal is connected to it and through it to all other customer terminals. This reduces the number of links in the work from $N(N-1)/2$ to $N-1$. In this manner switching control is exercised by T_S, and a two rank network results. Hierarchical ordering has been imposed.

An alternative method of introducing switching is to take the total set of original terminals and arrange them in clusters, N_{C_p}. A switching terminal T_{S_q} is added for each cluster of terminals T_{U_k}, $q = 1,2,...,P$ where P equals the number of clusters. Then each of the P switching terminals T_{S_m}, $m = 1,2,...,P$, is connected to all the other switching terminals T_{S_m}. This yields the network structure of Figure 4, which has been called the composite-centralized network N_{CC}. If there are P clusters of terminals in the network, then the number of crosspoints in the network is now $P(P-1)/2 + \sum j-1$ (where j is summed over N_{C_j} from 1 to P), where N as before was the number of customer or user terminals, T_U.

Although the number of links has been increased from that of the totally centralized network, the use factor of the $P(P-1)/2$ lines is greater than that of the N customer lines. If the N customer lines are made the short crosspoints and the P links between the local switching terminals are made the longer lines, then economies of cost are introduced. In the United States, there are 18,500 local switching terminals (corresponding to the T_S) serving approximately 1×10^8 or 100,000,000 customers (corresponding to the T_U).

By adding additional ranks of switching terminals, the hierarchical ordering is increased. Figure 5 shows a hierarchical network of order 3, i.e., with three rank orders of terminals. The customer or user terminals are always designated as rank order 1.

Hierarchical networks have a structure that has considerable utility. It is the only practical way in which alternate routing between terminals can be handled. This can be considered as redundancy in the interconnection set which increases the reliability of the network as a whole. It also can be considered as a means of attaining economy of scale through obtaining higher use factors for individual crosspoints or links of the connection set. The complexity of the control system of the network of course increases with hierarchical structure and demands for alternate routing or maximizing use factors of lines.

Hierarchical network structures allow more network states. Concomitantly, there are more equivalent network states in the sense of interconnection of a combination of terminals. That is, there are many ways in which connections can be made between any given set terminals. In a completely centralized network, N_C, there was only one possible means of interconnection between combinations of terminals. This was also true of the composite-centralized network, N_{CC}, when no control function was assigned to the central terminals, T_C. The same statement can be made concerning the completely decentralized network structure, N_D.

In this discussion hierarchical network structures have been built up on the basis of introducing versatility along with alternate usage of the connection set of a network. They could just as easily have been introduced on the basis of organizational ranking. Terminals whose activity is of lower priority are assigned a lower rank in the network. Then their access to the connection set or the links of the network is less than those of terminals of higher rank or with activities of higher priority. Control of access to the network connection set by terminals of rank N always is exercised by terminals of rank $r + 1$.

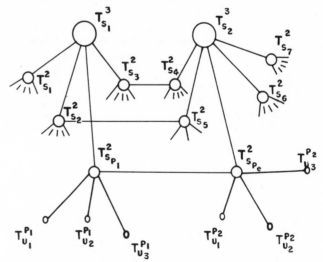

Figure 5   A Hierarchical Network of Rank

In organizational networks, information networks, management networks, and others, priority of activity is more often the cause for the use of hierarchical network structure than is versatility of the interconnection set. In cases of structure governed by priority of terminal activity, one normally finds access to the connection set governed by activity priority where such priority is exercised by funding limitations on the use of connecting links. In many existing automated networks, remote terminals only can gain access to computer terminals during certain periods of a day. Or, they can only use so many hours of connection time to a computer terminal per month.

As mentioned earlier, however, organizational considerations usually dictate that national networks such as the Biomedical Communications Network utilize the structure of the composite-centralized networks.

THE STRUCTURE AND COMPOSITION OF THE MEDICAL COMMUNITY RELEVANT TO NETWORK DESIGN

The planning and implementation of a biomedical communications network to serve the medical community assumes a special-interest audience and a content-dominant communications policy. The network begins to take form when its geographical coverage, its media, and its content are describable.

The medical community typifies the special-interest audience — a social phenomenon which is attracting considerable attention in this decade. Its homogeneity of scientific interests, its desire to be a self-regulated community, its tradition of performing its own research, and its intent to educate its own members is matched against the wide geographical dispersion of its members and their customer audience — the American patient. The communications needs of such a special-interest audience are not yet clearly understood or voiced. There is a growing recognition that to maintain itself as an entity the medical community must be a highly communicative community. Further, the medical world generally assumes an obligation to generate and assess the content of its internal communications, and to prescribe the amount and timing of its interactive communications.

There are presumably a number of ways to characterize an audience as "special." All of these result in bounding its interests to something less than those of the general public. Considered in this light, the medical community as a professional group is a special-interest audience.

In addition, there are more implications to the phrase than this, and these implications deserve explicit attention. This especially is true when we are attempting to determine the communications necessary to meet the needs of a special-interest audience.

Let us consider the elusive matter of content. Its limitation of range and domain are what makes the medical community a special-interest audience in the first place. More important is:

Who determines the range of interest? Do assigned groups in the medical community, itself, or the suppliers of information do it? The action of passive rejection of unwanted information always has been used effectively by special-interest audiences as a protective device. It is not conducive, however, to any planning process and operates well only when time is of little importance in achieving objectives. One must assume in planning that it is possible to assign responsibilities for selecting, assessing, and producing the content of the communications which *de facto* defines the special interests of the medical community. In most cases these responsibilities will be assumed by groups within the

medical community. In some cases, such as patient health care and health status records, groups external to the medical community which administer health service plans will play an important role. In a few cases external groups will probably continue to take the sole responsibility. A case in point is drug information generated and supplied by drug companies.

Who determines who receives what information? This responsibility has many facets. Denial of information is one of the most effective means of control. One can assume this practice is not being employed by the medical community. Instead, one assumes the communications policy of the medical community to be characterized by:

1. Permissive availability to the entire community of all educational-, research-, product-, and procedure-oriented information

2. A capability for individuals to be selective about the information they receive through the use of communications networks that allow selectivity and rejection although this capability presently does not exist

3. Availability after proper authorization of patient health-status records and patient health-service records

4. Communitywide accessibility (after authorization) to patient records so that appropriate records "follow" patients as they move about the country

5. Communitywide accessibility to directories, indexes, or guides listing available information, means of acquisition, and its credibility as assessed by recognized groups

6. Sufficient standardization of language and format so that information may be exchanged without the need for manual interpretation and changes at each step in the dissemination process

7. Selection of appropriate types of equipment and media with recommendations for their use by members of the medical community so that information can be effectively transmitted

8. Continual assessment and evaluation of content to permit purging, replacement, and description of material for dissemination purposes.

A *content-dominant* communications policy such as that just delineated is the first goal against which one plans communications for the medical community. The communication network or system which is implemented may differ from that desired because of the imposition of: (1) intellectual constraints, (2) technological constraints, (3) funding constraints, or (4) managerial constraints. For example, we run into difficulties intellectually when we try to select the content of educational materials for the first two years of medical school. We run into both technological and intellectual problems when we try to formalize clinical decision making. Neither the logic of problem-solving nor the data needed is currently adequate.

The technology that allows for self-paced learning either in medical schools or as part of continuing medical education does not exist today. Funding is not the fundamental problem. Electronic memories, film memories, selective retrieval strategies, and control logic are key technical problems barring self-paced learning from being a reality.

Costs augmented by technical problems force us to pay $15 an hour for use of interactive terminals connected to computers. Their widespread use to aid the communication of information is dependent upon at least a 500 percent reduction in their cost.

Communications costs currently preclude us from extending nationwide medical telelecture systems such as that of the University of Wisconsin. Known as the "Dial-Access System," it enables medical professionals to dial the University of Wisconsin, request a three-to-five-minute telelecture by number, and then listen to it on the telephone.

Managerial constraints are felt more subtly. They generally affect the permissible means by which one can proceed to achieve goals. Their universality suggests that we need not deal with them specifically for the medical community.

One important input to this network is the structure and composition of the medical community. The "medical community" as used here is assumed to be comprised of the 317,000 individuals who have obtained the degree of M.D. or D.O. (medicine, osteopathy).

There are 7,172 hospitals listed by the American Hospital Association. The majority of practicing physicians are affiliated with some hospital so that hospitals can serve as distribution points to the physician for materials and education. The Council of Teaching Hospitals represents 334 hospitals directly affiliated with medical schools. These latter hospitals serve the clinical practice needs of medical students and should be excellent points for the collection of patient and clinical data, and recorded experience.

Some 6,000 health-related libraries serve the medical community. They are capped by the National Library of Medicine, the only national library authorized by public law. The Medical Library Association is the group that represents medical librarians.

The medical community presently has organized its practicing members into thirty-five different specialty groups and nineteen specialty boards. Presumably the numbers of physicians associated with each gives an indication of the size audience to be expected for communications in each of these specialized areas of interest.

Once knowledge exists of the structure and composition of the medical community, different approaches to network design may be followed. Several were attempted by the Lister Hill National Center for Biomedical Communications.

The first approach was a comprehensive examination of the types and frequency of services to be provided by the BCN. The lack of detailed policy for or experience with such a network make this approach relatively unproductive. The second approach was to gather statistics on the location of individual and institutional members of the biomedical community, and to attempt to construct network models as tools for comparing various methods of network interconnection. Suggested networks were then developed as a basis for estimating the cost of the various interconnection schemes. The third approach was to investigate all potentially attractive communication links which could be applied to meeting the communications requirements of the models developed in the second approach.

The problem of interconnecting a wide variety of users and information resources even for a special-interest audience is not unlike that of developing a multiple access communication scheme such as the national telephone system. The problem of distributing information to users in a metropolitan area is quite different from the distribution of information between and among the metropolitan areas. For the BCN and especially the educational TV segment, local distribution means that have been considered are: (1) common carrier broadband coaxial lines, (2) utilization of broadcast techniques through either dedicated or the shared use of educational television facilities, (3) privately owned coaxial cables similar to community antenna distribution systems, (4) point-to-point dedicated microwave links, and (5) possibly, direct reception from a dedicated, relatively high-powered satellite. The choice among these will depend upon the number of users in the metropolitan area, the number of hours of use per day, the topological configuration of the users, as well as the intervening terrain, the number of years it is expected the network will exist, and the expected network growth. Cost is the principal criterion in considering and choosing among the options.

A somewhat different set of link options has to be considered for connecting the major metropolitan areas and the isolated users. One link option is supplied by the common carriers, utilizing coaxial cables, microwave links, and/or potentially, communication satellites. The existing rate structure does not differentiate between the different links and therefore, all combinations of these, when provided through a common carrier, can be considered as a single-link category. The second alternative is to utilize a dedicated network equivalent to those which the common carriers operate. Although it is doubtful whether such a network should truly be competitive with common carrier service, owing to the increased efficiency with which a common carrier can operate by serving a broad and diversified set of customers, the rate structure for a common carrier's services may nevertheless favor a dedicated transmission system.

A number of sources have been examined in an effort to determine the location of potential users of the BCN. Census statistics, organized by states, gave limited insight into the geographical distribution of the biomedical community. Locations of hospitals and medical schools help to further suggest the detailed structure of the geographical distribution. All of the sources indicate that the medical community is concentrated in about the same manner as the general population, with a tendency to be even more concentrated in central metropolitan areas.

The distribution of medical personnel and facilities is geographically uneven. In general, the distribution tends to follow the distribution of population in the United States, and one finds the heaviest concentration of medical practitioners and facilities in the heavily populated areas. For example, the ten most populated states, California, New York, Pennsylvania, Illinois, Texas, Ohio, Michigan, New Jersey, Florida, and Massachusetts, which account for about 55 percent of the total U.S. population, have among them 62 percent of the physicians, 61 percent of the dentists, 59.5 percent of the nurses, 46.5 percent of the hospitals, and 58 percent of the hospital beds in the nation. When considering regional distribution, the Middle Atlantic region has by far the largest number of physicians, dentists, nurses, hospital beds, and health-related professional schools. This results from grouping three heavily populated states (New York, New Jersey, and Pennsylvania) into one division. The Middle Atlantic region is followed by the East-North Central and Pacific regions. The South Atlantic ranks next in size, while the East-South Central and the Mountain regions are lowest, both in terms of facilities and personnel. Another pattern which is discerned in this analysis is that large metropolitan areas serve as the sites for most medical, dental, and other professional schools, research institutes, large hospitals, and medical societies of various specialties. These metropolitan areas are largely in the Northeast, Midwest, and in California. The distribution of physicians, dentists, hospitals, and hospital beds is such that in twenty-eight metropolitan areas, each of which will have a projected population of one million or more in 1980, will be more than 50 percent of the biomedical personnel in the United States. Although their share of the total number of hospitals and hospital beds is far less, they do have more than 40 percent of the hospitals with 300 or more beds. Since the large medical centers, research institutes, and educational schools are concentrated around great metropolitan areas, perhaps most of the educational programs should originate from and be distributed over these areas.

A variety of types of communications are envisioned in the BCN. Many of the objectives of the BCN will be accomplished with conventional nonelectronic communication means such as physical transportation of printed material, film, and video tape. The network will also require the real-time communications such as telephone, teletype, facsimile, and television. Television will be the pacing requirement because of its wide bandwidth requirements. Television standards similar to those used in present commercial television in the United States have been assumed in the planning.

COST ANALYSES OF BIOMEDICAL COMMUNICATIONS AND INFORMATION NETWORK SERVICE

The desirability of a service or product is normally highly dependent upon its cost. Choices between alternative services or products, all of them desirable or needed, are usually made on the basis of what can be afforded. Asking someone to choose between services or products without indicating costs is unrealistic. Making such a choice without knowing costs should be avoided except in those instances where it is agreed that "cost is no object." However, cost analyses for information networks are almost nonexistent in the literature.

There are many ways of presenting costs. Similarly, there are many premises underlying statements concerning cost-effectiveness or cost/benefits of services or products. Some of the more important of these are:

1. Cost should be stated in terms of funds, time, or manpower.

2. Cost/benefits may be realized by shifting manpower requirements from a scarce skill to a more available skill. For example, health manpower is an extremely scarce skill. If services now demanding the time of health professionals can be satisfactorily provided utilizing other less scarce professional skills and technologies then cost/benefits accrue. It is a fruitless endeavor to attempt to increase available health manpower through the initiation of services heavily reliant upon the health manpower one is attempting to conserve.

3. Cost/benefits may be realized through: (1) providing equivalent services or products at lower cost (dollars, manpower, or time); (2) providing better services or products at a less than proportional increase in cost; (3) providing services or products presently not available against a known objective expressed as savings in dollars, time, or manpower.

4. The continuing costs of maintaining network services are significant and should be explicitly calculated. Services and products differ in concept in this respect. A "product" does not carry with it the implication of continuing maintenance.

5. Savings in time for health professionals is a recognizable cost/benefit.

6. Recognized or expected improvements in quality of health services are not readily translated into cost/benefits. The results of changes in quality of health services demand measurement on the patient population which are generally statistical in nature and thus long term. No predictive techniques in this regard appear applicable because of the lack of usable patient or medical records.

7. Ideally costs should be stated in terms of: (1) intellectual effort required of the customer, of the producers, of the maintenance group, of the supporting technical groups; (2) equipment required for the customer, for the

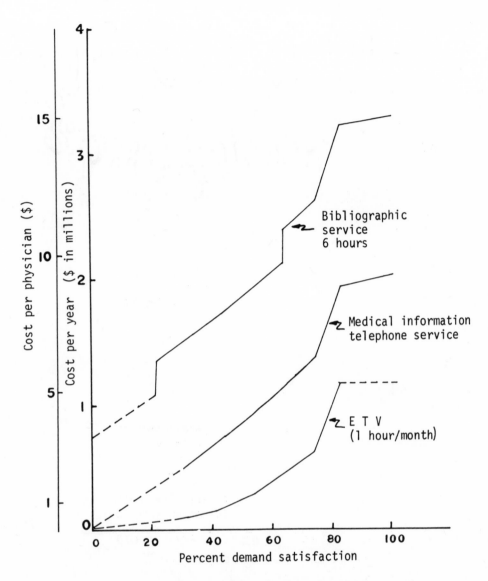

Figure 6   Cumulative Cost of ETV Services (1 hour/month), Medical Information Services and Bibliographic Access Services

production, for the maintenance, for the distribution or provision, for the technical support group; (3) manpower required by the customer, in the production, in the maintenance, in the distribution, in the design, development, test, evaluation, and control; (4) tariffs or costs for externally provided services such as common carrier costs.

Practically, data is spotty covering only a few of the above costs.

Some considerable effort has been devoted to the collection, analysis, and interpretation of cost data for selected biomedical communications services and products. It will be a continuing effort which will become more satisfying as cost record-keeping is improved within the medical community.

The remainder of this section addresses certain cost aspects of three biomedical communications network services, namely: (1) an audio-access system for medical information (Medical Information Telephone Service), (2) a medical ETV service, and (3) an on-line bibliographic access system to medical literature.

Two illustrative groups of services have been graphed in Figures 6 and 7. Figure 6 shows a cumulative cost of ETV services at one hour per month, of medical information services, and of bibliographic access services. Figure 7 shows the Medical Information Telephone Service, the Bibliographic Access Service, and the Medical ETV Service at one hour per week usage. Cost data are shown on a double scale along the vertical axis. The total annual cost is shown on the left side; the annual cost per American Medical Association member (assuming 219,000 members) is shown on the right side as a measure of cost per physician.

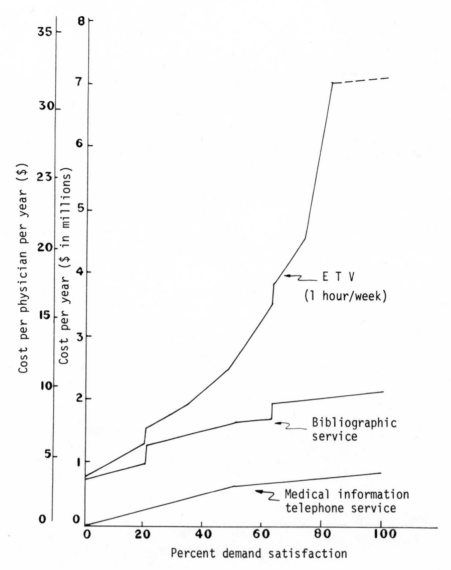

Figure 7   Medical Information Telephone Service, the Bibliographic Access Service, and the Medical ETV Service (1hour/week)

with the smallest physician population) in the number of stations included in the network will cause only about a 10 percent decrease in the size of the potential physician audience.

The cost for networking TV, using AT&T facilities and services, has three separate components: (1) an interexchange channel charge based on the airline distance between cities and the amount of broadcasting time; (2) a station connection charge, a fixed charge plus a rate based on the amount of broadcasting time for connecting the local station to the AT&T network; (3) a local channel charge based on mileage between the ETV station and the AT&T facility. It should be noted that the costs do not include TV sets for individual customers.

The phone access, audio message center service analyzed is from a library of recorded messages providing brief summaries of new developments and current practice in various areas of medicine. The messages would be four to six minutes in length

The percent of demand on the horizontal axis of the curve in Figures 6 and 7 necessarily has different meanings for different services. In general, an attempt to estimate the total reasonable demand was made, and demand levels were then expressed as a percent of this total. For the Medical ETV Service, the measure was simply the percent of the physician population reached.

By the end of 1969 there were 183 ETV stations operating in the United States. Of these, 135 can be considered distinct for purposes of networking. The remaining are either in statewide networks or in cities with multiple stations.

One hundred and six of these 135 stations reach about 97 percent of all the physicians residing in Standard Metropolitan Statistical Areas, SMSAs. Since about 85 percent of all physicians reside in SMSAs, the 106 station networks can reach about 82 percent of the total physician population of the U.S. In addition, the population distribution of physicians is quite skewed: About 30 percent of the physician population is in the five largest SMSAs. A 45 percent decrease (excluding the cities with the smallest physician population) in the number of stations included in the network will cause only about a 10 percent decrease in the size of the potential physician audience.

The cost for networking TV, using AT&T facilities and services, has three separate components: (1) an interexchange channel charge based on the airline distance between cities and the amount of broadcasting time; (2) a station connection charge, a fixed charge plus a rate based on the amount of broadcasting time for connecting the local station to the AT&T network; (3) a local channel charge based on mileage between the ETV station and the AT&T facility. It should be noted that the costs do not include TV sets for individual customers.

The phone access, audio message center service analyzed is from a library of recorded messages providing brief summaries of new developments and current practice in various areas of medicine. The messages would be four to six minutes in length and be available by telephone on twenty-four-hour, seven-day-week basis. Free access to the message library would be available to physicians by means of Inward Wide Area Telephone Service, In-WATS.

The contemplated service would provide some 300 to 1,000 separate information packets or messages from which the user can select. Costs include distribution of descriptive catalogs of the available service and other means of bringing the service to the attention of potential customers.

The analysis of the data from the Wisconsin Dial Access System has shown that utilization or demand experience can be explained reasonably well in terms of three basic variables: promotion policy (number of promotions or reminders per year), the size of the reachable population, and library size measured in numbers of messages. Given that the proposed center is to serve the nation as a whole, population must essentially be taken as given. This leaves two major policy or design variables which can be varied to affect utilization, promotion policy, and library size.

The Medical On-Line Bibliographic Access Service provides a MEDLARS data base on-line to users who have a TWX terminal or a teletype connected to the telephone system. It allows search of the most current two and a-half years of MEDLARS information on (1) use of the NLM data base for the *Abridged Index Medicus*, with slight augmentation to cover the bibliographic information and the most used medical literature; (2) use of part of a large, time-shared computer system rather than all of a smaller one; (3) connection of this system to the TWX network, thus providing potential access through terminals already existing in some 500 institutions in the medical community at no cost to the government. Medical libraries now use the TWX network; NLM receives over 1,200 requests for interlibrary loans per month over this network. These come from several hundred different libraries across the nation. A review of the directory of the TWX network indicates that there are 120 hospitals on the network; 150 pharmaceutical firms; 125 schools, including many medical schools; and a sprinkling of clinics and physicians.

The National Library of Medicine has contracted with System Development Corporation, SDC, to provide such an experimental service in bibliographic access. It is possible for either teletypes on the telephone network with standard 103A2 data sets or Model 33 or 35 Teletypes in the TWX network to access the computer system in Santa Monica. Five special lines have been installed by the General Telephone Company to connect the IBM 360/67 to the TWX network. SDC provides the computer time and an additional disc storage unit to allow the provision of bibliographic access to about 150,000 citations out of the MEDLARS data base. This available storage space is adequate to provide access to a consensus list of medical journals over the five-year period covered by MEDLARS.

Service started in June 1970. This service is provided each weekday from 11:00 A.M. to 3:00 P.M. EST/EDT. The cost of calling the system would be borne by the user, and TWX charges from twenty to sixty cents per minute depending on whether the station is calling from across the continent or from fifty miles away. In addition, SDC provides on-site training at a designated set of locations to selected users (physicians, hospitals, and libraries) of the system and will run a spot survey on organizations that will use the system without training. The SDC system can be used without training, and instructions are provided from the terminal giving a minimum amount of information about how to call in to the system. In addition, the language interface, the way the user phrases his request, is variable and can be modified to be more effective during the service period as a result of the experience gained in the use of the system.

The costs covered are hardware and interconnection costs. The cost of content development is not included. It is singled out for separate treatment. In addition, there are several hardware and interconnection costs not covered. The most important are the cost of placing a call in the bibliographic access service and the cost of a TV set in the Medical Education TV Service. Costs of placing a call vary with the location of the customer and the length of time the teletype terminal is connected. These have not been included in the service in order to leave an incentive to rapid effective use of the computer system. The costs of TV sets can be added to the cost estimates provided here as a fixed increment.

The available data for bibliographic access was much less suitable for demand estimation. The New York data for three cities, not including the "home" of the SUNY Biomedical Communication Network, showed an annual request rate of 2.3 requests per physician; the state as a whole showed .65 per physician. On the basis of this experience, it seems that one might expect as a conservative maximum about 1.0 requests per year per physician. Percent demand satisfaction is then percent of a request per physician.

The SUNY service time is about 1.2 minutes. A service goal of 90 percent of searches being processed in five minutes or less was adopted because it seems reasonable and corresponds to the maximum use of the SUNY system. Given this service criterion, the maximum search demand rates can be computed. These can be translated to numbers of processors required to derive cost and to requests per physician to reflect demand satisfaction. For example, consider a line at 48 percent. The graph shows that this demand level could be met for $2.5 million per year, or about $11.50 per physician. Of this $11.50, about $3.00 would provide dial-access service to a minimum library of 300 messages promoted only twice a year. An additional $4.40 would provide searches to half the physicians (actually one search for up to 63 percent of the physicians could be accommodated). And finally, $4.10 would provide for networking enough ETV stations and for the broadcast time to beam special programs to 48 percent of the physicians in the country one hour a week.

CONCLUDING COMMENTS

There are many reasons for the existence and growth of networks. The basic one — to communicate information — is as old as one desires to consider it, and it is expressed in a variety of forms from interlibrary loan services to the founding of the Royal Society (or "invisible colleges") and the Autodin networks of today. A second major reason is the increasing interdependence of the computer and communication technologies themselves.

Computers and mechanized data banks have most recently again highlighted networks as a means of communication. The circumstances which appear to call for the establishment of physical networks (as opposed to logical networks) are as cited earlier:

1. The existence of special data banks or special collections of information located at a single institution but useful to an audience geographically dispersed

2. The inadequacy of local general data banks or general collections of information to meet local needs where remote resources can be used in a complementary fashion to fulfill the needs of the clientele

3. The centralization of programming services, processing capabilities, reproduction facilities, or scientific resources with a geographically dispersed need

4. The need for interpersonal (including intergroup) direct communication. This includes teleconferencing and educational activities such as continuing medical educational TV

5. A justification on economic, security, or social grounds for distribution of responsibility for load-sharing among organizations or geographical regions

6. The need for intergovernmental interaction as by federal, state, and local authorities on law enforcement and/or the processing of social security and Medicare information.

In planning networks there is an hypothesis — in many cases proven — that communication services are the most effective means for joining customers to information where effectiveness is measured against established criteria.

The core of any information network involving automated data banks or communicable information (e.g., educational material, video or audio information) is a system of communication channels which serve network participants and provide for information exchange. The participating centers in the network interconnect with the the communications system through buffer or "translator": equipment frequently referred to as a network interface. Each interface is connected (generally electronically) to the communications system of the network at a node. The communications system is simply a means for information exchange, and the interfaces are required to accommodate the many terminal devices, with their multiplicity of frequencies, electronic languages, etc., to the standardized mode of operation of the communications system.

The types of network communication system node variations which may be envisaged encompass:

1. Terminal-to-terminal communication (this includes single-transmitter to multireceivers, multitransmitters to multireceivers, multitransmitters to single-receiver, and one-to-one transmit receive situations)

2. Terminal-to-computer communication with and without interaction

3. Computer-to-computer communication with the total spectrum of allowable control mechanisms.

Network transmission itself may be by voice, through record or message exchange, or by facsimile and video transmission. These communication types are classified into low-grade teletype, voice-grade data and record transmission, TELEX, TELPAK, narrowband or slow-scan TV and facsimile transmission, and wideband or standard video and TV transmission.

The communication media envisaged can be grouped in several ways such as: ground links or satellite; common carrier, private or dedicated; cable or free space.

There is no question that there is a strong interdependence between the planning for a network communications system and other aspects of network design. A much abbreviated set of questions that impact on communication system planning is as follows:

1. What is the scope of the network? Geographical coverage; services to be provided by and to whom; location and facilities of participants; existing capabilities available; required rate of development; the subject scope of the information exchange; data bank media, e.g., document, data, information, etc.

2. What are the relevant software and data characteristics? Privacy requirements, accessibility and/or availability of program services, system management programs, compatibility-convertibility

3.	What are the network management and control requirements? Standardization, membership, information and program manipulation, feedback, documentation, costs of services, priorities and scheduling

4.	What are the pertinent legal regulations and practices? FCC regulations, carrier rate structures, common carrier use, responsibilities for information content, privacy versus broadcast methods, federal agency jurisdiction e.g., DOT, DTM, HUD, FCC, HEW, DOD, etc.), copyright regulations, antitrust regulations

5.	What are the technological constraints?

6.	What are the budgetary constraints and financially allowable rate of development?

A number of the questions listed in 2, 3, and 5 above could readily be considered as technological problems. A recently published report by Mary E. Stevens gives an excellent survey of the relevant literature. However, there is no question that the

problems of network design and operation are intellectual and managerial as well as technological in nature. Most are still pending and awaiting attention and resolution. Experience with networks already existing or in advanced planning stages, whose development proceeded without benefit of such answers, will help solve the unanswered questions. The National Biomedical Communications Network is one of these.

NOTES

1. Ruth M. Davis, "Man-computer network" (unpublished documentation from a course presented at the University of Pittsburgh, April 1969).

2. This and all other factual material in the remainder of this section is from Ruth M. Davis, *Communications for the medical community--a prototype of a special interest audience,* American Institute of Aeronautics and Astronautics, paper no. 69-1072 (New York: 1969).

3. Ruth M. Davis, "Cost-benefit analyses of biomedical information and communications service" (Paper delivered at the Thirty-seventh National Meeting of the Operations Research Society of America, Washington, DC., April 20-22, 1970).

4. Mary E. Stevens, *Standardization, compatibility and/or convertibility requirements in network planning* (Unpublished report prepared for the Lister Hill National Center for Biomedical Communications).

A Hypothetical Plan
for a Library-Information Network

J.C.R. Licklider

INTRODUCTION

The public purpose of this paper is to formulate a plan to serve as a framework for discussion or as a target for criticism. It is a plan for a network to facilitate interaction among libraries and between libraries and other parts of the universe of information and knowledge.

The private purpose of the paper — or better, my reason for being happy to undertake to write it — is to give myself the pleasure of reflecting (again, after a few years of absence from the field) upon the new technology of information and how it might contribute to significant improvements in the preservation and organization of knowledge, and in its retrieval, communication, and application. It is obvious that the technology has much more raw power to contribute than is being refined, specialized, and exploited in library and library-related applications. It is obvious that the technology is continuing to advance (in terms of raw power) at such a rate that one decade's dreams are more likely to become the next decade's missed opportunities than to become its operational systems. But it is not obvious how to get things organized to grasp and develop the opportunities presented by the burgeoning technology of information. The "pleasure of reflecting" may therefore turn into frustration as I write, but even if it does, there is sure to be some joy in contemplating, for the library, in its relation to the body of knowledge and the human intellect, has had an increase in effectiveness much as in the past decade the computer increased the effectiveness of the comptroller's office vis-a-vis the payroll and the inventory.

A simple plan is a pair of models. One model represents how the planned process will work at some future time or times. The other model is a hypothesis about how to get from now to then in such a way that the first model will then obtain. A complex plan with contingencies may involve alternates to or conditionalities within each of the two models.

The plan to be described in this paper is forced into unrealistic simplicity by the pressures of space and time. Even so, it is complex in three ways. First, it deals with an extended future, and although it concentrates on the decade at hand, it anticipates continuation into the 1980s and 1990s when the main "payoff" will be or will probably be collected. Second, it recognizes that there are several ways to proceed toward more or less the same desideratum and therefore, does involve a few alternatives and conditionalities. And third, it deals with a highly pluralistic activity and a very complex technology — and must therefore be "read complexly" even though stated in oversimplified paragraphs.

Instead of proceeding immediately to set forth a plan, I am going to interpose three more introductory sections. I want to make sure that we all have in mind at least a few of the technical images that are essential components of constructive thought on the subject. The first interposed section briefly describes a library-information network of the kind that I think will exist at the end of this century — or at least could by then be brought into existence if society gave it a priority not often given to knowledge and understanding. I think it is important to consider where we may be going in the long run in order to round out the context — presumably we know approximately where we are now — for a five- or ten-year plan. The second interposed section suggests that what the present library-information "system" most obviously lacks and most critically needs is the analog of a nervous system — which is to say, of course, an appropriate computer-communication network. I think that there is enough validity in that analogy to risk a quick venture into rather hazardous metaphor. The third interposed section briefly describes the ARPA network. I think that this network, which is now coming into being, sharpens many of the technical concepts that must figure in a plan for a library-information network.

A LIBRARY-INFORMATION NETWORK OF THE DISTANT FUTURE

One of the difficulties of network planning at the present time stems from the fact that while "realistic" planning is limited by external factors to a time span of five or ten years, computer-based information networks will be developing and evolving for two or three times five or ten years. Networks planned now can be no more than way stations and checkpoints on a long road. But the road itself and where it goes are of the very greatest importance for the future of mankind. It may well be that networks planned now will be significant more because of their influence on the laying out and building of the road than because of their improvement of library and information services.

It is easier to see and describe the information networks of two or three decades hence, I think, than the course that network efforts will follow in the decade now beginning. Surely there will be a time when most serious intellectual work is done "on-line," with the aid of and in the medium of an electronic information network. Desks will be consoles. Pens and pencils will be position-sensitive styli. If paper plays a significant role, it will be because paper supports clear images that can be handled conveniently — not because print on paper lasts for years. Most business and professional conversations, and many meetings will involve computer support and take place through the network. Many conversations will be between a person on the one hand and the network (or a computer program in it) on the other. Memoranda, papers, books, tapes, films, data sets, and programs will be "published" by being submitted to and accepted at some level by the network. Both public and proprietary information will exist within the network — or within parts of it, for it will be a network of networks, continually changing in respect of detailed configuration — and there will be elaborate (though doubtless not wholly effective) mechanisms for maintenance of privacy, security, and control of access. Libraries will not only interact with their users and one another through the network but will exist primarily within the network and constitute not one but several of its most important subsystems. Computer-based relational nets will have become more important than documents and data sets as media for the representation and organization of knowledge. There will be transformations from computer-based relational nets to natural and mathematical language, and other modes of expression, and people will communicate with computer-based relational nets much as with other people.

The situation just described may well be transitory, its network of networks a way station on the road to some knowledge system based even more heavily on "artificial intelligence." But the situation just described is not the one the present plans are intended to achieve. The present plans lead in the general direction of the situation described, but they pertain to a nearer term. They do not assume as much help from computer programs that attempt to "understand" and "organize" the body of knowledge. They rely almost exclusively on human initative, comprehension, and control, but they depend much more upon digital computers for routine processing and digital transmission channels for communication than most of the recent plans for "national systems" have depended.

THE ELECTRONIC NERVOUS SYSTEM

The present "library system" and the present "system for scientific and technical communication" are not to any large degree the results of deliberate centralized planning, design, or organization. They are the results of evolution under the diverse influences that operate in a pluralistic society. It takes evolution a long time to create a nervous system. The systems just mentioned do not have advanced nervous systems. Perhaps they are rudimentary nerve nets: Their various parts do communicate with one another in a somewhat-faster-than-chemical way, but they do not yet have ganglionic or central nervous systems. Such nervous systems are, in my judgment, most important if systems are to "get organized" and cope successfully with the pressures and demands that are being imposed

upon them by the crescendo of technology with its alarming side effects and the "information explosion."

Biological evolution apparently encountered difficulties in incorporating central nervous systems into organismic structures already operating without central nervous systems. For one thing, the best material for making nerves was on the outside whereas the best place to put the nervous systems was inside; it took a major revision of the animal body plan to correct the matter. Fortunately, social evolution does not face this problem. The choice material for making a library nervous system is on the outside, it is true, but that is where libraries need a nervous system — between one library and another, between each library and other parts of the overall information complex.

Biological evolution developed coganglionic nervous systems before it developed nervous systems on the human paradigm with one dominant ganglion. I think that nature was wise to follow that course but wise also to move right on to greater specialization of function and centralization of control. For the library-information organism, I advocate a multiganglionic system, but I think control of most of the planning and much of the research and development should be vested in a central ganglion — or to break away from the biological-evolution analogy just in time to fall into another one of no higher calibre, a central organization. Too many cooks spoil the soup if they all use the same pot without a recipe. On the other hand, it takes a lot of cooks to make a lot of soup. Therefore, if there are many people to feed, a choice must be made among letting them go hungry, serving them bad soup, and getting organized. In my opinion, the most important step toward getting the world of libraries and information organized is to develop for it and in it an electronic nervous system with some, but not too much, centralization of function — with strong centralization of planning, moderate centralization of research and development, and continued distribution among diverse organizations of most of the operational functions.

THE ARPA NETWORK

The most important current development in the network field, I believe, is the multicomputer network that is now a focus of research and engineering by the Advanced Research Projects Agency, ARPA, and about a dozen of its contractors in the field of information processing. The ARPA network is bringing into reality many of the dreams and implementing many of the technical concepts that figure in plans for a library-information network. The multicomputer network is incorporating ideas that only recently were widely regarded as fanciful. In two or three years, enough of them will have been tested — and I am confident, proven — to shift the argument from one of feasibility to one of optimization. In any event, it seems very likely that the ARPA network will provide an existence proof for interactive multicomputer networks, and it is conceivable that the prototype network, suitably extended, will serve the library-information field as its initial electronic nervous system.

The main motive force, both technical and fiscal, behind the ARPA network has been Lawrence G. Roberts, director for Information Processing Techniques of the Advanced Research Projects Agency. He has recently described the overall concept and the status of its implementation. Here I can give only a quick summary, but I believe the ARPA network is of crucial importance for library-information network planning.

At the end of its initial development phase, the ARPA network will embrace about twenty-five "host" computers at about fifteen locations from California to Massachusetts. At each location there will be, in addition to one or more host computers, an Interface Message Processor, IMP, a small computer modified to facilitate connection to host computers on the one hand and telephone lines (or other transmission links) on the other. The IMPs will communicate with one another through 50,000-bit-per-second (50-kilobaud) lines, and with those lines (mainly leased), they will constitute a store-and-forward net responsible for delivering intact to any specified host computer, via one route or another, with retransmission if necessary, any message — consisting of packets of bits with suitable "headers" — presented by any host computer. The redundancy of interconnection will be such that each node will have at least two, and usually three, avenues into the network — and that at no latitude will there be fewer than three parallel communication channels. The IMPs were designed and developed from Honeywell 516 computers by Bolt Beranek and Newman, Inc. Nine IMPs are installed as of 1 August 1970. The lines are leased from the telephone common carriers, mainly the Bell System. All the installed IMPs are in continual communication with one another, testing, checking, and making records when not busy with actual messages, and it is evident from performance to date that the network will be able to handle about a trillion character-miles per day, day in and day out. Perhaps a more immediately meaningful measure is given by the approximately correct assumptions that there are typically three 50-kilobaud channels to or from a location and that a typical message will be relayed twice between source and destination. According to those assumptions there will be fifteen locations, each with the capability of sending or receiving about one-sixth of 20,000 characters per second, which amounts to about one typewritten page of text per second or if the peak rate could be sustained, 86,000 typewritten pages of text per day.

Most of the twenty-five host computers of the ARPA network are interactive time-shared computers. All together, they support about 1,500 terminals, most still just teletypewriters but an increasing number equipped with cathode-ray-tube displays. The host computers are diverse in manufacture, size, speed, language, and style of programming. Representatives of the several groups have been working together as a "network working group" to define a standard communication protocol and to lay out specifications for the "network control programs" that will operate in the host computers and make it possible for remote users (people or programs) to "log in" and use the host's resources within limits set by the host's provisions for access control and (in due course) billing.

The ARPA network will be used mainly to give research workers access to:

1. Computer programs or subprograms that have been prepared and tested in one computer environment but would be expensive and time-consuming to transfer to another

2. Specialized computer hardware, such as the very fast and highly parallel processor currently under development, Illiac IV, that would be prohibitively expensive to reproduce at many locations

3. Remote or even geographically distributed files of data that are updated frequently

4. Remote colleagues, together with programs and data, in geographically separated team research or in computer-supported "teleconferences."

There is not yet much research within the ARPA network groups that is directly and specifically oriented toward library-information problems, but it is obvious that the network itself and the kinds of application envisioned for it have strong relevance to library-information networks.

In the present paradigm of the ARPA network, the IMPs interface only with one another and with the host computer. All the consoles and all the data files in the network are associated directly with one or another of the host computers. In the future, however, there may be special "console computers," modified IMPs that connect arrays of consoles into the network but do not do substantial computing themselves, and "data computers," modified IMPs or specialized hosts that serve only the functions associated with data bases, do no substantial computing, and (perhaps even) have no consoles. Indeed, there will be experimentation with various equipment configurations and various specializations of function, some of which could well have direct bearing upon library-information applications.

When other networks begin to appear, interest will probably focus upon still other kinds of IMP, e.g., "multinetwork interfaces" to match host computers to several networks at once and "internetwork interfaces" to interconnect two or more networks for selected functions. If multinetwork and internetwork interfacing is handled properly, small networks will be able to join together or to attach themselves to large networks to serve certain functions without losing their individualities in respect to other functions.

For example, in the absence of legal and regulatory constraints, the internal networks of several pharmaceutical firms could remain separate insofar as proprietary information is concerned yet join together to serve a nonproprietary pharmaceutical information system. At the same time they could link into a general library network on the one hand and a multiairline reservation system on the other — not to mention their separate links to banks and to the digital text-communication system that will largely supplant the postal service insofar as interbusiness mail is concerned.

The thoughts of the preceding paragraph in one sense go far beyond the ARPA network, yet in another sense, they represent only obvious extensions of it. I think they suggest fairly accurately the context within which library-information networks will evolve. There will be somewhat diverse but also somewhat compatible and interlocking computer-communication networks throughout business and government, and hopefully, also the educational and professional domains. Much of the stimulus toward compatibility and aggregation could and should come from the library-information sector.

A LIBRARY-INFORMATION NETWORK MODEL FOR 1980

The generalization that most people overestimate what can be accomplished in one year and underestimate what can be accomplished in ten is a self-destructive generalization, but thus far it appears to remain true. Perhaps most people have not yet discovered this; I have, and I believe it, but nevertheless, the following model of a library-information network for 1980 probably represents an underestimate. In an effort to make the model plausible, I shall no doubt scale down the aspiration level.

NODES AND BRANCH OF THE NETWORK

The model assumes that in 1980 libraries and other components of the library-information system of the United States and several other countries are interconnected by an electronic nervous system of the kind described. The main centers, of which there are perhaps a thousand, are connected to one another by permanent channels (leased lines, microwave circuits, satellite links) more or less according to the ARPA network paradigm. This library-information network is one of many extant networks, and as suggested earlier, most of them are capable of interconnecting themselves selectively to serve broad and largely nonproprietary functions such as the library-information function. Subordinate centers are connected into the library-information network in many instances through main centers, but in many other instances several subordinate centers constitute a subordinate network and share an IMP that is a node in the main network. Some of the communication channels are dial-up Data-phone channels. Some are TELEX teletype channels. There is indeed considerable flexibility and great diversity in the pattern of approach to the main net, but at the same time, economics serves as a driving force to get messages into the main net where the channels are wide, the traffic density is high, the accesses are quick, and the unit transmission costs are low.

Major libraries are of course conspicuously present in the list of main centers—about 50 libraries having IMPs (as well as host computers) of their own, and some 250 using university or other organizational computers that are interfaced to IMPs. Most of the libraries that have or share IMPs and thus constitute major nodes of the network, however, are not major libraries. They are the libraries of organizations that are associated with the network primarily as users of information. There are about 600 of these organizations: business firms, nonprofit organizations, government agencies, universities, international organizations, and importantly, associations and consortia of various kinds. Most of the 600 organizations have internal computer-communication networks that serve several functions, the library-information function being an important one of the several. Because this multifunctional arrangement is the dominant one, only 10 or 15 percent of the cost of consoles and internal communication facilities — overall — is allocated to library information.

The remaining nodes of the main library-information network, approximately 100 in number, are associated with publishing houses, indexing and abstracting organizations, information analysis centers, organizations specializing in management of data bases, standards organizations, a few journals, and a few organizations concerned primarily with network research and development. Thus, many of the organizations intensely involved in interaction with the body of knowledge have broad and direct channels of communication with one another and with the digital information resources of the network. Because of the prevalence of associations and consortia among the 1,000 major "centers," far more than 1,000 organizations are effectively "in the network" and "on-line" to its computers. To illustrate this point with a specific example, I shall hypothesize — without that organization's blessing but with hope that such a thing will come to pass — that (in 1980) the Interuniversity Communications Council, EDUCOM, operates as one of its services a hierarchical network that brings 500 small-to-medium-size educational institutions into the library-information network through IMPs located at thirty major universities. The local and regional interconnections involve a complex of dial-up and leased facilities, EDUCOM-owned microwave links, state-owned microwave links and cable, and experimental satellite channels.

FUNCTIONS OF THE LIBRARY INFORMATION NETWORK

The library-information network of 1980 is involved to a greater or lesser degree in almost every aspect of generating, publishing, organizing, preserving, retrieving, disseminating, and using the body of knowledge, but some of its functions are well established and widely exploited whereas others are still experimental or otherwise not yet cost-effective. Among the main established functions are:

1. *Distribution of papers, prior to publication, within what in the 1960s had been called "invisible colleges": (In 1980, such groupings are clearly visible in the records of computer-communication networks.) In the digitally advanced countries, most articles and reports are written and edited on-line. Almost nothing of less than ten typewritten pages equivalent length is mailed within the United States.*

2. *Submission of papers to journal editors; reviewing and revision of papers.*

3. *Submission of programs and data sets to data-base editors; documentation, reviewing, revision, storage, organization, retrieval, and dissemination of programs and data sets.*

4. *Keeping bibliographic track of the status of all accessions (documents, programs, data sets, films, and other forms — including the emerging form here called "relational nets") to the corpus: One of the computer-processible data bases associated*

with the library-information network is a composite catalog that records each significant bibliographic fact and event (e.g., accepted for publication, published, stored in microimage form, filed in digital form, indexed, abstracted, reviewed) for every published entity.

5. *Indexing and "descriptorizing" (and coordination of the indexing and "descriptorizing" performed by different agencies) of published entities:* There are many indexes, catalogs, and directories within the network, prepared and maintained by diverse agencies but with a fairly high degree of compatibility. (They are all computer processible. The basic incompatibilities that prevailed during early phases of the development of the network caused so much trouble that they had to be eliminated.) The organization of the indexes is hierarchical: There are indexes to indexes, etc. A study is being made of the feasibility and desirability of integrating all the indexes into one comprehensive index.

6. *Abstracting of published entities:* Abstracting is now (in 1980) being done mainly in a syntactically and lexically constrained form of natural language that can be processed and fairly deeply "understood" by computer. The new abstracts are compatible with relational nets and promise in due course to displace indexes based on descriptors in most retrieval and dissemination functions. Abstracting is performed mainly by the several large field-oriented abstracting services. Abstracts are maintained in computer-processable form in network data bases and searched mainly with the aid of proprietary search programs available (for a fee) through the network on an "execute-only" basis.

7. *Current awareness services.*

8. *Retrospective search services.*

9. *Specialized bibliographic consultation and support:* Inasmuch as the network makes it possible, given the knowhow, to exploit a vast array of sophisticated bibliographic techniques, entrepreneurial bibliographic consulting and support services have sprung up within the network, and many organizations have hired librarians to work with users of information, e.g., as part of research teams.

10. *Research on the organization of knowledge:* The hottest research topic in the library field is relational nets. Most thesis problems in

library science are concerned with transformations between natural language and relational nets, and most theses are full of rewrite rules, transition networks, and pointer structures.

11. *Acquisition procedures and records:* All the "paperwork" of ordering, receiving, paying, and so on is done through the network. In the larger libraries, much of the decision making about what documents to acquire is done "by formula," i.e., by computer program. That procedure works fairly well because much information about each paper and film-based document is available prior to the time of its publication, because the selecting programs take many factors into account and because much experience has been incorporated over the years into the programs.

12. *"Circulation control":* There is not much actual circulation any more. What is called "circulation control" is actually execution of procedures concerned with copying, delivering and billing for copies, and paying copyright fees. The largest single part of "circulation" is keeping track of the actual use of "videoform." Videoform is microform from the publisher to the using organization's library, then cable video to the individual who actually reads it from a screen with intrinsic storage, without retrace, yet with quick erase. Videoform requires much record-keeping because the publisher is paid not on the basis of the number of microform copies delivered to the using organization but on the basis of the number of video copies actually displayed to a viewing individual.

13. *Delivery of full text:* Even though the library-information network of 1980 cannot handle the bulk of the document-delivery function, it is called upon to deliver large amounts of full text. Almost all documents newly acquired from organizational sources in the digitally advanced countries enter the publication system in digital form and are stored in that form in laser-beam or electron-beam storage devices. Such storage is compact and inexpensive. Even the processing, transmission, and display costs are affordable for high-priority access to short texts. Main drawbacks are that many old and many foreign documents do not exist in full-text digital form; that only quite recently acquired charts, diagrams, and graphs are well encoded; that gray-scale and

color photographs cannot yet been handled economically in digital code; and that there is still a shortage of transmission channels that severely limits the amount of retrospective full text one can call for without a special priority. (As mentioned earlier, however, almost all business "mail" is transmitted digitally in the United States.)

14. *Standardization:* The network is of course a strong force toward standardization. As suggested earlier, incompatibility becomes untenable when it can be directly perceived to be the only remaining obstacle to a desired advance. Several working groups operate continually within the network in the overlapping areas of compatibility, standards, languages, formats, and protocol. All established standards are of course immediately available within the network, and there are programs that are fairly effective in monitoring compliance.

15. *Record-keeping:* The network monitors itself and keeps records of its performance and of evaluations made by users.

16. *Instruction in "how to use":* The network of course provides instructions, part automated and part not, in use of the network.

17. *Modeling the library-information system:* In 1980 every system worthy of the name contains a model of itself, and the library-information system is no exception. The model is a sophisticated computer-program model. It incorporates the records of the use of the system that are accumulated by and through the network. An important aspect of the planning and research associated with the network involves varying the parameters — and from time to time the structure — of the model and studying the effects upon the model's performance.

HOW TO GET FROM HERE TO THERE

As I see it, there are six elements that are vital to any plan for realizing the model described in the foregoing section or any other model essentially similar to it. The six vital elements are:

1. Successful completion and extension of the ARPA network research and development program

2. Participation by library and information scientists in research on and development of computer-communication networks, such as the ARPA network, or reliance upon one or more system contractors to learn the essentially pertinent things about libraries and information systems

3. Mounting of a much stronger research and development effort than now exists in the field of library and information sciences; effort with strong bases in modern linguistics and computer science and technology

4. Intensification of efforts in standards and related fields, and orientation of those efforts toward networks

5. Development of an overall plan in terms of computer-program models; from the end of this Conference onward, no one — no individual, committee, commission, or company — should be allowed to propose a project plan that is not cast in the form of a computer-program model

6. Funding. There is no way to bring a library-information network into existence without subsidizing the research, development, and initial operating phases. I agree with the prevalent feeling that such a network should be self-supporting in mature operation, but I do not expect any leveling-off point that would clearly mark maturity to come in the next twenty years. I think that only a comprehensive model has any chance of handling the economic aspects of this question.

The foregoing six elements are not the only prerequisites for success. Help has to come from certain external sources over which library-information network planners have little or no control. The performance and cost trends of the computer technology must continue almost unchanged — and that is asking a lot — an increase by a factor of approximately 30 in processing power, for example, in one decade. The performance and cost trends of the communication technology must not be any worse than they have been. The FCC must continue to encourage (or at any rate to allow) competition in information-processing parts of the computer-communication complex that come fairly close to the boundaries of the regulated natural-monopoly area, e.g., the "modems" through which consoles are connected to telephone lines. And Congress must resist the pressures of book publishers to protect the print-and-paper status quo with copyright legislation that would, for example, require one to pay a copyright fee before putting copyrighted information into a computer-communication system, even if the probability were very low that anyone would ever ask to get it out. It is difficult to assess these four extrinsic factors, but I am more optimistic about them than about some of the six elements listed earlier.

SOME THOUGHTS ABOUT INITIAL STEPS

PARTICIPATION IN NETWORK RESEARCH AND DEVELOPMENT

Psychologically, the first question about an initial step is whether to take it ever, and the next question is whether to take it now. For myself, I can answer the first question in the affirmative without even deciding what the step should be, but I am uncertain about the second question. No doubt it is evident that I consider the ARPA network to have a crucial importance for interactive computer-communication networks in general and thus, for the library-information network under consideration here. I think it may take the ARPA network two or three years to demonstrate its feasibility, economy, and effectiveness in several applications, and I suspect that there will be many skeptics in the interim and few thereafter. Why do I not therefore conclude that the library-information network movement should simply cool it for two or three years, wait for the ARPA network to prove or disprove itself, and jump on the bandwagon when and if the bandwagon starts to roll?

There are three reasons: (1) Problems of a library-information nature, e.g., how to let users know what its resources are and how to exploit them — are intrinsic to the ARPA network, and ideas about how to solve them seem ripe and ready to contribute to the success of the ARPA network; (2) two or three years from now may be too late for library-information people to influence significantly the development of computer-communication networks: The pattern will have been determined so predominantly by considerations of programs and programming that the network may not be very hospitable, for example, to natural language text and bibliographic data; (3) the library world has been on the whole somewhat laggard in adopting and exploiting modern information technology, and it would be very bad for it to drop two or three years further behind. For those reasons I strongly urge a few library and information people to get into the general-purpose interactive computer-communication game now.

A PLAN IN THE FORM OF COMPUTER PROGRAM MODELS

In the present state of the nation and the world, I do not truly expect any massive response to a plea — even from a highly competent, widely respected, and quite powerful organization

— for massive funding on a five- or ten-year basis for the purpose of turning a paper plan into a library-information network. Paper plans are no longer convincing. In the library-information field enough of them have accumulated to neutralize one another. Moreover, if they are detailed enough to be definitive, they are too long to read and if read, too complex to understand. The development of a comprehensive computer-program model of a proposed library-information network — an interactive, multilevel simulation with a data base, a control language, graphical displays, and so on — would greatly clarify many of the problems; demonstrating it might convince the world that the planners had done their homework.

A MAJOR PLANNING RESEARCH AND DEVELOPMENT EFFORT in LIBRARY INFORMATION SYSTEM

Except for the fact that the mood of the country is not conducive, all the factors seem ripe for a major effort of planning, research, and development in the library-information field. Modern information technology offers tremendous raw power, but it will have to be adapted before it will solve library-information problems. Almost everyone has now sensed the fact that there is an information flood — if not explosion. There is at the top of the Establishment as much impatience about lack of progress toward a solution as ten years ago there was unawareness and unconcern. In short, the situation calls for a significant step — but a safe and inexpensive one.

On that note, it seems to me, an immediate course of action shapes itself: mount an effort to develop the computer-program model over a period of, say, three years. Combine this with carefully organized participation in network research and development. Choose a "neutral" lead organization to manage a summer study to get things organized. Pull representatives of all the major library and information organizations into the action. Set up a committee for each identifiable subproblem, not because committees are efficient but because interaction across the boundaries of established organizations is the essence of networking and prerequisite to the achievement of anything that can properly be called a system. Finally, be sure to make the effort multidisciplinary because the competencies required to develop a model are scattered — and be sure to make it informally international because knowledge is essentially international and because no formal international organization could complete a computer-program model in three years.

Worldwide Information Networks

Kjell Samuelson

INTRODUCTION

This report on international information transfer and network communication is focused primarily on the intricate problems of goal-setting and far-sighted planning. The need for such an approach has become apparent to me as a result of earlier work during the last few years.

It is admittedly not until recently that teleprocessing and computer technology suitable for undertaking worldwide network planning have become a reality. Now that such planning has been initiated in several nations, it is obvious that the real obstacles to face will be matters of methodology and principles, which must yield harmonious solutions to ill-defined tasks. The difficulties sometimes have been termed as socioeconomic problems and political or psychological barriers. Fortunately, a new set of systems analysis tools or methods and formalized procedures have come into existence which can be applied to these problems. Therefore, the development situation for global information networks again seems bright throughout the 1970s.

AUTOMATED INFORMATION NETWORKS

Several schemes have been outlined for networks where at least some information processing occurs. A few of these networks are already operational, at least nationally if not on a global scale. This document makes a conceptual distinction between more than a half dozen different network types, say:

1. Data base networks: for information retrieval from data bases

2. Communication networks: for messages, e.g., person-to-person

3. Library networks: for interlibrary exchange

4. Computer networks: for remote computation

5. Transportation networks: for airlines, trains, shipping

6. Mass media networks: for TV, radio, newspapers

7. Discipline/mission-oriented networks: for legal, police, automobile, corporate, hotel, ticket, educational, military, etc., purposes

These networks and others to come, plus all kinds of hybrids, will be partially overlapping, sometimes embedded in each other and often using the same time-shared computer utilities. The following text is confined mainly to the first and second kinds of networks: "information networks," therefore, is used to mean mixed-media networks between data bases, and multiple users and producers of full information, anywhere, at any time. This kind of information network may still become a functional part of those other networks which will use data bases and communications.

Given these criteria for automated information networks, let us explore the following questions:

1. Do they exist?

2. What are they?

3. What should they be?

4. What are the differences between national, international, and worldwide networks?

5. How can far-sighted planning be provided?

As late as 1968 it was stated that no operating information network actually existed.[1] Now, two years later, one may confirm that automated information networks, in accordance with our definitions, still do not exist, either nationally or internationally.

Yes, there are networks of other kinds, either in operation or in planning stages. A quick survey reveals their nature:

1. Communications

2. Libraries

3. Computers

4.   Mass media

5.   Legal, federal

6.   Educational

7.   Military

8.   Corporate

9.   Information transfer (nonautomated)

In fact, there are even real-time pilot projects and on-going experiments in information transfer from one point to another, which might serve as an embryo for future network growth.

The remaining three questions on "do's" and "don'ts," and divergencies in planning for worldwide automated information networks will be described in the remainder of this document. We shall assume that the moderately early history of information transfer and the large-scale traditional operations for bibliographical records or document-handling are familiar to our readers to the extent covered by the 1967, 1968, and 1969 volumes of the *Annual Review of Information Science and Technology,* edited by Carlos A. Cuadra. The principal discussion is centered around information and documentation (I&D) for science and technology (S&T) or research and development (R&D).

GOAL-SETTING AND PRIORITIES FOR WORLDWIDE INFORMATION NETWORKS

For a number of years the International Federation for Documentation/Theory of Machine Techniques and Systems, FID/TM, Committee has focused its studies on cooperation and work toward worldwide information networks. During the American Society for Information Science, ASIS, annual meeting in San Francisco in October 1969, FID/TM sponsored a technical session and panel on automated international information networks with emphasis on systems design concepts, goal-setting, and priorities. (The resulting papers appear in the ASIS 1969, *Proceedings.*) The panelists were FID/TM members, international systems analysts, and information systems experts, plus representatives of different countries and organizational bodies, projects, or programs such as OECD, INIS, and UNESCO/ ICSU's UNISIST.

Before the FID/TM network session, the panelists were asked to submit to the chairman their comments on goal-setting and ranked priorities for systems design concepts. As a result it proved quite feasible to follow formalized procedures in expressing objectives and preferences. It also became apparent that a striking need exists to consult and co-opt systems analysts at policy-making levels at an early planning stage and not only during the systems design phase. In other words, it appears necessary to use "the systems approach" to extract ultimate desires, which can then be translated into performance objectives and design tasks for implementation which takes into consideration assigned priorities as well as nondesirable effects.

When dealing with the problems of long-range, midterm, and short-period planning for worldwide automated information networks, one is faced with a multigoal situation in an imperceivable international environment.[2] The use of recent methods for technological forecasting can be applied to some degree.[3] However, there also exists the problem of fitting the integrated international ultimate goals for information transfer into the frame of overall national goals. Very few countries indeed have yet used systems analysis procedures for such formalization.[4] This might be one reason why some policy makers tend to avoid a workable declaration of higher goals and instead, express somewhat vague general directives which can be interpreted in the way that is most convenient at a particular, future occasion.

A similar case occurred at a recent FID/TM symposium on "Performance Evaluation of Information Retrieval Systems," organized in Stockholm in June 1970.[5] The theme for the panel discussion was intended to be focused on goal-setting, ultimate desires, design objectives versus nondesirable effects, preferences, priorities, and short- to long-term improvements. About thirty of the participants were representing "users" of information while a dozen were managers of information systems. The same experience remains, i.e., there exists a resistance against the explicit declaration of goals through formalized procedures. However, by listening to the taped discussion, it seems possible to extrapolate ultimate desires from several samples of implicit wording, understanding, and antithesis. To yield ultimate goals, it might be feasible to rephrase the formulations and arrange a second exposure in a dialogue for reconsideration.

Instead of enumerating and discussing each national and international network, we shall examine an arbitrary nonexhaustive "menu" of formulated goals, objectives, and primary purposes for information as they appear in available literature. The examples were chosen by scanning schemes from OECD, INIS, UNESCO/ICSU's UNISIST, COMECON, ESRO/RECON, COSATI, NAL, MEDLARS, EDUCOM's EDUNET, ERIC, and EUDISED, plus outlines from Canada, Japan, France, United Kingdom, Netherlands, Germany, Hungary, Czechoslovakia, Poland, Yugoslavia, and Scandinavian countries. The following list actually represents a mixture of a few higher objectives, some preliminarily criteria and operational goals, many intended modes of operation, and several presumptive means of eventually achieving some aims of immediate concern.[6]

1.   Information services of sciences primarily are intended for scientists, and it should be possible to collect from these all the data that are required –wishes, habits, needs, etc. –to determine a mutually agreed upon "ideal" information system.

2.   Users are an integral part of the information transfer chain since they alone should determine its goals and select the appropriate media. Moreover, the users of scientific information are also to a large extent the producers so that they can exercise a great deal of influence over the form in which it is generated and directed

toward the different channels of information transfer. Users do not form a homogeneous group with similar patterns of action and common requirements.

3. The goal is to connect the generators of spoken, written, or other symbolic data with potential users, whoever and wherever they may be.

4. The objective can be summarized in one sentence: to bring about an on-going reallocation of responsibilities and resources in the switching process from producers to users of S&T information, on the basis of a continuing scrutiny of the world information complex with regard to unproductive duplications and detrimental gaps.

5. Convertibility will be the more general immediate goal, to establish interconnections between systems that are not directly compatible.

6. The ultimate goal is to provide individual users in all parts of the world with comparable conditions of remote access to scientific information.

7. Decentralization of responsibilities.

8. Maximum use of existing organizations and resources.

9. Minimum additional bureaucracy.

10. Flexibility and interpretation in local distributions of functions within the proposed organizational pattern.

11. Develop special need-group services, as close to users as possible.

12. The goal must be to assure authoritative, accurate, objective, and technically sound information to governments and to industry (OECD).

13. The ultimate technical goal of the EDUCOM system should be to make available answers to standard types of questions in an abbreviated form and with shortest possible turn-around time. The ultimate goal should be a conversational system with relatively short access to answers.

14. Sharing of resources.

15. Equalizing access to information.

16. Accelerating information processing.

17. Facilitating long-distance interpersonal interactions.

18. Providing better bibliographical services.

19. Making life-saving information instantaneously available.

20. Decreasing production of unused copies.

21. Decreasing copyright infringement.

22. Providing information in a format appropriate for the user.

23. Improving continuing education.

24. Decreasing administrative delays in higher education.

25. Provision of all significant special fields in the country (Hungary) with information.

26. Centralized control.

27. Planned structure, a rational division of labor and tasks.

28. Flow of information in determined directions and ways.

29. Technical implements suitable for the tasks.

30. Progressive development both of the extension of the network and of the enlargement of the technical implement.

31. Prevention of uneconomical parallelism in work.

32. Information services for everybody, but first and foremost for the specialists of their own network.

33. Professional control of the institutions of their network.

34. Covering by the nationwide (Poland) information system of all domains of S&T and economy, and adaptation of information activity and its development to the changeable needs of users.

35. Documents should be systematized according to UDC symbols; parallel using of center's own classification is admitted.

36. Author's summaries, made out according to rules accepted by the documentation service, will be published together with any articles inserted in S&T periodicals as well as in books.

37. The rules for coordination of foreign (outside Poland) literature purchases will be set, as well as those for making use of literature purchased or acquired in another way.

38. The nationwide (Poland) system should ensure the full informational communication among the scientific and economic posts.

39. The international cooperation can be initiated and carried on directly by the center's of all categories but with the knowledge of ministerial centers and the CIINTE.

40. The S&T associations will enter into cooperation with the appropriate links of the information network.

41. A national (Yugoslavia) network of information and communication services with rational and functional subsystems (regional and local), and with a direct link to international and large national information centers, mainly in Europe.

42. International-national-local mutually interlinked complexes as a referral seen for emission, storage, selection, transmission activities.

43. Management and quality control of the indexing inputs.

44. Vocabulary development control.

45. One level of the (agricultural) network will be nationally (USA) oriented, the other will consist of national or supranational centers which will serve as members of the international network. Each of these also will serve as the principal mode in a national or regional network.

46. Control of the system (at NAL) as a whole.

47. Main storage for a national (USA) archival collection of documents (in the agricultural field).

48. Provision of timely and effective information and document retrieval capability.

49. An information center producing bibliographic tools of national (USA) and as assigned, international importance.

50. The (agricultural) information network should be a dynamic system responsive to user requirements.

51. The organizational arrangements of INIS do serve as a model for future activities of this kind (agricultural network).

52. Specific characteristics of an international network are free information flow and access to data bases for current awareness and retrospective search.

53. NAL would be a node to EDUCOM's EDUNET.

54. Further modernization, expansion, and reinforcement of national and language-area I&D services for education by working out and implementing development plans (for EUDISED) similar to those in the field of S&T.

55. Preparation of specialized national and regional educational I&D services to become partners in a regional and international cooperative system.

56. EUDISED should be considered as one of a number of regional systems within a UNESCO-sponsored worldwide educational documentation and information system.

57. Further development of the already existing forms of cooperation in the area of I&D in order to promote S&T economic progress in socialist countries (COMECON).

58. Concentration on coordination of efforts to speed up solutions to problems of methodological and technical nature in documentation and information.

59. Improvement of economic effectiveness of I&D activities.

60. Training of qualified personnel for I&D work.

61. Promoting broad international cooperation through active participation in the work of the appropriate international organizations.

62. Joint research projects in the area of I&D.

63. Participation in conferences on I&D.

64. It should be a national (USA) objective to attain economical and easy access to every significant article produced by the world's scientific community.

65. Our system (COSATI) should be capable of telling what is available in the world, pointing out the data store that offers the best data pertinent to one's problem, and explaining how to gain access to this store.

66. For the sake of progress, we need to agree on who should have the national (USA) responsibility for the formulation of national policies with respect to the scientific and technical information systems.

67. Centralization of basic abstracting and indexing services for the world of S&T literature.

68. Improvement of I&D delivery through the development of regional services adapted to the interest profiles of local research institutes and industrial organizations, and the use of modern techniques (e.g., SDI).

69. Development of consolidation services.

70. Special libraries for S&T.

71. Translation services.

72. Extensive use of sophisticated indexing languages, using UDC for broad subject categorization.

73. Development of the All-Union Information Center on R&D in progress.

74. State service of standards data.

75. Emphasis on the advantage of mechanized techniques.

76. Support of further research on many components of information switching.

77. Utility of special programs for the popularization of science.

78. Improvements of the status and proficiency of information scientists.

This list of course contains several overlapping statements, some of which represent means rather than ends. In addition, quite a few declarations have aspects that are controversial, i.e., centralization versus decentralization, regional or national versus supranational data bases, control and capping versus free flow of information, monolithic versus multilateral management supervision, institutionalization versus bureaucracy reduction, enlargement of existing organizations versus on-going reallocation of responsibilities and resources.

Although the human elements of information networks are mentioned in brief, the majority of items represents management's operational criteria: coverage, availability, accessibility, response time, overlap avoidance, switching, cost reduction.

In addition, design objectives would have to be developed which incorporate such users' constraints as: timeliness, serviceability, convenience, presentation, form of output, privacy, urgency, priorities, recall, precision, quality, motivation, instructiveness.

For the matter of overall network problems, the listed formulations give partial answers; the questions what, how, why, where, when, for whom, and by whom remain open to discussion.

Research on users' needs and behavior remains an important challenge explored partly in earlier work.[7] There also exist explicit declarations on principles for improving engineer/scientist productivity[8] and several ways to prevent inhibition of creative research.[9] The following obstacles were claimed nondesirable: publications imperialism; planning imperialism; organizational imperialism; mathematical imperialism; inadequate communications; data storage, reduction, and filing; repetitive, standardized procedures which are out of date; administration and organization of details; handling service calls; redundant paperwork: keeping and maintaining historical records, memos, jobs status, etc.; superfluous reporting: nontechnical progress reports, routine reports required by government, rewrite of corrected reports, preparation of preliminarily reports, time-consuming documentation of communications; management's lack of decisive goals and of steady progress toward them, confused definition of company policies, arbitrary attitudes of administrators who have not made investigation and refuse to listen to those who have.

Those are some of the items which should be considered in a well-defined goal structure and means-end analysis for automated information networks, communications, and future computer utilities in order to improve the S&T users' situation.

CURRENT INTERNATIONAL NETWORK PLANNING

Among the many reasons which have been claimed to prove the feasibility[10] of information networks is the fact that among specialized literature a 75 percent overlap of document-indexed input for storage has been estimated.[11] A brief survey of the fifty-one most common secondary services for tapes with surrogates (descriptors, abstracts, titles, citations, etc.) reveals that the major bulk of machine-readable material comes from thirty-one U.S. packages while a smaller volume is found among twenty varieties from the western world (see Table 1).

Besides this list of secondary services[12] there exists a full spectrum of primary processors-services-publishers, mediators-searchers-editors-procurists, and tertiary repackaging (synthesis-consolidation-IR-SDI) all the way to "n"--ary reprocessors. The multitude of transducers might result in such

Table 1.
Sources of Machine-Readable Material for Tapes with Surrogates

Package or Institution	Country	Package or Institution	Country
AERESS	UK	INIS	Austria
API	USA	INSPEC	UK
ASM	USA	INTREDIS	USA
BNB	UK	ISI (citation)	USA
BIOSIS	USA	ISI (source)	USA
BJA	USA	MARC	USA
CAC	USA	MEDLARS	USA
CBAC	USA	MRGRBI	USA
CCM	USA	MSDC	UK
CFSTI	USA	NAL	USA
CITE	USA	NDC	USA
COMPENDEX	USA	NISP	USA
CREDOC	Belgium	NSA	USA
CT	USA	NSL	Canada
DCST	Sweden	PANDEX	USA
DDC	USA	PLASDOC	UK
DTL	Denmark	POST	USA
EM	Netherlands	PULSP	USA
EMCDL	Netherlands	RINGDOC	UK
ENDS	Luxemburg	SIE	USA
ERIC	USA	SRD	Germany
GCL	USA	STIMS	USA
HRP	USA	STUR	Germany
IBS	UK	UCL	UK
IC	USA	ZAR	Germany
IDC	Germany		

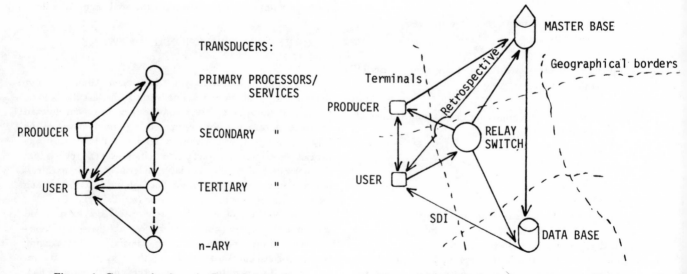

Figure 1 Communication via Recorded Media   Figure 2 Current Minimal Information Network

complexity that several users prefer to interact directly with information producers/sources (see Figure 1). It is not at all self-evident that interlinkage and growth of existing services[13] into networks will yield benefits and favorable procedures even if feasible. Perhaps S&T information users are served better by direct relations through communicators such as radio, TV, ETV, ITV, ITFS, picture-phones, and AV media.[14]

Compatibility-convertibility for hardware, telecommunications, and formats may possibly come of age, but it is not certain that contents overlap will disappear. The current picture of network interconnections between user terminals and data bases tapped from master bases has been described in previous studies.[15] There is an obvious need for relay switches and referral directories to serve as locators among the many diversified bases. As we proceed toward a general computer utility, we may compare the ever-changing placing of installations with electrical power supply,[16] which always will be available for plug-in usage even though new computer generations arrive and disappear.[17] Because of the more complicated procedures for maintenance-housekeeping and purging-updating-downdating the physical location of master bases, data bases, and personnel is more of a basic problem.

The major distinctions between national and worldwide information networks are due to global time-zone and geolinguistic factors. At present the minimum number of components may interact, as shown in Figure 2. In order to provide for fallback and economize toward "infinite" storage, a configuration trend such as Figure 3 is possible. The drawbacks of global time-zone differences could be turned into an advantage of triple fall-back facilities (see Figure 4). A manifold of hybrid structures is plausible in worldwide network thinking, based on the use of relay switches and referral directories. At an advanced stage this could lead to service-routing (see Figure 5) and explosive searches through data bases which are operational in widely separated geographical areas (see Figure 6).

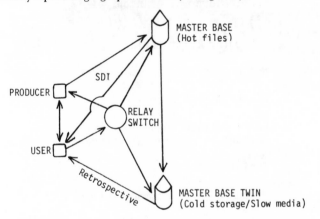

Figure 3 Supranational Allocation of Information Resources

The work toward a network structural solution is not to be considered as an optimizing task but rather as a problem of satisfying or creating executively optimal conditions. Traditional simulation, transportation theory, and graph theoretical methods[18] or recent algorithms used for library networks[19] seem less applicable in an international environment. Therefore, heuristics, bargaining,[20] and a systems

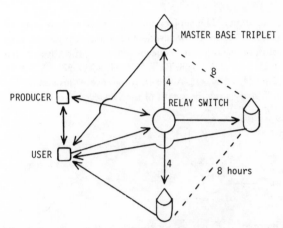

Figure 4. Triple Fall-back and Eight-hour Global Time Zone Difference Between Master Bases

approach in policy-making would be feasible when economy is not the single crucial factor, but prevailing instead are political science parameters and less tangible constraints such as: strategic value of information, financial responsibility, patronage-ownership-possessiveness, national prestige-pride, disciplinary esteem-envy.

Were it not for the strategic[21] nature of information, worldwide network planning could be approached by treating the usual factors: time, cost, volume, capacity, and geographical distance. In our early studies there were more than eighty formalized systems design concepts, parameters, and variables for automated international information networks,[22] and this number will increase.

While data bases, their structuring and management, have been described repeatedly,[23] the two locator components, relay switches and referral directories, deserve a closer description.[24] To find one's way between interconnected master bases and data bases, one needs devices and rules-of-thumb to determine: Who has how much of what; where it is; and how to obtain it. The relay switch is a frequently updated specialized data base of locator files which can be run close to or at a distance from some other master base or data base. The function is basically a table look-up in a referral directory which also is released as a shorter, hard-copy version. It indicates year span and approximate

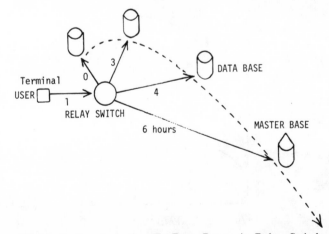

Figure 5 Search-routing To Data Bases via Relay Switch

number of items. The subject contents are described at meta-level entries which allow crude concordances between diversified multiclassificatory concept notations and thesauri featuring UDC, LC, COSATI, EURATOM, ALD, NASA, TEST, IEEE, MeSH, LEX, etc. A recent book cover[25] proclaims "the modern library and the death of the Dewey decimal system,"

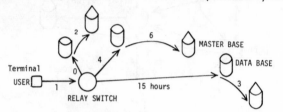

Figure 6   Expanded Search-routing via Relay Switch and Referral Directories

which may eventually occur. However, a revenant classification, ordering, or organizing principle is bound to "walk the earth's future mediatheques" by a different pseudonym as publishers and other primary services supply microforms and newer media which are preindexed at the source to facilitate detailed searches. History will recur and again logistics, topology, or file-usage frequency call for practical, task-oriented, class-partitioning and pragmatic, functional grouping into "fuzzy" subsystems[26] so that the computer operators/technicians at least can read "mnemo-labels" and load-requested, interchangable disc-packs, tape reels, strips, and other recorded information carriers.

Due to rapid changes and growing complexity, it becomes practically impossible to handle an unsurveyable global maintenance of thesauri and vocabularies with universally consistent procedures. The updating/housekeeping jobs are manageable

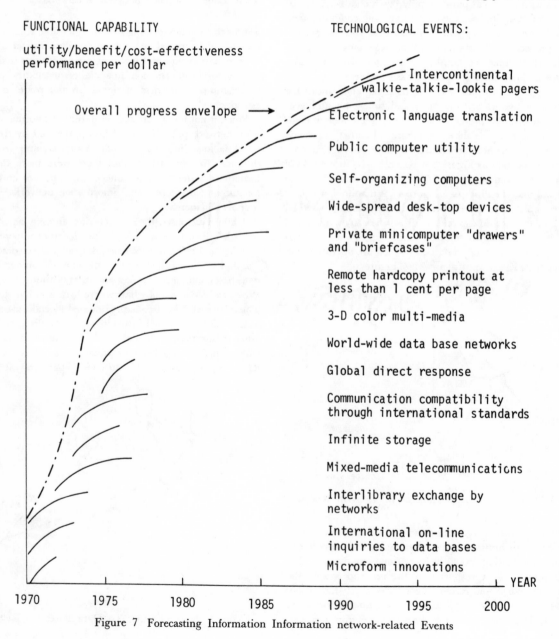

Figure 7   Forecasting Information Information network-related Events

when performed at the particular master bases within each discipline. It is of little practical use to look for detailed concordances, transformations, conversions, and distinct relators between all the vocabularies. Instead, it is imperative to arrive at crisp, formalized definitions of coupling points for subsystems linkage. The task of finding, knowing, and identifying these points so that they become perceivable is another matter of interdisciplinary systems analysis.

TOWARD GLOBAL INFORMATION TRANSFER AND NETWORK COMMUNICATION

The planning and course of action for worldwide information networks and the implementation of proposed solutions should be pursued in agreement both with overall objectives and technological forecasting. This means that the evolutionary steps of chained events has to occur at a pace which takes into consideration not only feasibility but also desirability.[27] A crude picture (see Figure 7) of the major information science events for the next twenty-five years can be summarized by examining available Delphi studies and other predictions.[28] It is emphasized that it will be partially up to our own choice to influence the development rate by sponsoring a particular R&D phase in the future. By linkage of many different national information systems into networks, a whole world might be bound to a technology which will be passe before an overall integrated, operational stage has been reached.

Insert Figure 7 Forecasting information network-related events

On the other hand, we could, and should, listen to the ultimate desires of the users –and there is a difference between the individual user and large user groups.[29] This can lead to decisions such as: "Let us do R&D and run experimental operations and test implementation in national/regional areas while we save our resources from being spent exhaustively on today's premature surrogate techniques." Quite obviously, users agree that neither abstracts with bibliographic references nor microforms are final operational goals, and therefore, increased sponsoring of the "invisible colleges" would be welcome by using intercontinental TV conferences and other new media in addition to quarterly travels. One will necessarily have to present substantial facts as counterevidence before labeling as "unrealistic" or "impractical" the following statements by a "Devil's Advocate" scientist or engineer (goal numbers 1, 2, 3, 9, 17, 20, 23, 24, 52, 59, 63, 77, 78, of the previous list):

1.   Increase the support of "invisible colleges" from existing research funds.

2.   Allocate 40 percent of the scientist's yearly income to conference participation, travel, personal book and journal copies, intercontinental phone calls.[30] These actions might cut his work time spent on literature and search from 40 to 5 percent and eventually, almost turn him into a "nonreader."

3.   "Tear off" a lot of "red tape" and stop "personal prestige and game-playing" within hierarchical organizations so that informal communication and personal contacts are improved.[31]

4.   Organize regional, professional TV conferences and mixed-media workshops for large professional groups.[32] Thus, to the benefits of information search will be added an "on-the-spot" learning effect. In addition, inquiries by future scientists searching for information could be referred to recent conference participants to facilitate information availability and accessibility.

Given these kinds of support, scientific groups are goal-seeking, self-organizing, and highly efficient information utilizers.

While waiting for the requested goal structure, facts, and figures, one may say that global S&T information is still only a subset of the entire world information and perhaps, could be handled partially in such an informal manner with full information and be cost-effective. The first on-line information networks to come tend mainly to be operational only for bibliographic references or abstracts rather than for full information. A higher level of ambition will comprise full, mixed-media transfer and justify the term "automated knowledge network." Until then, the "invisible colleges" do call for better sponsoring. Networking of full information at the relay switches will require pragmatic, mission-oriented tags and structural organization segmented so as to allocate "unit information."[33] This aspect of information has been investigated in a similar philosophical way by a few different scientists:

1.   "Elementary message" consists of the identification of the system point, the moment of time, and measure of one of the state variables of the system in the point, as well as identification of the kind of this state variable (e-messages constituting e-concepts on e-records in e-files).[34]

2.   "Informon" is a quantum of information, and flow of information for decisionmaking gives an uncertainty reduction.[35]

3.   "Information chunk" is the smallest identifiable unit of task-required information which, if further segmented, would lose its identification and meaning with respect to the task.[36]

The possibilities of carrying into effect the higher aspirations for information networks is very much a function of how fast global telecommunication progresses as agreed by the many bodies involved: INTELSAT, COMSAT, CCIT, OECD, CEPT of EEC, ITU, EBU, IEC, ISO, etc. When an agreement on ten-year planning becomes substantial, it will be feasible to schedule the implementation of information network innovations. Adequate committee representation by information scientists and systems analysts might actually make it possible to formalize an information policy which can plan on "skipping" a few evolutionary low-ambition events which have too short a life cycle (see Figure 7), e.g., reduce the ever-increasing card catalog printing. Meanwhile, it will be possible to increase the cost-effectiveness of existing installations (libraries, data bases, computers, communication traffic, service hours, etc.) to their tolerable level of maximum performance. This action is recommendable prior to an expansion of buildings, staff, and other nonmodular investments which represent point rationalization and vain efforts to handle the ever-growing workload by means of dated facilities. Committee representatives also could forward warnings against widespread exploitation of future bottlenecks, i.e., picture-phone with undersized display screens, insufficient resolution, and too few bits per square inch.

Trend watching can be hazardous, as trends are not always beneficial or right. Furthermore, any institution, building, center, staff, computer, standardized format, periodical, or "n"--ary service is a commitment. Why institutionalize when information will flow freely anyway? Unimaginative planning could lead to an overly ambitious establishment of surrogate productions and hierarchical[37] bureaucracies whereby the evolutionary benefit curve is flattened to the degree of deterioration, i.e., according to Parkinson, paper feeds paper (and the printing offices). The innovation steps and product life-cycles are partially chained in the sense that investments and support come from the same global budget set aside for I & D. Looking back only five years to 1965, one may recall that an extensive number of projects (symbol manipulation, parsing, tape-handling, compilers, homemade languages) were never implemented. How many of today's semiautomated network dreams in capping agencies and administrative boards will ever come true? In fact, how many personal-institutional relationships will last actively more than five years? Implementation of operational services may be an important decision, but it is equally important to know when to give up dated routines, surrogates, and storage. Marketing and promotion cannot sell inferior products and poor service when there exist more convenient ways for scientists to obtain paper less knowledge availability. Many of the jog trot ways in hierarchical corporate structures are symptomatic and cause excessive reporting which enters the public S&T information domain and is never downdated by the authors, themselves, or eliminated through quality control procedures. Thus far in most existing network schemes, the authors and producers have been left out of but should be brought into the scene. Apparently, there exists a whole set of missing links which have to be traced, discovered, and integrated by means of systems analysis and formalized procedures.

It has been claimed too often that overlap of information should be avoided. Some costs will be saved if a reduction of overlapping information input can be achieved, but certain overlapping (regional, interscientific, unidisciplinary) could be turned into an asset for quality control, checking, and parallel systems performance evaluation. Overlapping information storage and service are quite desirable and if eliminated, could lead to a negative chain reaction:[38]

Decreased overlap → Increased relay-switching → Longer routing-search time → Growing complexity → Heavy station workload → Increased communication costs.

The existence of master base twins and triplets will help to relieve political tensions as well, but the decisions on location will remain crucial. It is understandable that the decentralized build-up of INIS has had such an enthusiastic international reception.[39] Even in decentralized planning[40] the general question remains of whether master bases, relay switches, "n"--ary information processors and nodes for consolidation should be placed near technology transfer centers[41] in developing areas or rather with respect to operations economic constraints like communication and geolinguistic or geopolitical factors. An intended progression will be inhibited if one continues to squeeze a majority of information through computers, teletypes, and keyboards instead of promoting multiple, mixed telemedia. A picture can say more than a thousand words of textual strings. Considering the networking task in light of corporate structuring and management science, it appears that construction at the operational level from modular, decentralized subsystems is theoretically correct even when integrated control is an aim[42]—a design principle which is preferred to branching off from a primarily centralized directive hierarchy. This principle applies to supranational bodies, capping agencies, or steering units as well.

In summary, the international list of goal-oriented statements, which "ad hoc" has more than seventy-eight items, will have to be thoroughly structured by using systems analysis methods.[43] An exhaustive list of ultimate desires is essential and must be made subject to structure and comparison with crude goals through iterated procedures. There exist various approaches for outlining goal functions, one[44] of which will serve as an example: performance goals, coordination goals, development potential goals, constraints.

Our previous seventy-eight item list lends itself well to such partitioning. The next step will be to determine priorities and formalize priorities scheduling.

Most of the objectives listed thus far are normative from a management standpoint whereas user viewpoints are left for future exploratory studies. The set of performance goals from an overall interdisciplinary user population is probably smaller and more definitive than the set of contradictory and divergent subgoals in a multitude of existing managements, hierarchical official bodies, and organizational artifacts.

The universal case for worldwide, automated information networks is realistic considering manager/producer feasibility. Approximate scheduling can be estimated by using systems analysis and technological forecasting as previously outlined so that implementation will concur in pace with future innovations. Satisfactory efforts and sufficient support in order to meet desirability as indicated by the users of information remain open-ended challenges. Hopefully, there will be a harmonious balance between feasibility and desirability for worldwide information networks by the end of this decade.

NOTES

1. Joseph Becker and Wallace C. Olsen, "Information networks," in C.A. Cuadra, ed., *Annual review of information science and technology* (Chicago: Britannica, 1968), p.289-327.

2. See: B. Langefors, *Total objectives, ultimate and non-ultimate desires*, 1B-ADB 68, No. 27 (Stockholm: Royal Institute of Technology, 1968). ...., *Decision and control in a multi-object environment* 1B-ADB 70, No. 3 (Stockholm: Royal Institute of Technology, 1970), 4p. ...., *Integrated control by information system, effectiveness and corporate goals*, 1B-ADB 70, No. 23 (Stockholm: Royal Institute of Technology, 1970), 14p. H. Raiffa, *Preferences for multi-attributed alternatives*, RM-5868-DOTRC (Santa Monica, Calif.: Rand Corp., 1969), 108p. Kjell Samuelson, "Information structure and decision sequence," in K. Samuelson, ed., *Mechanized information storage, retrieval and dissemination* (Amsterdam: North-Holland, 1968), p.622-636.

3. See: R. U. Ayres, *Technological forecasting and long-range planning* (New York: McGraw-Hill, 1969), 237p. E. Jantsch, *Technological forecasting in perspective* (Paris: OECD, 1967) 401p. ...., ed., *Perspectives of planning* (Paris: OECD, 1969), 528p. B. N Tardov, *Method for scientific technical progress forecasting as based on dynamics of documental information* Paper presented at the FID/II Symposium in Rome, Oct. 1969. (Prague: UTEIN, 1969), 22p. G. Wills, D. Ashton, and B. Taylor, eds., *Technological forecasting and corporate strategy* (London: Bradford/Crosby Lockwood, 1969), 273p.

4. Richard M. Nixon "Re-establishment of a national goals research staff" *Technological forecasting* 1:217-218 (1969).

5. Kjell Samuelson, FID/TM Symposium on performance evaluation of information retrieval systems, Panel Discussion, Stockholm, 17 June 1970.

6. Statements 1-12 in: J.C. Gardin, *UNISIST: Report on the feasibility of a science information system* (Paris: UNESCO/ICSU, 1969), 345p. Statements 13-24 in: G.W. Brown, J.G. Miller and T.A. Keenan, eds., *EDUNET - Report of the summer study on information networks*, conducted by the Interuniversity Council (EDUCOM), (New York: Wiley, 1967), 440p. Statements 25-33 In: S. Balazs and G. Orosz, "Mechanized information network for small countries," in K. Samuelson, ed., *Mechanized information storage, retrieval and dissemination* (Amsterdam: North-Holland, 1968), p.407-417. Statements 34-40 in: E. Malkiewicz and A. Leszczyk, "Nation-wide information system in Poland," in A. I. Milhailov, et al., eds., *International forum on informatics,* (Moscow:VINITI, 1969), p.217-238. Statements 41-42 in: B. Tezak, "The role of small countries in international systems with special reference to Yugoslavia," in A. I. Mikhailov, *ibid.*, p.412-421. Statements 43-44 in: Scott Adams, "MEDLARS as a national and international system," in A. I. Milhailov, *ibid.*, p.377-387. Statements 45-53 in: A. I. Lebowitz, "Preliminary specifications for a network for agricultural knowledge," in A. I. Milhailov, *ibid.*, p.470-483. Statements 54-56 in: *EUDISED report of the working party of the applicltion of computer techniques to educational documentation and information*, vol. I, II, III (Strasbourg, Dec. 1969). Statements 57-63 in: P. Zunde, "Co-operation of the information agencies of the CMEA countries," *International Library Revue*, Statements 64-66 in: A.G. Hoshovsky "COSATI information studies - what results," in J. B. North, ed., *Proceedings of the ASIS annual meeting* (Westport: Greenwood, 1969), p.57-67. Statements 67-78 in: N. B. Arutiunov, "Dal nejsie Razvitie Sistemy Nancno-Tekniceskoj Informatsii v SSSR," NTI, *Organizatsija i metodika* 11:1-12 (1967).

7. See: L.H. Berul and A. Karson, "An evaluation of the methodology of the DOD user needs study," in *Proceedings of the FID 1965 Congress, vol. 2* (Washington, D.C.: Macmillan. 1966), p.151-157. A. F. Goodman, *Flow of scientific and technical information: the results of a recent major investigation*, Douglas paper 4516 (Calif.: McDonnel Douglas Astronautics Comp.-Western Div., April 1969. A. Wysocki, "Study of users' information needs - subjects and methods," in *On theoretical problems of informatics*, FID No. 435, FID/RI (Moscow: VINITI, 1969), p.80-92.

8. "Paperwork and nonprofessionals - improving engineer productivity," *Machine design* 36:83-6 (Jan. 1964).

9. L. B. Doyle, "Seven ways to inhibit creative research," *Datamation* 11:52-60 (Feb. 1965).

10. J. C. Gardin, *UNISIST....*

11. F. Levy, "Towards an exchange project in information science," in A. I. Mikhailov. et al., eds., *International forum on informatics* (Moscow: VINITI, 1969), p.151-68.

12. See: E. M. Housman, "Survey of current systems for selective dissemination of information (SDI)," in J. B. North, ed., *Proceedings of the American Society for Information Science annual meeting, vol.6* (Westport: Greenwood, 1969), p.57-67. South African Council for Scientific and Industrial Research, *Computer tape services in science and technology* (Pretoria: UDC, 1970), 24p.

13. J. W. Murdock and D. M. Liston, Jr., "A general model of information transfer; theme paper 1968 annual convention," *American documentation* 18:197-208 (Oct. 1967).

14. See: Rudolf Bretz, *Communication media: properties and uses*, National Library of Medicine and United States Air Force Project RM-6070-NLM/PR (Santa Monica, Calif.: Rand Corp., 1969), 113p. J. A. Farquhar and J. A. Dei Rossi, *Alternative technologies for information networks* (Santa Monica, Calif.: Rand Corp., Dec. 1969), 8p.

15. See: Kjell Samuelson, *Automated international information networks, systems design concepts, goal-setting and priorities*, 1B-ADB 70, no. 21 (Stockholm: Royal Inst. of Technology, 1970), 58p. ...., "Systems design concepts for automated international information networks," in J. B. Worth, ed., *Proceedings of the ASIS...*, p.431-5.

16. N. Cohn, et al., "On-line computer applications in the electric power industry," in *Proceedings of the IEEE* 58:78-87 (Jan, 1970).

17. See: Fred Gruenberger, *Computer and communications - toward a computer utility* (Englewood Cliffs, N.J.: Prentice-Hall, 1969), 219p. L. G. Roberts and B. D. Wessler, "Computer network development to achieve resource sharing," in *AFIPS Conference proceedings* (Montvale, N.J.: AFIPS Press, 1970) p.543-9.

18. F. Harary, *Graph theory* (Reading: Addison-Wesley, 1969), 274p.

19. See: Norman Baker and Richard Nance, "Organizational analyses and simulation studies of university libraries: a methodological overview," *Information storage and retrieval* 5:153-68 (Feb. 1970). W. A. Creager, "The application of simulation techniques to the design and management of information systems," in R. R. Freeman, et al., eds., *Information in the language sciences* (New York: Elsevier, 1968), p.115-25. Maryann Duggan, "Library network analysis and planning (LibNAT)," *Journal of library automation* 2:157-175 (Sept. 1969). Norman Meise, *Conceptual design of an automated national library system* (Metuchen, N.J.: Scarecrow, 1969), 324p. Philip M. Morse, *Library effectiveness: a system approach* (Cambridge: MIT Pr., 1969), 207p. Richard E. Nance, "An analytical model of a library network," *ASIS journal* 21:56-66 (Jan.-Feb. 1970).

20. Kjell Samuelson, "Fast-response and special-purpose usage in general information systems," in A. I. Mikhailov, et al., eds., *International forum on informatics, vol. 2* (Moscow: VINITI, 1969), p.420-37.

21. See: ...., "Information structure and decision sequence," in K. Samuelson, ed., *Mechanized information storage...*, p.622-36. ...., "Fast response and special-purpose usage...," p.420-37. M. C. Yovits and R. L. Ernst, *Generalized information systems: some consequences for information transfer* Columbus: Ohio State Univ., Dept. of Computer and Information Science, 1968.

22. See: Kjell Samuelson, *Automated international information networks....* ...., "Coordination of diversified data bases and information networks through multiclassificatory concept notation in relay-switches and referral directories," in *Proceedings second Seminar on UDC and Mechanized Information Systems (1970)*.

23. See: Fred Gruenberger, *Computers and communications....* B. Langefors, *Theoretical analysis of information systems* (Lund: Studentlitteratur, 1966), 402p. James Martin, *Telecommunications and the computer* (Englewood Cliffs, N.J.: Prentice-Hall, 1969), 470p.

24. Kjell Samuelson, "Coordination of diversified data bases and information networks...." in *Proceedings second seminar on UDC....*

25. Roger Meetham, *Information retrieval: the essential technology* (New York: Doubleday, 1970), 192p.

26. See: Kjell Samuelson, "Information structure..." in K. Samuelson, ed., *Mechanized information storage........*, "Coordination of diversified data bases and information networks...." in *Proceedings second seminar on UDC....*

27. See: Robert U. Ayres, *Technological forecasting....* E. Jantsch, *Technological forecasting.... ....*, ed., *Perspectives of planning....* Herman Kahn and A. J. Wiener, *The year 2000: a framework for speculation on the next thirty-three years* (London: Macmillan, 1969), 431p.

28. See: Robert U. Ayres, *Technological forecasting....* G. B. Bernstein and M. J. Cetron, "SEER: a delphic approach applied to information processing," *Technological forecasting* 1:33-54 (1969). C. Hammer, *The future: interactive electronic systems* (Paper presented at American Society of Cybernetics 3rd Annual Symposium, Oct. 1969), p.5. Herman Kahn and A. J. Wiener, *The Year 2000....* Parsons & Williams, Inc., *Forecast 1968-2000 of computer development and application* (Copenhagen: Parsons & Williams, 1968), 44p. G. Wills, D. Ashton, and B. Taylor, eds., *Technological forecasting and corporate....*

29. J. C. Gardin, *UNISIST...*

30. Currie S. Downie, "Legal and policy impediments to federal technical information transfer," in J. B. Worth, ed., *Proceedings of the ASIS...., vol. 6,* (New York: Elsevier, 1969) p.411-15.

31. See: George H. Grimes, "The regional information system in education: its background, structure, development, and implementation," in J. B. North, ed., *Proceedings of ASIS..., vol. 6* (Westport: Greenwood, 1969), p.387-97. L. J. Peter and R. Hull, *The peter principle,* (New York: Morrow, 1969), 179p.

32. J. A. Farquhar and J. A. Dei Rossi, *Alternative technologies....*

33. Kjell Samuelson, "Information structure...," in K. Samuelson, ed., *Mechanized information storage....*

34. B. Langefors, *Theoretical analysis....*

35. M. C. Yovitz and R. L. Ernst, *Generalized information systems....*

36. L. H. Berul and A. Karson, "An Evaluation...," in *Proceedings of the FID 1965....*

37. See: L. J. Peter and R. Hull, *The peter principle.* Kjell Samuelson, "Management information systems and nervous systems - a comparison of design concepts," in *Proceedings IEEE systems and cybernetics conference* (Philadelphia, Oct. 1969) p.90-8. L. L. Whyte, A. G. Wilson, and D. Wilson, eds., *Hierarchical structures* (New York: Elsevier, 1969), 322p.

38. Michiro Maruyama, "Mutual causality in general systems," in J. H. Milsum, ed., *Positive feedback* (Oxford: Pergamon Pr., 1968), p.80-100.

39. See: Herbert Coblans, "INIS - an international project for the control of the literature of the nuclear sciences," in A. I. Mikhailov, et al., eds., *International forum on informatics, vol. 1* (Moscow: VINITI, 1969), p.422-26. C. M. Gottschalk, "System analysis considerations in a decentralized international information system," in J. B. North, ed., *Proceedings of the American Society for Information Science, vol. 7* (Washington, D.C.: ASIS, 1970), p.211-213. M. Komurka, "International nuclear information system," in J. B. North, ed., *Proceedings of the ASIS..., vol. 6,* p.441-46.

40. See: Allen Kent, "Centralization, decentralization, and specialization - a problem in resource allocation," in A. Kent, et al., *Electronic handling of information: testing and evaluation* (Washington, D.C.: Thompson, 1967), p.25-40. W. T. Morris, *Decentralization in management systems* (Columbus: Ohio State Univ. Pr, 1968), 209p. J. A. Perlman, "Centralization vs. decentralization," *Datamation* 11:24-8 (Sept. 1965).

41. J. C. Gardin, *UNISIST....*

42. See: Russell L. Ackoff, *A concept of corporate planning* (New York: Wiley-Interscience, 1970), 158p. E. Jantsch, ed., *Perspectives of planning....* Kjell Samuelson, "Management information systems and nervous systems...," in Proceedings IEEE....

43. See: Russell L. Ackoff, *...corporate planning....* Harold Borko, *Utilizing systems analysis and operations research to facilitate the transfer of scientific and technical information,* paper submitted to the FID/II Symposium in Moscow, Sept. 1968 (Prague: UTEIN, 1968), 11p. E. Jantsch, *Technological forecasting.... ....*, ed., *Perspectives of planning........*, *Decision and control.... ....*, *Integrated control by information system...* B. Langefors, *Total objectives, ultimate and nonultimate desires* IB-ADB 68, No. 27 (Stockholm: Royal Institute of Technology, 1968). E. S. Quade and W. I. Boucher, eds., *Systems analysis and policy planning* (New York: Elsevier, 1968), 453p. H. Raiffa, *Preferences for multi-attributed....*

44. B. Langefors, *Integrated control....*

Bibliography

Abraham, C. "Evaluation of clusters on the basis of random graph theory," *IBM research memo* Nov. 1962.

..... "Survey of the theory of probabilistic graphs," in M. Kochen, ed., *Some problems in information science*, Metuchen, N.J.: Scarecrow Pr., 1965.

Ackoff, Russell L. *A concept of corporate planning*. New York: Wiley-Interscience, 1970. 158p.

Adams, Scott. "Facsimile for federal libraries," *Special libraries* 44:169-72 (May-June 1953).

..... "MEDLARS as a national and international system," in A. I. Mikhailov, et al. eds. *International forum on informatics, vol. 1*, p.377-87. Moscow: VINITI, 1969.

Aiken, H. *Synthesis of electronic computing and control circuits*, Ann. Computer Laboratory, Cambridge, Mass.: Harvard Univ. Pr., 1951.

Aines, Andrew A. "The promise of national information systems," *Library trends* 16:410-18 (Jan. 1968).

Allen, Layman, and Caldwell, Marye, ed. *Communication science and law*. Indianapolis: Bobbs-merrill, 1965. 442p.

Allen, Thomas J. "Information needs and uses," in C. A. Cuadra, ed. *Annual review of information science and technology, vol. 4*. p.3-29. Chicago: Britannica, 1969.

Amdahl, L.D. "Architectural questions of the seventies," *Datamation* 16:66-68 (Jan. 1970).

American Association of Law Libraries, *Recruitment check list 1969* Chicago: The Association, 1969. p.36-38.

American Council of Learned Societies. *Report on cooperation between the New York Public Library, the City University of New York and the State University of New York*, New York, 1968.

American Library Association. American Association of School Librarians. *Standards for school library programs*. Chicago: ALA, 1960. 132p.

..... American Association of School Librarians and National Education Association. *Standards for school media programs*. Chicago: ALA, 1969. 66p.

..... American Association of State Libraries. Survey and Standards Committee. *Standards for library functions at the state level*. Chicago: ALA, 1963. 37p.

..... American Association of State Libraries. Standards Revision Committee. *Standards for library functions at the state level*. Chicago: ALA, 1970. 48p. Revision of the 1963 edition.

..... Association of College & Research Libraries. Standards Committee. "Standards for college libraries," *College and research libraries* 20:274-80 (July 1959).

..... Association of College & Research Libraries. Standards Committee. "Standards for junior college libraries," *College and research libraries* 21:200-06 (May 1969).

..... Committee on Library Extension. *A study of public library conditions and needs*. Chicago: ALA, 1926. 163p.

..... Commission on a National Plan for Library Education. "Report," *ALA bulletin* 61:419-422 (April 1967).

..... Public Library Association. *Interlibrary cooperation*. Chicago: ALA, 1967.

..... Public Library Association. *Minimum standards for public library systems, 1966*. Chicago: ALA, 1967. 69p.

..... Public Library Association. *Public library service: A guide to evaluation with minimum standards*. Chicago: ALA, 1956. 74p.

..... Reference Services Division. Interlibrary Loan Committee. "Draft of a model interlibrary loan code for regional, state, local or other special groups of libraries," *Special libraries* 59:528-30 (Sept. 1968).

..... Reference Services Division. Science and Technology Reference Services Committee. *A guide to a selection of computer-based science and technology reference services in the U.S.A.* Chicago: The Committee, 1969. 29p.

..... *Student use of libraries: an inquiry into the needs of students, libraries and the educational process*. Chicago: ALA, 1964. 212p.

..... Reference Services Division. Interlibrary Loan Committee. *National interlibrary loan code*. Chicago: ALA, 1968.

American Psychological Association. *Reports of the American Psychological Association's project on scientific information exchange in psychology*. Washington, D.C.: The Association, Dec. 1965. vol. 1, nos. 1-9 Dec. 1963; vol. 2, nos. 10-15 Dec. 1965.

Amey, Gerald. X. "Channel hierarchies for matching information sources to users' needs," in *Proceedings of the American Society for Information Science annual meeting, vol. 5, p.11-14. New York: Greenwood, 1968*.

Aron, J.D. "Real-time systems in perspective," *IBM systems journal* 6:49-67 (1967).

Anglo-American cataloging rules. British text (Prepared by the American Library Association, the Library of Congress, the Library Association, and the Canadian Library Association.) London: Library Association, 1967. 327p.

..... *North American text*. (Prepared jointly by the American Library Association, the Library of Congress, the Library Association, and the Canadian Library Association.) Chicago: ALA, 1967. 400p.

Armstrong, Charles M. *Development of library services in New York state*. Albany: Univ. of the state of New York, 1949.

Aron, J. D. "Real-time systems in perspective," *IBM systems journal* 6:49-67 (1967).

"ASIS information program developments," *Newsletter of the American Society for Information Science* 9:1,6 (Jan.-Feb. 1970).

Association of Research Libraries. *Minutes of 73rd annual meeting, January 26, 1969, Washington, D.C.* Princeton: The Association, 1969.

..... *Minutes of the annual meeting* (sixteenth to the seventy-fifth). Chicago: The Association, 1940-1970.

..... "Position statement...on model interlibrary loan code for regional, state or other special groups of libraries," in Genevieve M. Casey, *Structuring the Indiana State Library for interlibrary coordination*, p.97-100. Indiana Library Studies, #16. Peter Hiatt, ed. Bloomington, Ind. Indiana State Library, 1970.

Atherton, Pauline, and Tessier, Judith. "Teaching with MARC tapes," *Journal of library automation* 3:23-35 (March 1970).

Austin, C.J. *MEDLARS 1963-1967.* (National Library of Medicine, Public Health Service, U.S. Dept. of Health, Education, and Welfare) Washington, D.C.: Gov. Print. Off., 1968. 76p.

Avram, Henriette D. "Bibliographic and technical problems in implementing a national library network," *Library trends* 18:487-502 (April 1970).

..... "The RECON pilot project: a progress report," *Journal of library automation* 3:102-114 (June 1970).

..... "Using computer technology - frustrations abound," in *AFIPS proceedings spring joint computer conference, vol. 34*, p.42-44. Montvale, N.J.: AFIPS Pr., 1969.

Axner, David H. "The facts about facsimile," *Data processing magazine* 10:42 (May 1968).

Ayres, Robert U. *Technological forecasting and long-range planning.* New York: McGraw-Hill, 1969. 237p.

Bailey, Jr., Herbert S. "Book publishing and the new technologies," *Saturday review* 49:41-3 (11 June 1966).

Baker, Norman, and Nance, Richard. "Organizational analyses and simulation studies of university libraries: a methodological overview," *Information storage and retrieval*, 5:153-68 (Feb. 1970).

Baker, William O. "The dynamism of science and technology" in Eli Ginzberg, ed., *Technology and social change*, p.82-107. New York: Columbia Univ. Pr., 1964.

Balazs, S., and Orosz, G. "Mechanized information network for small countries," in K. Samuelson, ed., *Mechanized information storage, retrieval and dissemination*, p.407-14. Amsterdam: North-Holland, 1968.

Barnett, Harold J. and Greenberg, Edward. "A proposal for wired city television." *Washington University Law Quaterly.* 1968: 1-25 (Winter 1968).

Baruch, Jordon J. "Interactive television: a mass medium for individual," *EDUCOM position paper* (Oct. 1969).

Bavelas, A. "A mathematical model for group structures," *Applied anthropology* 7:16-30 (Dec. 1943).

..... "Communication patterns in task-oriented groups," *The journal of the Acoustical Society of America* 22:725-730 (Nov. 1950).

Beasley, Kenneth E. "Social and political factors," *ALA bulletin* 60:1146-55 (Dec. 1966).

Becker, Joseph. "The future of library automation and information networks," in S. R. Salmon, ed., *Library automation; a state of the art review.* p.1-6. Chicago: ALA, 1969.

..... "Telecommunications primer," *Journal of library automation* 2:48-56 (Sept. 1969).

..... "Tomorrow's library services today," *News notes of California libraries* 63:429-40 (Fall 1968).

..... "How library automation may influence new building plans," in S.R. Salmon, ed., *Library automation - a state of the art review*, p.30-32. Chicago: ALA, Nov. 1969.

..... "Information networks prospects in the United States," *Library trends* 17:306-317 (Jan. 1969).

..... "Telecommunications primer," *Journal of library automation* 2:148-156 (Sept. 1969).

...., and Hayes, Robert M. *A proposed library network for Washington State: working paper for the Washington State Library.* Olympia: Washington State Library, 1967. 50p.

...., and Olsen, Wallace C. "Information networks," in C. A. Cuadra, ed., *Annual review of information science and technology, vol. 3*, p.289-327. Chicago: Britannica, 1968.

Bell, Daniel. "The measurement of knowledge and technology," in E. B. Sheldon and W. E. Moore, eds. . *Indicators of social change*, p.145-246. New York: Russell Sage Foundation, 1968.

Bell System. *Medical interlibrary communications exchange service (MICES). A pilot project to determine the usefulness of the teletypewriter exchange service for interlibrary communications.* (Participants: National Library of Medicine, Duke University Medical Library, University of Virginia Medical Library, Bowman Gray School of Medicine Medical Library, Medical College of Virginia Medical Library, University of North Carolina Health Affairs Library.) [n.p.] 1965.

Bernstein, G. B., and Cetron, M. J. "SEER: a delphic approach applied to information processing," *Technological forecasting* 1:33-54 (1969).

Bertalanffy, Ludwig von. "General systems theory," in *General systems, vol. 1.* (Yearbook of the Society for General Systems Research.) Ann Arbor: Braun-Brumfield, 1956.

Berthold, Arthur Benedict. "Directory of union catalogs in the United States," in R. B. Downs, ed., *Union catalogs in the United States*, p.349-91. Chicago: ALA, 1942.

Berul, Lawrence, "Document retrieval," in C. A. Cuadra, ed., *Annual review of information science and technology, vol. 4*, p.203-27. Chicago: Britannica, 1969.

..... "Technical means for national information systems," in A. I. Mikhailov, et al. eds., *International forum on informatics, vol. 2*, p.149-67. Moscow: VINITI, 1969.

...., and Karson A. "An evaluation of the methodology of the DOD user needs study," in *Proceedings of the 1965 congress, vol. 2*, p.151-57. Washington: Macmillan, 1966.

Bhushan, A.K., and Stotz, R.H. "Procedures and standards for inter-computer communications," in *AFIPS proceedings spring joint computer conference, vol. 32*, p.95-104. Washington, D.C.: Thompson Book Co., 1968.

"The Bibliographic Center for Research," *Library of Congress information bulletin* 28:246 (8 May 1969).

...., Rocky Mountain Region, Inc. *The basis for the support of the bibliographical center.* [Denver: The Center, 1951. 2p.]

...., ... *Membership fee schedule.* [Denver: The Center, 1961, 1963.] 1p.

...., ... *1970 fee schedule.* [Denver: The Center] 1969. 3p.

Bierman, Kenneth J. and Blue, Betty J. "Processing of MARC tapes for cooperative use," *Journal of automation* 3:36-64 (March 1970).

Billouin, L. "Information theory and most efficient codings for communication or memory devices." *Journal of applied physics* 22:1108-1111 (Sept. 1951).

"Biomedical communication network," *Bookmark* 28:105-7 (Jan. 1969).

Bird, Warren, "TWX and interlibrary loans," *Bulletin of the Medical Library Association* 57:125-129 (April 1969).

Bisco, R. L. "Social science data archives: progress and prospects," *Social science information* 6:39-74 (1967).

..... "Social science data archives: technical considerations," *Social science information* 4:129-150 (1965).

Blasingame, Ralph. *Survey of Ohio libraries and state library services.* Columbus: State Library of Ohio, 1968. 188p.

...., and Deprospo, Ernest R., Jr. "Effectiveness in cooperation and consolidation in public libraries," in M. J. Voight, ed. p.189-206 *Advances in librarianship, vol. 1.* New York: Academic Pr., 1970.

Block, Victor. "Inside the FCC common carrier bureau," *Telephony* 178:17- (15 August 1970).

Boaz, Martha. *Strength through cooperation in southern California libraries, a survey.* Los Angeles, [Univ. of Southern California?] 1965. 175p.

Bolt, Beranek and Newman, Inc. *Toward the library of the 21st Century; a report on progress made in a program of research sponsored by the Council on Library Resources.* Cambridge, Mass.: The Author, 1964. 41p.

Bone, Lary Earl, ed. *Library education: an international survey.* (International Conference on Education for Librarianship, 1967) Champaign: Univ. of Illinois. Graduate School of Library Science, 1968. 388p.

Borko, Harold. *Utilizing systems analysis and operations research to facilitate the transfer of scientific and technical information.* (Paper submitted to the FID/II symposium in Moscow, Sept. 1968.) Prague: UTEIN, 1968. 11p.

Bregzis, Ritvars. "Library networks of the future," *Drexel library quarterly* 4:261-70 (Oct. 1968).

..... "The bibliographic information network; some suggestions for a different view of the library catalogue," in *Anglo-American conference on the mechanization of library services...30 June-3 July 1966,* p.128-142. Oxford: Mansell Information/Publishing Ltd., 1967.

Bretz, Rudolf. *Communication media: properties and uses.* (National Library of Medicine and United States Air Force Project RM-6070-NLM/PR) Santa Monica, Calif.: Rand Corp. 113p.

Brewster, Beverly J. "International library school programs," *Journal of education for librarianship* 9:138-143 (Fall 1968).

Bridegam, Wallis E., Jr., and Meyerhoff, Erich. "Library participation in a biomedical communications and information network," *Bulletin of the Medical Library Association* 58:103-11 (April 1970).

Brillouin, L. "Information theory and most efficient codings for communication or memory devices," *Journal of applied physics* 22:1108-1111 (Sept. 1951).

Brodman, Estelle. "The professional user: the library and informational service needs of practioners." in D. M. Knight and E. S. Nourse, eds., *Libraries at large,* p.152-157. New York: Bowker, 1969.

Brooks, Harvey, and Bowers, Raymond. "The assessment of technology," *Scientific American* 222:13-20 (Feb. 1970).

Brown, G. W., Miller, J. G., and Keenan, T. A. eds. *EDUNET, report of the summer study on information networks.* (Conducted by the Interuniversity Communications Council; EDUCOM). New York: Wiley, 1967. 440p.

Brown, Karl. "The Library Services Act, Public Law 597," in *American library annual.* p.121-131. New York: Bowker, 1958.

Bucci, W. "Pcm: A global scramble for systems compatibility," *Electronics* 42:94-102 (23 June 1969).

Budington, William S. "Interrelations among special libraries," *Library quarterly* 39:64-77 (Jan. 1969).

Budington, William S. "Interrelations among special libraries," in L. Carnovsky, ed., *Library networks -- promise and performance, the 33rd Conference...July 29-31, 1968,* p.64-77. Chicago: Univ. of Chicago Pr., 1969.

Bunge, Charles A. *Professional education and reference efficiency.* (Research Series, no. 11) Springfield: Illinois State Library, Sept. 1967. 101p.

Bush, Vannevar. "As we may think," *Atlantic monthly* 175:101-108 (July 1945).

Cadwallader, G., et al. *Format compatibility and conversion among bibliographic data bases.* (Tech. Rept. No. 1582-100-TR-7) Philadelphia: Auerbach Corp., 24 June 1969. 16p.

Campbell, H. C. *Metropolitan public library planning throughout the world.* (International Series of Monographs in Library and Information Science, no. 5) Oxford: Pergamon, 1967. 168p.

Carey, James W., and Quirk, John J. "The mythos of the electronic revolution," *The American scholar* 39:219-241, 395-425 (Spring, Summer 1970).

Carey, R. J. P. *Finding and using technical information.* London: Arnold, 1966. 153p.

Carl, Herbert A., ed. *Statewide long-range planning for libraries.* (report of a conference, Sept. 19-22, 1965, Chicago, Illinois.) [Washington, D.C.]: U.S. Department of Health, Education, and Welfare, [1966.] 59p.

Carnegie Commission on Educational Television, *Public television, a program for action,* New York: Harper & Row, 1967. 254p.

Carlen, Sister M. Claudia. "Expanding resources: the explosion of the sixties," *Library trends* 18:48-56 (July 1969).

Carnovsky, Leon, ed. *Library networks - promise and performance: the 33rd Conference of the Graduate Library School, July 29-31, 1968.* Chicago: Univ. of Chicago Pr., 1969. 110p. (Also published in *Library quarterly* 39:1-108 (Jan. 1969).

Carnovsky, Leon, ed. *Library networks - promise and performance, 33rd Conference...July 1968.* Chicago: Univ. of Chicago Pr., 1969.

Carr, C. S.; Crocker, S. D.; and Cerf, V. G. "HOST-HOST communication protocol in the ARPA network," in *AFIPS proceedings spring joint computer conference, vol. 36,* p.589-597. Montvale, N.J.: AFIPS Pr., 1970.

Carter, Launor F., et al. *National-document handling systems for science and technology.* New York: Wiley, 1967. 344p.

..... "What are the major national issues in the development of library networks," *News notes of California libraries* 63:405-17 (Fall 1968).

Casey, Genevieve. *The future role and financial structure of the Bibliographical Center for Research, Rocky Mountain Region: a reconnaisance study.* (Wayne State Univ. Office of Urban Library Research, Research Report no. 6.) Denver: The Center, 1969. 134p.

..... *OTIS: an evaluation of the Oklahoma Teletypewriter Interlibrary System.* Oklahoma City: Oklahoma Dept. of Libraries, 1969. 116p.

"Circulation policy," *Newsletter [Center for Research Libraries]* 109:6 (Jan. 1969).

Clapp, Verner W. *The future of the research library.* Urbana: Univ. of Illinois Pr., 1964. 114p.

..... "Public libraries and the network idea," *Library journal* 95:121-24 (Jan. 1970).

..... "Public library systems and the national library networks," in B. Hoyt and L. Dudgeon, eds., *Realities of the public library systems concept in Wisconsin*, p.103-11. Madison: Wisconsin Div. for Library Services, 1968.

..... "Some thoughts on the present status and future prospects of reference work," in W. B. Linderman, ed., *The present status and future prospects of reference/information service*, p.1-11. Chicago: ALA, 1967.

Clason, A. *The flow of information in the enterprise.* (Paper submitted to the FID/II Symposium in Moscow, Sept. 1968) Prague: UTEIN, 1968. 5p.

Coblans, Herbert. "INIS - an international project for the control of the literature of the nuclear sciences," in A. I. Mikhailov, et al. eds., *International forum on informatics, vol.1*, p.422-26. Moscow: VINITI, 1969.

Coenenberg, Richard. "Synergizing reference service in the San Francisco Bay Region," *ALA bulletin* 62:1379-84 (Dec. 1968).

Cohen, Morris. "Research habits of lawyers," *Jurimetrics* 9:183-194 (1969).

Cohen, Nathan M. "Library Services and Construction Act, as amended," in *The Bowker annual of library and book trade information.* New York: Bowker, 1968. p.208-213.

Cohn, N., et al. "On-line computer applications in the electric power industry," in *Proceedings of the IEEE* 58:78-87 (Jan. 1970).

Colah, M. S., and Strunk, R. W. *Civil defense communication studies: data transmission standards.* Menlo Park, Calif.: Stanford Research Institute, April 1969. 131p.

"College Library Center to be created in Ohio," *Library journal* 92:726 (15 Feb. 1967).

Colman, William G. "Federal and state financial interests in the performance and promise of library networks," in L. Carnovsky, ed., *Library networks - promise and performance; the 33rd Conference... July 29-31, 1968*, p.99-108. Chicago: Univ. of Chicago Pr., 1969.

Committee on National Library and Information Systems (CONLIS). *Improving access to information; a recommendation for a national library/information program.* Chicago: ALA, 1967. [23p.]

"Communication problems in biomedical research; report of a study," *Federation of American Societies for Experimental Biology proceedings* 23:1117-1176 (1964).

Communication systems and resources in the behavioral sciences. (Publication 1575) Washington, D.C.: National Academy of Sciences, 1967. 67p.

"A comparison of fees charged by the Colorado Technical Reference Center and by centers in other states," *CTRC newsletter* 2:3 (Nov.-Dec. 1969).

Connor, Jean L. "Stages in and fields for interlibrary cooperation," *Bookmark* 27:13-18 (Oct. 1967).

"Consortium (of Minnesota college libraries)," *Library journal* 94:2548 (July 1969).

Coonan, Margaret E. "The opportunities law librarians are missing," *Law library journal* 54:218-22 (Aug. 1961).

"Cooperation among law libraries: a panel" *Law library journal* 52:418-34 (1959).

"Cooperation in law library service: a panel," *Law library journal* 49:413-36 (1956).

Corbett, L. "Computer-based information services, including the use of UDC at IKAEA Aldermaston," in R. Molgaard-Hansen and M. Rigby, eds., *Proceedings of first seminar on UDC in a mechanized retrieval system.* (FID/CR Report No. 9.) Copenhagen: Danish Centre for Documentation, 1969.

Cordtz, Dan. "The coming shake-up in telecommunications." *Fortune* 81:69 (April 1970).

Cory, John Mackenzie. "The network in a major metropolitan center," in L. Carnovsky, ed., *Library networks - promise and performance.* Chicago: Univ. of Chicago Pr., 1969.

..... "The network in a major metropolitan center (METRO, New York)," *Library quarterly* 39:90-98 (Jan. 1969).

Cox, Carl R. "Library cooperation in a state university system," *Bookmark* 28:114-17 (Jan. 1969).

Cox, Kenneth A. "Carterfone and the computer utility," *Law and computer technology* 2:2-8 (April 1969).

Cox, Nigel S. *The computer and the library.* (University Library publication No. 4.) [Newcastle]: Univ. of Newcastle upon Tyne Library, 1966. 95p.

Creager, W. A. "The application of simulation techniques to the design and management of information systems," in R. R. Freeman, et al., eds., *Information in the language sciences*, p.115-25. New York: Elsevier, 1968.

Cronin, John W. "The National Union and Library of Congress Catalogs: problems and prospects," *Library quarterly* 34:77-96 (Jan. 1964).

Cruzat, Gwendolyn S., and Pings, Vern M. *An evaluation of the interlibrary loan service, Wayne State University Medical Library: III: determination of cost for processing interlibrary loans.* (Rept. no. 17) Detroit: Wayne State Univ., School of Medicine, Library and Biomedical Information Center, March 1966. 31p.

Curran, Ann T., and Avram, Henriette D. *The identification of data elements in bibliographic records;* (Final Report of the Special Project on Data Elements for the Subcommittee on Machine Input Records (SC-2) of the Sectional Committee on Library Work and Documentation (Z39) of the United States of America Standards Institute.) [New York]: The Institute 1967.

"Current notices on the Farmington Plan," *Farmington plan newsletter* 29:6-7 (May 1969).

Currier, Lura G. *Sharing resources in the Pacific Northwest.* Olympia: Washington State Library, 1969. 335p.

Dammers, H. F. "Integrated information processing and the case for a national network," *Information storage and retrieval* 4:113-31 (June 1968).

Dantine, D. J. "Communications needs of the user for management information systems," in *AFIPS Proceedings fall joint computer conference, vol. 29*, p.403-411. Washington, D.C.: Spartan Books, 1966.

Darling, Louise. "Regional services for medical libraries," *California librarian* 21:46-52 (Jan. 1970).

Davies, D. W. "Communication networks to serve rapid-response computers", in *Proceedings IFIP Conference in Edinburgh*, p.72-8. (D11-5) Amsterdam: North-Holland, 1968.

..... "The principles of a data communication network for computers and remote peripherals" in *Proceedings of the IFIP Conference in Edinburgh*. Amsterdam: North-Holland, 1968.

..... "Information systems in a community - the communication requirements," in K. Samuelson, ed., *Mechanized information storage, retrieval and dissemination*, p.600-7. Amsterdam: North-Holland, 1968.

Davis, M. S. "Economics - point of view of designer & operator," (in preprints of papers) *Interdisciplinary conference on multiple access computer networks*, Austin, Tex., 20-22 Apr. 1970. p.4-1-1 to 4-1-7.

Davis, Richard A. and Bailey, Catherine A. *Bibliography of use studies.* (Prepared under Grant Number GN-170 [From the National Science Foundation] for the Office of Science Information Service, National Science Foundation) [Philadelphia], 1964. 98p.

Davis, Ruth M. *Communications for the medical community - a prototype of a special interest audience.* (AIAA Paper no. 69-1072) New York: American Institute of Aeronautics and Astronautics, 1969. 14p.

..... "Cost-benefit analyses of biomedical information communications services." (Paper read at the Thirty-seventh National Meeting of the Operations Research Society of America, 20-22 April 1970, at Washington, D.C.).

..... "Relationship of regional networks to the National Library of Medicine's Biomedical Communications Network," *Bookmark* 28:109-13 (Jan. 1969).

Dawson, John M. "The Library of Congress: its role in cooperative and centralized cataloging," *Library trends* 16:85-96 (July 1967).

Dean, Sidney. "Hitches in the cable," *Nation*, 210:45 (20 July 1970).

DeGennaro, Richard. "The development and administration of automated systems in academic libraries," *Journal of library automation* 1:75-91 (March 1968).

Dennis, J. B. "A position paper on computing and communications," *Communications of the ACM* 11:370-377 (May 1968).

Deutsch, Karl. W. "On communication models in the social sciences," *Public opinion quarterly* 16:355-380 (Fall 1952).

"Developing partnerships for California Libraries." in *News notes of California libraries*, 63:263 (Fall 1968).

Dickie, P. M., and Arya, N. S. "MIS and international business," *Journal of systems management* 2:8-12 (June 1970).

Dinter, H. "Design criteria for a man-machine information transfer system," in L. Schultz, ed., *The information bazaar*, p.15-22. Philadelphia: The College of Physicians of Philadelphia. Medical Doc. Service, 1969.

Dix, William S. "Centralized cataloging and university libraries - Title II, Part C of the Higher Education Act of 1965," *Library trends* 16:97-111 (July 1967).

"Document vs. digital storage of textual materials for network operations," *EDUCOM bulletin* 2:6 (Dec. 1967).

Dordick, H.S.; Chesler, L. G.; Firstman, S.I.; and Bretz, R. *Telecommunications in urban development* (Memorandum RM-6069-RC). Santa Monica: Rand Corp., July 1969.

Downie, Currie S. "Legal and policy impediments to federal technical information transfer," in J. B. North, ed. *Proceedings of the American Society for Information Science, vol. 6*, p.411-15. Westport, Conn.: Greenwood Publishing, 1969.

Downs, Robert B. "American library cooperation in review," *College and research libraries* 6:407-15 (Sept. 1945).

..... "Future prospects of library acquisitions," *Library trends* 18:412-421 (Jan. 1970).

..... *A survey of cooperating libraries for the Kansas City Regional Council of Higher Education.* Kansas City, Mo.: Kansas City Regional Council, 1964. 60p.

..... *University library statistics.* Chicago: ALA, 1970. 129p.

...., and Jenkins, Frances B., eds. "Bibliography: current state and future trends," *Library trends* 15:337-908 (Jan., Apr. 1967).

Doyle, L. B. "Semantic road maps for literature searches," *Journal of the Association for Computing Machinery* 8: (Oct. 1961).

..... "Seven ways to inhibit creative research," *Datamation* 11:52-60 (Feb. 1965).

Dougherty, Richard M. "Library technology; a panel discussion," *Law library journal* 61:413-18 (1968).

Drennan, Henry T. "Public library program goals in the decade of the 1970's," in *The Bowker annual of library and book trade information, 1969*, p.14-22. New York: Bowker, 1969.

Drewry, Virginia. "Georgia state catalog card service," *Library resources and technical services* 2:176-180 (Summer 1958).

Dror, Y. *A general systems approach to uses of behavioral sciences for better policymaking.* (P-4091) Santa Monica, Calif.: Rand Corp., 1969. 29p.

Drucker, Peter F. *The age of discontinuity; guidelines to our changing society.* New York: Harper and Row, 1968. 402p.

Dubon, R. J. "Implementation of an international information retrieval center," *Proceedings of the American Documentation Institute*, p.339-46. Santa Monica, Calif.: Adriadne, 1966.

Duggan, Maryann. "Library network analysis and planning (Lib-NAT)" *Journal of library automation* 2:157-75 (Sept. 1969).

Dunlop, Robert A. *The emerging technology of information utilities.* (Paper presented at the Conference on Information Utility and Social Choice, University of Chicago, December 1969.) unpub.

Dunn, Donald A. *Policy issues presented by the interdependence of computer and communications services.* (Rept. No. 7379B-1) Menlo Park, Calif.: Stanford Research Institute, Feb, 1969. 72p.

Dupuy, T. N. *Ferment in college libraries: the impact of information technology.* Washington, D.C.: Communication Service Corporation, 1968.

Duzs, J. "The technical and methodical complexity of the national information system and some of its international aspects," in A. I. Mikhailov, et al., eds. *International forum on informatics, vol.1*, p.255-70. Moscow: VINITI, 1969.

Eatough, Clair L. "What tomorrow's library will look like," *Nation's schools* 77:107-09 (March 1966).

Edelman, Hendrik. *Shared Acquisitions and Retention System (SHARE) for the New York metropolitan area: a proposal for cooperation among Metro libraries.* (Metro Miscellaneous Publication No. 3) New York: Metropolitan Reference and Research Library Agency, 1969.

Egan, M. E. "Education for librarianship of the future," in J. Sherra, et al., eds., *Documentation in action,* (Based on 1956 Conference on Documentation at Western Reserve University) New York: Reinhold Publishing Corp., 1956.

Einhaus, H. W. *UNIDO industrial information service.* (Paper submitted to the FID/II Symposium in Moscow, Sept. 1968) Prague: UTEIN, 1968. 13p.

Eisner, Joseph. *Suggested recommendations for interlibrary cooperation in the state of New Jersey.* Plainview, New York: The Author, 1968.

Electronic Industries Association, Industrial Electronics Division. *Comments on Docket No. 18397, Part V* (before the U.S. Federal Communications Commission) Washington, D.C.: The Association, 27 Oct. 1969. Unpublished.

..... Industrial Electronics Division *The future of broadband communications.* Response to FCC Docket 18397, Part V. (29 Oct. 1969).

..... *In the matter of use of the Carterphone device in message toll telephone service.* 13 FCC 2d. 423.

..... Industrial Electronics Division. Satellite Telecommunications Subdivision, ad hoc group. *Future communications systems via satellites using low cost earth stations.* Washington, D.C.: EIA, July 1968.

Emling, J. W.; Harris, J. R.; and McMains, H. J. "Library communications," in B. Markuson, ed., *Libraries and automation, proceedings,* p.203-19. Washington, D.C.: Gov. Print. Off., 1964.

"ERIC files," *JOLA technical communications* 1:6 (May 1970).

Ertell, Merton W. *Interinstitutional cooperation in higher education; a study of experience with reference to New York State.* Albany, N.Y.: State Education Dept., 1957. 118p.

Esau, L. R., and Williams, K. C. "On teleprocessing system part II - a method for approximating the optimal network," *IBM systems journal* 5:142-147 (1966).

Esterquest, Ralph T., ed., "Building library resources through cooperation," *Library trends* 6:255-383 (Jan. 1958).

..... "Cooperation in library services" *Library quarterly* 31:71-89 (Jan. 1961).

..... "The medical librarian's view" *Bulletin of the Medical Library Association* 56:52-55 (Jan. 1968).

EUDISED report of the working party of the application of computer techniques to educational documentation and information. vol. I, II, III. Strasbourg, Dec. 1969.

Farquhar, J. A., and Dei Rossi, J. A. *Alternative technologies for information networks.* Santa Monica, Calif.: Rand Corp., Dec. 1969. 8p.

Fasana, Paul. "The collaborative library systems development project: a mechanism for inter-university cooperation," *Proceedings of the Conference on Library Automation, Jan. 6, 1970.* Albany, N.Y.: Education Div. of the State of New York. (to be published).

Fava, James A. "A framework for future data centers," in J. B. North, ed. *Proceedings of the American Society for Information Science, vol. 6,* p.417-29. Westport, Conn.: Greenwood Publishing, 1969.

Federal Communications Commission. *Federal register* 33:247 20 Dec. 1968 p.18977 (Docket No. 18397).

..... *Notice of proposed rule making.* 24 June 1970. (Docket number: 18894.)

..... "Procedures and policies for handling microwave applications for specialized common carrier services proposed by FCC." Report No. 90(51530), 15 July 1970, p.2.

Felter, Jacqueline W. "The Medical Library Center of New York: a progress report." *Bulletin of the Medical Library Association* 56:15-20 (Jan. 1968).

Feordalisi, Vincent, et al. "Project lawsearch" *Law library journal* 60:42-63 (Feb. 1967).

"Financial status of the Union Library Catalogue of Pennsylvania, October 1, 1968-September 30, 1969," *Union Library Catalogue of Pennsylvania newsletter* 112:4 (March 1970).

Finn, James D. "Technology and the instructional process," *AV communication review* 41:371-8 (June 1960).

Fischer, Margaret Mary. "Library cooperation," *Catholic library world* 39:332-37 (Jan. 1968).

Fishburn, P. C., "Additivity in utility theory with denumerable product sets," *Econometrica* 34:500-03 (1964).

Five Associated University Libraries, Systems Committee and Masfile Input Group. *An experimental holdings list of selected research monographs in the Five Associated University Libraries. Book trade and library science.* (Companion Volume to Masfile-I Pilot Project) Syracuse, N.Y.: FAUL, Jan. 1969.

..... *Masfile-I pilot project. Final report.* Syracuse, N.Y.: FAUL., April 1969.

Foote, Nelson N. "The new media and our total society," in P. H. Rossi and B. J. Biddle *The new media and education: their impact on society.* Garden City, New York: Doubleday, 1967. 460p.

Forrester, G. "Mechanizing a bibliographic data bank, a pilot project for the public libraries of metropolitan Toronto, Canada," in K. Samuelson, ed., *Mechanized information storage, retrieval and dissemination,* p.676-82. Amsterdam: North-Holland, 1968.

Frantz, Jack C. "Big city libraries: strategy and tactics for change," *Library journal* 93:1968-70 (15 May 1968).

Freeman, R. R. "Evaluation of the retrieval of metallurgical document references using UDC as the index language in a computer-based system," in R. Molgaard-Hansen and M. Rigby, eds., *Proceedings of first seminar on UDC in a mechanized retrieval system* (FID/CR Report No. 9.) Copenhagen: Danish Centre for Documentation, 1969.

Freiser, L., "Reconstruction of library services," in W. B. Linderman, ed., *The present and future prospects of reference/information services, p.48-58.* Chicago: ALA, 1967.

Friedman, D. C. *Global information handling system - aspects of the formatting problems.* (unpublished report, National Bureau of Standards) Nov. 1963. 25p.

Furth, Stephen E. "[Conference Speech]" in North Country Reference and Research Resources council *New developments in information services, p.22-25.* (Summer Conference, Potsdam, New York, June 12-13, 1969.)

Fussler, Herman H., and Simon, Julian C. *Patterns in the use of books in large research libraries.* Chicago: Univ. of Chicago Library, 1961. 210p.

Gagne, Robert M. "Educational technology as technique," *Educational technology* 8:5-13 (15 Nov. 1968).

Gaines, Ervin J. "The large municipal library as a network," *Library quarterly* 39:41-51. (Jan. 1969).

Galbraith, John Kenneth. *The new industrial state.* Boston: Houghton Mifflin, 1967. 427p.

Gallagher, Marian G. "The law libraries of the Pacific Northwest," in M. Kroll, ed., *College, university and special libraries of the Pacific Northwest, vol. 3*, p.131-141. Seattle: Univ. of Washington Pr., 1961.

Gardin, J. C. *UNISIST: report on the feasibility of a science information system.* Paris: UNESCO/ICSU, 1969. 345p.

Garfield, Eugene. "The role of the medical librarian in SDI systems," *Bulletin of the Medical Library Association* 57:348-51 (Oct. 1969).

Gillette, Virginia, et al. "The Indiana biomedical information program," *Bulletin of the Medical Library Association* 58:60-64 (Jan. 1970).

Giuliano, V. E., and Jones, P. E. "Linear associative in P. W. Howerton, D., *Information handling*, p.30-54. Washington, D.C.: Spartan Books, 1963.

Glaser, W. A., and Bisco, R. L. "Plans of the Council of Social Science Data Archives, *Social science information* 5:71-96 (1966).

Goderich, Mario. "Cooperative acquisitions: the experience of general libraries and prospects for law libraries," *Law library journal* 63:57-61 (Feb. 1970).

Goldstein, B. "The case for networks," *Datamation* 16:62-4 (March 1970).

Goodman, A. F. *Flow of scientific and technical information: the results of a recent major investigation.* (Douglas Paper 4516, rev. Sept. 1968). Huntington Beach, Calif.: McDonnell Douglas Astronautics Co., 1968.

Gordon, G. "A general purpose systems simulator," *IBM systems journal* 1962.

Gottschalk, C. M. "System analysis considerations in a decentralized international information system," in J. B. North, ed., *Proceedings of the American Society for Information Science, vol.7*, p.211-213. Washington, D.C.: ASIS, 1970.

Grant, E. L., and Ireson, W. G., *Principles of engineering economy* 5th ed. New York: Ronald Press, 1970.

"Grant to Library of Congress RECON pilot project," *Publishers' weekly* 197:34-5 (6 April 1970).

Greenspan, Stephen H. *Central library services in Monroe County. The problem of fiscal equity.* Rochester: Rochester Bureau of Municipal Research, 1968.

Gould, Jack. "Books reproduced on TV cartridges," *New York times* (14 April 1970).

Grant, E. L., and Ireson, W. G., *Principles of engineering economy* 5th ed. New York: Ronald Press, 1970.

"Grant to Library of Congress RECON pilot project," *Publishers' weekly* 197:34-5 (6 April 1970).

Gray, J. C. "The scientific and technical information network in the United Kingdom," in D. J. Foskett, et al. eds., *Library systems and information services, p.23-31.* London: Crosby Lockwood, 1970.

Great Britain. National Libraries Committee. *Report of the National Libraries Committee.* London: Her Majesty's Stationery Office, 1969. 320p.

Green, Thomas F. *Education and schooling in post-industrial America: some direction for policy.* (Presented before the Committee on Science and Astronautics, United States House of Representatives at its 11th Meeting with the Panel on Science and Technology, January 27-29, 1970 at Washington, D.C.)

Greenup, Nadine. "System-level reference service: a case study," *California librarian* 30:237-38 (Oct. 1969).

Greenspan, Stephen H. *Central library services in Monroe County. The problem of fiscal equity.* Rochester: Rochester Bureau of Municipal Research, 1968.

Griffith, J., and Boehm, E. M., "A method for multiplexing computers," *IBM memos*, Parts I-VIII (Dec. 1958-June 1959).

Grimes, George H. *Information services; a survey of the history and present status of the field.* Detroit: Michigan-Ohio Regional Educational Laboratory, 1969. 35p.

..... "The regional information system in education: its background, structure, development, and implementation," in J. B. North, ed., *Proceedings of the American Society for Information Science, vol. 6*, p.387-98. Westport, Conn.: Greenwood, 1969.

Grogan, D., *Case studies in reference work.* London: Archon Books and Clive Bingley, 1967. 166p.

Gruenberger, Fred. *Computers and communications - toward a computer utility.* Englewood Cliffs, N.J.: Prentice-Hall, 1969. 219p.

Haas, Warren J. "Statewide and regional reference service," *Library trends* 12:405-412 (Jan. 1964).

Halkin, J. *Justification for a more simple approach to communication of information for use in industry.* Prague: UTEIN, 1969. 9p.

Hall, A. Rupert. "The changing technical act," in Carl Stover ed., *The technological order.* Detroit: Wayne State Univ. Pr., 1963. 280p.

Hamilton, Clark L. "The computer and the legal profession," *Law and computer technology* Part I 3:58-65; Part II 3:97-10, 1970.

Hammer, C. *The future: interactive electronic systems.* (Paper presented at American Society of Cybernetics 3rd Annual Symposium, Oct. 1969). p.5

Hammer, Donald P. "National information issues and trends," in C. A. Cuadra, ed., *Annual review of information science and technology, vol.2*, p.385- 417. New York: Wiley, 1967.

Hamsher, D. H., ed. *Communication system engineering handbook.* New York: McGraw-Hill, 1967.

Harary, F. *Graph theory.* Reading: Addison-Wesley, 1969. 274p.

Harrar, Helen Joanne. "Cooperative storage warehouses," *College and research libraries* 25:37-43 (Jan. 1964).

Harvard University. Graduate School of Business Administration. Division of Research. *Structure and performance of the U.S. communications industry.* Cambridge, Mass: Harvard Univ. School of Business Administration. Div. of Research, 1970.

..... Program on Technology and Society. *Technology and work.* (Research Review No. 2.) Cambridge, Mass.: Harvard Univ., 1969. 47p.

Havlik, Robert J. "Law libraries at the state level," *Law library journal* 60:64-68 (Feb. 1967).

Hawaii. Department of Education. Office of Library Services. *Planning for libraries in Hawaii.* (Prepared by Boos, Allen and Hamilton). Honolulu, Hawaii: The Author, 1968. 290p.

Hayes, Phoebe. "The PNBC of the future," *PNLA quarterly* 32:4-7 (Jan. 1968).

Hays, David G. et al. *A billion books for education in America and the world: a proposal.* Santa Monica, Calif.: Rand Corp., 1968. 79p.

Heinich, Robert. *Technology and the management of instruction.* Washington, D.C.: Association for Educational Communications and Technology, 1970. 198p.

Helmer, Olaf. *Social technology.* New York: Basic Books, 1966. 108p.

Henderson, M. M.; Moats, J. S.; Stevens, M. E.; and Newman, S. M. *Cooperation, convertibility, and compatibility among informaion systems: a literature review.* (National Bureau of Standards Misc. Pub. 276) Washington, D.C.: Gov. Print. Off., 15 June 1966. 140p.

Herner and Company. *A recommended design for the United States medical library and information system, vol. I and II.* rev. ed. Washington: The Author, 1966. medical library and information system, v.I and II. rev. ed. Washington: the author, 1966.

Herner, Saul. "The place of the small library in the national network," *Journal of chemical documentation* 6:171-73 (Jan. 1966).

Heron, David. "Telefacsimile in libraries: progress and prospects," *UNESCO bulletin for libraries* 23:8-13 (Jan.-Feb. 1969).

Hiatt, Peter. "Cooperative processing centers for public libraries," *Library trends* 16:67-83 (July 1967).

Hirsch, Phillip. "Multi-access computer networks," *Datamation* 16:153-4 (June 1970).

Hodges, T. M.; Colby, C. C; and Bloomquest, Harold. "NERMLS: the first year," *Bulletin of the Medical Library Association* 57:329-37 (Oct. 1969).

Hoshovsky, A. G. "COSATI information studies--what results," in J. B. North, ed. *Proceedings of the American Society for Information Science, vol. 6;* p.401-09. Westport, Conn.: Greenwood Publishing, 1969.

Houseman, E. M. "Survey of current systems for selective dissemination of information (SDI)," in J. B. North, ed., *Proceedings of the American Society for Information Science annual meeting, vol.6,* p.57-67. Westport: Greenwood, 1969.

Houston Research Institute. *Facsimile transmittal of technical information.* (Presented to National Science Foundation.) Houston, Texas, May 1965. 45p.

van Houten, R. *Scientific and technical information for industry.* (Paper submitted to the FID/II Symposium in Moscow, Sept. 1968) Prague: UTEIN, 1968. 25p.

Howard, R. A. "Bayesian decision models for system engineering," *IEEE transactions systems science and cybernetics* SSC-1:36-40 (Nov. 1965).

..... "Information value theory," *IEEE transactions systems science and cybernetics* SSC-2:22-26 (Aug. 1966).

..... "Value of information lotteries," *IEEE transactions systems science and cybernetics* SSC-3:54-60 (June 1967).

Husen, Torsten and Boalt, Gunnar. *Educational research and educational change: The case of Sweden.* New York: John Wiley, 1967. 233p.

Hutchins, Margaret. *Introduction to reference work.* Chicago: ALA, 1944. 214p.

Igoe, James G. "The 'Hotline' in Michigan," *Library journal* 93:521-23 (1 Feb. 1968).

Illinois. *Telecommunication study.* Santa Monica, Calif.: System Development Corp. 15 Feb. 1969.

"Indiana installs teletype facility," *Bulletin of the Medical Library Association* 55:237-238 (April 1967).

"The Indiana library studies: a list," *Focus on Indiana libraries* 24:86-88 (June 1970).

"Information center profile: chemical abstracts service," *Scientific information notes* 2:79-81 (Mar.-Apr. 1970).

"Information center profile: computer search center (CSC)," *Scientific information notes* 1:107-10 (May-June 1969).

International Meeting of Cataloguing Experts. Working Group on the International Standard Bibliographic Description. *Standard bibliographic description (for single volume and multi-volume monographs)* (prepared by Michael German.) July 1970. Unpaged.

Interuniversity Communications Council (EDUCOM). *Agricultural sciences information network.* Boston: EDUCOM, 1969. 74p.

...., *Agricultural sciences information network development plan.* (Research Report 169.) Boston: EDUCOM, 1969. [94]p.

"Iowa University libraries coordinate automation," *Library journal* 94:2546 (July 1969).

Isner, J. E. "ANYLTS - what it is, what it plans to do," *Bookmark* 29:87-91 (Dec. 1969).

Isotta, N. E. C. "Europe's first information retrieval network," *ESRO/ELDO bulletin,* p.9-17. (1970).

Jackson, Eugene B. "The General Motors research laboratories library: a case study," *Library trends* 14:353-362 (Jan. 1966).

de Jaeger, H. *National center for scientific and technical documentation.* Prague: UTEIN, 1969. 10p.

Janson, Donald. "Picture-telephone service is started in Pittsburgh," *New York times* (1 July 1970).

Jantsch, E. *Technological forecasting in perspective.* Paris: OECD, 1967. 401p. Jantsch, E. *Perspectives of planning, Proceedings of the OECD Symposium Oct.-Nov. 1968.* Paris: OECD, 1969. 528p.

Jefferson, George. *Library co-operation.* rev. ed. London: Andre Deutsch, 1968. 172p.

Joeckel, Carleton B., ed. *Library extension problems and solutions.* Chicago: Univ. of Chicago Pr., 1946. 160p.

Johnson, Elmer D. *A history of libraries in the western world.* New York: Scarecrow, 1965. 418p.

Johnson, Leland L. The future of cable television: some problems of federal regulation. (Memorandum RM-6199-FF.) Santa Monica, Calif: Rand Corp., Jan. 1970.

Johnson, Lyndon B. *Public papers of the presidents 1967.* Washington, D.C.: Gov. Print. Off., 1968.

Johnston, Harold S. *Detroit metropolitan library research and demonstration project.* Detroit: Wayne State Univ. Libraries, 1969. 173p.

Johnston, W. Dawson. "The library resources of New York City and their increase," *The Columbia University quarterly* 13:163-72 (March 1911).

Jones, S. O. "User needs: a local response," in *Proceedings of the American Society for Information Science annual meeting, vol. 5,* p.338. New York: Greenwood publishing Corp., 1968.

Jones, Stacy V. "Illustrated lessons sent by an FM System," *New York times* (20 June 1970).

Josey, E. J. "Community use of academic libraries," *Library trends* 18:66-74 (July 1969).

..... "A summary of the Reference and Research Library Resources Systems progress reports," *Bookmark* 29:294-8 (May 1970).

..... "Systems development for reference and research library service in New York state," *British Columbia library quarterly* 31:3-21 (April 1968).

Judge, P. J. *Government responsibilities in information for industry.* (Paper presented at the FID/II Symposium in Rome, Oct. 1969). Prague: UTEIN, 1969. 12p.

Jurkins, Jacquelyn. "Development of the county law library," *Law library journal* 62:140-152 (May 1969).

Kahn, Alfred. *Neighborhood information centers: a study and some proposals.* New York: Columbia Univ. School of Social Work, 1966. 150p.

Kahn, Herman, and Wiener, A. J. *The year 2000: a framework for speculation on the next thirty-three years.* London: Macmillan, 1969. 431p.

Keenan, Elizabeth L. "Interlibrary loan, 1952-62; ten years of progress?" *Bulletin of the Medical Library Association* 52:307-315 (Jan. 1964).

Keenan, Stella. "Abstracting and indexing services in science and technology," in C. A. Cuadra, ed., *Annual review of information science and technology, vol. 4,* p.273-303. Chicago: Britannica, 1969.

Kennedy, R. A. "Bell Laboratories' library real-time loan system (BELLREL)" *Journal of library automation* 1:128-146 (1968).

Kenney, Brigitte L. *A review of interlibrary communications developments.* (Presented at the Conference on Image Storage and Transmission Systems for Libraries, Dec. 1-2, 1969, sponsored by the National Bureau of Standards, and others.) Unpublished. 19p.

..... *A survey of Indiana special libraries and information centers.* (Prepared for the Indiana Library Studies and the Indiana State Library.) Indianapolis: Indiana State Library, 1970. 44p.

..... *Health sciences libraries today.* (Prepared for the National Library of Medicine under contract with the University of Pittsburgh, NIH Contract No. PH-43-67-1152.) Boston, Mass.: EDUCOM, Dec. 1967. 179p.

..... *Survey of interlibrary communications systems.* (Prepared for the National Library of Medicine under contract with the University of Pittsburgh, NIH Contract No. PH-43-67-1152.) Boston, Mass.: EDUCOM, April 1967. 74p.

Kent, Allen. "Centralization, decentralization, and specialization - a problem in resource allocation," in A. Kent, et al., *Electronic handling of information: testing and evaluation,* p.25-40. Washington, D.C.: Thompson, 1967.

Kilgour, Fredrick G. "A regional network - Ohio College Library Center," *Datamation* 16:87-9 (Feb. 1970).

..... "Research libraries in information networks," in M. Rubinoff, ed., *Toward a national information system,* p.147-54. (National Colloquium on Information Retrieval, 1965) New York: Spartan, 1965.

King, Gilbert W., et al. *Automation and the Library of Congress: a survey sponsored by the Council on Library Resources.* Washington, D.C.: Library of Congress, 1963. 88p.

..... "The automation of library systems," in B. Markuson, ed., *Libraries and automation, proceedings,* p.233-42. Washington: Gov. Print. Off., 1964.

Klintoe, K. *Scientific and technical information at enterprise level.* (Paper submitted to the FID/II Symposium in Moscow, Sept. 1968). Prague: UTEIN, 1968. 10p.

Knight, Douglas M. and Nourse, E. Shepley. *Libraries at large; the resource book based on the materials of the National Advisory Commission on Libraries.* New York: Bowker, 1969. 664p.

Knox, William T. "National information networks and special libraries," *Special libraries* 57:627-30 (Nov, 1966).

..... "Toward national information networks: 1. The government makes plans. " *Physics today* 19:39-44 (Jan. 1966).

Koch, H. W., and Harschman, A. *A network for physics information.* (ID 68-13) New York: American Institute of Physics, 1968. 16p.

Kochen, Manfred. "An information-theoretic model of organization," *Transactions of the Institute for Radio Engineers,* (Professional Group on Information Theory) 4:67-75 (Sept. 1954).

..... "Decentralization by function and location," (MHRI preprint 267, Univ. of Michigan, April 1970.) Submitted for publication to *Econometrica.*

..... "Toward a rational theory of decentralization: some implications of a mathematical approach," *American political science review* 63:734-49 (Sept. 1969).

..... "Organized systems with discrete information transfer," *General systems* 2:30-47 (1958).

..... "Referential consulting networks," in C. Rawski, ed., *Toward a theory of librarianship.* Cleveland: Case Western Reserve Univ. Pr., 1970.

...., and Deutsch, K. W. "Decentralization and uneven service loads," *Journal of regional science* 10:153-73 (Aug. 1970).

...., and Flood, M. M., "Some bibliographic and sociological devices to improve maintenance of current awareness about literature," in M. Kochen, ed., *Some problems in information science* Metuchen, N.J.: Scarecrow, 1965.

...., and Wong, E. "Concerning the possibility of a cooperative information exchange" *IBM journal of research and development* (April 1962).

Koltay, Emery. "International standard book numbering," *Bowker annual of library and book trade information* p.71-74 New York: Bowker, 1970.

Komurka, M. "International nuclear information system," in J. B. North, ed., *Proceedings of the American Society for Information Science annual meeting, vol.6,* p.441-46. Westport: Greenwood, 1969.

Krause, L. I. *Analysis of policy issues in the responses to the FCC computer inquiry.* (Rept. No. 7379B-2) Menlo Park, Calif.: Stanford Research Institute, Feb. 1969. 199p.

Kromer, Charles. *Establishing the information system.* Detroit: Michigan-Ohio Regional Educational Laboratory, 1969.

Kuljian, Maynard J. "A random-access audio-picture retrieval system," *Journal of the Society of Motion Picture and Television Engineers* (Oct. 1969).

Kuhn, Thomas S. *The structure of scientific revolutions.* Chicago: Univ. of Chicago Pr., 1962. 172p.

Kuncaitus, Yadwiga. *Comparitive study of the Cleveland and Columbus union catalogs.* Cleveland: Case Western Reserve Univ. School of Library Science, 1967.

..... *Union catalogs and bibliographic centers: a state of the art review.* Columbus: Ohio State Library, 1968. 20p.

Kurth, William H. *Survey of the interlibrary loan operation of the National Library of Medicine.* [n.p.]: U.S. Dept. of Health, Education, and Welfare. Public Health Service, 1962. 49p.

de Laclemandiere, J. *Information et strategie d'entreprise.* (Paper submitted to the FID/II Symposium in Moscow, Sept. 1968). Prague: UTEIN, 1968. 57p.

Lacy, Dan. *Freedom and communication.* Urbana: Univ. of Illinois Pr., 1965. 108p.

..... "Social change and the library: 1945-1980," in D. M. Knight and E. S. nourse, eds., *Libraries at large...,* p.3-21 New York: Knight and E. S. Nourse, eds., *Libraries at large...* New York: Bowker, 1969.

Lancaster, F. W. *Evaluation of the MEDLARS demand search service.* Washington: U.S. Department of Health, Education, and Welfare. Public Health Service, 1968. 276p.

..... *Information retrieval systems.* New York: Wiley, 1968. 222p.

Landau, Herbert B. "Design criteria for a multi-input data base for the National Agricultural Library" in J. B. North, ed., *Cooperating information societies, proceedings of the American Society for Information Science, vol. 6,* p.101-04. Westport, Conn.: Greenwood, 1969.

Langefors, B. *Decision and control in a multi-object environment.* (IB-ADB 70, No 3.) Stockholm: Royal Institute of Technology, 1970. 4p.

..... *Integrated control by information system, effectiveness and corporate goals.* (IB-ADB 70, No 23) Stockholm: Royal Institute of Technology, 1970. 14p.

..... *Theoretical analysis of information systems.*

..... *Total objectives, ultimate and nonultimate desires.*

..... *Total objectives, ultimate and nonultimate desires.* (IB-ADB 68, No 27,) Stockholm: Royal Institute of Technology, 1968.

Lawlor, Reed C. "Computers, law, and society: where do we go from here?" *Jurimetrics* 8:54-58 (1966).

Lazerow, Samuel. "The U.S. National Libraries Task Force: an instrument for national library cooperation," *Special libraries* 59:698-703 (Nov. 1968).

Leavitt, H. J., "Some effects of certain communication patterns upon group performance," *Journal of abnormal social psychology* 46:38-50 (1951).

Lebowitz, A. I. "Preliminary specifications for a network for agricultural knowledge," in A. I. Mikhailov, et al., eds., *International forum on informatics, vol. 1,* p.470-83. Moscow: VINITI, 1969.

"Legislation and grants," in *The Bowker annual of library and book trade information, 1970,* p.77-147. New York: Bowker, 1970.

Leonard, Lawrence E. "Colorado academic libraries book processing center: a feasibility study," *College and research libraries* 29:393-99 (Sept. 1968).

Levy, F. "Towards an exchange project in information science," in A. I. Mikhailov, et al, eds., *International forum on informatics,* p.151-68. Moscow: VINITI, 1969.

Lewis, Alfred J. "1969 statistical survey of law school libraries and librarians," *Law library journal* 63:267-272 (1970).

"Library education and manpower, ALA policy proposal," *American libraries* 1:341-345 (April 1970).

"Library systems for the 1970's," *News notes of California libraries* 65:283-436 (1970).

Lichtenstein, Walter. "Book experience in Europe," *Library journal* 38:77-81 (Feb. 1913).

Licklider, J. C. R. *Libraries of the future.* Cambridge, Mass.: MIT Pr., 1965. 219p.

..... "Man-computer interaction in information systems," in M. Rubinoff, ed., *Toward a national information system,* p.63-75. Washington, D.C.: Spartan Books, 1965.

Linderman, W. B., ed. *The present and future prospects of reference/information service,* (Proceedings of the Conference held at the School of Library Service, Columbia University, 1966.) Chicago: ALA, 1967. 195p.

Little, J. L., and Mooers, C. N. "Standards for user procedures and data formats in automated information systems and networks," in *AFIPS proceedings spring joint computer conference, vol. 32,* p.89-94. Washington, D.C.: Thompson Book Co., 1968.

Liu, H., and Holmes, D. W. "Teleprocessing systems software for a large corporate information system," in *AFIPS proceedings spring joint computer conference, vol. 36,* p.697-709. Montvale, N.J.: AFIPS Pr., 1970.

Livingston, L. G. "Computer utilities and the three national libraries," (preprint of paper prepared for the *Symposium on the computer utility - implications for higher education,* Manchester, N.H., May 5-7, 1969. 13p).

Lloyd, G. A. "An FID viewpoint on the role of UDC in a world science information system," in R. Molgaard-Hansen and M. Rigby, eds., *Proceedings of first seminar on UDC in a mechanized retrieval system.* (FID/CR Report No. 9) Copenhagen: Danish Center for Documentation, 1969.

Locke, William N. "Computer costs for large libraries," *Datamation* 16:69-74 (Feb. 1970).

Longenecker, Henry C. "Financial support of the Union Library Catalogue," [Union Library Catalogue of Pennsylvania] *Newsletter* 85:[8-11] (Feb. 1962).

Lorenz, John G. "International transfer of information," in C. A. Cuadra, ed., *Annual review of information science and technology, vol.4,* p.379-402. Chicago: Britannica, 1969.

..... "Networks for knowledge," *Mountain-Plains library quarterly* 14:3-6 (Spring 1969).

..... "Regional and state systems," in W. B. Linderman, ed., *The present and future prospects of reference/information service,* p.73-82. Chicago: ALA, 1967.

Lowell, Mildred H. *College and university library consolidation.* Eugene: Oregon State System of Higher Education, 1942. 136p.

MacCrimmon, K. R. *Decisionmaking among multiple-attribute alternatives: a survey and consolidated approach.* (RM-4823-ARPA) Santa Monica, Calif.: Rand Corp., 1968.

Malkiewicz, E., and Leszczyk, A. "Nation-wide information system in Poland," in A. I. Mikhailov, et al., *International forum on informatics, vol.1,* p.217-38. Moscow: VINITI, 1969.

Markowitz, H. M.; Hausner, Bernard; and Karr, H. W., *SIMSCRIPT: a simulation programming language.* Englewood Cliffs, N.J.: Prentice-Hall, 1963. 138p.

Marill, T., and Roberts, L. G. "Toward a cooperative network of time-shared computers," in *AFIPS proceedings fall joint computer conference, vol. 29,* p.425-431. Washington, DC.: Spartan Books, 1966.

Marron, Harvey. "Information network development, cost data for the operation of a decentralized information network: educational resources information center," in B. Fry, ed., storage retrieval vol. 6, p.221-7. Oxford: Pergamon Press, 1970.

Marschak, J., *Elements for a theory of teams,* (Cowles Commission for Research in Economics), Chicago: Univ. of Chicago, 1955.

Martin, James S. "The audio-visual department comes of age," *American school and university* 40:24 (Feb. 1968).

..... *Telecommunications and the computer,* Englewood Cliffs, N.J.: Prentice-Hall, 1969. 470p.

..... *Teleprocessing network organization.* Englewood Cliffs, N.J.: Prentice-Hall, 1970. 270p.

Maruyama, Michiro "Mutual causality in general systems," in J. H. Milsum, ed. *Positive feedback.* Oxford: Pergamon., 1968. p.80-100.

..... "The second cybernetics: deviation-amplifying mutual causal processes," in W. Buckley, ed., *Modern systems research for the behavioral scientist,* p.304-13. Chicago: Aldine, 1968.

Marx, Stephen M. "Citation networks in law," *Jurimetrics journal* 10:121-37 (June 1970).

Mayeda, T. "Methodology in presentation - a new objective: the multi-media network," (draft of lecture delivered to the Washington, D.C. Chapter, The Institute of Management Sciences, Nov. 1, 1967. 20p.)

McAnally, Arthur M. "Recent developments in cooperation," *College and research libraries* 12:123-32 (April 1951).

McBurney, R. E. *Technical information services in canada.* (Paper submitted to the FID/II Symposium in Moscow, Sept. 1968.) Prague: UTEIN, 1968. 13p.

McCarn, Davis B. "Biomedical communications network," *Bulletin of the Medical Library Association* 57:323-328 (Oct. 1969).

McCarthy, Stephen A. "Research library cooperation," *Bookmark* 28:75-80 (Dec. 1968).

McCleland, C. A. *Theory and the international system.* N.Y.: Macmillan, 1966. 138p. 198p.

McCulloch, W. S., and Pitts, W. "A logical calculus of the ideas immanent in nervous activity," *Bulletin of mathematical biophysics* 5:115 (1943).

McMains, H. J., and Bromleigh, Jr., G. L. "Telephony and the library," paper prepared for the *Conference on image storage and transmission systems for libraries,* Gaithersburg, Md., Dec. 1-2, 1969. 19p. (unpublished.)

McMurrey, Katherine, and Funk, Ralph, *Legal, organizational, and financial aspects of interstate, interlibrary cooperation in the southwest.* (Presented at SWLA Working Conference, 17 September 1970, Arlington, Texas).

McNamara, Mary E. *Establishing a medical library network for the Detroit metropolitan area.* (Rep. No. 20) Detroit: Wayne State Univ. School of Medicine. Library and Biomedical Information Center, May 1966.

Maier, Joan M. *The Bibliographical Center for Research, Rocky Mountain Region: a cost study of the Center's present operations.* (Prepared by...Project Leader and Consultant and a Project Team from the Institute on Library System Design and Analysis, Graduate School of Librarianship, University of Denver.) Denver: The Center, 1969. 89p.

Mansfield, Edwin. *The economics of technological change.* New York: Norton, 1968. 257p.

"The MARC editorial office," *Library of Congress information bulletin* 29:178 (16 April 1970).

Markuson, Barbara E., ed. *libraries and automation, proceedings.* (Conference on Libraries and Automation, Airlie Foundation, 1963.) Washington, D.C.: Library of Congress, 1964. 268p.

..... "The system implications of interlibrary cooperation," *PNLA quarterly* 33:4-13 (Winter 1969).

Martin, Lowell A. *Library response to urban change.* Chicago: ALA, 1969. 323p.

..... *Progress and problems of Pennsylvania libraries.* Harrisburg, Pa.: Pennsylvania State Library, 1967. 59p.

Massachusetts Institute of Technology. Project INTREX Staff. *Semiannual activity report.* Cambridge, Mass.: MIT. (15 March and 15 Sept. 1966 to 1970).

Master plan for total library service. Sacramento: California Library Association, 1969. Mimeo.

Meadows, Paul. "Models, systems, and science," *American sociological review* 22:3-9 (1957).

Meetham, Roger. *Information retrieval: the essential technology.* New York: Doubleday, 1970. 192p.

Meise, Norman R. *Conceptual design of an automated national library system.* Metuchen, N.J.: Scarecrow, 1969. 324p.

Menou, M. J. "Problematics of the international systems for the transfer of scientific and technical knowledge," in A. I. Mikhailov, et al. eds., *International forum on informatics, vol.1,* p.217-38. Moscow: VINITI, 1969.

Merritt, R. L., and Lane, R. E., "The training functions of a data library," *Social science information* 4:118-126 (1965).

Merskey, R. "Progress in law librarianship," *The Bowker annual of library and book trade information, 1970,* p.278-79. New York: Bowker, 1970.

Merta, A. "National system of scientific, technical and economic information in Czechoslovakia," in A. I. Mikhailov, et al. eds., *International forum on informatics, vol.1, p.377-87.* Moscow: VINITI, 1969.

Mesthene, Emmanuel G. From an address delivered at the American Management Association's Second International Conference and Exhibit, "Educational realities," New York. August 9-12, 1966.

Mesthene, Emmanuel G. *Technological change: its impact on man and society.* Cambridge: Harvard Univ. Pr., 1970. 127p.

Metcalf, Keyes D. "The New England deposit library," *Library quarterly* 12:622-28 (July 1942).

Meyer, Thomas C. "Communication - a supplement to medical library service," *Bulletin of the Medical Library Association* 57:338-42 (Oct. 1969).

Meyerhoff, Erich. "Medical Library Center of New York," *Bulletin of the Medical Library Association* 51:501-506 (Oct. 1963).

Midler, J. L. *Investment in network expansion under uncertainty.* (RM-5920-PR) Santa Monica, Calif.: Rand Corporation, 1969. 24p.

Mikhailov, A. I. *Scientific and technical information and international cooperation.* Prague: UTEIN, 1969. 10p.

Miller, James G. "Living systems," *Behavioral science* 10:193-411 (1965).

Miller, Joan. "The New York State special education instructional materials centers networks," *Bookmark* 29:58-9 (Nov. 1969).

Miller, R. K. "Quick access to land documents via 16mm microfilm file system," *Electrical world* (4 Aug. 1969).

Miller, Ted. "Six Minneapolis 'insiders' build unique cooperative," *Special libraries* 54:295-97 (May-June 1963).

"Model interlibrary loan code for regional, state, local, or other special groups of libraries," *ALA bulletin* 63:513-516 (April 1969).

Mohrhardt, Foster E. "The library kaleidoscope: national plans and planning," in W. B. Linderman, ed. *The present status and future prospects of reference/information service,* p.83-92. Chicago: ALA, 1967.

..... "A challenge to habit: some views on library systems analysis," in B. Markuson, ed., *Libraries and automation, proceedings,* p.244-48. Washington, D.C.: Gov. Print. Off., 1964.

Monroe, Margaret E. "AIM: an independent study program in library science," *Journal of education for librarianship* 6:95-102 (Fall 1965).

..... "Core course at Wisconsin," *Journal of education for librarianship* 9:116-122 (Fall 1968).

Montgomery, K. L.; Slater, F. L.; and Belzer, J. "The library automation network at the University of Pittsburgh," in L. Schultz, ed., *The information bazaar,* p.155-71. Philadelphia: The College of Physicians of Philadelphia, Medical Documentation Service, 1969.

Moody, Myrtle A. "Opportunities for library cooperation," *Law library journal* 54:223-226 (Aug. 1961).

Mooers, Calvin N. *Standards for user procedures and data formats in automated information systems and networks: part I, the need for standardization and the manner in which standardization can be accomplished.* unpublished report, 5 July 1967. 45p.

Moore, Raymond S. *Consortiums in American higher education: 1965-66; report of an exploratory study.* Washington, D.C.: U.S. Office of Education, 1968. 47p.

Morgan, Eleanor Hitt. "The county library," in C. B. Joeckel, *Library extension problems and solutions,* p.59-74. Chicago: Univ. of Chicago Pr., 1946.

Morris, Albert J. "University-industry television, radio and telephone links," *Educational broadcasting review* 4:44- (Feb. 1970).

Morris, W. T. *Decentralization in management systems.* Columbus: Ohio State Univ. Pr., 1968. 209p.

Morse, Elliott H. "Regional plans for medical library service: medical library cooperation in Philadelphia," *Bulletin of the Medical Library Association* 52:509-513 (July 1964).

Morse, Phillip M. *Library effectiveness: a systems approach.* Cambridge: MIT Pr., 1969. 207p.

Mumford, L. Quincy. "International co-operation in shared cataloging," *UNESCO bulletin for libraries* 22:9-12 (Jan.-Feb. 1968).

Murdock, J. W., and Liston Jr., D. M. "A general model of information transfer: theme paper 1968 annual convention," *American documentation* 18:197-208 (Oct. 1967).

Myers, Wilbur C. *PCMI technology and potential applications.* Hawthorne, California: National Cash Register Co., May, 1964. 125p.

Murphy, W. D.; Horty, J. F.; and Budington, W. S. "Libraries of the future, a panel discussion," *Law library journal* 60:379-397 (Nov. 1967).

Myers, Wilbur C. *PCMI technology and potential applications.* Hawthorne, California: National Cash Register Co., May, 1964. 125p.

"NAL/land-grant network plan completed," *EDUCOM bulletin* 4:1-3 (Oct. 1969).

Nance, Richard E. "An analytical model of a library network," *ASIS journal* 21:56-66 (Jan.-Feb. 1970).

Nasatir, D. *Social science data libraries* (Publication A-89) Berkeley: Univ. of Calif., Survey Research Center, Nov. 1967.

National Academy of Sciences - National Academy of Engineering. Committee on Scientific and Technical Communication. *Scientific and technical communication; a pressing national problem and recommendations for its solution.* Washington, D.C.: The Academy, 1969. 322p.

National Advisory Commission on Libraries. "Library services for the nation's needs: the report of the National Advisory Commission on Libraries," in D. M. Knight and E. S. Nourse, ed. *Libraries at large,* p.495-521. New York: Bowker, 1969.

"National Commission on Libraries and Information Science," *LC information bulletin* 29:374-77 (30 July 1970).

National Cable Television Association. *Membership bulletin* II:32 (19 Aug. 1969).

National Film Board of Canada. *The living machine.* (Motion) Picture). 60 min. sd, b&w, 16mm.

Nebraska. Government Consolidated Communications Committee. *The feasibility of a statewide communication network.* Kansas City, Mo.: 1965. (mimeo.)

Nelson Associates, Inc. *A reference and research library resources plan for the Rochester area: An analysis of the proposals of the Commissioner's Committee on Reference and Research Library Resources as applied to a selected region.* New York: The Author, 1962. 58p.

..... *An evaluation of the New York State Library's NYSILL pilot program.* New York: The Author, 1968. 150p.

..... *Interlibrary loan in New York State Library, 1969. 300p.*

..... *Interlibrary loan in New York state* New York, 1969. 1v. (loose-leaf) tables.

..... *Implementing centralized processing for the public libraries of New York State* [New York]: The Author, 1967. 35p.

..... *Interlibrary loan in New York State; a report prepared for the Division of Library Development of the New York State Library.* New York: The Author, 1969. 208p.

..... *Public library systems in the United States; a survey of multijurisdictional systems.* Chicago: ALA, 1969. 368p.

..... *The New York State Library's pilot program in facsimile transmission of library materials. A summary report.* New York: The Author, June 1968. 85p.

..... *Prospects for library cooperation in New York city: planning for more effective utilization of reference and research resources.* New York: The Author, 1963. v.p.

..... *Possibilities for a reference and research library system in the Buffalo-Niagara region.* Tarrytown, N.Y.: A. & M. Printing, 1966. 54p.

..... *Reference and research library needs in Michigan.* Lansing: Michigan State Univ., 1968.

..... *Strengthening and coordinating reference and research library resources in New York State.* New York: The Author, 1963. 98p.

..... *News from the State Library.* 108 (8 July 1970).

NERMLS News, no. 1, Jan.-Mar. 1970.

New Hampshire. State Library. *A plan for library cooperation in New Hampshire,* Concord: Arthur D. Little, 1967. 68p.

"New IIS fee schedules," *IIS [Industrial Information Service, Southern Methodist University, Dallas] newsletter* 4:2 (28 July 1970).

"New interlibrary loan code drafted," *ALA bulletin* 62:409-411 (Apr. 1968).

New York (City.) Mayors Advisory Task Force on CATV & Telecommunications. *A report on cable television and cable telecommunications in New York City.* New York: City Hall 14 Sept. 1968. 75p. (mimeo.)

"New York facsimile project judged a failure," *Library journal* 93:1564-1566 (15 April 1968).

New York Metropolitan Reference and Research Library Agency. *METRO: what it is and what it does.* [New York: 1968?] folder.

New York (State). Governor's Library Conference. *Proceedings of the first Governor's Library Conference, June 24-25, 1965.* Albany, NY: [n.p.] 67p.

..... Governor's Committee on Library Aid. *Library service for all.* (Report 1950.) Albany: The State of New York, 1951. 103p.

..... Commissioners Committee on Reference and Research Library Resources. *Report to James E. Allen, Jr., Commissioner of Education.* Albany: New York State Library, 1961. 43p. (mimeo.)

..... *Report of the Commissioner of Education's Committee on Public Library Service, 1957.* Albany, N.Y.: State Education Dept., 1958. 66p.

..... Office of Research and Evaluation. *Emerging library systems; the 1963-66 evaluation of the New York State public library systems.* Albany, N.Y.: State Education Dept., 1967. 291p.

..... State Library. Division of Library Development. *A directory of New York State public library systems.* Albany, N.Y.: State Education Dept., 1969. 71p.

..... *A directory of reference and research library resources systems in New York State.* 3rd ed. Albany, N.Y.: State Education Dept., 1969.

..... *A primer of public library systems in New York State.* Rev. ed. Albany, N.Y.: State Education Dept., 1966.

..... *Profiles of the public library systems in New York State (Reprinted from the Bookmark, 1963-66.)* 2d ed. Albany, N.Y.: State Education Dept., 1966.

..... State Education Department. Division of Evaluation. *Emerging library systems: the 1963-1966 evaluation of the New York State public library system.* Albany: State Education Dept., Div. of Evaluation, 1967. 291p.

New York (State) University. *Short summary of papers and proceedings.* (Conference on the bibliographic control of library science literature, State University of New York at Albany, April 19-20, 1968). Manuscript.

Nicholson, Natalie. "Service to industry and research parks by college and university libraries," *Library trends* 14:262-72 (Jan. 1966).

Nimmer, Melville B. "Project new technology and the law of copyright: reprography and computers," *UCLA law review* (April 1968).

Nixon, President Richard M. *Message on educational reform to the Congress of the United States.* Washington, D.C.: Office of the White House Press Secretary, March 3, 1970. 11p. (mimeo.)

..... "Re-establishment of a national goals research staff: statement by the president of the USA," *Technological forecasting* 1:217-18 (1969).

..... *Statement by the President on S. 1519.* Washington, D.C.: Office of the White House Press Secretary, 21 July 1970. 2p. (mimeo.)

Noon, Paul A. T. "The role of the state agency in library extension," in C. B. Joeckel, *Library extension problems and solutions.* p.160-170 Chicago: ALA, 1967.

North, Jeanne B. "A look at the new COSATI standard," *Special libraries* 58:582-584 (Oct. 1969).

North, W., "A tutorial introduction to decision theory," IEEE transactions systems science and cybernetics SSC-4:200-210 (Sept. 1968).

Nourse, E. Shepley. "Areas of inadequacy in serving multiple needs," in D. M. Knight, and E. S. Nourse, eds. *Libraries at large,* p.161-167. New York: Bowker, 1969.

Nugent, William R. *NELINET: the New England Library Information Network.* Cambridge, Mass.: Inforonics, Inc., 1968. 4p.

Nyren, K. E. "Cooperation strategy for evolution," *Library journal* 94:2743-51 (Aug. 1969).

Ohio State Library. *Meeting information needs in Ohio: a report on a TWX experiment and elements that will assist in designing a reference and information network.* Columbus: Ohio State Library, 1970. 21p.

"Of note," *American libraries* 1:510 (June 1970).

Olney, J. C., *Building a concept network to retrieve information from large libraries* (Rep. TM634) Santa Monica, Calif.: System Development Corp.

Oppenheimer, Robert. "Physics and man's understanding," in P. H. Oehser ed., *Knowledge among men,* p.143-155 New York: Simon and Schuster, 1966.

Oregon, State University. *Bulletin, catalog issue, 1968/69* (Corvallis: Oregon State Univ., 1968. p.10.

Orne, Jerrold, ed. "Current trends in collection development in university libraries," *Library trends* 15:197-334 (Oct. 1966).

Orr, Richard H., et al. "Development of methodologic tools for planning and managing library services. Pt.I: Project goals. Pt.II: Measuring a library's capability for providing documents. Pt.III: Development of methodological tools for planning and managing library services," *Bulletin of the Medical Library Association* 56:235-267, 380-403 (July 1968).

...., and Pings, Vern M. "Document retrieval: the national biomedical library system and interlibrary loans," *Federation of American societies for Experimental Biology proceedings* 23:1155-1163 (Sept. 1964).

Ottawa. National Library. System Development Project. *An integrated information system for the National Library of Canada vol. 1, The report.* Ottawa: Bureau of Management and Consulting Services, Dept. of Supply and Services, June 1970. 210p.

Overhage, Carl F. J. "Information networks," in C. A. Cuadra, ed., *Annual review of information science and technology, vol. 4,* p.339-77. Chicago: Britannica, 1969.

...., and Harman, R. Joyce. *INTREX: report of planning conference on information transfer experiments.* Cambridge: MIT Pr., 1965. 276p.

Paisley, William J. "Information needs and uses," in C. A. Cuadra, ed., *Annual review of information science and technology, vol. 3,* p.1-30. Chicago: Britannica, 1968.

...., and Parker, E. B. "Information retrieval as a receiver-controlled communication system," in L.B. Heilprin, et al. eds., *Proceedings of the symposium on education for information science,* p.23-31. Washington, D.C.: Spartan Books, 1965.

...., ... "Research for psychologists at the interface of the scientist and his information system," *American psychologist* 21:1061-1071 (1966).

"Paperwork and nonprofessionals - improving engineer productivity," *Machine design* 36:83-6 (Jan. 1964).

Parker, Edwin B. "The effects of television on public library circulation," *Public opinion quarterly* 27:578-589 (1963).

..... "Technological change and the mass media," *Conference on information utilities and social choice.* Univ. of Chicago. (Dec. 1969).

Parsons & Williams, Inc., *Forecast 1968-2000 of computer development and application.* Copenhagen: Parsons & Williams, 1968. 44p.

Paulson, Peter J. "Networks, automation, and technical services: experience and experiments in New York State," *Library resources and technical services* 13:156-9 (Fall 1969).

Perlman, J. A. "Centralization vs. decentralization," *Datamation* 11:24-8 (Sept. 1965).

Perraton, H. D.; Wade, D. A. L.; and Fox, V. W. R. *Linking universities by technology.* Cambridge, England: National Extension College. 1969.

Peter, L. J., and Hull, R. *The peter principle.* New York: Morrow, 1969. 179p.

Phister, Montgomery, Jr. *Logical design of digital computers.* New York: Wiley, 1958. 408p.

Pings, Vern M. *Interlibrary loans: A review of the library literature, 1965.* (Biomedical Information Center, Report #23). Detroit: Wayne State Univ. Pr., 1966.

..... *Study of interlibrary loan policies of midwest biomedical libraries.* (Rep. No. 15) Detroit: Wayne State Univ. School of Medicine. Library and Biomedical Information Center, Sept. 1965. 13p.

..... "The interlibrary loan transaction," *Bulletin of the Medical Library Association* 53:204-214 (April 1965).

Pizer, Irwin H. "Biomedical communication network," *Bookmark* 28:105-8 (Jan. 1969).

..... "A regional medical library network," *Bulletin of the Medical Library Association* 57:101-15 (April 1969).

Pohlman, L. Dawn. "Special libraries and METRO," *Bookmark* 28:183-84 (Mar. 1969).

Poole, Harold Albert. "AALL classification survey 1968," *Law library journal* 61:255-58 (Aug. 1968).

Poole, Herbert. "Teletypewriters in libraries: a state of the art report." *College and research libraries* 27:283-6 (July 1966).

"Possibilities of innovations in research methods for law, a panel," *Law library journal* 53:346-368 (Nov. 1960).

Prentiss, S. Gilbert. "Networks; promise and performance," in L. Carnovsky, ed., *Networks - promise and performance.* Chicago: Univ. of Chicago Pr., 1969.

..... "The evolution of the library system (New York)," *Library quarterly* 39:78-89 (Jan. 1969).

"The President's message to the Congress, 14 August 1967." *Weekly compilation of presidential documents* 3:33, p.1146-1154.

President's Task Force on Communication Policy: Final report. Washington, D.C.: Gov. Print. Off., 1968), Chaps. v, vi, and ix.

Price, Miles O. "The Anglo-American law," *Library trends* 15:616-627 (1967).

...., and Bitner, Harry. *Effective legal research.* 3d ed. Boston: Little, Brown, 1969. 503p.

Proceedings of the librarians' convention, (New York, Sept. 15-17, 1853.) Reprinted for W. H. Murray. Cedar Rapids, Iowa: The Torch Press, 1915. 63p.

"Program for 1970/71 fiscal year," *For reference* [New York Metropolitan Reference and Research Library Agency, Inc.] 16:1 (June 1970).

"A proposal for experimental use of ATS," in J. W. Meaney and C. R. Carpenter, eds., *Telecommunications: toward national policies for education* (Washington, D.C.: Joint Council on Educational Telecommunications, 1970).

Purdy, G. Flint. "Interrelations among public, school, and academic libraries," in L. Carnovsky, ed., *Library networks - promise and performance* p.52-63. Chicago: Univ. of Chicago Pr., 1969.

..... "Interrelations among public, school, and academic libraries." *Library quarterly* 39:52-63 (Jan. 1969).

Quade, E. S., and Boucher, W. I., eds. *Systems analysis and policy planning.* New York: Elsevier, 1968. 453p.

Rahilly, J. P. *Ground and satellite telecommunications networks for global information systems.* (Paper presented at the AIAA Communications Satellite Systems Conf. in Washington, D. C., May 1966. AIAA Paper No. 66-331).

Raiffa, H. *Preferences for multi-attributed alternatives.* (Memorandum RM-5868-DOT/RC) Santa Monica, Calif.: Rand Corp., April 1969. 108p.

..... *Decision analyses.* Reading: Addison-Wesley, 1968.

...., and Schlaifer, R. *Applied statistical decision theory.* Cambridge: Harvard Press, 1961. 356p.

Rand Corporation. *Satellites and technology for communication: shaping the future.* (Report P-3760) Santa Monica, Calif.: Rand, Jan. 1968. 30p.

Rathbone, Robert R. *Communicating technical information.* Reading, Mass.: Addison-Wesley, 1967. 104p.

Raymont, Henry. "Publishers report a decline in sales of textbooks," New York times (14 May 1970).

"RCA achieves major technological breakthrough in development of color-TV tape player employing lasers and holography," *RCA news release* (30 Sept. 1969).

RECON Working Task Force. "Levels of machine-readable records," *Journal of library automation* 3:122-127 (June 1970).

..... *Conversion of retrospective catalog records to machine-readable form: a study of the feasibility of a national bibliographic service.* Washington, D.C.: Library of Congress, 1969. 230p.

Rees, Alan M. "Broadening the spectrum," in W. B. Linderman, ed., *The present status and future prospects of reference/information service,* p.57-65. Chicago: ALA, 1967.

"A reference round-up: developments in communications, resources, cooperation, personnel, research, use of computers and financing," *Library journal* 92:1582-5 (April 1967).

Regional Information Network Group [Denver]. *Academic library teletype experiment; letter of intent.* [Denver: The Group] 1970. 2p.

"Regional Medical Library quarterly statistical report, interlibrary loans, July-Sept. 1969," *Library networks/MEDLARS technical bulletin* 9:4 (Jan. 1970).

Reimers, Paul R., and Avram, Henriette D. "Automation and the Library of Congress: 1970," *Datamation* 16:138-43 (June 1970).

"Report of Ad Hoc Joint Committee on National Library Information Systems (CONLIS)," *ALA bulletin* 62:255-265 (Mar. 1968).

Richardson, B. E. "Trends in cooperative ventures among college libraries," *Library trends* 18:85-92 (July 1969).

Richardson, Ernest C. *General library cooperation and American research books.* Yardley, Pa.: Cook, 1930. 144p.

Ridenour, Louis N. et al. *Bibliography in an age of science.* Urbana: Univ. of Illinois Pr., 1951. 90p.

Rider, Fremont. *The scholar and the future of the research library.* New York: Hadham Pr., 1944. 236p.

Rigby, M. "Selective dissemination of information using UDC in international information networks," in R. Molgaard-Hansen and M. Rigby, eds., *Proceedings first seminar on UDC in a mechanized retrieval system* (FID/CR Report No. 9) Copenhagen: Danish Center for Documentation, 1969.

Rike, Galen. *Statewide library surveys and development plans: an automated bibliography, 1956-1967.* Springfield: Illinois State Library, 1968. 105p.

Ringer, Barbara A. "Copyright law revision: history and prospects" in *Automated information systems and copyright law, a symposium of the American University.* Reprint from the Congressional Record, vol. 114, no. 102, June 11-14, 1968. p.2.

Rippon, J. S. *The industrial information specialist as a mediator in the information transfer process.* (Paper submitted to the FID/II Symposium in Moscow, Sept. 1968). Prague: UTEIN, 1968. 14p.

Roalfe, William R. *The libraries of the legal profession.* St. Paul, Minn.: West, 1953. 471p.

Roberts, L. G., and Wessler, B. D. "Computer network development to achieve resource sharing," in *AFIPS proceedings spring joint computer conference, vol. 36,* p.543-549. Montvale, N.J.: AFIPS Pr., 1970.

Rohlf, Robert H. "A plan for public library development in Illinois," *Illinois libraries* 46:217-53 (March 1964).

Rokkan, Stein, and Aarebrot, F., "The Norwegian archive of historical ecological data: progress report. August 1969," *Social science information* 8:77-84 (1969).

...., ed. *Data archives for the social sciences.* Paris: Mouton, 1966. 213p.

"The role of local-state-regional cooperation," in D. M. Knight and E. S. Nourse eds. *Libraries at large,* p.399-434. New York: Bowker, 1969.

Rollins, Jane G. "A summary of reference and research library resource systems programs," *Bookmark* 29:102-5 (Dec. 1969).

Ross, Virginia L. "Review of *Interlibrary cooperation under Title III of the Library Services and Construction Act,*" *News notes of California libraries* 65:367-75 (Winter 1970).

Rossi, Peter H., and Biddle, Bruce J., eds. *The new media and education: their impact on society.* Garden City, N.Y.: Doubleday and Co., Inc., 1967.

Rothstein, J. "Information, organization and system," *Transactions of the Institute for Radio Engineers* (PGIT-4) Sept. 1954.

Rothwell, G. J. "The performance concept: a basis for standards development," reprint from *ASTME vectors* (1969/2), 3p.

Rozsa, G. "The particular role of libraries and documentation networks within a national information system," in A. I. Mikhailov, et al. eds., *International forum on informatics,* vol.2, p.565-76. Moscow: VINITI, 1969.

Sackman, H. "Current methodological research," [position paper for sessions on managing the economics of computer programming], in *Proceedings 23rd national conference of the ACM,* p.349-352. Princeton, N.J.: Brandon/Systems Press, Inc., 1968.

Salton, Gerard. *Automatic information organization and retrieval.* New York: McGraw-Hill, 1968. 514p.

Samuelson, Kjell. *Automated international information networks, systems design concepts, goal-setting and propities.* (FID/TM Panel at the ASIS meeting, San Francisco, Oct. 1969. IB-ADB 70, No. 21.) Stockholm: Royal Inst. of Technology, 1970. 58p.

..... "Coordination of diversified data bases and information networks through multiclassificatory concept notation in relay-switches and referral directories," in *Procedings second seminar on UDC and mechanized information systems,* 1970.

..... "Fast-response and special-purpose usage in general information systems," in A. I. Mikhailov, et al. eds., *International forum on informatics, vol.2.* Moscow: VINITI, 1969. p.420-37.

..... *FID/TM symposium on performance evaluation of information retrieval systems.* (Panel Discussion on goal-setting, ultimate desires, preferences and non-desireable effects. Stockholm, 17 June 1970).

..... "Information structure and decision sequence," in K. Samuelson, ed., *Mechanized information storage, retrieval and dissemination,* p.622-36. Amsterdam: North-Holland, 1968.

..... "Management information systems and nervous systems - a comparison of design concepts," in *Proceedings IEEE systems and cybernetics conference,* p.90-8. Oct. 1969, Philadelphia.

..... "Systems design concepts for automated international information networks," in J. B. North, ed., *Proceedings of the American Society for Information Science, vol. 6, p.431-5. Westport: Greenwood, 1969.*

Sanford, Daniel S., Jr. *Inter-institutional agreements in higher education; an analysis of the documents relating to inter-institutional agreements with special reference to coordination.* New York: Columbia Univ. Teachers College, Bureau of Publications, 1934. 112p.

dos Santos, M. L., and Greybourne, S. *Directorate for scientific affairs computer utilisation in member countries an examination of surveys carried out in member countries on computer systems and personnel as of Oct. 1969. (Paper submitted to the group of experts on computer utilisation for information.) DAS/SPR/69,11.*

Saracevic, Tefko. "Linking research and teaching," *American documentation* 19:398-403 (Oct. 1968).

Savary, M. J. *The Latin American Cooperative Acquisitions Program...an imaginative venture.* New York: Hafner, 1968. 144p.

Scherr, A. L. "An analysis of time-shared computer systems." Ph.D. dissertation. (Rept. No. MAC-TR-18) Cambridge, Mass.: MIT Pr., June 1965. 178p.

Schick, Frank L. "The century gap of law library statistics," *Law library journal* 61:1-6 (1968).

..... "A century of U.S. library statistics of national scope," in *The Bowker annual of library and book trade information, 1970,* p.5-11. New York: Bowker, 1970.

Schieber, William D., and Shoffner, Ralph M. *Telefacsimile in libraries. A report of an experiment in facsimile transmission and an analysis of implications for interlibrary loan service.* Berkeley, Calif.: Univ. of California. Institute for Library Research, Feb. 1968. 137p.

Schwegmann, George A., Jr. "The National Union Catalog in the Library of Congress," in R. B. Downs, ed., *Union catalogs in the United States,* p.226-63. Chicago: ALA, 1942.

Scientific and technical communication: a pressing national problem and recommendations for its solution. A synopsis of the report of the on scientific and technical communication of the national academy of sciences-national academy of engineering.) Washington, D.C.: The Academy, 1969. 30p.

Shachtman, Bella E. "Other federal activities (in centralized cataloging and cataloging cooperation)," *Library trends* 16:112-26 (July 1967).

Shank, Russell. "Cooperation between special libraries and other types of libraries," in C. E. Thomasen, ed., *Cooperation between types of libraries: the beginnings of a state plan for library services in Illinois,* p.60-72. (Allerton Park Institute,,no. 15) Urbana: Univ. of Illinois, Graduate School of Library Science, 1969.

..... "Library service to industry: a view from New York City," *Bookmark* 27:269-73 (Apr. 1968).

..... "Networks," in *The Bowker annual of library and book trade information, 1970.* p.291-296. New York: Bowker, 1970.

..... *Regional access to scientific and technical information: a report on a Shared Acquisitions and Retention System for Metro Libraries.* (Metro Miscellaneous Publication No. 5) New York: Metropolitan Reference and Research Library Agency, 1970.

Shannon, Claude, and Weaver, W. *The mathematical theory of communication.* Urbana: Univ. of Illinois Pr., 1949. 125p.

Shannon, C. E. and Moore, E. F. "Reliable circuits using less reliable relays," *J. Franklin Institute* 262:191-208, 281-297 (Sept., Oct. 1956).

Shannon, D. E. "A mathematical theory of communications," in *Bell system technical journal* 17:379-423 (July-Oct. 1948). System Journal 17: (July-Oct. 1948).

Shaw, Ralph R. "Using advances in technology to make library resources more available." in ALA *Student use of libraries,* p.72-82. Chicago: ALA, 1964.

Sheehan, Sister Helen. "The library-college idea: trend of the future," *Library trends* 18:93-102 (July 1968).

Sheffield, England. Libraries, Art Galleries and Museums Committee. *The city libraries of Sheffield 1856-1956.* Sheffield, England: City of Sheffield Printing and Stationery Dept., 1956.

Shepard, Marietta. D. "Cooperative acquisitions of Latin American materials," *Library resources and technical services* 13:347-60 (Summer 1969).

Shera, Jesse H. "The challenging role of the reference librarian," in Texas Library Association, *Reference research and regionalism,* p.21-34. Austin: Texas Library Association, 1966.

..... "Foundations of a theory of reference service," in Texas Library Association, *Reference research and regionalism,* p.13-20. Austin: Texas Library Association, 1966.

Simms, R. L. Jr. "Trends in computer/communication systems," *Computers & automation* 17:22-25 (May 1968).

Simon, Herbert A. "Some strategic considerations in the construction of social science models," in P. Lazarsfeld, ed., *Mathematical thinking in the social sciences.* New York: The Free Press, 1954.

Skipper, James E. "National planning for resource development," *Library trends* 15:321-34 (Oct. 1966).

"Sky's the limit on satellite bids." *Broadcasting* 78:42 (30 March 1970).

Slamecka, Vladimir. "Methods and research for design of information networks," *Library trends* 18:551-68 (Apr. 1970).

....; Zunde, P.; and Kraus, D. H. "On the structure of six national science information systems," in A. I. Mikhailov, et al. eds., *International forum on informatics, vol.1, p.318-34. Moscow: VINITI, 1969.*

Slavens, Thomas P. *The development and testing of materials for computer-assisted instruction in the education of reference librarians.* (Final Report, Project No. 8-0560, OEC-5-9-320560-0043.) Washington, D.C.: U.S. Office of Education, Bureau of Research, 1970. 178p.

Smith, Dorothy. "Cooperative efforts," *Association of Hospital and Institutional Libraries quarterly* 9:93-9 (Summer 1969).

Smith, Hayden R. "Media men arise: what if McLuhan is right?" *Educational screen and audiovisual guide* 47:18-19 (June 1968).

Smith, Ralph Lee, "The wired nation," *Nation magazine* 210:582-606 (18 May 1970).

Snook, Helen A. "Cooperative effort in cataloging," *Law library journal* 53:115-117 (May 1960).

South African Council for Scientific and Industrial Research. *Computer tape services in science and technology.* Pretoria: UDC, 1970. 24p.

South Dakota. Governor's Ad Hoc State Communications Committee. *Communication system planning for the state of South Dakota.* 1965. (mimeo.)

"Southwest academic library consortium," *Mountain plains library quarterly* 13:28 (Spring 1968).

Special Libraries Association. *Special Libraries Association - its first fifty years, 1909-1959.* New York: SLA, 1959. 120p.

Standard book numbering. New York: Bowker, The Standard Book Numbering Agency, 1968. 13p.

Stanford University. Institute for Communication Research. *SPIRES annual report. A report of the Stanford public information retrieval system.* Stanford, Calif.: Stanford Univ. Institute for Communication Research. 1970.

Steinberg, Charles A. "Information storage and retrieval system," *Information display* (Feb. 1970).

Steinke, Eleanor G., and Tannehill, Robert S. "Regional medical library planning in the southeastern United States," *College and research libraries* 30:327-34 (July 1969).

Stevens, M. E. *Research and development in the computer and information sciences, vol. 3. Overall system design considerations --- a selective literature review.* (National Bureau of Standards monograph 113, vol. 3) Washington, D.C.: Gov. Print. Off., June 1970. 143p.

Stevens, Mary E. *Standarization, compatibility and/or convertibility requirements in network planning.* (Unpublished report prepared for the Lister Hill National Center for Biomedical Communications.)

Stevenson, Chris G. "A librarian looks at the State Technical Services Act," *Special libraries* 59:183-85 (March 1968).

Stewart, D. K. *Social implications of social science data archives.* (Technical memorandum 3724/000/000) Santa Monica, Calif.: System Development Corp., 7 Nov. 1967.

Stimler, Saul. *Real-time data-processing systems; a methodology for design and cost/performance analysis.* New York: McGraw-Hill, 1969. 259p.

Stone, C. Walter. "The library function redefined," *Library trends* 16:181-96 (Oct. 1967).

Sukhov, V. I. "A global information system," in A. I. Mikhailov, et al. eds., *International forum on informatics, vol.1, p.521-3. Moscow: VINITI, 1969.*

Swank, R. C. *Interlibrary cooperation under Title III of the Library Services and Construction Act...* Sacramento: California State Library, 1967. 78p.

..... "Partnerships in California: how can books and information be mobilized for every Californian," *News notes of California libraries* 63:419-28 (Fall 1968).

Swanson, Don R. "Design requirements for a future library," in B. Markuson, ed., *Libraries and automation, proceedings,* p.11-21 Washington, D.C.: Gov. Print. Off., 1964.

Swanson, Robert W. "Information systems networks - let's profit from what we know," in G. Schechter, ed., *Information retrieval - a critical view,* p.1-52. Washington, D.C.: Thompson, 1967.

"Symposium on video-tape recording standardization," *Society of Motion Picture and Television Engineers journal* 7:757- (July 1968).

System Development Corporation. *National document-handling systems for science ar.d technology.* New York: Wiley, 1967. 334p.

Tapper, Colin. "World cooperation in the mechanization of legal information retrieval," *Jurimetrics* 9:1-11 (1968).

Tardov, B. N. *Method for scientific technical progress forecasting as based on dynamics of documental information.* (Paper presented at the FID/II Symposium in Rome, Oct. 1969). Prague: UTEIN, 1969. 22p.

Tauber, Alfred S. "A review of microphotographic techniques and graphic storage and retrieval systems," *Drexel library quarterly* 5:234-240 (Oct. 1969).

Taylor, Robert S. *Curriculum for the information sciences; Report No. 12: Recommended courses and curricula.* (NSF Grant No. GE-2569) Bethlehem, Pa.: Lehigh University, Center for the Information Sciences, 1967. 48p.

..... *Question-negotiation and information-seeking in libraries.* (Studies in the man-system interface in libraries, no. 3) Bethlehem, Pa.: Lehigh Univ., Center for the Information Sciences, 1967. 99p.

..... "Technology and libraries." *EDUCOM bulletin* 5:4-5 (May 1970).

Texas. State Library. *Evaluation number two: Texas state library communications network.* Austin: Texas State Library, 1970.

..... *Major resources center communication network study.* (Prepared by Management Research International.) Austin: Texas State Library, 1967.

Tezak, B. "The role of small countries in international systems with special reference to Yugoslavia," in A. I. Mikhailov, et al. eds., *International forum on informatics,* p.412-21. Moscow: VINITI, 1969.

The Three R's: Reference and Research Resources Library Systems. Albany, N.Y.: State Education Dept., Div. of Library Development, 1969.

Timpano, Doris M. "Copyright legislation and you," *NEA journal,* (April 1969).

..... "The copyright law revision and ETV: an alternative to the wasteland?" *Rutgers law review* 1:112-113 (Fall 1968).

..... "International copyright - a world view," *Bulletin of the copyright society of the U.S.A.* 17:14, 149 (Feb. 1970).

Tribus, Myron. *Rational descriptions, decisions, and designs.* New York: Pergamon, 1969. 478p.

Troy, Frank J., "Ohio bar automated research--a practical system of computerized legal research," *Jurimetrics journal* p.62-69 (1969).

Truelson, Stanley D. Jr., "Planning for a library system: Connecticut regional medical program" *Bulletin of the Medical Library Association* 57:239-43 (July 1969).

Trueswell, Richard W. "A quantitative measure of user circulation requirements and its possible effect on stack thinning and multiple copy determination," *American documentation* 15:20-25 (Jan. 1965).

Uniform system of citation. 11th ed. Cambridge, Mass.: Harvard Law Review Assoc., 1967. 117p.

Union Library Catalogue of Pennsylvania. *Contract for service.* [Philadelphia: The Catalogue, n.d.] [1]p.

Union Library Catalogue of Pennsylvania. *Schedule of subscriptions for academic and related non-profit institutions voluntary support of the catalogue.* [Philadelphia: The Catalogue] 1966. [1]p.

United Nations. Educational, Scientific, and Cultural Organization. *Communication in the space age.* Paris: UNESCO, 1968. 200p.

..... Educational, Scientific, and Cultural Organization. "Plans for a world science information system," *UNESCO bulletin for libraries* 23:55-61, 1969.

"Ups and downs of information retrieval," *Datamation* 14:129 (Jan. 1968).

Uridge, Margaret D. "Interlibrary lending and similar extension services," *Library trends* 6:66-86 (July 1957).

U.S. Congress. House. Committee on Education and Labor. *To improve education. A report to the President and the Congress of the United States by the Commission on Instructional Technology.* Washington, D.C.: Gov. Print. Off., 1970. 124p.

..... Committee on Foreign Affairs. National Security Policy and Scientific Developments. *Satellite broadcasting: implications for foreign policy.* Hearings, 91st Cong., 2d sess., 13, 14, 15, 22 May 1969.

..... Committee on Science and Astronautics. Subcommittee on Space Science and Applications. *Assessment of space communications technology.* Hearings, 91st Cong., 1st sess., 16, 17, 18, 19 Dec. 1969.

..... Joint Economic Committee. Subcommittee on Fiscal Policy. *Revenue sharing and its alternatives: what future for fiscal federalism?* (90th Cong., 1st Sess. Jt. Com. Print.) Washington, D.C.: Gov. Print. Off., 1967. 3v. Vol.1, Break: 140-45; Harriss: 146-55; Maxwell: 102-39; Mushkin: 76-101; Mushkin and Adams: 171-94; Robinson: 61-75; and Senate Committee on Government Operations: 257-67. Vol.2, Adams: 1060-68; Break: 816-59; 1-69-99; Nathan: 666-84; Rafuse: 1053-59; Reuss: 977-90. Vol.3. Morss: 1423-31; Tax Foundation: 1277-1331.

..... Senate Committee on Labor and Public Welfare. Hearings before the Sub-Committee on Education. 90th Congress 2d Session (Washington, D.C.: Gov. Print. Off., 1968). Part 1295-1306.

..... Senate. Committee on Labor and Public Welfare. *National Commission on Libraries and Information Science: hearings on S. 1519.* 91st Cong., 1st sess., 24 April 1969.

..... Senate. *National Commission on Libraries and Information Science Act. Report to accompany S. 1519,* 91st Cong., 1st sess., 20 May 1969.

U.S. Department of Commerce. Telecommunication Science Panel of the Commerce Technical Advisory Board. *Electromagnetic spectrum utilization - the silent crises.* Washington, D.C.: Gov. Print. Off., 1966. 87p.

U.S. Department of Health, Education and Welfare. Office of Education. *Consortiums in American higher education: 1965-66; report of an exploratory study,* (by Raymond S. Moore...) Washington, D.C.: Gov. Print. Off., 1968. 47p.

U.S. Executive Office of the President. Office of Telecommunications Management. *The radio frequency spectrum, United States use and management.* Washington, D.C.: Gov. Print. Off., 1969.

..... *A report on frequency management within the executive branch of the government.* Washington, D.C.: Gov. Print. Off., 1966.

..... *Technological trends in telecommunications.* Washington, D.C. 22 Jan. 1968. (Mimeo.)

U.S. Federal Bureau of Investigation. "The FBI's computer network" *Datamation* 16:146-51. (June 1970).

U.S. Federal Council for Science and Technology. Committee on Scientific and Technical Information. *Standards for descriptive cataloging of government scientific and technical reports.* (Rev. no. 1.) Washington, D.C.: Clearinghouse for Federal Scientific and Technical Information, October 1966. 50p.

U.S. Library of Congress. *The MARC pilot project,* (Prepared by Henriette Avram.) Washington, D.C.: Gov. Print. Off., 1968. 183p.

..... "The Library of Congress as the national library: potentialities for service," in D. M. Knight and E. S. Nourse, eds. *Libraries at large,* p.435-65. New York: Bowker, 1969.

..... Information Systems Office. *The MARC pilot project: final report on a project sponsored by the Council on Library Resources, Inc.* (Prepared by Henriette D. Avram) Washington, D.C.: Gov. Print. Off., 1968. 183p.

..... Information Systems Office. *Format recognition process for MARC records: a logical design.* Chicago: ALA, 1970.

..... Processing Dept. *The Cataloging-in-Source experiment: a report to the Librarian of Congress by the Director of the Processing Department.* Washington, D.C.: Library of Congress, 1960. 199p.

..... Processing Dept. *National program for acquisitions and cataloging, progress report.* (No. 10) Washington, D.C.: Library of Congress, 1970. 8p.

..... Processing Dept. *The role of the library in the international exchange of official publications: a brief history.* Washington, D.C.: Library of Congress, 1953. 85p.

..... "The Library of Congress as the national library: potentialities for service," in D. M. Knight and E. S. Nourse, eds., *Libraries at large,* p.435-465. New York: Bowker, 1969.

U.S. Office of Education. Library Services Branch. *State plans under the Library Services Act, supplement 3: a progress report - the first five fiscal years, 1957-61.* (Bulletin 1963, no. 14) Washington, D.C.: Gov. Print. Off., 1963. 187p.

U.S. Office of the White House Press Secretary, The White House. *Announcement of administration's recommendations on the utilization of communications satellites for domestic telecommunications services.* Washington, D.C. 23 Jan. 1970. (Mimeo.)

..... "Memorandum for the Honorable Dean Burch, Chairman of the Federal Communications Commission from Peter Flanigan, Assistant to the President." Washington, D.C. 23 Jan. 1970. (Mimeo.)

U.S. Veterans Administration. *Professional services: medical and general reference library staff.* (Veterans Administration, Dept. of Medicine and Surgery Manual M-2, pt. 13) Washington: Gov. Print. Off., Feb. 1966.

Utley, George. *Fifty years of the American Library Association.* Chicago: ALA, 1936. 29p.

Vambery, Joseph T. "The new scope and content of cooperative cataloguing for law libraries," *Law library journal* 60:244-48 (Aug. 1967).

Vann, Sarah K. "Southeastern Pennsylvania Processing Center feasibility study: a summary," *Library resources and technical services* 10:461-78 (Fall 1966).

Vavrek, Bernard. "The theory of reference service," *College and research libraries* 29:508-510 (Nov. 1968).

Veaner, Allen B., and Fasana, Paul J., eds. *Proceedings the conference on collaborative library systems development, 1968.* Stanford, Calif.: Stanford Univ. Libraries, 1969. 233p.

Vlannes, P. "requirements for information retrieval networks," in B. F. Cheydleur, ed. *Colloquium on technical preconditions for retrieval center operations,* p.3-6. Washington, D.C.: Spartan Books, 1965.

von Neumann, J. "Probabilistic logics and the synthesis of reliable organisms from unreliable components," *Automata studies* (Annals of Mathematics Studies, No. 34) Princeton: Princeton Univ. Pr., 1956. p.43.

Voracek, J. "Centralized and decentralized abstracting and indexing in the light of Czechoslovak experience," in D. J. Foskett, eds., *Library systems and information services,* p.95-102. London: Crosby Lockwood, 1970.

Vosper, Robert et al. "Library cooperation for reference and Technological trends in telecommunications. Washington, D.C. 22 Jan. 1968. (Mimeo.)

Walker, Richard D. "Independent study materials in library science instruction," *Journal of education for librarianship* 10:44-52 (Summer 1969).

Wall, Eugene. "Possibilities of articulation of information systems into a network," *American documentation* 19:181-87 (April 1958).

Ward, J. E. "Systems engineering problems in computer-driven CRT displays for man-machine communication," *IEEE transactions systems science & cybernetics* SSC-3:47-54 (June 1967).

Warren, Peter A.; Vinken, P. J.; and van der Walle, F. "Design and operation of an advanced computer system for the storage, retrieval and dissemination of the world's biomedical information," in J. B. North, ed., *Proceedings of the American Society for Information Science,* vol. 6, p.423-29. Westport: Greenwood, 1969.

Weber, David C. "Foreign newspaper microfilm project, 1938-1955," *Harvard library bulletin* 10:275-81 (Spring 1956).

..... "Off-campus library service by private universities," in Association of Research Libraries, *Minutes of the sixty-second meeting,* p.25-38. Chicago: The Association, 1963.

Weinstock, Melvin. "Network concepts in scientific and technical libraries," *Special libraries* 58:328-34 (May-June 1967).

Wendell, Mitchell. "An interstate compact for libraries," *ALA bulletin* 58:132-34 (Feb. 1964).

Westby, Barbara M. "Commercial services," *Library trends* 16:46-57 (July 1967).

Western Union Telegraph Company. "Advanced record system, system description." (Prepared for U.S. General Services Administration.) Oct. 1964. (Mimeo.)

Whyte, L. L.; Wilson, A. G.; and Wilson, D., eds. *Hierarchical structures.* New York: Elsevier, 1969. 322p.

Wigington, Ronald L., and Wood, James L. "Standardization requirements of a national program for information transfer," *Library trends* 18:432-447 (April 1970).

Williams, Edwin E. *Farmington plan handbook, revised to 1961 and abridged.* Ithaca, N.Y.: ARL, 1961. 141p.

Williams, Gordon R. "History of the National Union Catalog Pre-1956 Imprints," in *The National Union Catalog 1956 imprints,* p.vii-x. Chicago: Mansell, 1968.

...., et al. *Library cost models: owning versus borrowing serial publications.* (Prepared under Grant Number GN-532 for the Office of Science Information Service, National Science Foundation.) [Philadelphia], 1968. 161p.

Wills, G.; Ashton, D.; and Taylor, B., eds. *Technological forecasting and corporate strategy.* London: Bradford/Crosby Lockwood, 1969. 273p.

Winchell, Constance. *Locating books for interlibrary loan, with a bibliography of printed aids which show location of books in American libraries.* New York: Wilson, 1930. 170p.

Winograd, S., and Cowan, J. D. *Reliable computation in the presence of noise.* Cambridge, Mass.: MIT Pr., 1963. 96p.

Witherspoon, John P. et al. *Educational communications system: phase III,* (Final report of Project 450 A) Washington, D.C.: U.S. Office of Education, Bureau of Research, October 1966). 300p.

van der Wolk, L. J. "National and international co-operation in library automation," in D. J. Foskett, et al. eds., *Library systems and information services,* p.52-6. London: Crosby Lockwood, 1970.

Wolpert, Bernard M. "A working library network," *American libraries* 1:570-72 (June 1970).

Woolston, John E. "The international nuclear information system (INIS)," *UNESCO bulletin for libraries* 23:125-38+ (May-June 1969).

Wormann, Curt D. "Aspects of international library cooperation - historical and contemporary," *Library quarterly* 38:338-51 (Oct. 1968).

Wysocki, A. "Study of users' information needs - subjects and methods," in *On theoretical problems of informatics,* p.80-92 (FID No 435, FID/RI) Moscow: VINITI, 1969.

..... *UNISIST (The present state).* Prague: UTEIN, 1969. 7p.

Yerkes, C. P. "Microfiche, a new information media", in H. P. Luhn, ed., *Automation and scientific communication, short papers, pt. 2,* p.129. Washington, D.C.: Am. Doc. Inst., 1963.

Yovitz, M. C., and Ernst, R. L. *Generalized information systems: some consequences for information transfer.* Columbus: The Ohio State University. Dept. of Computer and Information Science, 1968.

Zunde, Pranas. "Co-operation of the information agencies of the CMEA countries," *International library review* 1:487-509 (1969).

EPILOGUE

Hiawatha's Network

By the shores of Airlie House pond
In the hillsides of Virginia
Met a group of data experts,
Experts in the use of knowledge.

Working through the mists of evening,
Toiling in the late Fall sunshine,
Striving to define a network
And create a plan for action.

Said their leader, "Who will use it?
How will they input their questions?
Will there be a master center
Which will gather all the data?

Is technology developed
That can do the things demanded?
Must machines still be invented
Which can tie the parts together?"

Into groups they were divided,
So as to approach the problems
But their purposes collided
As they groped toward solutions.

Long they labored, argued, reasoned,
Tried to bring about consensus,
Tried to find a mode of action
Which would be quite universal.

Hiawatha came upon them
At the endpoint of their struggle
As they wrestled with their charges
Looking for the higher vision.

Their conclusions were quite startling!!!
People are of key importance.

Networks are indeed required.
Duplication is anathema.

Hiawatha nodded sagely
As he listened with attention.
And he marveled at their wisdom
Bringing order out of chaos.

And he said, "Your basic findings
Are so vital to all persons
That I will assist the telling
Of your plans and hopes and goals."

Strode he to the highest hillside,
Gathered wood and lit a fire.
Taking off his thick, warm blanket
He sent forth a coded message.

Thus it reached throughout his nation
And the others got the message.
Networks are the coming fashion.
Let us join and shout HOSANNAH!

As they wended homeward, weary,
From the site at which they pondered,
All the people had the feeling
They had from the topic wandered.

And they hoped that the *Proceedings*
Stenocomp would later issue
Could make sense from all their sayings
Make of the truth a tissue.

So the end was the beginning
Of a networks formulation
With the nations' users winning
New control of information.

This poem was written by Irwin H. Pizer, Director, Library of SUNY Upstate Medical Center. Mr. Pizer read it at the Friday Plenary Session and following thunderous applause, the Conference unanimously dubbed him the "Airlie Bard."